The Archaeology and Ethnology of St Kilda No. 1

Archaeological Excavations on Hirta 1986–1990

Norman Emery

The Archaeology and Ethnology of St Kilda no. 1

EDINBURGH: HMSO

First published 1996

British Library Cataloguing in Publication Data.
A catalogue record for this book is available from the British Library.

ISBN 0 11 495715 0

HMSO Bookshops
71 Lothian Road, Edinburgh EH3 9AZ
0131-228 4181 Fax 0131-229 2734
49 High Holborn, London WC1V 6HB
(counter service only)
0171-873 0011 Fax 0171-831 1326
68–69 Bull Street, Birmingham B4 6AD
0121-236 9696 Fax 0121-236 9699
33 Wine Street, Bristol BS1 2BQ
0117 9264306 Fax 0117 9294515
9-21 Princess Street, Manchester M60 8AS
0161-834 7201 Fax 0161-833 0634
16 Arthur Street, Belfast BT1 4GD
01232 238451 Fax 01232 235401
The HMSO Oriel Bookshop, The Friary, Cardiff CF1 4AA
01222 395548 Fax 01222 384347

HMSO publications are available from:

HMSO Publications Centre
(Mail, fax and telephone orders only)
PO Box 276, London SW8 5DT
Telephone orders 0171-873 9090
General enquiries 0171-873 0011
(queuing system in operation for both numbers)
Fax orders 0171-873 8200

HMSO's Accredited Agents
(see Yellow Pages)

and through good booksellers

CONTENTS

List of Illustrations

Unless otherwise stated, line drawings and photographs are by the author.

List of Plates

List of Tables

Acknowledgements

The archaeological investigations on St Kilda were initiated by the National Trust for Scotland, and it was through the efforts of Professor Rosemary Cramp that the project was undertaken by Durham University. Mr Alexander Bennett, of the NTS, set the project in motion, arranging the first exploratory visits from which proposals for archaeological investigations were produced, and took part in the first season of excavations at House 8.

He was succeeded by Mr Philip Schreiber, who took on the Trust's administration of the archipelago, and who has staunchly supported the archaeological project throughout. His organisational and practical skills, and his love of St Kilda, has made the running of this project a great pleasure.

The project, since its establishment, has been overseen by a committee comprising Professor Cramp, Mr (subsequently Professor) C.D. Morris, Dr C.E. Batey, Mr A. Bennett followed by Mr P. Schreiber, Mrs M. Buchanan, Miss M. Harman, Mr G. Stell and the author. Through the efforts of the committee the running of the project has been carried through, and the results of excavation brought to publication.

Scheduled Monument Consent to excavate the sites recorded in this work was given by the Inspectorate of Ancient Monuments, and particular thanks must go to Mr Patrick Ashmore for his involvement and practical assistance towards the project.

The archaeological work was financed through the generosity of the National Trust for Scotland, the British Academy, the Russell Trust, the St Kilda Club, the Hunter Trust and Glasgow Archaeological Society.

The practical excavation work was supervised by a small group of skilled, highly professional archaeologists — in 1986, Mr Christopher Morris and Dr Colleen Batey; in 1987, Dr Batey and Mr Mike Rains; in 1988, Mr Rains and Miss Gillian Quine; and 1989–90, Miss Amanda Clarke and Miss Gillian Quine. To them I owe a special debt of thanks, for their expertise, friendship and good humour. The members of the National Trust for Scotland's work parties played a vital practical role in the project, assisting in the excavation and recording work, under the supervision of their party leaders — Mr Philip Schreiber, Mr Alexander Bennett, Ms Angela Cartledge, Dr Jeffrey Stone, Mr George Thompson and Mrs Meg Buchanan. The administration of the work parties was in the capable hands of Susan Adair Brown.

The supply of equipment and land transport was arranged by Mr Harvey Watt of the Department of Archaeology, Durham University. Sea travel was initially on the *MV Kylebahn,* and subsequently on the *MV Monaco,* skippered in both instances by Mr Cubbie MacKinnon, assisted by his wife, Kate. I offer a special thanks to them for their skill, caring and kindness. On St Kilda we received invaluable help from the Officer Commanding and troops of the St Kilda Detachment, who made our visits particularly enjoyable.

The analysis of the material recovered by excavation, and the research involved, was greatly assisted by the following people —

Dr E.P. Allison (Environmental Archaeology Unit, York University), Mr J.H. Andrews (Birmingham Museum), Mr Robert Annan (Forbo-Nairn Ltd), Mr Ian Bailiff (TL Dating Laboratory, Durham University), Dr Colleen Batey (Glasgow Museum), Mr William Brannan (Blue Circle Industries plc), Ms Sallie Bassham (Dept. Mathematics, Salford University), Mr W. Burnett (United Distillers Co. Ltd), Mr G.M. Clarke (Eley Hawk Ltd), Dr John Coulson (Dept. Biological Sciences, Durham University), Mr Anthony Crawshaw (York Archaeological Trust), Mr Arthur Credland (Town Docks Museum, Hull), Dr L. Davies (Dept. Biological Sciences, Durham University), Dr Zakaria Erzinclioglu (Dept. Zoology, Cambridge University), Firmin and Sons (Birmingham), Mr A.R. Hall (Environmental Archaeology Unit, York University), Mr Ron Hardy (Dept. Geological Science, Durham University), Miss Mary Harman, Mr William Hartman (RAOB Grand Lodge of England), Mr William Hay (William Hay and Sons [Aberdeen] Ltd), Dr Elizabeth Healey, Mr R. Hindmarsh, Dr Jacqui Huntley (Dept. Archaeology Biological Laboratory, Durham University), Dr A.K.G. Jones (Environmental Archaeology Unit, York University), Ms Barbara Jones (Lloyds Register), Ms Jennifer Jones (Conservation Laboratory, Durham University), Mr Henry Kelly, Dr Harry Kenward (Environmental Archaeology Unit, York University), Mr Ron Lang (Rylands Whitecross Ltd), Dr Ann MacSween (AOC (Scotland) Ltd), Ms Sarah Moynihan, Mr Hugh Nicholson (Dept. Geology, Edinburgh University), Dr Rebecca Nicholson (Dept. Archaeological Sciences, Bradford University), Mrs Sonia O'Connor (York Archaeological Trust), Mr Maurice Pattison (Terry's Group), Mr D. Proctor (Sterling Winthrop Products Ltd), Mr Ian Read (Terry's Group Ltd), Mr Roy Rodwell (GEC-Marconi Ltd), Dr John Senior (Dept. Adult Education, Durham University), Mrs Caroline Shaw, Ms Clare Thomas, Ms Penny Walton (Textile Research Associates, York), Mr Trevor Woods (Photographic Unit, Dept. Archaeology, Durham University).

Dr Richard Hingley and Bill Lawson have kindly read and commented upon the text. The report has been sub-edited by Lyn Turner; and Robin Turner of the National Trust for Scotland has helped in the final stages of production. Alistair Holmes and Liz Fergusson guided the book through the HMSO production procedure.

Finally, thanks must go to the CBA, the Rosemary Cramp Fund, the St Kilda Club, and the National Trust for Scotland for grants and financial assistance towards publication.

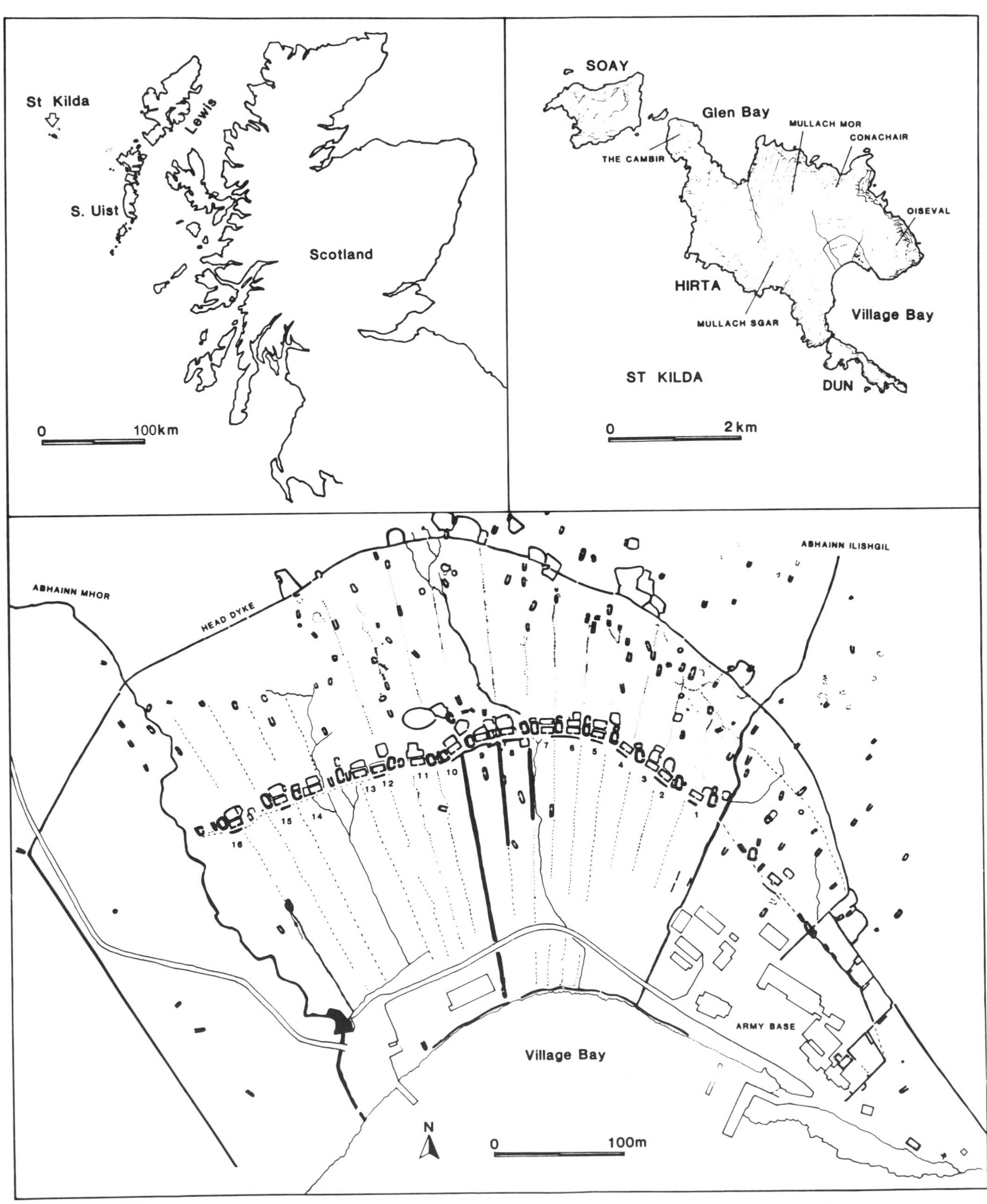

FIG. 1
Location map

CHAPTER 1

GENERAL INTRODUCTION

Location and geology

St Kilda is a 'World Heritage Site', lying in the North Atlantic, 160km west of the Scottish mainland (Fig. 1). It comprises the main island of Hirta, accompanied by Dun and Soay, along with Boreray, Stac Lee, Stac an Armin and Stac Levenish, forming the remnants of an early Tertiary (Palaeocene–early Eocene) volcano, some 60 million years old, one of the outer volcanic centres in the North-West Scotland Tertiary Volcanic Province.

Erosion has resulted in the removal of all the fine-grained volcanic rock cover from the volcano (Fig. 2), exposing the deep interior of the structure which consists of coarse-grained (plutonic) and medium-grained (Hypabyassal) intrusive rocks ranging in composition from basic gabbros and dolerites to acid granophyres and drusy granites (Harding *et al.* 1984).

During the Quaternary the island of Hirta was affected by a series of cold periods, initially indicated by the presence of exotic erratics, probably deposited by an ice sheet; then the emplacement of till in the early Devensian. The formation of an organic sand with the growth of grasses and sedges during an inter-stadial was followed by a deterioration to extreme cold, with glaciation, till and moraine formation by the late Devensian. Two protalus ramparts in Village Bay, post-dating the glacier, are associated with the Loch Lomond stadial (Sutherland *et al.* 1984, 270).

The glacial erosion of the Quaternary era produced the characteristic topography of the island. Hirta is roughly H-shaped, with the Cambir, Mullach Bi, Ruaival and Dun forming the west side; a central ridge of Mullach Sgar and Mullach Mor; and the towering peak of Conachair (426m) and Oiseval at the east. Between are the two bays — Village Bay at the south-east, and Gleann Mhor at the north.

The rock chemistry has influenced soil form and character (Fig. 2). Podzolic soils are found, with peaty rankers, peaty gleys, peaty gleyed podzols, anthropic gleys, and patches of Brown Earths, along with blanket and plantago peat, and man-made soils produced through cultivation (Gwynne *et al.* 1974, 70–87). This range of soil types, and a number of other variables, including the effects of salt sea spray and bird activity, has affected the range of vegetation (Fig. 3), with areas of *Luzula*, *Holcus*, *Agrostis*, *Festuca*, *Poa*, *Nardus* and *Molinia* grassland, dwarf shrub heath, bog and maritime communities (Gwynne *et al.* 1974, 36–70).

Climate

The location of St Kilda, far out in the Atlantic, and its topography are major factors affecting climatic conditions. Atlantic depressions tracking eastwards bring often heavy rain, and the high peaks of St Kilda affect cloud formations. High rainfall can occur fairly evenly during the year. The driest months throughout the Hebrides are generally April to June (Hudson *et al.* 1982, 14).

The Great Glen is drained by the Abhainn a Ghlinne Mhoir, which flows into a bay prone to uncomfortable swells, while the Abhainn Mhor runs into Village Bay. During certain weather conditions the Abhainn Ilishgil ('Dry Burn') drains water from An Lag. Village Bay itself has well-drained sand and a boulder storm beach. This bay is the main landing place. The island has several freshwater springs.

Sea fog also affects the archipelago, its effect like a blanket sinking into both bays. Associated with deep Atlantic depressions are the strong circulating winds which can hit St Kilda with extreme violence. On the 3rd October 1860, several of the 1830s blackhouse roofs were seriously damaged in gales, and in January 1962 there were 17 consecutive days of gales (Stone 1988, 4).

Records of temperature on St Kilda are limited. With the Atlantic Drift most of the Outer Hebrides are considered fairly warm in terms of accumulated temperature, although throughout north-west Scotland there is a low value of average bright sunshine, often less than 3.3 hours per day (Gilchrist 1966, 88).

History of human settlement

Hirta supported a farming and fowling community up to the Evacuation in 1930. Since 1957 the entire island group has been owned inalienably by the National Trust for Scotland — a total of 853ha (Hirta 637ha, Soay 99ha, Boreray 77ha, Dun 32ha, and the stacks 8ha). The group is leased to Scottish Natural Heritage (formerly the Nature Conservancy Council) as a National Nature Reserve. Responsibility for issues concerning natural history is devolved to SNH, whilst the Trust retains responsibility for the cultural interests on the islands. An area of 4.49ha is sub-leased by SNH to the Ministry of Defence for their radar and support facilities (P. Schreiber, pers. comm.).

The history of human settlement of St Kilda has been documented from the 16th century, by Sir Donald Munro in 1549 (Munro 1774), to the 1930 Evacuation, by authors like MacGregor (1931) and Steel (1977). However, much of the history before the 19th century is extremely patchy.

Structural remains and stray finds indicated that Hirta had been occupied in prehistoric times, but there is a substantial time gap in the historical record until a *Saga* reference and artefacts revealed some form of Norse presence on the island. It is unclear, however, whether the Scandinavians had landed on a deserted island, or one still populated. Several centuries then elapsed before Martin Martin visited St Kilda in 1697. He referred to structures in use in Gleann Mhor which were of great age, and to three early churches in Village Bay; but he also gave an important account of the existing population and their distinctive way of life. The islanders lived in a small village of thatched dwellings, and the recent survey by Stell and Harman (1988) has identified a number of pre-1830 structures in the vicinity of the spring, Tobar Childa.

Martin believed that St Kilda had been settled by islanders from Lewis, Harris, the Uists and Skye, and estimated the population at around 180. In the 1720s, however, the islanders were decimated by smallpox, introduced from Harris, when only four adults and 26 children remained alive. The island missionary, Rev. Kenneth Macaulay, found their numbers had increased to about 80 in 1758 (Macaulay 1764, 196–8).

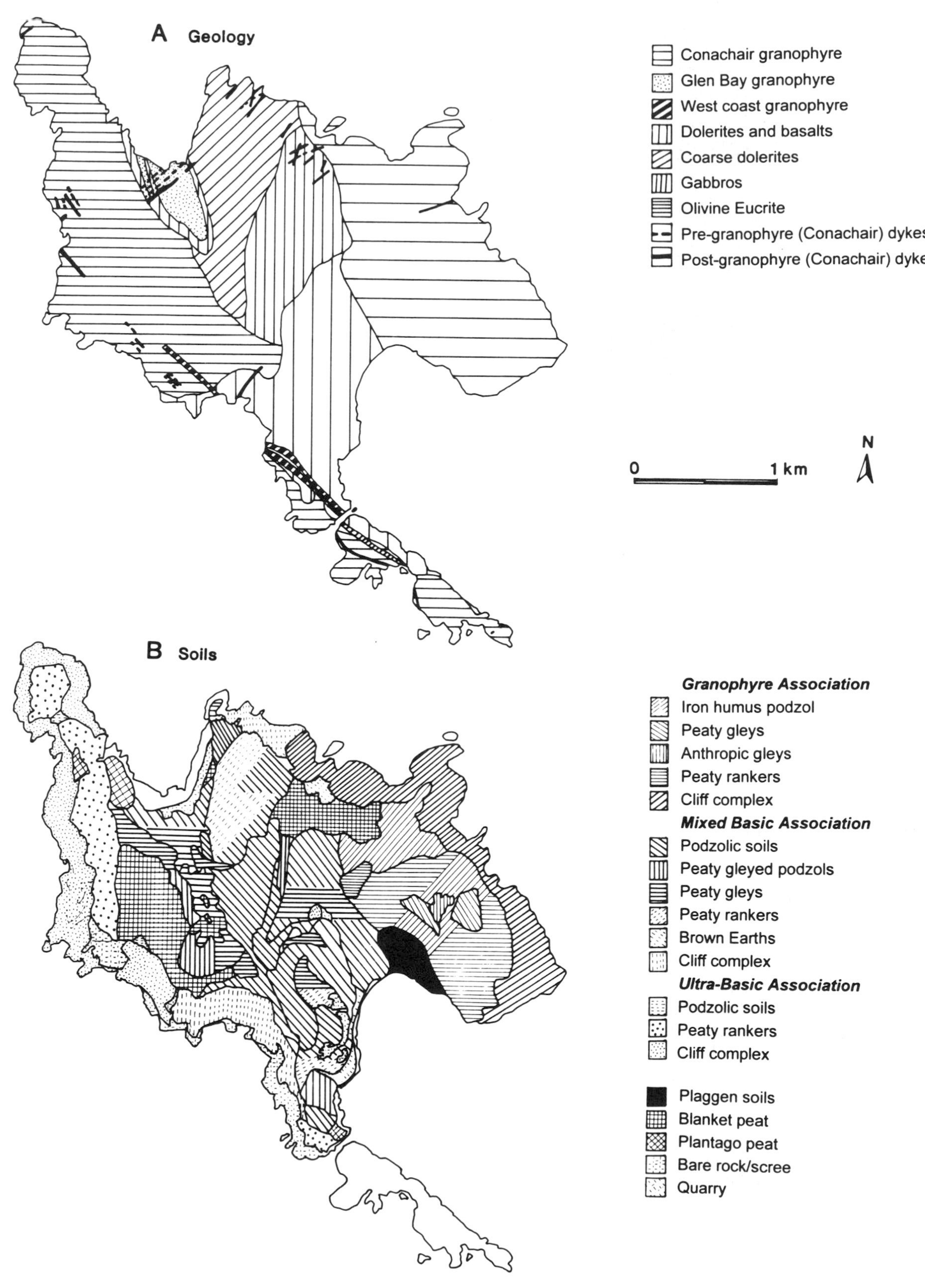

FIG. 2
The geology and soils of St Kilda

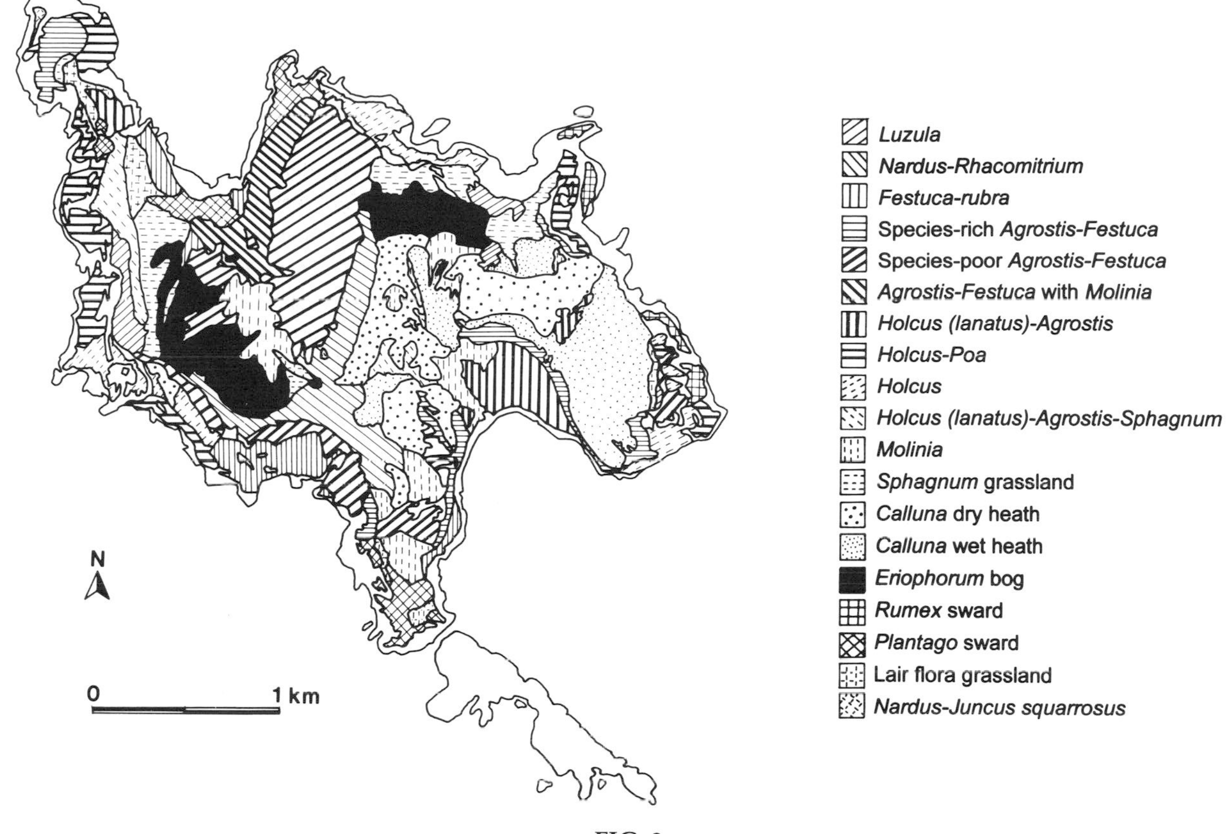

FIG. 3
The vegetation of St Kilda

This recovery seems to have been the result of a deliberate re-settlement policy, probably with eight or more immigrant families (Lawson 1981).

In the 1830s the village was re-located down-slope, with blackhouses set along a street. James Wilson found that there were 96 islanders in this new village in 1841, divided into 28 familial groups (Wilson 1842, 18). In addition, the minister, Rev. Neil Mackenzie, and his family increased the overall population to 105. By 1851 the census enumerators returns recorded that the population totalled 110, all islanders (the manse was temporarily unoccupied). From this date the decennial data shows a population dominated by females — only in 1911 was there equality in male–female numbers. By 1861 the numbers had fallen to 78, as a result of the emigration of 36 people to Australia in 1852; but in subsequent decades the figures remained fairly stable, never falling below 70. This was probably due to the eradication of neonatal tetanus in the latter half of the 19th century, which reduced the death rate; being offset by falling marriage rates and a reduction in fertility (Clegg 1977). By the turn of the century there was some stabilisation in the population structure, and by 1911 numbers had risen to 80. Outside influences and emigrations, however, reduced the population to 67 residents in 1921, before falling to 36 people at the time of the Evacuation in 1930.

Excavation history

Sporadic excavation has taken place on Hirta. Accidental discoveries of an early human presence were made in the 1830s and '40s during housing and agricultural changes. Examination of the earth-house — *Tigh an t' sithiche* — was begun by Sands in 1876 (Sands 1878a, 186–7), followed by the Keartons and John Mackenzie in the 1890s (Kearton 1897, 13–17), Mathieson and Cockburn in the 1920s (Mathieson 1928a, 125–6), and most recently by R. Ritchie (Stell and Harman 1988).

A small trench was dug into a mound underlying a sheep fank on An Lag bho Tuath in 1966. The findings confirmed that there had been cultivation in the area, and some dark coarse pottery was found (Celoria 1966, 4). One of the 'boat-shaped settings', close by, was excavated by Cottam in 1973, though the findings were inconclusive (Cottam 1973, 22–4). Most recently, Timothy Quine of the Department of Geography, University of Strathclyde, carried out small-scale excavations in 1983 at House 16 and Blackhouse U, as part of a soil analysis research project (Quine 1983). Aspects of the construction, use and decay of these buildings were recorded, along with details of primary soil formation and evidence of cultivated soils.

In 1983, the National Trust for Scotland proposed instigating an organised programme of archaeological investigation on Hirta. The Department of Archaeology at Durham University, under Prof. R.J. Cramp, was accepted by the NTS as their agent for the project. An initial reconnaissance of Hirta led to the production of an agreed programme for excavating problem areas, beginning with recent remains and working back in time, to elucidate more of the island's history.

The first site chosen for examination was a mound underlying the east gable of House 8, in the Village Street (Fig. 4). It was suspected that this might be the remains of an 1830s blackhouse, and excavations

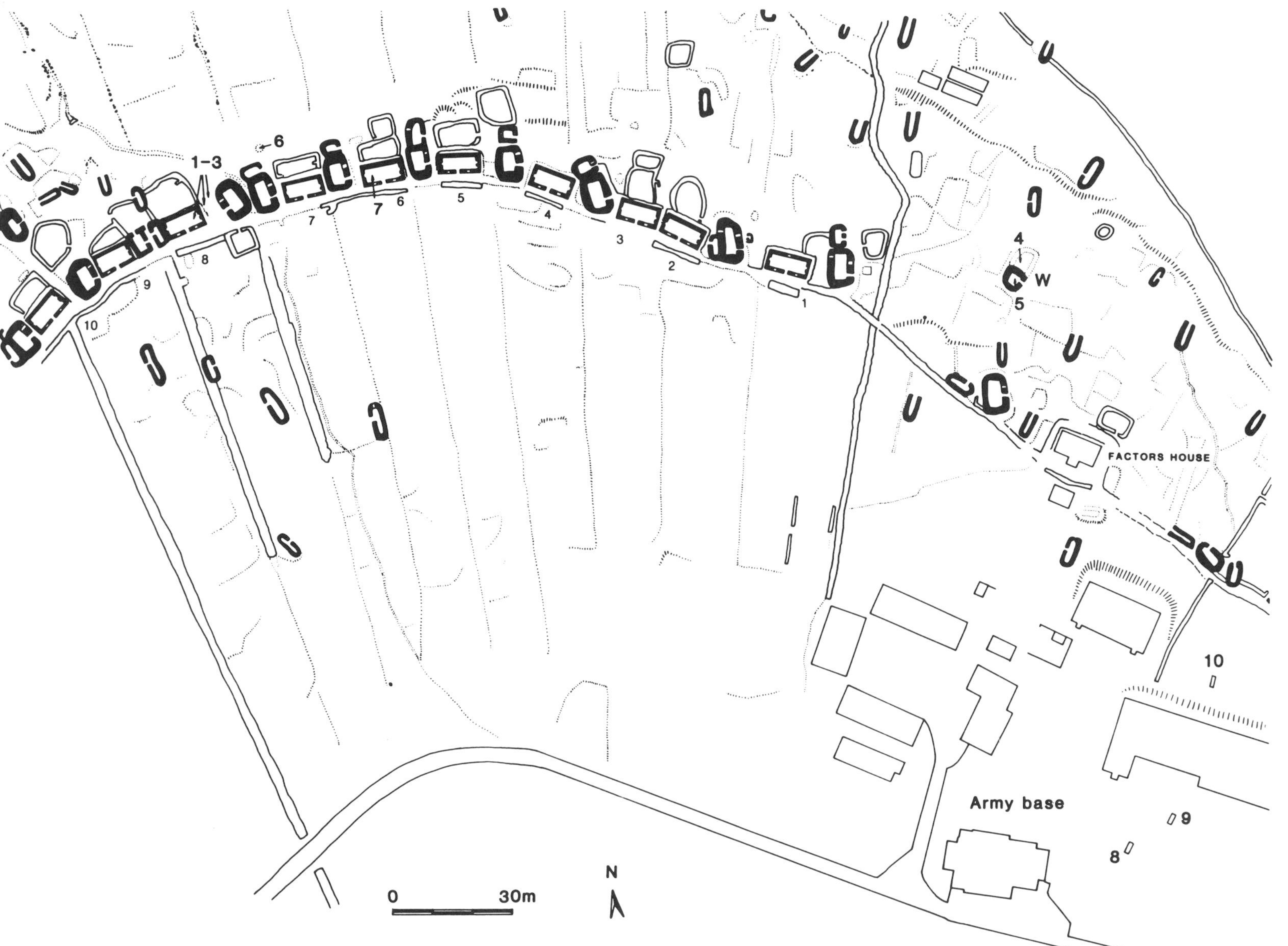

FIG. 4
The excavation areas in relation to the Village Street

were carried out in 1986–8 (Areas 1–3). In 1989, Blackhouse W and a ruined structure attached to its north side were then examined (Areas 4–5). A start was also made on the investigation of a viscera/rubbish pit behind Blackhouse G in 1989 (Area 6), and this was completed in 1990. In the latter year alterations to the excavation programme were made as a result of proposed development work at House 6 and the army base. The NTS proposal to convert the house into a museum necessitated an archaeological investigation before building work started (Area 7). As the theoretical aim of the project was to work back in time, the excavation of the 1860s House 6 is considered first in the report. Trial excavations were also carried out around the army base (Areas 8–10), to examine the state of the stratigraphy in advance of proposed redevelopment by the Ministry of Defence. The results are reported in Appendix A.

Format of the report

The record of each archaeological area examined has been sub-divided into four sections — the excavated evidence, detailed studies of the artefacts, and the ecofactual material, with a concluding summary, including site-specific documentary material and comparative evidence, principally for the artefacts. The finds reports cover objects dating from the prehistoric to the 20th century, with the studies giving equal value to both ancient and modern pieces. While the study and publication of 19th-century artefacts, like crockery, bottles and paraffin lamps, is rare in British archaeological reports, being more common in the 'historical archaeology' studies of the USA, Canada and elsewhere, the St Kilda report has pursued this subject, for the material recovered has illustrated quite dramatically the impact of the products of industrialised Britain on a materially 'primitive' society. In Chapter 6, the material included in the area summaries is brought together with other archaeological and documentary evidence, setting it into the St Kildan, and generally Hebridean, historical framework, while using ethnographic material to link the living conditions and way of life of the St Kildans to those of people in highland and island Scotland, and the North Atlantic area.

The results cover the five-year period 1986–90. The following phase of archaeological survey and excavation, including work beyond The Street, will be undertaken by Dr Alex Morrison of the Department of Archaeology, Glasgow University.

CHAPTER 2

EXCAVATIONS AT HOUSE 6

The National Trust for Scotland's proposal to reconstruct House 6, and to furnish it as it would have been around the turn of the century, necessitated structural work. This included the laying of a new floor, and excavations were carried out in advance of this work.

2:1 The Excavation Area (Fig. 5)

The whole of the interior of the house, roughly 9.15m x 4m, was excavated in 1990, and designated as Area 7 (see Fig. 4).

2:2 The Stratigraphic Sequence

Phase 1 (Fig. 6)

The primary surface consisted of an irregular area of granite (22, 41) with two boulders (42, 43) set in a matrix of this local material at the east end of the site. The surface appeared to be weathered bedrock, although two embedded pieces of green fine-grained dolerite with a few feldspar phenocrysts (J.R. Senior,

Size	% age	Description
<6.3mm	62.60	Large clasts of rotten coarse Conachair-Oiseval granite, angular fragments not water worn.
4.0mm	3.36	Ditto, smaller clasts.
2.0mm	3.83	Ditto, with some iron hydroxide aggregates with sand-sized grains.
1.0mm	4.88	Ditto, with some organic root debris and arthropod carapace material.
500µm	7.12	Ditto, with organic root debris and arthropod carapace material.
250µm	9.06	A 50/50 mixture of granite clasts and iron hydroxide aggregates with root debris and arthropod carapace material.
125µm	5.32	Ditto.
45µm	3.25	Ditto.
>45µm	0.90	*c.* 50/50 mixture of clasts derived from the granite source and the iron hydroxide aggregates.

TABLE 1
House 6: sediment, sieved fractions

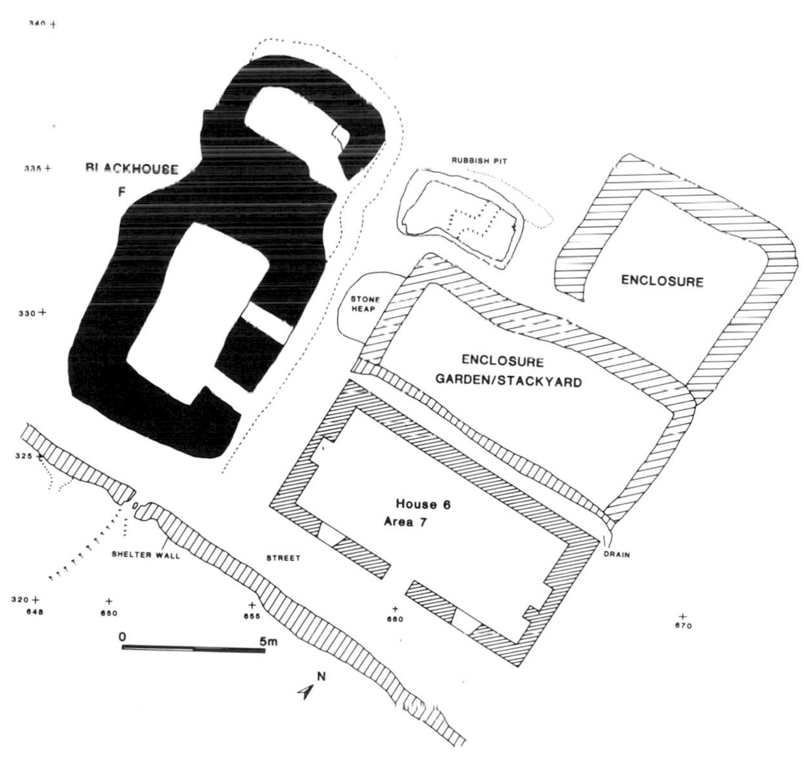

FIG. 5
House 6 and its surroundings

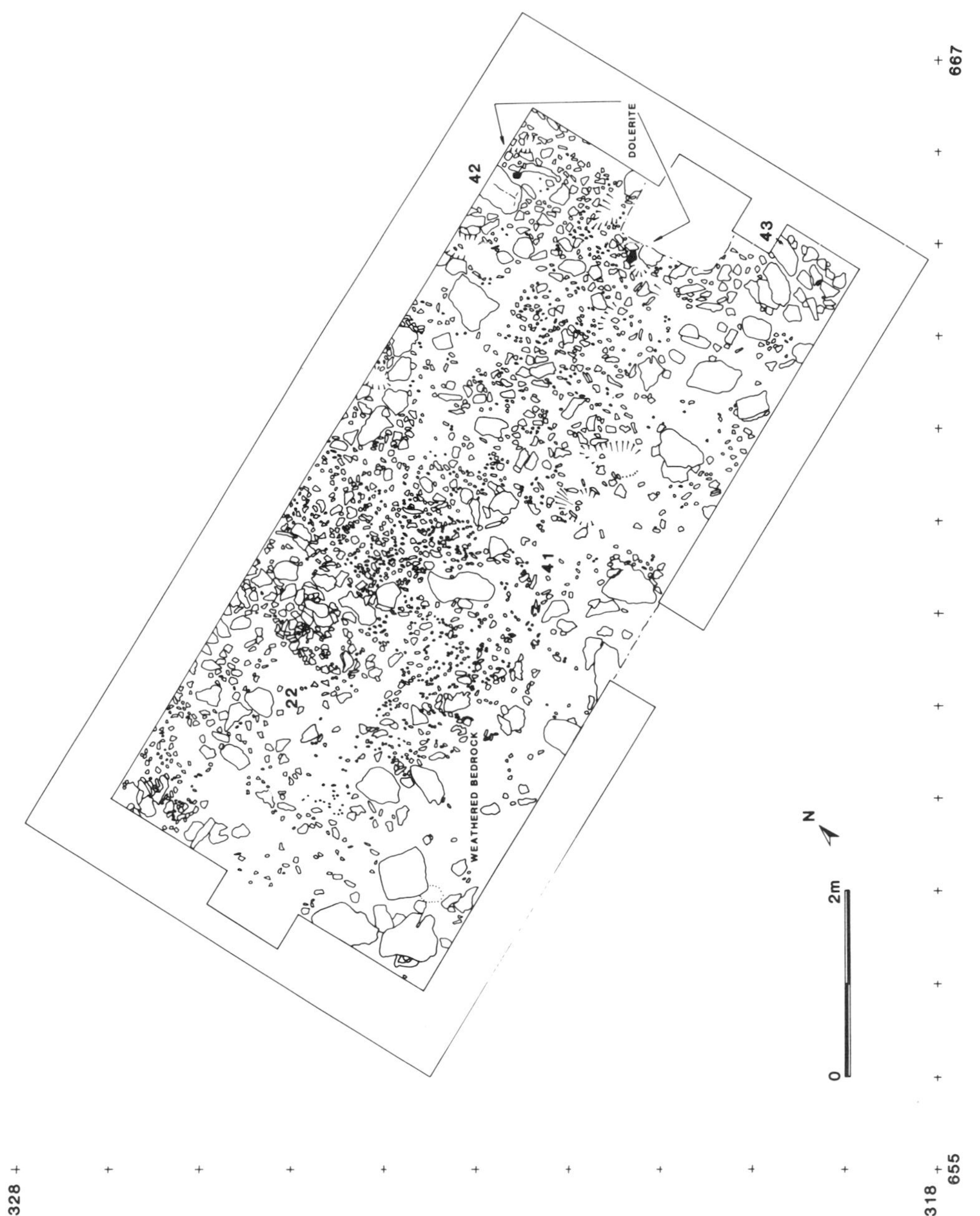

FIG. 6
House 6: Phase 1

pers. comm.) in the east end may suggest some glacial deposition onto the natural bedrock, although the material was angular and hardly abraded.

Within a cavity in the rock surface was a small patch of soil; 154.4g of this material was air dried and examined by Dr J.R. Senior. The analysis of the sieve fractions is given in Table 1, and displayed in histogram form in Figure 7. The analysis is consistent with an *in situ* soil developed on the granite substratum; rotten granite clasts form an important constituent of the soil, with the addition of chemical deposits of iron hydroxide aggregates associated with organic root debris. The association suggests an acid heather moorland soil development, with the iron hydroxides being derived from the granite parent material in the acid conditions, that is, a Brown Earth-type soil.

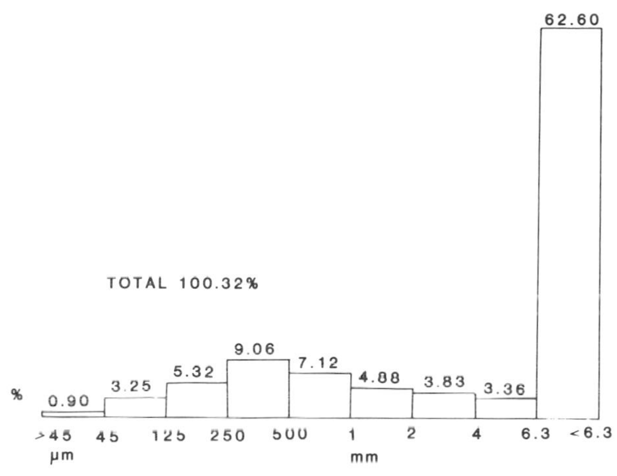

FIG. 7
House 6: sediment analysis

Phase 2 (Fig. 8)

The granite was covered by a dark reddish-brown friable gritty soil (19), noticeably thick towards the west and south, but thinning out towards the east. The soil contained two nails (sfs 207, 208) which were presumably associated with plank flooring (16) of Phase 5, an iron strip (sf. 143), probably a roof stay, and a pierced copper disc (sf. 226), although there was some doubt as to the object's exact position. More significantly, the layer produced seven fragments of coarse pottery (sfs 216, 221, 224, 229, 231, 240–41); 22 pebbles, including flakes, brought to the site from beyond the Abhainn Mhor (sfs 210–15, 217–19, 220, 222–3, 227–8, 230, 232–3, 235–9); a cinder-like fragment (sf. 234), and a fire-shattered pebble (sf. 209).

Phase 3 (Fig. 9)

The soil deposit was cut by a sub-rectangular pit (63 — Pl. 1), roughly 2.60m x 1.50m by 0.30m deep. The cut was sharpest at the west and south, with the presence of rock and pebbles creating more sloping faces at the other sides, and giving the base an uneven surface, deepest at the south-west.

The pit was filled with a compact, very dark greyish-brown, gritty, silty soil with some granitic pebbles (62). The rich quality of the soil was apparent in the noticeable earthworm content. The fill produced nine fragments of coarse pottery (sfs 195–99, 201–4) and a stone tool (sf. 200).

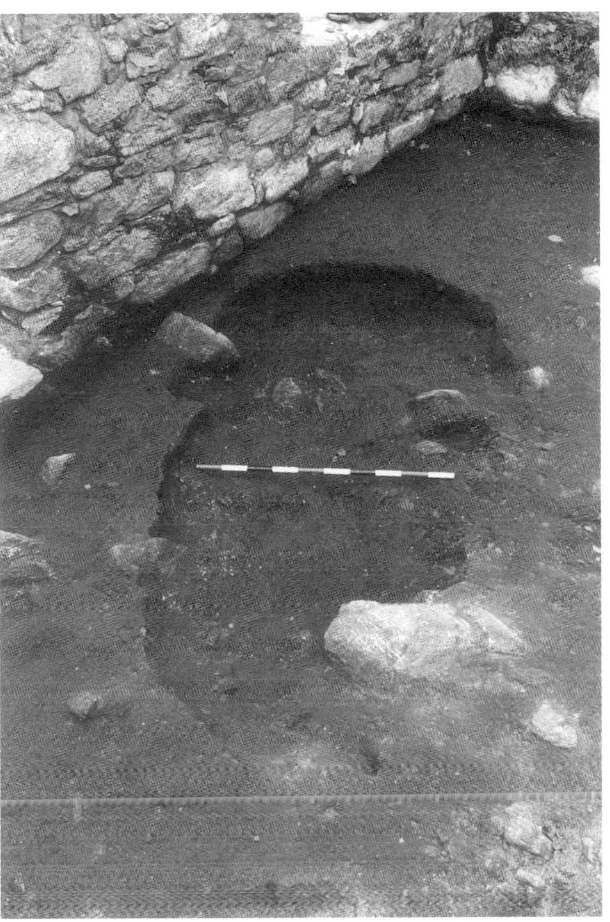

PLATE 1
House 6: the cultivation pit, looking west

The soil found in the pit was also found spread over the surface and some way beyond the feature (60). A number of small stones, apparently forming two lines (56, 57), may represent the fragmentary remains of a small drain cutting into the soil spread. The very dark brown to very dark greyish-brown, slightly gritty plastic soil (58) between the 'lines' of stones was somewhat more silty than the surrounding material.

Some thin patches of a very dark grey to black fine greasy silt (65) were found in the western half of the site, immediately over the reddish-brown soil (19) of Phase 2, and seems to have been associated with Phase 3 activity.

Phase 4 (Fig. 10)

During the period 1861–2 a rectangular cottage, House 6, was built (7–11). It is 10.48m by 5.26m (34' x 17'3") externally, with walls of mortared miarolitic granite rubble on stone footings. The longitudinal walls are 0.61m (2') wide; the south wall being pierced by a central door 0.98m (3'2") wide, with an internally splayed window, 0.62m and 0.82m (2'1" and 2'8") wide, to each side. The broader gable walls have fireplaces, each 0.92m (3') wide, and there is a mural cupboard, also 3' wide, in the south-east corner. During the construction work a number of small spreads of soil, mortar and sand were laid down (28, 46, 47, 61). Context 28 produced a clay pipe bowl fragment (sf. 194); two pieces of linoleum (sfs 182, 184), and copper alloy (sfs 180, 183) were found in

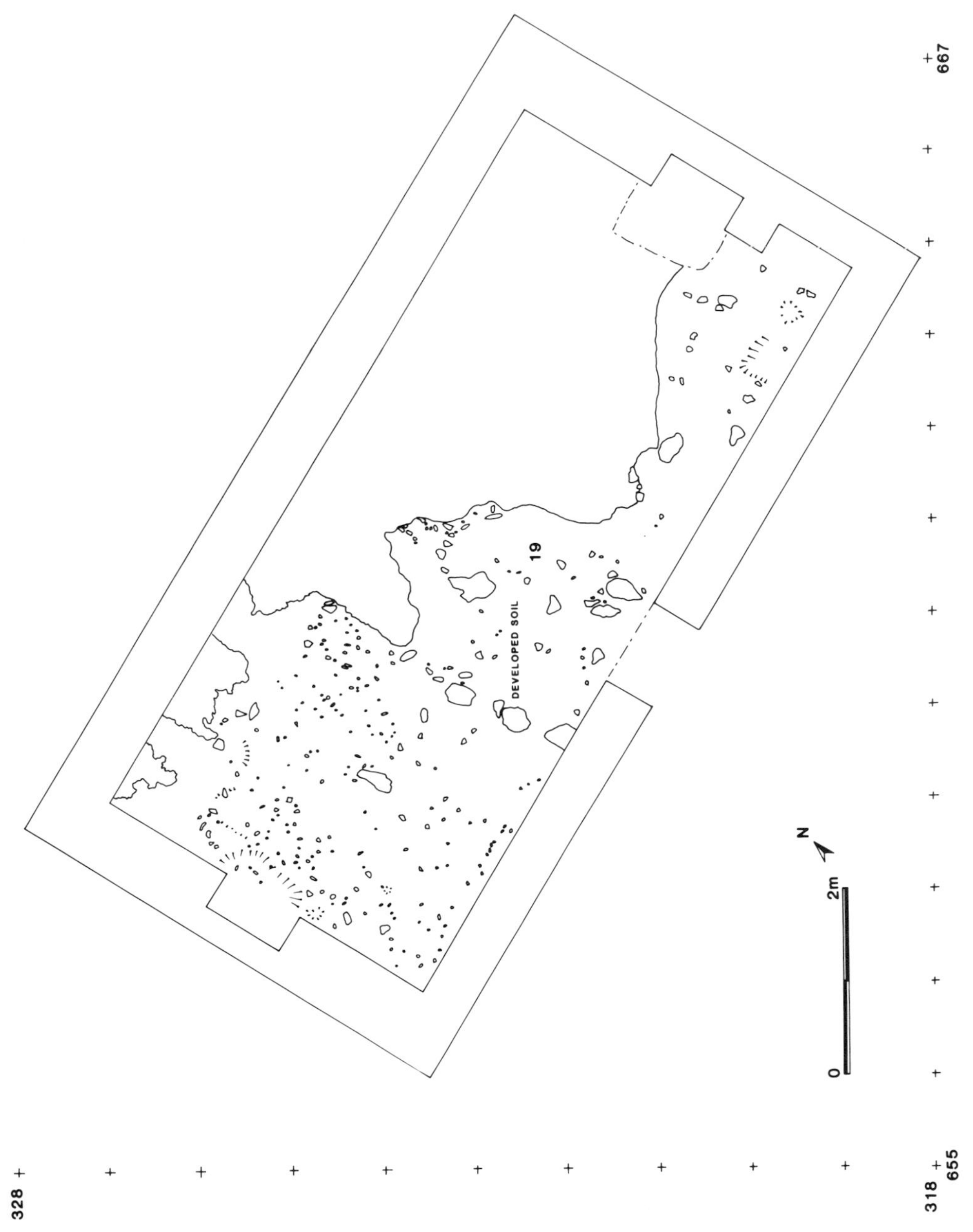

FIG. 8
House 6: Phase 2

FIG. 9
House 6: Phase 3

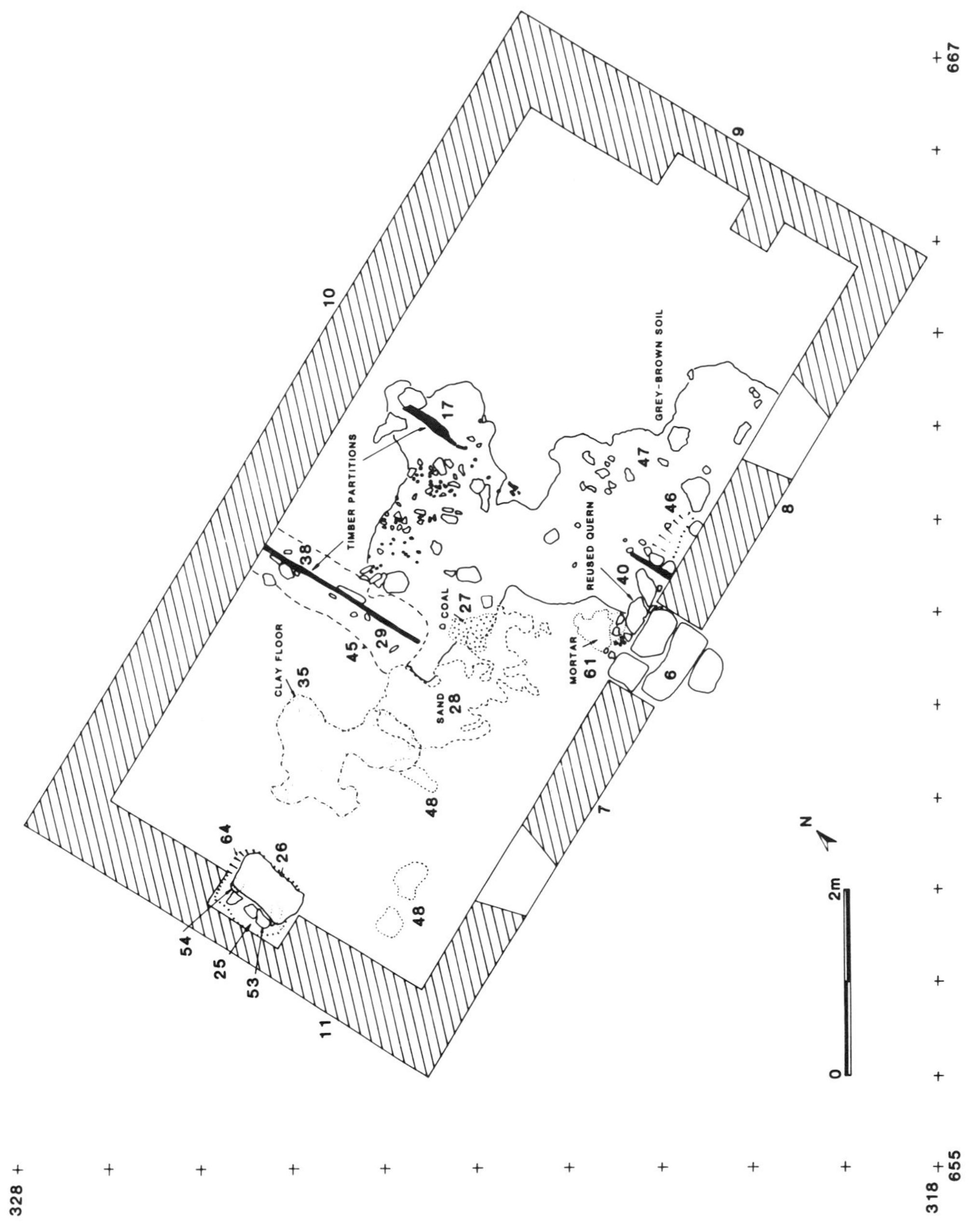

FIG. 10
House 6: Phase 4

context 46; and a clay pipe mouth piece (sf. 193) was found in context 61. Also during construction a stone threshold (6) was inserted for the door, and a small patch of paving (40) was laid inside, made up of broken quern fragments (sfs 187, 188 Fig. 24, Pl. 2).

PLATE 2
House 6: a re-used quern fragment at the house entrance

Probably from the beginning, and certainly by 1877 (MacDiarmid 1877, 12), the houses were divided internally by wooden partitions into two main rooms — a west kitchen and an east bedroom/living-room, flanking a small store-bedroom, and entrance lobby (Pl. 3).

A groove (45) was dug into the weathered granite to take the timber base rail or beam (38) of the west division. This was 65mm x 30mm (2½" x 1"), set vertically on its narrow face, and packed around with a fine silty black soil (29); 1.92m of the partition survived, and there were iron stains on the west face indicating the position of attached vertical planks. If projected, the line of the partition would be 0.71m (2'4") from the door. No trace was found of the vertical posts set at either end of the beam, but the evidence from gaps in the concrete flooring of the entrance lobby of House 7 would suggest that they were 77mm x 51mm (3" x 2"). With a top beam and other rails, these timbers would have formed the basic framework of the partition on which the planks were nailed. Two copper-alloy nails (sfs 150, 192) were recovered from context 38.

The partition for the east room survived as three fragmentary lengths of timber (17) set 0.30m (1') from the door, and lying on the grey-brown soil (60) of Phase 3. No clear evidence was found for the division between the entrance lobby and the back store/bedroom. A nail (sf. 181) was found in timber 17.

The primary floor was a hard yellow clay (35), though only a patch of it was found in the west end.

Of the two fires, only the west hearth was examined in detail. A hollow (64) was cut into the red-brown earth (19) of Phase 2, and a hearth slab (26) inserted. At an early stage peat or turf was burnt on the fire, and some (54) had spread down the back of the slab. Amongst context 54 was a worked stone (sf. 205) and a fire-reddened stone (sf. 206). This area was subsequently filled by three irregular pieces of granite (53). Further peat burning (25) took place on the hearth. The main slab projected out beyond the wall and gave a fireplace height from hearth to lintel of 1.12m (3'8").

Phase 5 (Fig. 11)

At a later stage, a timber floor was laid in the house. In the west room thin battens were laid down over the old clay floor to provide a base for the planks. The three surviving battens, aligned east-west, were around

PLATE 3
House 6: the central chamber and wooden partitions, looking east

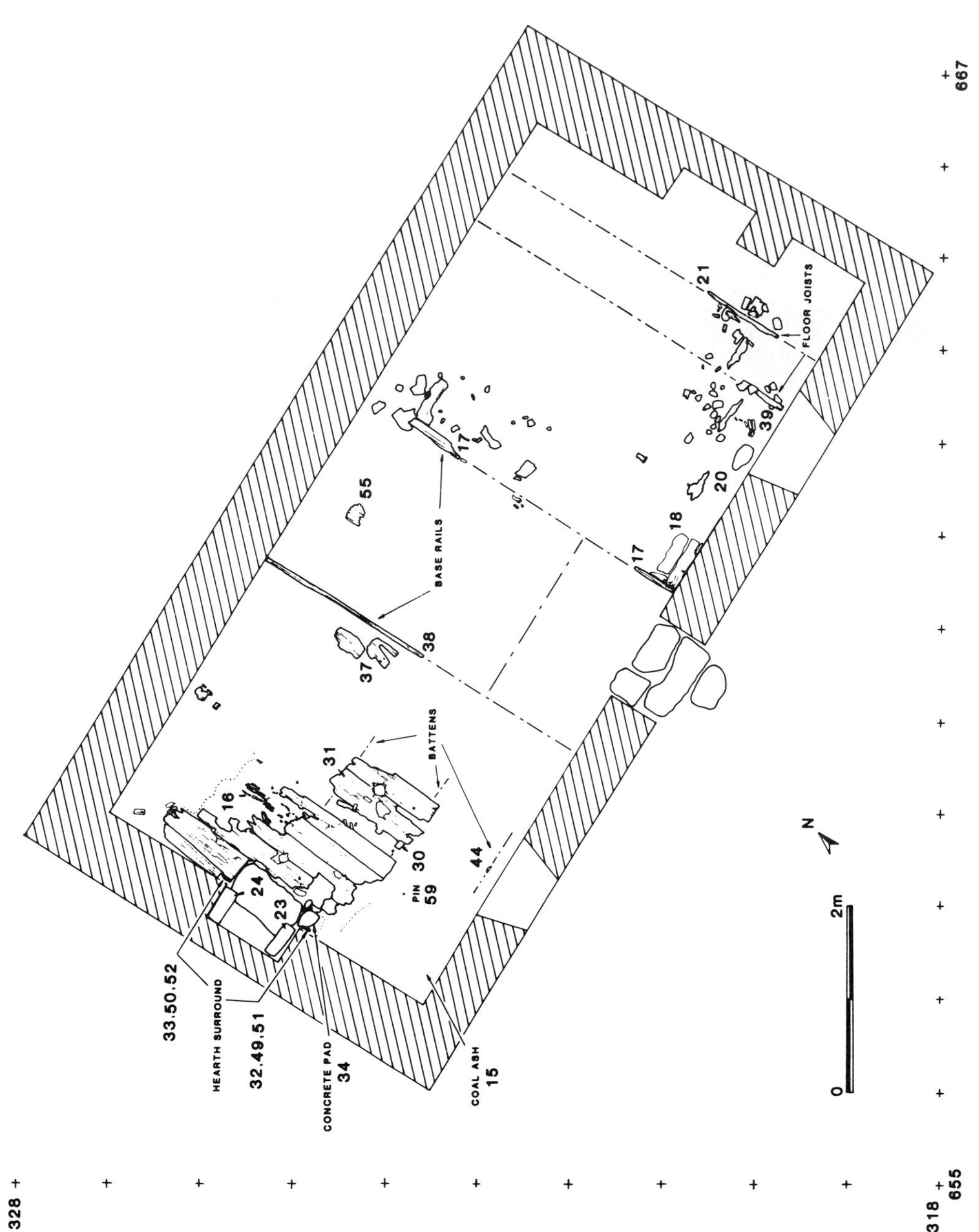

FIG. 11
House 6: Phase 5

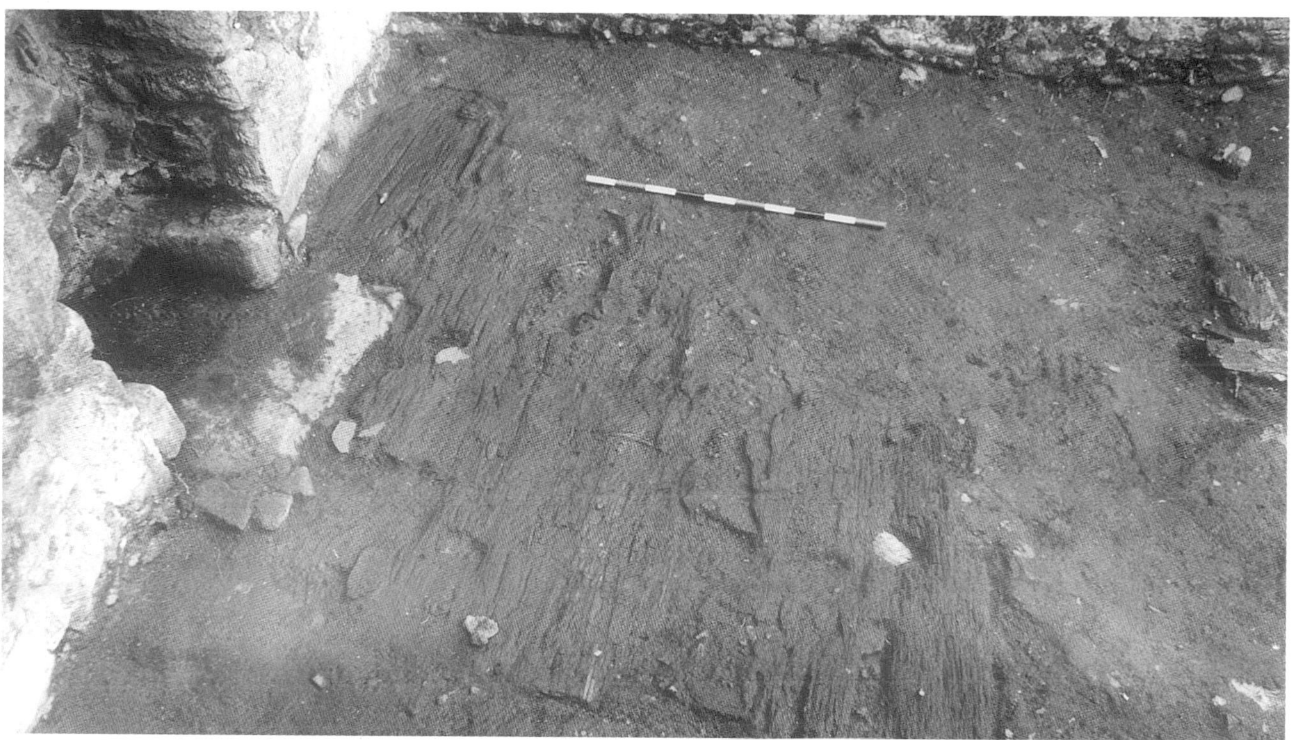

PLATE 4
House 6: the plank flooring in the west room, looking north

PLATE 5
House 6: detail of the flooring around the west hearth

60mm wide and 3mm thick (2¼" x ⅒"). The first (44) was placed 0.153m (6") from the south wall, while the other two (30, 31) were spaced at 0.91m (3') intervals.

Onto the battens were nailed north-south aligned wooden planks (16 — Pl. 4). These were 0.229m (9") butt-jointed planks, but were not placed perfectly parallel to the gable wall, and consequently there must have been some gaps when the planks reached the partition. In one case, a nail had been hammered through the planking directly into the underlying clay floor. However, some care had been taken to lay the planks around the hearth slab (Pl. 5). Of the plank fragments (37) nearest to the partition, one had been pierced by a nail (sf. 179), and traces of cork (sf. 177) and some wood with ?paint (sf. 178) were found by them. A single vertical wooden pin (59) was found 0.915m (3') from the south wall.

In the back store/bedroom only one small fragment of plank (55) remained, but it had clearly lain north-south.

In the east room the surface of the rock was somewhat lower, and it had been necessary to insert a suspended plank floor. Joists were inserted, of which fragments of two survived in the east end. The first of these (21), though presumably the second in the original line of joists, was placed 0.61m (2') from the fireplace, and the following joist (39) was placed a further 2' along. Onto them were laid east-west planks (18, 20). Unfortunately these had not survived as well as those in the west room. The most intact fragments (18) survived near the partition (17), and were clearly 0.15m (6") wide.

At the west hearth, the south-east corner of the slab was extended slightly by laying a small pad of concrete (34), which was secured to the underlying deposit by means of two copper-alloy pins (sfs 185–6).

Within the fire area two blocks of granite (23, 24) were set to support a grid-iron on which kettles and pans could be placed over the heat. Two holes (49, 50)

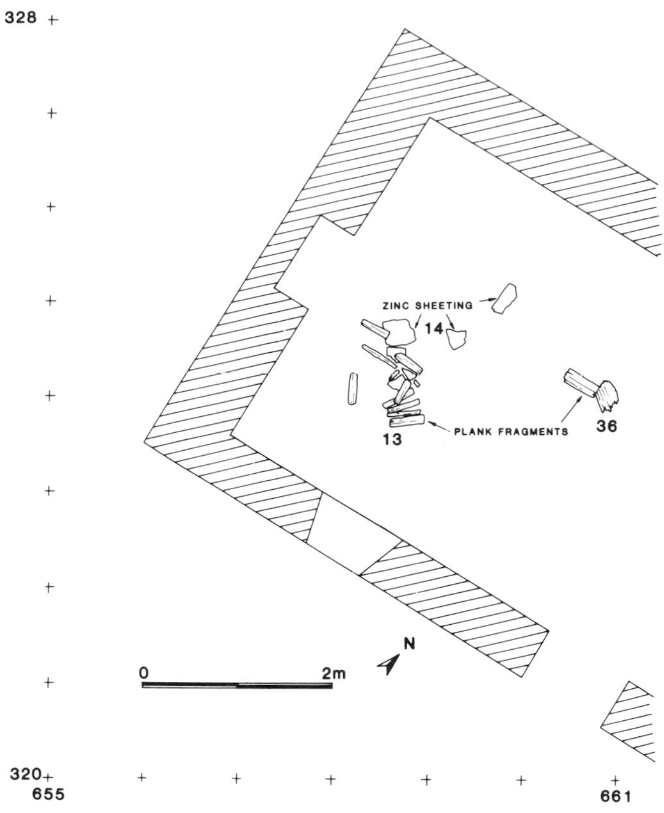

FIG. 12
House 6: Phase 6

were also dug either side of the hearth slab, by the gable wall. Into them were placed vertical pieces of timber (32, 33), of which only fragmentary stubs remained. They were packed around with a friable very dark greyish-brown silty soil (51, 52). These timbers formed the vertical upright of a fire surround, which probably had a mantelpiece to go with it. More recent pointing has, unfortunately, sealed any sockets which would have accommodated dooks, on which the timbers would have been nailed.

Some pink peat ash was found in the hearth, but the majority of the remaining ash was derived from coal (15). Some sand was found amongst the coal. The plank flooring closest to the fire showed evidence of having been slightly charred.

Phase 6 (Fig. 12)

The cold ash from the last fire spilt out from the fireplace onto the plank flooring. Pieces of plank (36), possibly from the roof, fell onto the west floor by the partition, while some zinc sheeting (14) and short wooden spars (13) were dumped onto the floor.

Phase 7 (Fig. 13)

The whole interior of the house was covered by lumps of mortar mixed in a very dark grey to dark reddish-brown friable, gritty, silty soil (2). This layer contained a vast number of artefacts, including textiles (sfs 1, 38, 148); Mother of Pearl buttons (sfs 11, 21, 39); metal buttons (sfs 12, 14, 153); a bone button (sf. 107); a leather offcut (sf. 18); a plastic comb (sf. 127); a padlock and key (sfs 20, 23); a bed caster from the east room (sf. 13); a spoon (sf. 22), fork (sf. 174) and knife handles (sfs 36, 173); iron bands and straps (sfs 17, 103, 105, 140–41), loops (sfs 81, 191), handles (sfs 73, 115), rods (sfs 59, 62, 64, 125, 133, 136–8), a fitting (sf. 101), a ?tube (sf. 119), a vessel rim and lid (sfs 16, 60), a cold chisel (sf. 109), a plate fragment (sf. 190), wire (sf. 144), spikes (sfs 74, 139, 189); nails of zinc, copper alloy, and principally iron (sfs 24–33, 40–54, 56–8, 61, 63, 65–7, 69–72, 75–80, 82–5, 89–91, 93, 95–100, 102, 106, 108, 110–12, 116–18, 121–2, 124, 128–30, 135, 145–7, 151–2, 154–5, 157–62, 164–72, 175–6); boat nails (sfs 19, 142); a screw (sf. 104); iron fragments (sfs 131–2); fragments of two lamps (sfs 149, 242); a lock-plate (sf. 244); a pierced copper-alloy bar (sf. 247); a copper-alloy fitting (sf. 55); a copper-alloy ring (sf. 156); a lead sheet (sf. 245); a pharmaceutical tin (sf. 248); a glass bottle (sf. 68); stone tools (sfs 15, 123); a piece of painted plaster (sf. 114); and several wooden pegs.

Phase 8 (Fig. 14)

Over the mortary surface was a small patch of very dark grey, gritty soil (12) in the west room. It produced a large 'Indestructible' plastic comb (sf. 6), a small fruit juice bottle from Maidstone (sf. 7), and a tiny fragment of coarse pottery (sf. 225). Over the layer was some clean soft yellow beach sand (4), and some large fragments of

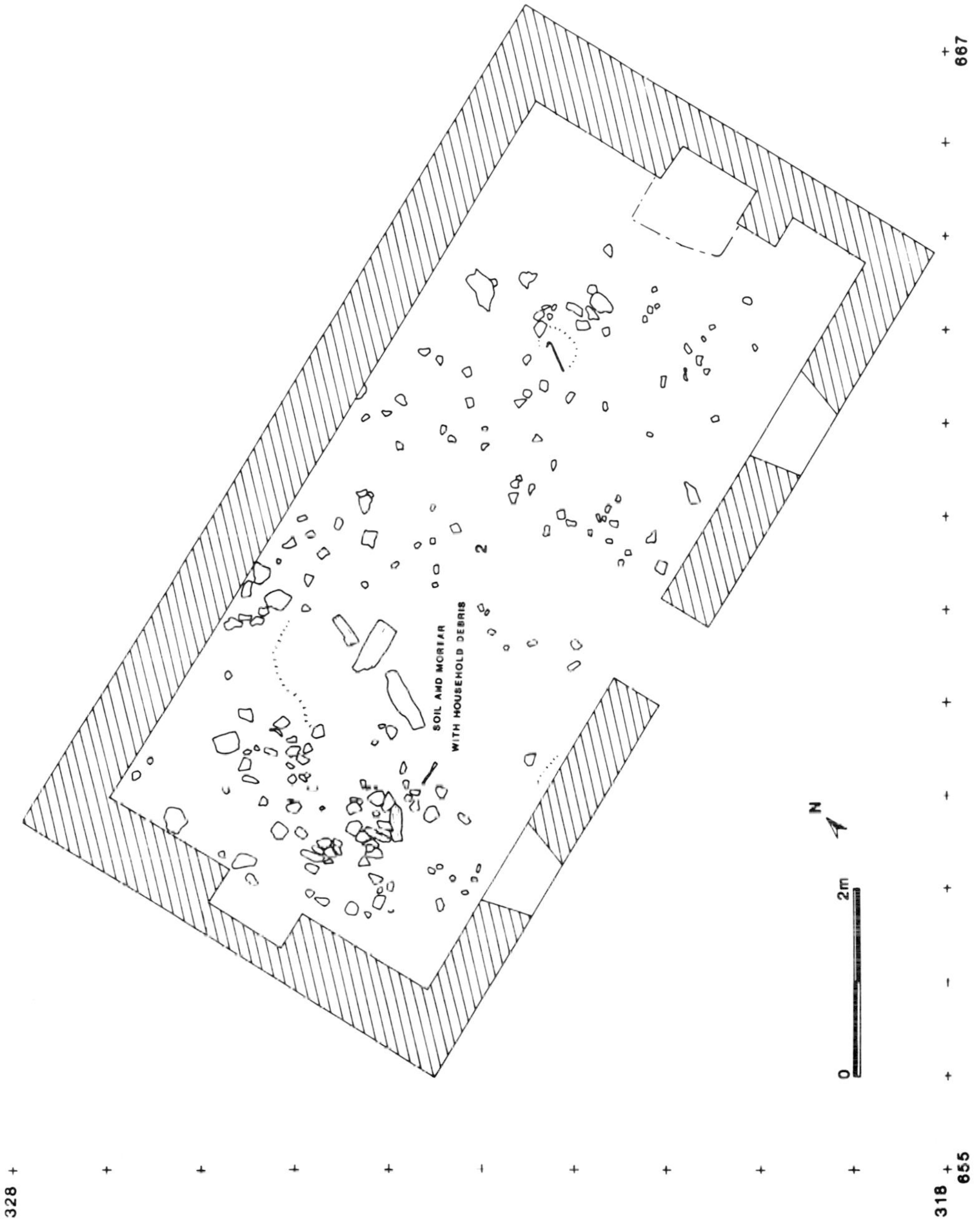

FIG. 13
House 6: Phase 7

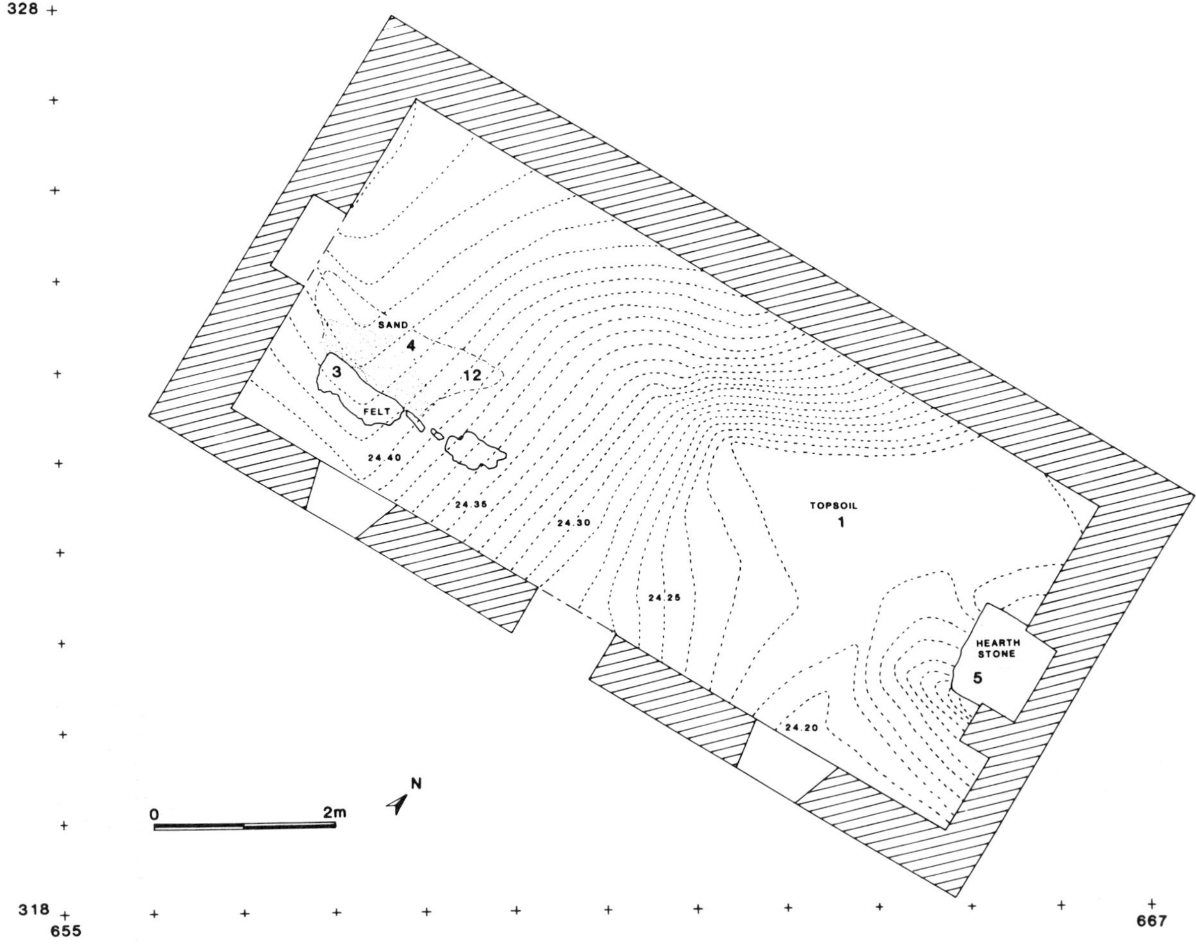

FIG. 14
House 6: Phases 8 and 9, and contours

roofing felt (3). The hearth slab (5) in the east room also appeared to have been reset. It lay over the mortar layer (2) of Phase 7, and had recently been used for a fire, the surface being covered with solidified tar.

Phase 9 (Fig. 14)

Apart from the east hearth slab (5), the interior of the house was covered by a very dark grey, gritty topsoil (1), which produced a fishing weight (sf. 2); a lead sheet (sf. 3); three lamp fragments (sfs 4, 243, 246); two copper-alloy boat nails (sf. 5); two bottles (sfs 8, 9); three leather offcuts (sfs 34–5, 37); and a bone button (sf. 10).

2:3 The Artefactual Evidence

Throughout this work objects specially recorded on site are discussed, with identifiable general finds, by their material type. Small finds are referred to in the text by a sf. number, and general finds by context number and phase number, e.g. gf. 1/9. Unless otherwise stated, the artefact reports are by the author. Where reports do not have catalogues, or have only partial catalogues, these are available in archive form.

FN	No.	F	M	T	R	BY	BS	D	S	FAB	MAN	SOOT
Phase 2												
216	1			*								*
221	1		*									
224	3		*							10		*
240	1											
241	1			*								
Phase 3												
195	2		*									*
196	3			*		c			s			*
199	1		*									
201	1											*
203	1		*									*
204	1	*										
Phase 8												
225	1									10		

KEY:

FN = finds number of catalogue entry
No. = number of sherds represented
F = fine; sherds less than 4mm thick
M = medium; sherds between 5–9mm thick
T = thick; sherds over 10mm thick
R = Rim type: p — plain; f — flattened; e — everted; i — inward sloping; o — outward sloping.
BY = Body: g — globular; c — corrugated; s — straight sided; n — necked
BS = Base: pa — plain, angled; fa — footed, angled; pr — plain, rounded
D = Decoration: co — undecorated cordon; dc — decorated cordon; ca — carination; r — rilling
S = Surface finish: b — burnished; s — smoothed; p — perforated
FAB = Fabric: a percentage indicates the presence of organic tempering
MAN = Manufacture: cl — coil (type undetermined); n — N-shaped coil; u — U-shaped coil; sl — slab-built
SOOT = * indicates that either the exterior, interior, or both surfaces of a sherd are sooted

TABLE 2
House 6: summary of coarse pottery

2:3:1 Coarse Pottery (A. MacSween)

Seventeen sherds of coarse pottery were recovered from Area 7, and all are body sherds. The majority are small and abraded and show signs of secondary burning. The pottery is all undecorated, and there is no indication of any surface treatment.

Microscopic examination shows that the fabric is very similar to that of sherds recovered at the House 8 site (3:3:1), where thin-section analysis of fifteen sherds indicated local production. The proportions of large inclusions present in the sherds from the Area 7 excavation are so small that temper addition is not suspected. Only four sherds (sfs 224, 225, 229, 231), three of them probably from the same vessel, have fragments in a proportion (10%) which indicates that temper was deliberately added.

Catalogue

Only the illustrated pottery is described in the catalogue; summary details of all pottery found from this area is contained in Table 2. The pottery in the table has been grouped by the phase to which it relates. If a vessel comprising sherds from different phases is represented, it is included in the phase in which the majority of finds were made. If there were the same number of finds from each phase, the vessel is included with the earliest phase represented.

Phase 3 (context 62)

sf. 196. Body sherd. Brown. Fabric — hard; quartz/black igneous inclusions, up to 1mm — natural. Slightly corrugated on exterior, smoothed on interior. Exterior and interior sooted. Th. 10mm. Fig. 15.

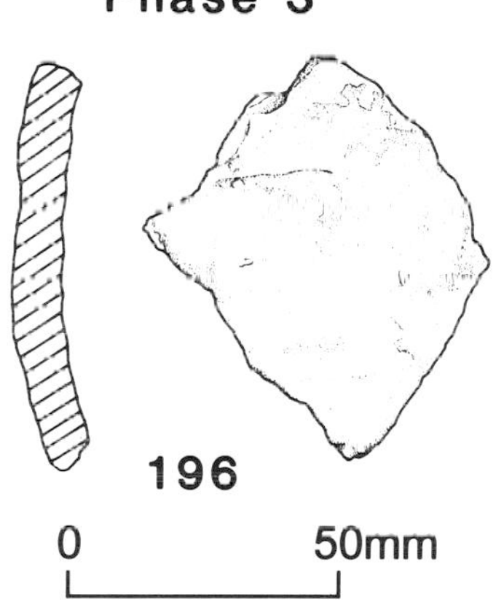

FIG. 15
House 6: coarse pottery (Phase 3). Scale 1:2

2:3:2 Crockery — Red and White Earthenware (H. Kelly)

The sherds from this area form a consistent whole as to dating since the vast majority of them come from the second half of the 19th century, most probably from its last quarter, and some way into the 20th century. The main exception to this are sherds of a small bowl with painted 'chrysanthemum'-type flowers on it, but hand-painted ware was very often treasured above all other pottery and kept on a shelf to be looked at rather than used.

The stoneware is all Bristol-glazed except for a few sherds which have a later, more glassy, type of glaze on them; this brings them close to 1900, if not slightly beyond it. The stoneware types are interesting as they would all have contained something useful: whisky or varnish in the case of the 'whisky jars', probably jam in the case of the 'jam jars', and the 'meat loaf jars' would also have contained some foodstuff.

The china is all of the cheapest variety, whose only decoration is painted gold lines, and is continental rather than British from the shape of the body. It is likely that it was one of the cheap lines which were being shipped over to Britain from the 1870s onwards to be sold for what they could get on the market.

Such goods destroyed a great part of the British industry, but the makers themselves did not survive either.

The sponge-printed ware all looks Scottish, but such wares are notoriously hard to attribute with any accuracy. The presence of so much grey sponge-printing and the 'Grecian' pattern points to a date after 1875, which is the beginning of the taste for grey-printed wares either in sponge or transfer printing. It coincides with the introduction of 'Japanese' patterns, but these seem to be missing from this group of sherds. Coloured spongeware pieces also fit in well with this dating.

A painted bowl with possible 'Persian Rose' pattern is found from the first half of the 19th century to the present day, and in several countries.

Rockingham glazed teapots, which are also represented, are widely made in both time and area, since they are made by the whiteware potteries as well as the firebrick potteries. The sherds present are too generalised to be of any help in attribution or dating.

There are a few sherds of redware, in marked contrast to the large numbers from the other excavated areas.

The most likely place of manufacture of most of the pieces represented here is Scotland, but the china looks like a European import, and the later pieces of stoneware could easily be of English origin.

2:3:3 Glass

A total of 861 fragments of glass were found, divided between Phases 2–4 and 6–9. The majority come from Phases 7 (495 fragments) and 9 (325 fragments), and were confined to only two layers — the overall mortary deposit (2) of Phase 7, and the topsoil (1) of Phase 9.

Catalogue

Phase 2

This phase produced a single 2mm thick fragment of window glass (gf. 19/2), which must represent disturbance.

Phase 3

Two fragments of 1mm window glass (gf. 62/3).

Phase 4

There are two bottle fragments — a sherd of light green bottle body, with a slight patination (gf. 61/4); and a thick green cylindrical bottle neck with a vertical mould scar (gf. 28/4).

Twelve fragments of clear glass (gf. 29/4) may have come from a phial or lamp.

One fragment of 2mm window glass (gf. 29/4) was also recovered.

Phase 6

A splinter of clear vessel glass (gf. 13/6) was found.

Phase 7

A total of 495 fragments of glass were recovered: 276 from bottles, 32 from jars, 23 fine 'vessel' sherds, 66 other containers, 1 closure, 88 pieces of sheet glass, and 9 unidentified flakes.

The bottles may be divided by form into round-based (208 sherds), round with flat sides (1) and rectangular (67).

The round-based bottle fragments represent approximately 44 vessels, in green (pale to turquoise, copper, and dark green), clear and amber glass. The green bottles appear to be for alcohol or other beverages. There are remains of eight bases, with rounded or flat resting points and slightly domed push-ups — one having a small mamelon and embossed letters 'AQ' (Fig. 16D). The majority of fragments are from the body, and some retain horizontal and vertical mould scars, with evidence for body/shoulder divisions. Shoulders are rounded, and necks cylindrical or slightly bulging, with some stretch marks and gas bubbles. Seven necks have a 2-piece finish with a string rim, principally V-shaped, with one instance of a straight-sided string. One V-shaped string rim has an internal screw thread (Fig. 16C) — a form used for glass and composition stoppers from the 1840s. Only three examples of embossing, using lettered plates, were found — the base 'AQ' (Fig. 16D) — dating to after 1821, and the letters 'WO . . .' from the shoulder of a thick, clear glass bottle, dating from the last third of the 19th century onwards. The round bottle with flat sides (sf. 68, Fig. 16A) has a flat indentation on the base with the embossed mark '00105' and an 'F' within a square. The neck is round-sectioned, with a straight finish, and is fire-polished.

The rectangular-sectioned bottle fragments represent approximately seven vessels, ranging in colour from clear, turquoise and pale blue to amber. The corners are generally chamfered or rounded. In two cases the sides are indented, and there is one instance of a slightly concave push-up. One body sherd in clear glass with a slight turquoise hue has a corrugated surface, and there are two examples of moulding — remnants of trailing, and the letters 'M' and 'O'. These vessels were most probably for pharmaceutical products, like liquid medicines and lotions.

The 32 jar fragments are from around seven containers. Although fragmentary, they appear to represent the common 'jam jar' form (which may have contained a range of foods), and two low food jars, possibly for extracts or pastes (Fig. 16E). They are of clear glass, one having a slight turquoise hue. The jar fragments include a short neck with a small out-turned rounded lip; a straight body with heel and shoulder division, a short rounded shoulder, short vertical neck and flanged rim with central horizontal mould scar; a rounded shoulder with 2-part neck and beaded, slightly flattened lip; a body/shoulder with 3-part mould scars, a low rounded shoulder and vertical neck; and a round faceted heel with shallow concave push-up, embossed numbers '604' (Fig. 16F), low rounded shoulder, short neck and bead rim.

Twenty-three sherds of clear glass are curved and extremely fine, and may have come from phials, or perhaps the globe or chimney of a lamp.

Sixty-six fragments of glass represent the remains of at least 15 other containers, although they are of such a size as to be undiagnostic of vessel type and function. They are principally of clear glass, some with a slight turquoise hue, and of varying thickness.

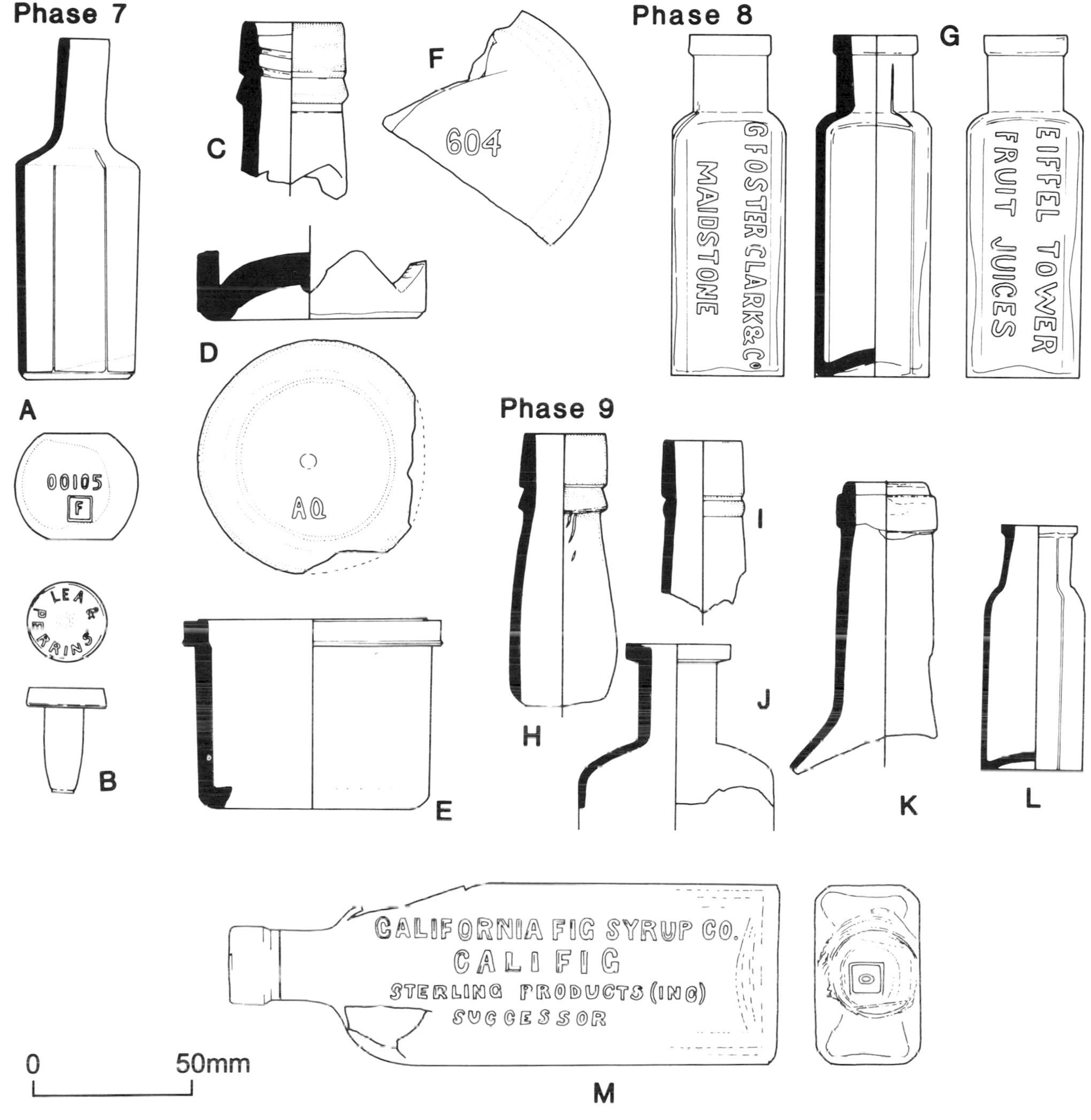

FIG. 16
House 6: glass (Phases 7–9). Scale 1:2

One fragment was probably produced in a 3-part mould, and another shows a horizontal mould scar.

The closure is a club sauce type (Fig. 16B), with a flat round head and round tapered shank, with cracked-off end, to fit a bottle with a 12mm diameter bore. The upper surface of the finial bears an embossed commercial mark — 'LEA & PERRINS'. This firm has produced Worcestershire Sauce, in Worcester, since 1837. Club sauce type stoppers were held in place by a wire tie or cap.

The 88 flat or sheet fragments range in thickness from 1mm (8 sherds), 2mm (71 sherds), 3mm (7 sherds), and 4mm (2 sherds). One incomplete 2mm fragment has been cut to a pane 37mm wide, with rounded corners; and a 3mm sherd has one press-moulded surface. A similar fragment was found in Phase 9.

It was not possible to categorise the nine splinters of glass which were also found in this phase.

Phase 8

This phase produced a complete juice bottle, seventeen other bottle fragments, and four fine ?lamp glass sherds.

The bottle (sf. 7 — Fig. 16G) is turquoise, and square with flat chamfered corners, a shallow circular press-up, vertical body, almost horizontal shoulder, broad round vertical neck finish, and patent lip. The body is embossed on two sides — 'G. FOSTER CLARK & Co/MAIDSTONE' and 'EIFFEL TOWER/FRUIT JUICES'. The bottle must have been produced after 1889, the date of the construction of the Eiffel Tower for the World Fair in Paris; G. Foster Clark produced a similar bottle for lemonade. The size, 106mm in height, suggests that it may have held essence.

The other bottle sherds comprise fifteen fragments of a copper green circular-sectioned type, with rounded shoulders and body/shoulder mould scar (gf. 4/8); a fragment of pale green neck finish by the shoulder (gf. 4/8); and a dark green shoulder (gf. 4/8).

The four very thin clear glass fragments (gf. 4/8) may be from a phial or lamp.

Phase 9

One complete bottle and 324 glass fragments were found in layers of this phase. The 325 items may be divided into 246 from bottles, 5 from jars, 19 from other containers, 15 possibly from lamps, 35 pieces of flat glass, and 5 unidentifiable flakes.

The 246 bottle pieces represent the remains of around 25 vessels, 141 from round bottles and 105 from rectangular or square forms. Seventy-one of the round bottle sherds are of clear glass, and 70 are pale, copper or dark green. The complete bottle (sf. 9 — Fig. 16L) is a clear round-based pharmaceutical type, with a shallow press-up, vertical body, rounded shoulder, short vertical neck and patent lip. There are vertical mould scars from the base to the finish. It would have been closed with a cork.

The majority of round bottle fragments are from the body, though there is evidence for four of the bottles having 2-part finishes, with V-shaped and applied flattened string rims (Fig. 16H, I, K). In addition, there is a dark green heel/resting point, and two instances of embossing — an 'm' and 's'. One body sherd shows a vertical mould scar, and another fragment has been heavily water-worn.

The square or rectangular bottle fragments comprise 75 in clear glass and 30 in amber. Sixty-two of the clear fragments form the majority of a pharmaceutical bottle (sf. 8 — Fig. 16M), a rectangular-sectioned bottle with flat chamfers, and a vertical body with an embossed panel on one side — 'CALIFORNIA FIG SYRUP CO./CALIFIG/ STERLING PRODUCTS (INC)/SUCCESSOR'. This type of Califig bottle dates from around the 1920s (D. Proctor, Sterling-Winthrop Products Division, pers. comm.). The feather-like pattern on the base probably represents a suction scar from an automatic machine, probably an Owen type.

Some of the amber glass comes from a bottle that was square, with rounded corners and shoulder, a round vertical neck, with a patent lip (Fig. 16J). This may be a pharmaceutical bottle, although the fragments found may represent more than one bottle. There is a fragment of amber glass embossed 'LO' within a triangle, and remnants of angled letters '[?T or K] ORY' — possibly chicory.

The five jar sherds are from three vessels, comprising a flat-based fragment; a thick body sherd; and three pieces from a vertical-sided jar, with a flat-sided and topped lip with an inner ridge, probably of the type closed with a metal cap. All five fragments are in clear glass.

The nineteen 'container' fragments represent approximately seven vessels. All are body sherds, and are clear, green and amber.

Fifteen fine, clear glass fragments may have come from phials or formed elements of a lamp.

Thirty-five fragments of window glass range in size from 1mm (3 sherds), 2mm (25 sherds), 3mm (6 sherds), and 4mm (1 sherd). One 3mm fragment has a moulded undersurface, similar to examples from Phase 7.

2:3:4 Copper Alloy

Buttons

Phase 7

sf. 12. Rimmed disc, with depressed centre pierced by 4 holes. The upper surface bears motto 'NE PLUS ULTRA', while depression on undersurface is enclosed within scored diamond design. Buttons of similar type are known, with marks including 'Excelsior' and 'Suspender', which may give a possible explanation of its function. Diam. 17mm. Fig. 17.

sf. 153. A 4-hole, sew-through type, dished, with traces of gilding. Upper surface has broad border, within which is ring of pellets. Undersurface bears punched mark of 'SMITH & WRIGHT LTD./BIRM'M'. Smith & Wright were established some time in the 18th century, and were, throughout their history, Birmingham based. The company now forms part of the London-based Firmin & Sons Group. Diam. 16mm. Fig. 17.

Discs

Phase 2

sf. 226. Small disc, punctured by roughly central hole. Diam. 15mm. Fig. 17.

Phase 4

sf. 180. ⅜" washer. Diam. 20mm. Fig. 17.

Tube

Phase 7

sf. 156. Copper-alloy tube, cut into broad ring. One end has beaten surface. L. 25mm, w. 13mm, th. 2mm. Fig. 17.

Knife

Phase 7

sf. 173. Heavy brass scale pierced by four holes, one still containing iron rivet. L. 109mm, w. 18–22mm, th. 2mm. Fig. 17.

Rods

Phase 5

sfs 185, 186. Two heavy rods or pins were used to secure concrete pad extension of west hearth to old earth floor. Sf. 186 is still attached to a piece of concrete. Sf. 185 — L. 140mm, diam. 16mm.

Nails

Phases 4–7

Nine copper-alloy nails were found, Phase 4 (sfs 150, 183, 192 — Fig. 17); Phase 5 (sf. 179); Phase 7 (sfs 19, 79 — Fig. 17, 106 — Fig. 17, 142, 172), conforming to six imperial sizes — 1½", 1¾", 2", 2¼", 3" and 3¾" (38–95mm). They are square-sectioned, and mainly pointed, although sf. 106 has a chisel-shaped tip. The head is either flat, 'T', or rose form.

Phase 9

Two rivet nails (sf. 5) were used for tying the strakes of a clinker-built boat (Fig. 17). The nails are each 3¾" (95mm) long, square-sectioned, with a round head. The other end has been burred over a concave rove ½" (13mm) in diameter.

Screw

Phase 7

sf. 104. One 1½" (38mm) countersunk wood screw, with slotted head, was found. Fig. 17.

Lamps

Phase 7

sf. 149. Small vertical wick lamp burner, comprising perforated plate with milled rim; decorated chimney seating; remnants of flat wick tube; three of original four plain round-ended chimney prongs; screw mount; and thumb wheel. Wheel is decorated with two-pronged four-arm cross. Plate shows slot, possibly for hinged deflector. Certainly post-1868, and if in combination with hinged deflector, post-1873. Plate diam. 43mm (1¾"), 22mm (⅞") screw mount, 13mm (½") wick tube. Fig. 18.

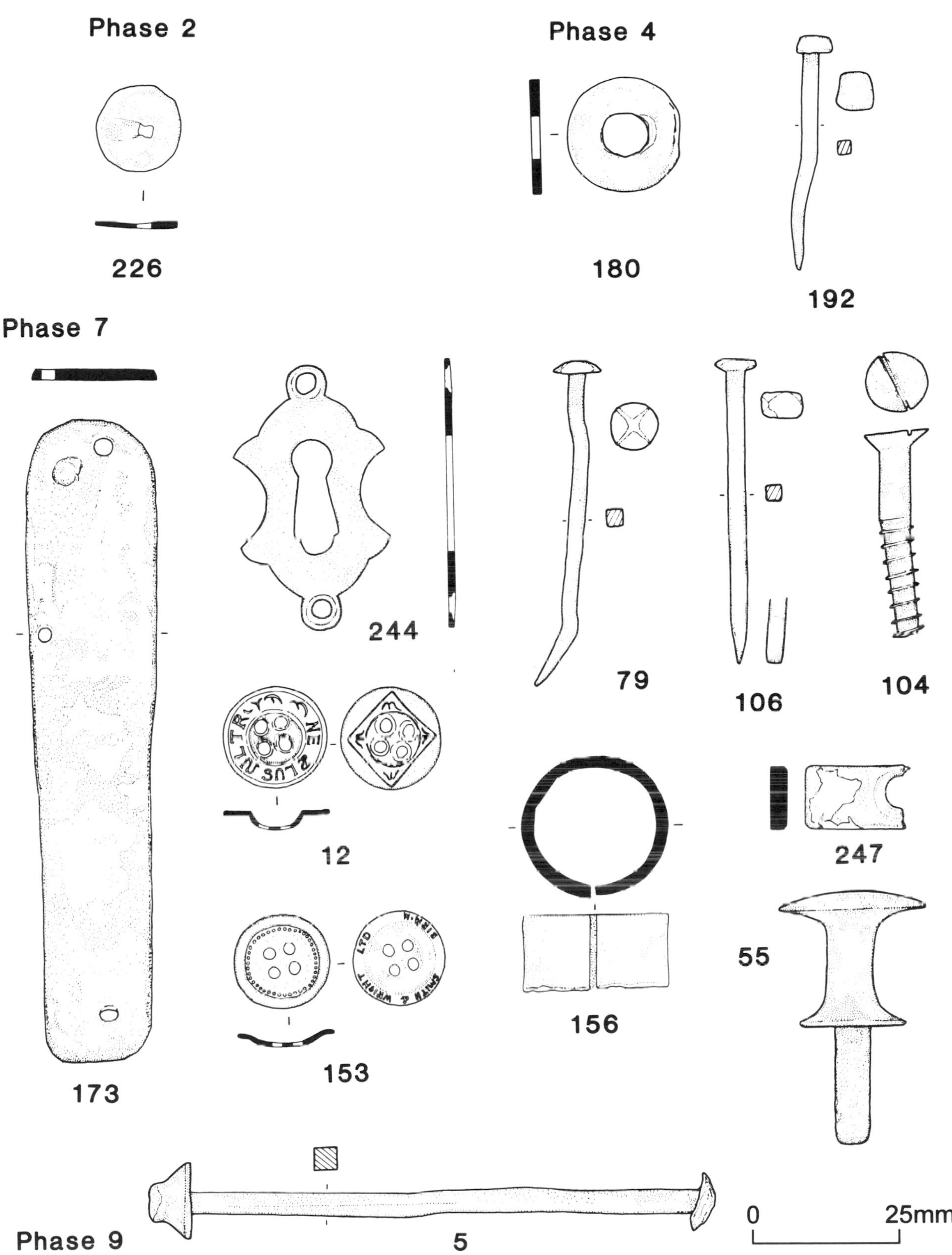

FIG. 17
House 6: copper alloy (Phases 2, 4, 7 and 9). Scale 1:1

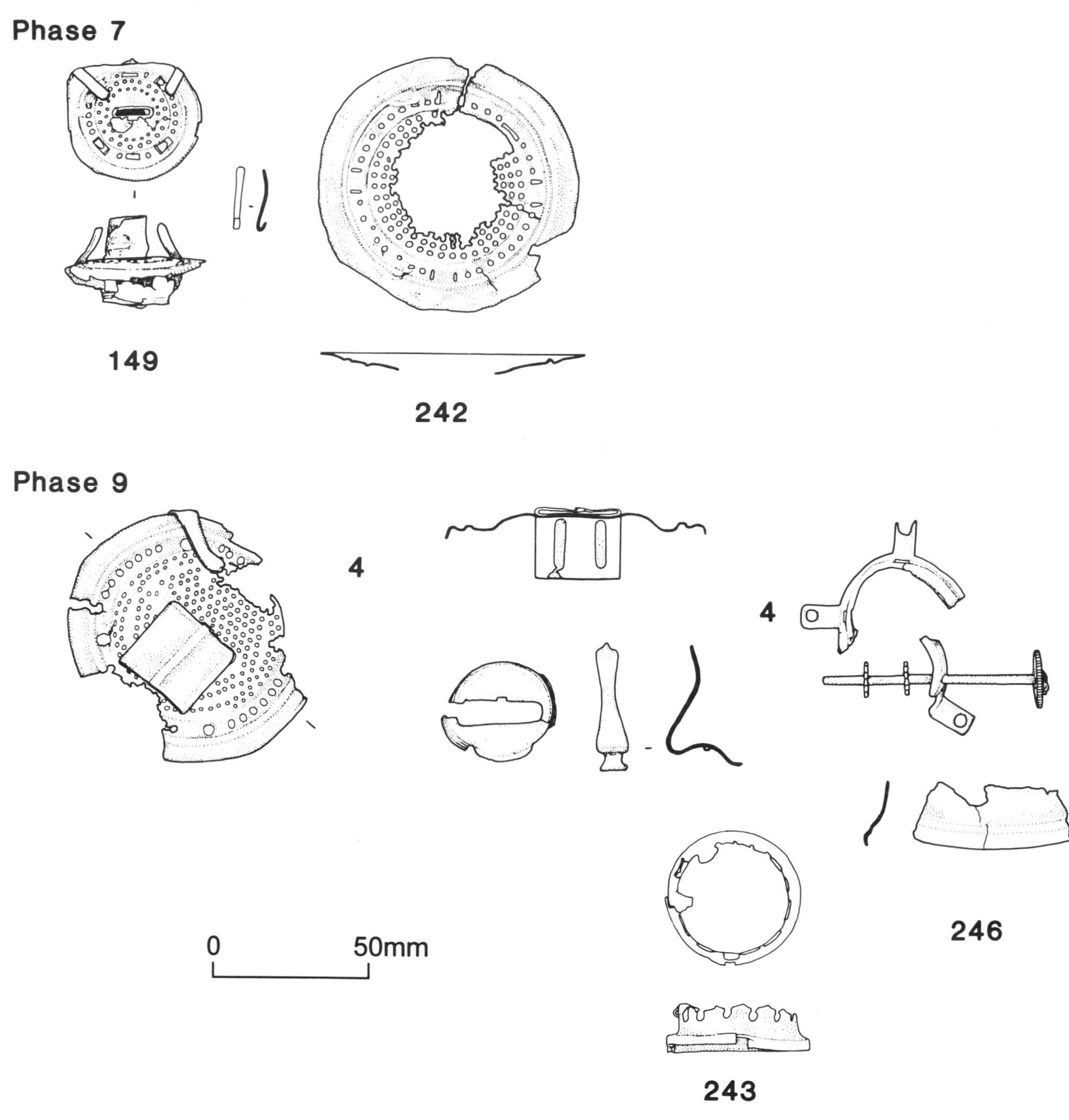

FIG. 18
House 6: copper-alloy lamps (Phases 7 and 9). Scale 1:2

sf. 242. Flattened perforated lamp plate, with damaged centre. Slot probably for hinged deflector. Similar size to sf. 4. Post-1873. Diam. 83mm. Fig. 18.

Phase 9

sf. 4. Seven fragments of vertical wick lamp burner, comprising perforated air intake-distributor plate; flat wick tube; screw mount to reservoir; thumb wheel wick adjuster with two spurred wick wheels; and two of original four chimney prongs. Prongs are similar in size to sf. 135a from House 8 (3:3:6), although that example has fretted chimney prongs, and finer holes to plate. No. 2 1" wick tube and No. 1 1" collar mount. No deflector. Maker's mark on thumb wheel — 'YOUNG'S/TIN/ WICK/COMET BURNER'. Some tin corrosion on adjuster rod. Post-1868. Plate diam. 83mm (3¼"). Fig. 18.

sf. 243. Three fragments of domed deflector, and decorated chimney seat from vertical wick lamp burner. Diam. 43mm, ht 15mm, th. 1mm. Fig. 18.

sf. 246. Fragment of deflector with rimmed base. L. 52mm, ht 20mm, th. 1mm. Fig. 18.

Furniture fittings

Phase 7

sf. 55. Finial with iron shank, perhaps knob from drawer or door. L. 43mm, diam. 24mm. Fig. 17.

sf. 244. Escutcheon with scalloped edges and two countersunk lugs for attachment. Found in west room and is possibly from a dresser drawer. L. 45mm, w. 25mm, th. 1mm. Fig. 17.

Miscellaneous

Phase 7

sf. 247. Small fragment of heavy copper bar or plate, with chamfered end. Pierced by one surviving hole. L. 18mm, w. 11mm, th. 3mm. Fig. 17.

2:3:5 Iron and Steel

Items of clothing

Phase 7

sf. 14. Corroded, 4-hole, sew-through type button, with slightly curved undersurface. Diam. 19mm. Fig. 20.

Cutlery

Phase 7

sf. 22. Incomplete spoon, with part of circular bowl and all-in-one handle, which is expanded near bowl. Fig. 20.

sf. 36. 4" square-ended bone table knife handle, with rounded edges and remnants of iron bolster. Tang has been secured into handle by means of fine pin. L. 103mm. Fig. 20.

sf. 174. Three fragments of 4-pronged fork, probably plated. Spatulate end of handle bears very worn elliptical stamp mark 'MADE IN GERMANY/BEST QUALITY'. The fork presumably post-dates the formation of the German Empire in 1871. The labelling of items with their country of origin followed the Merchandised Marks Act of 1887 (50 and 51 Vict. c.28) and American legislation of 1891. By the early years of the 20th century German cutlery was competing with Sheffield products. Fig. 22.

Lids and containers

Phase 7

sf. 16. Two fragments of domed cast-iron vessel lid, with seat and moulded knob. Probably from a kettle or small cooking pot. Max. diam. 130mm (6"). Fig. 20.

sf. 60. Fragment of cast-iron vessel with slight vertical rim. Mouth diam. 127mm (5"). Fig. 20.

sf. 248. Fragments of container for Andrews Liver Salts. Artwork consists of dark blue background with light green lettering and border. This product was originally marketed in about 1900, though the artwork seems to date from around the 1920s (D. Proctor, Sterling-Winthrop Products Division, pers. comm.). Fig. 22.

gf. 2/7. Corroded fragment of enamelled container.

Phase 9

gf. 1/9. Fragment of enamelled container.

gf. 1/9. Corroded fragment of kettle lid. Diam. 76mm (3").

Tools

Phase 7

sf. 109. Cold chisel, with round head and octagonal-sectioned shank. Normally used in rough working cold metal. L. 192mm (7½"), head diam. and blade w. 26mm (1"). Fig. 20.

sf. 119. Heavily corroded fragment of tube, ?haft of spade. L. 108mm, diam. 28mm.

sf. 138. Large, incomplete iron hook, rectangular sectioned. L. 146mm, w. 8mm, th. 7mm. Fig. 20.

Phase 9

gf. 1/9. Corroded cold chisel with round head and round-sectioned shank. L. 159mm, head diam. 30mm, blade w. 22mm.

gf. 1/9. Corroded drill bit, now 13mm (½") diam.

gf. 1/9. Corroded knife handle, slightly curved, possibly with folding blade, and two fragments of bone facing with iron pins. Surviving l. 60mm, w. 23mm, th. 16mm.

gf. 1/9. Corroded blade and finger loop from pair of scissors. Surviving l. 158mm, max. blade w. 16mm, loop 42 x 29 x 6mm.

Locks and keys

Phase 7

sf. 20. Heart-shaped padlock with simple plate escutcheon, but no cover. Padlocks were certainly in use in the 15th century, but the heart-shaped form came in during the 18th century. Willenhall in the West Midlands became the centre of the British lock-making industry. The internal mechanism has, unfortunately, disintegrated. W. 60mm, ht 94mm, max. th. 26mm. Fig. 20.

sf. 23. Padlock key with missing bow. Hollow stem. L. 40mm, ht 18mm. Fig. 20.

Handles, fittings and fastenings

Phase 7

sf. 13. Bedstead caster with glazed pottery wheel, from east room. Ht 100mm, shaft diam. 50mm, wheel diam. 39mm. Fig. 20.

sf. 73. Two fragments of round sectioned wrought-iron handle. Upper end is beaten to produce an attachment plate, while

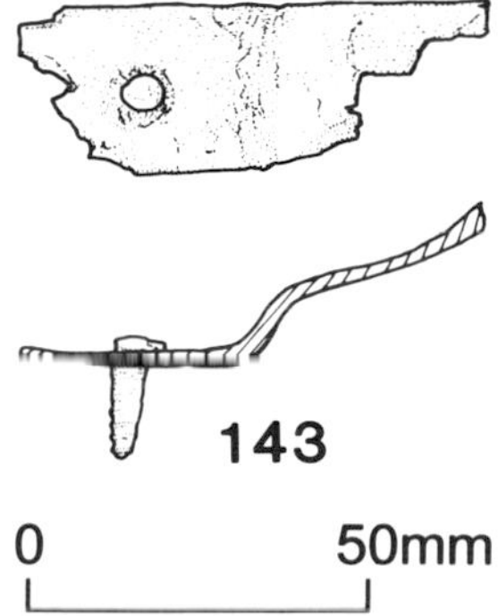

FIG. 19
House 6: iron (Phase 2). Scale 1:2

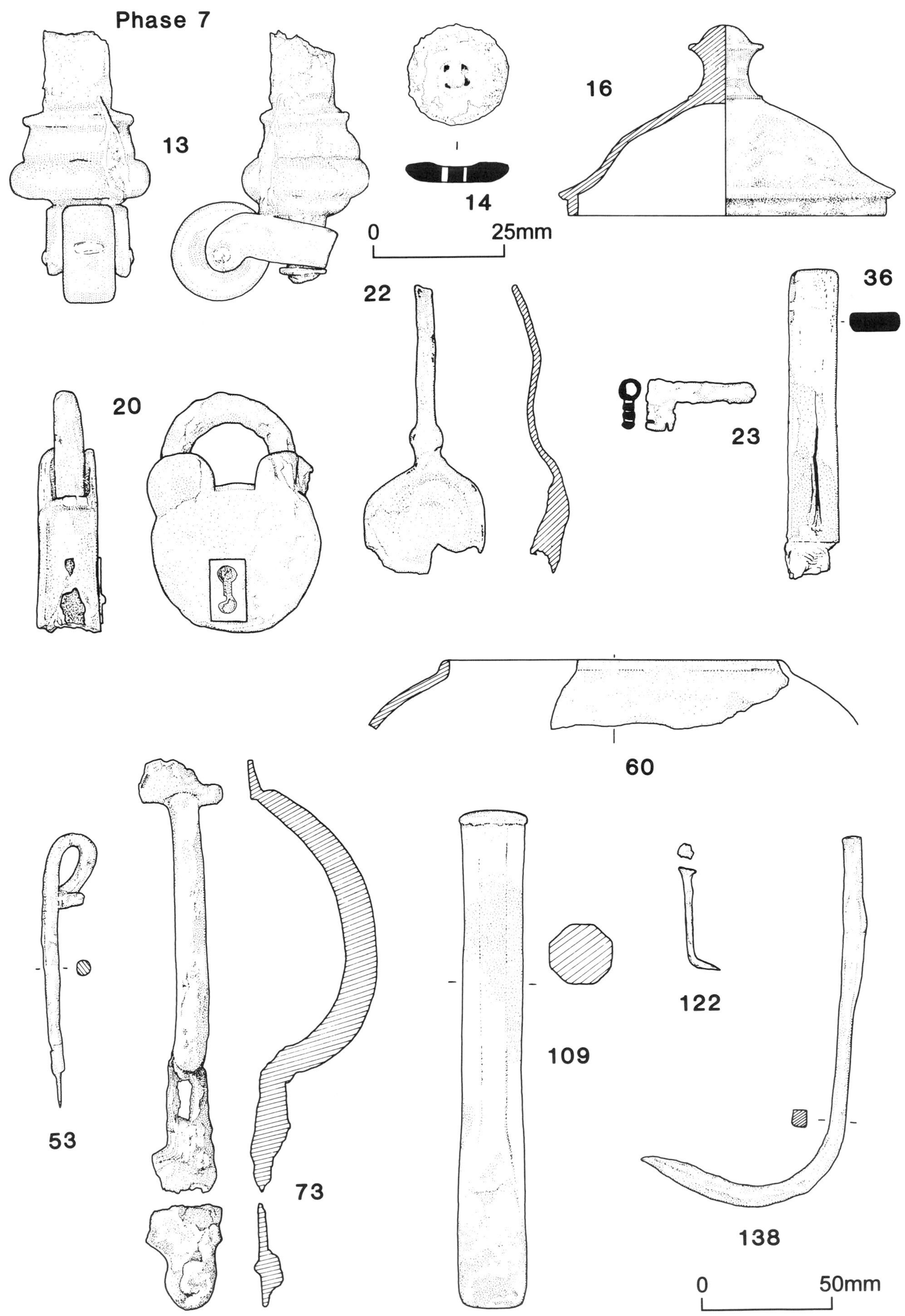

FIG. 20
House 6: iron (Phase 7). Scale 1:2; sf. 14 1:1

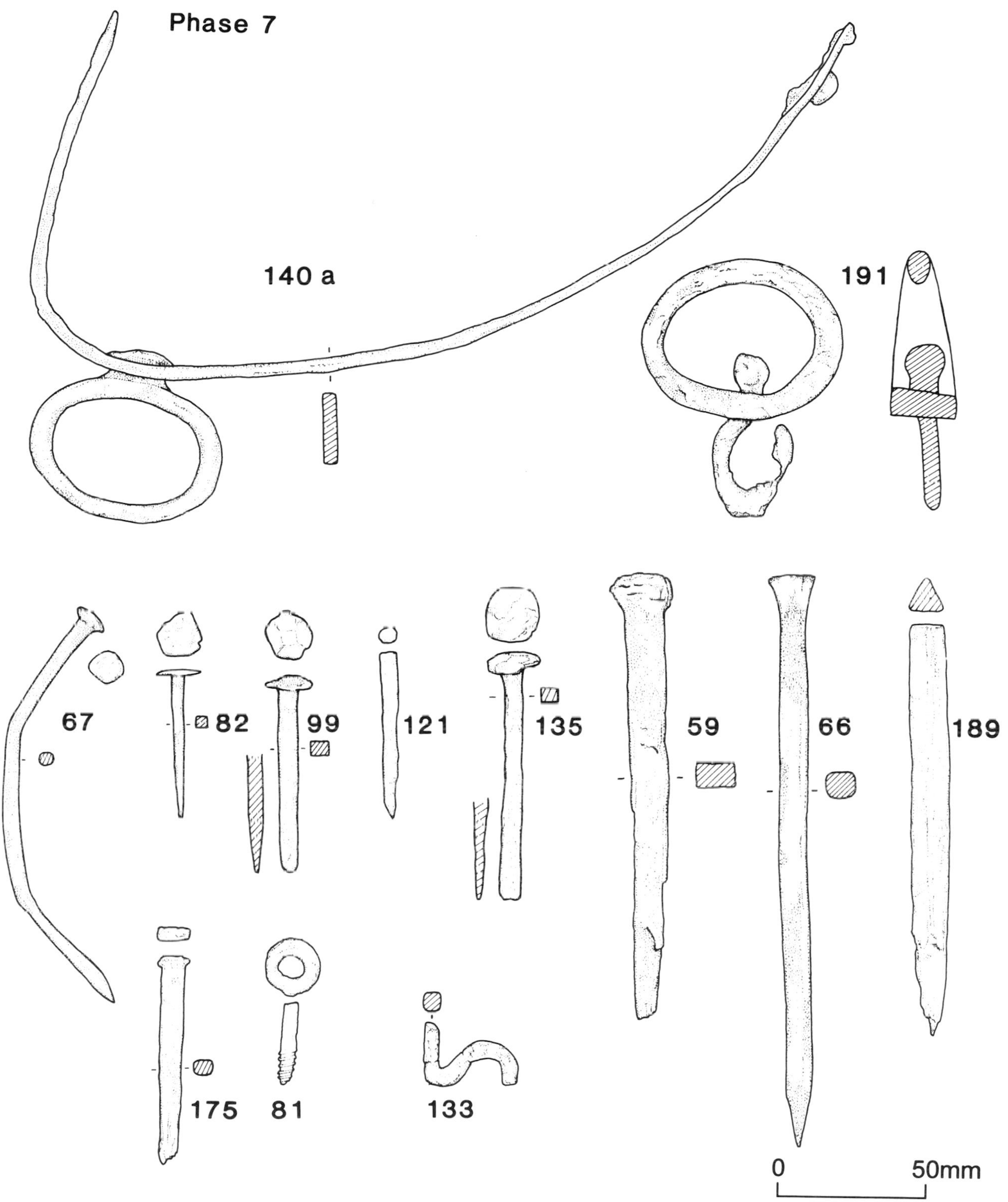

FIG. 21
House 6: iron (Phase 7). Scale 1:2

lower part has been beaten into a bar, pierced by an elliptical hole, and the end flattened into a moulded attachment plate. L. 166mm (incomplete), handle diam. 14mm. Fig. 20.

sf. 81. ¾" screw eye. L. 46mm, ring ext. diam. 18mm. Fig. 21.

sf. 101. Corner plate, comprising bar with two ridges on underside, and attached thin metal plate forming a corner. There are two support bars, and plate is edged with copper-alloy band with two semi-circular flaps. Corner plate is pierced by nail. L. 118mm, w. 25mm, ht 32mm. Fig. 22.

sf. 105. Incomplete plate tapering to round attachment. L. 108mm, max. w. 18mm. Fig. 22.

sf. 115. Part of corroded elliptical-sectioned handle. L. 59mm, w. 10mm, th. 9mm.

sf. 137. Incomplete curved rod, ?handle. L. 118mm, diam. 8mm.

sf. 140b. Rod ?handle and moulded plate with two holes for attachment. Plate l. 48mm, w. 36mm, th. 3mm. Rod diam. 8mm.

gf. 2/7. Stud securing ends of small leather flap, looped around remains of iron ring. Stud top marked 'CLIMAX/PATENT'. No patent number. Stud diam. 10mm, th. 7mm.

gf. 2/7. Catch bar from cupboard door. L. 52mm, w. 13mm, th. 6mm, central screw hole diam. 4mm.

gf. 2/7. Bedstead caster with glazed pottery wheel, as sf. 13.

Phase 9

gf. 1/9. Pot or cauldron handle. Rod, with looped ends, one having a spur. Diam. *c.* 267mm, ht *c.* 220mm, rod th. 6mm.

gf. 1/9. Incomplete strap handle. Surviving l. 107mm, w. 26mm, ht 44mm.

gf. 1/9. Fragment of 6" pipe or down-comer. Diam. 153mm.

Nails

Seventy-one samples of nails were recorded as small finds. The majority uncovered are of wrought iron, and have undergone serious decay in the soil. The information recoverable is, therefore, limited.

Most of the nails were found in Phase 7, in the east room. Ten nails have traces of wood in the corrosion products — sfs 29, 61, 65, 69, 76, 83, 89, 132, 165, 176, and may represent nails from the roof carcase, ceiling or floor. It was not possible to tell if any were specifically brads.

Of those nails which were identifiable, three are rose-head cut nails (sfs 99 — Fig. 21, 135 — Fig. 21, 154). They are square-

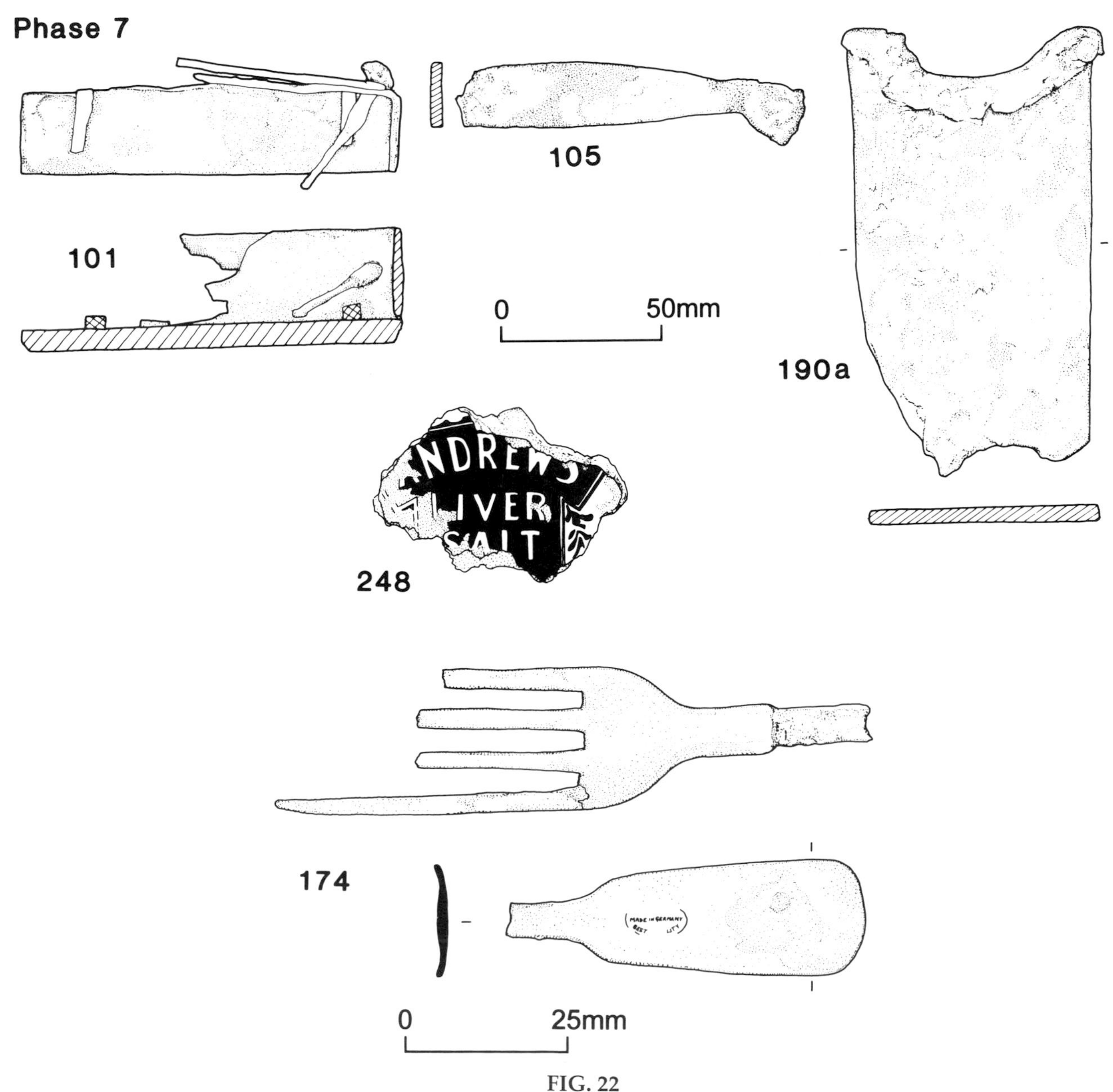

FIG. 22
House 6: iron (Phase 7). Scale 1:2; sfs 174 and 248 1:1

sectioned and tapered, with a rounded end, and ranging from 1¾" to 3¼" (43–83mm) in length. These nails are heavy duty, used for major structural work.

Ten complete nails (sfs 24, 31, 41–2, 50, 71, 80, 82 — Fig. 21, 97, 170) are of the large head clout variety, generally used for attaching roof covering. They are 1½", 1¾" and 2" (38, 43, 51mm) long, with square-sectioned shank, pointed end, and ½" (13mm) diameter flat head. All have been galvanised. One apparently ungalvanised incomplete clout (sf. 158) was also found. Two square-sectioned pointed shanks (sfs 25, 32) may have been from clouts.

One complete 6" (153mm) wire nail (sf. 67 — Fig. 21), and a rod which might have been part of the shank of another (sf. 63) were found.

A complete 2" (51mm) fine round-headed wire nail with the end bent (sf. 122 — Fig. 19), and two incomplete shanks (sfs 44, 46) from Phase 7 would have been used for general woodworking purposes.

One iron nail has a T-head (sf. 175 — Fig. 21) and sf. 121, a 2¼" (58mm) round-sectioned nail, has no head (Fig. 21).

Nails were made by hand up to the 17th century, but there is evidence that there was equipment for splitting nail rods at an iron mill in Saugus, Massachusetts about 1645. The first to form cut nail blanks from cold iron was believed to be Jeremiah Wilkinson of Cumberland, Rhode Island, in about 1777. The heads were formed by gripping the slit metal in a vice and upsetting the head with a hammer.

About this time Jacob Perkins of Newbunyport, Massachusetts, invented a nail cutting machine — small sections of nail plate were fed into the machine by hand, the machine cutting off short tapering lengths of iron, then forming the heads. By 1873 there were ten major nail mills on the Ohio river making 3½ million kegs of nails per year, approximately 190 billion nails. Nails had been made from wire during this period, the first recorded being a French invention about 1840.

The first nail machine to make nails from wire was produced in the USA in 1851 by Morton and Bremner, to a design by William Hassell.

The decline of the cut nail was brought about by the introduction of the Bessemer steel-making process. A combination of good quality steel wire, and the introduction of an improved nail machine by John Hassell, resulted in steel wire nail production exceeding cut nail production by 1888, and from then on the decline was rapid.

Spikes

Phase 7

sf. 59. Rectangular-sectioned form with square head. L. 150mm (incomplete), head 18mm sq. Fig. 21.

sf. 66. Round countersunk head, round-sectioned shank tapering to point. L. 194mm, head diam. 16mm. Fig. 21.

sf. 74. Rectangular-sectioned spike with T-shaped head. L. 158mm, shank 9 x 7mm.

sf. 139. Incomplete, heavily corroded wrought-iron spike. L. 140mm, w. 10mm, th. 8mm.

sf. 141b. Spike found with strap sf. 141a. L. 80mm (incomplete), diam. 6mm.

sf. 189. Triangular-sectioned type. L. 140mm (incomplete), w. 12mm. Fig. 21.

Plates, straps, rings and loops

Phase 2

sf. 143. Three fragments of thin strip, probably roof stay. W. 26mm (1"). Fig. 19.

Phase 7

sf. 53. Thin rod with end bent into loop. L. 105mm (incomplete), diam. 5mm. Fig. 20.

sf. 103. Very corroded thin plate frag. L. 45mm, w. 38mm, th. 0.5mm.

sf. 140a. Incomplete strap from container, with outer elliptical loop handle, and remnants of attached rivetted strap. L. 434mm, w. 24mm, th. 3mm. Loop 67 x 48mm. Fig. 21.

sf. 141a. Flat band, with two holes for attachment. L. 142mm (incomplete), w. 31mm, th. 3mm.

sf. 190a. Incomplete heavy plate with U-shaped beaten end. L. 137mm, max. w. 82mm, th. 5mm. Fig. 22.

sf. 190b. Incomplete band/ring, fused by corrosion products to sf. 190a. Now elliptical. L. 62mm, w. 48mm, ht 18mm, th. 2mm.

sf. 191. Elliptical ring with attached swivel hook. Ring L. 67mm, w. 52mm, th. 8-22mm. Hook max. l. 58mm. Fig. 21.

Rods/wire

Phase 7

sf. 64. Bent incomplete length of fine rod/wire. L. 348mm, diam. 3mm.

sf. 133. Small S-shaped fragment of bent rod. Uncertain function. L. 38mm, diam. 5mm. Fig. 21.

sf. 144. Bent rod/wire. Overall l. 167mm, diam. 3mm.

2:3:6 Lead

Catalogue

Phase 7

sf. 245. Thin folded sheet. L. 31mm, w. 13mm, th. 0.5mm. Fig. 23.

Phase 9

sf. 2. Lead fishing weight, comprising bar, tapered and notched at both ends, with hole close to each end. This is probably for a hand line, enabling the baited end to be thrown out from a boat or from on the shore. The line would presumably have run through the two holes and be wrapped around from end to end, resting in the notches when not in use (A. Credland, Town Docks Museum, Hull, pers. comm.). L. 110mm, w. 20mm, th. 15mm, wt 235g. Fig. 23.

sf. 3. Sheet with holes for securement round the edges. It may have been forced off the surface to which it had been attached. One edge is folded over, and the corners are folded or bent. L. 150mm, w. 108mm, th. 1mm. Fig. 23.

2:3:7 Zinc

Twenty-three zinc nails were recorded as small finds, all from Phase 7 — sfs 33, 40, 43, 47, 48, 70, 78, 84 — Fig. 23, 91, 95–6, 118, 124, 128–30, 135, 152, 155, 159, 162, 168, 171; and fragments of eight others were noted as general finds (gfs 1/9, 2/7, 29/4). The majority are damaged, but at least two sizes are indicated — 1¼" (30mm) and 1½" (38mm), with a ⅜" (9mm) head. Examination by Mr R. Lomas of the Nail Department of Rylands Whitecross Ltd (Warrington) showed that the heads had been upset in a split die or set, the underside of the head showing the fins or flash where the two halves came together. The taper could have been pressed by the die or swaged on in a separate operation before heading; the taper on the nail is more pronounced on one side. The nails are of the clout variety. Moulded letters 'V M' were noted on two heads (e.g. sf. 84 — Fig. 23). It is just conceivable

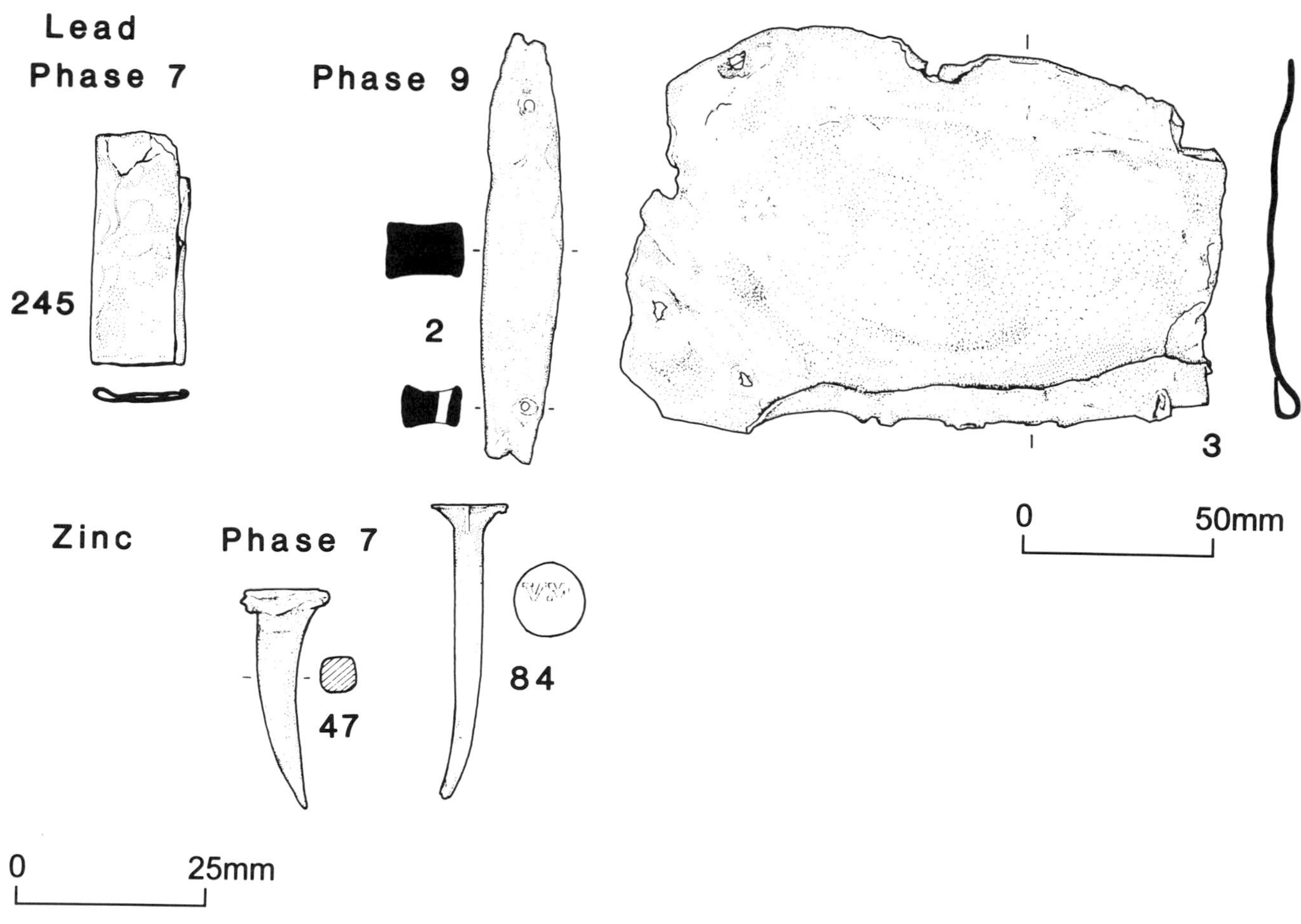

FIG. 23
House 6: lead (Phases 7 and 9) and zinc (Phase 7). Scale 1:1; sfs 2 and 3 1:2

that the 'V M' may be associated with a fragmentary commercial mark MONTAGNE on a piece of zinc roof sheeting found earlier on Hirta (Glasgow Museum, 622). One 1¼" nail retains traces of zinc around the head, while others have tar on the head.

2:3:8 Clay Pipe

Three fragments were found.

Catalogue

Phase 4

sf. 193. Stem mouth-piece. Diam. 6mm. Fig. 26A.

sf. 194. Part of the back of pipe bowl with mould-imparted letters 'TW' in an ellipse. This may be the mark of the Edinburgh pipemakers Thomas White (1823–67) or Thomas White & Co. (*c.* 1880–82); though it is a type also used by D. McDougall & Co. of Glasgow. The latter firm, a partnership of Donald McDougall and Campbell Rodger, emerged in 1871 following the bankruptcy and death of the pipemaker Duncan McDougall (Gallagher 1987, 67–8). The firm became a limited company in 1909 and continued until 1965. The 'TW' was certainly used by the company around 1900. Fig. 26B.

Phase 7

gf. 2/7. Stem fragment with impressed mark on one side 'SCOTLAN(D)'. Fig. 26C.

2:3:9 Plaster

Catalogue

Phase 7

sf. 114. One piece of wallplaster with streak of dark blue paint or colour.

2:3:10 Stone (J.R. Senior)

Catalogue

Phase 2

This phase produced the greatest quantity of stones — 23 small finds and 55 general finds, all from context 19.

sf. 209. Burnt, reddened, shattered pebble in fine-grained miarolitic granophyre from the Conachair-Oiseval Complex.

sf. 210. ?Dolerite with iron stains and coating.

sf. 211. Hammer stone with two worked ends in grey-green fine-grained dolerite with granophyre veinlets, from margins of the Mullach Sgar Complex.

sf. 212. Worked pebble in grey-green fine-grained Mullach Sgar dolerite with granophyre veinlets. Fig. 24.

sf. 213. Burnt, pink-coloured, fire-shattered pebble in medium-grained Mullach Sgar dolerite.

sf. 214. Burnt, fire-fractured pebble in reddened miarolitic Conachair-Oiseval granite with drusy cavities.

sf. 215. Fragment of pebble in grey-green fine-grained dolerite of the Mullach Sgar Complex.

sf. 217. Worked pebble in grey-green fine-grained Mullach Sgar dolerite. Fig. 24.

sf. 218. Burnt, reddened, fire-shattered pebble in medium-grained diorite. This pebble has been extensively and repeatedly burnt.

sf. 220. Fragment of 'blade' in medium-grained porphyritic dolerite from the Mullach Sgar Complex. Reddened by leached materials from a fire source, but not burnt. Fig. 24

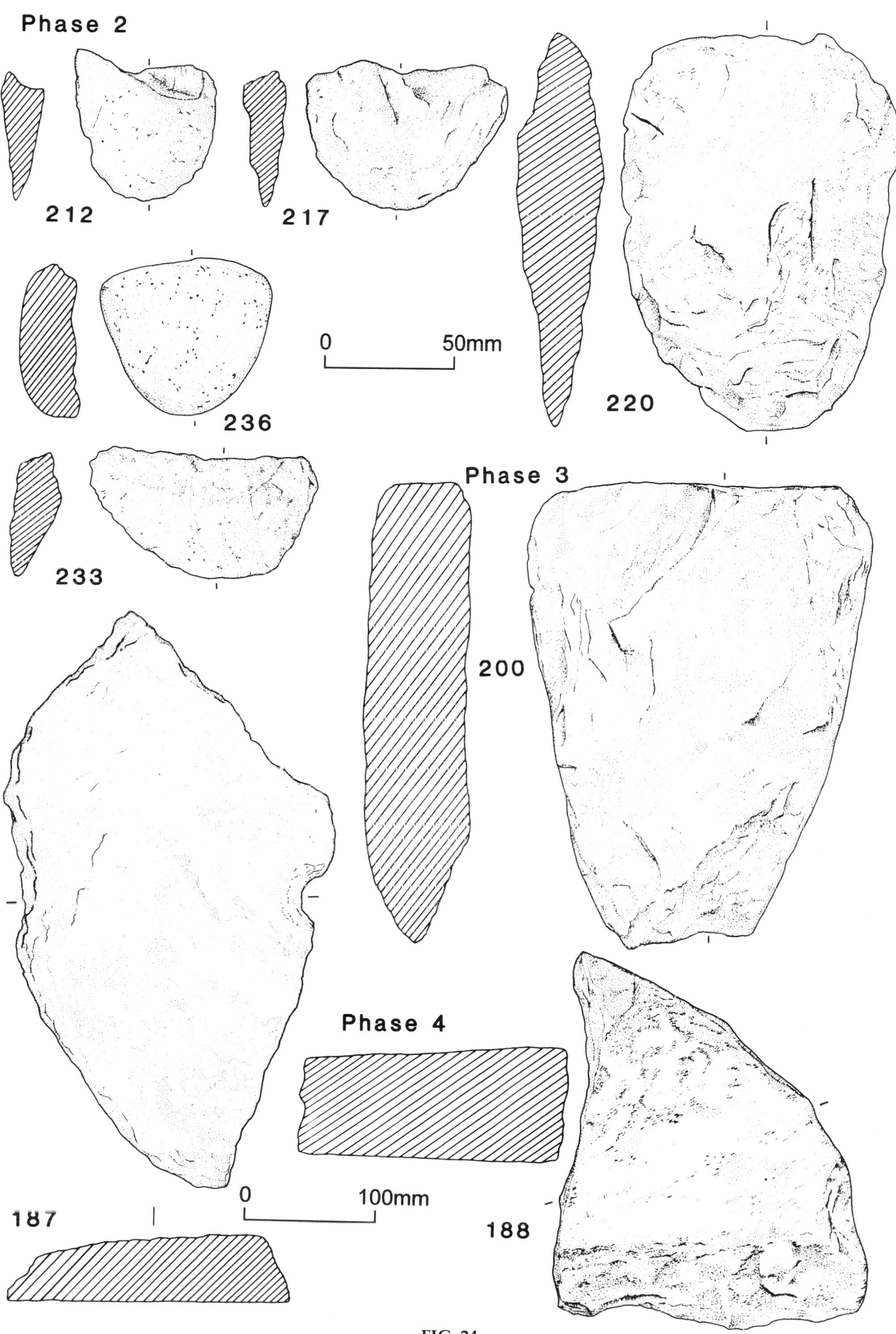

FIG. 24
House 6: stone (Phases 2–4). Scale 1:2; sf. 187 1:4

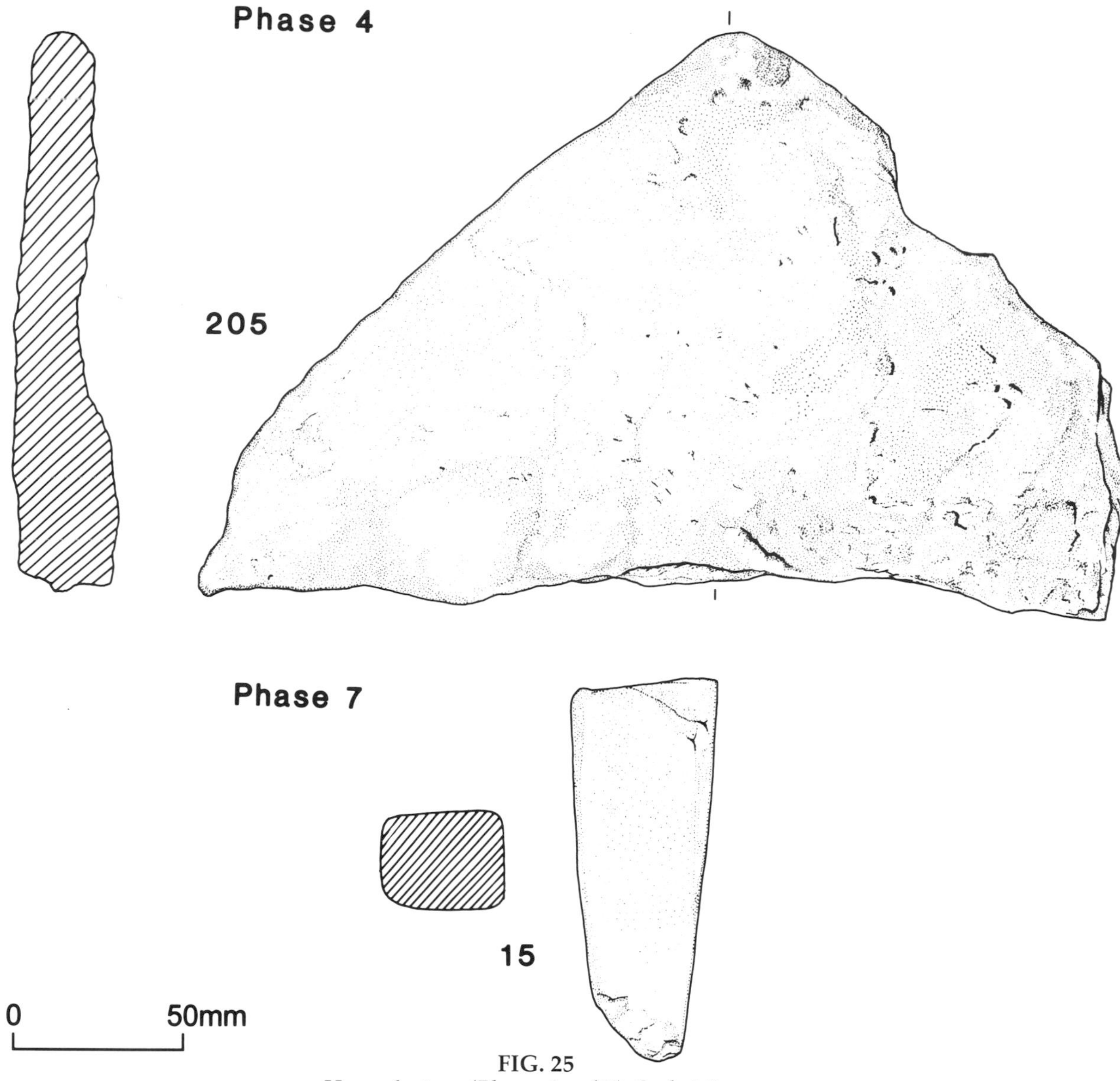

FIG. 25
House 6: stone (Phases 4 and 7). Scale 1:2

sf. 222. Burnt, reddened, fire-shattered biotite diorite pebble.

sf. 223. Porphyritic dolerite from the Mullach Sgar Complex with secondary iron pan coatings.

sf. 227. Burnt, fire-shattered pebble in pink-coloured, fine-grained diorite with coarse biotite diorite veins.

sf. 228. Fire-shattered, reddened pebble fragment in grey-green fine-grained dolerite from the Mullach Sgar Complex.

sf. 230. Burnt, fire-shattered pebble in pink medium-grained biotite diorite from the Mullach Sgar Complex.

sf. 232. Pebble in fine-grained grey-green dolerite with granophyre veinlets from the Mullach Sgar Complex.

sf. 233. Worked pebble in grey-green fine-grained Mullach Sgar dolerite with granophyre veinlets. Fig. 24.

sf. 234. Clinker/coke from coal fire.

sf. 235. Burnt, reddened, fire-shattered pebble in medium-grained diorite.

sf. 236. Grey-green fine-grained porphyritic dolerite from the Mullach Sgar Complex. Worked, with unnatural scratches and abrasions. Fig. 24.

sf. 237. Burnt, fire-fractured fragment of pebble in reddened medium-grained diorite from the Mullach Sgar Complex.

sf. 238. Burnt, pink-coloured, fire-shattered fragment in Mullach Sgar medium-grained diorite.

sf. 239. Burnt, reddened, fire-shattered pebble in fine-grained porphyritic Mullach Sgar dolerite.

General finds

a. Two samples of basaltic material of uncertain origin.

b. Three pieces of medium-grained gabbro, two certainly from the Western Gabbro Complex, the third of uncertain source.

c. Four coarse porphyritic dolerite pieces, and 20 fragments of fine and medium-grained dolerite from the Mullach Sgar Complex.

d. Five fine-grained dolerite pieces, four with granophyre veinlets, from the margins of the Mullach Sgar Complex.

e. One medium-grained fragment of diorite with granophyre veins from margins of the Mullach Sgar Complex.

f. A flake of hybrid diorite/granophyre from same complex.

g. Six pieces of granite/granophyre from the Conachair-Oiseval Complex.

h. Two fragments of porphyritic rhyolite, one from same source as g., the other of uncertain source.

i. Quartz vein material, from same source as g.

j. Weathered marble fragment of ?Durness limestone.

k. Five fragments of fine-grained sandstone of uncertain origin.
l. A lump of sand-sized grains cemented with iron pan and three unidentifiable pieces.

Phase 3

sf. 200. Stone 'blade' in grey-green fine-grained porphyritic dolerite from the Mullach Sgar Complex. Fig. 24.

Phase 4

sf. 187. Large quern fragment in biotite mica schist. Probably Moinian (Late Pre-Cambrian) material imported from Western Scotland. Fig. 24.

sf. 188. Quern fragment in quartzo-feldspathic layer in imported biotite mica schist, from a source on the west coast of Scotland. Fig. 24.

sf. 205. Large curved stone in porphyritic hybrid rock, mixed Conachair-Oiseval granite and Mullach Sgar diorite. Prominent alkali feldspar phenocrysts. It seems to have been worked into rectangular shape (now broken), and may have been slightly burnt as the feldspars now a reddish colour. Conceivably a plough stone. Fig. 25.

sf. 206. An intensely fire-reddened fine-grained gabbro from the Western Gabbro Complex.

General finds

a. Burnt fragment of fine-grained (indeterminate) basic rock with granophyre veinlets, probably from margins of the Mullach Sgar Complex.
b. Fragment of coral material, either recent or fossil, and imported.

Phase 7

sf. 15. Broken medium-grained micaceous sandstone artefact with four worked faces, probably Upper Carboniferous, from mainland Scotland. Fig. 25.

sf. 123. Hammer stone with two worked ends (not smoothed) in medium-grained dark porphyritic dolerite with granophyre veinlets at one end. Mullach Sgar Complex.

General finds

a. Corroded marble, possibly Cambrian Durness limestone.

b. Upper Carboniferous Coal Measures siltstone with fossil plant debris, possibly discarded contaminant from imported coal, possibly from the Central Valley of Scotland.

c. Quartzo-feldspathic veinstone from the Conachair-Oiseval Complex.

d. Percussion flake of fine-grained basic igneous rock, probably basalt of uncertain origin.

e. Fine-grained granophyre pebble from the Conachair-Oiseval Complex.

f. Low grade metamorphic rock, spotted hornfels, sawn and worked on four faces, possibly from a mainland source, and probably used as good-quality whetstone for woodworking tools. Associated with fragment a. in Phase 9.
g. Nine pieces of imported Ballachulish Slate.

Phase 8

Four general finds were taken.

a. Smoke-blackened coarse-grained miarolitic granite from the Conachair-Oiseval Complex.
b. Three pieces of imported Ballachulish Slate.

Phase 9

Eighteen general finds were taken.

a. Low grade metamorphic rock, spotted hornfels, sawn and worked on four edges, main face broken on natural cleavage planes. Part of a good-quality whetstone, associated with fragment f. in Phase 7.
b. Tar and smoke-blackened coarse gabbro, with feldspars burnt to pink colour. From the Western Gabbro Complex. Has been in vicinity of coal fire.
c. Medium-grained gabbro, ?from the West Gabbro Complex.
d. Small weathered clast of concentrated melanocratic minerals, ?from the Western Gabbro.
e. Fine-grained dolerite with granophyre vein from margins of the Mullach Sgar Complex.
f. Rock of same type as e., with one end impacts suggesting it was used as hammer.
g. Grey-green medium-grained dolerite from the Mullach Sgar Complex, not used as tool.
h. Three pieces of miarolitic granite from the Conachair-Oiseval Complex.
i. Vein quartz from the Conachair-Oiseval Complex.
j. Burnt indeterminate fine-grained rock.
k. Six pieces of imported Ballachulish Slate.

2:3:11 Bone Objects

Buttons

Phase 7

sf. 107. Bone button, with worn surface, of 4-hole, sew-through type. Upper surface has flat centre containing holes, and surrounding groove with broad rim. Undersurface is plain and slightly curved. Diam. 19mm. Fig. 26E.

Phase 9

sf. 10. Bone button with polished surface of basically same form as that above, but with surrounding groove further from holes. Diam. 15mm. Fig. 26D.

2:3:12 Leather (C. Thomas)

Only four offcuts were found here; these represent, however, shoe-working or repairing waste. For a full discussion of all the leather found during the excavations see pp 166–7.

Catalogue

Phase 7

sf. 18. Triangular offcut; *c*. 55 x 25 x 5mm.

Phase 9

sf. 34. Offcut, long triangular strip; *c*. 105 x 18 x 6mm.

sf. 35. Triangular offcut, very thick; *c*. 90 x 15 x 8mm.

sf. 37. Triangular offcut; *c*. 80 x 30 x 5 7mm.

2:3:13 Shell Objects

Three Mother of Pearl buttons were found.

Catalogue

Phase 7

sf. 11. 2-hole button, holes having joined. Both faces flat. Diam. 10mm. Fig. 26F.

sf. 21. 4-hole, sew-through type. Traces of groove around holes. Worn. Diam. 15mm. Fig. 26G.

sf. 39. 4-hole, sew-through type. One dished surface. Diam. 10mm. Fig. 26H.

2:3:14 Textiles (P. Walton)

Six textiles were recovered from Area 7, from levels dating to the late 19th or early 20th century (Phase 7). All are wool twills, five of them in plain, dark colours and one patterned in two colours (T112).

Catalogue

It is planned to publish a more detailed catalogue and report elsewhere.

Notes:
'coarse' – less than 10 threads per cm in warp and weft
'medium' = 10–20 threads per cm
'medium-fine' = 20–30 threads per cm

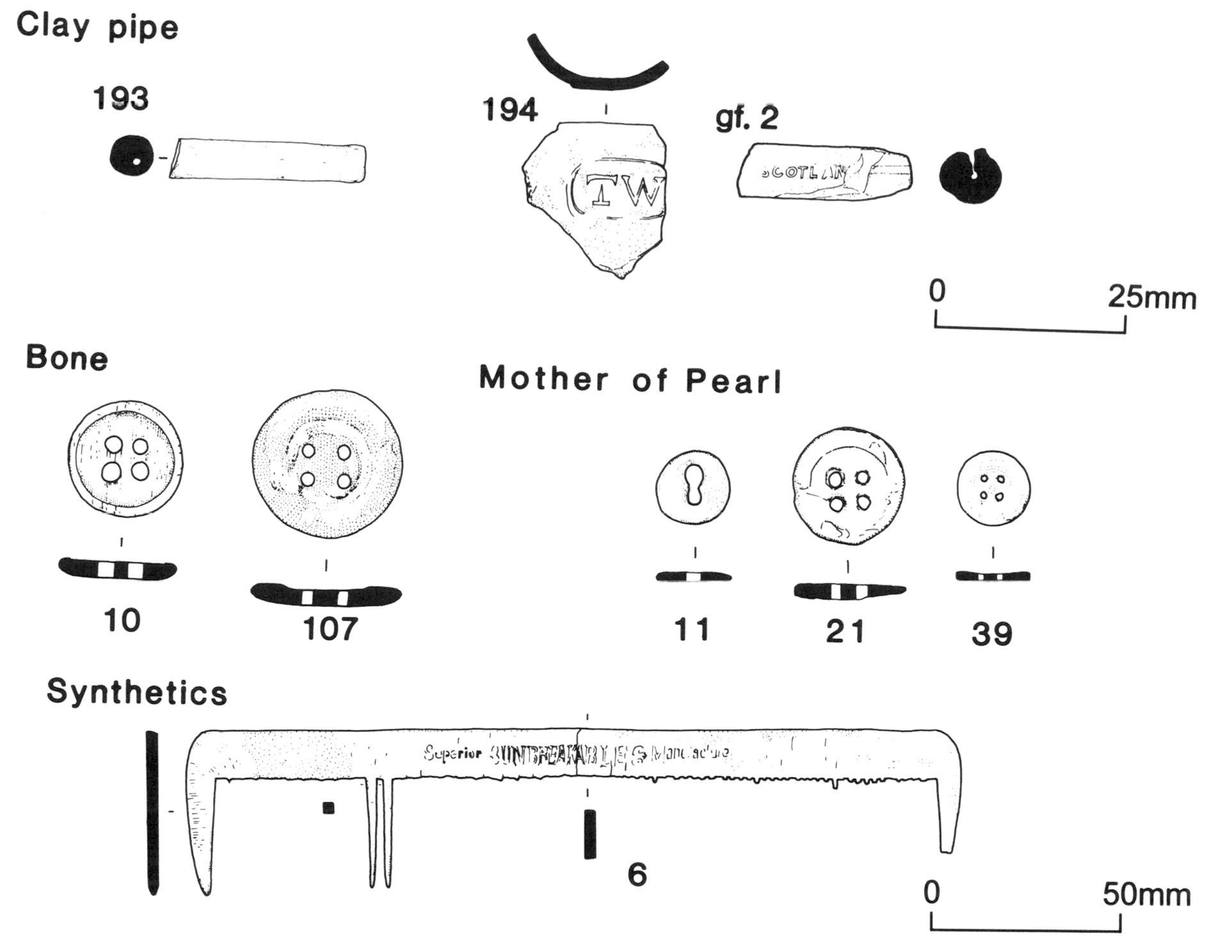

FIG. 26
House 6: clay pipe (Phases 4 and 7), bone (Phases 7 and 9), mother of pearl (Phase 7) and synthetics (Phase 8). Scale 1:1; comb 1:2

Phase 7
sf. 1 (T111). Medium purplish-blue wool twill in 2/2 structure.

sf. 38 (T115). Medium-fine brown-black wool twill in 2/2 structure; trimmed with pieces of T116.

sf. 38 (T116). Medium-fine grey-brown wool twill in 2/2 structure; trimming T115.

sf. 148 (T112). Medium or medium-coarse brown wool textile in interrupted chevron pattern worked on 2/2 base; one system dark, other light; slightly matted.

sf. 148 (T113). Medium-fine dark brown wool twill in 2/2 structure; yarn of worsted type; flimsy, lightweight fabric.

sf. 148 (T114). Medium black wool twill in 2/2 structure; reinforced selvedge constructed from paired warp threads in tabby weave.

2:3:15 Miscellaneous

Cork
Phase 5
sf. 177. Irregular lump of cork. L. 58mm, w. 34mm, th. 20mm.

Linoleum
Phase 4
sfs 182, 184. Comprising tiny fragments of floor cover, with pink ribbed undersurface, and green chequered pattern on top surface.

Synthetics
Two plastic combs were recovered.

Phase 7
sf. 127. Fragment of creamy coloured single-edged straight-backed comb, with fine teeth. L. 67mm, w. 30mm, th. 3mm.

Phase 8
sf. 6. Complete long cream-coloured single-edged comb, with straight back and division of coarse and fine teeth. Marked on one side 'Superior UNBREAKABLE Manufacture'. L. 207mm, w. 42mm, th. 3mm. Fig. 26I.

2:4 The Ecofactual Material

2:4:1 Plant Remains (Jacqueline P. Huntley)

Bulk samples of two buckets or more were floated to 500 microns on-site during excavation. In a few cases the material was sufficiently organic that flotation was inappropriate — it being a method to concentrate organic material in an essentially mineral matrix — and the sample was therefore wet-sieved to 500 microns. In the laboratory the flots or wet-sieved material were described and all identifiable plant material was hand-picked from them. This material was identified by comparison with modern reference material held in the Biological Laboratory, Department of Archaeology, University of Durham. The numbers of carbonised items were counted. For the waterlogged taxa up to five individuals were counted and then further quantities estimated, thus, in the tables, '+' refers to a few being present, '++' to moderate numbers, and '***' to extremely large numbers. In the tables the data are presented at context level, amalgamating information from several samples as appropriate, and by phase; the taxa are presented within preservation category and then broad ecological category; the latter was subjectively derived.

Description of samples (Table 3)

Phase 3

Fill of a sub-rectangular pit cut into soil over the bedrock.

Context 62 (flots 16 and 17). Flot 16 was the upper fill of the pit and consisted of a compact dark grey-brown silty soil. The flot was minute and consisted principally of charcoal fragments. Four carbonised oat grains and two fragments of barley grains were recovered. No waterlogged seeds at all were seen and it is suggested that preservation conditions are the cause. The presence of many earthworms would, indeed, have brought about well-drained, aerobic conditions. Flot 17, the lower fill of the pit, was very similar in typology and content to that of the upper fill.

Phase 4

The building of House 6.

Context 25 (flot 9). West fireplace. Four samples were analysed from this material — all labelled flot 9. In the first, amorphous carbonised material predominated, although there were a few fragments from monocotyledons such as grasses or sedges, and some bryophyte fragments. One germinated hulled barley grain was recovered. The second sample contained large numbers of small grass stems, bryophyte stems and leaves. Seeds from small grasses were recovered and these, too, were burnt. There was a little conifer charcoal, but more or less no waterlogged material. The third sample was very similar to the others but there were also a few heather shoots present. Other than seeds of small grasses one immature hulled barley grain was all that was recovered. The fourth and final sample was more or less pure clinker from coal or similar material. It also contained fine woody twigs, but not from heather, and some burnt grass and bryophyte stems. There were no seeds.

Context 28 (flot 9). This was one of the primary spreads laid down during the construction of the cottage. The flot from the sample was of moderate size and consisted of charcoal and carbonised material — leaves, bryophyte stems, etc., but no burnt seeds. Only a few waterlogged sorrel seeds were present.

Context 54 (flot 15). This was an example from the early fuel from the back of the west hearth. The flot consisted of amorphous charcoal and burnt material with a few bryophyte stems. Two indeterminable cereal grains were present although not sorted out.

Phase 8

The grey, gritty soil over the mortar of Phase 7.

Context 12. This was the grey, gritty soil lying over and around slab 5 (flot 8, tub 3). The two flots from it consisted entirely of clinker and coke with a small amount of coniferous charcoal, some of which formed quite large chunks, and the occasional fragment of burnt monocot. stem base. The second flot, although again predominantly coke/clinker, did contain some waterlogged seeds. Nettles, chickweed, small grass and *Sphagnum* were all represented.

The seeds throughout this area are sparse and suggest that the building as a whole was kept clear of accumulated rubbish. The plant remains do, however, give some specific information about the fuel used. The heather may have been kindling or the fuel itself, giving rather rapidly burning fires, although most of the burnt material was sufficiently amorphous to suggest that it was probably well-humified peat. Remnants of such material can today be found on the slopes of Conachair above An Lag. The wood and monocot. remains may well have been used as kindling too, the former being collected as rare driftwood. The botanical results overall indicate that well-humified peat was being burnt in the earlier phases, whereas principally raw peat or grass turf were being burnt during the later phases, as well as coal.

2:4:2 Mammal and Bird Bones (M. Harman)

There are a small number of bones from this site. Almost all of the bones came from context 1 (topsoil, Phase 9), and 2, a mortary deposit which accumulated as the

Area number	7	7	7	7	7
Context number	**62**	**25**	**28**	**54**	**12**
Phase	**3**	**4**	**4**	**4**	**8**
Carbonised:					
[c]*Avena* grain (oats)	5				
[c]Cerealia undiff.	3			2	
[c]*Hordeum* hulled (barley)	1	2			
[c]*Hordeum* indet. (barley)	2				
[x]Gramineae <2mm (small grasses)	4				
Waterlogged:					
[a]*Stellaria media* (chickweed)					3
[g]*Rumex acetosa* (sorrel)			+		
[r]*Urtica dioica* (nettle)					+
[w]*Eriophorum latifolium/ angustifolium* (cotton grass)					1
[w]*Sphagnum* sp(p). (bog moss)					+
[x]Gramineae <2mm (small grasses)					+

KEY

The taxa have been put into broad ecological category. The latter was subjectively derived and the prefix codes are as follows:

a = arable weeds
c = cereal grain
g = grassland
r = ruderals/disturbed ground
w = wet ground
x = broad, unclassified

For the waterlogged taxa up to five individuals were counted and then further quantities estimated thus:

+ = a few being present
++ = moderate numbers
*** = extremely large numbers

TABLE 3

House 6: plant remains

house was decaying after its last occupation (Phase 7). This latter layer includes many items abandoned by the people, and this is reflected in the bones.

The mammal bones

The only mammal represented is sheep, and most of the bones (Table 4) are from animals of Soay sheep size, and are undoubtedly oddments from carcases of sheep which died in or near House 6. There are, however, a few bones of a size indicating that they are from animals larger than a Soay; these are likely to be from domestic refuse. These are a lumbar vertebra with parts cut off it, probably during butchering, parts of a sternum, and a radius. Unless they are quite recent refuse from visitors, abandoned perhaps by scavenging gulls in the ruins of the house, they must have been left by the last occupants. Accounts of the Evacuation suggest that the last few days were very busy, and the bones from hurried meals might well have been left inside, or possibly tucked away by a dog for future use and overlooked.

There is one fragment of burnt knee joint from the pit (63), from a lamb. This was probably an odd bone thrown on the fire and then deposited outside with the ashes when this area was garden, before the house was built.

The bird bones

The bones from contexts 1 and 2 are summarised in Table 5. The bones of starling, herring gull and snipe were probably deposited naturally.

The puffin and Manx shearwater bones are very unlikely to be natural casualties in this situation and are probably food refuse, as are the fulmar bones. This is complemented in the bones from the refuse deposits in Area 6 (see 5:5:2) and the blackhouse ruins of Area 1 (see 3:4:2), where the emphasis is on the wings. However, there is also a clear emphasis in this group on gannet wing tips, a part of the bird with no meat at all. At least five left and five right wings are represented; three have cuts into the proximal end of the carpometacarpus or wrist joint. The only other gannet bones are a carpal and the distal end of an ulna, which were undoubtedly attached to a wing tip, and an immature tibiotarsus which is probably gannet.

The use of a bird's wing as a stiff feather brush in the house is known in the Western Isles, and the terminal part of the gannet's wing with the primaries attached would serve this purpose well. There was obviously a ready supply of these brushes, which would probably wear fairly rapidly with use. Sands (1878b, 14–15) mentions a person who brought him water and milk, and who swept his hearth with a bundle of solan goose wings, and Mrs S. Ogilvie (Alexander Ferguson's daughter) remembers her aunt (Mrs Anne Ferguson of No. 5) using the wing of a large bird to clean the girdle before using it for baking. Mrs Ogilvie stayed with her aunt and uncle at various times up to 1915 (pers. comm.). These excavated bones, then, should be seen as the remains of household utensils, a by-product of harvesting gannets for food.

The only other bird bones were another gannet wing bone in context 27, a patch of coal in the west room, probably part of another brush; and a fulmar leg bone associated with context 17, the east room timber partition.

	Context 1	Context 2
Skull	3	1
Tooth	5	
Vertebra	3	2
Rib	1	8
Scapula	1	
Radius	2	1
Ulna	2	
Metacarpal	1	
Pelvis		2
Femur	1	1
Tibia		1
Phalanx	1	2

TABLE 4
House 6: sheep bones and fragments of bone

2:4:3 Fish Bones (R. Nicholson)

Four bones were recovered from Area 7, Phases 8 and 9. All proved to be from large fish from *Gadidae* (cod family), and those identifiable to species were from cod *(Gadus morhua)* and saithe or pollack *(Pollachius* sp*)*.

Catalogue

Phase 8

One cod *(Gadus morhua)* prevomer, from a fish of total length in excess of 0.70m.

	Context 1		Context 2	
	Gannet	Fulmar	Gannet	Fulmar
Ulna			1	
Carpal			1	
Carpometacarpus	6		4	
Wing 1st phalanx	2		5	
Wing phalanx	1		3	
Femur		1		1
Tibiotarsus	?1	2		2
Fibula		1		

Context 1	Context 2
Also: Puffin: maxilla Starling: mandible	Also: Manx shearwater: humerus Puffin: carpometacarpus; ulna Snipe: humerus; 2 ulnae (Waders): sternum; humerus; carpometacarpus Herring Gull: 2 humeri; ulna; tibiotarsus Starling: skull; sternum; 2 femora; tarsometatarsus

TABLE 5
House 6: numbers of bird bones from different species

Phase 9

One cod *(Gadus morhua)* cleithrum, left side, proximal half of the bone, from a fish of total length in excess of 0.70m. This bone appears to have been nicked on the dorsal aspect, a cut probably resulting from filleting.

One saithe or pollack *(Pollachius* sp.*)* left ceratohyal, from a fish of estimated length 0.60–0.75m.

One cod *(Gadus morhua)* abdominal vertebra.

2:5 Discussion

The earliest human presence was noted in Phase 2, with the discovery of coarse pottery and stone tools. The pottery has no diagnostic features with which it could be dated, and is, unfortunately, too small and abraded to be suitable for thermoluminescence dating. The majority of stone artefacts are worked local rocks, and include examples used as hammers, which could be of any date. The 'blades' (sf. 220 in Phase 2, and sf. 200 in Phase 3) are heavy, flat, rectangular stones, shaped to a roughly rounded blade at one end, and flat or broken at the other. It is conceivable that they may have been used for ploughing, though they are not ard points in the accepted sense of that term. They do, however, show similarities with the 'rectangular tools' noted at Scord of Brouster in Shetland (Rees 1986, 81), which were utilitarian, though possibly used for preparing the land, and were associated with Neolithic occupation. The St Kilda bladed tools may belong to this period of time, but this cannot be said with any degree of certainty. All that can safely be said is that they are pre-1830.

The first reliable date for occupation on the site is when this strip of land was initially allotted to the Fergusons in the 1830s. Malcolm Ferguson was the first occupant. He had married Catherine MacDonald in 1846 (GROS OPR 111/2, Marriages, 7.8.1846), and they had a daughter, Mary. The family emigrated to Australia, with other islanders, on board the *Priscilla* in 1852 (Holohan 1986). Only Malcolm survived the journey. The plot on St Kilda was transferred to Malcolm's brother, Finlay (born 1816). Sharbau's plan of 1858/60 (SRO RHP 6778) shows Finlay's blackhouse and manure cleit in a line along the street. The blackhouse remains today (F), but no trace was found in excavation of the cleit.

The pit found in Phase 3, with its rich soil fill, is marked on Sharbau's plan as being a 'cabbage enclosure'. Although no stonework was found around the pit, it is possible that it was associated with small walled enclosures found elsewhere, within and just beyond the head-dyke. Those within the village area lie on the strips of dwellings X, 2, 3, 9, 10, Q and 13, and are rectangular, sub-rectangular, elliptical or roughly circular in plan. They vary in size from 1.75m x 1.65m (13) to 3.10m x 2.15m (X) internally, and have walls *c.* 0.80m wide, and from 1.10m to 2m high. In some cases the walls tend to lean outwards, but in every case there is no opening for access. The walls form a protection for the plants from wind and animals.

The enclosure was cleared and replaced by House 6 in the early 1860s. The Fergusons — Finlay, Betsy and Mary — moved into their new home. Mary (later Mrs Neil MacKinnon) died in 1871, followed by her mother in 1883, and Finlay left for Australia the next year. MacDiarmid, in 1877, confirmed that Finlay and his wife were still there, though he noted that their daughter had died (MacDiarmid 1878, 238). By 1886, however, the cottage was occupied by Angus Gillies and his wife Annie (Murray 1886–7, MS). In 1883 Gillies was 35 years old, and clearly a respected member of the community, for when Lord Napier and the other members of the Crofters Commission arrived on Hirta, he was asked to give evidence (Report 1884, 27).

The house follows a fairly standard form — a basic rectangular plan with the width half the length (17' x 34'); roughly coursed miarolitic granite rubble walls, lime mortared, on projecting footings; a central door in the 2' thick south long wall; gable fireplaces; and a mural cupboard in the south-east corner. Internally, the cottage was divided by wooden partitions into two rooms, one on either side of an entrance lobby, and a back store/bedroom. The west room would have been 3.20m x 3.96m, and the east room 3.50m x 3.96m, with the central area 2m wide. Although no division was found between the lobby and the back closet, evidence from other houses in the street indicate that it could range from 0.99m (3'3") in breadth (House 11), to 1.22m (4') in House 13.

The primary flooring of the cottages was hard yellow clay, and this surface was still used in the 1890s, for John Ross said that:

> I myself heard one man expressing a desire to have one end of his house floored with wood so as to make it more comfortable, but he had to give up the idea, some of the others coming down on him with most peculiar arguments leading him to understand the folly of his plan. (Ross *c.* 1890, MS).

Sometime after 1890 timber flooring was inserted into House 6. It is conceivable that the stimulus for this change was the arrival of masons and carpenters to the island from Dunvegan in 1898 to build the schoolroom and repair and wainscot the kirk (Heathcote 1900, 92–6). Although the islanders had a saw-pit for cutting up the very limited supplies of driftwood washed up in Village Bay, the quantity of planking required in flooring the cottages, and the standard imperial dimensions of the planks would tend to suggest that they were imported. Equally, the idea of suspended plank flooring must also have been imported.

A wooden chimney-piece was set up in the west room, and stones were laid at the corners to take the grid-iron. Although peat/turf was used, coal was later burnt, and ashes and unburnt coal were found in the room. Many visitors to St Kilda reported on the damaging practice of cutting turf for fuel, and by the beginning of the 20th century coal was imported. Supplies were given by trawler skippers (Heathcote 1900, 208), and the captain of 'The Big Whaler' gave 5 tons of coal to the islanders as a gift in 1906 (McLachlan, A., in Quine 1988, 56).

When Angus Gillies and his wife died (1924 and 1925 respectively), the cottage was not taken over and occupied by others, and was empty at the Evacuation in 1930, along with Houses 3, 4, 8, 10 and 12. The shell of House 6 was strewn with a wide range of personal and household possessions, which became mixed with soil and mortar. Within eight years of the Evacuation the house had lost its roof.

Following the takeover of the island by the National Trust for Scotland, the cottage underwent initial repairs. Some work seems to have taken place at the east fireplace, and the discovery of sand and felt in Phase 8 may relate to this work. For a time the building was used as a temporary store for materials. Immediately prior to this excavation, NTS work party members cut and set a new door lintel, stripped turf from the cottage interior, and rebuilt the west chimney.

CHAPTER 3

Excavations at House 8

3:1 The Excavation Areas (Fig. 27)

A rectangular area (Area 1), 4m by a maximum of 9.10m, was opened up in 1986 by the east gable of House 8, over a grass-covered mound. A small square area inside the south-east corner of the house was also examined in 1986, but later expanded in 1987 and 1988 to take in most of the interior of the house (Area 2). A baulk was retained across the building at the entrance. In addition, a triangular area (Area 3), 5 x 4 x 3m, was dug to examine a roughly circular mound, just north-east of the house.

3:2 The Stratigraphic Sequence

Phase 1 (Fig. 28)

During the Quaternary there is evidence for glaciation in Village Bay with a small ice sheet, its margins indicated by boulder deposition around the western edges of Oiseval, and by elongated moraines at the side of Mullach Sgar (Sutherland *et al.* 1984, 262). Glacially deposited boulders are found from the arcuate rampart below Conachair to, and in some places beyond, the 50m contour. Periglacial formations, contemporary with the glacier, include the weathering of the granophyre east of the Abhainn Mhor, producing a bouldery detritus. Boulder deposition (273), possibly as a result of glacial action, is clustered in the north of Area 1, and in Area 3 (255) over the regolith, with scattered outliers elsewhere (132, 279).

Phase 2 (Fig. 29)

The boulders were covered by a massive accumulation of sediment — initially a dark brown gritty layer (274), followed by a reddish-brown deposit (202). The particle size distribution (Fig. 30) is consistent with a re-deposited, poorly sorted soil, and examination of the sediment fragments verifies this (J.R. Senior pers. comm.). There are angular fragments of granite/granophyre, both as composite agglomerations and grains; there are also individual angular grains of alkali feldspar and quartz. A sample subjected to liquid suspension showed no

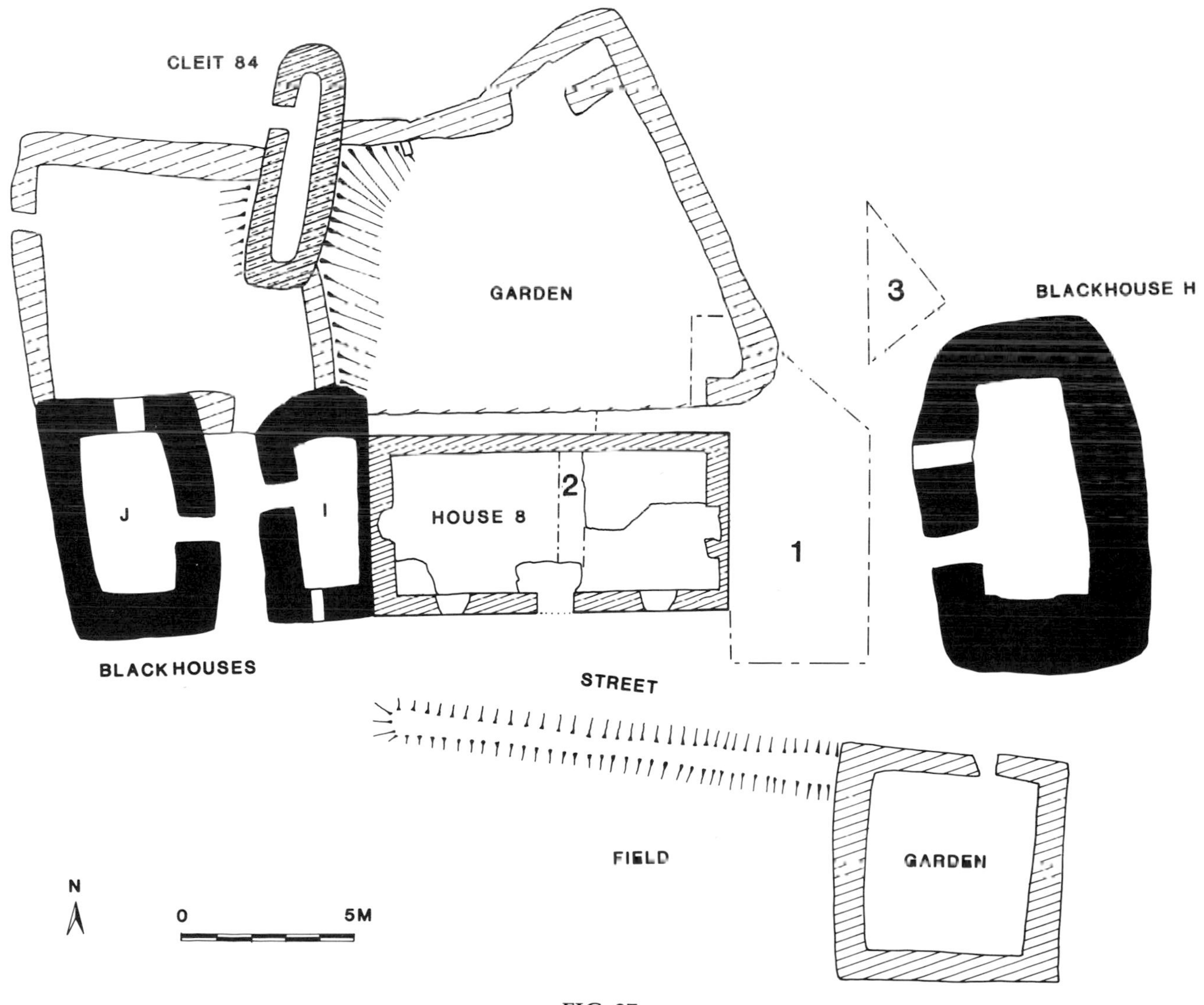

FIG. 27
House 8 and its surroundings

FIG. 28
House 8: Phase 1

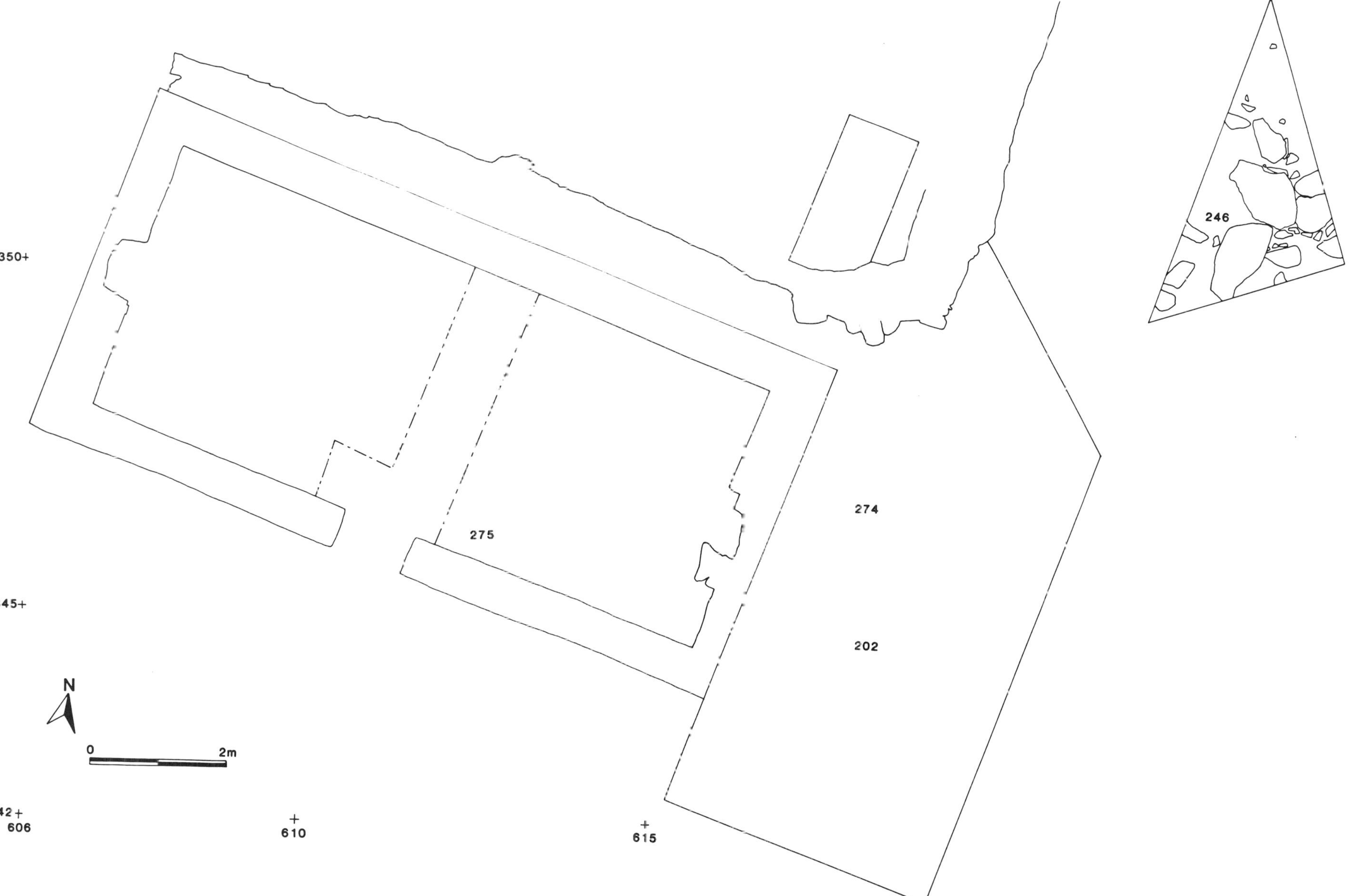

FIG. 29
House 8: Phase 2

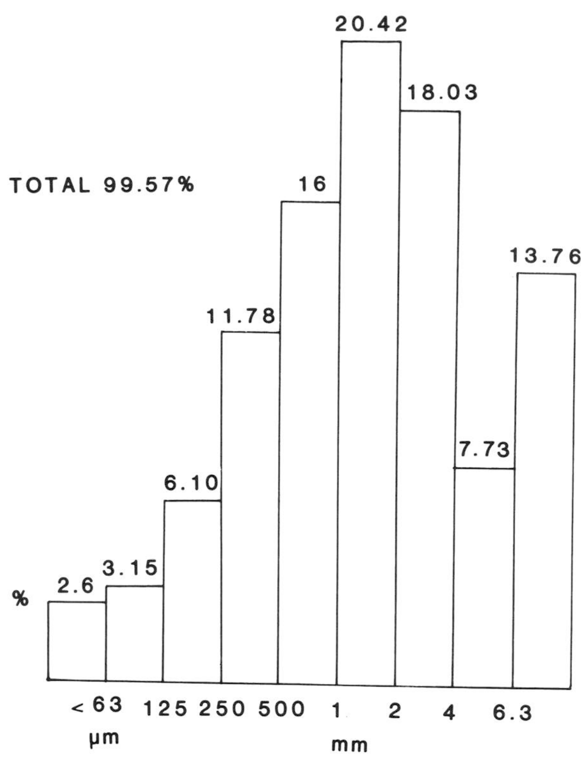

FIG. 30
House 8: sediment analysis

organic material. This, then, suggests that it is a poorly sorted sediment rapidly deposited from a stream, rather than a boulder clay-type sediment of glacial origin. Amongst these deposits were fourteen fragments of coarse pottery (sfs 664, 772–8, 780, 801–5). One fragment (sf. 775) has produced a thermoluminescence date of AD 190 ± 360 (Dur90TL142–1AS: the overall error is given at the 68% level of confidence). Gritty soil was also found in Area 2 (275). A dark brown soil, marked with patches of iron pan (246), was found over boulders in Area 3, and may be contemporary with this phase. It contained coarse pottery (sfs 702–5).

Phase 3 (Fig. 31)

The surface of the subsoil in Area 1 was scored by a stream channel (268) running down and curving towards the south-east. A slight ridge divided the broad, main channel from a narrow tributary (267) just to the east. They may have drained water flowing down from the spring 'Tobar Childa'. Traces of another stream were found in Area 3.

Phase 4 (Fig. 32)

In Area 1, black soil (232) spread over the southern end of the channels, containing nine fragments of coarse pottery (sfs 727, 748–50, 753–7); a flint (sf. 752); a stone disc (sf. 758) and pieces of bone. It was associated with a clogging accumulation of medium-sized stones (234)

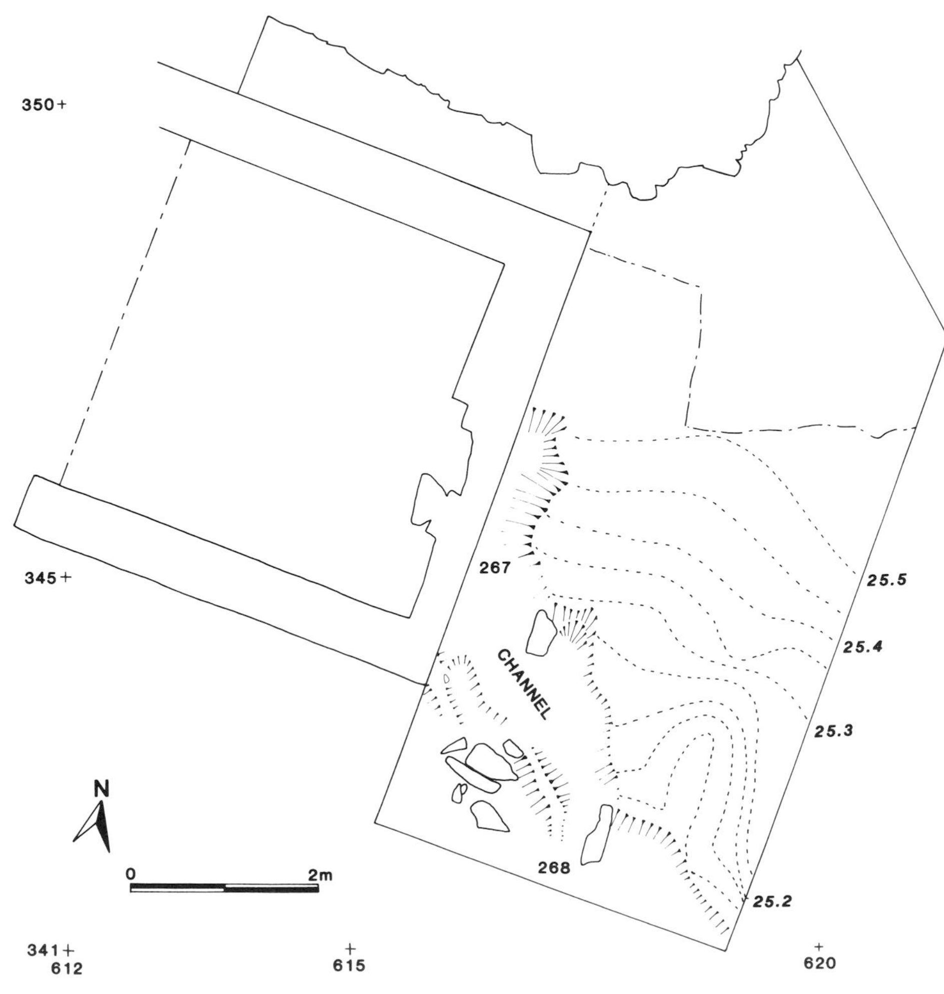

FIG. 31
House 8: Phase 3

FIG. 32
House 8: Phase 4

and dark brown soil (230) packed with tiny granophyre grits. This debris contained 41 fragments of coarse pottery (sfs 540–44, 546–50, 571, 636–8, 641, 643, 665–71, 673–8, 700–1, 726, 761–8, 771); steatite vessel fragments (sfs 545, 642, 672, 769); and stone objects (sfs 679, 760, 770). A fragment of coarse pottery (sf. 665) produced a thermoluminescence date of AD 1135 ± 170 (Dur90TL142–1AS: the error is given at the 68% level of confidence). A light brown gritty clayey soil (186) probably formed part of the north fill.

Evidence of the channel and fill was also found in Area 2, where a patch of grey gritty soil (272) was covered by a spread of dark reddish-brown gritty soil (243), brown gritty soil (266), stones (270), and mid-brown gritty soil (269). The grit layer (243) produced steatite (sf. 785); a schist fragment (sf. 789); coarse pottery (sfs 747, 786); and a fragment of iron (sf. 628). Soil 269 produced five fragments of coarse pottery (sfs 781–3, 787–8).

Included in this phase, on purely stratigraphical grounds, were two circular hollows (250, 253 — Pl. 6) dug into the surface of Area 1, on the east bank; in one case (250) down to the underlying boulders. They were roughly 0.84m and 1.12m in diameter, and 0.16m and 0.28m deep. Some burnt matter and yellow concretion was found in them, along with a general fill of reddish-brown soil (251, 254), but no artefacts. Also, close by, was a slight linear feature (258), containing a similar fill to the pits (259). Two fragments of pottery were recovered from this fill (sf. 751).

There was no direct stratigraphic link between Areas 1 and 3, but the deposits of Phase 2 in Area 3 were overlain by stones (224), and a dark gritty soil containing decayed stone (201). A copper-alloy needle (sf. 520) and 27 fragments of coarse pottery (sfs 395, 521, 529, 531, 573–86, 607–13, 634–5) came from this accumulation.

Phase 5 (Fig. 33)

Whatever human activity there was in this area ceased. Clean sand (235) spread over the black accumulation (232, Phase 4) by the channel, and this was sealed by a sandy dark grey-brown sticky clayey soil (176, 189) which developed over the site. Patches of decayed turf were noted, and this new surface was, in part, used as a dumping ground for waste. Fragments of coarse pottery were scattered around (sfs 421, 454, 461–5, 486–93, 495, 517–19, 522–3, 530, 532–9, 572, 639–40, 759), along with fire-shattered stones (sfs 456, 458, 524); stone tools (sfs 422, 460, 494); a flint (sf. 527); a possible peat sample (sf. 496); and animal bones. The skeleton of an adult dog (Pl. 7), *c.* 17" (437mm) at the shoulder, was found lying on the soil surface. It was largely intact, lying on its right side, though the hind limbs had been disturbed, possibly by scavengers. In part the bones were covered by a spread of medium to large stones.

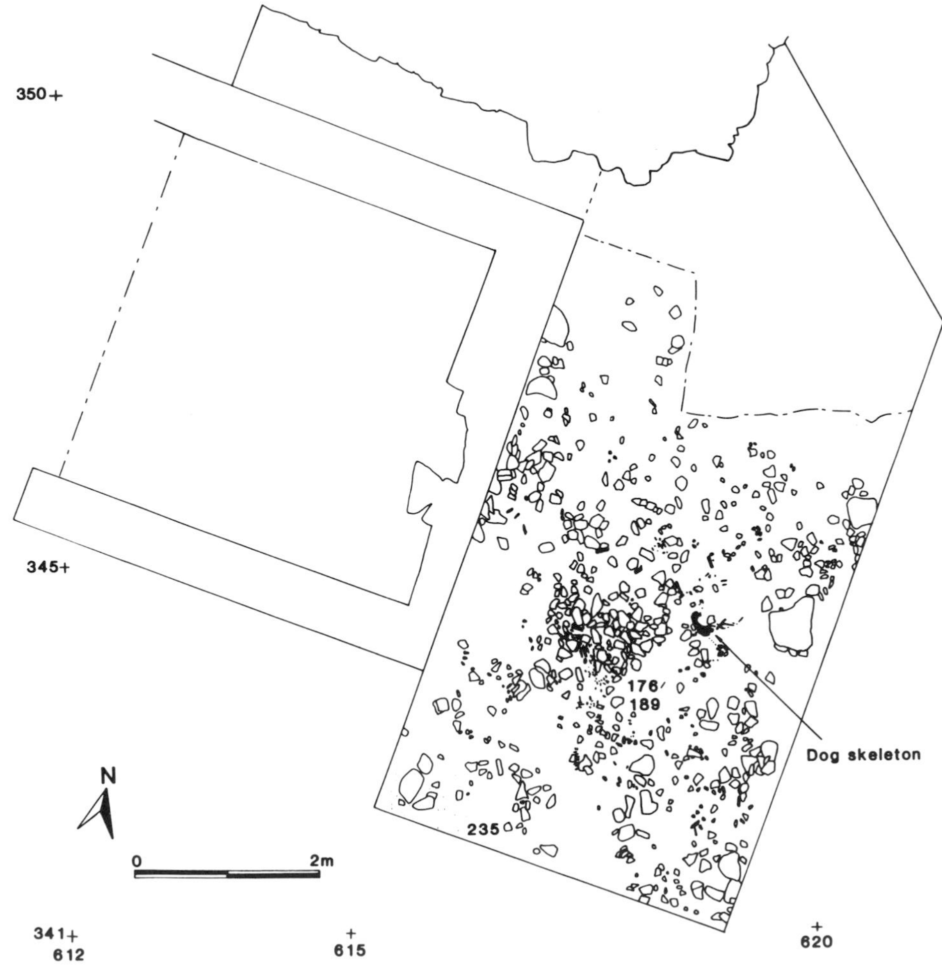

FIG. 33
House 8: Phase 6

PLATE 6
House 8: pits 250 and 253 with the stream bed, looking west

PLATE 7
House 8: a dog skeleton found in Phase 5

FIG. 34
House 8: Phase 7

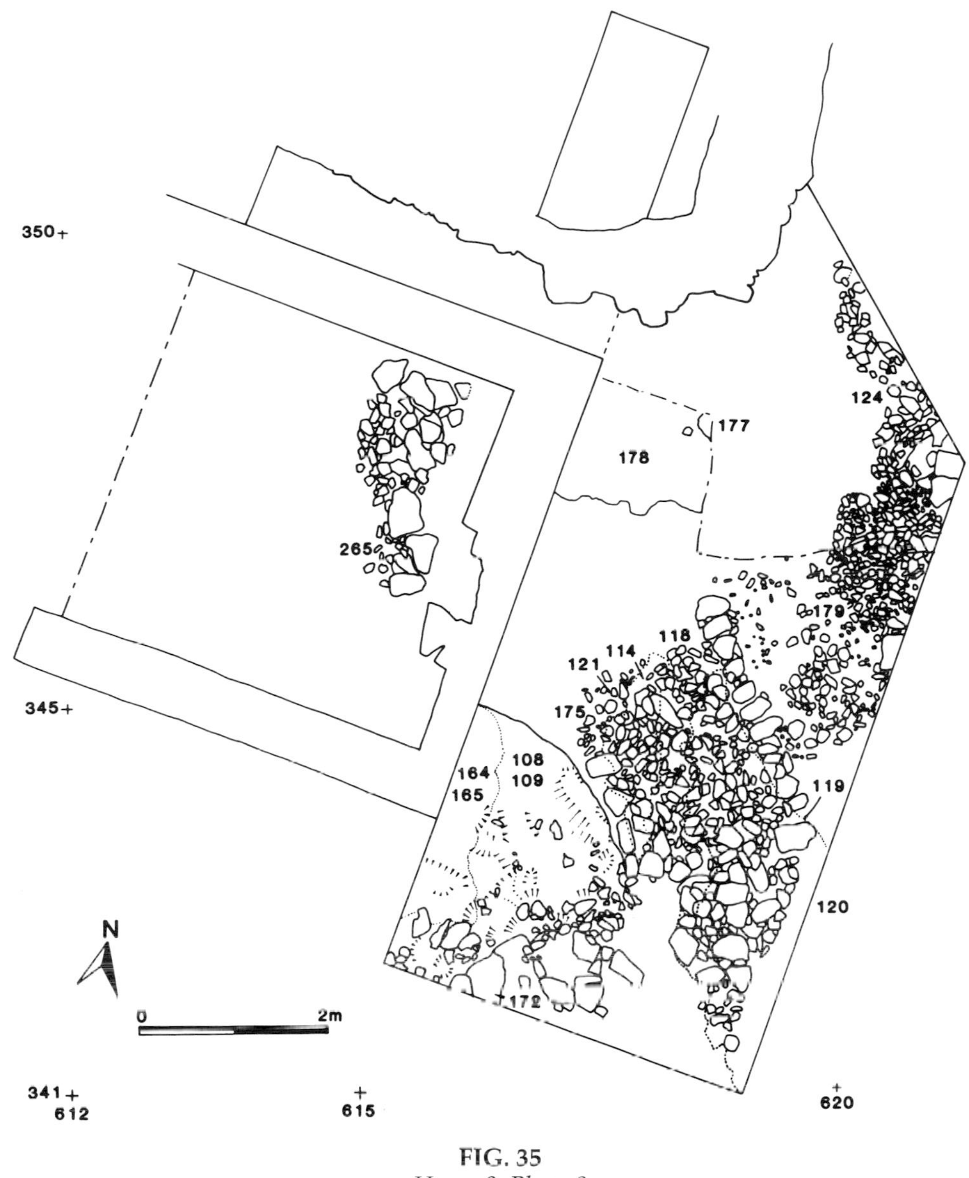

FIG. 35
House 8: Phase 8

Phase 6 (Fig. 34)

The soil was then worked, and possibly divided. A drainage system was laid out, the channel sides lined (218–23) and then capped (181–4), though there were no base stones. The channel connections were at slightly different levels, and at one junction there was a much larger capstone. All the drains contained a gritty silt (211–13), in which was found a fragment of coarse pottery (sf. 525) and two flints (sfs 526, 528).

Two parallel lines of stones (122, 123 — Pl. 8) ran across the site, 1.40m apart, on a north-west to south-east alignment. They were one stone broad; the southern line (122), although damaged, was clearly formed from larger stones, and they delimited the extent of the land drains, which were found to the south and west, but not beyond the stone lines. Possible traces of the lines were also noted in Area 2 (263, 264). A stone tool (sf. 457) was found in context 123.

Phase 7 (Fig. 35)

Later, rubble and soil filled into the space between the lines of the stones (175, 118, 120, 179, 178) in Area 1 and, in part, in Area 2 (265). Coarse pottery was found (sfs 327, 350, 355, 382, 397, 413, 433, 455), as well as an iron find (sf. 459), and a stone tool (sf. 380). The rubble was covered by gritty soils (109, 119, 121, 124), which produced a tiny quartz crystal (sf. 396), stone tools (sfs 248, 311) and coarse pottery (sfs 249–50, 253, 255, 322–4, 326, 352, 367, 401–2). One fragment (sf. 249, context 124) produced a thermoluminescence date of AD 1685 ± 60 (Dur88TL108–1BS: the overall error is given at the 68% level of confidence). The rubble fill and gritty soils were, to a certain extent, contaminated from above, with the presence of some glass, coal and mortar. A stone, initially interpreted as coarse pottery, was also found (sf. 254, context 124).

South and west of the stone lines there was a noticeable spread of peat/turf ash which overlay the drains of Phase 6. In parts it was apparent that three layers (165, 164, 108) had been tipped over the area. The ash contained a quartz chip (sf. 297); some concretion (sf. 301); a stone tool (sf. 306); and coarse pottery (sfs 298–300, 302–5, 308–9, 366). Associated with this burning was a further patch (172), composed of sticky dark brown soil and ash. This deposit contained a fragment of coarse pottery (sf. 349).

Phase 8 (Fig. 36)

Ultimately, these deposits were covered by sticky dark brown peaty clay (92) and dark brown gritty soils (130, 146), an overall dark reddish-brown silty soil (43, 55), and ash (40). Associated with these layers was a patch of sand (115), and some brown clayey soil (102). These layers were heavily disturbed by later activity. Context 43 produced crockery (sf. 73), coarse pottery (sf. 58), iron (sf. 60); context 55 produced a

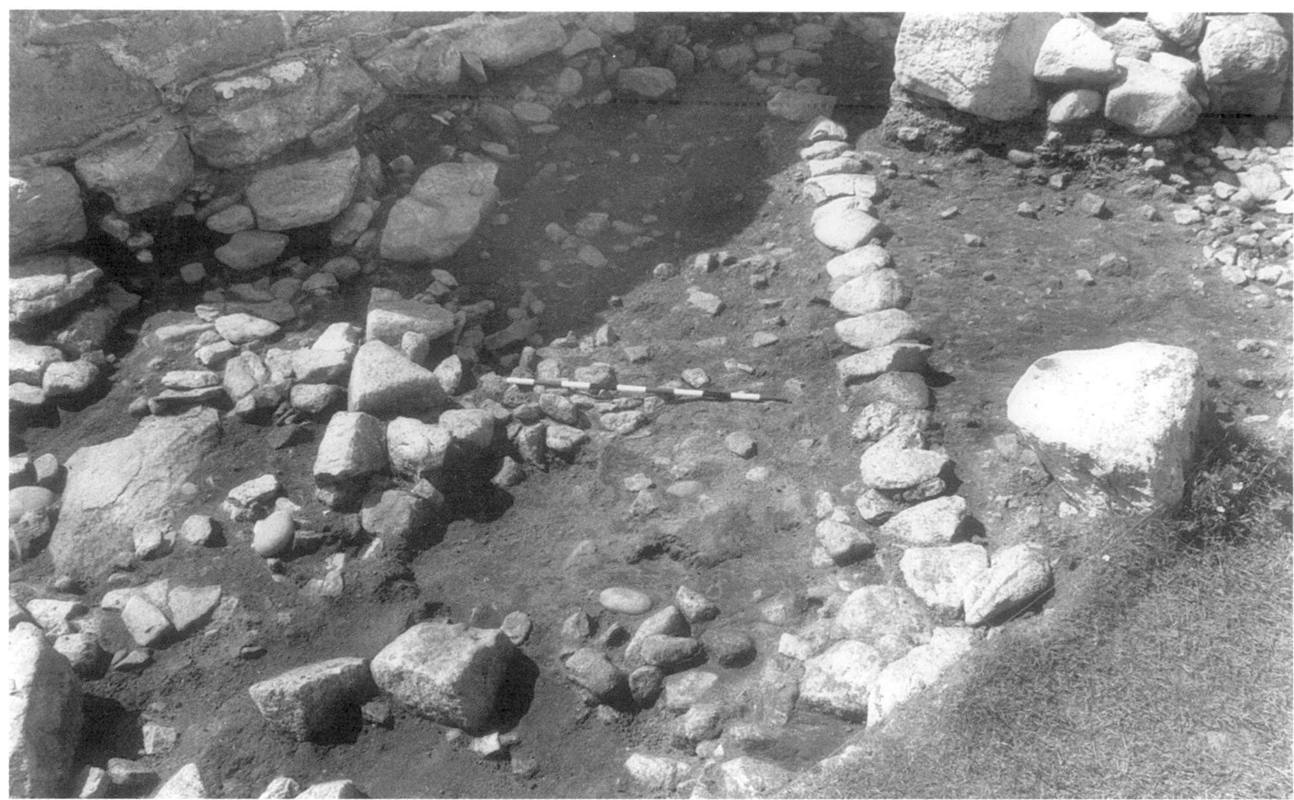

PLATE 8
House 8: parallel lines of stones 122 and 123, looking north-west

clay pipe (sf. 225), iron (sfs 53, 226), coarse pottery (sf. 227), glass (sf. 72) and a bead (sf. 140). Context 92 contained crockery (sfs 204, 206, 210–11), coarse pottery (sfs 209, 222, 238, 240, 246, 262), iron (sfs 202, 205, 207, 217), glass (sf. 223), stone (sf. 203) and wood (sf. 239); context 102 produced coarse pottery (sfs 230, 251–52), and iron (sf. 232); context 115 contained coarse pottery (sfs 359, 377); while context 146 produced a fragment of tile (sf. 307).

Possibly associated with this phase was a patch of brown soil (127), located in the garden trench, which pre-dated the construction of the blackhouse (Phase 10).

In Area 3, gritty brown soil and some small stones (197) had accumulated, possibly from Phase 5. There were no clear features which could be equated with the activity of Phase 6 onwards; the deposit appeared as a developed soil.

Phase 9 (Fig. 37)

The area subsequently underwent a major change of use, as the site for a blackhouse. To ensure dry conditions, an elaborate network of drains was constructed (Pl. 9), using fairly small side-stones (149, 150, 152, 153, 151, 154, 155, 156) and heavy caps (32, 30, 31, 85). An east-west drain line was laid at the top of the site (237, 238, 128, 239, 240, 229, 225–6, 190, 191), and a rough herringbone pattern of drains ran across the slope. Spores of mildew were noted on the side-stones. In some cases additional stones (148 on 146, 157, 44, 57, 159) were noted packed against the drain sides or as outliers. The drainage system also extended to the west end of Area 2 (277–8, 271, 276), with two additional drains (262, 260, 261, 215, 214 and 203, 204, 199). Context 204 produced some coarse pottery (sfs 698–9).

This drainage system was considerably more substantial than the land drains of Phase 6. The top drain had base stones (239), but the others did not.

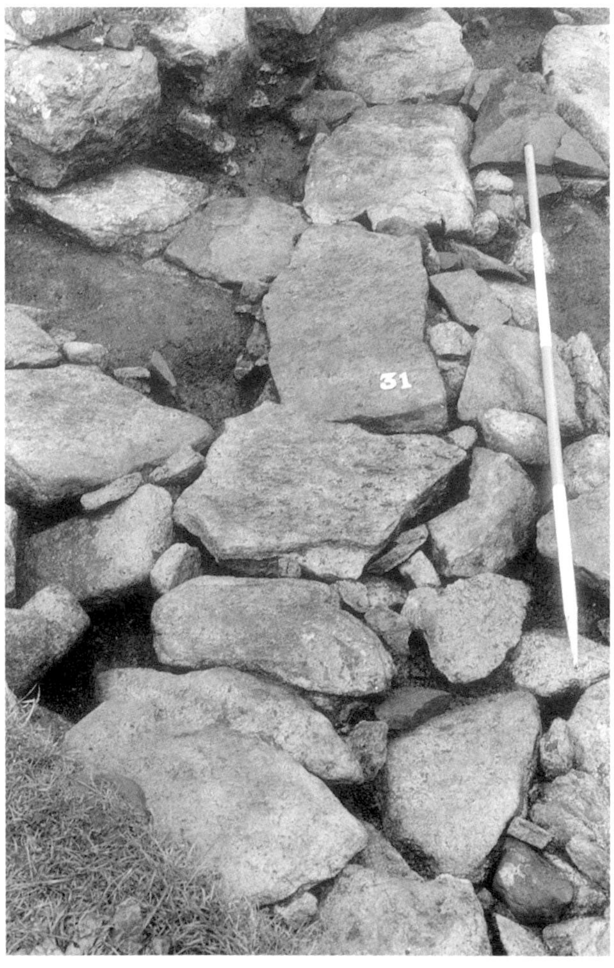

PLATE 9
House 8: stone-capped drains underlying the blackhouse, looking north-west

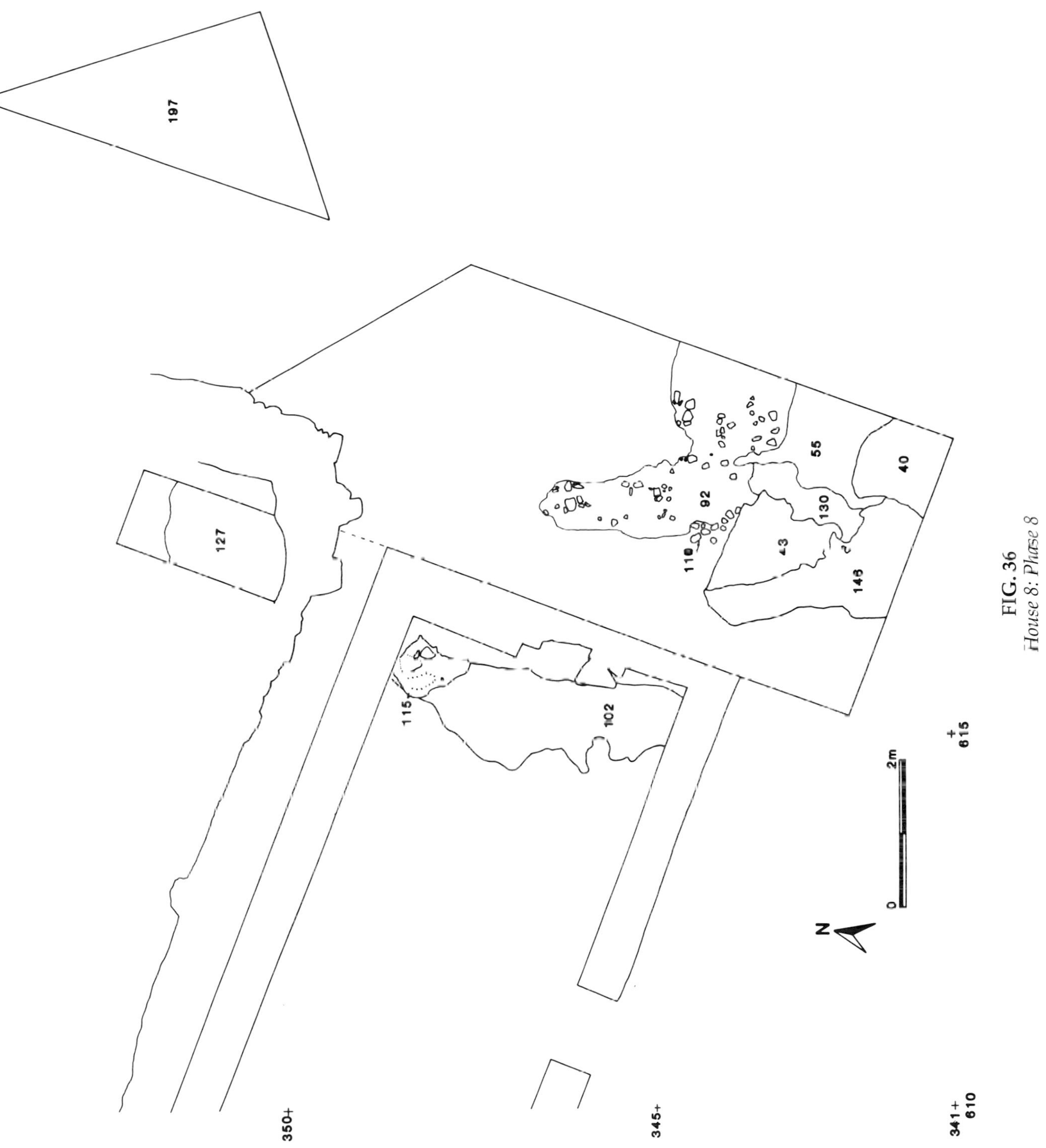

FIG. 36
House 8: Phase 8

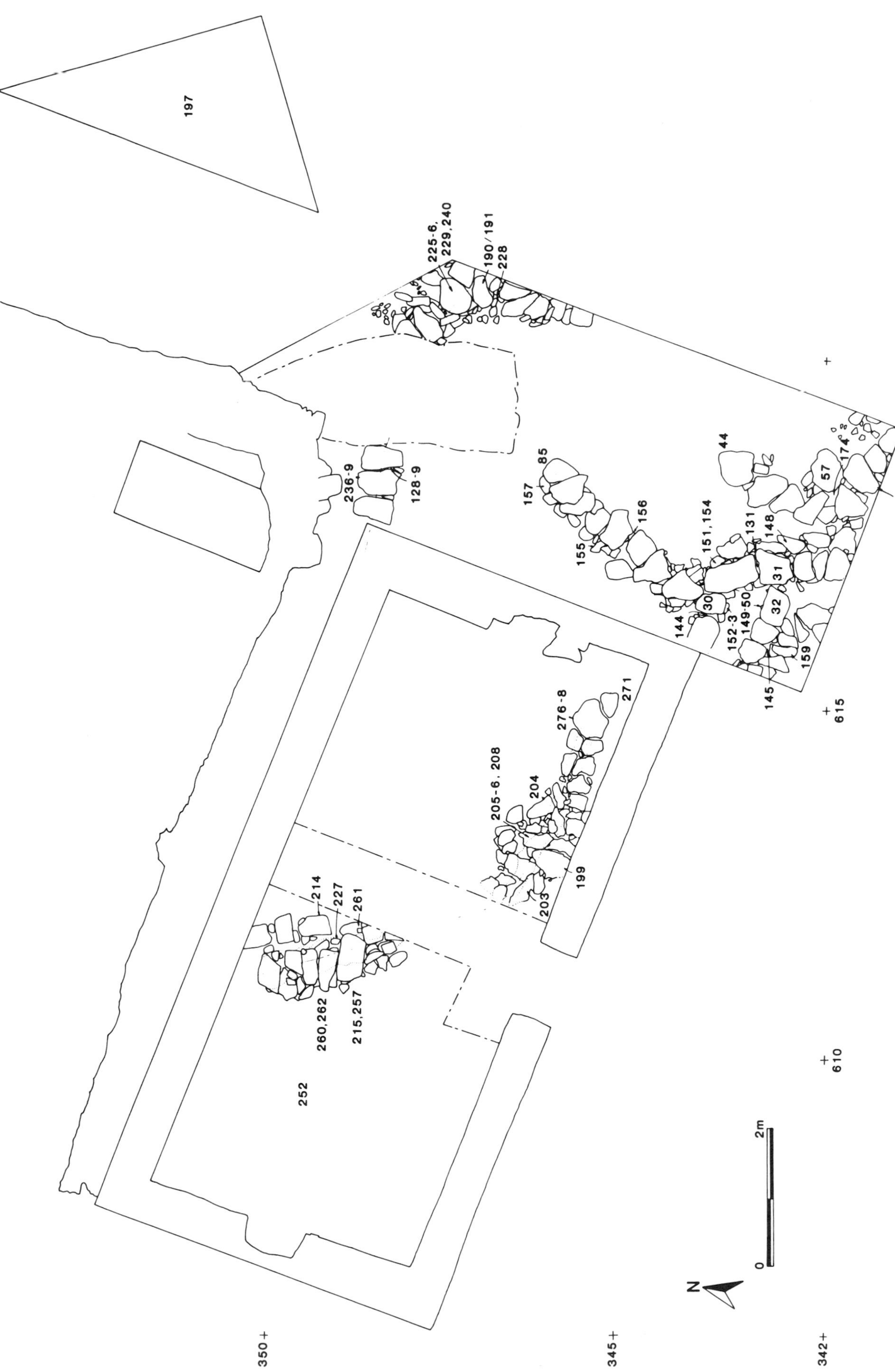

FIG. 37
House 8: Phase 9

Their fill was graded gritty silt (145, 144, 131, 129, 236, 228), in which was found a piece of coarse pottery (sf. 271), crockery (sf. 270), and burnt material (sf. 269). In the drains of Area 2, the fill comprised layers of sticky silty clay (257, 227, 208, 206, 205). They produced some coarse pottery (sfs 507, 651, 659, 720–21, 724–5, 745–6); iron (sf. 504); burnt material (sf. 505); and some garlic snail shells. The soil of Phase 8, cut by these drains, was used to cover them. A patch of sand (115) and brown clayey soil (102) also appears to have been used (see Phase 8). Some large stones (162, 174) lay between the drains and may be associated with this phase; some coarse pottery was found (sfs 414–18, 420). They clearly post-dated Phase 6.

In Area 3 there was no stratigraphic link with Area 1, but a gritty brown soil with some small stones (197) had developed over the area, and may be associated with this phase. It is possible that it had accumulated from Phase 5 onwards.

Phase 10 (Fig. 38)

The new house site lay between those of Blackhouses H and I. On it was built an 'improved' blackhouse. It was originally elliptical in plan, aligned north-south, with walls 1.70m thick (15, 68, 98, 100). These were set, in part, on a cobbled surface (39, 163) and built of heavy granite boulders forming facings for a soil and stone core. Only fragmentary remains survived, particularly at the northern end. Amongst the cobbles (39) were fragments of coarse pottery (sfs 328, 353–4, 379, 393, 398); a nail head (sf. 394); stone tools (sfs 378, 399, 400); and a disturbed steatite spindle whorl (sf. 325). On the west side, in Area 2, only a few large stones (103, 76 and ?126) remained, seemingly set on cobbles (200) associated with a black silt (196/231). Coarse pottery (sf. 443) and a stone tool (sf. 470) were found with stones 103. Context 196 produced coarse pottery (sfs 471–3, 480, 503, 508–10, 512, 555–8, 562, 569, 588, 590–602, 616–18, 620–22, 624–7, 632–3, 644, 646–50, 657, 660, 680–82, 688–93, 696–7, 706, 708–9, 711–12, 714–15, 717, 719, 728, 735–6, 740); iron (sfs 645, 784); stone tools (sfs 445–6, 806); and conglomerate (sf. 619). Context 231 contained a fragment of coarse pottery (sf. 710). On the east side there were some areas of stone (59, 83), covered by yellow-brown gritty soil (88), and a compact dump of bones (20). The layers had been disturbed, and it was unclear whether they were associated with the soil surface of Phase 8, or whether they had been dumped as a base for the blackhouse wall. The yellow-brown gritty layer produced coarse pottery (sfs 200, 241, 244–5, 261) and stone tools (sfs 242–3), but fragments of crockery (sf. 208) and glass were also found. Similarly, the bone dump produced coarse pottery (sf. 61); crockery (sf. 48); glass (sfs 47, 52); iron (sfs 51, 79); and a ?bone object (sf. 15).

The blackhouse interior was divided into two by a low stone wall or *talan* (21, 95, 56), 0.70m wide; to the north were the human quarters (Pl. 10), with a threshold (29) into a byre at the south.

Roughly in the centre of the north end a shallow hole (169) had been dug. In it was placed some brown clayey soil (161, 166, 160), which formed a bed for a hearth (78, 23, 25). It was probably originally box-shaped, with base and side-stones, propped up with small wedge-shaped stones (158), and packed around with stones and more clayey soil (167). The hearth was probably about 0.85m square (Pl. 11). Brown clayey soil (166) produced a fragment of coarse pottery (sf. 381), while context 160 also produced pottery (sf. 310). Yellow clay (38), from an uncertain source, though possibly dug from the banks of the Abhainn Mhor, was laid on a bedding of brown clayey soils (84, 81) around the hearth and lipping slightly over the

PLATE 10
House 8: interior of the blackhouse, looking north

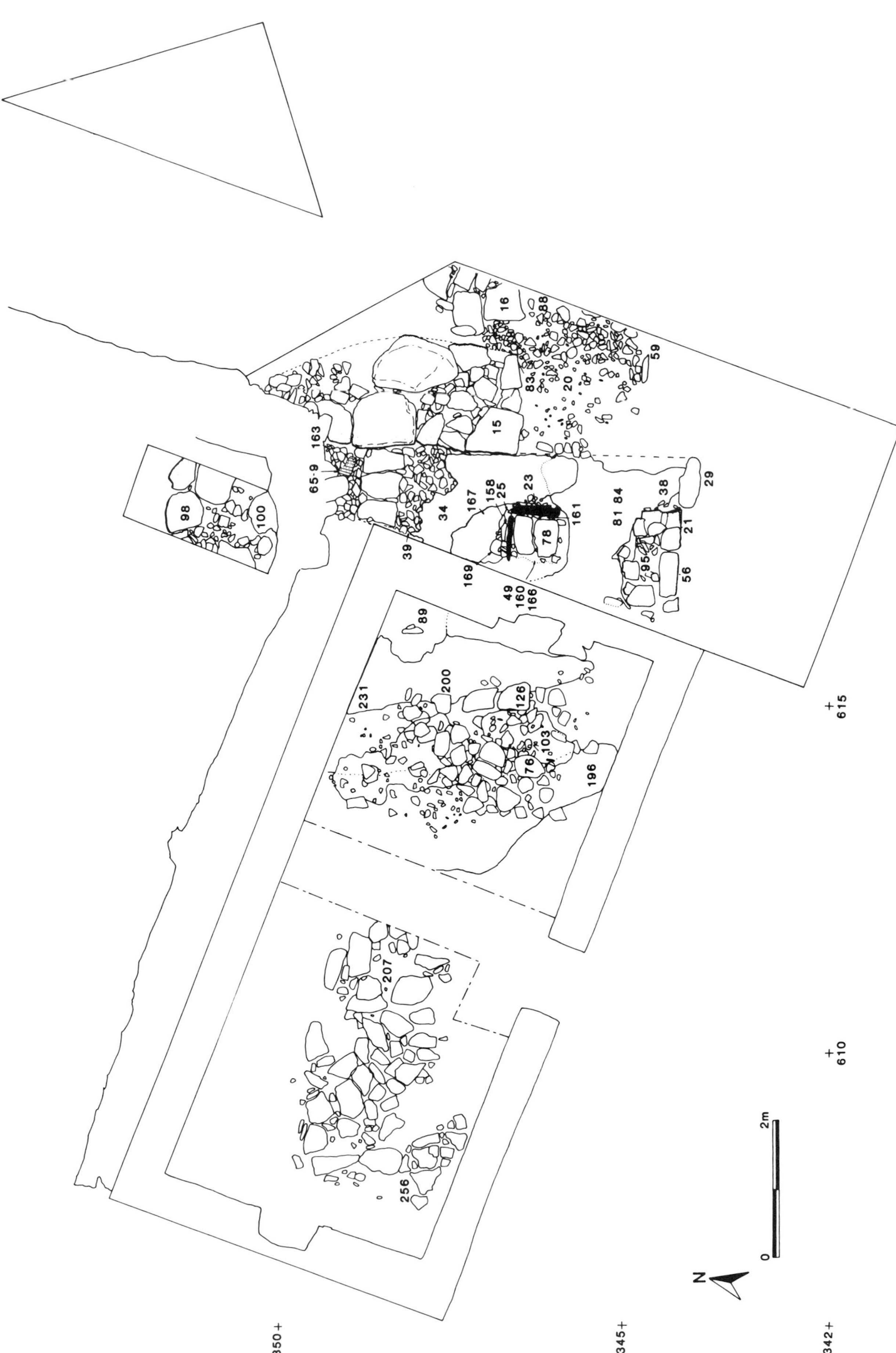

FIG. 38
House 8: Phase 10

PLATE 11
House 8: the blackhouse central hearth in the living area

threshold, and against the *talan*. This formed the beaten surface of the living area, though it was not found to extend fully to the north wall. Context 81 produced a sherd of coarse pottery (sf. 176), a clay pipe fragment (sf. 179), and iron (sf. 177). Traces of the floor also survived in Area 2 (89). Wear marks of human activity were visible, particularly around the hearth. Red ash (49), probably burnt peat or turf, was found on the hearth, and a dump of turf lumps (69, 67, 66, 65) were found at the back of the dwelling area. Amongst peat 69 was some wood (sf. 139) and a stone tool (sf. 260). Ash also seems to have been scattered over the floor, and at some late stage this was covered over with a patch of more yellow clay (34).

The byre at the southern end had, unfortunately, been largely removed by later activity. Just to the west of the blackhouse was a curving pattern of stones, set in a brown silty clay, forming the fragmentary remains of a cleit or store-shed (207). A few flat stones (256) to the south of it may represent part of a roughly paved surface. Amongst them were two fragments of coarse pottery (sfs 723, 790).

To the east of the blackhouse was a flagged surface (16), forming a path between the building and the facing Blackhouse H (Pl. 12).

Phase 11 (Fig. 39)

About 30 years later the blackhouse was largely removed, with only the lower courses around the north-east corner remaining. The byre was completely cleared, and only a few of the lower stones of the east wall were left in a jumbled mass (61, 41, 37, 99). A whetstone (sf. 20) and coarse pottery (sf. 19) were found in context 37. The *talan*, however, survived, as did the flooring and most of the hearth, though the west and east side-stones were ripped out (71). Two stones (54) that had been lying near the hearth were also disturbed.

Some dark reddish-brown silty clay (50) and ash (36) was spread around, and was covered by more disturbed clay and ash (48, 35) and black silt (26); contexts 36 and 48 produced some coarse pottery (sfs 127–8), and context 26 produced a copper-alloy nail (sf. 17). Sticky soil with ash (33) was found over this accumulation, and was associated with a similar soil (28) at the south end of the building. A glass button (sf. 26) was found in context 28.

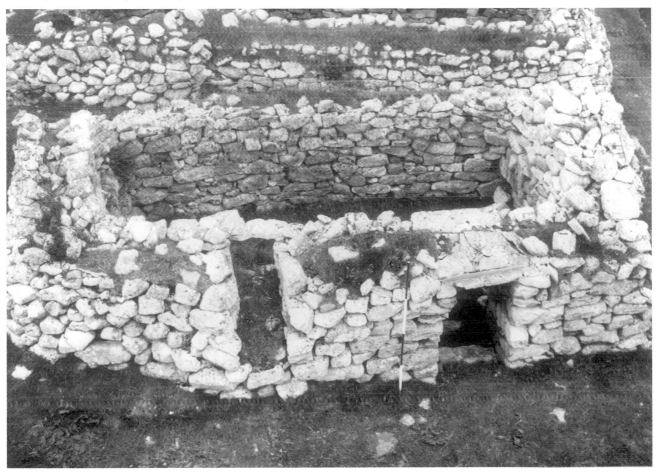

PLATE 12
Blackhouse H, looking east

FIG. 39
House 8: Phase 11

The cleit to the west of the blackhouse was demolished, and its ruins covered by an extensive dump of red peat/turf ash (91, 107, 112, 170). Associated with the ash (170) was a black silty layer with burnt material (216) and some stones (247–9). A hollow (217) was also noted in the ash, filled with more burnt material (209). The ash contained animal bone, including two pieces of whalebone (sfs 365, 427); bird and fish bones; a ?worked bone (sf. 442); coarse pottery (sfs 428–31, 434–6, 441, 444, 447–53, 466–9, 474–5, 481–2, 484–5, 497–502, 506, 513, 563, 662, 687, 694–5, 707, 713, 743–4); a piece of quartz (sf. 561); wood (sf. 432); and a stone tool (sf. 686). Preserved in the dump were pieces of egg membrane (sfs 483, 511, 514) and heather stalks. The burnt material (216) produced coarse pottery (sfs 515, 551, 554, 559, 565, 567–8, 587, 589, 614–15, 623, 630, 653–6, 729–34, 737–9, 742). Associated with the ash (107) was a greasy peaty soil (105), and a dark clayey soil with grits and small stones (116). The latter layer contained coarse pottery (sfs 234–7, 360–61, 425–6) and a stone tool (sf. 411).

The burnt material was covered by patchy areas of stones (187, 188), amongst which were fragments of coarse pottery (sfs 409, 476–8, 603–6) and a piece of egg membrane (sf. 479). These were, in turn, covered by midden material (194, 185). This contained animal and fish bones; more egg membrane (sfs 388, 391–2, 404, 406); and coarse pottery (sfs 423, 438–40). There were also distinctive clumps of limpet shells, stacked together and dumped. The accumulated dumps were sealed by black greasy, silty clay (139, 180), which contained a few fragments of coarse pottery (sfs 386–7, 390, 405); and a piece of copper alloy (sf. 403), and then sealed by small stones (173) and a spread of brown silt (168). This latter layer contained a dump of hammers and polishing stones (sfs 312, 315–17, 330–32, 334–6, 346); a quern fragment (sf. 383); and a stone sample (sf. 337), along with some coarse pottery (sfs 319–21, 329, 338, 343, 347, 364, 368–76, 384–5); iron (sfs 313, 318, 333, 339, 348); shell (sf. 314); bone (sf. 344), and large pieces of whalebone (sfs 345, 389). This was finally sealed by reddish-brown silty layers with stones (171, 244). Amongst context 171 were fragments of coarse pottery (sfs 357–8); iron (sfs 340–42, 356), and a quern fragment (sf. 408).

Perhaps associated with the midden dumps (194, 185) was more midden (104) over the walling (173). Context 104 produced coarse pottery (sfs 199, 228, 229b, 231, 263–5). Some linear stone features (117, 125) were also noted. Two fragments of coarse pottery (sf. 407, 437) and a stone tool (sf. 410) were found with stones 117. The midden was covered by irregular scatters of stones (27 on 42), which was sealed by dark reddish-brown soil (24, 64). This deposit also covered patches of ash (107) and sandy silt (106). Context 24 produced coarse pottery (sfs 185, 189, 229a); a glass stopper (sf. 184); a bead (sf. 186); iron (sfs 180–82, 190); zinc (sf. 196); and a bone button (sf. 187). Context 64 produced coarse pottery (sfs 114, 118, 188, 191); iron (sfs 116–17); a button (sf. 115); a slate pencil (sf. 183); wood (sf. 145); a bead (sf. 173); and a stone tool (sf. 131).

The east wall of Blackhouse I was also taken down, and into this space was built a new cottage, with a rear garden to be used for cultivation and as a stack-yard.

Phase 12 (Fig. 40)

House 8 is a rectangular-plan dwelling, 10.42m by 5.12m, aligned east-west, with a three-bay frontage and central entry, facing towards Village Bay. It would, like House 6, have been divided into two main rooms, with an entrance lobby and small back bedroom/store. Some traces of a prepared surface were noted, particularly a dark peaty silty layer (142), and below the north wall was a rough drain (245, 241, 242, 136, 233). The peaty silt layer (142) produced coarse pottery (sfs 276, 280, 296); iron (sfs 287, 292–3); zinc sheet (sf. 294); and leather (sf. 290). In the drain was some coarse pottery (sfs 570, 629, 631); a knife (sf. 560); iron (sf. 553); glass (sf. 564); a bead (sf. 566); a worked bone (sf. 722); textile (sf. 552); and some egg membrane (sf. 718). The walls were constructed with footings (13, 14, 74), on which the rubble coursing was laid with lime mortar (4, 5, 6, 75).

Within the house, layers of brown and reddish-brown soil formed a base for the first phase of flooring. In the west room the flooring had been heavily disturbed by later activity, but in the east room there were fragmentary remains of a wooden floor (58, 82). The decayed condition, unfortunately, made it impossible to identify the position of joists, or the direction of planking. Two pieces of wood showed evidence of sawing, and it was clear that, in part, the planks had been covered with patterned floorcloth. With the floor remnants were iron nails (sfs 87, 95, 97, 99, 102, 108–9); wood (sfs 94, 96, 98, 100–1, 103, 106); bone (sf. 88); and a button (sf. 107). At a later stage a new floor was laid, partly of cement and partly of wood. In the northern half of the east room a hard-core of very large, well-rounded stones (52), each *c.* 0.40m across, mainly of granophyre, was laid. The irregular surface was covered with a blind of crushed mortar (51), river-washed granophyre pebbles, some Ballachulish Slate, pantile, fish bones, and some pieces of metal. This material became graded as it settled into the voids, with pebbles (47) and some linoleum fragments (sf. 80); iron (sfs 32–3, 43, 46, 85); tar (sf. 45); shell (sf. 84); copper alloy (sf. 93); and wood (sf. 50); and formed a bed for a 0.05m thick cement/concrete floor (46). A scarcement provided support for a wooden floor, probably suspended, perhaps in part set on stones (9) over a dark brown to very dark greyish-brown soil (10), in the southern half of the room. The deposit was heavily contaminated with objects which entered the soil when the wooden flooring rotted (see Phase 13). Traces of cement/concrete flooring (134) were also found in the south-west corner of the house, set on reddish peaty silt (147); while in the entrance lobby a layer of sand (140) formed a bedding for a further patch of flooring. A fragment of coarse pottery (sf. 295) and a piece of iron (sf. 291) were found in context 147.

The gabled end walls accommodated fireplaces, with neat lintels and hearth stones. The west stone (135) remained *in situ*, and some ash (143) was found in front of it, containing ten pieces of iron (sfs 277–9, 282–6, 288–9). At the east fireplace, where an iron suspension bar is still *in situ*, a primary layer of stones, including a whetstone (sf. 195), had been laid down (97). These were covered with a bed of loose brown soil (96), in which a piece of iron was found (sf. 198); more stones (93), and a further pack of soil (94) to take the hearth stone (7). Here, however, there was some evidence to suggest that the hearth had

FIG. 40
House 8: Phase 12

FIG. 41
House 8: Phase 13

been re-set at some time. Turf was used as a fuel, and some red ash (195) was cleared and dumped outside, in the vicinity of Area 3. Amongst the ash was a slate pencil (sf. 779). Later, coal, of a poor quality, was used, and the ashes (193) were dumped in the same place. The peat ash may have built up over a long period, and there was no stratigraphic link with the sequence in Area 1. It could conceivably have built up since Phase 10.

A drainage channel was dug behind the house, its northern edge revetted with stones (87) overlain by reddish-brown gritty soil (86); and a garden wall (60) was erected, over a layer of dark reddish-brown silty loam (62). Context 86 produced coarse pottery (sfs 216, 218–21), while the loam (62) also produced coarse pottery (sfs 82–3, 89–91, 105, 110–11) and a flint (sf. 92).

Phase 13 (Fig. 41)

During the occupation of the house up to 1930, household rubbish and other material was dumped outside the east gable wall of the house, over the site of the ruined blackhouse.

A midden developed on a dark reddish-brown to black soil (19), which contained coarse pottery (sfs 12, 14), and a pottery whorl (sf. 13), and small and medium-sized stones (22), which covered the blackhouse interior. The blackhouse midden layer of reddish-brown soil (17) was dumped near the gable wall, and spread around the disturbed stones of the wrecked east wall of the blackhouse. It contained some coarse pottery (sfs 4–7, 9–10, 16), crockery, glass, iron, wood, zinc sheeting, slate, some animal bone and shell, and a piece of tailors' chalk (sf. 29).

Following this deposit, the southern end of Area 1 became part of a rough pathway (18), forming part of The Street, and devoid of any objects.

At a later stage, richer midden material was dumped — a dark reddish-brown soil (12), particularly stony around the ruined walls and byre area of the blackhouse, which contained a shoe sole, three fragments of coarse pottery (sfs 2–3, 11), more crockery and glass, iron — possibly from a bedstead, and an Eley shotgun cartridge (sf. 22). Finally, a grey-brown soil (2) accumulated, in which were larger quantities of crockery and glass, a fragment of coarse pottery (sf. 8), iron objects, zinc (sf. 31), tar, a button (sf. 27), leather (sf. 419), part of a doll (sf. 30), and the runner stone of a rotary quern (sf. 1). The soils of the upper layer may have been dumped in quick succession, or been subject to significant disturbance, for fragments of pottery and glass from the same vessels were found in several layers. In some cases this disturbance had, to a certain extent, led to contamination of layers from earlier phases.

In the trench between the house and garden, brown soil (113) accumulated, in which was found wooden plank fragments, zinc sheet, coarse pottery (sf. 266); leather (sf. 256) and cloth. A roughly level area of stone covered this material (101), and was, in turn, sealed by a brown turfy soil (72). The turf produced a stone tool (sf. 258). All of these layers of soil and stone had been splashed with tar, indicating that their deposition pre-dated 1930.

In the garden a fibrous soil (80) built up, and became the surface for a tar preparation site (77) used in coating the felt roof, which replaced the original zinc plate cover. The soil contained coarse pottery (sfs 141, 174–5, 178, 212–15) and stone tools (sfs 201, 224, 259).

Following the Evacuation in 1930 the condition of the house declined quickly. Plaster fell from the walls, and mortar from the wall-head. Patches of this material, contexts 8 and 11, were found in the south-east corner. Context 8 produced some iron objects (sfs 39–41, 62) and leather (sf. 44). The suspended plank flooring rotted, and the items left on the cottage floor fell through into the cavity below, and became mixed with the underlying soil. This heavily contaminated layer (10, see Phase 12) produced coins dating from 1903–11 (sfs 34, 156, 158, 171); a medallion of 1903 (sf. 169); iron objects (sfs 35–8, 54, 57, 65, 68, 71, 74, 76–7, 113, 119–21, 123–5, 132, 134, 138, 142–3, 146, 151–2, 159, 162, 166–7, 172, 193); leather (sfs 55, 66, 135b, 147); copper-alloy (sfs 49, 135a, 148, 160–61, 192); zinc (sfs 63–4, 122, 136, 150); lead (sf. 78); glass (sfs 56, 112, 129, 149, 165, 168); a button (sf. 67); collar stud (sf. 137); beads (sfs 69, 126, 133); bone (sf. 70); a slate pencil (sf. 130); pencil leads (sf. 157); clay pipe (sf. 144); crockery (sf. 153); combs (sfs 155, 164); plaster (sf. 154); wood (sf. 75); and textiles (sfs 163, 170).

Phase 14 (Fig. 42)

Sometime after 1957, NTS work parties began repair and consolidation work on the house. A patch of mixed mortar (137, sf. 275) was found inside by the north wall, and the east hearth stone appeared to have been re-set. A plastic comb was found in the disturbed soil close by.

The topsoil (1, 3, 73, 133, 192), containing zinc sheet, crockery, coarse pottery (sfs 42, 81), copper alloy (sfs 267–8), iron, glass, a button (sf. 28), slate (sfs 23–5), leather, wire and wood, finally formed the bed of a *Holcus (lanatus)-Agrostis* grassland; the mound over the blackhouse and midden marked by nettles.

3:3 The Artefactual Evidence

3:3:1 Coarse Pottery (A. MacSween)

The coarse pottery assemblage from House 8 and the area around comprises around 600 sherds, representing an estimated 185 vessels.

The majority of the sherds are undecorated body sherds, making it difficult to determine vessel shape and size, but fortunately there are some rims and bases which give an indication of the range of vessel types present.

All the pottery is 'hand thrown' — there is no indication that a wheel or tournette had been used. The predominant method of manufacture was coil construction (see Tables 7–16). Often the vessels had split along a junction, and where this was the case, the type of junction revealed was almost always 'N-type', with the coils joining obliquely in section.

The majority of vessels appear to have been used for cooking. The exteriors of many are heavily sooted (see Tables 7–16), and often there is a residue or further sooting on the interiors.

The task of matching up sherds which may have belonged to one vessel was complicated by the extent to which some sherds had been burnt or abraded once they had been discarded. Because of secondary burning, and also the use of the majority of vessels as cooking pots, colour was of little use in matching sherds, so fabric was the attribute relied on most heavily, backed up by a consideration of colour, thickness, and method of manufacture where possible.

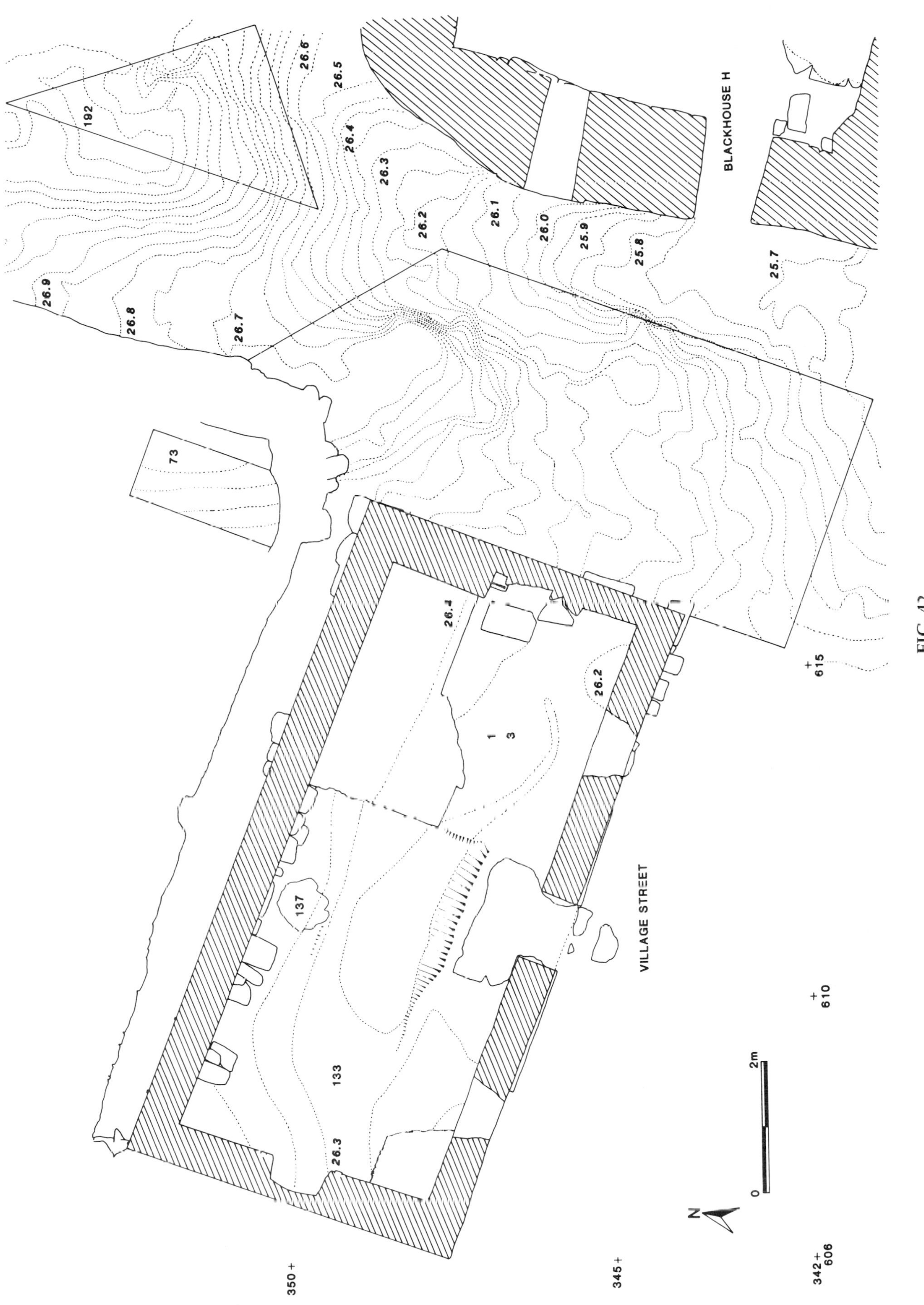

FIG. 42
House 8: Phase 14, and contours

Fifteen thin-sections from pottery of various phases were analysed by Hugh Nicholson (Dept. Geology, Edinburgh University). From the mixed nature of the inclusions in the sherds, and their relatively small size, it is probable that the inclusions were natural to the clays rather than deliberately added. Three sub-groups were identified:

1. *Clays containing inclusions from granitic rocks.*
2. *Clays containing inclusions from gabbroic/basaltic rocks.*
3. *Clays containing a mixture of gabbroic/basaltic and granitic rocks.*

SUB-GROUP 1		SUB-GROUP 2		SUB-GROUP 3	
Sample	*Phase*	*Sample*	*Phase*	*Sample*	*Phase*
772	2	775	2	538	5
521	4	213	13	209	8
582	4	199	11	556	10
488	5			690	10
308	7			498	11
652	9			744	11

TABLE 6

House 8: coarse pottery, clay inclusion analysis

The clays were probably stream-bed sediments. Too few samples were analysed to determine whether a particular source was favoured by certain groups on the site.

There is nothing to suggest that the pottery is anything other than what could have been manufactured on the island, nor do the fabrics change noticeably over the life of the site. The predominant fabric is a clay containing a large proportion of small quartz and black igneous inclusions, and sometimes a percentage of micaceous inclusions. Often quartzite is present in the sherds, and may in some cases have been deliberately added. In sherds from some of the larger vessels, gravel or crushed rock had been added — usually angular fragments in proportions ranging from 10–20%. By no means all the sherds from larger vessels have a component of rock fragments: some of the vessels seem to have been able to survive firing, and, from the soot build-up, many heatings and coolings, without the addition of large rock fragments. Occasionally, organics (apparently grass) had been added to the pottery (sfs 118, 374). Additions could be determined by looking for voids and impressions in the section of the sherd. These sherds can be distinguished from other sherds where the impressions were on one side of the sherd only (e.g. sf. 713), and were due to a damp pot resting on the grass during manufacture.

The majority of vessels have roughly smoothed surfaces, but there are some sherds (e.g. sf. 14) which indicate that the pot had been burnished, to lessen its porosity.

Catalogue

Only illustrated sherds are described. See Tables 7–16 for summary information on all the pottery found from House 8. The number in brackets after the sf. number refers to the find number in the tables. The pottery has been grouped by the phase to which it relates in the catalogue and tables. If a vessel comprising sherds from different phases is represented, it is included in the phase in which the majority of finds were made. If there were the same number of finds from more than one phase, the vessel is included with the earliest phase represented.

Phase 4 (Fig. 43)

sf. 548 (FN 377). Basal sherd. 25 sherds, including this one, thought to be of same vessel (sfs 541–3, 636, 643, 671, 765–6, 768, 782–3, 788 — Phase 4; 465, 486, 495, 518, 530, 536–7 — Phase 5; 377 — Phase 8). Form — plain rim, thinning to top; plain base, slightly footed, angled. Brown/red with grey core. Fabric — hard, coarse quartz/black igneous matrix, to 2mm, large angular rock fragments to 7mm (5%). Coil constructed — N-shaped coil junctions. Exterior and interior sooted. One sherd (sf. 542) is spalled along the coil junction. Th. 9-19mm, rim diam. 300mm, base diam. 240mm, wt 1540g.

sf. 537 (FN 377). See above.

Phase 5 (Fig. 43)

sf. 487 (FN 487). Rim sherd. 2 rim sherds, including this one, of the same vessel (also sf. 488). Everted rim, broadening out to shoulder. Brown exterior, black interior. Fabric — hard, small quartz/black igneous/mica matrix. Interior and exterior sooted. Th. 8mm, wt 78.8g.

sf. 492 (FN 326). Body sherd. 12 sherds, including this one, of the same vessel (also sfs 462–3, 491, 534 — Phase 5; 326, 433, 455 — Phase 7; 735 — Phase 10; 554, 630, 654 — Phase 11). Form — two of the body sherds have a carination (sfs 326, 492), pinched up from the side of the vessel; plain base, slightly rounded. Red/brown/grey. Fabric — hard, coarse quartz/black igneous matrix, to 3mm; large black igneous rock inclusions to 5mm (5%). Coil constructed. Exterior sooted. Th. 7–12mm, wt 257.8g.

sf. 639 (FN 461). Rim sherd. 3 sherds, including this one, of the same vessel (sfs 461 — Phase 5; 570 — Phase 12). Plain rim. Grey/red/black. Fabric — hard, small quartz/black igneous matrix; larger rock inclusions to 3mm (5%). Coil constructed. Exterior and interior sooted. Th. 10–12mm, wt 43.9g.

Phase 7 (Fig. 43)

sf. 303 (FN 250). Body sherd. 7 sherds, including this one, of the same vessel (also sfs 250, 255, 413 — Phase 7; 447–8, 567 — Phase 11). Form — plain rim, flattened; basal sherd slightly angled. Brown/red. Fabric — coarse quartz/black igneous matrix, to 2mm; occasional larger inclusions, to 7mm. Coil constructed. Exterior and interior sooted. Th. 10–11mm, wt 145.5g.

sf. 350 (FN 350). 1 perforated body sherd. Red exterior, black interior. Fabric — hard, coarse quartz matrix to 3mm. Coil constructed. Interior sooted. Th. 11mm, perforation diam. 6mm, wt 42.8g.

sf. 373 (FN 397). Body sherd. 3 sherds, including this one, from the same vessel (also sf. 397). One sherd is perforated with two holes, 6mm diam., 23mm apart. Grey. Fabric — hard, small quartz/black igneous/mica matrix; occasional large quartz to 8mm. Exterior and interior sooted. Th. 6–8mm, wt 54.2g.

Phase 8 (Fig. 43)

sf. 251 (FN 251). 1 decorated body sherd; with raised strip or beading, probably pinched up from the vessel side rather than applied. Black exterior, red interior. Fabric — hard, large quartz/black igneous matrix, to 2mm; very occasional larger inclusions to 7mm. Exterior sooted. Th. 11mm, wt 12.4g.

sf. 359 (FN 359). 2 basal sherds, probably from a globular vessel. Brown with grey core. Fabric — hard, coarse quartz/black igneous inclusions, to 5mm. Coil constructed. Sooting on exterior. Th. 10mm, base diam. 180mm, wt 144g.

Phase 9 (Fig. 43)

sf. 725 (FN 725). 1 rim sherd. Plain rim, probably from a straight-sided vessel. Brown. Fabric — hard, small quartz/black igneous matrix; coarse quartz, to 5mm (20%). Coil constructed. Exterior sooted. Th. 10mm, wt 119.9g.

KEY FOR TABLES 7–16 IS AS FOLLOWS:

FN = finds number of catalogue entry
No. = number of sherds represented
F = fine; sherds less than 4mm thick
M = medium; sherds between 5–9mm thick
T = thick; sherds over 10mm thick
R = Rim type: p — plain; f — flattened; e — everted; i — inward sloping; o — outward sloping.
BY = Body: g — globular; c — corrugated; s — straight sided; n — necked
BS = Base: pa — plain, angled; fa — footed, angled; pr — plain, rounded
D = Decoration: co — undecorated cordon; dc — decorated cordon; ca — carination; r — rilling
S = Surface finish: b — burnished; s — smoothed; p — perforated
FAB = Fabric: a percentage indicates the presence of organic tempering
MAN = Manufacture: cl — coil (type undetermined); n — N-shaped coil; u — U-shaped coil; sl — slab-built
SOOT = * indicates that either the exterior, interior, or both surfaces of a sherd are sooted

FN	No.	F	M	T	R	BY	BS	D	S	FAB	MAN	SOOT
533	3		*			n					cl	*
664	2			*						10	cl	*
702	1		*									*
703	2		*					co		10		
704	13			*				dc			cl	*
705	1			*								
773	2			*		g					cl	*
780	2		ab							10		

TABLE 7
House 8: summary of coarse pottery from Phase 2

FN	No.	F	M	T	R	BY	BS	D	S	FAB	MAN	SOOT
377	25			*	p		fa				n	*
395	10		*		e	g					cl	*
521	3			*						20		*
529	7			*							n	*
540	5		*									*
544	1		*									*
547	1			*								*
549	5			*			pr			10		*
550	2			*						10		*
571	2			*							n	*
576	4		*									*
577	1		*									*
585	3			*								
608	1		*									*
634	1		*									
638	2			*	f							*
666	3		*									
673	1		*									
675	2		*									
749	1		*									*
753	5		*								n	*
754	1		*									*
757	1		*									*
762	1		*									
763	1		*									
764	4		*									*
786	1		ab									
787	1		*								n	

TABLE 8
House 8: summary of coarse pottery from Phase 4

FN	No.	F	M	T	R	BY	BS	D	S	FAB	MAN	SOOT
326	12			*			pr	ca			cl	*
454	2		*									*
461	3			*	p						cl	*
464	2		*							10		*
487	2		*		e	g						*
489	1	*										*
493	1		*									*
519	1		*									*
522	1		*							20		
532	1		*							20		*
353	10		*									*
539	1		*									*
640a	1			*						10	cl	*
640b	1		*									*
781	1			*								*

TABLE 9
House 8: summary of coarse pottery from Phase 5

FN	No.	F	M	T	R	BY	BS	D	S	FAB	MAN	SOOT
230	8			*		g			b		n	*
250	7			*	f		pa				cl	*
302	4		*		p						cl	*
304	3			*			fa					*
308	5		*							or	n	
327	3			*					s		n	*
350	1			*					p		cl	*
397	3		*						p			*

TABLE 10
House 8: summary of coarse pottery from Phase 7

FN	No.	F	M	T	R	BY	BS	D	S	FAB	MAN	SOOT
21	1		*						s			
209	3			*						10	u	*
240	4			*								*
246	1		*									
251	1			*				r				*
359	2			*		g					cl	*

TABLE 11
House 8: summary of coarse pottery from Phase 8

FN	No.	F	M	T	R	BY	BS	D	S	FAB	MAN	SOOT
414	1		*									*
415	3		*								n	*
417	2		*		f							*
507	1		*									*
651	1		*									*
652	3			*			a					*
658	4		*								cl	*
661	4			*						10		*
663	1		*									*
716	1		*									*
725	1			*	p						cl	*
741	2			*						10		*
745	1		ab									
746	1		*									

TABLE 12
House 8: summary of coarse pottery from Phase 9

FN	No.	F	M	T	R	BY	BS	D	S	FAB	MAN	SOOT
61	7		*		e	g			b		n	*
176	19			*	o					20	n	*
329	11		*		f						cl	*
353	5			*			a					*
368	2		*									
398	1		*									*
437	9		*						s			*
472	1		*									*
473	1		*									*
474	1			*								*
477	11			*	p		a			10	n	*
516	1			*			p					*
555	15			*						20	cl	*
557	5		*									*
562	4			*	p	c					cl	*
588	13										u	*
599	1			*						10	cl	
600	2			*						10	cl	*
617	4									20		*
618	1									20	cl	*
626	1					c					cl	
627	3			*	p	c					cl	*
632	2			*	p		f				n	*
687a	1		*									
692	1									20		*
708a	1			*							cl	*
723d	1		*									*
723e	1	*										
740	1			*								
790	1			*								

TABLE 13
House 8: summary of coarse pottery from Phase 10

FN	No.	F	M	T	R	BY	BS	D	S	FAB	MAN	SOOT
19	14		*								n	*
58	8		*		e	g			s		n	*
114	1		*									
118	1		*							or		*
128	1			*								*
185	3		*								cl	*
191	2			*							cl	*
551	10			*			af				n	*
228	5		*						s		n	*
229b	4		*		is	g					n	*
234	1		*			g						*
253	12		*			s			b		n	*
263	24		*				pa			10	cl	*
265	3		*		p							
319	1		*									*
321	1	*										*
358	1		*									*
360	3		*				r				n	*
361	1		*									
369	4			*	p	c				20	n	*
370	1		*									
374	7		*							or		*
375	1			*								*
384	5		*									
386	1		*			g						*
405	7		*				r					*
430	1			*		s				10	cl	*
434	1			*	f	g						*
436	3		*		p						sl	*
450	1		*				r					*
451	2			*							n	*
452	5			*						10	cl	*
468	4			*								*
481	4			*		p						*
482	3			*						10		*
501	2			*								
513	1		*									*
606	1			*								*
615a	1		*								n	
615b	1			*						10		
662a	9			*		p					cl	*
662b	7		*								cl	*
662c	2		*			f					cl	*
662d	1			*						10	cl	*
687a	1		*									
695	2			*	f	c	fa				cl	*
732	2			*						30	cl	

TABLE 14
House 8: summary of coarse pottery from Phase 11

FN	No.	F	M	T	R	BY	BS	D	S	FAB	MAN	SOOT
82	1			*							cl	*
83	1		*									
89	2			*								
90	5			*								
105	3		*									
110	10		*			g	r		b		cl	*
111	2			*						10		*
220	2			*								*
221	1			*								
364	4		*		p				s		cl	*

TABLE 15
House 8: summary of coarse pottery from Phase 12

FN	No.	F	M	T	R	BY	BS	D	S	FAB	MAN	SOOT
Phase 13												
2	1		*									
3	4		*									*
4	1		*			g					cl	*
5	2		*									
6	1		*									
7	2			*								*
8	1		*									
9	1		*									
14	2		*						b			
16	2	*										
18	5		*								n	
81	2		*									*
175	1			*								
214	1		*									
215	1			*								*
Phase 14												
42	1										cl	*

TABLE 16

House 8: summary of coarse pottery from Phases 13 and 14

Phase 10 (Fig. 44)

sf. 471 (FN 329). Rim sherd. 11 sherds, including this one, from the same vessel (sfs 602, 644, 697, 706 — Phase 10; 329, 466, 499, 694 — Phase 11). Form — flattened rim; flat part of base, with grass impressions on underside (sf. 706). Black/brown/grey. Fabric — hard, coarse quartz matrix to 2mm; large quartz and siltstone to 4mm (5%). Coil constructed. Exterior and interior sooted. Th. 6–10mm, wt 165.1g.

sf. 562 (FN 562). Rim sherd. 4 rim sherds, including this one, from the same vessel (also sfs 592, 690 — Phase 10). Plain rim. Red exterior, brown interior. Fabric — hard, small quartz/black igneous matrix; large rock inclusions, to 7mm (5%), angular. Coil constructed — coils smoothed on interior, but not on exterior. Exterior sooted. Th. 20–22mm, rim diam. 320mm, wt 1510. 5g.

sf. 600 (FN 600). Basal sherd. Also one body sherd from same vessel (sf. 708b — Phase 10). Slightly angled base. Red exterior, grey interior. Fabric — hard, small quartz matrix; rock inclusions to 7mm (10%). Coil construction -- only smoothed on interior. Exterior and interior sooted. Th. 15mm, base diam. 140mm, wt 307.4g.

sf. 618 (FN 618). Rim sherd. Plain rim. Brown. Fabric — soft, coarse quartz/black igneous matrix, to 3mm. Coil constructed; coil joins still show on exterior, but not on interior. Exterior sooted. Th. 10mm, diam. 260mm, wt 108.3g.

sf. 627 (FN 627). 2 rim sherds. Also body sherd from same vessel (sf. 650 — Phase 10). Plain rim, thinning to top. Brown. Fabric — hard, small quartz/black igneous matrix; rock inclusions, to 5mm (5%), angular. Coil constructed; coils smoothed on interior, but not on exterior. Exterior sooted. Th. 13–25mm, diam. 260mm, wt 953.5g.

sf. 632 (FN 632). 1 basal sherd, 1 rim sherd. Plain base, slightly footed, probably from a straight-sided vessel; plain rim. Brown. Fabric — hard, coarse quartz/black igneous matrix, to 3mm. Coil constructed — N-shaped junctions. Exterior sooted. Th. 10–15mm, rim diam. 260mm, base diam. 220mm, wt 125.7g.

Phase 11 (Fig. 45)

sf. 369 (FN 369). Basal sherd. Also 2 body sherds (sfs 431, 738b) and 1 rim sherd (sf. 623) from same vessel. Form — plain base; plain rim. Grey/red/buff. Fabric — hard, small quartz/black igneous matrix; large siltstone, sandstone, black igneous rock inclusions, to 9mm (20%), round and angular. Coil constructed — N-shaped junctions. Exterior sooted. Th. 14–18mm, rim diam. 280mm, wt 779.8g.

sf. 386 (FN 386). 1 rim sherd, inward sloping, probably from globular vessel. Brown with black core. Fabric — hard, coarse quartz/black igneous, to 1mm. Exterior sooted. Th. 7mm, wt 16.8g.

sf. 407 (FN 229b). Rim sherd. Also 3 body sherds (sfs 229b, 264, 475 — Phase 11). Form — inward-sloping rim, from globular vessel. Grey interior, red exterior. Fabric — hard, small quartz/black igneous matrix; occasional larger inclusions to 7mm. Coil constructed — N-shaped junction. Exterior and interior sooted. Rim broken off at point of inflection. Th. 6–8mm, wt 78.2g.

sf. 434 (FN 434). 1 rim sherd, flat, probably from shouldered vessel. Grey with buff exterior margin, buff interior surface. Fabric — hard, matrix has relatively little quartz; occasional large quartz to 2mm. Exterior sooted. Th. 10mm, wt 16g.

sf. 565 (FN 477). Basal sherd. 11 sherds, including this one, from the same vessel (also sfs 477, 515, 655 — Phase 11). Form — plain rim; plain base, steeply angled. Brown. Fabric — hard, coarse quartz/black igneous matrix, to 1mm; larger quartz and rock inclusions in basal section, to 10mm (10%). Coil constructed — N-shaped junctions. Exterior sooted, residue. Th. 8–11mm, base diam. 200mm, wt 290g.

sf. 587 (FN 263). Basal sherd. 24 sherds, including this one, from the same vessel (sfs 263, 476, 500, 653, 737, 739 — Phase 11). Plain base, sharply angled. Red/brown/grey. Fabric — hard, coarse quartz/black igneous/mica matrix, to 2mm; large inclusions of quartzite and various rock inclusions, to 10mm (10%). One sherd (sf. 476) has a finger impression, probably from manufacture rather than decoration. Coil constructed; sf. 587 has a strengthening coil in the angle of its base. Exterior and interior sooted. Th. 8–10mm, base diam. 220mm, wt 540.5g.

sf. 623 (FN 369). See sf. 369.

sf. 695 (FN 695). Rim sherd. Also one basal sherd (sf. 744 — Phase 11) from this vessel. Form — flattened rim; slightly footed base, angled. Brown. Fabric — coarse quartz/black igneous, to 3mm. Coil constructed — coils smoothed on interior, unsmoothed on exterior. Exterior and interior sooted. Th. 15mm, rim diam. 250mm.

Pottery re-used as spindle whorls (Fig. 46)

Phase 8

sf. 227. Unfinished whorl from pottery sherd. A hole 12mm across has been started. Brown. Fabric — hard, small quartz matrix. Exterior sooted. Th. 8mm.

Phase 10

sf. 200. Part of whorl, possibly made from pottery sherd. Perforated with hole 7mm diam. Grey/brown. Fabric — hard, small quartz/black igneous matrix. Th. 6mm.

Phase 11

sf. 347. Pottery sherd with 7mm depression in one corner; does not go right through. Black. Fabric — hard, small quartz/black igneous matrix. Depression probably made by twisting a stick with a rounded point. Sooted on one side. Th. 5mm.

Phase 13

sf. 13. Part of pottery whorl — possibly fired as whorl. Brown. Fabric — hard, small quartz/black igneous matrix. Sooting on one side. Th. 7mm.

Vessel types by phase

Phase 2

The earliest phase containing pottery, Phase 2, is represented by eight vessels. There is one rim: sf. 805 (FN 773) which is from a globular vessel.

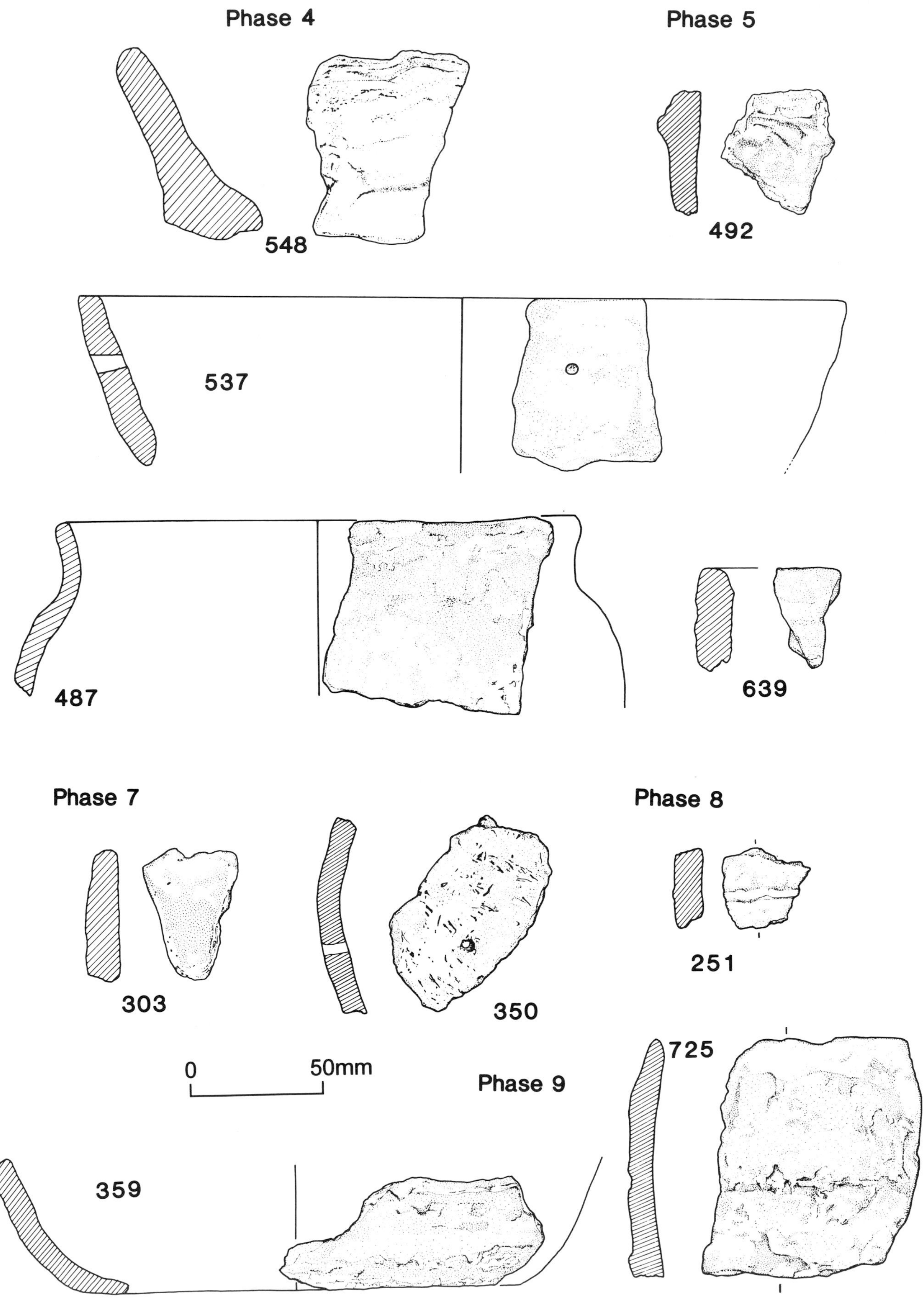

FIG. 43

House 8: coarse pottery (Phases 4–5 and 7–9). Sherds are illustrated under the phase in which they were found, not necessarily the phase to which they have been attributed. Sfs 548 and 537 are attributed to the same vessel. Scale 1:2

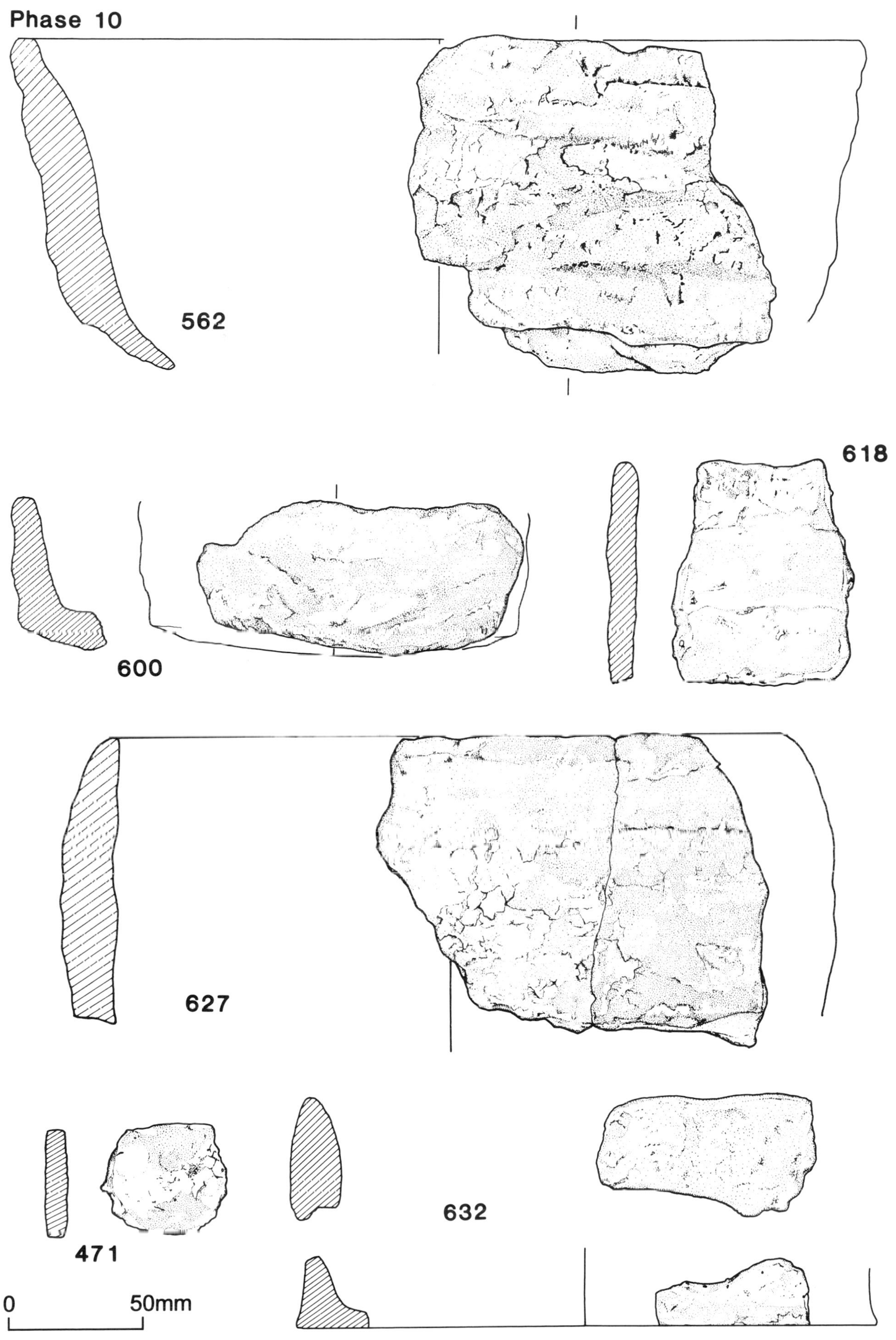

FIG. 44
House 8: coarse pottery (Phase 10). Scale 1:2

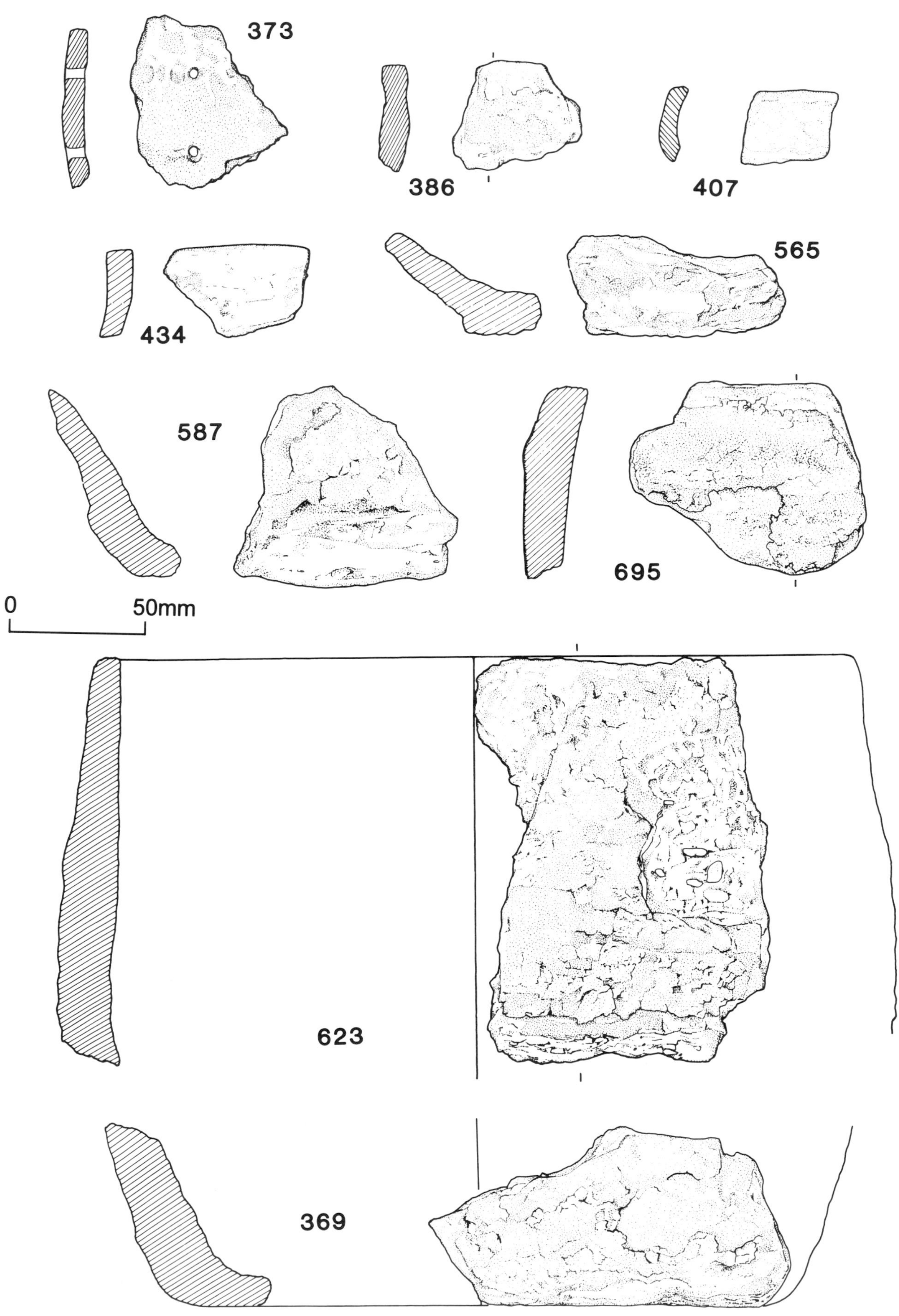

FIG. 45

House 8: coarse pottery (Phase 11). Sherds are illustrated under the phase in which they were found, not necessarily the phase to which they have been attributed. Sf. 373 is attributed to a vessel in Phase 7; sfs 369 and 623 are attributed to the same vessel. Scale 1:2

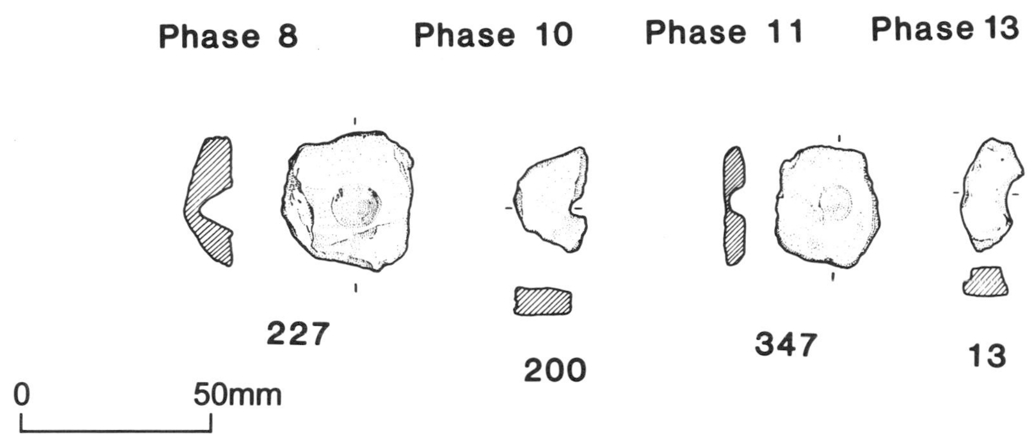

FIG. 46
House 8: coarse pottery whorls (Phases 8, 10–11 and 13). Scale 1:2

Sherd 804 (FN 703) has an undecorated cordon. The phase also produced the only examples of decorated cordons (sfs 774–5, FN 704), probably from the same vessel. Unfortunately, the sherds are too abraded to determine whether the decoration is zigzagging, or slanting incisions. If the cordon is decorated with a zigzag design, this would indicate an Iron Age date. Such decorations have been found on sherds from sites such as Dun Cuier, Barra (Young 1958, 307), and the earth-house at Foshigarry, North Uist (Beveridge 1931, 310). However, if the decoration on the cordon is impressed finger-decoration, this could imply either an Iron Age or a Late Bronze Age date. Finger-impressed cordons have been found at Iron Age sites, including Dun Cuier, but there are also Bronze Age examples, such as the urn from Trecklet in North Uist (Megaw and Simpson 1963, 67).

Phases 4–8

The majority of the 57 vessels represented in these phases are of medium coarseness — 7–10mm thick. Everted rims, probably from globular vessels (e.g. sf. 487, FN 487, Phase 5) are represented, as are larger vessels with angled sides narrowing in diameter towards the base (e.g. sf. 548, FN 377, Phase 4).

The only examples of decoration are on sf. 326 (FN 326, Phase 5), which has an undecorated carination, and sf. 251 (FN 251, Phase 8) which is decorated with a raised strip or 'beading'. Neither types of decoration are diagnostic of a particular period and cannot be used to date the pottery of these phases.

Phases 9–11

The remains of the 91 vessels associated with the building and occupation of the blackhouse in Phases 9 and 10, and the dumps of Phase 11, indicate the continued manufacture of globular vessels, and the appearance of thick 'corrugated' vessels.

The 'corrugated' vessels have plain rims, and flat bases (e.g. sf. 695, FN 695, Phase 11 — Fig. 45). Most of the other rims belonging to these phases are either plain, flattened, or everted.

A large proportion of the vessels from these phases are thick (over 10mm), and there are no decorated sherds.

Phases 12–14

From Phase 12 onwards there is a noticeable decrease in the amount of pottery present, and no new styles. It may be that the pottery from these later phases (mainly body sherds) is residual, probably reflecting an increasing reliance on imported crockery.

Discussion

Most of the pottery from the site came from the blackhouse phases (9–11). On sites of a similar age in the Western Isles, such as Barvas, Lewis (Cheape 1983) and Balevullin, Tiree (Holleyman 1947), the predominant form of vessel was the craggan, a round-based, globular-shaped vessel with an everted rim, varying in height from 360mm to only 100mm.

From records containing observations on the pottery, craggans were used for cooking, storing, and carrying food, and in the manufacture of fish liver oil (MacSween 1984, 5–6). Another use was in the churning of butter. Use as a churn required a vessel to be perforated. The perforations were plugged during churning, and opened occasionally to allow gases to escape (McLellan Mann 1908). The perforated sherds sf. 350 (Fig. 43) and sf. 373 (Fig. 45) from House 8 may have come from vessels used for churning, but the perforations are less than 10mm in diameter, and it is more likely that they were for fixing a lid or handle to the vessel.

The sherds from the blackhouse phases indicate that in addition to craggans, larger 'corrugated bucket-shaped vessels' (e.g. sf. 627 — Fig. 44) were also used. These vessels are 'corrugated' in the sense that their coils have been smoothed on the interior to a flat surface, while on the exterior they have not. This could have been the result of least effort — it would have been easier to smooth only the interior (the side in contact with food and requiring cleaning), while leaving the exterior the way it was manufactured. Alternatively, the corrugations could have been a form of decoration. A third possibility is that they were a deliberate functional trait, to increase the surface area of a vessel, which would have led to more effective heating — corrugation is only found on the larger cooking vessels.

From references to the manufacture of hand-made pottery of this period in the Western Isles, clay was collected from local sources and underwent very little preparation, apart from the removal of the larger gravel, before being shaped into vessels. The pots were left to dry for several days before being fired on the domestic hearth (Curwen 1938, 208).

From Phases 8–11 are three examples of sherds which were perforated and probably re-used as whorls (Fig. 46). The whorl from Phase 13 (sf. 13) was probably fired as such, rather than made from a sherd.

3:3:2 Crockery: Red and White Earthenware (H. Kelly)

The late pottery group from St Kilda shows several peculiarities. First and most evident is the surprisingly small size of the sherds from the excavation. Sherds discarded on a dump tend to be quite large and of an awkward shape. There are a few such sherds in the St Kilda assemblage, but they form a remarkably small percentage of the whole, and are mostly of large, thick, red earthenware dishes with slip decoration. The vast majority of the sherds are very small — the average must be under 50mm in diameter, perhaps under 25mm. This leads one to suspect that there has been disturbance on a fairly large scale.

A second curious feature is the almost total lack of backstamps on the sherds. Slipware and spongeware are certainly two of the commonest types and it is very unusual to find either of them marked. Rockingham glazed brown teapots are slightly more frequently marked but not so much as to make the lack of backstamps remarkable. On the other hand, there are large amounts of stoneware and transfer-printed ware present and these, especially the former, tend to be marked with some frequency. Yet the only approach to a backstamp is on a stoneware jam jar, and even from this the manufacturer's name is absent. The lack of backstamps is not due, either, to an absence of base sherds, which are present in quantity. Statistically this is impossible as a chance factor and again leads to the conclusion that there has been great and deliberate disturbance of the sherds in the past. Confirmation of this is given in the distribution of certain sherds, with some pieces, particularly of spongeware, recognisably distributed through several contexts and phases.

Shapes of pottery

The assemblage displays one peculiarity of Scottish peasant pottery of this period and that is the predominance of bowls over plates. Perhaps this belongs to Highland Zone Britain rather than to rural Scotland. There are plates present, and some, like Bell's 'Corea' pattern, are surprisingly fine, but the number of bowls, sponge-printed, hand-painted, or transfer-printed is far greater.

An almost incredible feature, though, is the total absence of jugs from the assemblage, and nothing speaks more eloquently of the isolation of St Kilda from the rest of Scotland.

In the second half of the 19th century jugs were undoubtedly the most popular form of crockery throughout Scotland. Their uses were, of course, many, but they were valued above all for their decorative qualities and were, in fact, decorated with an astonishing array of techniques and subjects. They were sometimes produced in identical pairs, or in sets of three in graduated sizes, and were so given as Christmas, birthday, or even wedding presents, often specially inscribed by the manufacturers or by a nearby dealer with a glost kiln.

Collections in the Lowlands of Scotland were widespread, but in the Highlands it often became a mania, and collections of over 100 jugs were not unknown. Even the humblest croft would have had a display of crockery in which jugs took pride of place. The only jug sherd from St Kilda is a spout fragment from a yellow ware cream jug.

Types of pottery

In view of the fact that many of the pottery types present on St Kilda are of the cheapest and least-studied types of wares, it seems convenient to discuss them here.

Slipware

This is really the name for a type of decoration which was applied to both white and red earthenware all over Europe for several centuries and is still widely used today. Clay is made into a 'slip' with water and is used to cover the biscuit body of the ware and allowed to dry. A variety of techniques can then be applied to decorate the ware further, finishing with a glaze. In the excavated samples the slip is usually white, brown or black, and the only further form of decoration applied is a white slip, trailed in a pattern over the brown. This is by far the commonest type of slipware made in Britain, and it is fully documented as being made from Aberdeen to Devon, and from Yorkshire to Ireland.

The red earthenware types present in the St Kilda group seem to be all fairly large bowls, or taller and narrower storage jars such as were used on the mainland for dairy work. Most have simply a plain slip in black or white on the inside, and brown on the outside, but a few are slip-trailed in white over brown. Unfortunately these sherds are very small and it is impossible to be sure of the pattern. Such patterns can be diagnostic of area of manufacture. In one or two sherds, however, the trailing would agree with a pattern of large round arches round the edge. This pattern is the typical design on Irish slipware. This is, however, far from certain and some of the sherds could agree with designs thought to be from Glaswegian potteries.

A finer type of slipware was popular from the 1840s for a decade or more. The body is white, and the bowls quite finely made. The slip is in several colours: brown, ochre, blue and white. The colours can be banded, slip-trailed, marbled, or even painted on. There are several tiny sherds from several small bowls of this kind, decorated in several patterns, in Phases 8, 11 and 14. One of the sherds has a hole bored inexplicably through it. The nearest known manufacturer of this ware is Verreville Pottery in Finnieston (at that time just outside Glasgow) under the ownership of Robert A. Kidston & Co. from *c.* 1838 to *c.* 1847, but the ware was certainly also made in other shapes by Harwood of Stockton, and in North Staffordshire.

Spongeware

There are two varieties of this: dabbed ware (in which the sponge is used to dab colour onto the biscuit piece), and sponge-printed ware. The latter is the only type represented on St Kilda.

Sponge-printing is a technique invented, probably in Scotland, *c.* 1835, but subsequently widely used in Western Europe and even in the USA. The hard root of a sponge is cut into a motif, glued to a little wooden handle, and then used to apply colour to the biscuit ware, rather in the manner of a child's potato print. Surprisingly complex motifs can be made by an experienced worker.

It was the first technique taught to young girls entering the painting department of potteries, and was generally applied to the coarsest of white earthenware bodies for the least opulent markets, e.g. export to Canada, the USA, South-East Asia, the Scottish Highlands, and rag and bone men.

It was commonest on small bowls but was applied to jugs, punch bowls, mugs, chamber pots, plates, etc. It was widely made in various centres in Britain: Glasgow, Greenock, Bo'ness, Fife, Newcastle/Sunderland and North Staffordshire, and, since it is seldom marked, it is extremely difficult to identify. Many of the St Kilda pieces can be paralleled by Glasgow sherds but, since motifs were widely copied and sponges were sold ready-made by some dealers, this evidence is by no means conclusive.

Brown teapots

There are several of these represented in the assemblage, but, as already stated, no backstamps are present. Unfortunately most of the teapots in the group are also of the least decorated and least recognisable forms. One tiny base sherd is from a rusticated pot, but this type was also manufactured over a large area, from Central Scotland to the Midlands. The type also has a long life-span, from *c.* 1850 until well into the 20th century.

Stoneware

This is abundantly present at all levels. Most of the sherds are from jam jars or 'meat loaf jars', but at least one whisky jar is present. Butter containers seem to be totally absent.

These pots were obviously greatly treasured since their shapes and toughness made them excellent storage jars.

All the sherds should date from after 1860, and the only clue to place of manufacture is part of an impressed mark on one jam jar indicating that Portobello was its place of origin. But with stoneware the place of origin of the product is more decisive of destination than the place of manufacture, and any of these pieces could have come from Glasgow, Bristol or London, though Portobello and Glasgow seem the most likely.

Disappointingly, the one whisky jar represented, which may not have contained whisky, has no dealer's mark on it, so its place of origin is unknown. 'Whisky jar' is a generic term; many of the jars could have contained other liquids, like varnish.

A unique object from context 10, Phase 12/13, is the knob from a hot water bottle in stoneware, known in Scotland as a 'pig'.

Transfer-printed ware

This was widely made from Central Scotland south to Bristol as well as in Northern Ireland and over much of North-West Europe.

None of the sherds present need be earlier than the 1840s, while some are distinctly later in date and are almost certainly from the 1910s. Among the patterns identified are:

Pattern	*Maker*	*Date*
Syria	Verreville and Britannia Potteries, Glasgow	1840s–1920s
Corea	J. & M. P. Bell & Co., Glasgow Pottery, Glasgow	*c.* 1875–*c.* 1890
Chinese Pheasant	Verreville Pottery, Glasgow	1838–1846
Apsley Plants	J. & M. P. Bell & Co., Glasgow	
Country Scenery	Victoria Pottery, Pollokshaws, now Glasgow	1854–*c.* 1870
The Lily of the Valley	Clyde Pottery, Greenock	*c.* 1880–*c.* 1900

Other patterns identified are 'Willow', 'Broseley', and 'Fibre' (in Scotland) or 'Weed' (in England), but all of these are so widely made in time and space as to be useless for dating or specifying origin.

Of the unidentified transfer patterns present, some are certainly English and seem to range in date from *c.* 1850 to *c.* 1910. English transfer ware of the second half of the 19th century has been little studied or published, and is largely ignored by museums.

Hand-painted ware

Very little of this is present, but especially notable are some comparatively luxurious sherds from at least two bowls with pink 'chrysanthemums' surrounded by green and brown leaf painting and pink lustre 'commas'. This type was widely made in Britain in the 1840s and 1850s.

Black basalte or Egyptian black

This consists of a fine red earthenware body stained with manganese and cobalt oxides to colour it black. It is fired at quite a high temperature so that no glaze is needed, and in England usually none was applied. In Scotland, however, the ware was generally burnished or given a thin layer of glaze.

The body was used for very ambitious ornaments by firms like Wedgwood and Bentley, but also for tea services (teapot, cream jug and sugar bowl) all over Britain. The one sherd of this type in the collection appears to be Scottish. In Scotland the ware was made principally, but not only, in Glasgow, and was very little made after 1860.

Date and attribution of the wares

So many of the types of pottery are of the cheapest and least studied that it is difficult to be precise about any dates.

There is very little, if anything, which could be before 1840. On the other hand the later types trail into the 1910s and could be from the 1920s in some cases.

The area from which the pottery came is very wide as one would expect. At the core of our area is Glasgow, which is almost certainly the principal emporium from which pots were obtained, but Portobello is certainly represented (perhaps in jam pots from Dundee), and the punch bowl in context 19, Phase 13 is almost certainly from Methven's of Kirkcaldy in Fife.

Most of the later transfer patterns look like English wares (probably from Staffordshire), and this agrees with the decline of many of the Scottish potteries in the late 19th century. Glasgow could still, however, have been the emporium from which the goods were bought.

The most likely area of origin of most of the spongeware is also Glasgow, but Bo'ness, particularly, must be borne in mind.

The slipware is more difficult. The most obvious place is Aberdeen, but while the more ornate slipware products of the Seaton Pottery are well known, no archaeological work has been done, and the commoner wares are virtually unknown. The same applies to Cumnock Pottery, Ayrshire. These are the two most widely known slipware potteries in Scotland. Again, slipware is known to have been made in Glasgow and Montrose, but very little is known about either. In England the most likely candidate would be a Yorkshire pottery.

3:3:3 Other Fired Clay

Twenty fragments of pantile, and three irregular fired clay lumps which could be tile, were found (sf. 307 — Phase 8; gfs 197/8, 190/9, 16/10, 24/11, 47/12, 62/12, 195/12, 2/13, 10/12–13, 18/13, 1/14). They have sanded undersurfaces, and have been fired to a good orangey-red colour. Pantiles were normally used in lowland Scotland, particularly on the east coast.

One baked clay marble (gf. 1/14) is a terracotta colour, and 17mm diameter. Marbles were introduced to St Kilda by a Mr Campbell of Sunderland around 1890 (Ross *c.* 1890).

3:3:4 Glass

A total of 837 fragments of glass were found, comprising vessel sherds (50.8%), sheet glass (46.3%), closures (0.8%), beads and buttons (1.1%), and unidentifiable flakes (1.0%).

Vessels

The containers include bottles for alcohol, food, and pharmaceuticals, along with fragments from other vessels.

One identifiable whisky bottle was found (gf. 3/14) — a square-sectioned base with rounded corners, and a very slightly domed central push-up, which bore the embossed lettering of 'WALKER/ WHISKY/KILMARNOCK'. The mould number 24A1 indicates that it was made between 1900 and 1910 (W. Burnet, pers. comm.).

A minimum of five wine bottles were found. They show some differences in manufacture, including hand-finished shoulders, necks, and applied finish of 3" diameter bottles, with neck stretch-marks, gas bubbles, and 'tears' (gfs 2/13, 12/13 — Fig. 47R); a well-formed, machine-made neck/finish in amber glass (sf. 149); and a straight neck with no mould seams and an applied finish (gf. 73/14). Eight base fragments were found and, where identifiable, were 3" or 4" diameter. All had domed push-ups, but they showed no clear pontil scarring. Alcohol was drunk in moderation, and was used mainly for medicinal purposes. Milk and port wine was given by the islanders to sick babies, and in 1877 *HMS Flirt* brought to the island two cases of brandy, sherry and port (MacDiarmid 1878, 233).

Several bottles could have contained processed foods or liquids other than alcohol. One body fragment (gf. 1/14) of a 'flat' bottle had the embossed letters 'CHICOR(Y)'. This presumably dates to after 1885 when coffee with chicory essence was introduced (Opie 1987, 56). Fragments of one other bottle, a cylindrical type, had embossed lettering on the body (gf. 1/14) — 'BRO...' Four bottle bases of this group were found. Two showed mould codes — a playing-card spade enclosing a 'P' with an accompanying '1', on a square base with expanded body, possibly a sauce bottle (gf. 10/12–13, Fig. 47P); and a ?2–piece moulded cylindrical bottle base with embossed numbers and letters — '7165 BLTK' (gf. 8/13). A fragment of square turquoise-green bottle base had a slightly domed push-up which probably once bore a mark (gf. 1/14). The only other base was from a 2" cylindrical vessel with rounded base edging and a moulded internal peak, not produced by a pontil (gf. 141/12).

A number of bottles probably contained pharmaceutical preparations. A 'flat' medicine bottle (sf. 112 — Fig. 47O) had the embossed lettering of 'KITCHIN/CHEMIST/GLASGOW'. This was probably G.S. Kitchin, who took over a Glasgow chemist's shop in 1894 and died in 1926 (C. Shaw, pers. comm.). An internal white deposit still remains on the base. A squat, cylindrical bottle (gf. 8/13 — Fig. 47Q), made in a 3-piece mould with a rolled lip, also retains a yellow internal deposit. Other bottles include a corked cylindrical transparent form (sf. 564 — Fig. 47L) made in a 3-piece mould, with a mould-code 'WT 1261'; a seamless cylindrical bottle with a rolled lip (sf. 129 — Fig. 47M); a 1" diameter cylindrical bottle fragment with embossed base number '1054' (gf. 1/14); a 2½" long glass phial (sf. 168 — Fig. 47N); and a flake of cobalt-blue glass, probably from a poison bottle (gf. 17/13). The 'Kitchin' bottle would originally have contained 4 fl. oz., and sf. 112, 1 fl. oz.

A number of other vessel fragments were recovered. Some pieces of milky-blue glass were found disturbed and scattered through several layers (gfs 10/12–13, 20/10, 24/11). They show traces of white and green applied paint in a leaf design, with a flaked red border. Similarly scattered were fragments of a bowl or globe with a ground-edged, 5" diameter, out-turned rim. Roughly etched on one of the body fragments is the code 'AC 6162 12/14, 11' (gfs 2/13, 12/13). Sixteen fragments of another bowl were found in the topsoil (gf. 1/14). Two fragments of a pressed glass ?bowl (gf. 10/12–13) incorporate a pointed ellipse, blob and stipple design.

Closures

The closures are turn-moulded stoppers. They include a clear peg with knob top (sf. 184 — Fig. 47H); part of a clear peg etched with the number '59' and a faceted neck (sf. 56 — Fig. 47J); and two club sauce-type green stoppers (sf. 165 — Fig. 47K, gf. 24/11 — Fig. 47I). They have turned and ground pegs, with the ends snapped off and left untrimmed, and there is an embossed 'E' on the undersurface of the finial of sf. 165, and the embossed mark 'C 14' on gf. 24/11.

Sheet glass

The 388 fragments of sheet glass varied in thickness from 1mm (71.8%), 2mm (23%), 3mm (4.3%), 4mm (0.6%), and 5mm (0.3%), and generally had a slight blue-green hue. Modern window glass is generally 4mm or more, though some sash window glass was often 3mm. MacDiarmid referred to 9-paned windows in 1878 (MacDiarmid 1878, 240), but 4-pane vertical sliding sash windows were also used. The majority of fragments found (e.g. sf. 47) are 1mm, which is picture-frame glass. Most glaziers now use 2mm glass for picture framing. The 5mm thick glass is plate glass.

Beads and buttons

A number of beads and buttons were also found. Four opaque orange standard truncated convex

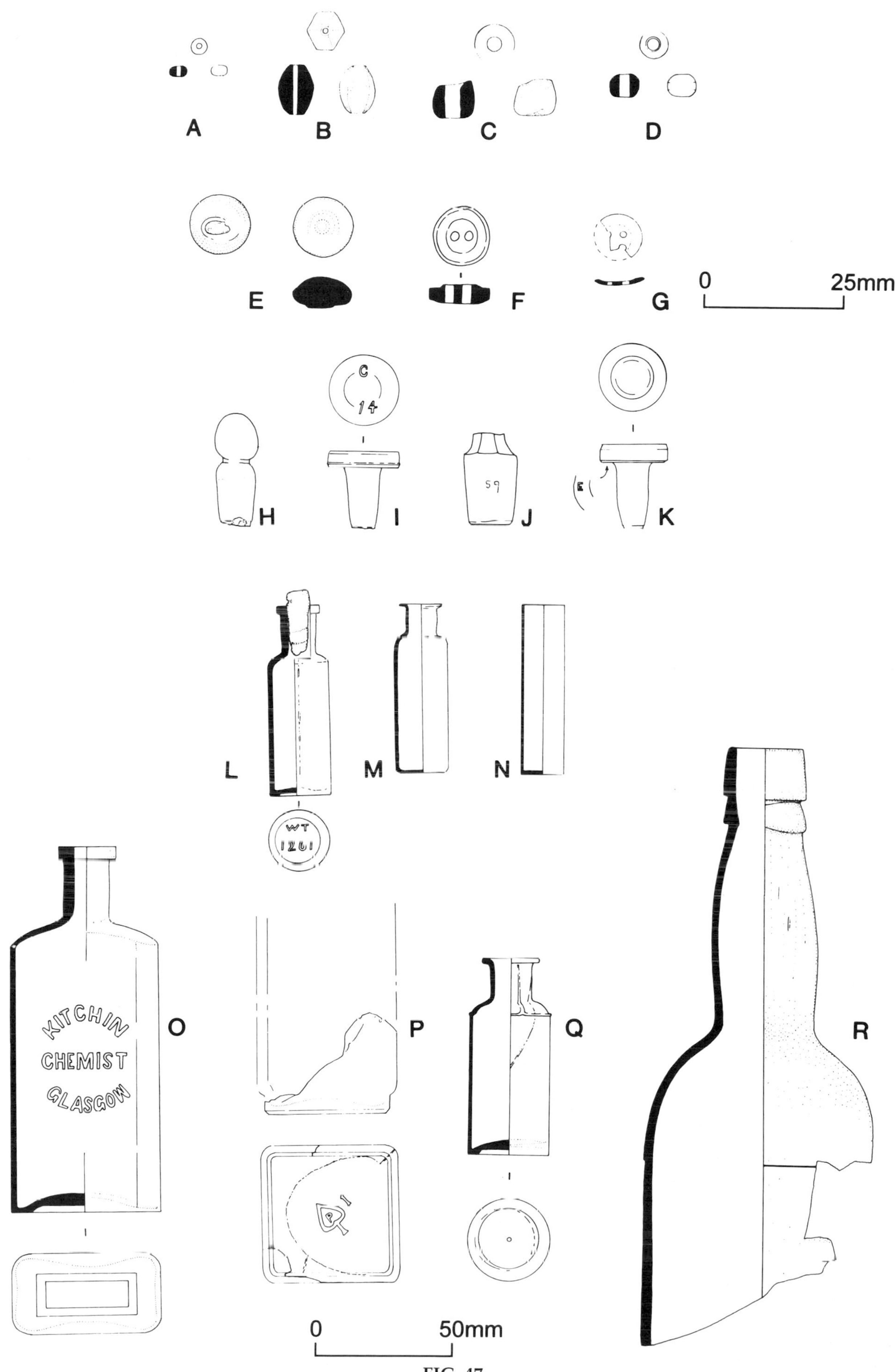

FIG. 47

House 8: glass — beads (Phases 11–13), buttons (Phases 11–13), closures (Phases 11–13) and bottles (Phases 12–13); mother of pearl button (G – Phase 12/13). Objects B, D, G, J-K and M-P were found in context 10, Phase 12/13. Scale 1:2; A-D 1:1

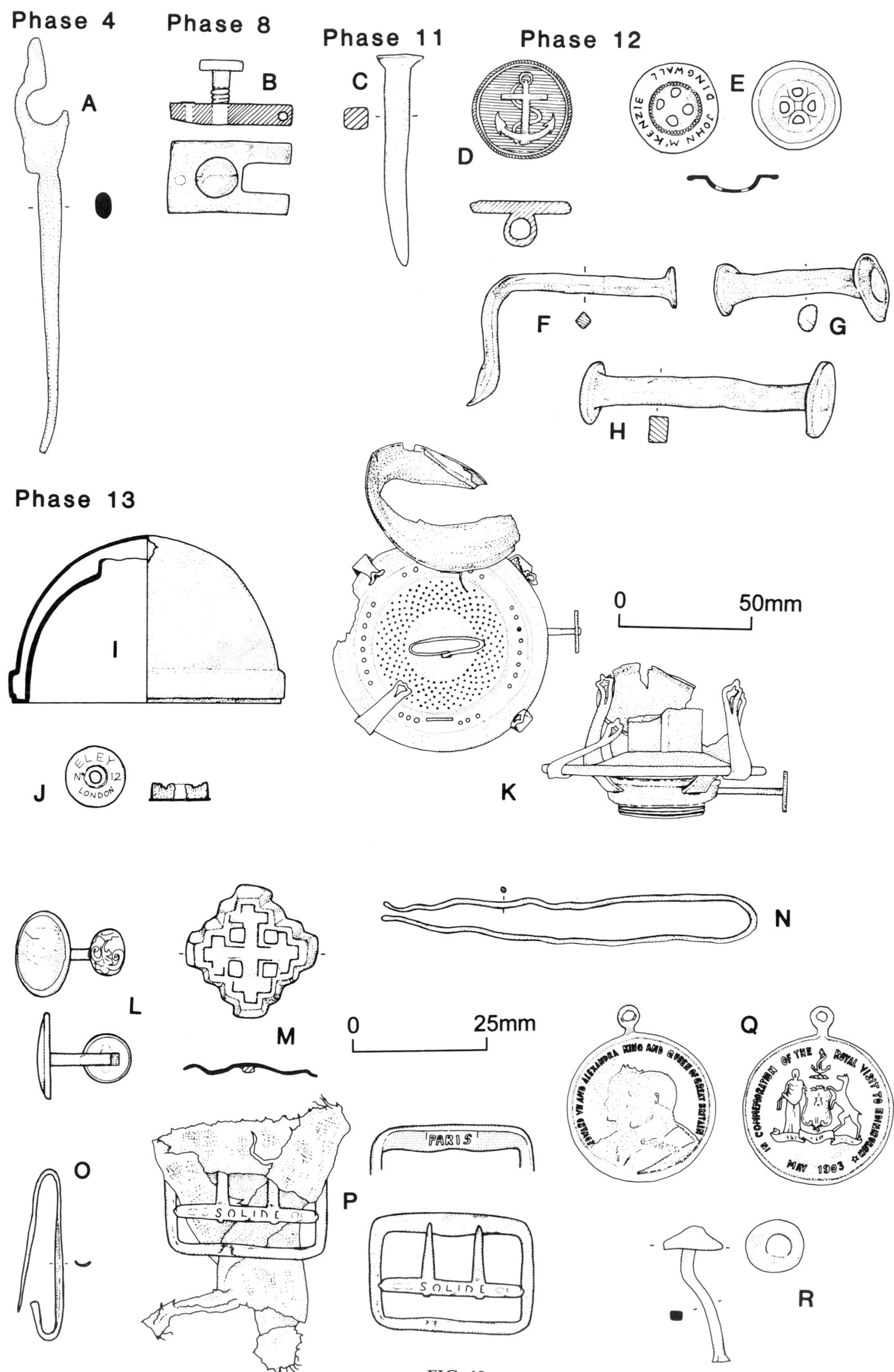

FIG. 48

House 8: copper alloy (Phases 4, 8 and 11–13). Objects K, M-O and Q were found in context 10, Phase 12/13. Scale 1:1; K 1:2

bicone beads came from Phases 11 (sf. 173) and 12/13 (sfs 69, 126 — Fig. 47D), and an unstratified general find from Area 2. Tiny opaque blue standard barrel-shaped beads were found in Phases 8 (sf. 140) and 11 (sf. 186 — Fig. 47A). One opaque milky-blue lenticular bead was found in Phase 12/13 (sf. 133 — Fig. 47B), along with a transparent blue truncated convex cone bead with a pitted surface from Phase 12 (sf. 566 — Fig. 47C). A late 19th-century dome-shaped cobalt-blue button (sf. 26 — Fig. 47E), with the remains of an embedded shank, was found in Phase 11. After *c.* 1920 metal shanks were often replaced with glass loops. The other buttons, sfs 27 (Phase 13, Fig. 47F), 28 (Phase 14) and gf. 24/11 were examined by Mrs Sonia O'Connor, of the York Archaeological Trust Laboratories. She found that they were moulded in a translucent white or cream glass. Under microscopic examination the glass was discovered to be speckled with spots of whiter, more opaque, glass. The backs of the buttons were puckered, and break surfaces revealed numerous minute bubbles. These features suggest that the buttons were formed by the fusion of powdered glass at a fairly low temperature.

3:3:5 *Coins*

Four pennies were found in Phase 12/13 of Edward VII — 1903 and 1907 (sfs 34, 171); one of George V — 1911 (sf. 158); and an unidentifiable example (sf. 156).

3:3:6 *Copper Alloy*

This material was used in part of a domestic utensil, containers, for items of personal adornment, securing a range of materials, and as plate or offcuts.

Domestic utensil

The domestic utensil was part of a vertical wick lamp burner (sf. 135a — Fig. 48K) with a screw cap, pierced air intake-distributor plate, wick tube and adjuster, and prongs for a globe. 'Tin' lamps were being used by the 1870s, but by the 1890s the paraffin lamp, with its globe and chimney, had largely replaced the traditional stone dish or *clach shoilse,* with its floating wick, and the iron crusie. Glass bowl lamps were used up to the Evacuation, and Atkinson found examples in the ruined cottages in 1938 (Atkinson 1949, 233).

Containers

Fragments of the end of a 5" (127mm) diameter container were found in Phase 13 (gf. 113). The base and sides are joined by a solder consisting of Cerussite $PbCO_3$, Hydrocerussite $Pb_3(CO_3)_2(OH)_2$, Barytes $BaSO_4$, and possibly Lead Stannate $PbSnO_3$ (R. Hardy, XRD analysis). It is unclear what this container was used for. It is unlikely to have been canned food. From 1810, food cooked by the Appert process was normally packed in containers of tinned wrought iron, though the sheets of these vessels were also joined by lead solder.

Personal items

The objects for clothing include two buttons from Phase 12 — sf. 93 (Fig. 48D) is a circular, slightly dome-topped, naval jacket type, with a fouled anchor design (no crown) on a hatched background, with rope edging and a ring or alpha shank. The other (sf. 107 — Fig. 48E) is a simple punched and 4-hole, sew-through button with depressed centre, possibly a trouser button, bearing the mark of John Mackenzie of Dingwall. A 15mm diameter disc (gf. 1/14 — Fig. 49D) may have been a button. Other fasteners include a collar stud (sf. 137 — Fig. 48L) with a bone setting, which may once have been covered with an enamel plate. It implies an attachable collar, and probably went at the back.

Phase 13 produced a two-pronged 'Solide'-type buckle (gf. 2 — Fig. 48P), possibly black japanned, and made in Paris. Very corroded fragments of another buckle (sf. 135b) were found with a strip of leather and coarse fibres.

Two pin types were found — an untinned wire with bulb head (sf. 268 — Fig. 49C), and a safety-pin (sf. 192 — Fig. 48O) of a very simple form, comprising a pointed rod, half beaten and bent, with the end curled and splayed. Photographs taken *c.* 1910 on St Kilda show examples of safety pins being used in fastening women's blouses (SSS 1909, DII 3.9b 7930; 7932). A long hairclip (sf. 161 — Fig. 48N) came from Phase 12/13, and a tie-clip (sf. 267 — Fig. 49B) from Phase 14.

One historic object (sf. 169 — Fig. 48Q) is a medallion depicting the conjoined busts of King Edward VII and Queen Alexandra on the obverse, and the coat of arms of the city of Edinburgh on the reverse. It commemorates a royal visit from the 11th–13th May 1903. This involved Court ceremony, presentation of South Africa war medals, and the laying of a foundation stone at Colinton Mains fever hospital (see *The Times* 11–13.5.1903). This was a public holiday, and the medallion was probably a mass-produced memento. A gilt example is in the Royal Museum of Scotland, Edinburgh (1963–59).

The earliest copper-alloy object is a damaged needle (sf. 520 — Fig. 48A) from Phase 4. It has an elliptical-sectioned shank, and a broad flat head pierced by a large hole.

One brass head of an Eley (London) 12-bore shotgun cartridge (sf. 22 — Fig. 48J) came from Phase 13. It was examined by G.M. Clarke of Eley Hawk Ltd (Birmingham). Eley (London) was in production from 1826 until the early 20th century; however, this form of centre-fire shotgun cartridge was not common until the 1890s. The base wad and tube would have been of paper. The cap is missing, but the size of the hole would date the case to the turn of the century. Firearms were used on St Kilda by visitors and the islanders. The Keartons used a double-barrelled fowling piece during their visit in 1896, and the factor used a gun during a boat trip in the same year (Kearton 1897, 99–101, 122). Donald MacDonald, when giving evidence to the Napier Commission, noted that it was forbidden to shoot birds during the hatching season (Report 1884, 26), and a photograph in the Janet Chalmers Collection, taken *c.* 1927 (see Buchanan 1983, 51), shows an islander with a double-barrelled shotgun.

Two tapering strips (gfs 197/8 and 2/13) may have been facings for a knife handle, and a clasp-knife (sf. 49 — Fig. 49A) was found in Phase 14. The damaged blade is hinged between brass 'scales', though the facings have gone. Knives were, obviously, of general use, but men sometimes carried clasp-knives suspended on a string around their necks when fowling (Connell 1887, 127). They were also used when 'rooing' the sheep.

Nails and screws

A number of objects were probably used as boat fittings. They include rivet nails (gfs 195/12 — Fig. 48H, 193/12

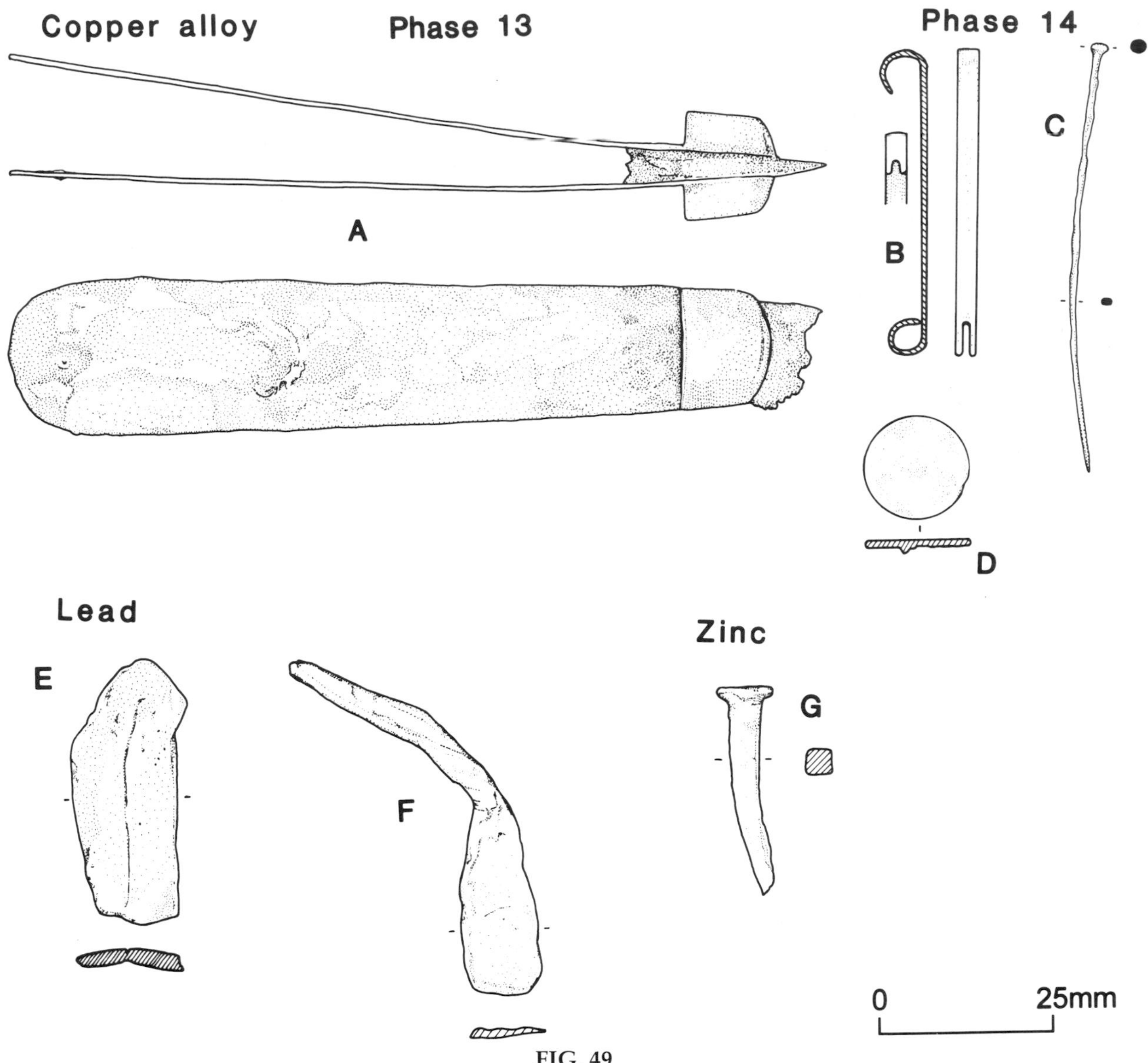

FIG. 49

House 8: copper alloy (Phases 13–14), lead (Phases 8 and 12/13), and zinc (Phase 13). Objects A and F were found in context 10, Phase 12/13. Scale 1:1

— Fig. 48F–G, 2/13 — Fig. 48R, 12/13, 1/14) which would have been secured through the planks, with the end burred, inside the boat, over a small circular rove. A number of copper-alloy nails with round heads and square-sectioned shanks (sf. 17 — Fig. 48C; gfs 92/8, 195/12) have been bent and hammered over, probably to clench the strakes. One 1¾" (43mm) pointed countersunk screw (gf. 1/14) may have been a general wood screw, but could also have been used on a boat. It was examined by J.H. Andrews, Keeper of Technology, Dept. Science and Industry, Birmingham Museum. He noted that the shape of the core of the screw, with a sharp transition from plain to threaded shank, and little tapering of the core at the point, might indicate that it was an early machine-cut screw. However, it could equally be the result of the state of cutting tools and adjustments of a later threading machine. It is a well-produced example, and is almost certainly post-1860.

Plate or offcuts

Copper-alloy sheet and plate was also found. This includes a possible mount (sf. 148 — Fig. 48M) in the form of a cross crosslet; a small rectangular strip bearing the punched numbers '6462' (gf. 2/13); a thin, possibly electro-plated, strip with traces of three Gothic letters, forming a decorative band, possibly for a briar pipe (gf. 2/13); and a flanged ring or 'eye' with traces of textile (gf. 2/13). General finds of folded copper-alloy sheet were found in Phase 12 (gf. 195), and an anvil-shaped fragment (gf. 18) from Phase 13 may be an offcut. A very corroded fragment (sf. 403) was located in Phase 11. A domed cap, 50mm in diameter and 34mm high, contained an inner cap (gf. 12/13 — Fig. 48I) and was of uncertain function.

Electrical equipment was examined by R. Hindmarsh (Institute of Electrical Engineers). It includes 2-strand copper wire, covered by a very finely woven textile, wrapped around with broad strand cotton, and sealed with lead, which was found in the topsoil (gf. 1/14). This is heavy load-carrying cable, presumably from the 1913–19 telegraph station, possibly from a variable resistance cable. The end of one fragment showed heat reddening of the textile, and hardening of the wire, suggesting an overloading of the system. Also in the topsoil were lengths of 5-strand, tinned copper wire, coated with shellac, then wrapped around with non-adhesive insulating 'Empire' tape, and sealed with an outer layer of shellac hardener. This must also have come from the station, but could have been used in a number of ways.

One curious object, clearly disturbed, is a small, solid, U-shaped piece of brass (gf. 197/8 — Fig. 48B), with a fixed screw on top, a partly chamfered undersurface, and holes for a fine spindle. It may be part of a telegraph Morse tapper, of the small size required to produce a finer quality signal.

3:3:7 Iron and Steel

Iron was the most seriously corroded of all the metals, and recoverable information was limited. Of the 865 fragments found, 157 were indeterminate. The majority of objects, 87.5%, came from Phases 12–14.

The identifiable objects include items of clothing, tools and other implements, containers, fittings, fastenings, bars, rods, and plate.

Items of clothing

A hook and eye (gf. 113/13 — Fig. 51D), used to secure the waistband of a pair of trousers, was made of stamped sheet metal, the hook bent to form and decorated with a heraldic boar's head and thistle design. The eye is a folded blank with spears at each end. It is an American type, patented in Britain by J. Blum of Baltimore in 1890 (patent 12, 420).

Tools and other implements

The tools include agricultural implements, like two examples of the *ceap*, or *ceaba*, the blade of a cas-chrom. They were found in Phases 10 (gf. 34) and 13 (gf. 2 — Fig. 50I). Reaping tools comprise a sickle blade and tang found in Phase 12/13 (sf. 113 — Fig. 50E); and the tang, riveted strengthening bar, and remains of the blade of a scythe (gf. 77/13 — Fig. 50J). A fragmentary shovel socket was found in Phase 13 (gf. 12).

One iron fish-hook (gf. 72 — Fig. 51C) was also found in the dump of Phase 13. Both ends were damaged, so that it was unclear whether it had originally been barbed. The diagnostic shape of the bend shows close similarities to the Harwich type of hook.

Textile tools comprise part of a thin rod, possibly once part of a knitting needle (gf. 12/13), and a heavily corroded thimble (sf. 36 — Fig. 50B), showing no visible size number or maker's mark. A short curved bar with spindle from Phase 8 (sf. 205) could be part of a spinning wheel, linking the wheel, via a wooden rod or cord, to the treadle.

One knife (sf. 560) was found in Phase 12 (but see also copper-alloy objects). It may have been a table knife with a blade fragment and broad tang, with black wooden facings secured by three rivets.

Three sections of ⅝" (15mm) diameter wire rope (gf. 80/13) may have been part of the guide ropes for a telegraph aerial. A 60mm diameter pulley wheel with a spindle (gf. 1/14 — Fig. 51F) has an uncertain function. Conceivably it may have been used with the wire rope on the telegraph aerial.

Containers

Thirty-three pieces of thin sheet metal, found in Phases 10–13, were container fragments (gfs 69/10, 193/12, 2/13, 19/13). These include part of a prise-off lid of a tan shoe-polish tin, and what may be the base, with the embossed stamp '(M)ILLS/LONDON', from the ash tip in Area 3 (gf. 195/12 — Fig. 50A); the base of a 127mm (5") diameter container (gf. 113/13); and a 51mm (2") diameter ?lid (sf. 172 — Fig. 50H).

Fragments of iron (gf. 19/13) may be part of a vessel base, and two sizes of U-sectioned pot or bucket handle came from Phase 13 (gfs 12 and 17 — Fig. 51A). Two pieces of barrel hoop (gf. 73) came from Phase 14, one part riveted together. Some barrels used on St Kilda had six hoops around the staves (SSS 1938, S265); those above and below the 'belly' were normally known in the trade as 'booges', 'quarters' and 'chimes'. The islanders stored salted fish in barrels for export, and some clearly had brand marks (SSS 1938, S290).

Fittings and fastenings

Fittings comprise a ⅞" (22mm) washer (gf. 17/13); a reinforced strap (sf. 38 — Fig. 50C); a pierced plate (sf. 68 — Fig. 50D); a heavy ring-base, pierced cap, and vertical spindle (sf. 119 — Fig. 50F) possibly from a bedstead; and a bedstead caster (sf. 120 — Fig. 50G) comprising a spindle, bell-shaped cap and plate, with the forks holding the wooden wheel core. There were two beds in the cottage in 1938, one in the east room, the other in the central back chamber.

A corroded length of chain (gf. 77/13) could have had a variety of functions, though it may have been the *slabhraid* which usually hung down from a ridge or tie-beam; and a hook (gf. 12/13) could have been the 'crook' or *dubhan* secured near the end of the chain, on which was hung a pot or kettle over a central fire.

A total of 289 nails were found, though most are fragmentary or fractured by corrosion. Standard imperial lengths were identified from 1½", 1¾", 2", 2½", up to 5". Head size varied from fine $\frac{3}{16}$" (5mm) to ¾" (20mm). Forged or cut nails (gf. 12/13 — Fig. 51B, gf. 1/14 — Fig. 51G) have 'T' or rose heads, and tapering square to rectangular-sectioned shanks, with rounded ends. Several examples have wood in the corrosion products. One uncorroded machine cut and formed French wire nail was found (gf. 17/13), and an extra large head clout nail used to secure roofing felt to sarking board (gf. 1/14). Six heavy square-headed spikes, from Phases 12/13 (gf. 10) and 13 (gfs 12, 77, 113 — Fig. 51E), were perhaps for masonry use. The other fasteners comprise two fragments of butt-hinge (gf. 1/14 — Fig. 51H), and part of a rectangular strap, pierced by at least one hole, with the undamaged end folded over. Conceivably this is part of a band and gudgeon hinge (gf. 12/13).

3:3:8 Lead

A spatulate scrap, partly twisted (sf. 78 — Fig. 49F), was found in Phase 12/13; and a roughly rectangular scrap of lead, with a scored surface and one end bent and beaten, was also found (gf. 197/8 — Fig. 49E).

3:3:9 Zinc

Twenty to twenty-two SWG zinc plates formed the primary roof covering of the cottage. Samples were found in Phases 12–14, but also in the disturbance of layers of Phases 8, 10 and 11. Seven examples were specially recorded (sfs 63–4, 122, 136, 150, 196, 294). They were secured to the sarking board with zinc nails (e.g. sf. 31 — Fig. 49G). Pierced sheeting shows holes of 4–5mm diameter, but a sheet fragment from Phase 13 (gf. 2) shows fine holes of 2.5mm and 2 x 1.5mm, possibly produced by puncturing with panel pins or fine tacks.

3:3:10 Tar (A. Crawshaw)

Tar was found in Phases 12–14, and in the disturbance of layers in Phases 10 and 11. A sample was treated

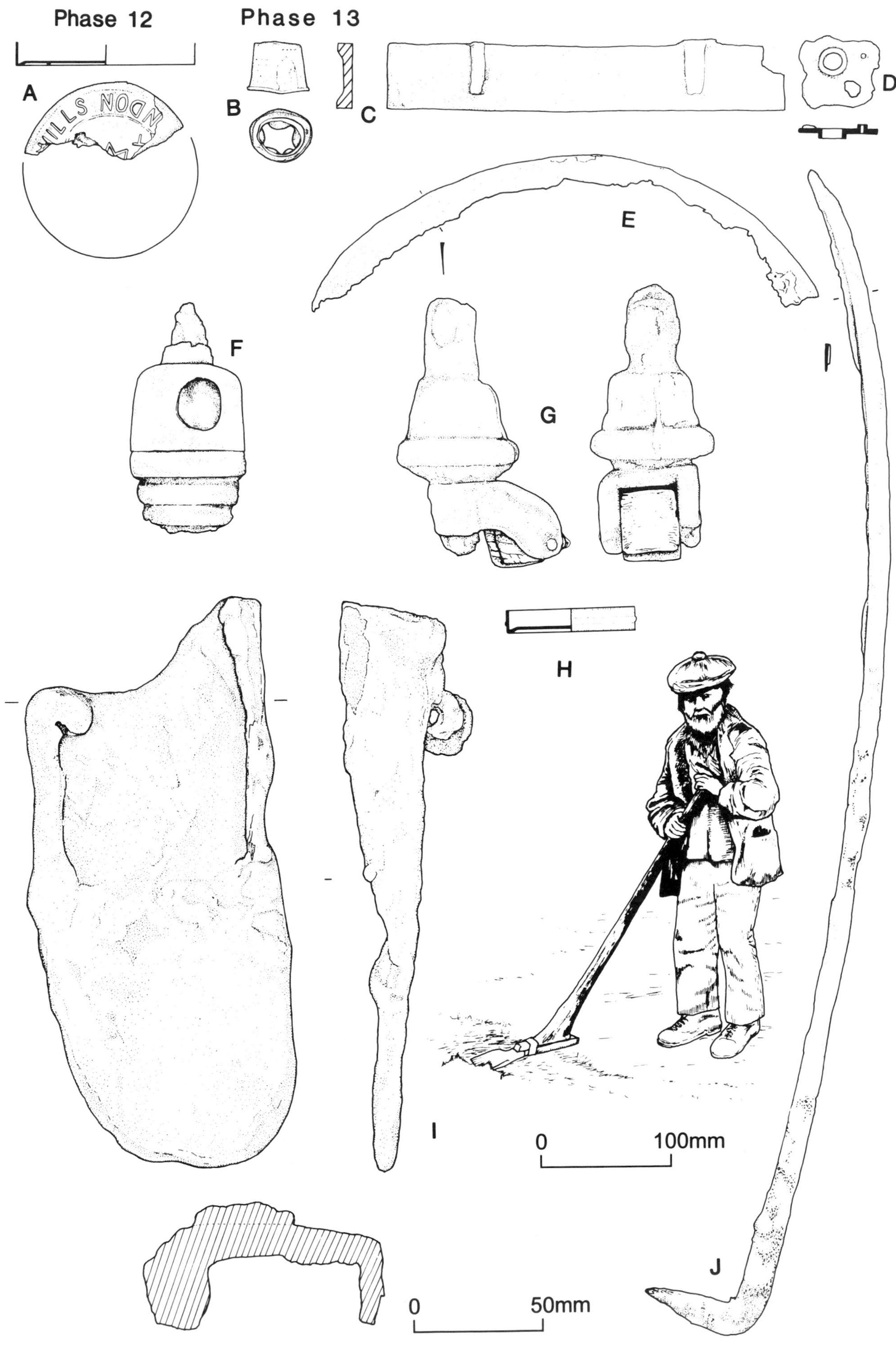

FIG. 50
House 8: iron (Phases 12–13). Objects B-F were found in context 10, Phase 12/13. Scale 1:2; E and J 1:4

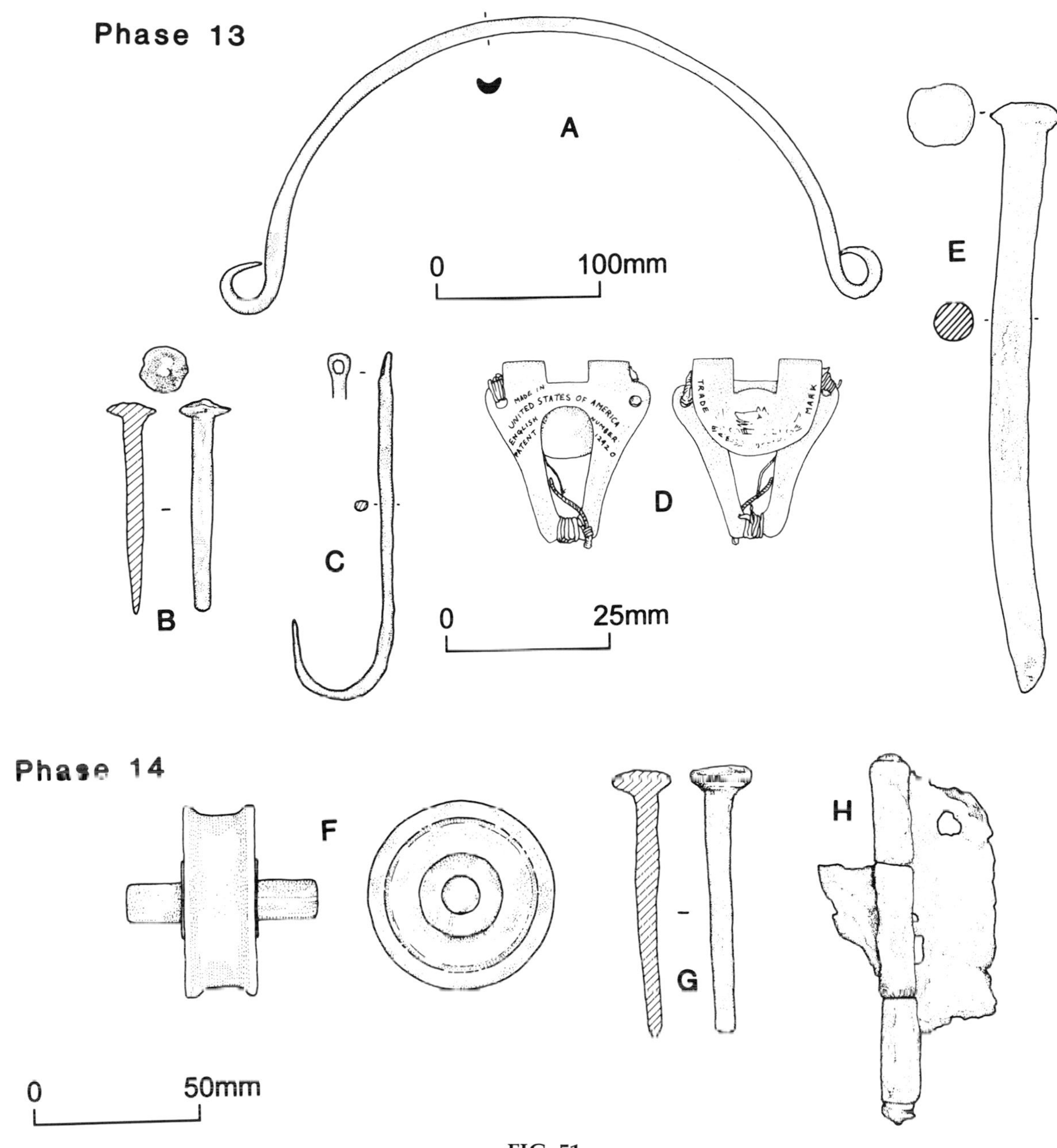

FIG. 51
House 8: iron (Phases 13–14). Scale 1:2; A 1:4, C and D 1:1

with chloroform, and the solution filtered and evaporated onto salt plates. The infrared spectra indicated it is a coal tar. It is a material used to coat and saturate felt laid on sarking boards, a roof covering which replaced zinc sheeting after 1896. An asphalted felt had been patented by F. McNeil of London in 1844.

3:3:11 Clay Pipes

Nine fragments of clay pipe were recovered. Two stem fragments from Phase 8 (sf. 225; gf. 92); a bowl fragment from Phase 10 (sf. 179); a marked stem fragment from Phase 12 (gf. 193/195); a decorated bowl from Phase 12/13 (sf. 144); bowl and mouth piece fragments (gf. 17), and a neck fragment (gf. 80) from Phase 13; and a marked stem fragment from Phase 14 (gf. 1).

Three stems had maker's marks, but only one (gf. 193/195 — Fig. 59G) is identifiable as Samuel McLardy, Manchester, 1869–1930 (Oswald 1975, 180), from disturbance in Phase 12. One bowl (sf. 144 — Fig. 59H) is decorated with the buffalo head and stamp of the Royal Antediluvian Order of Buffaloes. The Order started in London in 1822, but it was not until the mid-1860s that it became centrally administered and organised (W. Hartman, pers. comm.). A specially made RAOB pipe would probably not have been available until after the 1860s. They are found in many parts of Britain, depicting either horns or full head. The marked stem fragment from Phase 14 (gf. 1) was made in Glasgow, but the maker's name is indecipherable. The mouthpiece (gf. 17/13) was stained or glazed brown.

3:3:12 Plaster, Mortar and Cement (W. Brannan, J.R. Senior)

The wallplaster from the house appears to be 'render and set' work. There is no trace of animal hair binder. The first layer is around 18mm thick, and has been finished with a darby float, before a second, 10mm, setting coat was applied and smoothed. There are traces of brush finishing.

The mortar is probably largely from the wall-head, the lime content including numerous nodules due to poor reduction in the kiln.

A sample of the second-phase flooring in the house was examined by Mr W. Brannan of Blue Circle Industries plc. The mortar has been made using sand which contained a multiplicity of minerals and shells. It was also made with a high water content which has had two effects. First, it has enabled the cement particles to undergo a large degree of hydration, and secondly it has led to advanced carbonation of the cement paste. The residual unhydrated cement fragments contained some heterogeneity due to inefficient mixing of coal ash while the cement clinker was being fired. Some pieces of carbon from poorly burned coal was also present. These features point to the cement not having been made in a rotary kiln but in a shaft or chamber-type of kiln. In the latter, a dried cake of blended raw material and coal would be fed into the top and fired, the resultant clinker being drawn out of the bottom. This, coupled with the fineness of the cement (the largest particles probably being around 300 microns), would indicate by comparison with concretes of known age that the cement used was manufactured after 1900, and probably in the 1920s.

The degree of hydration and carbonation, together with the soluble calcium oxide and silica in the sand, make chemical analysis of cement content and composition virtually impossible. This, coupled with the knowledge that after 1900 cement was being shipped to the UK from the continent, makes identification of source impossible without documentation.

Although a hard, usable surface, it had not been well-tamped during the laying process, and air bubbling had resulted in the development of lacuna.

Samples of the flooring and aggregate, along with some plaster and mortar, were examined by Dr J.R. Senior. The aggregate was found to be miarolitic granite, and fine-grained and medium-grained dolerite pebbles.

The cement comprised 41% sand and 58% binding material, while the plaster was 37% to 62%, and the mortar 36% to 63%. The sand content was principally in the range 125–250 microns, and is shown in percentage form in Table 17.

Sample Size	Cement	Plaster	Mortar
2mm	2.05	2.60	–
1mm	1.33	0.64	–
710µm	0.32	0.97	0.39
500µm	0.82	1.59	3.60
355µm	6.58	10.05	5.14
250µm	46.09	43.36	44.09
125µm	42.07	35.82	46.11
60µm	0.58	3.65	0.37
32µm	–	0.30	–

TABLE 17
House 8: sand particle size in cement, plaster and mortar samples

The mineral content of the cement and mortar comprised:

feldspar — both alkaline feldspar and plagioclase feldspar in fresh, i.e. non-weathered, condition — Over 50%

quartz — freshly broken angular fragments — 30%

ferromagnesian minerals — unstable minerals chiefly pyroxene and amphibole often in composite grains with plagioclase or quartz — 10–20%

zircon — a few grains as an accessory mineral

The mineralic composition, with abundant fresh feldspars, a considerable content of other unstable minerals, combined with the angular and poorly sorted nature of the grains, suggests rapid deposition near to source. There is no degree of rounding of the grains, thus ruling out beach and dune sands. It is suggested that this material is derived from a pocket of river sand (either from a recent river or a periglacial outwash sand); mixed materials being derived from granitoid and gabbroic source rocks.

3:3:13 Stone (J.R. Senior, C.E. Batey, E. Healey)

Steatite (C.E. Batey)

Phase 4

sf. 545. Very poor-quality steatite, roughly constant thickness; one smooth outer face suggests that this was originally part of a ?vessel. Two striations on inner face, edges broken and irregular. L. 47mm, w. 38mm, th. 17mm. Fig. 52A.

sf. 642. Three amorphous fragments of rotten steatite. One has constant thickness and slightly curving profile, possibly suggesting that it was originally part of a vessel.

sf. 672. Re-used vessel sherd, now in form of narrow curving bar, indicating curvature of vessel wall. Traces of internal ?burnt deposit and burning on opposing face. Slight traces of striations on inner curving face along length of bar. L. 67mm, w. 23mm, th. 15mm. Fig. 52B.

sf. 769. Wall sherd with smooth, blackened internal surface. L. 53mm, w. 27mm, th. 16mm. Fig. 52C.

sf. 785. Substantial wall sherd in coarse-grained steatite, with external burning and traces of internal tooling. Very thick wall, differing from rest of assemblage. No burning along breaks. Very smooth external and internal faces. L. 65mm, w. 44mm, th. 22mm. Fig. 52D.

sf. 789. Flat piece of green-coloured actinolite schist, well crystalline West Coast Gabbro. ?Baking plate. L. 55mm, w. 29mm, th. 8mm. Fig. 52E.

Phase 10

sf. 325. Flat spindle whorl in coarse-grained steatite, slightly eccentric ?drilled perforation. Roughly circular, but slightly irregular and edges slightly squared-off by rubbing. Both flattened faces are damaged, one appears to have been cut. Diam. 37mm, th. 10–14mm, perforation diam. 13mm, wt 32.527g. Fig. 52F.

Steatite sf. 769 was thin sectioned, showing it to be a talc, antigonite rock with minor opaque oxides (?magnetite). It is almost identical to the steatite material found in Shetland. The actinolite schist (sf. 789) possibly also came from Shetland (J.R. Senior, pers. comm.).

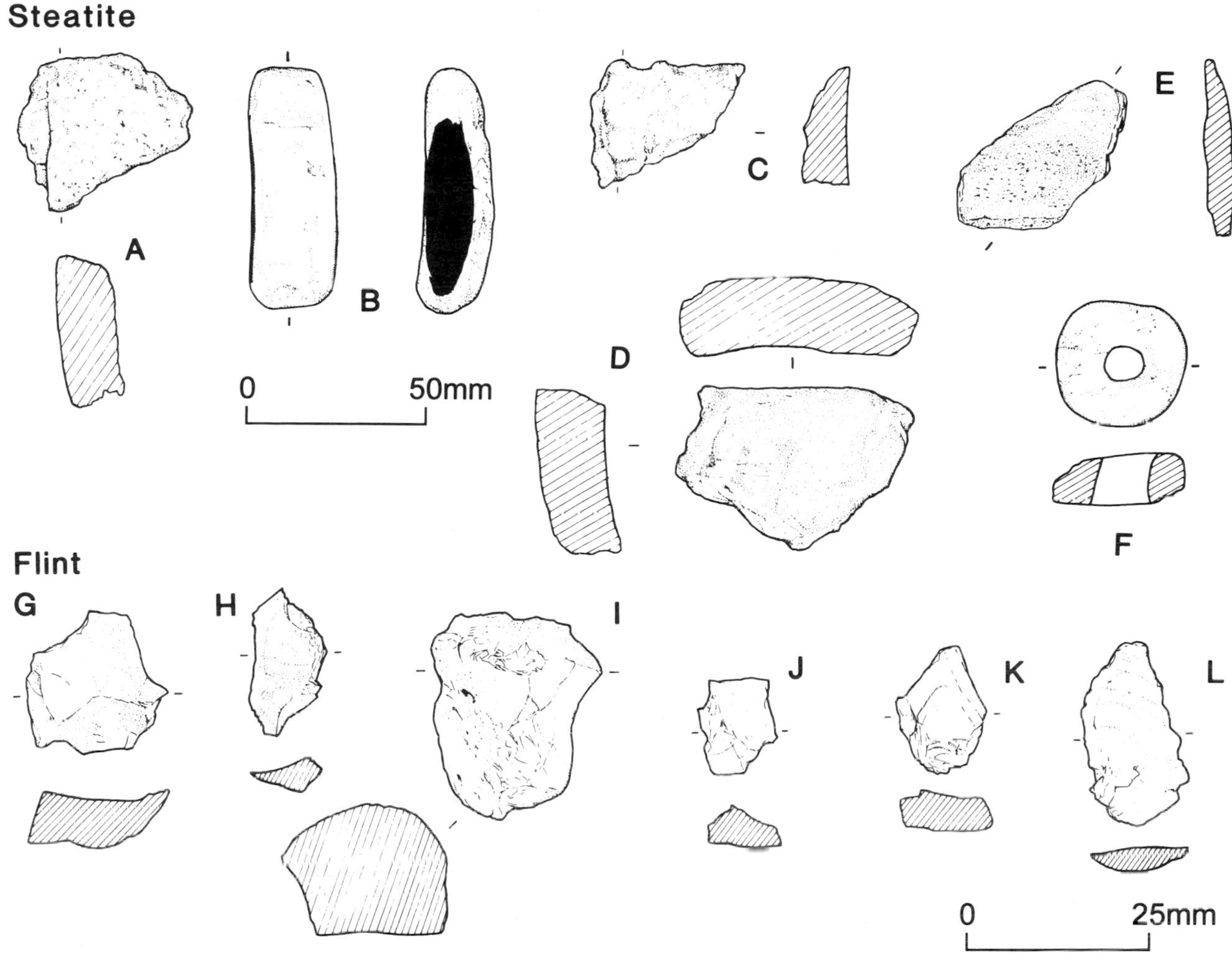

FIG. 52
House 8: steatite (Phases 4 and 10) and flint (Phases 4–6 and 12). Scale A-F 1:2; G-L 1:1

Of the nine pieces in this assemblage, four are identifiably parts of steatite vessels (sfs 545, possibly one of 642, 769, 785), with the spindle whorl (sf. 325) and bar (sf. 672) clearly also originally having been vessel sherds. It is not possible to make further comment on the other two pieces of material in sf. 642, although they do bear a resemblance to very burnt steatite recovered from Area 1 at Beachview, Orkney (Batey forthcoming).

The form of vessel represented by these sherds is not clear, but in the absence of contrary evidence it would seem that hemispherical bowls, which were the most commonly produced in the Viking period, are represented (Skjölsvold 1961, 15). Several Norse sites in Scotland have produced evidence for the use of these vessels, e.g. Brough of Birsay BB77 OX, SF no 2112 (Batey and Heggie forthcoming; also Hunter 1986, 188–9; Freswick Links, Caithness — Batey 1987, 157–61). The interest in this context lies not so much in the precise form of the vessel, but in the fact that the nearest outcrops of the rock which were exploited are in Shetland, and beyond that, Norway (Hamilton 1956, 206–10; Ritchie, P.R. 1984, 65–73). Although steatite vessels and sherds have been recovered in the Western Isles, e.g. at Drimore Machair, South Uist (MacLaren 1974, 15), they have been from Norse contexts. In Shetland, where there are several workable outcrops, steatite has been used extensively from prehistoric times (Hamilton 1956, 20, fig. 11). The form of the vessel in these cases is rather crucial, the prehistoric and medieval vessels having a more squared form, differing markedly from the Viking-period ones.

The fact that sherds have been re-used on St Kilda is not surprising: there must indeed have been a limited supply, although from the vessel thicknesses represented (*c.* 14–17mm and 22mm) it seems that in excess of two individual vessels might be represented. I think it is theoretically acceptable to see the bracket of 14–17mm being from a single vessel, 22mm is clearly from a very much more substantial vessel, although conceivably from elsewhere on the same bowl. The softness of the stone enables easy reworking and this is reinforced by the presence in this small assemblage of a bar (sf. 672) of unfortunately obscure function in its present form, and the spindle whorl (sf. 325).

The whorl, from Phase 10, is of ubiquitous form, and several sites have produced parallels — it need not be Norse however. Similar examples have been found at Freswick Links (Batey 1987, 179–80) and Jarlshof (Hamilton 1956, 119–20, fig. 16, no. 1), Buckquoy, Orkney (Ritchie 1979, 197, fig. 8, no. 86), Brough of Birsay, Orkney (Curle 1982, 67 and 68, Ill 43, nos 538, 540) and nearer to St Kilda, at Drimore Machair, where seven similar examples were recovered (MacLaren 1974, 18, nos 46–52). The heaviness of the whorl is perhaps surprising, given Ryder's suggestion that a whorl of 8g would be sufficient to

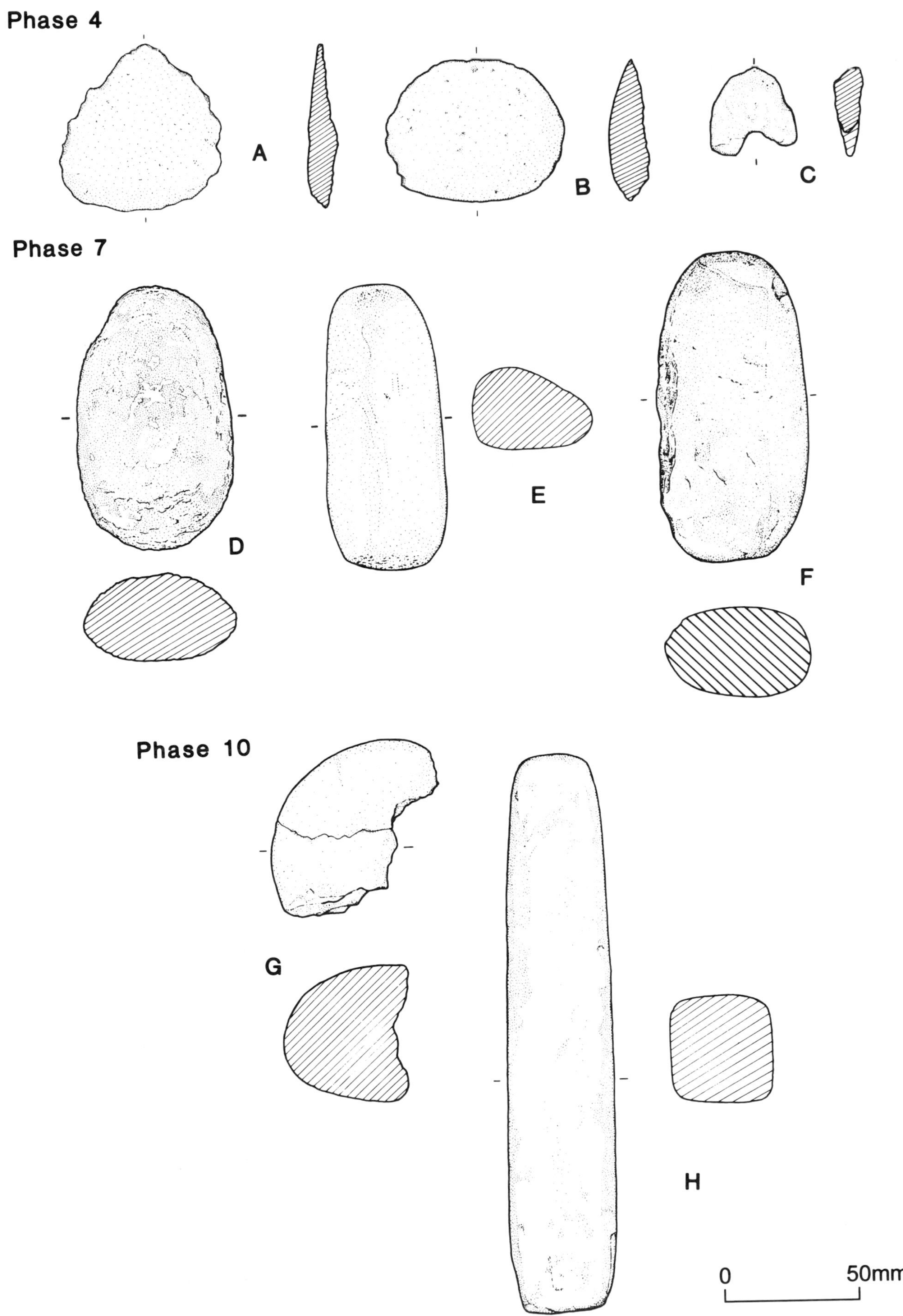

FIG. 53
House 8: stone (Phases 4, 7 and 10). Scale 1:2

spin Soay wool (Ryder 1968, 81), although work by MacGregor on the Brough of Burrian assemblage from N. Ronaldsay points out that weight is not critical (MacGregor 1975, 89).

Small find 789 might conceivably be part of a baking plate, as recorded at several sites in the north of Scotland, particularly Tuquoy, Westray (O.A. Owen, pers. comm.); Mounthoolie Lane, Kirkwall (Ross 1983, 419); Pool, Sanday (J.R. Hunter, pers. comm.); Underhoull, Unst, Shetland (Small 1967, 244); and at Da Biggins, Papa Stour, Shetland, Crawford notes examples in association with a 15th century hearth (Crawford 1985, 147); and in Norway, Weber notes the continued use up to as recently as *c.* 1700 (Weber 1984, 160).

The material so far discussed is notable for the fact that it appears to be rather worn, somewhat more so than perhaps to be expected from archaeological processes on an artefact, and it is just possible that some of the pieces might have been subject to either weathering or water wear. It is at present difficult to prove this, just as it is impossible to date these items themselves. We cannot judge the date of the re-use, particularly since the finished products are common to several centuries, even if we can support an origin for the stone in the form of steatite vessels.

Flint and quartz (E. Healey)

This small group comprises one flint core, five flakes, and three pieces of quartz.

Flint

Phase 4

sf. 701. Mid-brown translucent flake with crushed butt and diffuse bulb. Fig. 52H.

sf. 752. Mid-grey flake with irregular striking platform. Visible scar and diffuse bulb. Irregular. Fig. 52G.

Phase 5

sf. 527. Mid-grey matt core with fine white mottling. Two 'platforms', one a scar producing a flake, and one cortex where three or four flakes were struck. Cortex is thin and smooth. Scars are very mottled and edge, perhaps fortuitously, crushed. Wt 17.126g. Fig. 52I.

Phase 6

sf. 526. Mid-grey-white flake. Edge is crushed, possibly damaged. Fig. 52J.

sf. 528. Mid-grey flake fragment with splintered edge, probably resulting from striking an anvil. Fig. 52K.

Phase 12

sf. 92. Mid-brown-grey translucent flake. Edge is abruptly denticulated, cortex thin and hard, with double bulb. Shattered platform. Fig. 52L.

Quartz

Phase 7

sf. 297. Fragment of possibly flaked massive quartz.

sf. 396. Amethystine quartz.

Phase 11

sf. 561. Small quartz crystal.

The flint, from Cretaceous chalk, is probably derived from beach pebbles, since chalk is found in some of the off-shore sedimentary basins. The struck surfaces appear rather fresh. The flakes are irregular, and the crushed butt might indicate that they were struck on an anvil. The core is a 'non-standard' form and could be accidental, for the scars are different from the flakes, which are rather squat.

Slate (J.R. Senior)

Fragments of slate were found in contexts from Phases 8–14. They are derived from quarries at South Ballachulish, Argyll (NW 085583). These are slates of Dalradian (Late Pre-Cambrian to Early Cambrian) age, characterised by crenulated slaty cleavage planes and prominent idiomorphic pyrite porphyroblasts.

Originally they had curved heads, and the edges and tail trimmed with a bladed tool or *corc sgleit*. Only one was clearly identifiable as a 9" (229mm) slate. Pyrite cube inclusions prevented perfect cleaving, and thickness varies from 4–17mm. Slates were generally found on estate or community buildings like the church, school, manse, factor's house, and storehouse, though some slates were used on the wall-heads of the cottages, or for drip-courses.

Finer Welsh slate was used for school purposes. The examples (sfs 24–5, both from Phase 14) were neatly trimmed to fit into a wooden frame, with lines scored for text on one side, and squares for arithmetic on the other. They are probably post-1884. Slate pencils (sfs 23, 130, 183, 779 — Fig. 55A, from Phases 11–14), usually produced in slate districts where cross-cleavage occurs, were also found, along with graphite pencil 'slips' (leads) (sf. 157). The cedar or pine slats are missing. The slips were probably made by the Conte process and are HB.

Stone tools and other samples (J.R. Senior)

Phase 2

One fire-shattered pebble fragment in dark-coloured fine-grained dolerite (gf. 202) came from the Mullach Sgar Complex.

Phase 4

Twenty-two samples were recovered, predominantly of dark-coloured medium-grained Mullach Sgar dolerite. Some pebbles had been worked (sf. 770 — Fig. 53C), or polished (gfs 232, 243, 251). A few chips, also from this complex, may also have been polished (gf. 232), along with one piece from the same context, which is a porphyritic medium-grained dolerite mixed with granophyric material, which must have come from the margins of the complex.

Two discs with chipped edges (sfs 758 and 760 — Fig. 53A and B) are also dark-coloured medium-grained Mullach Sgar dolerite. These pebble edge-scrapers may have been used as 'knives'.

A hammer stone (gf. 232) and a polished tool (gf. 272) are in porphyritic West Coast Gabbro. A piece of amphibole-rich pegmatite (sf. 679) may also be from the West Coast Gabbros.

Phase 5

Twenty-four items were recovered, of which sixteen come from the Mullach Sgar Complex. These include grey-green fine-grained dolerites, such as sf. 422. Several of the examples from context 176 had been fire-reddened or shattered. One item had been polished (sf. 422), and another, of medium-grained dolerite with granophyre veinlets, had been used as a hammer, with two impact ends (gf. 176). Two pieces of fine-grained dolerite, also from context 176, had

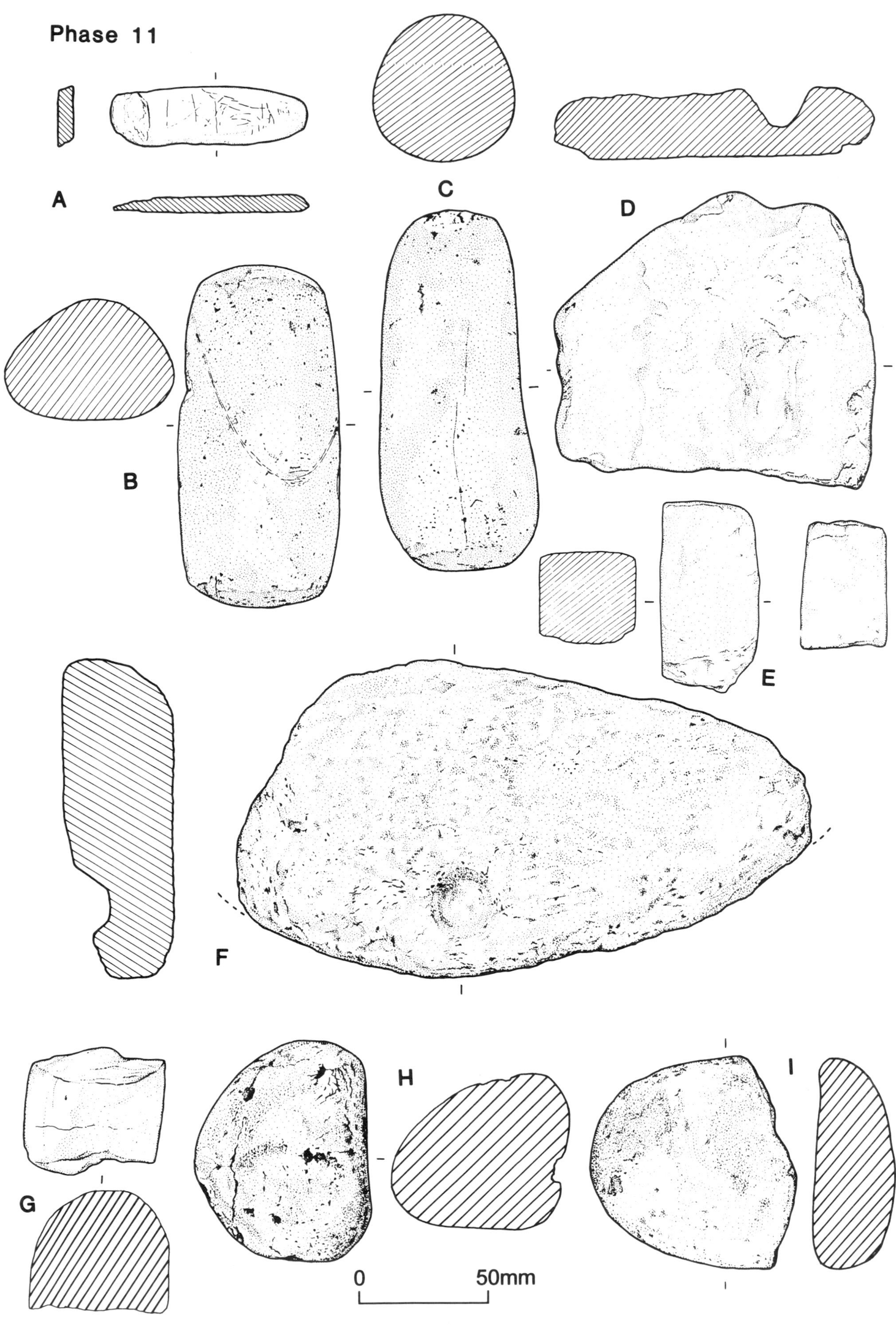

FIG. 54
House 8: stone (Phase 11). Scale 1:2

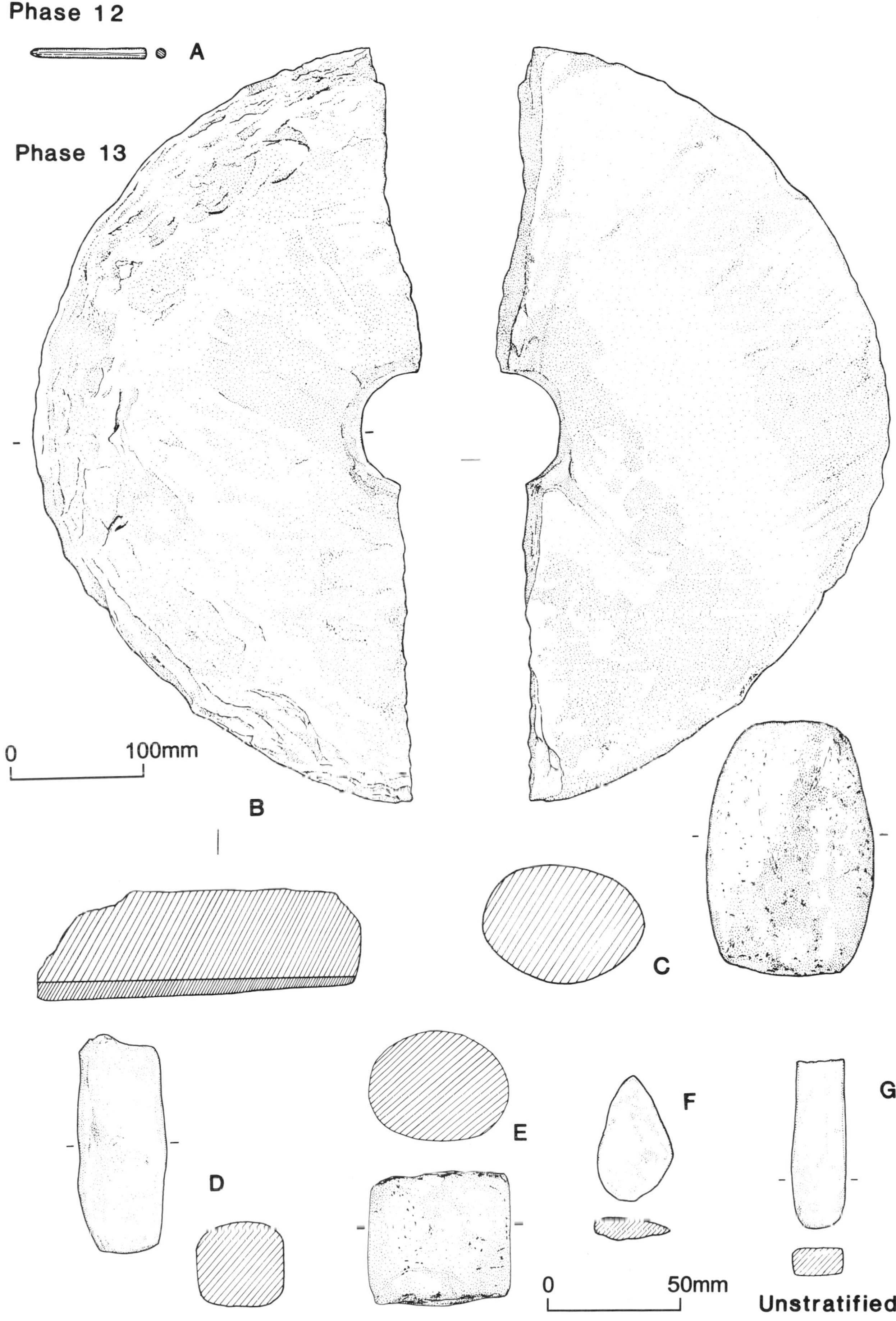

FIG. 55
House 8: stone (Phases 12–13 and unstratified). Scale 1:2; B 1:4

been used as possible scrapers. One shows granophyre veinlets, and mica patches.

Four samples of Conachair-Oiseval granite were recovered, including a burnt piece (sf. 456).

A piece of biotite schist grindstone (gf. 189) was work-polished, and clearly an import. A fire-shattered piece of well crystalline West Coast Gabbro (gf. 176) was also found, though it shows no signs of human use.

Phase 6

Two dark-coloured medium-grained dolerite fragments are from the Mullach Sgar Complex. One is roughly dressed (sf. 457), the other is not (gf. 198).

A burned capstone from the land-drains is a coarse-grained West Coast Gabbro.

Phase 7

Sixteen items were recovered, of which nine are dolerites from the Mullach Sgar Complex, though few were actually utilised. Those which were include hammers (sfs 306 — Fig. 53E, 311 — Fig. 53F); an unpolished hammer with two worked ends (sf. 380); a hammer with one broken end (gf. 175); and two scrapers (gf. 165).

One reddened fragment of coarse-grained miarolitic granite is derived from the Conachair-Oiseval Complex (gf. 165).

Imports consist of a friable piece of biotite schist (sf. 248 — Fig. 53D), probably of Moinian age (Late Pre-Cambrian), from a mainland source; and a small piece of gneiss (gf. 124), which may be an import.

Phase 8

Nine stones were collected. Five come from the Mullach Sgar Complex, of which two (both from context 55) have been polished, one (gf. 92) has been fire-shattered, and two others are unworked. Another fire-shattered stone, a coarse miarolitic granite, from context 92 is derived from the Conachair-Oiseval Complex.

A fine-grained, grey, igneous rock, possibly pumice, most probably an import. There was some disturbance, with a piece of burnt shale, possibly from coal, being found in context 92. A piece of Ballachulish Slate (gf. 146) is an import.

Phase 9

Nine samples. Three of the pieces come from the Conachair-Oiseval granites, one of which has been worked, and is reddened by burning (gf. 190). A grey-green fine-grained dolerite from the Mullach Sgar Complex has been polished.

Phase 10

Forty-six recorded samples, which come principally from the Mullach Sgar Complex, including rotten melanocratic segregation (sf. 619). Amongst the finds from this complex are four polished hammer stones (gf. 196); hammer stones (gfs 39, 196); polished stones (sfs 242, 260, 446, 470, 806 — Fig. 53H — a whetstone; gfs 88, 103, 196); and fire-reddened stones (sfs 399, 400 — Fig. 53G; gfs 103 (seven pieces), 231).

A sample from context 196 may be fine-grained dolerite or a fire-reddened sandstone.

Samples derived from the Conachair-Oiseval complex include a miarolitic microgranite (?granophyre, gf. 103); a miarolitic granite with drusy cavities (gf. 196); and a piece of rotten coarse miarolitic granite (gf. 200).

Phase 11

Seventy-one samples were recovered, again mainly from the Mullach Sgar Complex, including sf. 686, a rotten basaltic rock or more likely a very fine-grained doleritic contact rock. Other general samples include sfs 337 and 411. Artefacts comprise polished hammer stones (sfs 315 — Fig. 54C, 316–17, 604; gfs 28 (fire cracked) — Fig. 54G, 168 (three examples) — Fig. 54H–I, 216); hammer stones (sfs 312, 330–32, 334–5; gfs 117, 168, 170); polished stones (gf. 188 — two pieces); a whetstone (sf. 131 — Fig. 54B); burnt stone (gf. 170); and a ?pot boiler (gf. 168).

Material from the Conachair-Oiseval complex includes a sample (gf. 116); quartz (gf. 187); two hammer stones (gf. 168); and fire-blackened specimens (sfs 346, 410; gf. 117).

Imports include a worn-out biotite mica schist quern fragment (sf. 383 — Fig. 54D), which had been broken and re-used; a piece of muscovite biotite schist, possibly Moinian, from mainland Scotland, used as a drain cap (gf. 125); part of a garnet mica schist quern (sf. 408 — Fig. 54F), probably Moinian (Late Pre-Cambrian), from mainland Scotland; a fragment of burnt, rotten biotite or amphibolite schist (gf. 188); a polished slate whetstone (sf. 20 — Fig. 54A) with scratched incisions; three pieces of medium-grained sandstone (gfs 24, 116, 216), probably Carboniferous, from the Midland valley in Scotland (gfs 24 — Fig. 54E and 116 are probably whetstones); and two flints (gf. 187).

Phase 12

Nine samples were recovered. Four pieces come from the Mullach Sgar Complex, including a polished tool, probably a whetstone (sf. 195); and two polished stones (gf. 245). Four unworked specimens come from the Conachair-Oiseval granites. A soft, possibly Welsh, slate pencil (sf. 779 — Fig. 55A) was also recovered.

Phase 13

Twenty samples. Examples from the Mullach Sgar Complex were found in contexts 2, 8, 12, 18, 19 and 80. Three specimens (sfs 201, 224 — Fig. 55C (possibly a whetstone), 258; gf. 12) have been polished, two have been burnt (gfs 12, 19). A general sample (gf. 2) and a tool (sf. 259) come from the Conachair-Oiseval granites. One piece of vein quartz (gf. 80) was recovered.

Among the imports is a large quern top runner (sf. 1 — Fig. 55B) of ?Moine schist from a west Scottish mainland source. It is 576mm in diameter, and a maximum of 80mm thick, with a quartzose layer with garnets used as a harder base working-surface. Other imports comprise a large piece of biotite mica schist (gf. 19) from the Scottish mainland; two whetstones (gfs 12, 19 — Fig. 55D-E) of yellowish-brown medium-grained micaceous sandstone, probably Carboniferous in age, from the Midland valley of Scotland, and a triangle of creamy tailors' chalk (sf. 29 — Fig. 55F).

Phase 14

Nine samples, all from the Mullach Sgar Complex, including seven general specimens (gf. 1); a polished stone (gf. 1); and a fire-reddened ?bowl (gf. 1).

Unstratified

Three samples, comprising a dark-coloured medium-grained dolerite hammer stone; a flint core; and a polished, slightly metamorphosed, imported sandstone whetstone (sf. 257 — Fig. 55G).

3:3:14 Bone Objects

Some cetacean bone was found in Phase 11 (see also 3:4:2). Three conjoining fragments (sf. 345 — Fig. 56A) form a block pierced by a 20mm diameter hole (max. l. 212mm, w. 125mm, th. 70mm). There were also 40 small scraps (sf. 389), the largest being 47 x 39 x 27mm, and two other samples (sfs 389, 427). A pierced cetacean vertebra, from a bottle-nosed dolphin or young pilot whale, was found in excavations at Kirkwall, Orkney (McGavin 1983, 421). Such items were apparently used as household ornaments in Orkney, and the excavated example is dated to the 15th-16th century.

A thin, heavily scored strip of ?cattle ulna (sf. 722 — Fig. 56B) was found in Phase 12. It has one polished face, and is 111 x 3–8 x 8mm in size.

Three 4-hole, sew-through turned bone buttons were found, two in Phase 11 (sfs 115, 187), the other (sf. 363 — Fig. 56C) was unstratified. They had been stained brown. Examination by Sonia O'Connor at York revealed they are from dense compact tissue probably cut from cattle longbones, rather than scapulae. This form of clothes fastener, normally considered the product of peasant industry, was widely manufactured and extensively used in the 18th and 19th centuries, both in Britain and Europe (Peacock 1978, 56). Examples have been found in the Danish brigantine *Fraumetta Catherina*, which was carrying a cargo of Russian reindeer hides when it was wrecked in Portsmouth Sound in 1786 (Garbett and Skelton 1987, 18).

One bone from Phase 10 (sf. 15 — l. 14mm, diam. 9mm) may conceivably have been a bead. There were also bones recorded as a cluster (sf. 344), while two pieces (sfs 70, 88) were found not to be artefacts.

3:3:15 Leather (C. Thomas)

This assemblage comprises parts of six shoes, plus twenty-seven smaller shoe fragments, as well as two offcuts and twelve scraps. This includes the most detail of shoe construction and style.

Over half the leather came from Phase 14; the rest belonged mostly to Phase 13, while a few fragments were associated with Phase 12. For a full discussion on this assemblage and all the leather found during the excavations see pp 166-7.

Shoes

Phase 13

sf. 256. Fragments of shoe, comprising heel, composite sole (sole, mid-sole and insole) and toe-cap of vamp.

a. Composite fragment, comprising heel, sole, mid-sole and insole. Heel consists of two lifts, nailed together with iron hobnails. Sole includes seat, waist and rear of forepart. Row of grain to flesh slits adjacent to edge, stitch length 3.5mm.

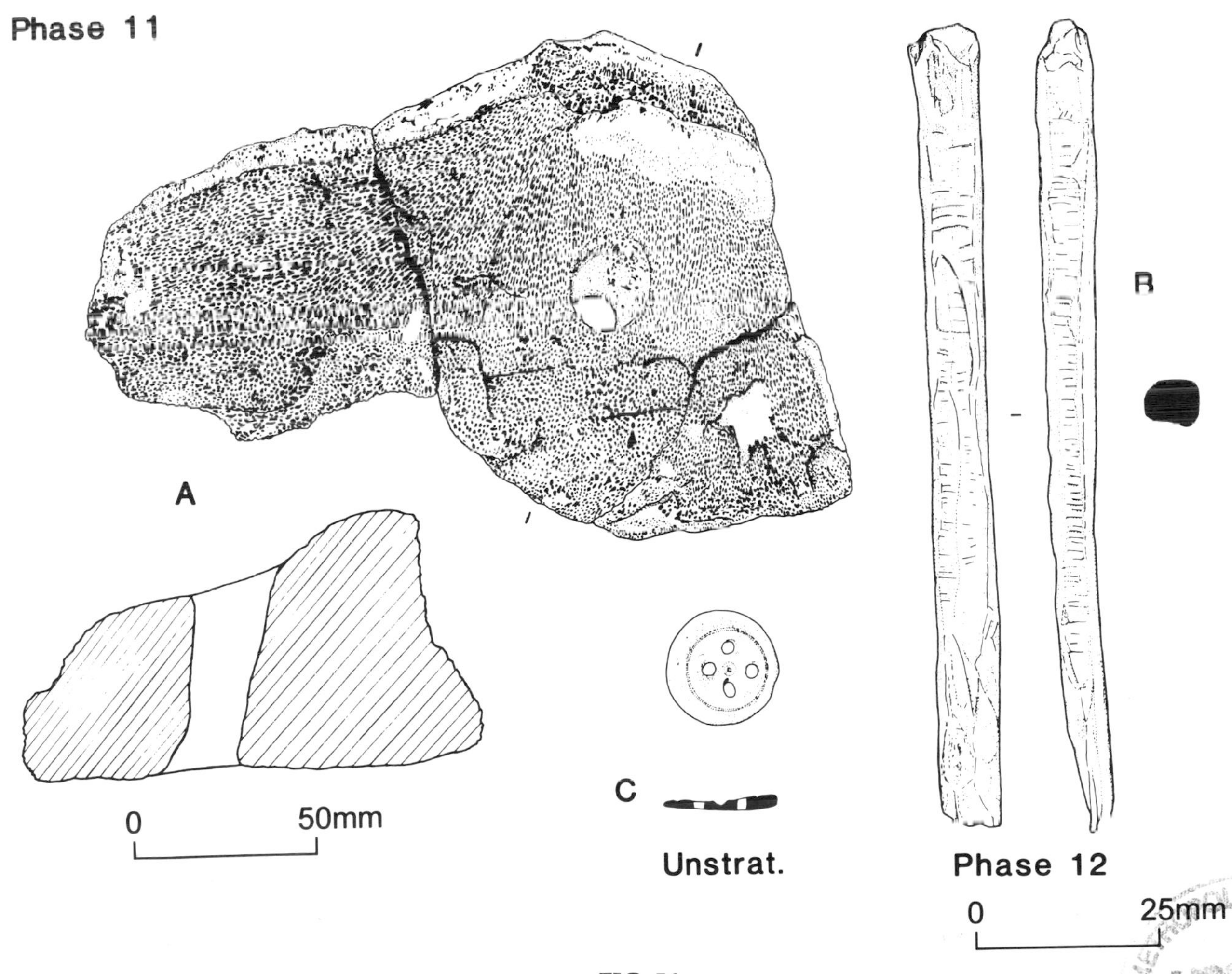

FIG. 56
House 8: bone objects (Phases 11–12 and unstratified). Scale A 1:2; B and C 1:1

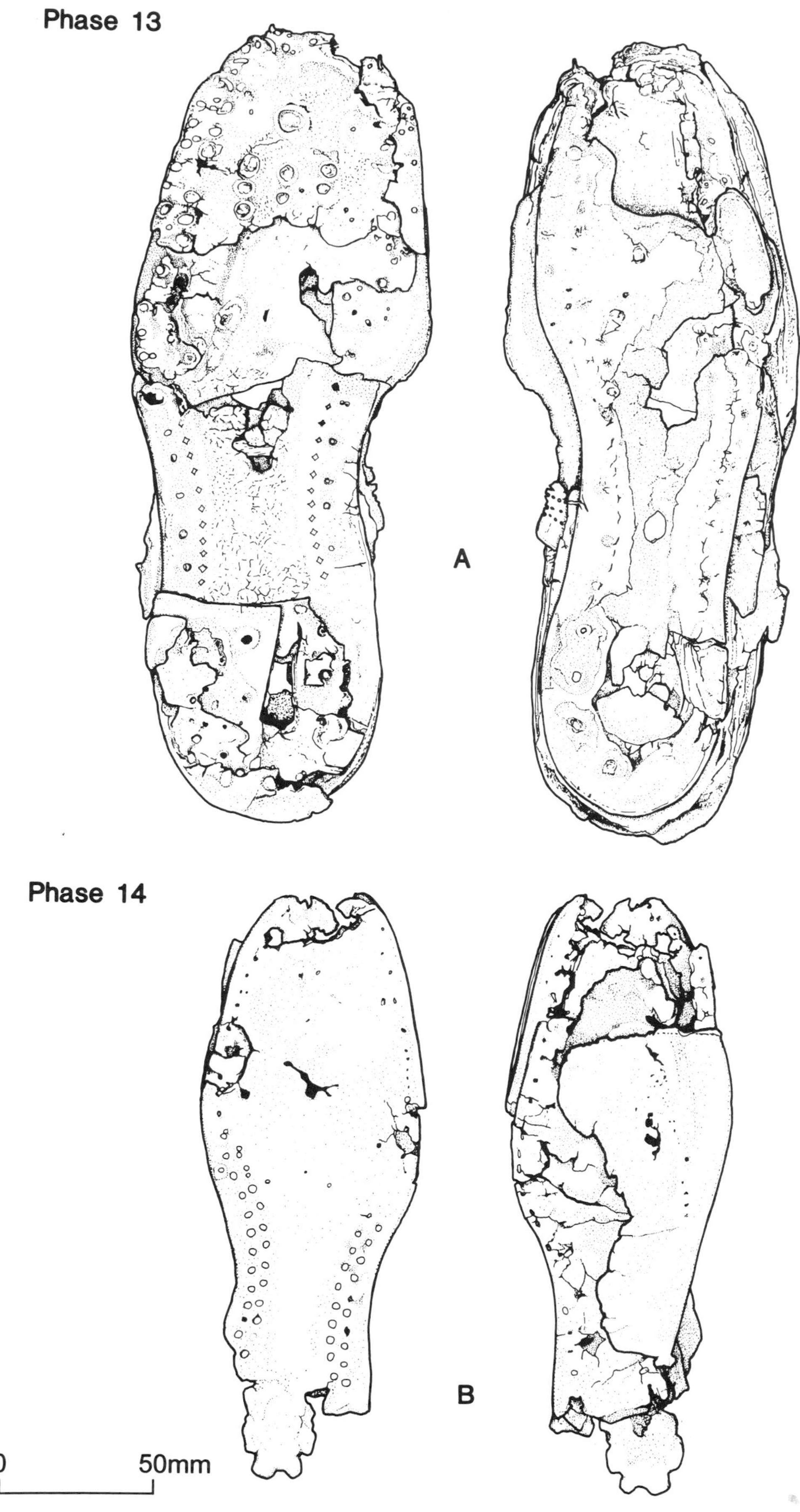

FIG. 57
House 8: leather footwear (Phases 13–14). Scale 1:2

b. Composite fragment, comprising sole and mid-sole. Joins a. and c. Grain to flesh slits as on a. Iron accretion on underside. *c.* 23 x 6 x 3mm.
c. Composite fragment, comprising something attached to ?outer sole-clump, outer sole, mid-sole, insole and semicircular toe-cap of vamp. Clump ?nailed to sole with iron hobnails. Mid-sole also nailed. At wide end of toe-cap, double grain to flesh stitching channel, hole diam. *c.* 0.25–0.5mm, between stitching channels, repeating pattern of one larger dot, diam. 2.5mm and two smaller ones, diam. 1mm. Toe-cap appears to have been attached to insole, mid-sole and sole by brass rivets.
d. Fragment of mid-sole. Approx. l. *c.* 200mm, max. w. of forepart *c.* 70mm, w. of seat *c.* 50mm, th. of outer sole *c.* 2mm, th. of toe-cap *c.* 1mm. Worn at toe. Upper probably cattlehide.

sf. 419. Left boot comprising heel, patched composite sole (sole, mid-sole and insole) and four fragments of upper. Heel consists of several lifts of leather, and iron nails. Details of construction are obscured by corrosion. Composite sole consists of outer sole, mid-sole and insole. Clump sole attached to inner forepart indicates that this part of sole has been patched. Wear on sole towards rear of clump suggests that the damage may have been caused by a bunion. Sole, mid-sole and insole were attached to each other, and to lasting margin of upper by brass rivets. Clump sole was attached by iron hobnails, which were also on rest of outer sole. Hobnail pattern consists of a row round the outside of sole, plus three in centre of forepart, apart from those securing the clump. L. *c.* 200mm, max. w. of forepart *c.* 80mm, w. of waist *c.* 35mm, w. of seat *c.* 55mm, surviving ht of heel *c.* 15mm.
a. Upper. Four fragments survive — toe-cap, part of vamp, one quarter, and backstrip. Toe-cap is riveted to sole. Rear of toe-cap is perforated by two grain to flesh stitching channels, 4.5mm apart, stitch length 1mm. Space between the two stitching channels is filled by repeating pattern of one large round hole, diam. 1.5mm, and one small round hole, diam. 0.5mm, 3.5mm apart. Toe-cap was joined by this double stitching channel to vamp. Rear edge of toe-cap folded underneath, and partially perforated by holes described above. Toe-cap length 45mm. Vamp is complete on outer side of foot, but not on inner. Riveted to sole, between insole and mid-sole. Joined to toe cap by double grain to flesh stitching channel, matching that on toe-cap, but without repeating pattern. Vamp wings are slightly curved, and vamp throat is slightly pointed. Double grain to flesh stitching channels, 2mm apart, stitch length 1mm, on vamp wings and throat, for attachment to quarters and to tongue respectively. Latter does not now survive.
b. Quarters. Outer portion, riveted to sole between insole and mid-sole. Edge joining vamp wing folded, both thicknesses perforated by double grain to flesh stitching channel, 2mm apart, stitch length 1mm. At rear of quarters, grain to flesh stitching channel, stitch length 1mm, parallel to vertical edge. Adjacent but not exactly parallel, a second grain to flesh stitching channel, stitch length 1mm. Second stitching channel is 11mm from first at lasting margin height, then tapers to 7mm, widens out again to 11mm, then tapers to 4mm, then, *c.* 23mm from the top, it joins first stitching channel — for attachment of missing quarters and backstrip. Top edge of quarters folded and stitched, with single grain to flesh stitching channel on outside, and double stitching channel on inside. Fifth edge has 14 lace-holes with eyelets, diam. 4mm, 5mm apart. Edge itself folded over. Two grain to flesh stitching channels, stitch length 1mm, both parallel to edge, 2mm and 16mm from edge — for attachment of lace-hole facing, part of which survives. Ht of quarters *c.* 125-130mm.
c. Backstrip. Riveted to sole, between upper and mid-sole. Both long edges folded, and perforated by grain to flesh stitching channels, stitch length 1mm, for attachment to quarters, and to missing fragment of quarters. Top edge torn. Surviving ht 33mm, plus lasting margin 13mm, w. 28mm at lasting margin, tapering to 12mm.
Condition. Wear on vamp and sole at inside joint suggests that the wearer may have had a bunion. This part of the vamp may have been patched. As noted above, this portion of the sole had been repaired with a clump sole. Fig. 58.

gf. 2/13a. Shoe, sole fragment. Small fragment with two brass rivets. Probably part of a shoe sole. *c.* 30 x 17 x 2mm.

gf. 2/13b. Shoe, sole fragment. Fragment of composite sole, comprising outer sole, mid-sole and insole, with upper sandwiched between insole and mid-sole. Held together with brass rivets, eight of which survive. *c.* 60 x 23 x 16mm.

gf. 2/13c. Shoe, sole fragment. Fragment of sole, with grain to flesh stitching channel, oval holes, *c.* 2.5 x 1.5mm, stitch length 5mm. Worn. Probably insole. Traces of iron corrosion possibly from hobnails.

gf. 2/13d. Shoe, sole fragment. Fragment of insole, with grain to flesh stitching channel. Stitch length 8–9mm, and with traces of rivet holes. Grain surface uppermost. Cattlehide. Surviving l. *c.* 125mm, surviving w. 46mm, th. *c.* 3mm.

gf. 2/13e. Shoe, upper fragment. Irregularly shaped fragment, with one curved cut edge, with double grain to flesh stitching channel, hole diam. *c.* 0.25mm, stitch length *c.* 1mm, rows are *c.* 1mm apart. Approx. 110 x 62 x 1mm.

Large iron accretion attached to one portion, *c.* 30 x 15 x 15mm. Three similar, smaller fragments, with folded edges and similar double grain to flesh stitching channels, one fragment also has a corroded lump of iron attached. Probably part of the vamp wing of an upper.

gf. 11/13. Shoe, sole fragment. Very small fragment of leather, *c.* 24 x 10 x 4mm, with three brass rivets. Almost certainly part of the sole of a shoe.

gf. 12/13. Right shoe comprising composite sole (sole, mid-sole, insole and heel) and at least four fragments of upper, with possible fragments of welt-like strips.
a. Heel consists of three surviving lifts of leather, attached to sole by iron hobnails, nailing pattern obscured by corrosion.
b. Composite sole consists of outer sole, mid-sole and insole. Mid-sole includes at least two pieces of wood in area of waist and seat. At least three leather scraps stuffed between forepart of mid sole and insole.
c. Outer sole has iron hobnails. Pattern appears to consist of a double row round outside, one large nail under front centre forepart, with three rows towards rear of forepart.
d. Insole has grain to flesh stitching channel, stitch length 4–5mm. Stitching channel is set in approx. 8–10mm from the edge, although at rear of inner forepart it is set in *c.* 12–13mm. Stitching may have been for attachment of upper, although brass rivets were used as well. Brass rivets survive, particularly on outer sole and mid-sole.
e. Four fragments survive, sandwiched between insole and mid-sole — these appear to consist of two vamp wings and two quarters. They do not survive for more than 15mm beyond insole. Vamp wings and quarters sewn together by lapped seams, consisting of triple grain to flesh stitching channels, 2mm apart, stitch length 2.5mm. Second piece of leather is sandwiched between quarters and insole — this may have been a narrow welt-like strip. L. 255mm, max. w. of forepart 76mm (insole), *c.* 85mm (outer sole), w. of seat 58mm (insole), 67mm (outer sole), w. of waist 48mm (insole), 65mm (outer sole), th. of insole 2.5mm, th. of whole sole *c.* 21mm.
Condition. Outer sole worn at front and rear of forepart, front of insole missing. Hole in seat of insole, and in outer rear of forepart. Fig. 57A.

gf. 17/13. Shoe upper — toe-cap. Delaminated fragment of upper, consisting of toe-cap of vamp. Lasting margin with round grain to flesh holes, diam. *c.* 1mm, *c.* 6.5mm apart. Not possible to decide whether holes had been used for stitching or riveting. Across rear of toe cap is a double grain to flesh stitching channel, 1mm apart, stitch length 1mm — for attachment to vamp wings. Very worn.

Phase 14

gf. 1/14a. Fragment of left shoe, comprising sole (outer sole, mid-sole, insole) and part of inner vamp wing.

Phase 13

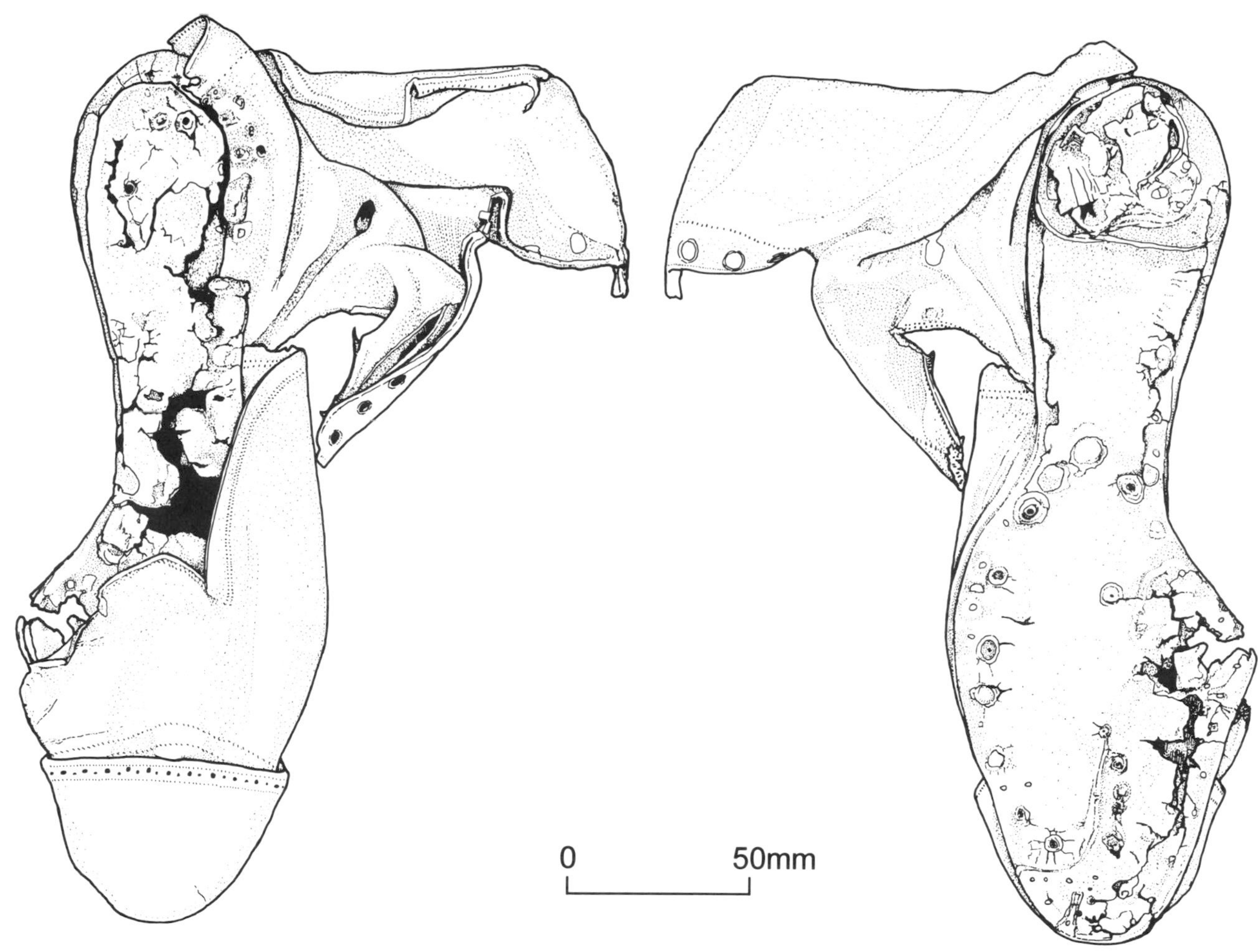

FIG. 58
House 8: leather footwear (Phase 13). Scale 1:2

a. Composite sole, with forepart, waist and rear of seat surviving. Outer sole is 4mm thick. Mid-sole consists of wood, two forepart-shaped pieces of leather (possibly originally one, now delaminated) and a smaller third piece of leather in centre of the tread. Welt-like strip survives on rear inner and outer edge of forepart. Insole now delaminated, th. 2mm. Sole held together, and to upper, with brass rivets. Only slight suggestion of hobnails on outer sole — impression of small ?rust stain, and three holes possibly made by hobnails — suggests that this sole was not hobnailed. However, clear traces and remains of iron nails on the lasting margin of the upper may represent a repair.
b. Upper consists of inner vamp wing, with traces of single grain to flesh stitching channel for attachment to toe-cap. Stitch length 1.5mm. Small holes near a worn patch suggest that upper might have been repaired.
c. Second fragment of upper, very small, still riveted to lasting margin of larger piece. Probably part of quarters. Surviving l. 195mm, surviving w. of seat *c.* 50mm, surviving w. of waist *c.* 45mm, max. w. of forepart 74mm, overall th. of sole *c.* 13mm.
Condition. Very worn; missing seat and heel, and toe of sole, toe-cap, second vamp wing and both quarters. Partially delaminated. Fig. 57B.

gf. 1/14b. Boot upper — latchet. Fragment of upper of boot, consisting of latchet with five lace-holes with eyelets, and with lace-hole facing, originally sewn onto latchet. Top edge of latchet has also been stitched. Extremely faint suggestion of stitching on vertical edge opposite that with lace-holes. Also, short row of grain to flesh stitching, 13mm long, stitch length 1mm, at right-angles to top edge. Worn. Max. dimensions *c.* 70 x 45mm.

gf. 1/14c. Shoe, sole fragment. Small fragment of leather with eleven brass rivets. Almost certainly part of the sole of a shoe. *c.* 60 x 22 x 4mm.

gf. 1/14d. Shoe, sole fragment. Small fragment with four rivet holes, and with traces of iron. Probably part of a shoe sole. *c.* 40 x 35 x 3mm.

gf. 1/14e. Shoe, sole fragment. Small fragment with two brass rivets and with traces of other rivet holes. Probably part of shoe sole. *c.* 31 x 13 x 3mm.

gf. 1/14f. Shoe, two sole fragments. Two fragments of sole, one with a brass rivet. *c.* 28 x 22 x 3mm, and *c.* 80 x 60 x 3mm.

gf. 1/14g. Shoe, sole fragment. Fragment of insole or mid-sole, probably from waist, with grain to flesh stitching channel, stitch length 5mm. One stitch hole survives from opposite edge. Also two rivet holes, one with brass rivet surviving *in situ*. Stitch holes appear to have been used — ?rivets for repair. Surviving l. 98mm, w. 69mm, th. 3mm.

gf. 1/14h. Shoe, sole fragment. Fragment of composite sole, with outer sole, mid-sole and insole, held together by brass rivets, at least ten of which survive. *c.* 85 x 30 x 10mm.

gf. 1/14i. Shoe, sole fragment. Fragment of mid-sole or insole with grain to flesh stitching channel. Stitch length 5.5mm, and with one brass rivet. *c.* 65 x 25 x 4mm.

gf. 1/14j. Shoe, sole fragment. Small fragment of sole of a shoe, with two rivet holes, *c.* 16 x 20 x 2mm.

gf. 1/14k. Shoe, sole fragments. Four small scraps of sole(s). *c.* 55 x 40 x 2mm, 40 x 25 x 2mm, 37 x 18 x 2mm, 12 x 13 x 2mm.

gf. 1/14l. Shoe, sole fragment. Fragment of composite sole, comprising outer sole and delaminated mid-sole, riveted together with brass rivets, ten of which survive. L. *c.* 115mm, w. 30mm, th. *c.* 6mm.

gf. 1/14m. Shoe, sole fragment. Small fragment of sole, with rivet holes, and with one surviving rivet. *c.* 52 x 16 x 2mm.

gf. 1/14n. Shoe, sole fragment. Small sole fragment with rivet holes. Delaminated. *c.* 28 x 20mm.

gf. 1/14o. Shoe, two sole fragments. Two small sole scraps. *c.* 20 x 10 x 1.5mm, 10 x 11 x 1.5mm.

gf. 1/14p. Shoe, sole fragments. Waist fragment of sole, possibly delaminated fragment of outer sole or mid-sole, with eight surviving bronze rivets, and with grain to flesh stitching channel. Hole diam. *c.* 1mm, stitch length 2.5mm, immediately adjacent to the edge, some holes right on the edge, implying that edge has worn away. Stitching possibly for attachment of an upper. Two small fragments of mid-sole or insole still attached by rivets. Delaminated. Surviving l. *c.* 113mm, max. surviving w. *c.* 40mm.

gf. 1/14q. Shoe, ?sole fragment. Short curved strip, with two grain to flesh stitching channels, one with hole diam. *c.* 0.25mm, the other with hole diam. *c.* 1.5mm, stitch length *c.* 7mm. Probably part of a sole. *c.* 35 x 4 x 3mm.

gf. 1/14r. Shoe, upper fragment. Small delaminated fragment with traces of stitching. Probably part of upper. *c.* 22 x 23mm.

gf. 1/14s. Shoe, upper fragment. Irregularly shaped fragment, with one slightly scalloped edge, with triple grain to flesh stitching channel, hole diam. *c.* 0.25mm, stitch length 1mm, 3mm, and 2.5mm. Rows of stitching are 3mm and 4.5mm apart. Probably fragment of upper. Partially delaminated. *c.* 60 x 30 x 1.5mm.

Scraps and offcuts

Phase 12

sf. 290. Offcut or scrap. Small, irregularly shaped fragment, approximately oval with one straight cut edge. Worn. *c.* 52 x 35 x 2mm.

Phase 12/13

sf. 55. ?Offcut. Triangular fragment, with cut edges, one slightly curved. Worn. Cattlehide. *c.* 73 x 40 x 7mm.

sf. 66. Offcut or scrap. Small, approximately triangular fragment with one straight and one slightly curved cut edges, meeting in a point. Third edge torn. *c.* 38 x 22 x 5mm.

sf. 147. Offcut. Irregularly shaped fragment, three sides of rectangle with curved area cut out. Worn. *c.* 75 x 8–42–45 x 5mm.

gf. 10/12–13a. Scrap. Small fragment, approximately rectangular. Exceedingly worn and missing most of the grain. *c.* 82 x 22 x 2mm.

gf. 10/12-13b. Small scraps. About 15 small scraps of leather, largest 22 x 15 x 1mm. ?Part of a mid-sole.

Phase 13

sf. 44. Offcut or scrap. Small fragment of leather. Grain surface quite well preserved. Cattlehide. *c.* 55 x 4–35 x 5mm.

gf. 2/13. Scrap. Fragment with corroded lump of iron and fragment of textile attached. *c.* 20 x 23mm.

gf. 113/13. Offcut or scrap. Triangular fragment, with two cut and one worn or torn edges. Cattlehide. *c.* 95 x 73 x 3mm.

Phase 14

gf. 1/14a. ?Scrap. Irregularly shaped fragment, with one cut edge. *c.* 40 x 33 x 2mm.

gf. 1/14b. Offcut or scrap. Irregularly shaped fragment, with five cut and one torn edges, and with three round holes, diam. 1.5mm. *c.* 76 x 21–39 x 1.5mm.

gf. 1/14c. Scrap. Irregularly shaped scrap, worn. *c.* 92 x 50 x 2mm.

gf. 1/14d. Scrap. *c.* 59 x 29 x 2mm.

gf. 1/14e. Scrap or ?part of mid-sole. *c.* 15 x 15 x 2mm.

gf. 1/14f. Fragment of bronze rivet.

gf. 1/14g. Fragment of iron hobnail.

gf. 1/14h. Miscellaneous fragments with iron corrosion.

3:3:16 Shell Objects

A 2-hole Mother of Pearl button (sf. 67 — Fig. 47G) was found in Phase 12/13. The chief centre of production of this type of button was Birmingham, where they were mass-produced throughout the 19th century, though production was affected by the establishment of an American industry after the Civil War (White 1977, 71–2). Examples of Mother of Pearl buttons have, for instance, been found on the shirt of leading stoker John Torrington, a member of the 1845–8 Franklin expedition, whose preserved body was found in ice at Beechy Island, Canadian North West Territories (Beattie and Geiger 1987, 105).

3:3:17 Textiles (P. Walton)

The excavation of House 8 yielded 38 finds of textile (T1–38) and five of raw fibre (F1–5). One fragment (T17) is from Phase 8 (pre-1830), but the majority come from Phases 12–13, and date to between 1860 and 1930. One find from the topmost levels (T1) can be matched with a pre-1930 textile and may have been up-cast from earlier levels.

Fibres: Most of the pieces are made from wool. A few, however, were clearly once linen-wool union cloths, from which the linen has decayed away. This is a common feature of archaeological textile finds from damp northern climates, where linens are attacked by fungi and acid soils. Those textiles which were originally made in linen alone have presumably decomposed and left no trace in the archaeological record.

A few rare examples of silk, including a large silk bow (T38), show that the St Kilda community was not without access to some luxuries. Man-made fibres, which began to be developed commercially in the 1890s, do not appear to be represented in the collection.

Five examples of raw wool, still in the staples in which they came from the fleece, have been examined by Dr M.L. Ryder. His preliminary report suggests that the wool is most like that of the Hebridean Blackface on Boreray.

Structures: The textiles range from fine to coarse and there is a considerable variety of weave. St Kilda is known to have produced its own hand-spun tweed, but only a handful of the excavated textiles are coarse twills of tweed-like quality (e.g. T24, T27, T36). Many of the remaining fabrics are woven in compound twills of some sophistication; satin-weave also occurs in some of the lightweight jacket fabrics. These fabrics may be machine-woven and presumably imported from the mainland.

Costume: Some of the larger fragments show details of cut and stitching. One group in satin-weave, felted on one face, appear to be pieces from a woman's jacket, with a cuffed sleeve, front buttoning and pocket slits. In another example, a short band of wool twill is in position in a two-prong buckle, of the type used to gather a waistcoat. The silk bow mentioned above is mounted on a metal bar or clip, and may be a hair or dress decoration.

Colour: Traces of colour are still visible in some of the fragments, for example in a wool twill with fine line-checks of red, black and natural (T25). A differently coloured warp and weft has been used in other pieces, including a herringbone twill of red and grey (T35). Most commonly, however, the textiles are one uniform colour, mostly shades of blue and black — or brown, where dye has leached away.

Dr G.W. Taylor (Textile Research Associates, York) has analysed the dyes by absorption spectrophotometry and thin-layer chromatography and his work has confirmed that dark blue and black were common colours. The chemical identified most frequently is indigotin, which may be from natural or synthetic indigo. Aniline black, invented in 1863, has also been tentatively identified in T22, which is part of a jacket. The silk (T21) was dyed with indigodisulfonic acid, a man-made indigo derivative, but not truly a synthetic. It was introduced as 'Saxe Blue' in the 18th century and continued in use until synthetic indigo was invented in 1880, when it was rapidly ousted. This tallies with the relatively early date for this textile, contemporary with the cottage building of the 1860s.

Further research on the textiles, including the weaves, wool, raw fibres, dyes, and costume details, is being carried out, and a more detailed report will be published separately.

Catalogue

Notes:
'coarse' = less than 10 threads per cm in warp and weft
'medium' = 10–20 threads per cm
'medium-fine' = 20–30 threads per cm
'fine' = more than 30 threads per cm

Phase 8
gf. 55/8 (T17). Medium quality red-brown wool tabby.

Phase 11
gf. 71/11 (T19). Medium quality brown wool 2/2 twill.

Phase 12
sf. 552 (T38). A bow made up of two strips of fine silk ?twill: broad inner strip black and narrow outer strip light brown.

gf. 96/12 (T21). Fine black silk ?twill.

gf. 195/12 (T36). Coarse green-grey wool 2/2 twill.

gf. 195/12 (T37). Parallel wool threads, possibly part of a linen-wool union cloth; in association with a leather belt and belt fittings; also a feather.

Phase 12/13
sf. 35 (F5). Wool staples, 50mm long, pointed.

sf. 135 (T12). Many large fragments, largest 670 x 200mm, of a fine grey ribbed weave made from 2/1 twill combined with 5/1 twill.

sf. 163 (T13). More fragments of T12.

sf. 170 (T14). More fragments of T12–13.

Phase 13
gf. 2/13 (F1). Wool staple, 230mm long, wavy.

gf. 2/13 (F2). Wool staples, 60–75mm long, crimpy.

gf. 2/13 (T2). Band of medium-fine brown 2/2 twill, slotted through square, two pronged buckle.

gf. 2/13 (T3). Parallel wool threads, probably from a linen-wool union cloth.

gf. 2/13 (T4). Medium-fine blue-black wool satin, similar to T22.

gf. 2/13 (T5). Medium-fine brown/black wool tabby.

gf. 2/13 (T6). Remains of a jacket/coat revere in medium-fine black wool satin, similar to T22.

gf. 2/13 (T7). Tattered fragments of wool satin, similar to T22.

gf. 2/13 (T8). Threads of ?silk, probably remains of lining to T7.

gf. 2/13 (T9). Small fragments of wool satin, similar to T22.

gf. 2/13 (T10). Threads of ?lining to T9.

gf. 2/13 (T11). Black wool satin, similar to T22, with parallel rows of stitching.

gf. 12/13 (T15). Medium-fine blue-black wool satin similar to T22.

gf. 17/13 (T16). Medium-fine light brown compound twill.

gf. 17/13 (F3). Wool staple, light brown, 85mm long, wavy.

gf. 17/13 (F4). Wool staple, dark brown, 75mm long, wavy.

gf. 80/13 (T20). Brown-black textile, made up of parallel wool threads, matted together: probably originally a linen-wool union cloth.

gf. 113/13 (T22). Several large fragments, making up the right side of a woman's jacket in blue-black wool 5-end satin.

gf. 113/13 (T23). Greenish-grey open-weave satin, lining of binding to T22.

gf. 113/13 (T24). Coarse black wool 2/2 twill.

gf. 113/13 (T25). Medium-fine wool twill patterned with fine line-check in red, black and natural.

gf. 113/13 (T26). Parallel light brown threads, matted together: probably originally part of a linen-wool union cloth.

gf. 113/13 (T27). Coarse brown-black wool 2/2 twill.

gf. 113/13 (T28). Coarse green-grey wool 2/2 twill.

gf. 113/13 (T29). Coarse light brown wool 2/2 twill.

gf. 113/13 (T30). Fine, light brown fabric, poorly preserved, possibly a double-faced twill.

gf. 113/13 (T31). Very tattered remains, weave not identified.

gf. 113/13 (T32). Coarse green-grey wool 2/2 twill, possibly more of T28.

gf. 113/13 (T33). ?Pocket flap in blue-black satin, possibly part of T22.

gf. 113/13 (T34). Compound twill similar to T12.

gf. 113/13 (T35). Coarse herringbone twill in red and grey.

Phase 14

gf. 1/14 (T1). Medium-fine blue-black wool satin, similar to T22.

gf. 73/14 (T18). Parallel fine dark brown threads, probably once part of a linen-wool union cloth.

3:3:18 Wood

A total of 3365 fragments of wood were recovered. Although four small fragments were found in Phases 4–9, the bulk came from the construction, use and decay of the cottage. A few solid pieces were probably from joists, but the vast majority came from boards. These include floor-boards, wainscotting and sarking boards. At least some of the boards had been united by machine-cut tongue-and-groove jointing (sf. 98 — Fig. 59A-B), though lap-boarding, with grooved and moulded ends, probably came from the walls (sf. 100).

Traces of floor-cloth were still found attached to fragments of boarding of the first-phase floor (see 3:3:19). The sarking board was *c.* 8mm thick, with a finely woven cloth cover, coated with tar. Some heavy rippling of tar by the edge of the board contained trapped plant remains (gf. 113/13).

Although most of the wood was fragmented, some boarding had clearly been cut across the grain with a very sharp knife, probably post-use, leaving at least 55 rectangular flakes. Four fragments of disturbed wood from Phase 8 were heavily charred (sf. 239).

Three pieces of wood were non-structural and had been worked. One was part of a bobbin-like object found in Phase 10, 38mm diameter (sf. 139 — Fig. 59D); the others were 105mm and 67mm long pointed rods or pegs, one from Phase 12/13 (sf. 75) and one from Phase 13 (gf. 80/13 — Fig. 59C).

3:3:19 Miscellaneous

Fragments of 1mm thick floorcloth (sf. 80 — Fig. 59E) were found associated with the first wooden floor of the cottage (Phase 12). The woven fabric, either calico or probably jute, has decayed, though the pattern can still be seen in section and in damaged flakes. The warp and weft threads are of different sizes, spaced about 2mm apart. In factory production a full web was often 150 x 8yd (137.16 x 7.32m) cut into 24yd

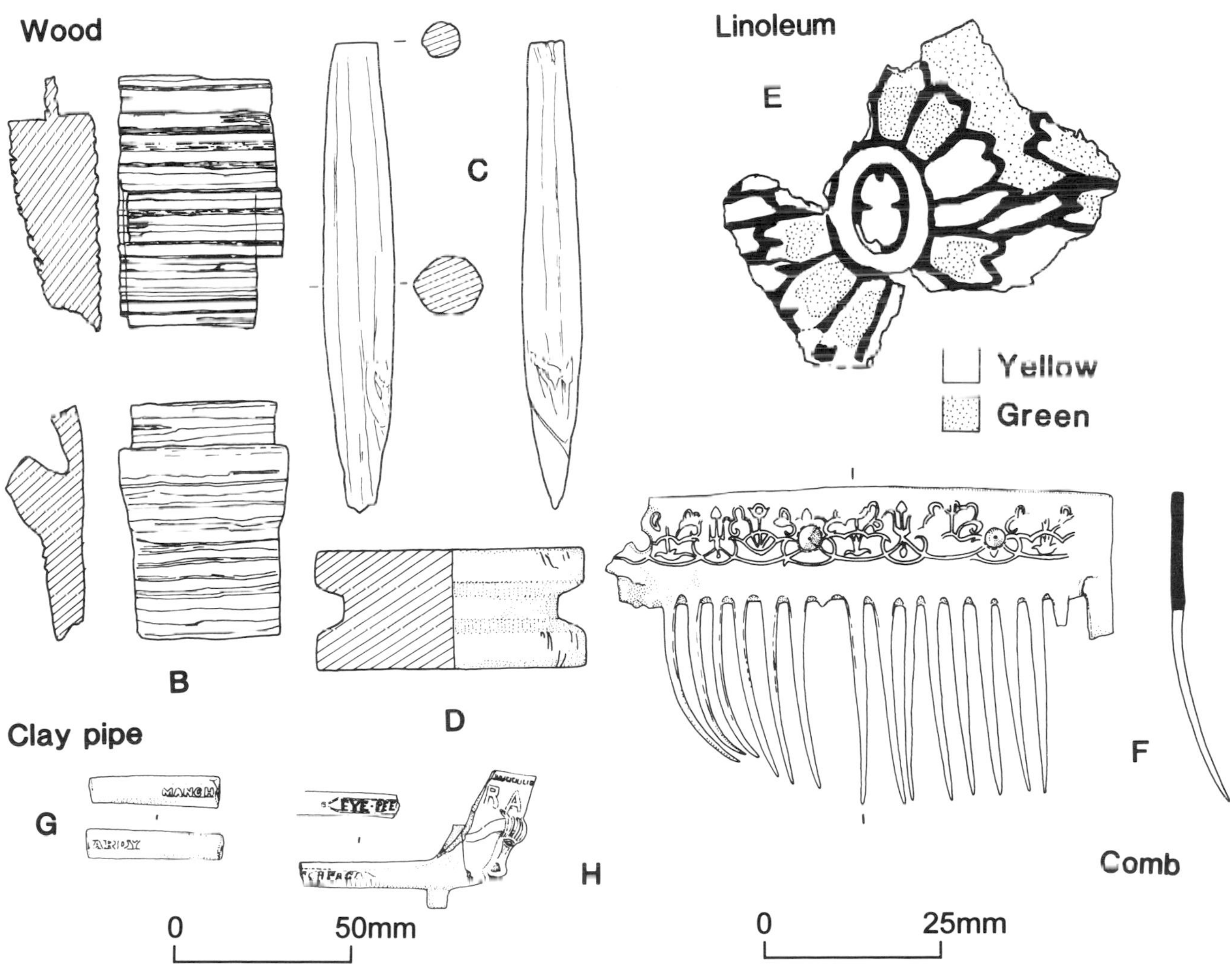

FIG. 59

House 8: wood (Phases 10 and 12–13), linoleum (Phase 12/13), clay pipe (Phases 12–13) and comb (Phase 12/13). Scale 1:1

(21.95m) lengths. The lengths would be held taut in the frame room, and the fragments show that it was coated on the undersurface with a pink-orange paint, and white on the upper surface. The latter surface was then given a thin coat of pink colour as a background for a floral decoration. The design is made up in three stages — a yellow basic shape for the flower head and stalks, etc., green patches on the petals, and a black viscous outline. The printing of floorcloth was normally done using 18" (457mm) square blocks, with a block for each colour, stamped by a printer (with the aid of a 'tear boy') onto the 8yd cloth. There are no obvious dots in the colours, usually associated with the paint retaining pattern cut on a block. From 1847, Nairns of Kirkcaldy were the chief manufacturers of floorcloth in Scotland, with an extensive market elsewhere (Muir 1956). Many of their printing blocks were cut in Glasgow.

Synthetic materials include a bun comb (sf. 155 — Fig. 59F); and a recent matt-black hair comb (sf. 164), both from Phase 12/13. The bun comb was examined by Sonia O'Connor at York, who found that it is made from a brittle, brown-coloured material of varying colour and translucency. The surface is very much eroded although in strong reflected light the remains of an intricate relief decoration can be seen on the surface of the comb front, and the remains of machine tooling marks are visible on the back. A broken surface reveals a smooth, almost glassy fracture, with little evidence of any internal structure. Three pits in the top of the comb probably originally took decorative metal studs. The texturing and bubbling of the surface of the pits are consistent with a technique used on thermosoftening materials where the heated metal studs are pushed into the surface.

Although this comb has a passing resemblance to tortoise-shell, the characteristics of the pigmentation of the material, and the decayed and freshly fractured surfaces are not those of an object made from tortoise-shell. On the same grounds this is not horn or baleen, both of which have been used in imitation of tortoise-shell. Although these natural plastics were often highly modified during the manufacture of combs (by dyeing and staining, heating and pressing, powdering and melting or by modifying their chemical structure), the resultant material usually retains some characteristics of the original material.

It would appear that this comb is made from a synthetic plastic. Many of the early plastics used to imitate tortoise-shell are acetone soluble, this object is not. However, if the style of decoration suggests a date early this century, a very wide range of plastics with differing solubility characteristics would have been available.

One other item was the moulded end of an object, possibly part of a child's toy (sf. 30).

3:4 The Ecofactual Material

3:4:1 Plant Remains (Jacqueline P. Huntley)

The sampling and processing methods follow those used for the other areas and are described above (see 2:4:1).

Description of the samples (Table 18)

Phase 2

Context 246 (flot 152), Area 3. This was a layer of soil accumulation. The sample produced both barley and oat grains although none were well preserved.

Phase 4

Context 230 (flot 151), Area 1. This was a dark brown silty layer in the stream channel covering context 232 (see below). It contained a single oat grain.

Context 232 (flot 156), Area 1. This was a black soil at the southern end of the stream channel and covered by context 230 (see above). It contained modern roots and waterlogged seeds of nettles, sedges and *Polygonum* spp. including black bindweed, redshank and knotweed. Carbonised indeterminate cereal, barley and oats were also present in moderate numbers, although preservation was poor.

Context 251 (flots 153 and 154), Area 1. This context was the reddish-brown soil in pit 250. The first flot was tiny and barren. The second was small and consisted of charcoal fragments with barley grains, one of which was immature and hulled.

Phase 6

Context 211 (flot 133), Area 1. This was a gritty silt filling the drainage system and produced a tiny flot containing only a few fragments of small mammal bone, with one each of barley and, possibly, rye.

Context 213 (flot 132), Area 1. This was also a fill of a land drainage system. Its flot was small and contained the occasional fragment of bone and insect but no seeds.

Phase 7

Context 108 (flot 96), Area 1. This was one of three dump layers of peat ash underlying the south-east corner of the cottage. Although it produced only a small flot there were considerable numbers of burnt fucoid frond fragments present as well as a few modern unburnt seeds and earthworm egg cases. One barley and one possible breadwheat grain were recorded.

Context 175 (flot 110), Area 1. This was a sample from the rubble and soil between stone lines. It produced one oat grain and two indeterminate cereal grains.

Phase 8

Context 55, Area 1. This context covered soil layers which were heavily disturbed by the drain-laying operations of Phase 9. Two samples were analysed. One contained several modern dock/knotweed *(Rumex/ Polygonum)* seeds as well as burnt heather shoots and occasional fragments of charcoal. The other consisted primarily of modern rootlets and earthworm egg cases with a few pieces of miscellaneous burnt stem.

Context 130 (flot 84), Area 1. This was a further heavily disturbed soil layer. The sample contained plenty of modern seeds but more or less no charcoal. Earthworm egg cases and insect fragments were common.

Context 197 (flot 124), Area 3. This was a gritty brown soil, with scattered stones, which had developed over the whole area. The small flot produced a selection of seeds mostly relating to wet ground taxa, although oat grains and awns were present.

Phase 9

Context 129 (flot 83), Area 1. This was the fill of a drain constructed during preparation of the site for a blackhouse in the 1830s. It only produced a tiny flot

AREA No.	3	1	1	1	1	1	1	1	3	1	1	1	1	2				1		1	2	1	2	2
CONTEXT No.	246	230	232	251	211	108	175	55	197	129	131	145	150	205	81	84	88	166	36	170	185	194	209	10
PHASE	2	4	4	4	6	7	7	8	8	9	9	9	9	9	10	10	10	10	11	11	11	11	11	13
[a]*Centaurea cyanus* (cornflower)																								1
[a]*Chrysanthemum segetum* (corn marigold)																		1		1				
[c]*Avena* grain (oats)	2	1	1				1		2			2	4	1	4		7		9	7	6	5		
[c]Cerealia undiff.	2		8	2	2		2						1	2			6		3		2	1	1	
[c]cf. *Secale cerealia* (?rye)					1																			
[c]*Hordeum* hulled (barley)				1						1			4		1	1	1	3					1	
[c]*Hordeum* indet.	4		17	11	1	1					1	1					1			6		1		
[c]*Hordeum* straight hulled																							1	
[c]*Hordeum* twisted hulled												1							1				1	
[c]*Triticum* cf. *aestivum* (bread wheat)						1																		
[c]*Triticum* sp(p). grain (wheat)										1									1		1	1		
[g]*Rumex acetosa* (sorrel)																					1			
[h]*Calluna vulgaris* twigs (heather)								+		1								+	+					
[h]*Calluna vulgaris* wood																	+	+		+				
[h]*Erica tetralix* (cross-leaved heath)							1																	
[h]*Sieglingia decumbens* (heath-grass)						1							1											
[m]*Fucus* — thallus/frond (brown seaweed)						++						+	++				+	+					+	
[r]*Rumex obtusifolius*-type (docken)																						1		
[s]*Avena* awn (oat chaff)									1															
[s]Culm nodes (straw)																					1			
[t]*Luzula sylvatica* (woodrush)											1													
[w]*Carex* (lenticular) (sedges)									1			1												
[w]*Carex* (trigonous) (sedges)									3									1	1					
[w]*Juncus* (rush)																				+				
[w]*Montia font.* ssp. *chondr.* (blinks)				1																				
[x]Gramineae culm node (grass 'straw')																	1							
[x]Gramineae undiff.									1				2				1			1				
[x]*Luzula* sp(p).									1															
[x]*Ranunculus repens*-type (buttercup)																				1				

TABLE 18
House 8: carbonised plant remains

KEY
The taxa have been put into broad ecological category. The latter was subjectively derived and the prefix codes are as follows:
a = arable weeds c = cereal grain g = grassland h = heathland m = maritime/coastal r = ruderals/disturbed ground s = cereal chaff and straw fragments t = scrub/woodland w = wet ground x = broad, unclassified

with three carbonised fragments of material — barley, wheat and a heather shoot.

Context 131 (flot 85), Area 1. This was the fill from another part of the drain of context 129 above. The small flot contained considerable numbers of modern rootlets and seeds — mainly from black bindweed *(Polygonum convolvulus)*. In addition, there were moderate numbers of insect fragments from several species and a single snail, and one carbonised barley grain.

Context 145 (flot 86), Area 1. A further fill of the drain. It contained much well-preserved root material and a few fragments of insect. One extremely well-preserved hulled twisted barley grain was recovered, as well as two oat grains and one poorly preserved barley grain.

Context 150 (flot 95), Area 1. A layer associated with drain construction prior to the 1830s blackhouse. The small flot contained waterlogged blinks seeds, chunks of charcoal and quite a few burnt fragments of fucoid seaweed including a probable holdfast. Four each of hulled barley and oat grains were present.

Context 205 (flot 128), Area 2. This was a layer of drain fill in the soil later prepared for the 1830s blackhouse. The sample contained modern rootlets and earthworm egg cases, with one oat and indeterminate cereal grains.

Context 228 (flot 139), Area 1. The fill of the drain underlying the area upon which the 1830s blackhouse was built; the sample contained a few modern seeds — violet, black bindweed — and insect fragments only.

Phase 10

Context 81. This sample was taken from the grey-brown soil spread around the threshold between the human and animal occupation areas of the blackhouse. It produced only a tiny flot of charcoal fragments which, nonetheless, contained four oats and one hulled barley grain.

Context 84. This was a more clay-rich sample from the threshold area as described in context 81 above. The sample produced a tiny flot with a single exceptionally well-preserved hulled barley grain still having its palea/lemmas attached.

Context 88 (flot 175 and second sample). These samples were associated with the blackhouse and produced a number of bone fragments. Many seem to derive from birds although the majority were highly comminuted. Oat and barley grains in moderate numbers make it one of the richest contexts analysed.

Context 166 (flot 101), Area 1. This was a layer of clay soil within the hearth of the blackhouse. It produced a moderate-sized flot consisting of fucoid fragments and heather twigs. It almost certainly reflects material being burnt in the hearth. The clay itself may represent the fabric of the hearth. Three barley grains were present. One seed of corn marigold represents a weed of the cereal fields.

Phase 11

Context 36. This was a deposit of peat ash from the decay and demolition phase. The flot consisted of primarily modern rootlets and peat fragments with modern, unburnt blinks and rush seeds. A variety of cereals, barley, oats and wheat were present.

Context 106 (flot 178). This formed a layer of sandy silt overlying the dark brown soil of context 24, itself sealing the midden material of contexts 194 and 185 (see below). The small flot consisted of charcoal fragments and carbonised grass stems but no seeds were recovered.

Context 168 (flot 111), Area 2. A layer from the decay and demolition phase of the blackhouse but whose sample contained only earthworm egg cases.

Context 170 (flot 125), Area 1. An ash tip over a cleit wall which produced a moderate-sized flot containing many tiny fragments of clean charcoal. Oats and barley were common and there were indications of arable weeds from the presence of corn marigold seeds.

Context 185 (flot 11 and bag 1). This was a midden dump of shell and bone. The first sample produced a moderate flot with large numbers of fish scales, a few fish vertebrae and teeth. Lots of modern nettle (*Urtica dioica*) seeds were recovered as were some fly puparia fragments. Odd bits of carbonised vegetative fragments were present. The second sample produced a very small flot with nettle seeds and modern roots only. Oats were common and one grain of wheat was recorded.

Context 194 (flot 114), Area 2. This midden dump of shell and bone produced a tiny flot, with oats, barley and possibly wheat.

Context 209 (flot 131), Area 2. A sample was taken of burnt material filling a hollow, which was in a black silty layer covering the cleit area. The flot produced a few fragments of charcoal with some fucoid fragments and barley grains.

Phase 12/13

Context 10 (flot 171). This sample produced a small flot containing only wood fragments, a single snail shell, and a cornflower seed.

Discussion

Cereals are the only potential food plant remains found, with barley and oats the most abundant, although no samples had large amounts of grain in them. This may be due to the small volume of material originally floated or may be a 'real' low level of occurrence. In some cases the grains were sufficiently well preserved to determine that the barley was hulled and at least some was the 6-rowed *Hordeum vulgare*. This latter is evidenced by the twisted embryos of the lateral grains. With six grains at each rachis node, four show a twisted character and two a straight character. This is in comparison with the 2-row *H. distichon* where all of the grains have straight embryos. The 6-row barley, or bere barley, was the most commonly found species in the north of Scotland until recent times, and, indeed, can still be found in the extreme north of the mainland and upon the islands of the Orkneys today growing in a few fields. It is still common in Scandinavia.

Somewhat surprising is that no rachis fragments of barley were recovered. These, in quantity, would indicate local production of the cereal. However, their absence may simply indicate that the samples were not large enough, that they were not from a suitable area or that the chaff was used for some other purpose such as chicken feed and that none was preserved.

Oats were the other abundant cereal grain recovered and, likewise, no chaff was present, with the exception of one awn. This means that no distinction could be made as to whether the oats were the cultivated or wild species, although the former is presumed.

Both of these cereals could have been grown locally in small, protected fields and used for human consumption.

Almost certain to have been imported are the few grains of wheat recovered as well as the one, tentatively identified, rye grain. Preservation is generally not good and the sharp embryo and overall shape, although rye-like, could be a wheat species. If these had been for human consumption they may, perhaps, be expected to have been imported ready-ground as flour; could their presence as grain indicate animal fodder? The interpretation of such overall low numbers has to be highly speculative.

The associated weed seeds are also low in numbers and are from the expected weeds of cereal crops in the north — corn marigold *(Chrysanthemum segetum)* and sheep's sorrel *(Rumex acetosella)*. The other weed seeds indicate grassland and wet ground in the vicinity — the former probably grazed. Of particular interest is the cornflower *(Centaurea cyanus)*. This is traditionally associated with rye cultivation — here perhaps being imported as a weed amongst the rye grain although the two were not recovered from the same context.

Heathland representatives are common in most of the samples in the form of wood, shoots and flowers of heather *(Calluna vulgaris)*. The plant is found on the acid peats in drier regions of the island and would probably have been gathered as bedding and conceivably for thatching as well as for making *simmens* (rope), with waste or damaged material subsequently burnt. Indeed, its moderate numbers in a few contexts may indicate a demolition phase when heather roofs had collapsed. The peat underlying such heather moorland would almost certainly have been exploited as a fuel and some of the heather fragments could have originated this way.

In a few contexts there were abundant fragments of fucoid seaweed — the so-called 'brown' seaweeds which form the wracks of the middle shore and the kelp beds of the lower shore. Both their fronds and their holdfasts were present, all of which were carbonised. They demonstrate the use of local resources and have been found in other archaeological localities such as Birsay, Orkney (Donaldson *et al.* 1981) and Freswick, Caithness (Huntley 1986). They are a recognised fertiliser and are used in the manufacture of 'lazy beds' in the West of Ireland even today. Why their remains should have been burnt is not clear since, in the lazy beds, they are gathered from the shore and dug straight away into the peat. Although they may have been accidentally burnt, the relatively large numbers, compared with anything else, tend to indicate a deliberate policy of burning. Perhaps the ash was used as the fertiliser if an organic but mineral soil had already been produced over time. They were also used in the manufacture of potash and this was carried out in pits. This function of the material is rather unlikely given the lack of abundance of raw material around this island. The wracks grow in a restricted, with respect to tide levels, band around a shore and this is itself a very restricted zone in the case of St Kilda with its steep and high cliffs.

Although the overall numbers of seeds were low and therefore patterns of distribution would be meaningless, nonetheless they should be discussed against their archaeological background.

Only one sample from Phase 2 was analysed. It contained both barley and oat grains as well as two badly preserved indeterminate cereal grains. Its context type as a re-deposited soil through stream action makes any interpretation doubtful.

The samples from Phase 4 showed barley as the most common species with a little oat. Only one weed seed was found and this is from a species, blinks, which is also characteristic of muddy, trampled ground. Samples from context 251 were pit fill layers, but unfortunately the evidence does not indicate their function. The sample with the most grain was from a silt layer in the stream channel, and possibly indicates a small concentration of grain through water action. The layer overlying this one contained only one oat grain.

Phase 6 contexts contain only a few cereal grains. The samples were from a silty fill in a land drainage system and this was perhaps very rapidly deposited.

The very species-poor context 175, from Phase 7, was a rubble layer between stone lines and therefore would not necessarily be expected to contain many remains. The second sample from this phase contains relatively large numbers of fucoid fragments, as well as evidence of heathland and cereals. This was from a dumped layer of peat ash (108) and probably gives evidence of domestic rubbish, in a very limited way.

Phase 8 produced evidence of wet ground taxa and two burnt oat grains only.

During Phase 9 a wider variety of other species is represented. This partly may be due to the fact that more samples have been processed although not as many as for Phases 2, 4, 6, 7 and 8 in total. In particular, plants of wet ground (sedges and rushes) and scrubland or inaccessible rocky areas are in evidence. The latter is represented by *Luzula sylvatica*, the woodrush, which is grazing-intolerant and hence only commonly found on steep, rocky ledges, or in grazing-free woodlands (which are not to be found on St Kilda). It forms a dense vegetation on the upper slopes of Conachair. The higher levels of wet ground species could indicate the use of such turfs as fuel. The seaweed fragments are scattered throughout this phase.

Phase 10 samples start a preponderance of oats although the wet ground plants are more or less absent. More remains of heather have been preserved than before; whilst this may reflect use as a fuel it may also indicate a period of dereliction where heather-thatched roofing material was burnt.

During Phase 11, oats were more abundant again and a few seeds of traditional cornfield weeds such as corn marigold were found. Scattered grains of wheat are found in samples from this phase.

Although the overall numbers of seeds were disappointingly low they do indicate something of the local cereals and natural plant communities. Barley and oats were most commonly consumed and were probably, at least partly, locally grown. It is unusual that so little evidence remains of chaff fragments since the people certainly grew, and dried, at least some of their cereal requirements. There is an indication that barley was the preferred cereal during the early phases of occupation but that from Phase 10 onwards oats were favoured. The wheat was almost certainly imported and tends to be more common in samples from the later phases. The local moorland was exploited and probably used as bedding, roofing and fuel. Other than cereals the most abundant evidence of usage of plant material is of the seaweeds thrown up upon the island or gathered from the intertidal zone around the island. This material seems to have been deliberately burnt, perhaps indicating the presence of established fields requiring continued fertilising, rather than new fields being developed from the peat.

3:4:2 *Mammal and Bird Bones (M. Harman)*

All the bones recovered were examined. Their condition varies, many of those from older deposits are poorly preserved: fragile and crumbly, while those from more recent deposits are in better condition. No bones survive from the three earliest phases and there are only small quantities from any of the other phases, before the establishment of the village on its present site in the late 1830s, so most of the bones are derived from deposits spanning about a century. Most of the pieces are identifiable. The volume of bird bones is about twice that of the animal bones. Estimation of age is based partly on figures given by Silver (1963). Dog sizes are calculated using Harcourt's formula (1974).

The mammal bones

Table 19 shows the number of bones present from each species recognised in each phase. This clearly demonstrates the scarcity of bones from deposits before about 1835, and brings out some other interesting characteristics. Apart from a single bone

PHASE	CATTLE	SHEEP	DOG	OTHER
4		3	11	?Cetacean fragment
	4 teeth	6–8 teeth		
5	1	2	31	
	1 tooth	5 teeth	3 teeth	
6		1	4	
7			5	
		2 teeth		
8	2	2		
	2 teeth	1 tooth		
9		2	2	
		4 teeth		
10	5	47	3	Horse: 1 tooth
	2 teeth	21 teeth		Woodmouse: 1 bone
11	11	107	2	Cat: 4 bones
	2 teeth	27 teeth		Cetacean: 2 fragments
12	3	22		
		8 teeth		
13	3	40		Cat: 1 bone
	1 tooth	10 teeth		
14	1	13		Pig: 1 bone

TABLE 19

House 8: numbers of bones and loose teeth from different species identified from different phases

— a piece of rib with sawn ends, which is clearly of recent origin — there are no pig bones. This is not surprising, as there is no record of swine ever having been kept on St Kilda, but their bones do occur on archaeological sites in the Western Isles, and they may have been taken out to St Kilda in earlier times.

Most of the bones are from cattle, sheep, and dog. Cattle and sheep are scantily represented in earlier phases, though the numbers of teeth suggest that had preservation been better there might have been more bones; some of the teeth were reduced to sheets of enamel. It is not until Phase 10 that the bones become more numerous; in this and later phases there are still considerably more bones from sheep than from cattle. This probably reflects the relative numbers of animals kept: many more sheep than cattle, and slaughtering a cattle beast would have been a much rarer event than the slaughtering of a sheep. Most of the bones from these early phases are from mature animals, though there are sheep teeth from Phases 5 and 7 from animals of about 1½ to 2½ years, and about 1 year respectively.

The few cattle bones from Phase 10 include two from a calf or calves. Most of the sheep bones are from skeletally mature animals, but there is a jaw from a very small lamb of a month or two, and jaws and teeth from three animals of between 1½ and 2½ years. There are a few bones with unfused epiphyses, from well-grown but immature sheep. Few of the sheep bones are measurable, but those that are are comparable in size with those of the modern Soay sheep now on the island. Several of the bones have cuts on them consistent with butchering: there is evidence for the cutting off of sheep's heads, the halving of the skull on the axial line, and removal of the toes and hooves. Two scapulae have cuts beside the spine, probably the result of cutting the meat off.

In Phase 11 the cattle bones include two teeth from a calf of about 6–9 months old, and a metatarsal from a well-grown animal aged between 1 and 2 years. One vertebra was halved. Most of the sheep bones are skeletally mature, but there are two jaws from lambs of 4–6 months old, and eleven bones with unfused epiphyses, some from quite small animals, others from sheep which were clearly at least a year old but not fully mature. Pieces from two or three skulls show that sheep heads were halved, and one horn core had been cut off a skull: it might be difficult to get a sheep's head into a pot with the horn still on it. A few sheep bones could be measured; several are at the upper end of the Soay sheep size range, and could be from improved sheep.

From Phase 12 there are mandibles from a lamb of 2 or 3 months, and a sheep in its second year, and three other bones from immature animals, one of which was a very small lamb. One sheep mandible has cuts on the ascending ramus: these might have resulted from the skinning of the animal or detaching the lower jaw from the skull. Two vertebrae were cut across. One sheep toe bone (a second phalanx) has a lot of extra bony growth around the proximal end. The articular surface is roughened, with a patch of eburnation, all signs of osteo-arthritis in the joint.

In Phase 13 two of the cattle bones and three of the sheep bones are from immature animals. One sheep skull fragment is halved, and a vertebra cut across. In Phase 14 there are two bones from immature sheep. In both the last two phases there are robust bones from sheep of a size incompatible with Soays.

It is probable that most of the cattle and sheep bones are from animals which were eaten, although some of the bones are from parts normally discarded at slaughtering, such as feet; so there are bones which have probably been cooked and discarded from the home, and others which were probably disposed of without entering the home. Cuts on some of the sheep bones indicate that the neck was cut across and the heads halved, and some sheep and cattle vertebrae have cuts which show that the carcase, or part of the carcase, might have been halved.

It is unlikely that dogs would have been eaten; there is certainly no documentary evidence for this, but it is possible they may be partly responsible for the scarcity of other bones. A collie can demolish bones such as vertebrae of sheep or young cattle, and reduce the denser sheep limb bones to collections of small fragments. The number of dog bones in the early phases is surprisingly large, particularly compared with those of cattle and sheep, and the later phases. It is possible that the inconsistency between the early and late phases in this respect has something to do with the transition from arable land to land immediately beside the dwellings; the dead dogs were probably disposed of some distance from the houses. The large number of dog bones in Phase 5 are from one animal, a partially complete skeleton of an adult dog: much of the skull is present, several vertebrae and ribs, most of both fore-limbs, and a few bones from the hind-limbs, all fairly fragile. Some of the bones were articulated when the burial was found; either it was buried as a carcase found elsewhere, or else it was lying exposed for some time, and various pieces were detached as it decayed. It was not disturbed by agricultural operations. The dog bones from other deposits could be from old carcases well disturbed by repeated digging over of the ground.

The dog in Phase 5 had a shoulder height of about 17" (437mm). One measurable bone from Phase 9 is from a dog with a shoulder height of about 14" (360mm). Most of the bones from all phases are from dogs of a similar size to these, but there are some from smaller animals, comparable with a reference skeleton of a dog with a shoulder height of about 10" (255mm). Nineteenth-century films and photographs show that there were a large number of dogs on the island. While there is no mention of numbers in earlier accounts, there were certainly dogs on the island in Martin's time (Martin 1753, 18), and many subsequent authors mention them. Clarke (1824, 270–71) and some later authors noted both sheep dogs and small terriers used for catching puffins.

Cats are mentioned, but less often; it is surprising that there are so few cat bones compared with those of dog. Those that were found are from well-grown but not fully mature animals.

No bones of house mice were found, but there is one jaw from a woodmouse or fieldmouse (*Apodemus sylvaticus*) from Phase 10; the fieldmouse is well known to most visitors to the island today.

There is one bone from an animal which has not been seen on St Kilda for over 150 years: a single horse tooth, a deciduous molar, was found in deposits attributable to Phase 10; it is almost certainly re-deposited from an earlier period.

There are no seal bones; these are more likely to occur in earlier deposits, and thus are less likely to be preserved. There are a few fragments of cetacean bone; a small lump of cancellous bone from Phase 4, and two pieces from Phase 11. One of these is large, a slab of bone about 210 x 125mm and 70mm thick (sf. 345; see also 3:3:14 and Fig. 56A); there is scarcely any trace of the natural exterior surface of the bone, which has been used for some purpose, having had a circular hole cut through it. It is most likely to be part of a vertebra, and the size indicates that it is from one of the large whales, either one of the baleen whales, or a sperm whale. The species most frequently caught round the Hebrides in the first quarter of this century were fin, sei and blue whales, with lesser numbers of right, sperm and humpback whales (Brown 1976, 28); any of these could have produced a bone of suitable size. As a worked bone, this may well be re-deposited from an earlier phase, though its fair condition suggests that it is of relatively recent origin, unlikely to be earlier than the 19th century.

The bird bones

There are very few of the smaller bird bones such as wing and foot phalanges, quadrates and vertebrae from smaller species such as the auks. The evidence from the rest of the bone assemblage suggests that some of these bones, such as puffin wing phalanges, should have been present on the site, and their absence from the bone collection is almost certainly due to their being missed on site; but these are very tiny bones, and only sieving through a fine mesh would retrieve them consistently. As there are so few, no attempt was made to identify vertebrae or foot phalanges.

Table 20 shows the number of bones present from each species recognised in each phase. It is

Phase	Gannet	Fulmar	Guillemot	Razorbill	Puffin	Other
4	3	3	1		6	
5	48	6	26	6	9	Shag: 4
6		1				
7		1	2	2	6	
	1		1		2	(all calcined)
8	12	36	8	2	20	Kittiwake: 1
9	7	4	7		6	
10	197	597	415	218	1512	Manx shearwater: 5
	7%	20%	14%	7%	51%	Shag: 2
						Kittiwake: 8
11	324	441	315	83	802	Manx shearwater: 7
	16%	22%	16%	4%	41%	Shag: 1
						Kittiwake: 2
12	53	73	31	13	84	Manx shearwater: 4
						Kittiwake: 1
13	10	47	17	5	99	Kittiwake: 2
						Starling: 2
14		5	1	1	1	Starling: 1

TABLE 20

House 8: numbers of bones from different bird species identified from different phases, with percentages where relevant

immediately clear that the bones are almost exclusively from the main species harvested for food: gannet, fulmar, guillemot, razorbill and puffin. As with the mammal bones, there is generally a scarcity of bones from deposits before about 1835, except for a single deposit (176) from Phase 5 which contained a comparatively large quantity, and a fairly large group in Phase 8 (mostly from context 102). The group from context 176 shows a strong emphasis on gannet and guillemot bones, and the greatest number of shag bones from any one phase; though the total number is not large, so this is unlikely to reflect truly any emphasis on particular species at this period. The bones in this deposit are almost exclusively from wings, except for several pieces of gannet skull and parts of the body and legs of guillemot; only these include good meat-bearing parts of the body. In Phase 8 there is greater emphasis on bones from fulmar and puffin than any other species; again nearly all the bones are waste bones, and the quantities are small.

Phases 10 and 11, covering the occupation and demolition of the blackhouse, contain the vast majority of the bird bones from the site; there are several large deposits: contexts 20, 88, 37, 90, 104, 168, 170, 185. In Phase 10 (Table 20) puffins account for just over half the bones; fulmar and guillemot were also important, gannet and razorbill less so numerically. In Phase 11, puffin bones still account for the majority, nearly twice as many as from any other bird; gannet, fulmar and guillemot are all roughly similarly important; razorbill relatively insignificant.

It should be remembered here that puffin, particularly, is probably under-represented: that the tiny carpometacarpi and wing phalanges were probably not so well recovered as the larger bones of gannet and fulmar. As far as food is concerned, bones from the head: skull, maxilla and mandible; the wing: humerus, ulna, radius, carpometacarpus and first phalanx; the foot: tarsometatarsus; and to a lesser extent the leg: tibiotarsus, are really all waste bones; it is the bones of the body: sternum, furcula, sacrum and pelvis, and the vertebrae, to which most of the meat is attached. Shoulder bones: coracoid and scapula; and the upper leg: femur, might be detached with wing or foot or retained with the body.

Tables 21 and 22 show that there are considerable inconsistencies between the number of different sorts of bones. Wing bones account for the majority of the bones from each of the main species; there are also quite a lot of bones from the head and leg, particularly the lower leg, and the foot. In Phase 10, there are numbers of bones from the body from gannet and puffin, though not as many as might be expected compared with other bones, particularly in the case of puffins. In Phase 11 there are body bones from gannet and the three auk species, but again not as many as the number of birds represented by wings, and there are scarcely any body bones from fulmar. Head and foot bones, in most cases more numerous than body bones, are fewer than wing bones. The lower legs and feet of all these birds have little value; there is no meat on them and no feathers. There are more feathers on the heads of large birds such as gannets, and gannet head and neck skins

	Gannet			Fulmar			Guillemot			Razorbill			Puffin		
	L		R	L		R	L		R	L		R	L		R
Skull		7			10			8						12	
Maxilla		6			4			3			5			3	
Mandible	7	4	4	13		12	11		13	2		1	9	3	14
Sternum		6			1									24	
Furcula		4			1			1			2			18	
Scapula	6		6	3		2				1		5	13		14
Coracoid	6		8	1		3	3	1	3	5		6	26		33
Humerus	12		12	80		102	72		72	38		30	246		229
Ulna	24		11	83		67	33		43	15		33	161		196
Radius	6		6	25		29	25		30	13		14	91		84
Carpo-metacarpus	6		14	37		42	23		24	10		9	81		75
Wing 1st phalange	4		11	16		7	6		5	2		4	20		28
Sacrum		5						2						14	
Pelvis	2		1	1		1	1		1				3		8
Femur	4		4				2		2	4		2	19		14
Tibio-tarsus	1		3	3		1	5		8	3		4	27		30
Tarso-metatarsus	6		1	31		22	4		14	5		5	9		8
Total		197			597			415			218			1512	

Also: Manx shearwater: humerus: 2L, R; ulna: L; carpometacarpus: R Shag: humerus: R; tibiotarsus: L; Kittiwake: humerus: 2L, R; ulna: 2L, 3R

TABLE 21

House 8: numbers of bones of different types from different species represented in Phase 10

	Gannet			Fulmar			Guillemot			Razorbill			Puffin		
	L		R	L		R	L		R	L		R	L		R
Skull		13			12			5						11	
Maxilla		8			6			2			2			7	
Mandible	15	2	19	9		16	2		5			1	1		1
Sternum		15						12			3			12	
Furcula		8			1			3			1			14	
Scapula	7		7	2		1	1		1				6		9
Coracoid	13		15	3		1	8		4	6		1	18		20
Humerus	36		24	61		59	52		48	9		10	130		148
Ulna	21	2	23	55		51	41		24	8		11	104		102
Radius	9		10	28		22	20		12	3		9	39		45
Carpo-metacarpus	10		14	29		30	17		12	3		3	26		25
Wing 1st phalange	7		7	8		4	5		2	1			1		
Sacrum		5			3			3			3			7	
Pelvis				1		1							1		1
Femur	11		4	1		2	5		4	2			8		7
Tibio-tarsus	4		7	2		4	11		4	1		3	29		15
Tarso-metatarsus	2		6	17		12	3		9			3	8		7
Total		324			441			315			83			802	

Also: Manx shearwater: humerus: R; ulna: R; radius 2R; carpometacarpus: R; wing 1st phalanx: L; femur: L. Shag: tibiotarsus: L; Kittiwake: humerus: R; ulna: R

TABLE 22

House 8: numbers of bones of different types from different species represented in Phase 11

were used, at least in the 17th century, as short-life shoes; but in auks, particularly, the neck is fairly short and it might be easiest to leave the head on the body. While wings of all species would have been important for feathers, they would probably have been discarded after plucking.

These deposits, then, seem to represent waste from an intermediate phase in the use of the birds; the lower legs and feet, wholly waste, have probably been removed from most of the birds and discarded elsewhere: fulmar feet seem to have been retained more often than those of any other birds; this is difficult to explain. Heads, similarly, may in some cases have been discarded elsewhere; both heads and feet may have been removed, and eaten by dogs, particularly the heads; indeed Wiglesworth (1903, 17–18) particularly noted their use as scavengers. Once plucked, the wings would have been discarded, and possibly some of the puffin carcases; they were very small and if there were plenty would be less worth preparing and cooking than those of larger birds. Connell (1887, 123) recorded that most of the puffins were killed for their feathers alone, and the carcases used as manure.

Both shag and Manx shearwater might well have been eaten, though less easy to catch than the other birds in any number; gulls are less usually eaten, but perhaps the odd kittiwake might have been taken more for its feathers than its meat. A few of the auk and the gannet bones are from immature birds; about one-third of the fulmar bones from Phase 10 and one-tenth from Phase 11 are from immature birds.

There are far fewer bones from Phases 12 and 13; they are generally similar to those in Phases 10 and 11. The proportions vary a little but with small numbers this is unlikely to be significant.

Not all the bones are well enough preserved for cuts to show, but despite that the number of clean cuts is surprisingly few. Most are on gannet bones: an upper bill cut off near the joint with the cranium; a coracoid with part of the distal end cut off (this could result from cutting off the wing near the shoulder joint); and two femora with cuts near the head are evidence for cutting off the legs at the hip joint. A gannet sternum has a cut on the mid-line on the inner surface; if the birds were cleaned by cutting into the body cavity from the back, then the inner surface of the breast bone might easily show cuts.

One fulmar humerus has cuts at the proximal end, again probably the result of cutting off the wing, while a radius has cuts at the distal end. A razorbill humerus shows signs of the wing having been cut off.

Though the total number of bird bones, just over 5500, seems impressive, considered as parts of individual birds it is less so; the greatest figure for the minimum number of birds from any phase would be about 250 puffins from Phase 10. As part of the catch for a family for the duration of that phase (a score or so of years), this number is quite insignificant, and all the bones from the site must represent a very small proportion of the bird harvest for even one family. The variation in the number of bones from different species in different phases could be related to dumping practices and seasonal variations in bird numbers, and not necessarily to changes in preference for particular species. In general, the numbers of bones do have some relationship to the abundance of species, no doubt also affected by ease of access to different birds. Modern counts of the main species harvested, made in 1977 (Harris and Murray 1978), 1985 (gannets only, Murray and Wanless 1986), and 1987 (Tasker *et al.* 1988) are:

Gannet:	(1973) 59,258 nests, (1985) 50,050 nests
Fulmar:	43,977 apparently occupied nest sites 62,786 apparently occupied sites
Guillemot:	22,085 individuals and 22,705 individuals
Razorbill:	over 500 pairs and 3,814 individuals
Puffin:	est. over 300,000 pairs est. 230,501 occupied burrows

It is difficult to make direct comparisons between these figures which refer to different counting units, but nevertheless it is clear that puffins far outnumber the other species; that numbers of gannet and fulmar nests are not very different; and that there are fewer guillemots and far fewer razorbills than anything else in the list. Annual harvesting would affect the numbers, but there is still some relationship between the figures. For instance, puffins are the most numerous and razorbills the least numerous of the five species, and this is the same with the total number of bones. There are only small numbers of shags: 52 nests in 1987, and in the same year there were 7829 sites apparently occupied by kittiwakes, so the scarcity of bones from these small gulls is more related to preference than availability. Numbers of Manx shearwaters are not known: Harris and Murray suggest that the population is 'probably not very large' and most of the birds nest in inaccessible sites (Harris and Murray 1978, 14).

The number of different birds taken gives no indication of the amount of flesh they would produce, and there are no figures for dressed carcase weights, but there are figures for live weights (Cramp and Simmons 1977, 128, 198; 1985, 183, 207, 243). These would vary seasonally, but average figures given are:

	Male (M)	Female (F)
Gannet:	3120g	2941g
Fulmar:	884g	706g
Guillemot:	853g	870g
Razorbill:	634g	
Puffin:	368g	

At fledging gannets weigh 3650g and fulmars 860g, but before fledging they can weigh up to 4250g and 1120g respectively, so that young gannets and fulmars would provide considerably more fat than adult birds. In live weights, gannets are far superior to any other bird in the list; fulmar and guillemot are similar, but three to four would be required to balance a gannet; razorbills are rather smaller and puffins very small, about eight to a gannet. This should be borne in mind when considering the figures in Tables 20–22.

There are two further observations arising from the bones, relevant not just to the history of St Kilda but the zoological history of the British Isles.

The fulmar is first mentioned in late 17th-century accounts of St Kilda; one collected by Robert Sibbald (Advocates Library Ms. 33.3.2) and Martin's book (1698, 30–31). There is every indication that the bird was well established on the islands at that time, though it is not known to be resident anywhere else in the British Isles. It is, therefore, important to find that there are several bones, from more than one bird, in both Phases 4 and 5; one of those from Phase 4 is from an immature bird, implying that the birds were breeding on the island at that time (between the 10th and 13th centuries), and wherever they came from to establish themselves on St Kilda, they must have arrived earlier than Phase 4.

No bones from garefowl were recognised. As most of the bones were from deposits of the 1830s and later this is not very surprising: the last recorded garefowl on St Kilda were single birds caught in 1821 (Grieve 1885, 8–9) and about 1840 (Harvie-Brown and Buckley 1888, 158–9).

3:4:3 Fish Bones and Scales (R. Nicholson)

Fish bones and scales were recovered from excavations at House 8. All the remains were recovered by hand from the deposits during excavation, which will introduce a bias in favour of large, more easily visible bones. The fish remains were recovered from Phases 10, 11, 12 and 14, although only two bones came from Phase 14.

A total of 212 bones and scales were identified to species or lower taxonomic level, from around 250 recovered remains. This high proportion of identified material is a result of the large size of the bones, and the relatively low species diversity. The bones and scales were identified using the comparative collection of fish skeletons held in the Environmental Archaeology Unit, University of York. The identifications are summarised in Table 23, and listed bone by bone in the archive record.

Species	**PHASE 10**	**PHASE 11**	**PHASE 12**	**PHASE 14**
Elasmobranch			1v	
Conger conger			2v	
Gadus morhua	1hb	1hb	2hb	1hb
Pollachius virens	3hb, 1v		1hb, 1v	
Pollachius pollachius	2v	2hb	1v	
Pollachius sp.	2hb, 1v			
Pollachius/Gadus	4hb, 2v 2o	2hb, 4v	1hb	
Molva cf. *molva*	1hb, 2v		26hb, 7v 10o	1v
Gadidae	4hb, 2v	1hb, 1v	4hb, 2v	
Pagellus bogaraveo		13hb, 39v 34scs, 31o	1v, 2o	
Trachurus trachurus	1v			
Pleuronectidae	2v			
Indeterminate	5o	9v, 3o	16o	
Total	15hb, 13v 7o	19hb, 53v 34scs, 34o	34hb, 15v 19o	1hb, 1v

KEY: hb = head bone(s); v = vertebra(e)
scs = scales; o = other (including spines, ribs and rays)

TABLE 23
House 8: fish remains by phase

The condition of the fish remains varied between contexts. In Phase 11, contexts 168 and 185 from an organic dump on the cleit site contained assemblages of well-preserved bone. Contexts from Phases 10 and 12, by contrast, contained few, more poorly preserved bones, which were frequently crumbly in texture. Phase 10 comprises the blackhouse and associated contexts, Phase 12 the new cottage. Two bones from Phase 12 — a conger eel *(Conger conger)* abdominal vertebra, and a ling *(Molva cf. molva)* supracleithrum, were embedded in cement flooring. Phase 14 represents the period of restoration of the cottage after 1957.

Preservation has been recorded by three criteria: texture, erosion and flaking. Texture is recorded on a scale of 1 (as fresh) to 5 (very crumbly), and erosion on a scale of 0 (none) to 5 (severe). The sum of these three categories is recorded as 'condition', providing a means of assessing the relative states of preservation between contexts (see Table 24). The minimum score for condition is 1 (as fresh) and in theory the maximum is 15, although this score is unlikely, as severe erosion and flaking are to a certain extent mutually exclusive. The amount of the bone represented by the recovered fragment has been recorded as an approximate percentage, for each fragment (except for large groups of spines, ribs, rays and scales).

		PHASE 10	**PHASE 11**	**PHASE 12**	**PHASE 14**
Mean %bone	*Gadid*	60 (n=30)	55 (n=13)	65 (n=44)	65 (n=2)
	Other species	75 (n=3)	75 (n=63)	85 (n=7)	–
Mean condition	*Gadid*	7 (n=30)	7 (n=13)	5 (n=44)	9 (n=2)
	Other species	6 (n=3)	3 (n=63)	3 (n=7)	–

TABLE 24
House 8: fish bones, preservation between phases

Table 24 compares the mean 'condition' and mean 'percentage bone' between gadid and other identified species, by phase. Only bones identified to taxon have been included. The fish have been grouped in this way because of the low numbers of bones present for many species. As illustrated, the mean percentage bone is fairly constant for the gadid remains (55–65% of the original skeletal element present in each fragment), indicating moderate levels of bone breakage, with the greatest fragmentation in Phase 11. The non-gadid bones were in all cases less fragmented (mean percentage bone of 75–85%). The non-gadid bones in Phase 11 (all from the red sea bream *(Pagellus bogaraveo)* were also in a better condition than the gadid bones from the same phase ('condition' score 3, compared with 7), and compared with the bones from Phases 10, 12, and 14. This may be a consequence of the burial environment: both bones and scales were recovered from an organic dump, grouped in Phase 11. The relatively poor condition and fragmented nature of the gadid bones from the same deposits could be explained in terms of their pre- and/or post-depositional history; for example, at least some of the gadid bones may have been re-deposited. However, recent research indicates that gadid bones may be less resistant to destruction than other, superficially more fragile, fish bones (Nicholson 1991; 1992).

The assemblage recovered from Phases 10, 12 and 14 differed from that from Phase 11 in species composition as well as in preservation. In the former three phases the dominant species were large gadids: cod *(Gadus morhua)*, saithe *(Pollachius virens)*, pollack *(Pollachius pollachius)* and ling *(Molva* cf. *molva)*. All these fish are commonly caught by hook and line offshore, both in fairly shallow water around rocks and in deep water. Measurements taken on the bones (after Morales and Rosenlund 1979; and Jones, pers. comm.), and comparison with bones of modern fish, indicate that most of the gadid bones were from fish of at least 0.75m in length, and some would have been over 1m. In Phase 10, 27/30 bones identified to taxon were from large gadids; in Phase 12, 46/52 bones were from large gadids, mainly from ling. In Phase 11, however, 117/128 fragments (bones and scales) were from the red sea bream *(Pagellus bogaraveo)*. The red sea bream is fairly commonly found in waters around northern Britain, although it is more common to the south and west. It is usually a summer visitor to more northern waters. Comparing the bones with those in the reference collection, a size range of about 0.38–0.45m total length was obtained for the fish. This is slightly larger than the average size caught today (0.35m; Wheeler 1978). Red sea bream of this size are usually found off-shore, at depths of up to 100–200m and can be caught by hook and line (Wheeler 1978).

Other fish represented in the assemblage include the conger eel *(Conger conger)*, the horse mackerel or scad *(Trachurus trachurus)*, small flatfish *(Pleuronectidae)* and, represented by one vertebra, an *elasmobranch* (sharks and rays), probably a small dogfish *(Scyliorhinidae)*. All these fish can be caught off-shore from boats by hook and line.

There is no indication of butchery on any of the bones, and only one brachiostegal ray has possible gnawing marks. From the species present, and the size of the fishes represented, it seems clear that all, or the majority, originated as human food refuse. From the bones present it appears that whole fish were prepared and disposed of.

Clearly it would be unwise to conclude much about fishing methods, dietary preferences, or rubbish disposal practices from such a small, and biased, assemblage of bones. While the presence of red sea bream may indicate a preference for this fish in Phase 11, its prevalence could just be a consequence of the advantageous conditions for bone preservation in the organic dump, compared with fairly poor conditions for organic preservation elsewhere.

3:4:4 Egg (J. Coulson)

Fragments of egg membrane, the material surrounding the yolk and albumen, and encased by shell, were found in Phases 11 (sfs 388, 391–2, 404, 406, 479, 483, 511, 514) and 12 (sf. 718). It is light brown in colour, with a tough leathery texture. Tiny flakes of shell were found with it, white, but discoloured yellow-brown, with no obvious markings. Fulmar (and other *Procellariformes*), puffin and gannet have white-shelled eggs, the gannet egg tending to become discoloured (Perrins 1987), though soil conditions may have affected pigment survival (see Keepax 1981). Membrane has been found at other sites, most recently at Annetwell Street, Carlisle, where fragments were found with food waste in Roman pits, and in a medieval well (K. Goodwin, pers. comm.).

3:4:5 Terrestrial Molluscs (T. Butterfield)

The land snails are confined to one family, the Zonitidae, with 102 examples of *Oxychilus alliarius* (Miller), found in Phases 10–12. The greatest number, 98, were found in Phase 12, of which a death assemblage of 71 were found among the small rounded pebbles which had been laid on boulders to provide a bed for a cement floor in the cottage east room. They are generally considered a 'woodland' species, but are found in more open habitats, on relatively undisturbed grassland, often on acid soils (Evans 1972, 188; Pfleger and Chatfield 1988, 194).

3:4:6 Marine Molluscs

The marine mollusc collection was dominated by the common limpet *(Patella vulgata)*. A total of 846 shells were found, based on intact apices, and 1754 fragments. Four of the 846 shells were found in Phase 8, the earliest period to produce limpets, but the majority, 658 (77.8%), came from the dumps over the ruined cleit of Phase 11.

The only other shells found were nine grey top shells *(Gibbula cineraria)*, and one fragment of dog whelk *(Nucella lapillus)* from Phase 11, and part of a great scallop *(Pecten maximus)* from Phase 13. The gill-breathing top shells are normally found around rocks and seaweed on the lower shore; the dog whelk usually coming from the middle or lower shore. The great scallop normally occurs off-shore, but could have been washed up.

3:4:7 Insect Remains (L. Davies and Z. Erzinclioglu)

A pupa of the blowfly *(Calliphora uralensis)* was found in Phase 8. It could have reached this stage in the life cycle at almost any month in the year, though probably not in January to March. The insect had not emerged, and death was due either to squashing or, conceivably, by asphyxiation through burial, though the deposit would have had to have been waterlogged, as the insect could have escaped through aerated soil. The species is widespread in Northern Europe and Eurasia, and is still found today on St Kilda. There is evidence that the fly will feed on faecal matter, but doesn't normally lay in latrines; the eggs would normally be laid in any rotting animal matter.

3:4:8 Dung (A.K.G. Jones, E.P. Allison, A.R. Hall and H.K. Kenward)

Three samples were submitted to the Environmental Archaeology Unit, University of York, for the analysis of animal and plant remains. The samples were examined visually, described and treated by a set of standard techniques used for the extraction of a wide range of animal and plant remains.

SK86 sample 1, collected from the wall of Blackhouse H. This sample consisted of 30g of a light yellow-brown dry matted herbaceous detritus which appeared to be compressed straw. On microscopic analysis, the plant material, although poorly preserved, was made up of plant epidermis fragments almost certainly of cereals, with a few Gramineae (grass) glumes. In addition, seeds of chickweed *(Stellaria media)* and fly puparia were recovered.

This sample also produced a small but distinctive assemblage of insects. Fragments of *Mycetaea hirta* and other mould-feeding beetles were present. This assemblage is typical of damp, open-textured, mouldering organic material and is typically found in buildings.

Other remains from this sample were small numbers of *Trichuris* eggs of a size consistent with those produced by *T. trichiura*, the human whipworm. However, the eggs were not common and were only found after the sample had been treated using a flotation procedure using saturated magnesium sulphate solution. Small numbers of human parasite eggs can be recovered from most occupation layers in settlements where the inhabitants are infested with *Trichuris*.

The animal and plant remains in this sample were typical of those commonly found in byres and other buildings provided with open-textured litter.

SK86 20 (Phase 10), sample 17. This consisted of 25.8g of mid to dark grey-brown dry crumbly humic silt, including fine and coarse sand particles. It was identified as ?dung. On disaggregation the sample proved to contain two poorly preserved ctenoid fish scales, probably from a spiny-rayed fish. Several families of fish, e.g. Percidae, Serranidae and Dicentrachidae, have ctenoid scales. In addition, there were fibres which were probably animal hair, possibly wool, but the cuticles were not sufficiently well preserved to make a more certain identification. There was one tiny fragment of ?wool which appeared to be woven.

A number of phytoliths were present, as were fly puparia, earthworm egg capsules, bone fragments and nutlets of a species of dock *(Rumex* sp.) and possibly an achene of corn marigold *(Chrysanthemum segetum),* a cornfield weed. It is possible that this sample was dung, but no faecal indicators were apparent.

SK86 10 (Phase 12/13), sample 19. This sample consisted of 232g of mid-grey-brown dry crumbly silt. Stones, 2–6mm in size, root voids and rootlets were also present. On microscopic examination the sample produced a few fragments of charcoal and poorly preserved ?toad rush *(Juncus* cf. *bufonius)* seeds. No parasite ova were recovered and the few beetle fragments present provided no insight into the nature of the deposit.

3:5 Discussion

The earliest datable evidence of a human presence on this site is represented by the small fragments of coarse pottery in Phase 2, one of which produced a thermoluminescence date of AD 190 ± 360.

The soil in which the fragments were found was then cut and scoured by a stream. Soil and other debris, along with some objects, accumulated in the channel until it was completely choked, and ceased functioning.

The steatite from the channel fill is the most diagnostic; the vessel fragments, and probably the spindle whorl, suggesting a Viking date, while the plate fragment (sf. 789) is more indicative of the Late Norse period. A pottery fragment (sf. 665), also from the fill, gave a Late Norse thermoluminescence date — AD 1135 ± 170.

Gradually soil built up and covered the old channels, until the 17th/early 18th century, when the ground was divided up by two lines of stones, and the area to the south was drained and cultivated. The dumping of rubble in the area, and the development of soil over the stone lines, indicates that by the early 19th century they had gone out of use.

In 1812, Sir Thomas Dyke Acland visited the island and recorded, in watercolours, the main settlement in Village Bay (Acland 1981, 50), apparently further up-slope than the area under excavation. In 1834 he returned, and was so appalled at the living conditions of the islanders, that he offered 20 guineas to the first person who would build a new house (Acland 1981, 63). Eventually the St Kildans agreed. Land which had been common was divided up, initially by a Mr MacDonald, but, following disputes, the land was parcelled out by the islanders themselves (Mackenzie 1911, 21). The new settlement was established further down the slope, about 200m from the shore, roughly in a crescent shape, and the area under investigation became the site of a new blackhouse.

The islanders were guided in their work by the Rev. Neil Mackenzie, who may have been the influence behind the important initial preparation of the ground. Water, which must still have flowed down from Tobar Childa, was channelled round the site, and also taken round the area which became the site of Blackhouse H.

The excavated 1830s blackhouse was the home of Finlay MacDonald's son, John, who was born in 1811 or 1812, the elder brother of Malcolm. The dwelling was divided internally by the stone *talan* into human quarters at the north, with a clay floor and open central hearth; and a byre at the south.

To the west of the blackhouse was a cleit to store MacDonald's seabird catch (SRO 1858/1860, RHP 6778). The practice of building cleitean to store bird carcases or other materials was referred to by Martin Martin. He said that they 'commonly keep yearly about twenty thousand young and old [birds] in their little stone Houses, of which there are some hundreds for preserving their Fowls, Eggs, etc.' (Martin 1716, 281). The number of cleitean in the St Kilda group is surprising — 1430 are known from the archipelago as a whole. Such structures are not unique. On Swona, in the Pentland Firth, the islanders caught dogfish in the 18th century, 'the former of which they dry in small houses made of rough stones, without any cement, so that the wind blows freely thro' the walls and cures them, but renders them much tougher than fish dried over a fire' (Low 1879, 28–9). In Shetland similar sheds, known as 'skeos', were also a common sight in the 18th century. They were used to air-dry mutton and beef, called 'vivda', but 'nothing can smell stronger than a number of these skeos placed near one another' (Low 1879, 90). Fish, cheese, butter and meal were also stored in skeos during the 17th century in Shetland, spaced apart to catch the drying currents of air (Fenton 1978a, 160, 581).

The blackhouse and cleit, like the others in Village Street, was set in its own strip of land. Some of the croft boundaries were marked by substantial consumption dykes, which stretched from near the shore to the newly constructed head-dyke. There was an opening here for access between the infield and hill grazing. Set into the west dyke, south of the blackhouse, was a cleit (no. 87) used for fish storage, and built before 1858.

The violent storm of October 1860 caused damage to the blackhouses, and MacLeod's masons built a new house for the MacDonald family. In most cases the new houses were spaced between the 1830s blackhouses. This arrangement did not work in the case of House 8, where it was necessary to carry out substantial demolition.

The demolition of the cleit was followed by the dumping of ash, either burnt peat or turf. Blanket peat is found between Mullach Mor and Conachair, and on Na Mullichean Mor (Gwynne *et al.* 1974, 82). The islanders cut the hill peat and took the half-dried blocks to the cleitean for storage. When needed, the women carried them down to the houses in creels (Mackenzie 1911, 100). It was used as a fuel, but some was also broken up and used as a powder deodoriser on the house floor. The islanders also cut turf from the pasture land, a destructive practice which continued up to the Evacuation (Mathieson 1928b, 78). The heather strands found in the dump may well have been associated with the cut fuel. Heather is found in both dry and wet heath areas on the slopes of Village Bay, outside the head dyke, particularly around Conachair and Gearraidh Ard (Gwynne *et al.* 1974, 38–44).

The shells in the midden material which covered the ash were predominantly common limpets. This species is found in both bays, and in Village Bay is abundant in both the eulittoral and the littoral fringe (Gauld *et al.* 1953, 33–4, 47). They may have formed a food resource, particularly in times of shortage, as was the practice elsewhere in Scotland (Devine 1988, 8), or served as bait for fishing. The careful stacking of many of the shells in the dump suggests that it was open for some time before the final greasy silty clay deposit was sealed by the base layer of the cottage.

The latter layer contained coarse pottery and stone tools, and, like the earlier dump, also produced several large pieces of cetacean bone. Hebridean whalebone finds have been discussed by Crawford (1967), but reference to actual strandings on St Kilda are rare. Clearly whales were to be found in the area, and in 1866 a dead whale was found floating off Hirta, and brought into the bay (Murray 1886–7, 6). One hundred and fifty gallons of oil was extracted, and part of its jaw was being used as a door prop at cleit 122 in 1897 (Kearton 1897, 46).

The blackhouse was replaced by a mortared stone cottage, House 8, which was similar in form to No. 6, divided into two main rooms, with an entrance lobby and a small back room. Two phases of flooring were noted. The rooms had been plastered up to wall-head level, and probably had a planked ceiling, above which was attic storage space. At a later stage, wooden battens had been nailed to the walls to take vertical matchboard wainscotting. Remains of the iron and copper nails were noted, particularly on the north wall. The splayed reveals of the windows were similarly lined.

The gabled end walls accommodated fireplaces, with neat lintels and hearth stones. Both had dooks inserted to hold fireplace surrounds, or, at least, mantelpieces. In the east wall of the cottage was a cupboard which, on comparison with others in the street, probably held three shelves. This has now gone, but a photograph taken in 1938 (SSS 1938, S265) shows it had a plank-built door hung on iron hinges, with a wooden sneck.

The roof cover changed from zinc plates nailed to boards, to a tarred felt cover over the sarking; and the excavated evidence indicated that the preparation of the tar was undertaken in the back garden.

John MacDonald moved into this new house with his family. He had married Christian MacKinnon in 1836 (GROS OPR 111/2, Marriages, 16.9.1836), and the baptismal register and census returns record their children — Donald (b. 1838; died in infancy), Margaret (b. 1839), Catherine (b. 1842), Mary Anne (b. 1844), Christian (b. 1853), Marion (b. 1857) and Kate (b. 1866). John had worked the croft, but by 1871 he was blind (GROS CEN/1871/111 3). Margaret, his eldest daughter, married, probably in the late 1850s,

PLATE 13
A photograph of House 8 in 1883 by D. Whyte (Ross 1893, facing p. 84)

but returned to the family home a widow some time in the 1860s, with her child, Malcolm, who had been born in 1863. By 1877 there were seven people in the house — the parents, four daughters and the grandson (MacDiarmid 1878, 238). Christian died in 1887, and John in 1889.

With John having no surviving sons, Malcolm succeeded as head of the household, and married Christina Gillies in the late 1880s. By 1891 they were living in the cottage with his widowed mother and two unmarried aunts — Catherine and Kate (GROS CEN/1891/111 4). Malcolm was alive in 1927 (in photograph by A. Cockburn; Quine 1988, 243), but seems to have died before the Evacuation in 1930.

Some changes were made to the croft during the late 19th century, particularly the erection of two cleitean south of The Street (nos 88 and 90), and one to the north (no. 53). Some time after 1883 a small garden was built in front of the house (Ross 1893, pl. facing 84 — see Pl. 13).

Debris and refuse accumulated over the ruins of the old blackhouse, and as the house became vacant, so refuse collected in it, and the process of decay began.

The cable and other electrical items found seem to be related to the St Kilda telegraph station. Bad weather and declining food stocks on the island in the winter of 1911 and spring of 1912 led to relief expeditions by the *Victor* and *HMS Achilles.* Subsequently, in 1912, a wireless telegraph station was established by the *Daily Mirror* and Mr Gordon Selfridge. A London contractor's foreman and two workmen went out from Glasgow on the *Hebrides* and erected two masts — one between House 1 and the Factor's House, the other near the church. The instrument, by Marconi and British Telegraph Instruments Ltd, was set up in a packing case in the Factor's House by Mr Ward-Miller (Pl. 14, *Daily Mirror* 7.7.1912). Once a licence had been granted, the first message was sent on the 29th July 1913 to the post office wireless station at Lochboisdale, South Uist (*Daily Mirror* 30.7.1913).

The system was put to use soon afterwards in August, when crewmen arrived on St Kilda in an open boat from the stricken *Bergenhaus,* which had been sailing from the Tyne to New Brunswick. A message was sent, and a Grimsby trawler towed the Olsen vessel to Lough Foyle, Northern Ireland (*Daily Mirror* 16.8.1913). However, by April 1914 the *Daily Mirror* gave up its interest in the station, and in 1915 it was taken over by the Admiralty. The station was shelled by a U-boat in May 1918, and was abandoned and dismantled in February 1919. It is possible that some cable may have been stored at the post office, near House 5, as it would have tended to affect transmission if it had been kept near the station, and then later dumped at House 8.

Following the Evacuation in 1930 the condition of the cottage declined quickly. Plaster fell from the walls, and mortar from the wall-head, while the plank flooring rotted and collapsed. By 1938 the roof cover had gone, as had most of the wainscotting (Pl. 15).

Following the takeover of the island by The National Trust for Scotland in 1957, work parties have consolidated the structure.

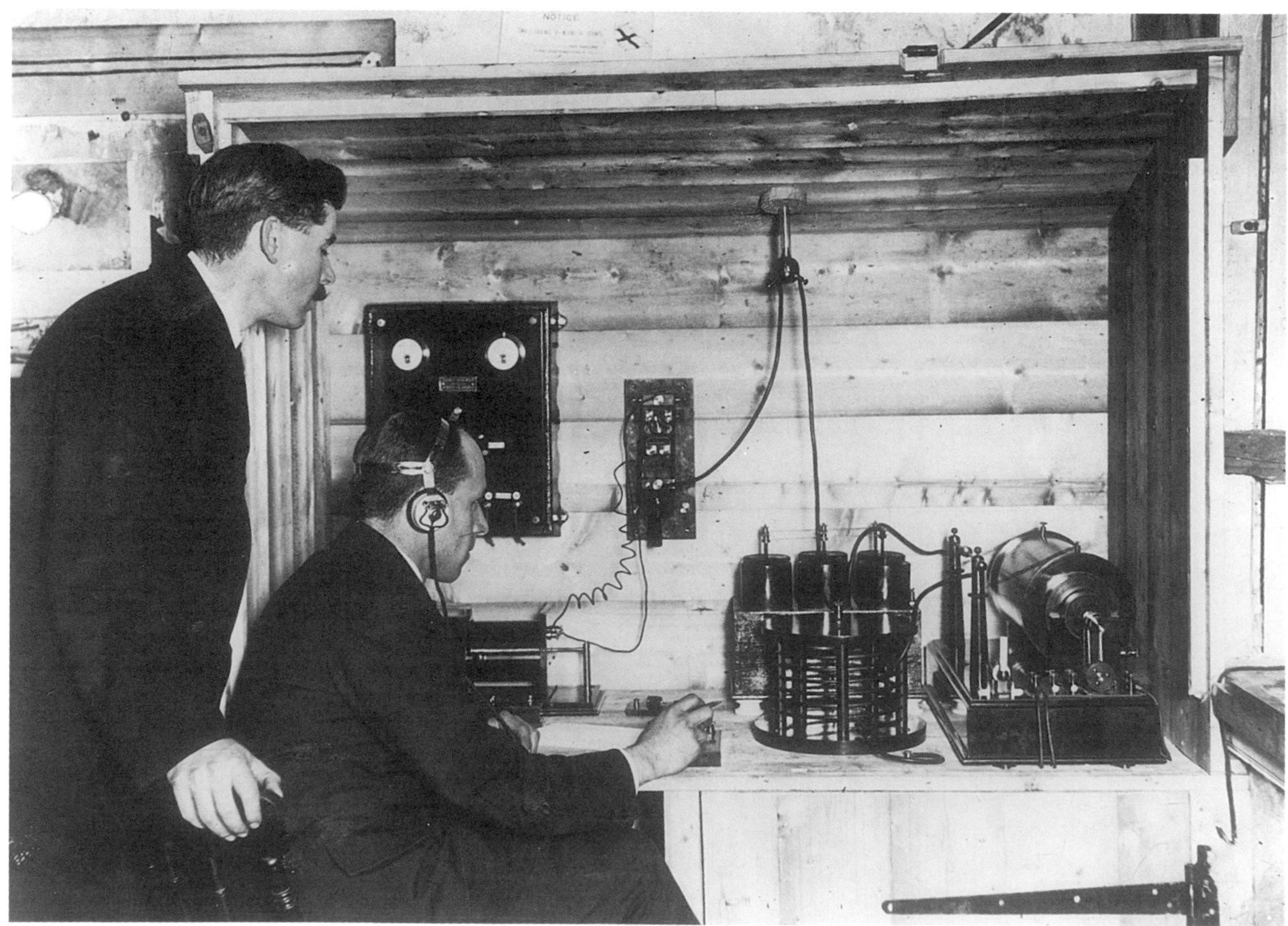

PLATE 14

The wireless station in the Factor's House, 1913, with Dudley Ward-Millar operating the transmitter, watched by Neil Ferguson. (Reproduced with permission from GEC-Marconi, 59279)

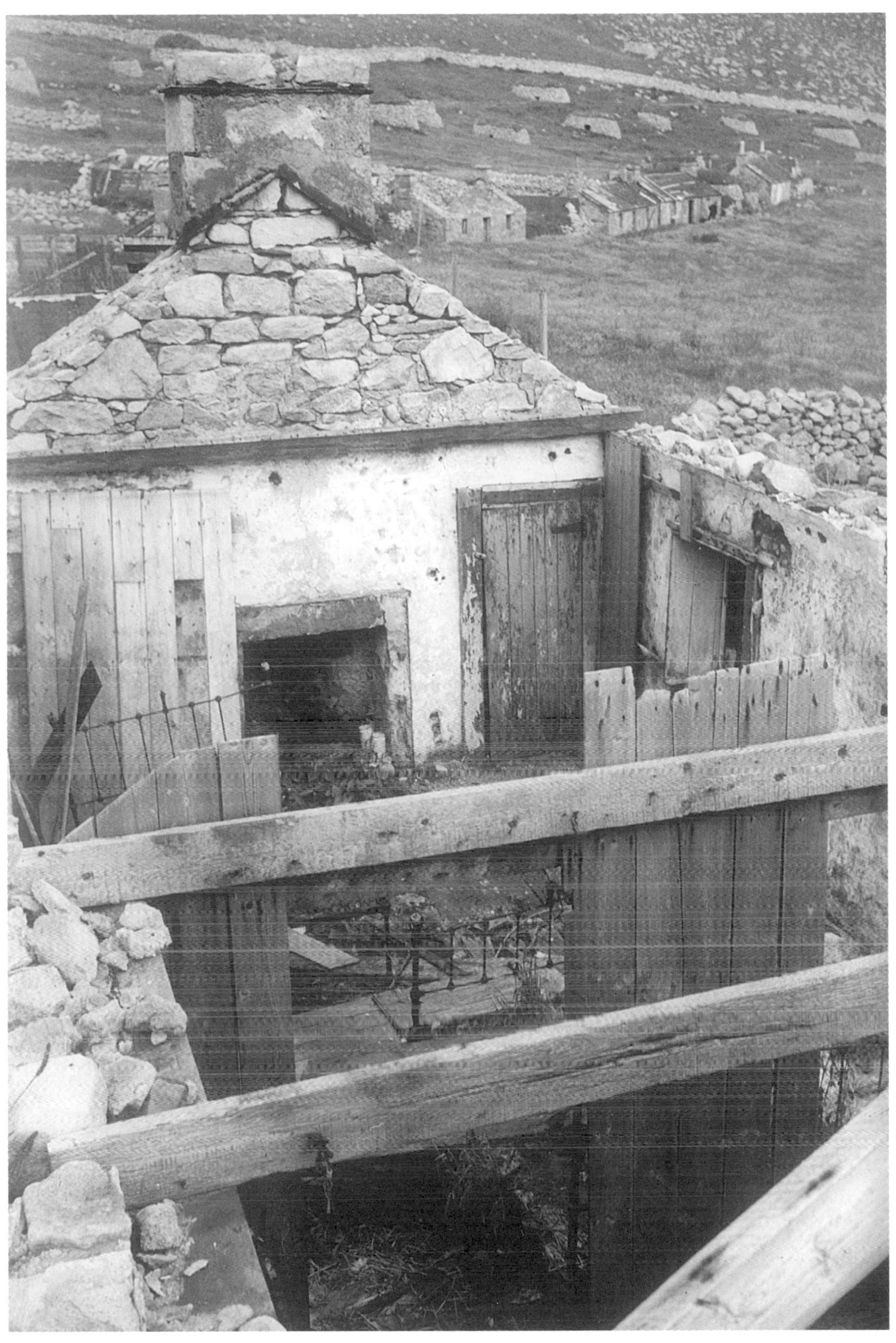

PLATE 15
House 8 in 1938 (R. Atkinson)

C H A P T E R 4

Excavations at Blackhouse W

4:1 The Excavation Areas (Fig. 60)

Excavations were carried out at Blackhouse W, to the north of the Factor's House, in June and July 1989. For logistical purposes the site was divided into two areas — Area 4 covering the turf-covered structural remains at the rear of the standing blackhouse, and Area 5 which included the interior of the building, and its surroundings to west, east, and south. For recording purposes, however, a single continuous number sequence, for layers, finds, etc., was used to cover both areas.

4:2 The Stratigraphic Sequence

Phase 1 (Fig. 61)

The fractured granite (139, 152) formed the geological base of the site. It was covered with a deposit of finer fractured rock (138, 114). This latter material had been slightly contaminated from above, as a fragment of crockery was found in context 114 (sf. 45).

Phase 2 (Fig. 62)

Due to the ground slope, deposits were thin at the north, up-slope in Area 4, and increased in thickness in Area 5, to the south. In both areas a thin black silty layer was found on top of the geological formations of Phase 1 (162 in Area 4, 136 in Area 5). To the east of the silt (162) was a grey-brown gritty soil (166). Covering these two soils was a dark grey gritty clayey soil (137), which was also located in Area 5 (135). On both areas was a distinct hard, crust-like, formation (156, 157 in Area 4, 86 in Area 5), similar in some ways to a pan. In Area 5 the pan was covered by a scatter of small stones (85), and a friable light brown humic sandy silt (113). A hollow (120) was noted in the surface, filled with a dark greyish brown gritty sandy silt (112). It contained charcoal flecks and some burnt clay or peat. It was sealed by a friable sticky greyish-brown sandy silt (81, 66) which formed a land surface, and seems to be equivalent to brown gritty soils (133, 153) in Area 4.

Around the edges of Area 5 was a further friable sticky dark brown clayey silty sand (117, 167), in part overlying some large stones (163). A piece of iron (sf. 48) was found in context 167.

A small number of objects was recovered from these layers, but probably represents contamination from above. Crockery was found in context 117 (sfs 60, 61); coarse pottery in 86 (sf. 46) and 133 (sf. 54); pebbles in 85 (sf. 38), 86 (sf. 47) and 166 (sf. 62); and wood in 133 (sf. 53).

Phase 3 (Fig. 63)

Channels were later dug into the ground surface for a drainage system. Two lines were cut down-slope; in Area 4, 169 at the west and 172 at the east, both curving in towards the north. These appear to have continued into Area 5 (94, 98), joining up in the southern end. A diagonal line (171) was cut across to connect the two channels, with remains of a roughly parallel line to the north (170). There were also traces of a north-south channel (96) in Area 5, though no evidence was found for it further north.

Into the cuts were laid fairly small side-stones, with large capstones (143, 144, 131, 41, 87, 151, 80 at the west; 148, 149, 150, 93, 132, 154, 99, 97, 84, 74 in the east; 146, 147, 130 on the main diagonal; 158, 159, 155 in the parallel channel; and 100, 95, 73 in the short southern channel). In some cases the slope of the ground required more than one course of side-stones. This was noted in drain 41 (west-side drain) where the initial lining (87) was covered by a second course of stones (151). In drain 99 there was also some soil (116) placed in the drain cut before the sides (97) were inserted.

The drains were covered, in part, by a hard-packed dark brown gritty soil (92).

The channels, during their use, acquired a gritty silty fill (67, 71, 72, 140, 160), though the fill of west drain 130 contained some flecks of yellow clay and pink ash (141), while the east drain (93) contained a dark reddish-brown gritty silty soil with flecks of pink and black ash (142). These fills clearly contained material which had entered the channels by some means after they had been sealed. Context 140 contained a fragment of window glass (sf. 51), and context 142 a sherd of crockery (sf. 52).

Phase 4 (Fig. 64)

The prepared site was then used for the construction of a corn-drying kiln (Pl. 16). The building was elliptical, 12.25m x 6.10m, aligned down-slope (i.e. north-south), with the top end cut into the ground. Here, two large boulders (24) had been levered up to produce massive walling blocks, 1.13 x 1.10 x 0.50m, and 1.03 x 0.96 x 0.37m. Elsewhere, large boulders up to 1.05 x 0.46 x 0.35m were used to form the wall facings, while the core was made up of soil and small rubble. The sections of walling were numbered 14, 15, 16 and 60, 61, 62, 102 on the east; 22, 23, 24 on the north; 25, 26, 27 and 55, 56, 57, 103 on the west, and 13, 53, 54, 104 on the south. At the north-west, large flat stones (33, 78) probably formed a levelling platform.

The south wall produced coarse pottery (sfs 6–7), two stone tools (sfs 49–50) and some leather fragments (sfs 84–6).

At the northern end of the chamber a large flat slab (165) was laid down as the base of the kiln, and a round tapering bowl of neatly laid granophyre walling, 0.70–0.85m broad (7), was built up on it (Pl. 17). There was no evidence of clay bonding between the stones, nor was there any lining. The bowl was 0.95m diameter at the top, 0.84m deep, and 0.70m diameter at the base. The kiln area was faced with large blocks (18), and the area between the facing, bowl, and walling was filled with soil and small rubble (134). This was then covered with a brown soil (126), containing a piece of iron (sf. 42) and a stone (sf. 43), and coated with yellow clay to produce a smooth surface (3, 4).

At the south-east edge of the kiln a flue was built (Pl. 18), with a heavy block (8) laid across the rim of the bowl to form a lintel. This produced a vent opening 0.40m wide and 0.49m high. Stonework (10) projected from the kiln facing to form the west side of the flue, while the east side (9) curved into, and markedly reduced, the thickness of the main wall to one stone in width. The flue would originally have been capped.

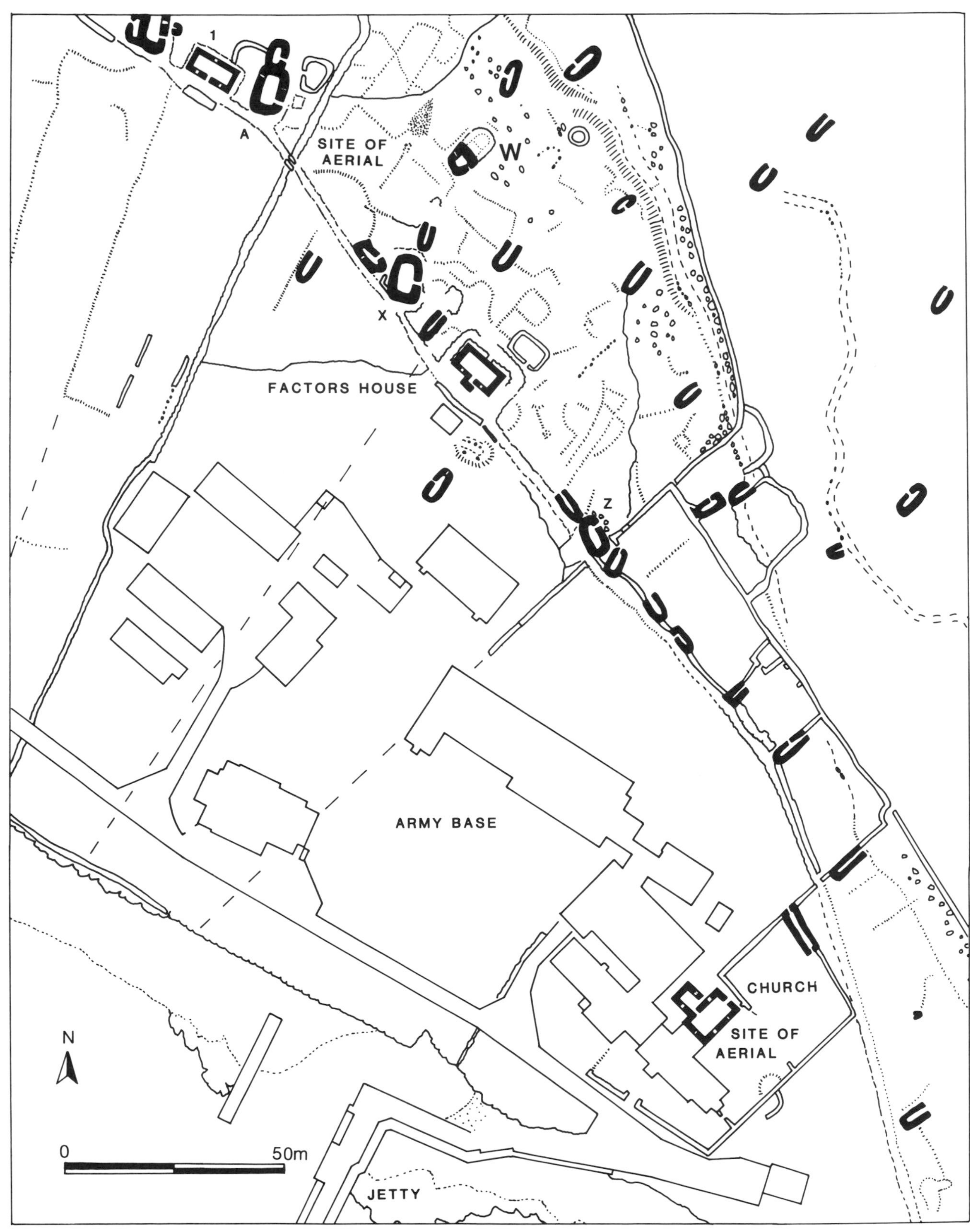

FIG. 60
Blackhouse W and its surroundings

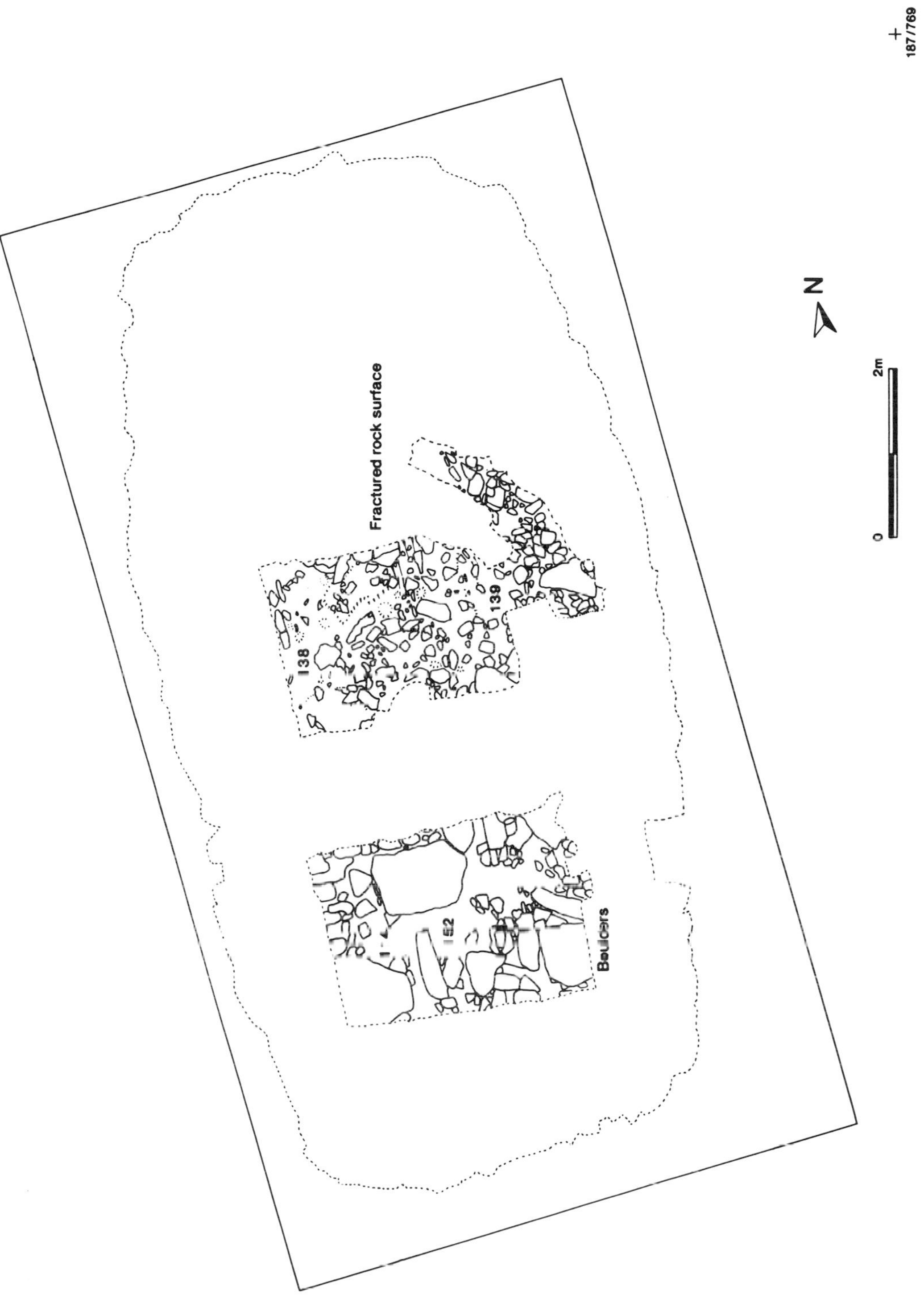

FIG. 61
Blackhouse W: Phase 1

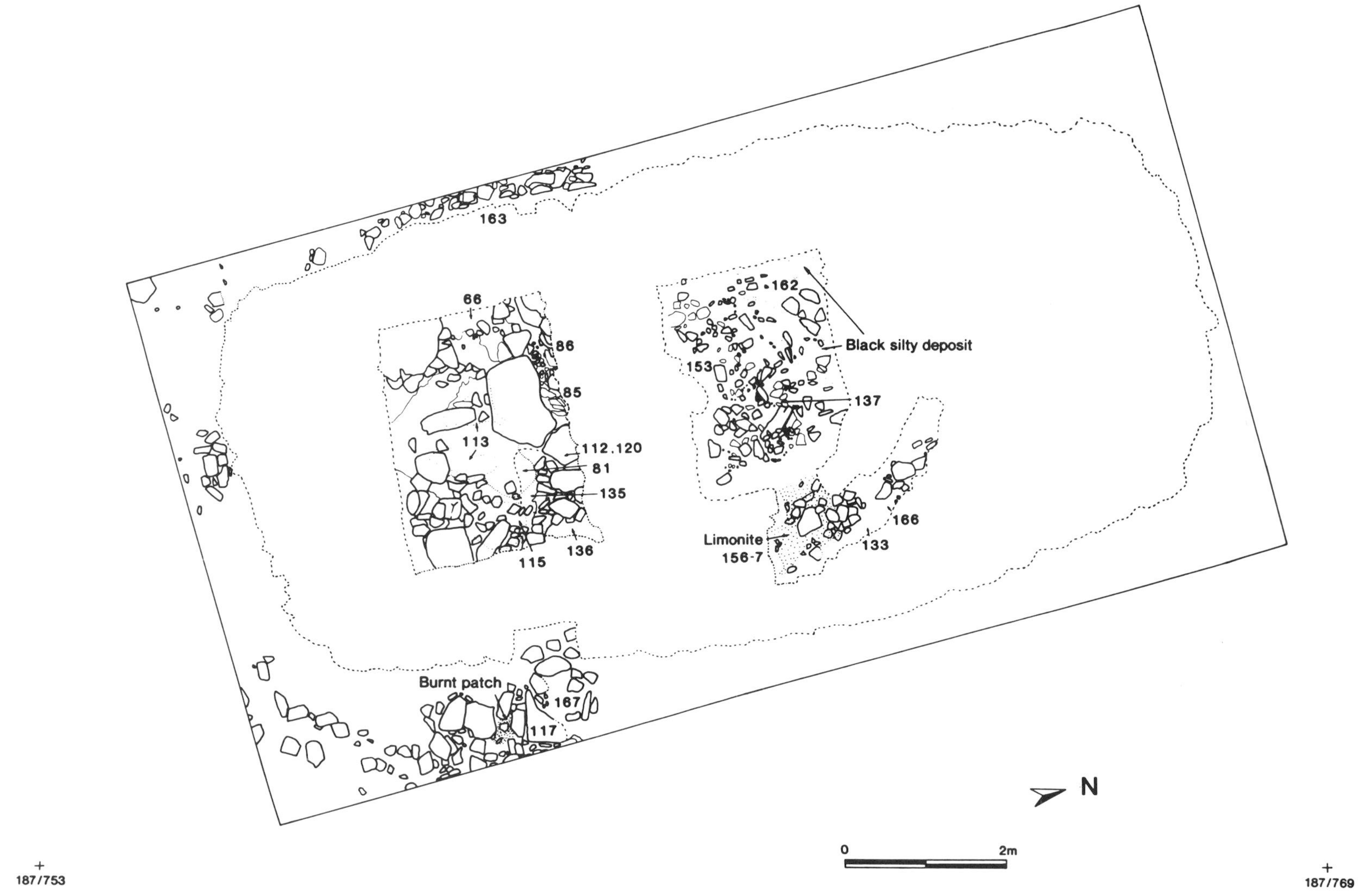

FIG. 62
Blackhouse W: Phase 2

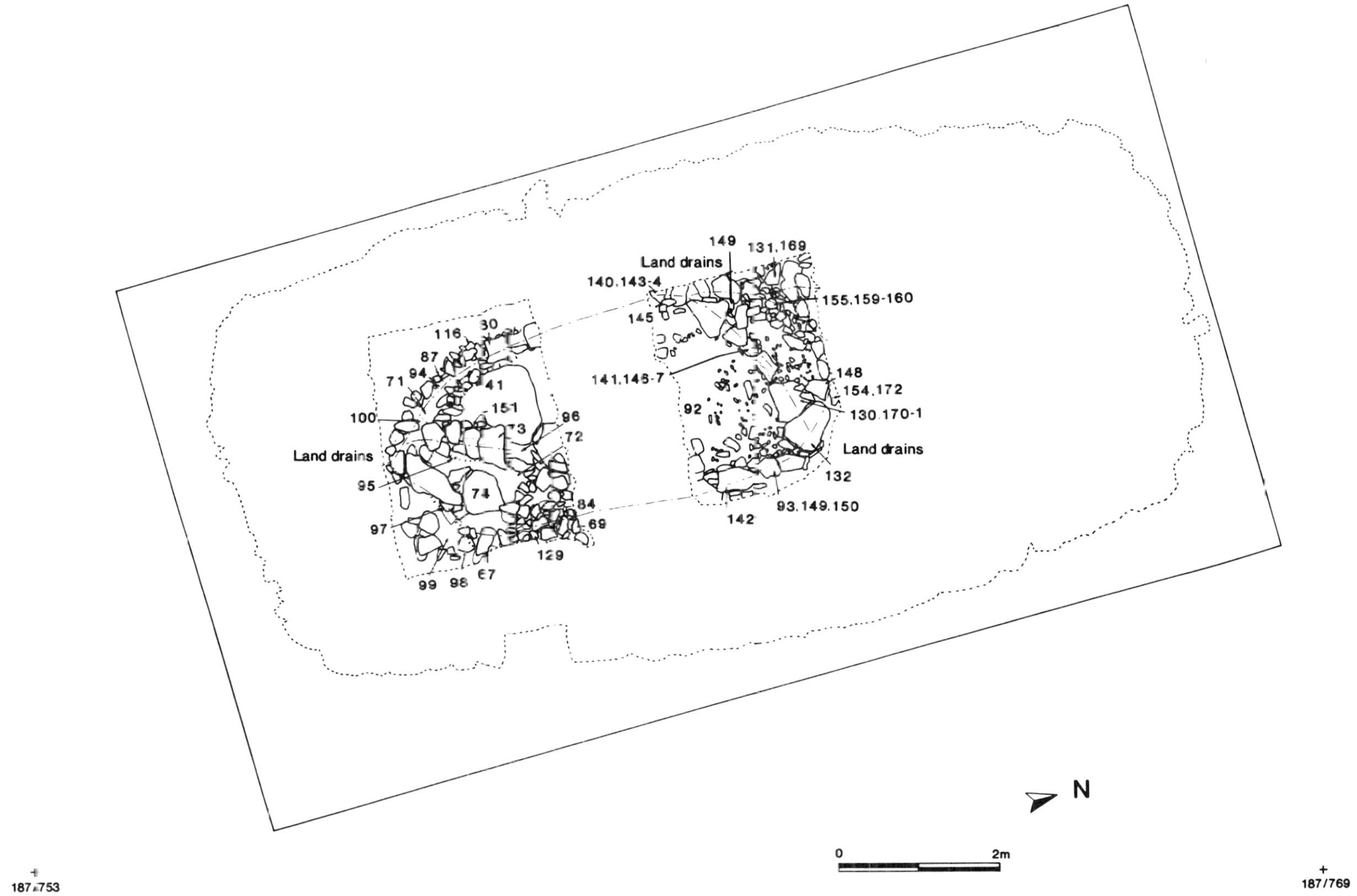

Fig. 63
Blackhouse W: Phase 3

PLATE 16
Blackhouse W: the kiln, looking north-west

PLATE 17
Blackhouse W: detail of the kiln bowl

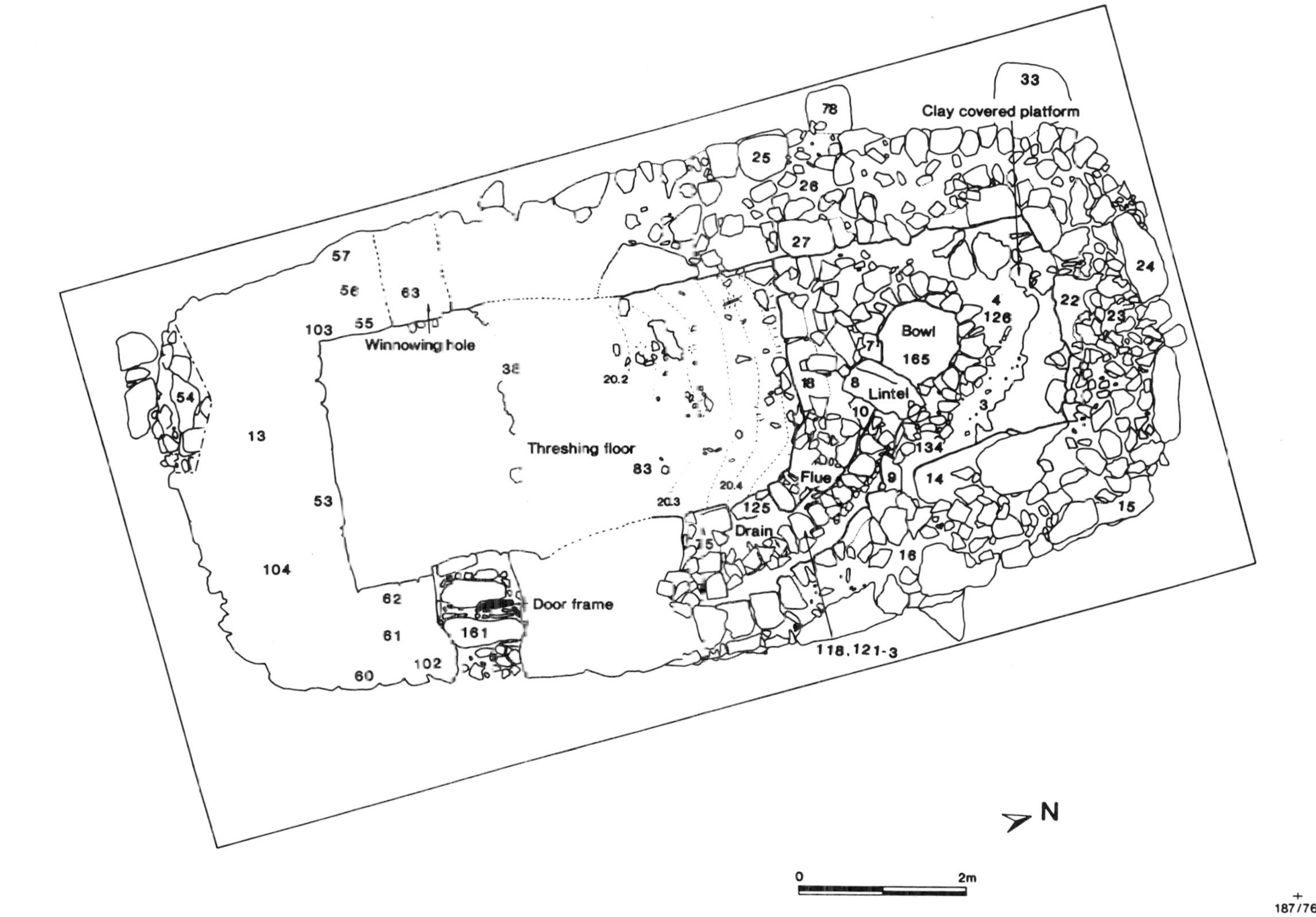

Fig. 64
Blackhouse W: Phase 4

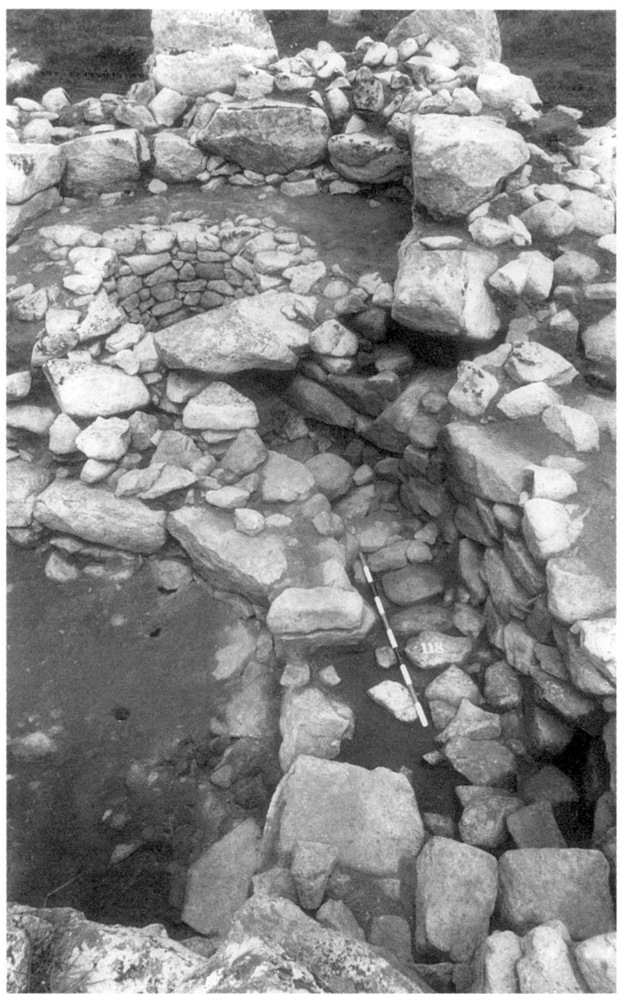

PLATE 18
Blackhouse W: the kiln bowl and flue, looking north

In the base of the flue, and running the length of it, was a small stone drain in a prepared surface of grey-brown gritty soil (123). It comprised side-stones (121, 122) and capstones (118).

The inner edge of the west side of the flue showed a noticeable indent at the outer end. Immediately in front of the flue was an open, but defined, area, edged on the west with stones (125). This was presumably the stoking place. At the southern side of this area was a loosely built block of stonework (75), which may have been part of the main walling of the building, or could have acted as a seat for the person tending the fire.

The 'seat' was faced with yellow clay, along with the lower edge of the kiln facing, and the west wall. Similarly, the main area of the kiln-barn was surfaced with a very hard yellow clay (83). Some samples of clay appeared to indicate that it had been laid in a series of layers or daubings to produce the final smooth surface. The floor sloped southward, and would have been used for threshing, though most of the clay at the lower end had been removed by later activity. Only patches (38) remained *in situ*.

In the east wall of the barn was the only door, and remains of the wooden frame lay across the centre of the threshold (161, sf. 56). Opposite the door, in the west wall was a winnowing hole (63).

Phase 5 (Fig. 65)

The kiln was then used for the drying of grain, using peat or turf as fuel, and grey-brown soil (119) containing some grain, and red peat ash (124), were found in the flue drain. The construction of the drain within the flue indicates that groundwater seepage was seen as a potential problem from an early stage. This problem seems to have continued, for the floor level in the bowl was raised. A brown silty soil (164)

PLATE 19
Blackhouse W: the east door

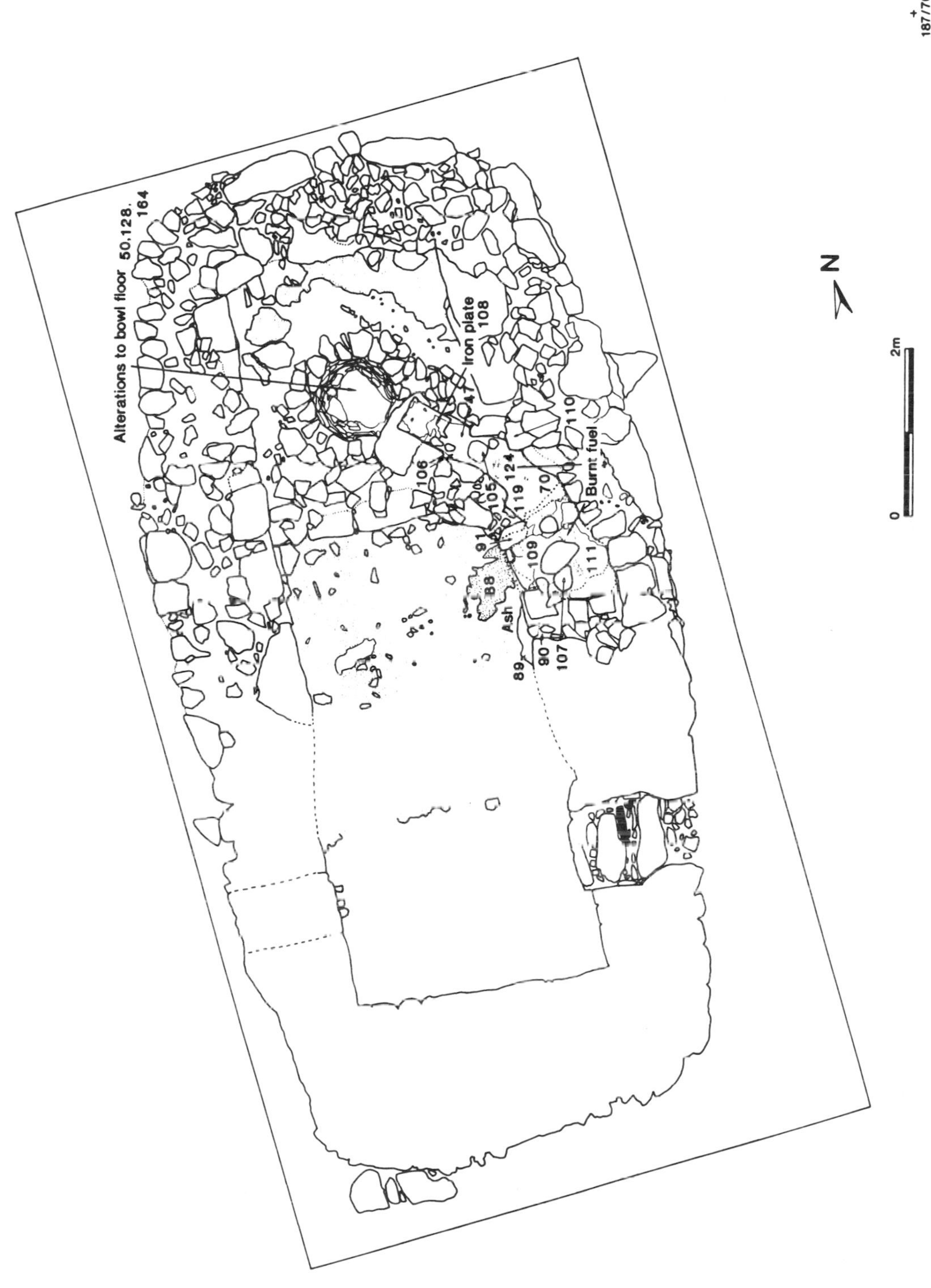

FIG. 65
Blackhouse W: Phase 5

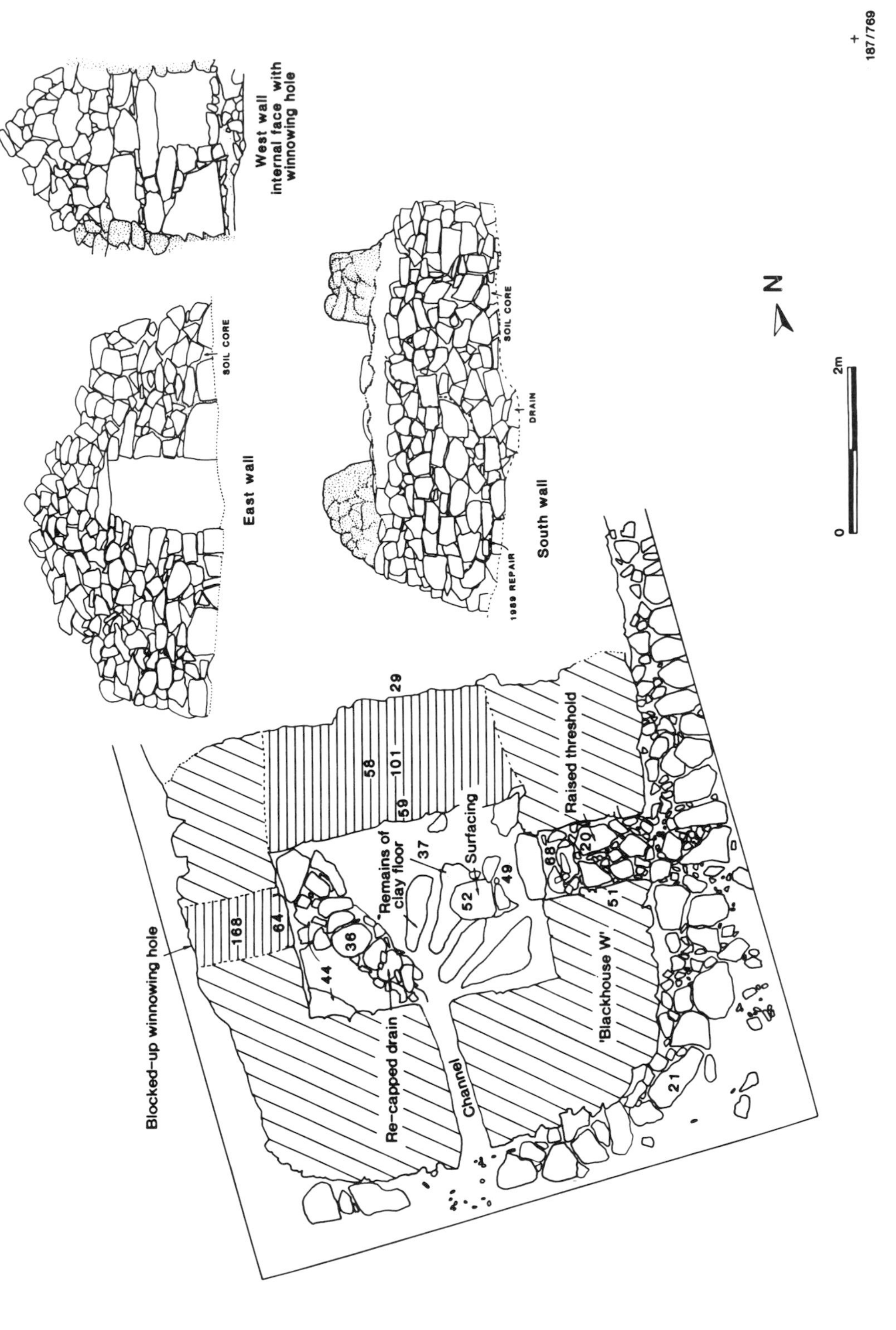

FIG. 66
Blackhouse W: Phase 6

was spread over the original base, and a flat slab (128) laid on it. This consequently reduced the size of the vent to a height of 0.38m. Apparently at the same time a heavy rectangular cast-iron plate (108) was placed in the flue, directly below the lintel. There were no marks on the plate, but it had chamfered edges, and had clearly come from a larger item, possibly a stove. Corrosion products had eventually bonded it to the stonework. Later still the floor was raised again, with a very dark greyish-brown clayey soil (127) spread over the base and covered with slabs (50). The vent was reduced still further to 0.29m in height.

Within the flue and stoking area were a complex series of layers of burnt fuel, much of it reduced to red ash. Some red ash (124) was found in the drain, and produced a fragment of crockery (sf. 44). Lying over the drain caps was a black peaty soil (111), containing two fragments of crockery (sfs 40–41). Over it were interleaved layers of pink and black ash (110, 109, 106, 91, 105). In context 109 was a piece of burnt iron (sf. 39). The heat from the kiln firings had been sufficient to redden the east face of the flue. At a late stage, a number of stones (107) had been scattered over the stoking area, before the final firing; this was marked by red ash (47) in the flue, and brown-black ash (70) containing lumps of ?peat, outside. Some ash (88) had spilt onto the barn floor.

Phase 6 (Fig. 66)

Perhaps because of the problems of dampness within the kiln, or for other reasons, it went out of use. The lower end of the building was converted into a smaller gabled structure, by building a wall (29, 58, 59, 101) across the barn, on the clay threshing floor and a layer of friable dark brown sandy silt (44). This wall formed the northern end of the new structure, and produced three pieces of leather from its make-up (sfs 31, 97–8). The west and east ends were built up fairly loosely, at some stage, to provide gables (Pl. 19). At the east side stones were laid as a paved edging (21), amongst which was a stone tool (sf. 57) and some crockery (sfs 58–9). The winnowing hole was filled up with a very loose crumbly mixed silty brown sand core (168) and stones (64 — Pl. 20). The east door was retained, though the surface was raised with stones (51, 68) laid north-south in the entrance, and covered by a threshold (20). These stones may represent a series of threshold surfaces. Amongst them was a stone tool (sf. 55).

Within the building, patches of the threshing floor (37) were still extant. On it was a dark brown silt (52), overlain by granophyre slabs, which must at one time have formed a surface throughout the room.

At this stage the western land drain (80 — Phase 3) appeared to have been examined and re-capped (36). It ran out through the south wall, where there was a byre slurry hole.

Phase 7 (Fig. 67)

The kiln structure was demolished, and the debris left to fill in the remains. The upper end of the barn floor was covered with dark reddish-brown soil (82), onto which a vast quantity of large rubble (65) had been tipped, principally from the east. This also included stone from the flue and kiln facing. A stone tool (sf. 35) was recovered from the rubble. Some yellow clay facing from the walls also fell onto the rubble. This was covered by more dark reddish-brown gritty clayey soil (17) with angular and sub-angular rocks, amongst which was coarse pottery (sfs 28, 32–4); crockery (sf. 29); textile (sf. 66); and leather (sfs 20, 87–8). This and the rubble layer also contained zinc sheeting. Later still, more rubble (40), along with two polished stones (sfs 13, 19), was dumped into the

PLATE 20
Blackhouse W: the blocked winnowing hole in the west wall

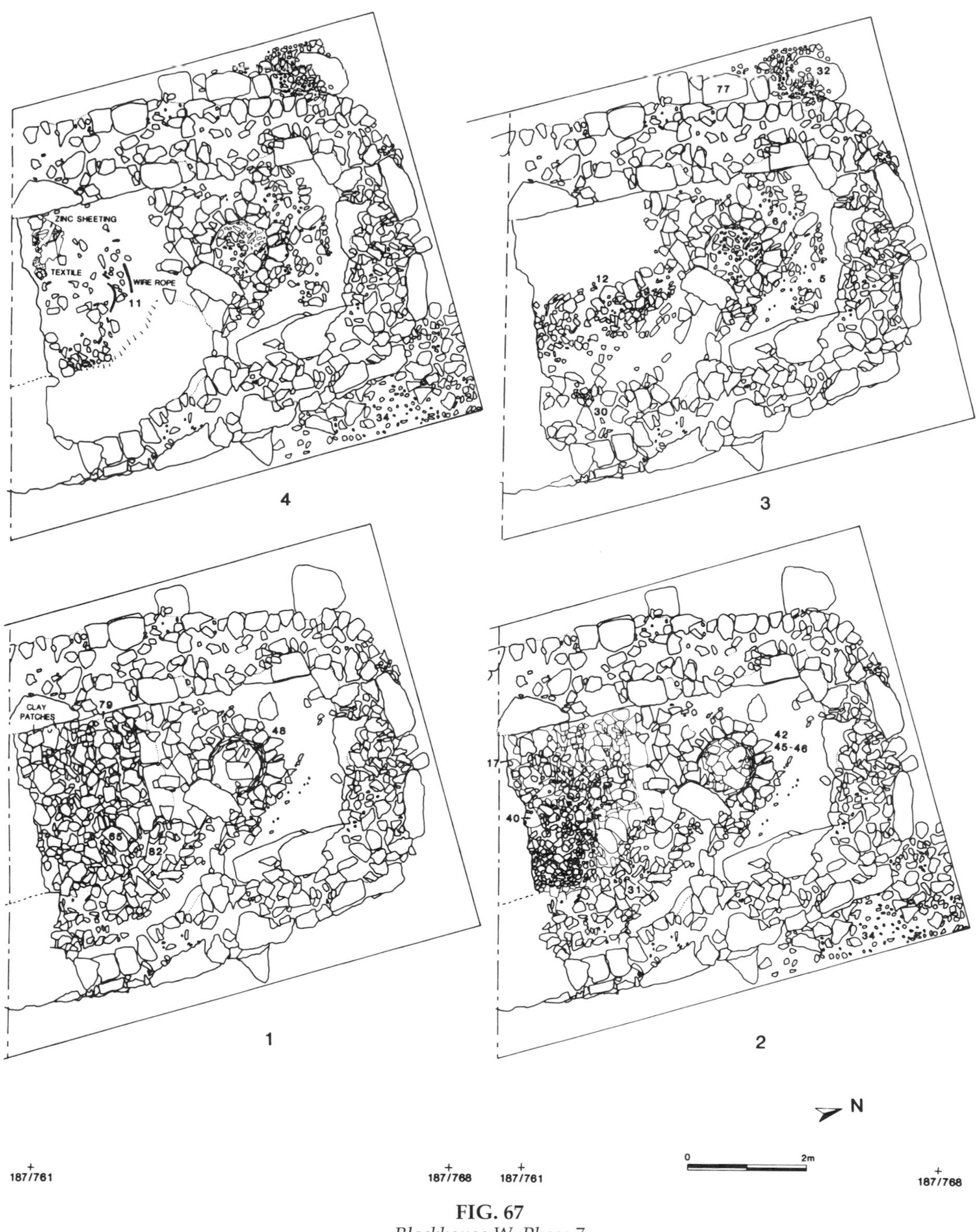

FIG. 67
Blackhouse W: Phase 7

upper end of the barn, and also into the flue and stoking area (31). In the latter area, two stone tools (sfs 14, 21) were recovered. Medium to large rocks (34) were also found in the north-east corner, along with a stone tool (sf. 24) and two pieces of coarse pottery (sfs 36–7). This was, in turn, covered by smaller rubble (12, 30), amongst which were two pieces of iron (sfs 10–11). A slip of small rubble (32) was also noted outside, by the north-west corner, amongst which were three pebbles (sfs 23, 25–6) and scraps of zinc sheet. With this were some sub-angular granophyre rocks (77).

A series of rubble layers (48, 46, 45, 42) also filled into the kiln bowl (Fig. 68), with contexts 6 and 5 spreading over the top of the kiln surface. Only the latter two tips could be linked to a rubble layer outside the bowl — the late accumulation (12, 30).

The debris-filled remains of the upper end of the barn were, at a late stage, covered by a tip (11) containing coal, glass bottles, a glass bead (sf. 8), crockery, textiles (sfs 16, 30, 63), leather (sfs 80–83), a slate (sf. 17), a stone tool (sf. 18), iron straps, and wire rope.

Phase 8 (Fig. 69)

The stone flooring of the blackhouse was sealed by a very dark brown clayey silt (39). Onto this had fallen medium to very large stones (35), representing the gradual collapse of the building. Amongst the stones were several offcuts of leather (sfs 90–95).

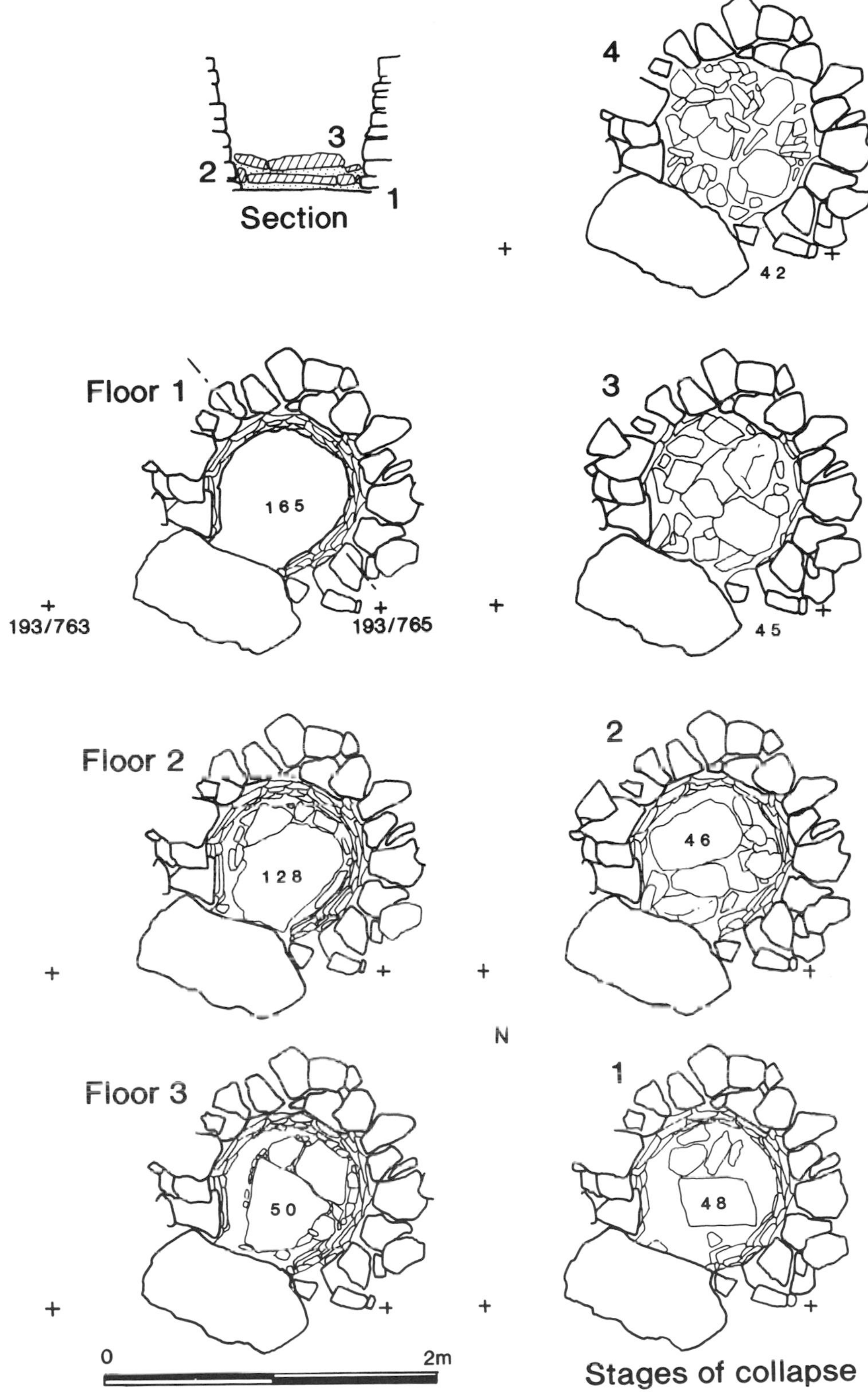

FIG. 68
Blackhouse W: details of kiln bowl flooring and infill

Phase 9 (Fig. 70)

The coal tip of Phase 7 (11) was finally covered by turf and topsoil (1). Within the soil were fragments of coarse pottery (sfs 1–2, 5, 9); a glass button (sf. 4); a manure fork by the mouth of the drain (sf. 15); a piece of iron (sf. 3); a stone tool (sf. 27); fragments of textile (sfs 22, 64–5); and leather (sfs 67–76). Within the blackhouse, the collapsed remains were covered by a clayey silt (28), which contained some fragments of leather (sf. 89) and a recent dump of stones (19). This was sealed by a sparse cover of turf with bracken roots (2), amongst which was some leather (sfs 77–9). It had been recently contaminated, when the room had been used as a temporary dump for sheep and seal carcases. Amongst this deposit was a slate pencil (sf. 12). Turf and topsoil (43) also covered the area around the blackhouse, from which a scrap of leather (sf. 96) was recovered.

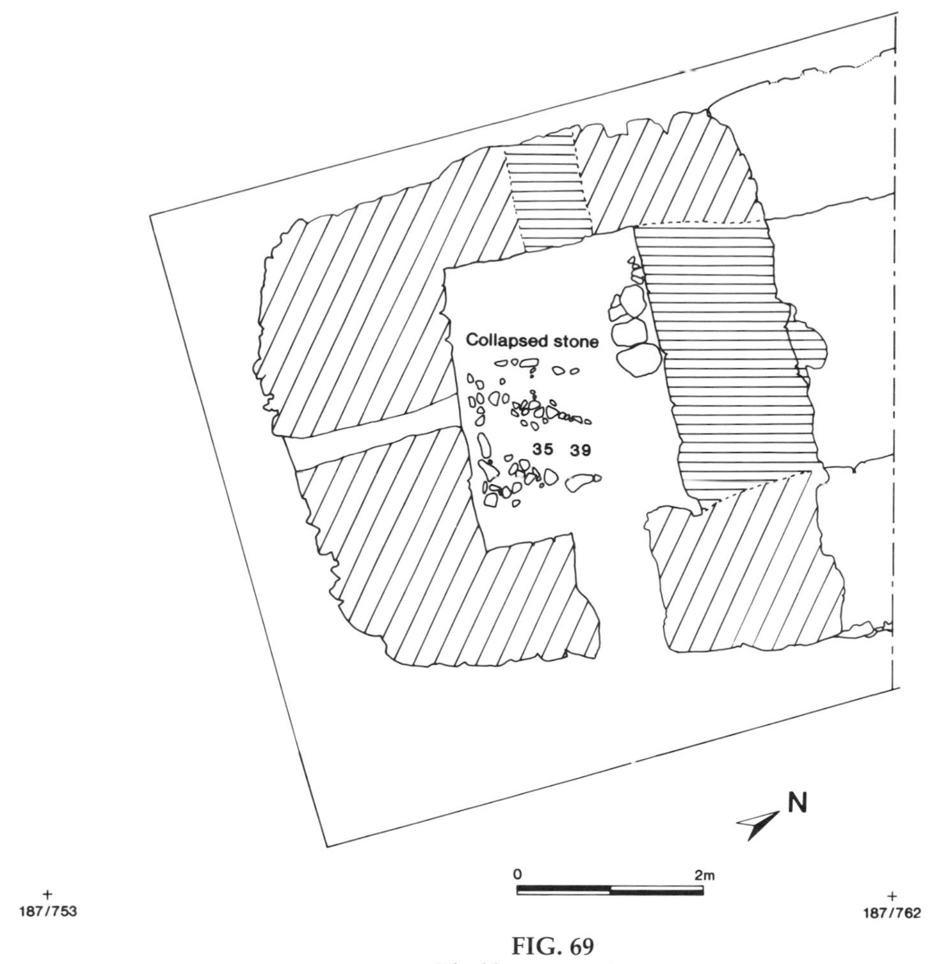

FIG. 69
Blackhouse W: Phase 8

4:3 The Artefactual Evidence

4:3:1 Coarse Pottery (A. MacSween)

The excavations at Blackhouse W produced a small pottery assemblage comprising 16 sherds, representing 11 vessels. There is only one rim, an everted rim from a globular vessel (sf. 7). Two basal sherds are from a rounded base (sf. 28) and a flat base (sf. 2).

Most of the body sherds are undiagnostic but one (sf. 46) is from a corrugated vessel similar to those from the blackhouse phase of House 8. In the report on that pottery it was noted that 'corrugations' (caused by leaving the coil junctions on the outer face of a vessel unsmoothed) are only found on large vessels. The thickness of the sherd from Blackhouse W suggests that it, too, was from a large cooking vessel. Globular vessels similar to sf. 7 are also common in the blackhouse phases of House 8. The diagnostic sherds from Blackhouse W indicate a 19th-century date.

All the pottery is well fired. Only one sherd (sf. 9) has added temper — in most cases the natural sand seems to have been adequate for the initial firing and the subsequent use of the vessels as cooking pots (indicated by the sooting). The pottery fabrics from Blackhouse W bear strong resemblances to those from House 8, which proved on thin sectioning to be local.

Catalogue

Only illustrated sherds are described. Table 25 gives summary details of all the pottery found from Blackhouse W. In the catalogue and table, the pottery has been grouped by the phase to which it relates. If a vessel comprising sherds from different phases is represented, it is included in the phase in which the majority of finds were made. If there were the same number of finds from each phase, the vessel is included with the earliest phase represented.

Phase 2

sf. 46. 1 body sherd. Red with brown core. Fabric — hard; clay has quartz, black igneous inclusions and rock fragments, up to 3mm — natural. Coil-constructed — N-shaped coil junctions. From a 'corrugated' vessel. Th. 18mm, wt 35.5g. Fig. 71.

Phase 4

sfs 6, 7. 1 body sherd, 1 rim sherd. Globular vessel with an everted rim. Black with a brown core. Fabric — hard; clay with quartz and black igneous inclusions, some up to 11mm — natural. Coil-constructed — N-shaped junctions. Interior and exterior sooted — exterior has an encrusted residue. Th. 7mm, ext. diam. 160mm, wt 112.4g. Fig. 71.

Phase 7

sf. 28. 1 basal sherd. Rounded base. Brown with a grey core. Fabric — hard; clay has quartz, black igneous inclusions and mica; added larger rock, up to 10mm (10%). Exterior and interior sooted. Th. 8mm, wt 28.6g. Fig. 71.

4:3:2 Crockery (H. Kelly)

All the sherds are surprisingly small and totally lacking in backstamps. A possible explanation of these two factors is that the island children may have used the sherds in play.

Almost all the pottery comes from the lower end of the market, if not from the lowest third. Types like

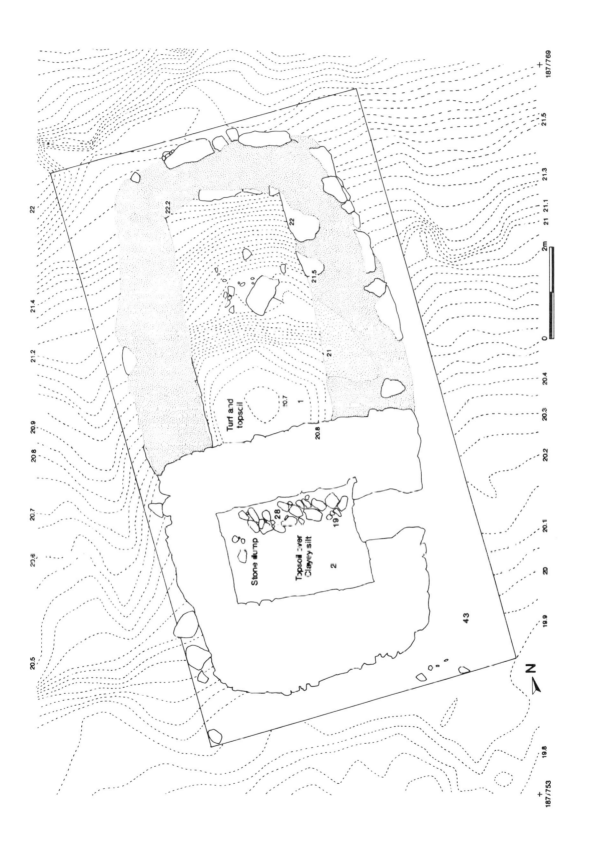

FIG. 70
Blackhouse W: Phase 9, and contours

Table 25
Blackhouse W: summary of coarse pottery

FN	No.	F	M	T	R	BY	BS	D	S	FAB	MAN	SOOT
Phase 2												
46	1			*		c					n	
54	1		*									*
Phase 4												
4	1			*								*
6	2		*		e						n	*
Phase 7												
28	1		*				pr			10		*
32	4		*									*
36	1		*									
Phase 9												
1	1		*								cl	*
2	1			*			pa					*
5	2			*								*
9	1		*									

KEY

FN = finds number of catalogue entry
No. = number of sherds represented
F = fine; sherds less than 4mm thick
M = medium; sherds between 5–9mm thick
T = thick; sherds over 10mm thick
R = Rim type: p — plain; f — flattened; e — everted; i — inward sloping; o — outward sloping
BY = Body: g — globular; c — corrugated; s — straight sided; n — necked
BS = Base: pa — plain, angled; fa — footed, angled; pr — plain, rounded
D = Decoration: co — undecorated cordon; dc — decorated cordon; ca — carination; r — rilling
S = Surface finish: b — burnished; s — smoothed; p — perforated
FAB = Fabric: a percentage indicates the presence of organic tempering
MAN = Manufacture: cl — coil (type undetermined); n — N-shaped coil; u — U-shaped coil; sl — slab-built
SOOT = * indicates that either the exterior, interior, or both surfaces of a sherd are sooted

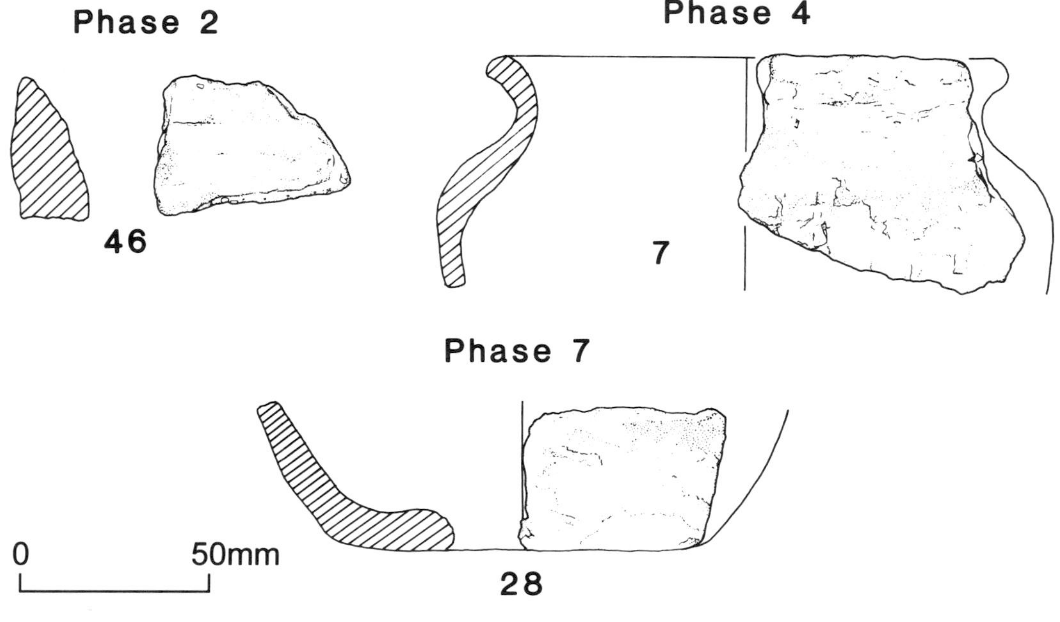

FIG. 71
Blackhouse W: coarse pottery (Phases 2, 4 and 7). Scale 1:2

slipware (sfs 29, 40–41, 45, 52, 58) and spongeware (sf. 60; gfs 17/7, 1/9) had a long life in the world of manufacture and have not been much studied in a serious way. Slipware of the white and brown or black type certainly dates back to the 18th century and is still being made; spongeware probably starts about 1835 and lasts for at least 100 years. Potteries which made spongeware were not anxious to acknowledge that they did so; so, unlike their grander products, it is seldom marked. Slipware potteries more commonly worked for a local market for which there was no need to mark their wares. Plain white earthenware and Rockingham glazed brown teapots have had a life of almost 200 years and are ubiquitous. The transfer patterns used here tend to be of early unattributable patterns or else to be, like 'Willow' (sf. 44) and 'Broseley' (gf. 34/7), so ubiquitous as to be useless for attribution. With the brown teapots in particular, the sherds are so small that provenancing by shape is out of the question.

There are a few helpful factors, however. All the stoneware (e.g. gf. 1/9) can be dated to after 1865, and much of it, indeed, can be dated to around the early years of this century. It is interesting that all the sherds seem to come from jam jars or 'meat loaf jars'; there are no whisky or varnish jars, no butter dishes, no hot water bottles, most of which are represented elsewhere on the island.

The jam jars almost certainly originally contained jam or marmalade, when brought to the island, but 'meat loaf jar' is a generic term, widely used, and those jars could have contained many things — or nothing — when imported.

All the spongeware could have been made in Scotland but could also have come from elsewhere; the date of manufacture seems to be varied. Several pieces are worth noting. 'Grecian' is represented. This pattern was widely made after *c.* 1875 in both Central Scotland

and the Sunderland/Newcastle area. It certainly continues till the turn of the century and perhaps a little beyond. Other grey-printed pieces with something like a Maltese cross are widely represented on the island. A teaset (gf. 17/7), decorated with a blue leaf pattern at the rim, is also widely represented and must date from the very late 19th century.

On the other hand, two sherds with lemon-yellow banding under sepia sponge-printing of poor design (sf. 60; gf. 43/9) look very early and should date from the 1840s or 50s. One of them (sf. 60) has a small hole bored through it, a phenomenon so far unexplained but already noted elsewhere on St Kilda. The effort involved in boring such a hole would have been great and it is unlikely to have been done casually.

Most of the slipware on a red earthenware body seems to come from bowls of various sizes and shapes, either with a white or black slip, sometimes simply slip-trailed in white over the red body. Such bowls were normally used in dairy work, like the cooling of milk or the separation of the cream which followed. The bottom half of such dishes would quite often be unglazed on the outside, but totally unglazed pieces or pieces with one part totally unglazed are less common and, unfortunately, the sherds from such pieces present in the assemblage are of too small a size to be useful in reconstructing the shape.

Slipware of this nature was made universally in Europe, but the sites most likely to be relevant are: Aberdeen, Montrose, Glasgow, Cumnock in Ayrshire, and various sites in Yorkshire and Northern Ireland. Again the slip-trailed sherds are too small to show diagnostic patterning to help with provenancing.

Another kind of slip decoration was used on a white or yellow body in the years around 1840. It consists of bands of coloured slip in brown, ochre, blue and sepia in various combinations and of various widths. Two sherds of this type are present in Area 4, one on a white body and one on a caneware fragment.

This type of slipware was also widely made. The nearest sites certainly known are Verreville Pottery in Glasgow and at least one pottery in Portobello in Lothian, but it was also made on a large scale in various places in England and was certainly made in Germany and Central Europe in the 19th century. A doll's arm (gf. 1/9) could well be German and tentatively dates from the early years of this century or perhaps a little earlier. The doll itself could not have been more than a couple of inches in height.

The potsherds found in Areas 4 and 5 have a timespan from about 1830 to 1910 and seem to be inextricably mixed. The places of origin are most likely to have been in Scotland, but there is a distinct possibility that some of the pieces came from England or even farther afield. From 1830 till the 1890s one would expect the area of origin of most of the pottery to be Scotland and most particularly Glasgow (from which some of the sherds certainly came), though Bo'ness and Kirkcaldy were also important centres for transfer-printed white ware. But after that the most likely source is North Staffordshire.

4:3:3 Glass

The glass comprises one bead, one button, 266 vessel fragments, 7 pieces of sheet glass, 5 melted lumps, 3 flakes, and a broken thermometer.

The short annular white bead (sf. 8) is 3mm diameter and 1.5mm long. The button (sf. 4) is of multi-faceted black glass, originally having an embedded metal shank. Black glass, like jet, became popular in the 1860s and '70s, and probably continued to be used into the 20th century. By *c.* 1920 the metal shank on glass buttons gave way to a glass shank (Banks 1978, 131).

Of the 266 vessel fragments, only six were found in the phases of construction and use of the kiln (Phases 3–6). No glass was found in the phases of use of Blackhouse W (Phase 8), but 260 fragments were recovered from the destruction of the kiln (Phase 7) and the decline of the site generally (Phase 9).

The fragments are from approximately 37 vessels, predominantly bottles for alcoholic beverages. Most were round in section, though two were 'flat' (gfs 1/9, 13/4). One hundred and seventy-three fragments were in green metal (84 dark, 89 light), 43 in a clear glass (sometimes having a slight pale green or turquoise hue), 40 in light brown-amber, and 10 in cobalt blue.

Two trade-marks were found — the embossed mark of William Hay on the body of a round aerated water bottle (gf. 11/7 — Fig. 72E); and A. & R. Vannan of Glasgow (gf. 1/9 — Fig. 72G) on the base of a pale green round bottle. William Hay began an aerated water business at Alford in 1843, but moved to Aberdeen in 1895. In 1902 the main works at Berryden Road were established, and are still in operation. Hay bought in bottles for filling with their soft drinks. The excavated bottle, minus the shoulder and neck, is a 'Rawlings' shape of 1910–25, probably originally around 230mm in height, with a blob top and internal screw stopper. A. & R. Vannan have, as yet, not been identified.

Although limited in number, the bottle finishes comprise two-part and crown types. The two-part finishes include applied V-shaped string rims (gfs 2/9, 17/7 — Fig. 72D), the latter on an olive-green wine bottle; a flat-topped and flattened-sided patent lip on a rectangular-sectioned bottle with rounded corners in a clear-pale turquoise metal (gf. 13/4 — Fig. 72B); and a flattened lip, where the side of the lip is high and flat — this was noted on a fragment of amber glass (gf. 1/9 — Fig. 72I).

The crown style of finish is designed to take a metal cap with crimped edges. The cap would originally have had a cork liner, to cover small mouthed bottles for beer and soft drinks. The crown finish and cap was patented in America by William Painter in 1892, and examples were found in Phases 7 (gf. 11/7) and 9 (gf. 1/9 — Fig. 72H).

Domed bases are found on dark green alcohol bottles (gf. 11/7), which have rounded resting points and a slight indent before the dome. The heel is either straight and abrupt to the resting point, or has a slight bulge or flare. An example of a small mamelon was noted on two of these bottles, and also on the Vannan bottle (see Fig. 72). Indented bases were found on rectangular-sectioned bottles with rounded corners (gfs 13/4 — Fig. 72A, 1/9); and in a double form on a clear-pale green round-sectioned bottle (gf. 1/9 — Fig. 72F) which was probably machine-made.

Cobalt blue body fragments (gfs 17/7, 40/7, 1/9, 2/9) presumably come from pharmaceutical bottles, particularly poisons. The glass exhibits stretch marks and gas bubbles. No chemists' product labels were found. In addition, two fragments of very fine clear glass tube or phial (gf. 2/9) may have contained pharmaceutical products, and a broken thermometer (gf. 13/4) was also found pushed into the wall of Blackhouse W at some very recent date.

A fragment of a 38mm (1½") diameter jar was found (gf. 31/7 — Fig. 72C), comprising the shoulder-neck-finish in clear glass. The neck is short, with a flared lip, and was produced in a contact mould, with the mould scar extending up the neck.

Two pieces of thin clear glass (gfs 36/6, 43/9) may have come from bowls, the latter possibly coming from a lamp.

Seven fragments of sheet glass include six of window glass, and one piece of a 20th-century white backed sheet. Four window glass fragments were 1mm thick (gfs 1/9, 43/9) and two were 2mm thick (sf. 51; gf. 2/9).

Five pieces of bottle had been melted and heavily distorted (gf. 124/5). Three undiagnostic flakes were also recovered (gfs 40/7, 1/9); one of them has been water-worn.

4:3:4 Copper Alloy

Five items of copper alloy were found.

Catalogue

Phase 7

gf. 11/7. Two identical fittings riveted to remnants of iron sheeting. They may be simple strap handles, a strap to secure some form of batten, or a strap on which something could be clipped. Fig. 73A.

gf. 11/7. A corroded nail head.

Phase 9

gf. 1/9. Two fittings as gf. 11/7 above.

4:3:5 Iron and Steel

A total of 437 iron objects were found, of which six were specially recorded on site.

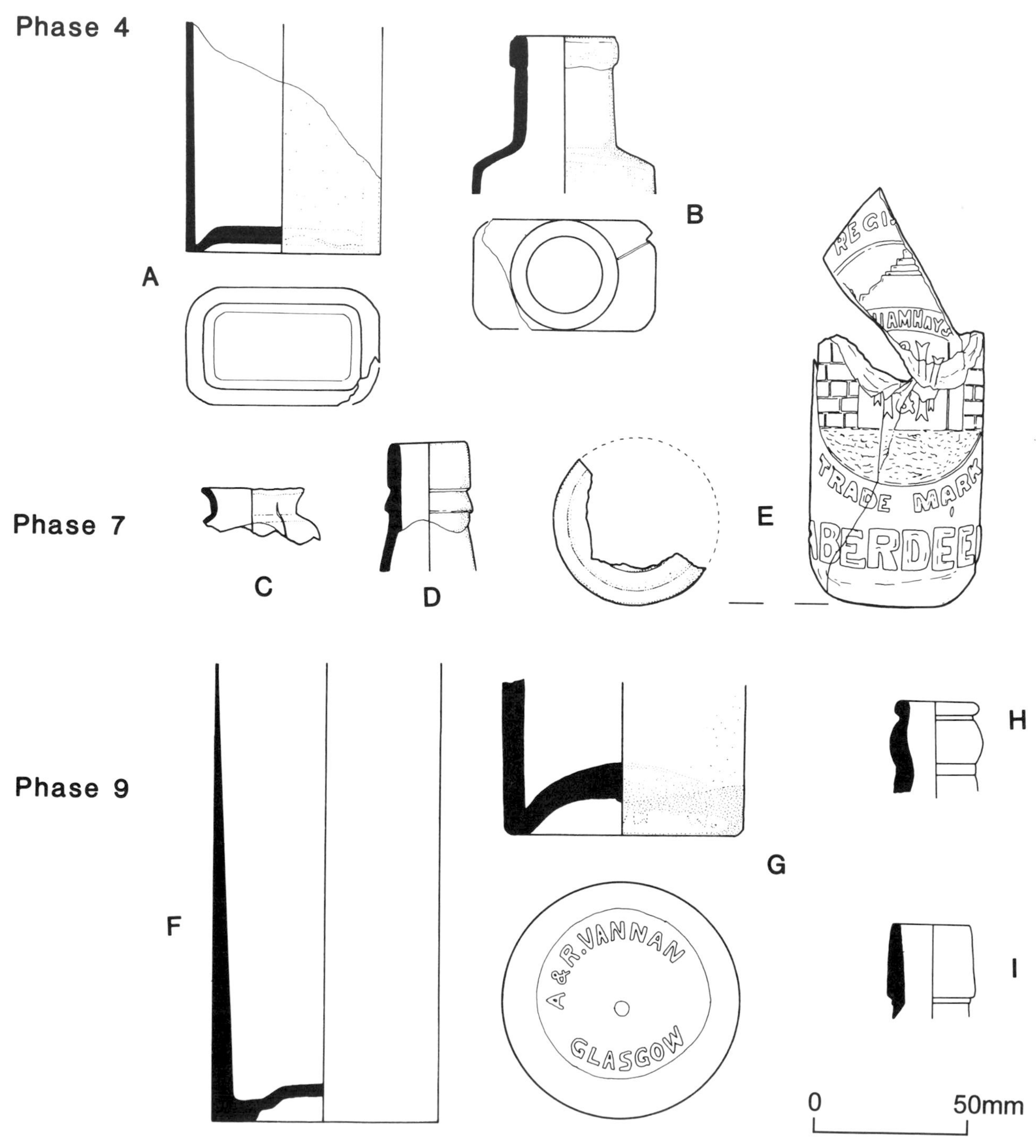

FIG. 72
Blackhouse W: glass (Phases 4, 7 and 9). Scale 1:2

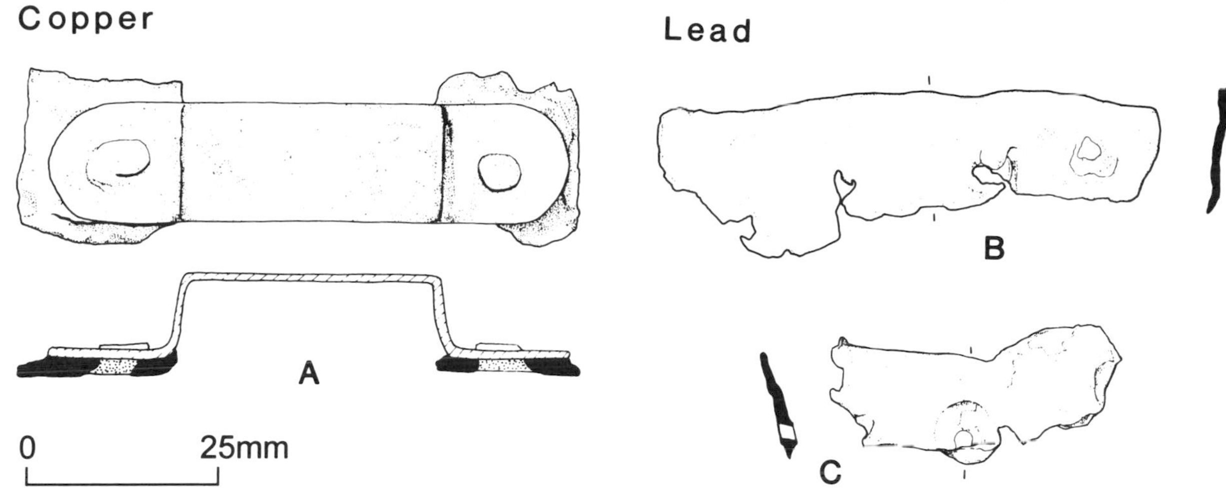

FIG. 73
Blackhouse W: copper alloy (Phase 7) and lead (Phase 9). Scale 1:1

Catalogue

Phase 2
Six items were found. A corroded sheet fragment (l. 170mm, w. 100mm, th. 35mm) fused to a granite block (sf. 48), and five indeterminate lumps.

Phase 3
One indeterminate lump was found.

Phase 4
Eighteen items were recovered. A fragment of sheet iron (sf. 42 — l. 81mm, w. 42mm, th. 31mm) heavily coated with clinker from a coal fire, and seventeen fragments of heavily corroded wire rope.

Phase 5
Thirty-six items, including a lump of corroded burnt iron (sf. 39, l. 65mm, w. 36mm, th. 19-24mm). A heavy rectangular plate (gf. 108, 500 x 364 x 11–26mm — Fig. 74A) was found laid at the junction of the kiln bowl and flue; it has chamfered edges forming a rim around three sides. On the upper face are three attachment plates and the mark of a fourth, and on the undersurface is a projecting bar. This may conceivably have come from a stove. Fourteen fragments of heavily corroded sheet flakes were associated with the plate. Twenty lumps of corrosion product were also recovered.

Phase 6
Three heavily corroded nail fragments and an indeterminate lump were found.

Phase 7
A total of 234 items were recovered. Items used for attachment include an incomplete wire nail, a corroded nail fragment, and a screw shank. An incomplete round-headed object with a forked shank may be a fastening or a decorative element.

Three straps were found (274 x 18 x 2mm; 502 x 32 x 2mm with a hole for attachment at both ends; and a fragment fused to coal), along with 166 pieces of sheet metal.

Fifty-six lengths of rope, possibly from the telegraph station, are of 6-strand broad and fine-gauge wire. Five indeterminate lumps were also recovered, including sfs 10–11.

Phase 9
Only one container was found, the rim seam from the top or base of a tin can.

Items for attachment comprise part of a ?bolt (sf. 3, l. 40mm, w. 25mm, th. 25mm — Fig. 74C); an indeterminate corroded nail fragment; a 4" (103mm) wood screw; a 25mm diam. disc head and remnants of the shank of a ?bolt; and a long tie-rod or bolt, 320mm long, with an attached hexagonal nut. A heavy loop with splayed sides (Fig. 74D) was also for attachment, along with an incomplete 22mm wide strap, pierced by two 6mm diam. holes. Fitments include a 5" (127mm) cast-iron pipe fragment, and 62 lengths of corroded rope of broad and fine gauge 6-strand wire.

Tools comprise a 650mm long rod with a splayed round head and blunt end; and a 3 prong muck fork (sf. 15, l. 115mm, ht 141mm — Fig. 74B), found in the topsoil by the exit of the slurry hole from the south wall of Blackhouse W. Other examples of the 3-prong type of byre graip have been found on Hirta in the past (Glasgow Museum 840–42), and one has recently been recovered in excavations at an 18th century longhouse at Lianach in Perthshire (Stewart and Stewart 1989, 313).

Fourteen pieces of sheet metal and 51 indeterminate lumps were also recovered, including small pieces associated with the textile/leather group in Phase 9 (sf. 22).

4:3:6 Lead

Two associated items were found in Phase 9 (gfs 1, 43 — Fig. 73B–C), parts of a distorted strap pierced by nail holes (65 x 19 x 2mm and 35 x 14 x 2mm).

4:3:7 Zinc

Two hundred and ten pieces of zinc were found, 205 in Area 4 and five in Area 5. One small fragment was found in Phase 6, but the majority were recovered from Phases 7–9. The pieces are generally flat sheeting, but many show damage through buckling, deliberate folding, or cutting. Twenty pieces are punctured by 46 nail holes, ranging in size from 3–10mm. Seven holes are irregular in shape, but the majority are 4mm diameter. One 4mm hole contains an iron nail with a 10mm diameter round head. An edge fragment (gf. 17/7) is punctured with a line of

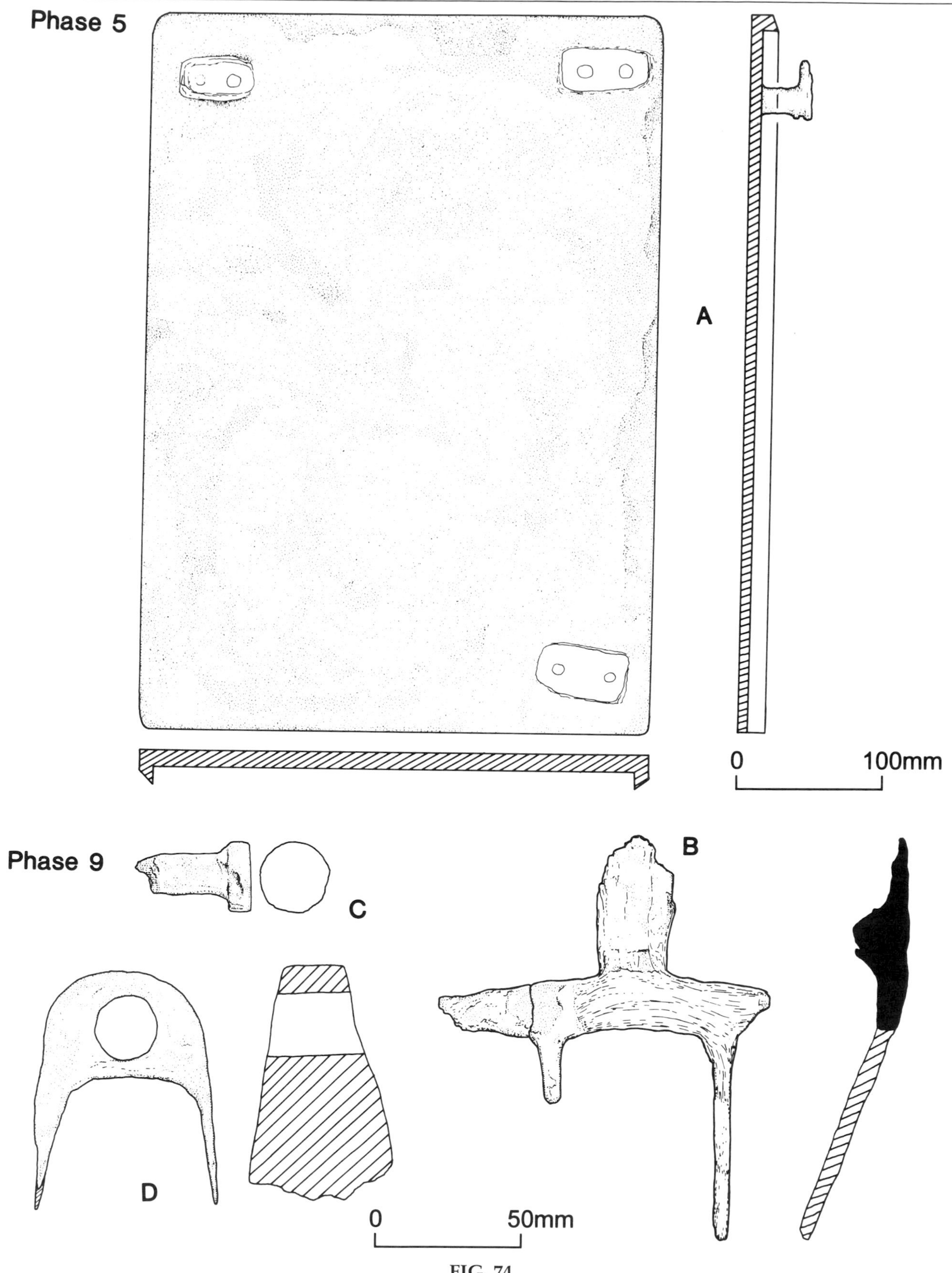

FIG. 74
Blackhouse W: iron (Phases 5 and 9). Scale 1:2; A 1:4

five holes, each 4mm diameter, centred about 36mm (1½") apart and 14mm (½") from the edge. Many of the fragments show some traces of tar coating or streaking. Zinc sheeting on the cottages was replaced around 1896 with tarred felt, but the sheeting was used as patches on the byre roofs when the thatch was replaced with tarred felt. Zinc pieces are often found over the blackhouse door lintels.

4:3:8 Plaster

Eight small pieces of plaster/mortar were found (gfs 71/3, 80/3, 91/5, 65/7, 43/9).

4:3:9 Stone (J.R. Senior)

Samples of stone were taken from layers belonging to Phases 2–9. A small number had been used as hammers, or as 'blades'. The majority of the stones come from either the Mullach Sgar Complex or the Conachair-Oiseval Complex. A number of imports were found in the collection, these being principally roofing slates from the large quarries at South Ballachulish. These are of Dalradian (Late Pre-Cambrian to Early Cambrian) age, often characterised by crenulated slaty cleavage and idiomorphic pyrite porphyroblasts. They were found in Phases 3 (gf. 97), 4 (gf. 7), 7 (gfs 11, 17, 30, 40, 82), and 9 (gfs 1, 43). One of the slates (sf. 17 — Fig. 76) shows evidence of a scratched doodle.

Recovered stones by phase

Phase 2

Three items are clearly tools — a grey-green fine-grained dolerite (sf. 38 — Fig. 75), which may have been used as a 'blade'; a hammer (sf. 47 — Fig. 75) in granophyric material, smoothed all around, with three worked surfaces; and a broken hammer stone (sf. 62 — Fig. 75) containing granophyre veinlets, which has one worked end surviving. They are derived from the Mullach Sgar Complex. Four other samples of fine to very fine-grained grey-green dolerite are also derived from the same source (gfs 66, 86). Two incorporate granophyre material.

Two pieces of smoke-blackened miarolitic granite, which have turned pink with burning (gf. 86), come from the Conachair-Oiseval Complex. A piece of vein quartz (gf. 86) probably comes from the same complex.

Phase 4

Two 'blades' were recovered from this phase (sfs 49 — Fig. 75, 50 — Fig. 75), both in grey-green fine grained dolerite, from the Mullach Sgar Complex. A piece of burnt and reddened fine-grained grey-green dolerite (gf. 4), from the same complex, was also found. In addition, there is a piece of probably fine-grained rhyolitic material (?burnt) from the Conachair-Oiseval Complex (sf. 43); and an indeterminate burnt and very reddened fine-grained igneous rock.

Phase 5

This phase produced two indeterminate flakes of igneous rock, and three samples of burnt coal residue with iron clinker.

Phase 6

This phase also produced worked stone 'blades' (sfs 55 — Fig. 76, 57 — Fig. 76), both in grey-green fine-grained dolerite from the Mullach Sgar Complex.

Phase 7

Four stones had been used as hammers (sfs 18 — Fig. 76, 19 — Fig. 76, 24 — Fig. 77, 35 — Fig. 77). Hammer sf. 19 has two worked ends and two smoothed faces in coarse-grained granophyre from the Conachair-Oiseval Complex. The same complex was the source of sf. 24, which is a miarolitic granophyre with one surviving worked end, and smoothed all around.

Hammer sf. 18, a porphyritic hybridised fine-grained dolerite from the Mullach Sgar Complex, has two worked ends and two smoothed faces. Hammer sf. 35 is a grey-green fine-grained dolerite with granophyre veinlets, also from the Mullach Sgar Complex. It has two worked ends.

Three items may have been human artefacts (sfs 14, 21, 23). They are fine-grained grey-green dolerite from the Mullach Sgar Complex. Artefact 23 is slightly pink in colour due to burning.

The Conachair-Oiseval Complex is the source of a number of stones collected in excavation, but not necessarily artefacts. These include samples of coarse miarolitic granite (gfs 11, 34, 40), including some with developed crystal-lined drusy cavities (gf. 17). Some vein quartz (gf. 11) and a quartz crystal (gf. 31), probably from a drusy cavity, also came from the granophyre.

Two other stones, specifically recorded on site, were found not to be artefacts (sfs 13, 25). Both are hybrid grey-green fine-grained dolerite with granophyre veinlets; sf. 13 has been fire shattered. Two general finds of fine-grained grey-green dolerite were also recovered (gfs 11, 40).

One piece of dense gabbroic rock (sf. 26), rich in ferro-magnesium minerals, may be derived from the early Western Gabbros.

Phase 8

This phase produced one piece of burnt fine-grained grey-green Mullach Sgar dolerite, and a burnt porphyritic rhyolite with granophyre veins from the Conachair-Oiseval Complex (gfs 35, 39).

Phase 9

Two hammer stones were recovered from this phase (sf. 27 — Fig. 77), a hybrid coarse Gabbro invaded by Mullach Sgar granophyre, with two worked ends and one smoothed side; and gf. 1, a hybridised fine-grained grey-green dolerite with granophyre veins, from the same complex, with two worked ends.

Nine pieces of burnt and reddened fine-grained dolerite from the Mullach Sgar Complex were also found (gfs 1, 43), along with a porphyritic sample of the same material (gf. 1).

Three samples of miarolitic granite from the Conachair-Oiseval Complex were also recovered (gfs 1, 2). Some have drusy cavities with developed crystals, and one (gf. 2) has been burnt and reddened. A piece of fine-grained rhyolite (gf. 1) from the same complex was also noted.

Imported items include a piece of fine-grained limestone (gf. 1) or low grade marble (probably marble), which may be from the Cambrian Durness limestone. It could have been imported either by glacier or man. A slate pencil (sf. 12 — Fig. 77) was imported, though the slate source could not be identified; and a piece of burnt and reddened slate may have come from the Ballachulish quarries.

4:3:10 Leather (C. Thomas)

The leather includes fragments of eight shoes, two strap loops, three miscellaneous stitched pieces, seventeen offcuts and eleven scraps. Both welted and riveted construction are represented here.

Nearly half of the leather belongs to Phase 9, with a substantial quantity from Phase 7, and smaller amounts from Phases 4, 6 and 8. For a full discussion of the leather from this and the other excavations see pp 166–7.

Shoes

Phase 7

sf. 20. Area 4. Fragment of shoe, with welted construction, comprising part of vamp, welt and fragment of insole.

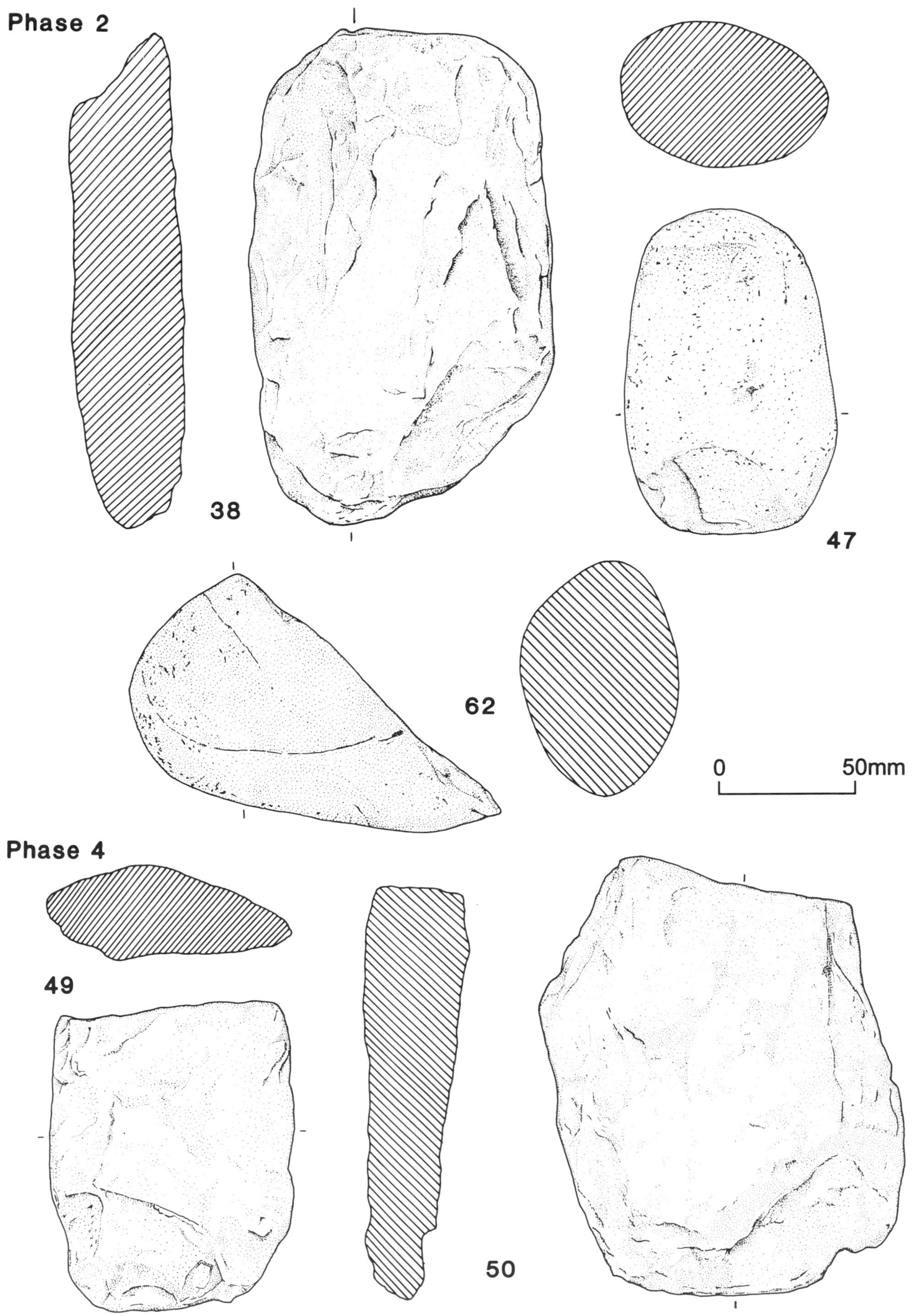

FIG. 75
Blackhouse W: stone (Phases 2 and 4). Scale 1:2

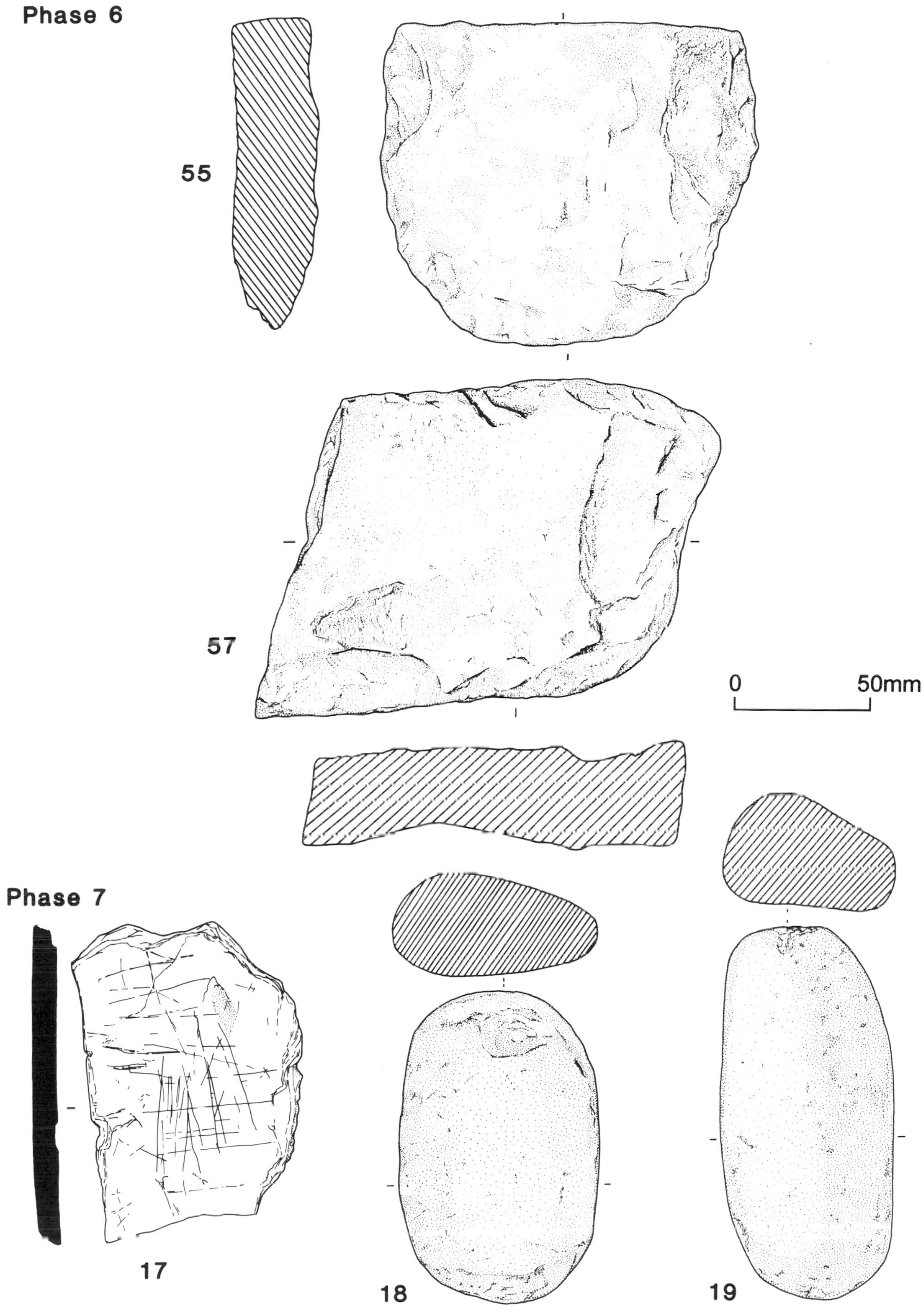

FIG. 76
Blackhouse W: stone (Phases 6–7). Scale 1:2

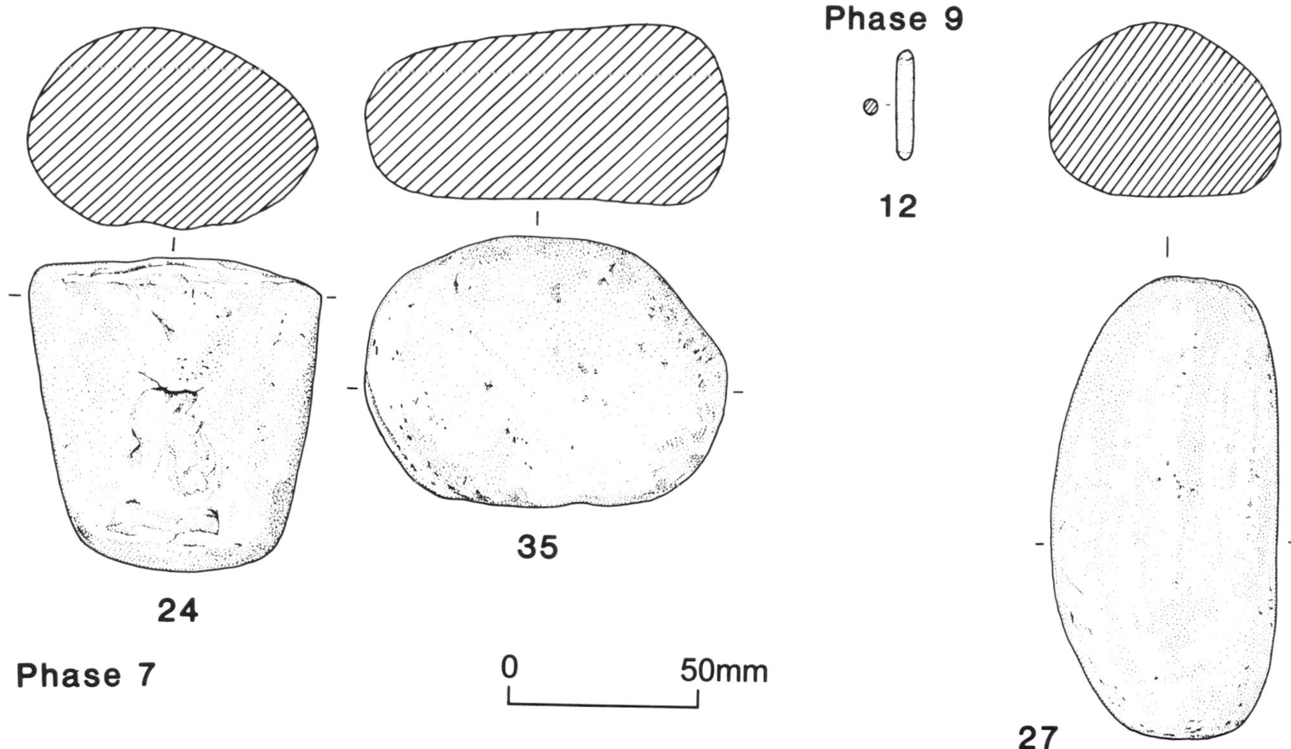

FIG. 77
Blackhouse W: stone (Phases 7 and 9). Scale 1:2

a. Vamp or toe-cap; with lasting margin with double grain to flesh stitching channel, pairs of oval holes 2 x 2.5mm, 5mm apart, forming tunnels, pairs are 9-10mm apart. Towards rear of vamp, traces of double grain to flesh stitching channel, crossing vamp diagonally; holes 1 x 0.5mm, stitch length 3mm, 4.5mm between stitching channels. No surviving grain surface. Worn. Max. surviving dimensions 130 x 76 x 1.5mm.
b. Welt; with two grain to flesh stitching channels. Inner stitching channel has oval holes, 5 x 2.5mm, stitch length 8.5–12.5mm Traces of leather thongs survive in holes, also in holes of lasting margin, suggesting that welt, lasting margin and insole were sewn together with thongs, or possibly repaired thus. Outer stitching channel is irregular, with stretched holes and extra holes, again suggesting repair. W. welt 11–18mm, mostly 14–15mm, th. *c.* 2mm.
c. Insole; only a narrow strip, 10–20mm wide, survives. Double grain to flesh stitching channel, forming tunnel stitches. Hole sizes and stitch lengths not measurable. Fig. 78.

sf. 82. Area 4. Fragment of shoe of riveted construction, comprising upper, seat of composite sole and heel or top-piece.
a. Upper; consists of bottom edge of quarters, with lasting margin with small holes for brass rivets. Also trace of vertical grain to flesh stitching channel, stitch length *c.* 1.5mm.
b. Insole; length *c.* 85mm, with large holes for iron nails and small holes for brass rivets.
c. Mid-sole; consists of two strips of leather, *c.* 15mm wide, nailed to upper and outer sole.
d. Sole; in two sections, rear of seat and front of seat, with iron nails and encrustations. Holes for iron nails and brass rivets.
e. Top-piece or heel; made of several thicknesses of leather nailed together with small brass rivets. No surviving grain pattern. W. *c.* 72mm, l. *c.* 75mm, surviving ht *c.* 15mm. Fig. 78.

sf. 83a. Area 4. Fragment of composite sole, probably part of infill of forepart of mid-sole. No surviving grain surface. *c.* 55 x 60 x 1.5mm.

sf. 87. Area 4. Fragment of boot with front lacing, comprising two latchets and two other pieces.
a. Two latchets; with linings, and eyelets, for front lacing. One latchet has complete set of 16 eyelets; 12 survive on the other. Diameter of eyelets 3.5mm. Eyelets enclosed in 15mm-wide band. Stitching channel on edge of latchet perforates both upper and lining. Second stitching channel only through upper; tiny stitch holes, 0.5 x 0.25mm, stitch length 1mm. Edge of upper cut and stitched. Edge of lining folded to form hem, then stitched. At bottom of latchet, two stitching channels, 5.5mm apart, curving slightly. Size of holes and stitch length as above. Top corner of latchet curved. Ht of latchets *c.* 250mm.
b. Approximately rectangular strip; 105 x 19–27 x 0.75mm, one end torn, tapering slightly with three cut and stitched edges. Grain to flesh stitching channels, stitch length 2mm, hole diam. *c.* 0.25mm. Possibly part of quarters.
c. Small fragment; possibly part of sole, with iron hobnails and with holes for brass rivets. Fig. 78.

sf. 88. Area 4. Fragment of shoe of riveted construction, with upper, mid-sole, sole and top-piece of heel.
a. Upper; small fragment of quarters.
b. Mid-sole; with grain to flesh stitching channel, stitch length 6.5mm.
c. Sole; attached to mid-sole and upper with brass rivets.
d. Top-piece or heel; consists of several layers of leather, all held together by iron nails. L. *c.* 65mm, max. w. *c.* 55mm. Extremely fragile, no surviving grain surface. Fig. 78.

Phase 9

sf. 68. Area 4. Fragment of shoe of riveted construction, comprising front of forepart and vamp. Forepart consists of two layers, probably mid-sole and insole. Mid-sole, insole and vamp held together by iron nails and brass rivets. Brass rivet heads on grain surface of vamp, suggesting repair. Very worn. L. *c.* 45mm, w. *c.* 70mm. Fig. 78.

sf. 77. Area 5. Three small fragments, probably from composite soles. No grain surface. *c.* 40 x 22 x 0.25mm, *c.* 70 x 30 x 0.5mm, *c.* 40 x 43 x 0.5mm.

sf. 78. Area 5. Fragment of composite sole of riveted construction. Two complete rivets, plus four rivet heads survive. Also, 5 small scraps, probably part of a sole. *c.* 40 x 50 x 3mm.

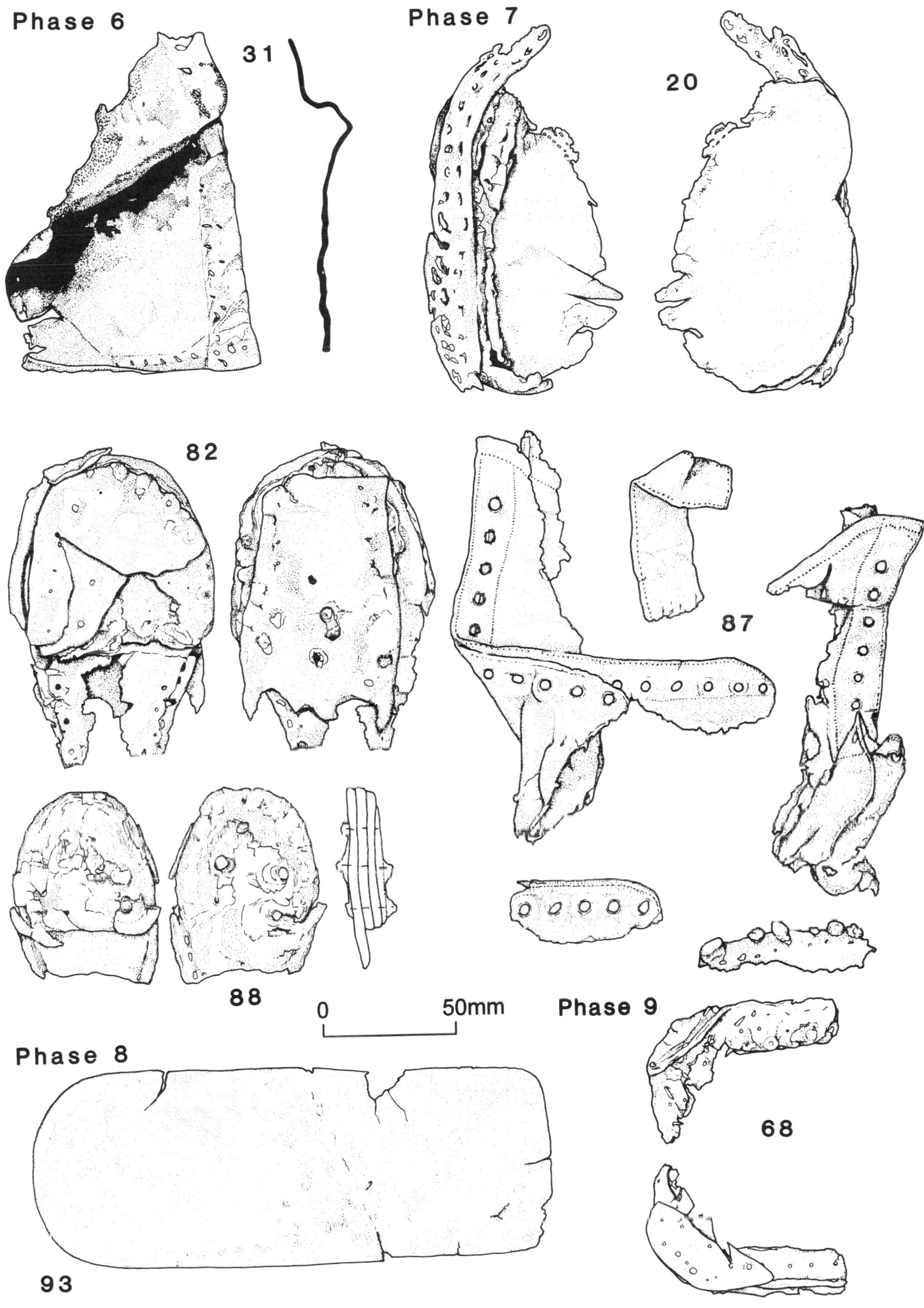

FIG. 78
Blackhouse W: leather (Phases 6–9). Scale 1:2

Straps

Phase 7

sf. 83b. Area 4. Strap loop, similar in shape to sf. 74. Inside polished smooth. No surviving grain surface. L. 38mm, w. at each end 42mm, w. of narrower part 31mm, th. 2mm.

Phase 9

sf. 74. Strap loop made of three thicknesses of leather, stitched together with grain to flesh stitching channels, stitch length *c.* 5mm. Each layer is 2mm thick. Inside of loop has been polished smooth. Grain very worn. L. of loop 67mm, l. of narrower part 25mm, w. at each end 42–47mm, w. of narrower part 30mm.

Other fragments with stitching

Phase 6

sf. 31. Approximately oblong fragment, with one rounded corner and three right angles, *c.* 130 x 92 x 1mm.

Grain to flesh stitching channels on all four edges. That on short edge with two right angles has oval holes, *c.* 2.5 x 1.5mm, stitch length 5.5–6mm; stitching channel set in 6mm from the edge, but continues right up to the long edges. Stitching channel on long edge with two right angles has oval holes, 3.5 x 1mm, stitch length 8–9.5mm, and is set in 14mm from edge; it also continues right up to the short edges. Also eight small round holes, diam. 1.5mm; irregularly spaced, *c.* 14–25mm apart and 8–13mm in from long edge. Thread marks or indentations. Stitching channel on short edge with one right angle has oval holes, 2.5 x 1.5mm, stitch length *c.* 7mm, and is set in 4.5mm from the edge. Stitching channel on long edge with one right angle has oval holes, 2.5 x 1.5mm, stitch length 6.5mm, and is set in 4mm from the edge. Holes continue round corner. Partially torn. Cattlehide. Fig. 78.

Phase 7

sf. 80. Area 4. Strip, with slight suggestion of stitching. Irregularly shaped, cut edges; six irregularly spaced holes in one edge, possibly remains of stitching. Grain slightly worn. *c.* 160 x 5–16 x 2mm.

sf. 83c. Area 4. Small fragment with possible stitch or nail holes. Irregularly shaped scrap, with five cut edges and other torn edges. Three small holes, possibly stitch or nail holes. Grain worn; delaminated. *c.* 60 x 40 x 1mm.

Offcuts

Phase 4

sf. 85. Area 5. Offcut, irregularly shaped. Vaguely sole-shaped, but with no waist and with an irregularly shaped seat. Cut and torn edges. Grain quite worn. Probably cattlehide. *c.* 230 x 78 x 1.5mm.

sf. 86. Area 5. Approximate triangular offcut; with one slightly curved cut edge and one straight cut edge, forming a right angle. Third edge torn. Grain slightly worn. Cattlehide. *c.* 370 x 195–250 x 1.5mm.

Phase 6

sf. 97. Area 5. Large offcut, irregularly shaped; with some cut and some torn edges. Not very worn. Cattlehide. *c.* 380 x 150 x 1mm.

Phase 7

sf. 81. Area 4. Large offcut, irregularly shaped; now folded, with some cut and some torn edges. Cattlehide. *c.* 230 x 160 x 1.5mm.

Phase 8

sf. 90. Area 5. Large offcut, irregularly shaped; three cut edges, rest torn. Grain slightly worn. Cattlehide. *c.* 220 x 130 x 1.5mm.

sf. 93. Area 5. Approximately rectangular fragment; with cut edges and one rounded end. No grain surface. *c.* 190 x 75 x 2mm. Fig. 78.

sf. 94. Area 5. Large offcut, irregularly shaped; some roughly cut edges, rest torn. Some scars on grain. ?Edge of hide. Grain worn. *c.* 250 x 115 x 1mm.

sf. 95. Area 5. Offcut, irregularly shaped; two straight cut edges, one irregularly cut edge, one torn edge, also a couple of score marks. Now folded. Cattlehide. *c.* 145 x 68 x 1mm.

Phase 9

sf. 67. Area 4. Large offcut, irregularly shaped; some cut edges, some torn. Now folded. Grain not very worn. Cattlehide. *c.* 370 x 50–380 x 1.5mm.

sf. 69. Area 4. Offcut, irregularly shaped; one slightly curved cut edge, rest torn. Grain not very worn. Cattlehide. *c.* 155 x 60–92 x 2mm.

sf. 70. Area 4. Offcut, irregularly shaped; four cut edges, two torn, now folded. Grain not very worn. Cattlehide. *c.* 160 x 230 x 1.5mm.

sf. 71. Area 4. Large offcut, irregularly shaped; one long and two short cut edges, two torn edges. Grain quite worn. Cattlehide. *c.* 240 x 110 x 2mm.

sf. 72. Area 4. Large offcut, irregularly shaped; one long straight cut edge, one curved, probably cut edge, and one long torn edge. No surviving grain surface. *c.* 390 x 150 x 1mm.

sf. 73. Area 4. Large triangular offcut; edges cut. Slight iron concretion on flesh side, near apex of triangle. Grain worn. ?Pigskin. Ht 210mm, base 106mm, th. 1.5mm.

sf. 75. Area 4. Narrow strip, irregularly cut. Grain very worn. *c.* 430 x 5–15 x 0.75mm.

sf. 76a. Area 5. Large offcut, irregularly shaped; three cut edges, two torn. ?Pigskin. *c.* 190 x 160 x 2mm.

sf. 89. Area 5. Approximately oblong offcut, irregularly shaped; with cut and torn edges and with two pairs of small holes, diam. *c.* 1.5mm.

Scraps

Phase 4

sf. 84. Area 5. Scrap; irregularly shaped; delaminated, edges torn. Very fragmentary. Irregular pattern of holes, just possibly stitching but more probably decay. Grain very worn. *c.* 100 x 70mm.

Phase 6

sf. 98. Area 5. Scrap; irregularly shaped; edges torn. Worn. *c.* 210 x 120 x 1mm.

Phase 8

sf. 91. Area 5. Scrap; small, irregularly shaped; delaminated, all edges torn. Cattlehide. *c.* 57 x 25mm.

sf. 92. Area 5. Scrap; small, irregularly shaped; delaminated, all edges torn. Cattlehide. *c.* 55 x 20mm.

Phase 9

sf. 22. Area 5. Scrap; small, irregularly shaped; all edges torn. Very fragmentary. *c.* 65 x 53 x 1mm.

sf. 76b. Area 5. Scrap; small irregular fragment; torn. Worn. c. 90 x 115mm.

sf. 79a. Area 5. Scrap. ?Pigskin. *c.* 80 x 125 x 2mm.

sf. 79b. Area 5. Scrap. ?Pigskin. *c.* 100 x 10–60 x 2mm.

sf. 79c. Area 5. Scrap. ?Pigskin. *c.* 130 x 5–30 x 2mm.

sf. 79d. Area 5. Scrap. ?Pigskin. *c.* 55 x 75 x 2mm.

sf. 96. Area 5. Scrap; small, all edges torn. *c.* 40 x 25 x 1mm.

4:3:11 Textiles (P. Walton)

Six textiles were recovered from Area 4 (T43, T57, T106–9) and one from Area 5 (T50). These textiles are from levels dated to the late 19th or early 20th century, with some late pieces (T107) from the topsoil of Area 4. There is also a piece of chained nylon yarn (T110), purportedly from late 19th/early 20th-century levels (see below).

All the textiles are of wool and in simple weaves, 2/2 twill and tabby. Some of the coarser twills, such as T108, probably represent the locally made tweed. One of the finer twills (T43) has missing and decayed threads forming a check pattern: it is possible that these threads were dyed a contrasting colour with a dyestuff which has attacked the fibre. The piece of chained nylon yarn seems to be detached machine stitching, of a kind commonly used nowadays to hold the hems of jersey T-shirts. Nylon was invented in America in 1930, but was not in regular use, except for stockings, until the late 1940s and it seems likely that this piece is a modern contaminant.

PLATE 21
Blackhouse W: jacket fragment, sf. 30 (T57)

Catalogue
It is intended to publish a more detailed catalogue and report elsewhere.

Notes:
'coarse' = less than 10 threads per cm in warp and weft
'medium' = 10–20 threads per cm
'medium-fine' = 20–30 threads per cm

Phase 7

sf. 16 (T43). Medium-fine brown wool twill, 2/2 structure, in poor condition; missing threads in warp and weft form a check pattern.

sf. 30 (T57). Remains of jacket front with interfacing, made from a coarse brown-black wool twill in 2/2 structure; both faces of twill have been given a matted finish, one face more than the other. Pl. 21.

sf. 63 (T106). Medium or medium-coarse dark brown wool twill in 2/2 structure; felted.

sf. 66 (T109). Medium dark brown wool twill in 2/2 structure; matted, in several layers, originally adhering to a leather boot.

Phase 9

sf. 22 (T50). Medium-fine yellow-brown wool twill in 2/2 structure; remains are arranged in compacted pads of fabric.

sf. 64 (T107). Medium-fine green textile in tabby weave; felted on one face, brushed pile on other.

sf. 65 (T108). Coarse brown wool twill in 2/2 structure.

gf. 2/9 (T110). A row of machine stitching in nylon thread; the fabric which it once sewed is no longer present.

4:4 The Ecofactual Material

4:4:1 Plant Remains (Jacqueline P. Huntley)

The sampling and processing methods followed those used for the other areas (see 2:4:1).

Description of samples from Area 4 (Table 26)
Phase 2
This phase contained generally thin soils overlying the natural granite.

Context 133 (flot 79). This was a brown gritty soil. Although small the flot was very rich in modern seeds, fly puparia and earthworm egg cases. Mainly seeds of sorrel, blinks and chickweed were present, but there was also a variety of other weeds represented. Strawberry and raspberry/blackberry seeds were present. Modern seeds reinforce the archaeological description as a soil, they suggest disturbed and, possibly, slightly nutrient-enriched ground. The strawberry and raspberry/blackberry are probably from fruit being grown on the site since none of these species are recorded from St Kilda in the Atlas of the British Flora (Perring and Walters 1976).

Phase 5
The kiln in use for drying corn.

Context 88 (flot 44). This sample contained odd fragments of wood only with one carbonised barley fragment and a few modern chickweed and blinks seeds.

Context 47 (flot 2 and second sample). Red ash in the flue. This was a small flot with fragments of carbonised monocot., a few burnt bryophyte stems and odd *Sphagnum* leaves. Waterlogged *Sphagnum* leaves and chickweed seeds were present, as were two extremely well-preserved hulled barley grains, one with a straight embryo. The base of the lemma on one was very clear and showed a nicked base. Although this was once considered to be diagnostic of dense-eared forms, subsequent detailed analyses of modern material has demonstrated that base shape is not necessarily definitive (Renfrew 1973). The fine remains of moss, etc., are probably the result of fly ash being drawn along the flue and suggest that peat was the source of fuel. The second flot was of wood and charcoal with some numbers of carbonised hulled barley and oat grains. There were also barley awns and two barley rachis internodes, unfortunately these latter were broken thus not allowing determination of whether two or three grains had been attached. There were also a few carbonised seeds from arable weeds including corn spurrey and corn marigold, both indicators of acidic and relatively dry soils.

Context 110 (flot 62). The flot consisted principally of charcoal, wood and monocot fragments, including the awns and fine stems of grasses — all burnt. Although few waterlogged seeds were recovered, relatively large numbers of carbonised seeds were. These were mainly oats with hulled barley and various associated weeds although no cereal chaff was recovered.

Phase 7
During this phase the kiln was demolished leaving the debris as infill. The floor of the barn was then covered with a variety of debris.

Context 17 (flots 17, 19 and 20). This was the dark reddish-brown gritty clay soil overlying rubble tipped onto the barn floor. Flot 17 contained many lumps of rock. Earthworm egg cases, rat-tailed maggots and a few fragments of insect leg were present but otherwise little else. Some numbers of waterlogged sorrel seeds were recorded. The maggot remains suggest that some rubbish was organic and left to moulder amongst the mineral rubble. The waterlogged sorrel seeds indicate that probably some soil was also brought in with the mineral rubble, or that the layer was left exposed to weathering for some time, thus allowing some plants to colonise it. Flot 19 contained predominantly fragments of dry wood, with large numbers of earthworm egg cases and odd fragments of fly puparia. Carbonised barley and oats were present but not too well preserved. Large amounts of modern black bindweed seeds were recovered. Flot 20 contained hulled barley grains, one straight-embryoed example in excellent condition.

Context 48 (flot 15). This was rubble from one of the layers within the kiln bowl following demolition of the kiln. The flot contained earthworm egg cases, one blinks' seed and a few sorrel seeds only. Sufficiently few seeds are present that it is suggested that the rubble layer was not left exposed for any length of time but neither did it consist of soil.

Although the numbers of carbonised seeds are disappointingly low, given that the main feature was a corn-drying kiln, this area does have moderate numbers of both barley and oats. Phase 5 contains more

Area No.	4	4	4	4	4	4
Context No.	**133**	**88**	**47**	**110**	**17**	**48**
Phase	**2**	**5**	**5**	**5**	**7**	**7**
Carbonised:						
[a]*Spergula arvensis* (corn spurrey)			1	1		
[a]*Stellaria media* (chickweed)				3		
[c]*Avena* grain (oats)			8	15	2	
[c]Cerealia undiff.						
[c]*Hordeum* hulled (hulled barley)		1	17	4	4	
[c]*Hordeum* indet.						
[c]*Hordeum* straight hulled			1		1	
[c]*Hordeum* twisted hulled					1	
[g]*Chrysanthemum segetum* (corn marigold)			2	1		
[g]Gramineae 2–4mm (medium grasses)				2		
[h]*Calluna vulgaris* wood (heather)		+				
[m]*Fucus* — thallus/frond (brown seaweed)		+				
[s]Culm nodes (straw)			1			
[s]*Hordeum* awn (barley chaff)			+			
[s]*Hordeum* rachis internode (barley chaff)			2			
[w]*Carex* (trigonous) (sedges)			1	3		
[x]Gramineae <2mm (small grasses)				3		
[x]Gramineae undiff.			2			
Waterlogged:						
[a]*Chrysanthemum segetum* (corn marigold)	+			1		
[a]*Galeopsis tetrahit* (hemp nettle)	1					
[a]*Spergula arvensis* (corn spurrey)	+					
[a]*Stellaria media* (chickweed)	++	+	++	+	+	
[g]*Rumex acetosa* (sorrel)	++			+	++	+
[r]*Fallopia convolvulus* (black bindweed)					++	
[r]*Polygonum aviculare* (knotgrass)					1	
[r]*Rumex acetosella* (sheep's sorrel)	+					
[r]*Tripleurospermum maritimum* (mayweed)			1			
[t]*Fragaria vesca* (strawberry)	+					
[t]*Rubus fruticosus* (blackberry)	1					
[w]*Carex* (lenticular) (sedges)	1		1			
[w]*Carex* (trigonous) (sedges)	+					
[w]*Montia font.* ssp. *chondr.* (blinks)	+	+			+	1
[w]*Sphagnum* sp(p). (bog moss)			1			

TABLE 26

Blackhouse W: Area 4 — plant remains

KEY

The taxa have been put into broad ecological category. The latter was subjectively derived and the prefix codes are as follows:

a = arable weeds c = cereal grain g = grassland h = heathland m = maritime/coastal
r = ruderals/disturbed ground s = cereal chaff and straw fragments t = scrub/woodland
w = wet ground x = broad, unclassified

For the waterlogged taxa up to five individuals were counted and then further quantities estimated thus:
+ = a few being present ++ = moderate numbers *** = extremely large numbers

chaff than during any other period and this is in accord with it being the period of use of the kiln. The cereals would have been cut and stooked in the field and then brought to the kiln for drying. During this process, inevitably some would be burnt leaving remains of grain, straw and ear fragments behind. The numbers of sedge, grass and weed seeds that were also burnt suggests that the cereals were growing in quite weedy fields and that these weeds were cut with the crops.

The numbers and species of waterlogged taxa represent remains similar throughout this area for all periods. Chickweed is, perhaps, slightly more common in the earlier phases, possibly representing plants growing around the doorway of a building, much as it does today around the cleitean. It is interesting to note that, although the seeds of black bindweed were recovered in abundance here, it is not recorded from the island today.

Description of samples from Area 5 (Table 27)

Phase 2

Original soil overlying natural.

Context 66 (flot 25). The old land surface of friable grey-brown silt. It contained worm egg cases and the occasional charcoal fragment. Waterlogged sorrel seeds and one carbonised oat grain were present. The sorrel seeds indicate cultivated soil as do the worm egg cases.

Context 86 (flots 47 and 61). A gritty soil overlying earlier soils which formed something akin to an iron pan. Flot 47 contained odd fragments of vegetation and clinker only. The clinker suggests that the layer was deliberately laid or that it as an area where ash was dumped. It leads to the question as to the origin of that clinker — presumably some coal was imported for fuel since the natural peat formations on the island are rather sparse, and evidence from earlier excavations suggests that at least some grass turf was burnt in earlier times. Flot 61 contained a few tiny fragments of charcoal and one fragment of a hulled barley grain.

Phase 4

During this phase the corn-drying kiln was built.

Context 13 (flot 1). The flot contained a few modern twigs and bracken fragments with earthworm egg cases. One fragment of hulled barley was recorded.

Phase 9

Turf and top soil covering the old coal tip.

Context 2 (flot 25) A sample of soil taken from around textile sf. 22. This consisted of only worm cases and a couple of fragments of wood and bracken. In addition, there were two chickweed seeds and about six fragments of insect and fly puparia.

Context 43 (flot 70). Although there were earthworm egg cases they were less numerous than usual. Quite a number of carbonised seeds were present — oats and hulled barley and one floret base from the cultivated oat. Moderate numbers of waterlogged taxa were represented — predominantly weeds of disturbed ground and nutrient-enriched ground.

The results overall show very sparse numbers of any types of seed, with the exception of context 43 which has a suite of barley and oats very similar to that from Area 4 (see above). They suggest that this area was kept generally clear throughout the phases analysed and that there was little build-up of soil or vegetation. There is limited evidence, however, for the dumping of clinker or ash. Bracken frond fragments are recorded for the first time. This is a plant that would have been used for bedding if it had been abundant enough. It is clearly spreading around Village Bay today, and the material in these samples may have been from some of the pioneer plants, although it could reflect modern contamination. There are always difficulties in determining whether non-carbonised material is contemporary with the archaeological deposit or is a modern intrusion. Such material is, however, still of interest in a situation such as St Kilda, when the archaeological deposits under

Area No.	**5**	**5**	**5**	**5**	**5**
Context No.	**66**	**86**	**13**	**2**	**43**
Phase	**2**	**2**	**4**	**9**	**9**
Carbonised:					
^{c}*Avena* grain (oats)	1				6
^{c}Cerealia undiff.					1
^{c}*Hordeum* hulled (barley)		1	1		4
^{c}*Hordeum* straight hulled					1
^{s}*Avena sativa* floret base (oat chaff)					1
Waterlogged:					
^{a}*Stellaria media* (chickweed)				2	+
^{g}*Potentilla erecta* (tormentil)					+
^{g}*Rumex acetosa* (sorrel)	+				+
^{h}*Pteridium aquilinum* — frond frag. (bracken)			++		
^{r}*Fallopia convolvulus* (black bindweed)			+		
^{r}*Rumex acetosella* (sheep's sorrel)					+
^{r}*Urtica dioica* (nettle)					+
^{t}*Rubus fruticosus* (blackberry)					+
^{w}*Carex* (trigonous) (sedges)					+
^{w}*Montia fontana* ssp. *chondr*. (blinks)					+
^{w}*Sphagnum* sp(p). (bog moss)					+
^{x}*Ranunculus repens-type* (buttercup)					1

TABLE 27

Blackhouse W: Area 5 — plant remains

KEY

The taxa have been put into broad ecological category. The latter was subjectively derived and the prefix codes are as follows:

a = arable weeds c = cereal grain g = grassland h = heathland m = maritime/coastal
r = ruderals/disturbed ground s = cereal chaff and straw fragments t = scrub/woodland
w = wet ground x = broad, unclassified

For the waterlogged taxa up to five individuals were counted and then further quantities estimated thus:

+ = a few being present ++ = moderate numbers *** = extremely large numbers

discussion here are themselves only 100–150 years old. In particular, there are questions to ask of the changing nature of the vegetation following the evacuation of the island's people. Modern vegetational studies (Huntley, in prep.) of the anthropogenic vegetation may answer some of these questions.

4:4:2 Mammal and Bird Bones (M. Harman)

Very few bones were found on this site. In Area 4, one sheep tooth occurred in Phase 5. In contexts attributed to Phase 7, there were further sheep bones: a skull fragment, three teeth, a scapula, humerus and tibia, all from mature animals, and two vertebrae from an immature bird of guillemot/fulmar size.

In Area 5, there are sheep bones from Phase 4, mostly tucked into the wall: in wall core 13 there were three eroded pieces, probably all from the same skull, of a sheep of Soay size. In wall core 53 there was part of a radius from a small animal. From another context there is a fragment of cartilage, probably from a sheep thorax.

In Area 5, Phase 6, there is one sheep tooth, one fragment of tibia, and one large foot phalanx from an immature bird, possibly a goose; though from a large bird, it is not a gannet.

In Phase 8 there are a left scapula, radius and ulna, and a phalanx, all rather eroded, quite possibly from one animal, a sheep of Soay size.

From Phase 9, there are three loose sheep teeth, a radius, metacarpal and phalanx, all of a size consistent with Soay sheep; one vertebra from a seal pup; and a fragment of bird bone. The seal bone is from a carcase 'cached' in the winter of 1988/9 in the building by a visiting naturalist. The sheep bones from this phase are almost certainly from Soays which have died in the structure since 1932.

Apart from the seal bone, there are no bones from mammals other than sheep. None of the sheep bones from the earlier phases would be incompatible with Soay sheep, so it seems unlikely that any of them are from the 'improved' breed which the islanders had from the late 19th century.

4:4:3 Marine Molluscs

Very few shells were found. They are all limpets, comprising one complete shell, three apices and four fragments. The complete shell came from Phase 2 in Area 5; an apex was found in Phase 7, Area 4; and the remainder were spread through both areas in Phase 9.

4:4:4 Fungi

A mature example of a puffball (*Bovista nigrescens*) was found in Area 5, Phase 6. It was 39mm in diameter, with a globular body and dark brown inner layer. It still contained part of the purplish-black spore mass. It is a type normally found on open grassland in autumn, though old examples can be found at any time of the year. *Bovista* is also to be found on Mullach Sgar.

4.5 Discussion

Kiln drying of grain on St Kilda is first mentioned by Martin Martin in 1697, when he said that 'They have only one common kiln, which serves them all by turns, as the lots fall to their share; he whose lot happens to be last does not resent it at all' (Martin 1753, 53). There is no evidence that the excavated kiln is this 17th-century example. Dating evidence is limited, but the coarse pottery and crockery suggest a 19th-century date, and there are also similarities between the land drains and the clay floor of the kiln barn with those found during the excavation of the blackhouse underlying House 8. That dwelling dates from the 1830s. The only potentially early items from the site are the seven stone tools, found in Phases 2, 4 and 6 (sfs 38, 47, 49, 50, 55, 57, 62). They could have been found while preparing the ground for the kiln, or could have been taken from elsewhere and re-used at the site. Similar items have been found on Hirta, in the souterrain, and elsewhere in northern Scotland on prehistoric sites.

Rev. Neil Mackenzie, who was minister on the island from 1829–43, referred to a communal kiln in use (Mackenzie 1911, 9), but does not specifically say that it was built during the period of his ministry, though this may be an oversight. The kiln was also referred to by Wilson in 1842, when it was still clearly in use (Wilson 1842, 2).

When Sharbau mapped the village in 1858 and 1860 his plan showed no kiln on the site, or Blackhouse W. This does not, however, mean that they were not there at that time. The site was then part of a broad swathe of ground marked by Sharbau as 'Common Property (Two families gone to Australia)' (SRO 1858/1860 RHP 6778). This strip is devoid of dwellings apart from one structure close to the boundary with the glebe land. This was occupied by Roderick Gillies. Three cleitean were also used by Norman Gillies and Finlay Ferguson. The 1851 census enumerators returns, prior to the emigration, begins its listing of heads of household with Roderick Gillies, and follows with Finlay Ferguson, Mary MacCrimmon, Effy MacCrimmon, Roderick MacDonald, John MacDonald, Lachlan MacKinnon, etc. Finlay Ferguson, John MacDonald and Lachlan MacKinnon are, however, shown on Sharbau's plan as living west of the Dry Burn. Roderick MacDonald did leave for Australia, though he and his wife died of diarrhoea after measles on the emigrant ship in November 1852. This leaves Mary and Effy MacCrimmon apparently living in this area, plus another family who emigrated in 1852. Mary was born in 1775, was a widow by 1851, and had died by 1861. Effy (Euphemia) was born in 1779 or 1780, and was also a widow by 1851. She was renowned as a poetess and was still alive, aged 82, in 1861. The other families who emigrated were headed by Catherine MacDonald, two Finlay MacQueens, Malcolm Ferguson, Hector Ferguson, Donald MacCrimmon and Mary Morrison.

A photograph of the east end of the village, taken about 1878 for Valentines of Dundee, shows what appears to be the thatched roof of Blackhouse W, and an area of rubble behind it, which must be the remains of the kiln (Stell and Harman 1988, 10, pl. B). The thatched building is also shown in a photograph taken for the George Washington Wilson studio in 1886, and it would appear that it was the building sketched by Norman Heathcote during his visit to St Kilda either in 1898 or 1899 (Heathcote 1900, 57). The sketch shows it thatched, and with a wooden door in place. A woman is shown standing near it, ladling something into, or from, a large cauldron, of the type often used for dye. It is not possible to tell whether the building was at that time being used as a dwelling. Clearly though, it had continued to be used after the death of Euphemia MacCrimmon. The archaeological remains suggest that it became a byre, possibly with the laying of the rough stone floor, and the use of the slurry hole in the south wall. Fragments of a muck fork were found in the channel.

In the 16th century, Munro said that St Kilda was 'abundant in corne and gressing' (Munro 1818, 142). Later sources indicate that barley and oats were the chief white crops grown. The barley, the hardiest of the cereal grains, was of the bere variety (*Hordeum vulgare*), and the oats seem to be the black form (*Avena sativa*). Martin, in 1697, noted that the grain was sown thickly, and produced a 16 to 20 fold yield (Martin 1753, 18), and Macaulay records that 'fifty bolls of . . . [barley] . . ., old Highland measure, are every year brought from there [St Kilda] to Harris, and all the western islands hardly produce anything so good of this kind' (Macaulay 1765, 35). Neither barley nor oats contain gluten from which bread could be produced, but they are both high in carbohydrates, with quantities of protein, calcium, and some vitamin B. Porridge, consequently, was an important part of the diet. The factor reported in 1898 that each person consumed on average 120lb of oatmeal per year, 28% more than most other Hebrideans (Kearton 1897, 9). Porridge was normally served at breakfast and supper. Oat cakes were also made.

By the 1820s it is clear that barley was the principal crop, and of fine quality, though the oats received little attention (MacCulloch 1824, 181). Planting continued to be done thickly, but by the 1870s there was a marked decline in the crop yields. MacDiarmid said of the land that 'with all this fine fertile appearance, the return it gives is miserable' (MacDiarmid 1878, 242). He noted that within living memory the returns for bere were double or treble what they were in 1878, and the oat crop was never more than 2½ times the quantity of the seed sown.

The stripping of turf for fuel, bad planting and cropping practices, and poor-quality seed saw agriculture on St Kilda continue to decline. By about 1890 the grain and straw from both white crops was being used for cattle fodder, as the islanders increasingly relied on imported flour; and in many other parts of the Hebrides there was a general decline in cereal production (Cameron 1986, 109). At the same time Ross said of the St Kildans that: 'Formerly they made meal of their grain but they say it is not worth making meal for all they have now, and no wonder, that is the justice the land is getting. It will very soon grow nothing but weeds under the same management' (Ross *c*. 1890). His prophesy proved correct; in 1928, only two years before the Evacuation, it was said 'only small patches, about two acres in all, are sown with potatoes and corn. The rest is so neglected that it chiefly grows docken and bracken' (Mathieson 1928b, 69).

The St Kildans prepared the ground for planting in March, and manured with dung, straw, household soot and ashes, urine, and bird carcases. Occasionally some seaweed was used (MacDiarmid 1878, 243), and in 1860–61 imported guano was spread on the fields (Seton 1878, 122). There was a tendency, perhaps only in later years, for the barley to receive more manuring than the oats. The seed was sown in early April. By June the plants were generally well on, and were pulled before September and the onset of the gales.

Although sickles were sometimes used, the normal method was to pull the plants up by the roots and leave them on the ground for a few days. This was a widespread practice, as farmers believed that sunshine, dew and rain mellowed barley and improved its colour. They were then tied into bundles ready for stack drying. Later the sheafs would be cut in two, the heads stacked for kiln drying and grinding, and the straw used for byre bedding and thatching material. Barley straw is soft and friable, while oat straw tends to be long and fine, and both are good for fodder, providing bulk roughage.

Where small quantities of dry grain were required for grinding, particularly at harvest time, the ears of corn would be cut from the stalks and graddaned. This involved setting fire to the attached straw, and drying the grain without actually burning it. When completed, the waste was removed and the grain ground in a quern, to be used for the harvesters' supper (Mackenzie 1911, 9). The meal was baked into cakes, and used for gruel and porridge (Sands 1878a, 190).

Some small-scale de-husking of barley was carried on at St Kilda using stone mortars. One is known to have stood outside House 8 (Mathieson 1928a, 131–2). It is a type known in Scotland as a 'knocking stone', and in northern England as a 'creeing trough'. The grain was placed in the mortar and beaten with a mallet. Water could then be introduced to float off the husk. Fenton records that, in the Northern Isles, kail and 'knocked corn' was a favourite supper dish (Fenton 1975), and in northern England crushed barley was often made into 'frumenty'. Mortars of this type were certainly in use from at least the 17th century, and continued to be used on certain English farms into the 19th century. A knocking stone was known to have been used at the Kirtomy kiln (Cheape 1984, 10).

The ears of corn were divided up into what was needed for seed corn, and that which was to be kiln-dried ready for grinding into meal. Kiln drying was necessary wherever and whenever the quota of sunshine was insufficient to dry the grain naturally. Consequently it was, and still is, practised in many parts of Britain; in the Western and Northern Isles, and also in the *sodnhús* of Faroe. In Scandinavia, grain drying is also carried out, with the kiln also being used for drying malt, flax and hemp. These *kjone,* in areas like Vestfold, Norway, tend to be two-storied wooden buildings, with a stone 'stove' on the ground floor, and the warm air rising to dry the grain laid on the upper floor (Norwegian Folkmuseum 1975, 23 and 35).

Kiln drying of grain has a long history. Scott suggests its use in prehistoric times, and gives Roman evidence (Scott 1951, 204–8). Post-Roman kilns have been found at Poundbury Camp, Dorset (Dorchester Excavation Committee 1973, 138), Victoria Street, Hereford (Rahtz 1971, 233) and Chester (Ward 1980, 219); with Norse evidence at Jarlshof, Shetland (Hamilton 1956, 190), Doarlish Cashen in the Isle of Man (Gelling 1971, 78–9) and Coileagan An Udail on North Uist (Crawford 1976, 176). By the 14th century, and a period of climatic deterioration, corn kilns, which had normally been a feature of the uplands, began to be found throughout much of Britain. An increasing number are being revealed by excavation, with examples at Back Silver Street, Durham (Clipson 1980, 110–12); Templars' Manor, Nuneaton, Warwickshire (Taylor 1972, 168); Grafton Regis (Mahany 1967, 202) and Wythemail (Hurst and Hurst 1971, 179) in Northamptonshire; Houndtor, Devon

(Beresford 1979, 140); Widows Tenement, Lundy (Gardner 1968, 302); and Streatham in Sussex (Hamilton 1966, 204). Kilns of the same period have also been uncovered in Ireland, at Kilferagh, Co. Kilkenny (Hurley 1983, 218), and at South Quay, Drogheda, Co. Louth (Campbell 1984, 256). Fifteenth-century examples have been found in towns, like Northampton (Williams 1979, 97), but they also occur in the uplands, like the field kiln at Collfryn, Llansantffraid Deuddwr, Powys (Britnell 1984). Seventeenth to eighteenth-century kilns again occur in upland areas, like that found at Belling Mill, Northumberland (Harbottle 1974, 135). Other late kilns have been found by fieldwork in mainland Scotland, the Northern and Western Isles, and northern England (Ramm *et al.* 1970, 84).

There is some variation in the forms of corn-drying kiln, but essentially two main types are found — the kiln with, or without, an associated room. The room may be simply a small loading area, or it may be a complete barn with threshing floor.

The first group are simple kilns, often dug into a bank or constructed in an hour-glass-shaped pit comprising a bowl with a long projecting flue, at the end of which is a stoking area. They may or may not have had a temporary cover. Medieval examples of this basic form have been excavated at Abercairny in Perthshire (12th century), and Capo in Kincardineshire (13th century — Fig. 79) (Gibson 1989, 226); Beere in Devon (Jope 1958, 123–4); and Wharram Percy in Yorkshire (Milne 1979, 272–3). Other kilns of this form have been found in parts of mainland Scotland — at Chapelton (Fig. 79) in the Lunan valley in Angus (Pollock 1987, 363–8); the Dairy Park (Fig. 79) at Dunrobin, Sutherland (Close-Brooks 1981, 336–8); Barbush Quarry (Fig. 79), Dunblane, Perthshire (Barclay *et al.* 1982); Glenvoidean (Fig. 79) in Bute (Marshall and Taylor 1979, 18–20); Braleckan (Fig. 80) in Argyll (Grant *et al.* 1983, 155); and, in Wales, Collfryn (Fig. 80) in Powys (Britnell 1984, 191). They have also been noted at Uragaig, Colonsay; Lussagiven and the Ardlussa area of Jura (Mercer 1972, 34); and Machrins (Fig. 80), on Colonsay (Ritchie 1981).

Kilns with integral small loading areas are known from Allt a' Bhurg (Fig. 81) in Caithness, where the kiln has been cut into an isolated bankside; on the promontory site at Poll Gorm, in the same county; at Rosal (Fig. 81), in Strath Naver, Sutherland (Fairhurst 1969, 151–2); and Port Henderson (Fig. 81), in Wester Ross (SSS BV 29d3 6423). In the Hebrides, kilns with small rooms have been found at Mannel, Tiree (RCAHMS 1980, 245); Eilean An Naoimh and Garbh Eileach on the Garvellachs (Mercer 1972, 27); and Fiola Meadhonach on Lunga (Mercer 1972, 30). On the Isle of Man, examples have been reported from the Sulby Glen, at Forrester's Lodge (Fig. 81) and Close (Cubbon and Megaw 1969; Emery 1985, 4–5).

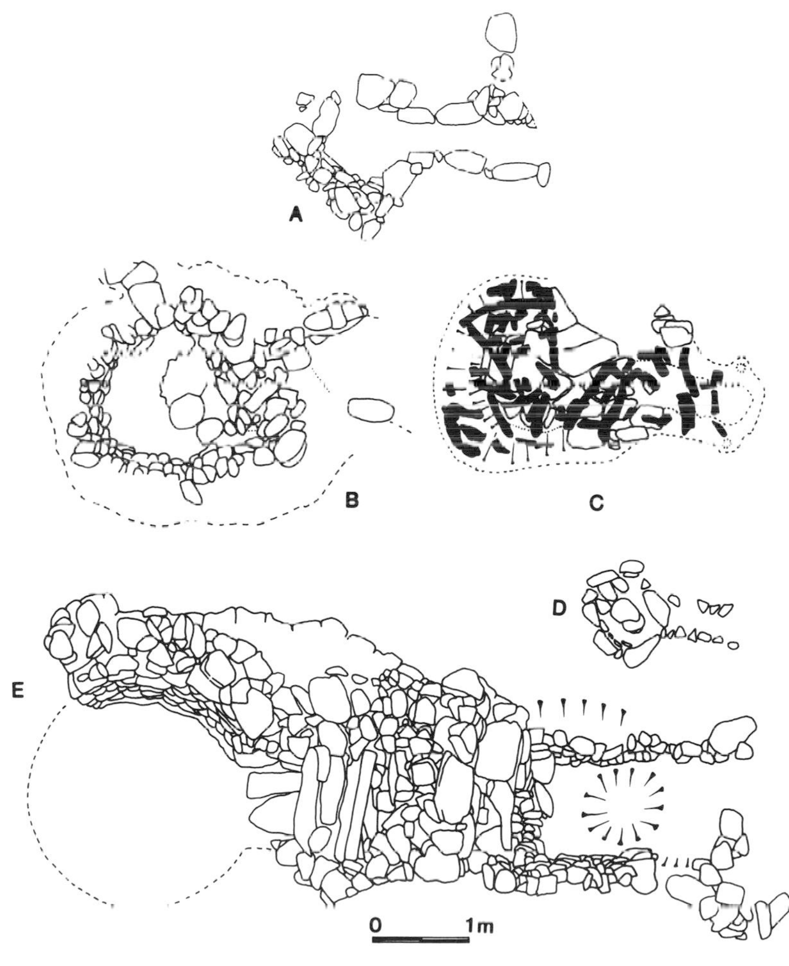

FIG. 79

Corn-drying kilns: A — Dairy Park, Dunrobin, Sutherland (after Close-Brooks 1981); B — Chapelton, Angus (after Pollock 1987); C – Capo, Kincardineshire (after Gibson 1989); D — Glenvoidean, Bute (after Marshall and Taylor 1979); E — Barbush Quarry, Perthshire (after Barclay et al. *1982)*

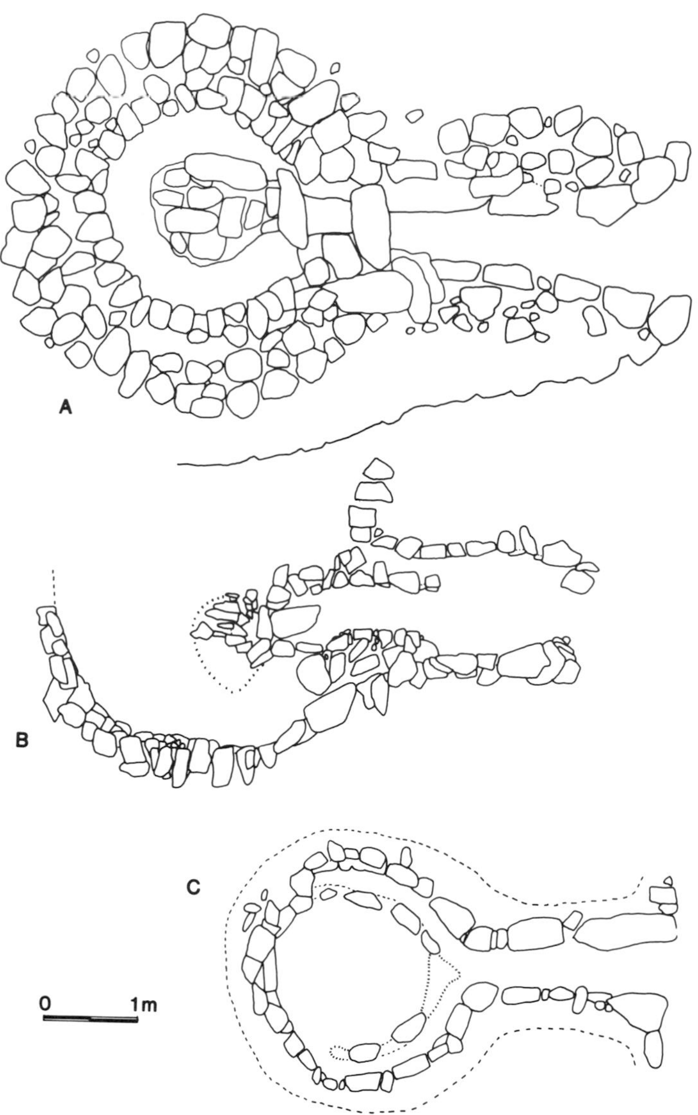

FIG. 80
Corn-drying kilns: A — Braleckan, Argyll (after Grant et al. *1983); B — Machrins, Colonsay (after Ritchie 1981); C — Collfryn, Powys (after Britnell 1984)*

Larger rooms — barns — have been located in the Hebrides, at South Galson, Lewis (Scott 1951, 200, 202); Peninerine (Fig. 82), on South Uist (Whitaker 1957); Griminish (Fig. 82), on North Uist (Whitaker 1957, 165); Hougarry (Fig. 82), on North Uist (SSS BV 33d3 6462–3); Sollas and Heisker (Fig. 82), also on North Uist (M. Harman, pers. comm.). On the Scottish mainland there are others in the Balmavicar township in Kintyre (RCAHMS 1971, 195–6); and at Ardmaleish (Fig. 82) in Bute (Milligan 1963). The excavated remains on Hirta fit into this group of kilns with associated barns.

Excavations at Houndtor and Hutholes in Devon have revealed kiln-barns of the 13th century (Beresford 1979, 140–42). Here the top end again accommodates the built-up kiln area, but these have two kiln bowls within the structure. In Caithness, Orkney and southern Shetland, kilns can still be seen built onto the end of a substantial gabled barn. In the latter two counties they are roughly bottle-shaped. Examples are found at Skaill (Fig. 83) and Brough, Rousay, Orkney; Dunrossness (Pl. 22), Mousa (Pls 23–5), and Fair Isle, Shetland (Hunter 1984, 26). Although the round kiln is common in southern Shetland, four-sided forms were also used. Excavations at Kebister, on the south side of Dales Voe, Shetland, revealed a rectangular kiln (Fig. 83, Pl. 26), with a bowl and flue, inserted into a deserted 16th-century building. This was re-used in the 18th century, with the addition of a loading room, new flue and loading steps (Owen 1987, 30–31). A four-sided, late 19th-century kiln can still be seen in the barn of the deserted croft of Northside, Birsay, Orkney (Fig. 83). At Kebister the bowl was round, while at Northside it was rectangular.

The basic elements are found throughout the kilns — a fire-place, flue and drying area. In the Caithness, Orkney and southern Shetland kilns the drying area is enclosed. The drying floor is set well above ground level, and is loaded through a doorway reached by a few steps or foot-holes. In many Hebridean kilns, including the St Kilda kiln, the drying area was open, and at the Creag an Starraig kiln on Lewis, people could actually walk on top of the stone platform (MacDonald 1984, 147). Wilson said of the St Kilda kiln: 'It consisted of two dark apartments, one within and of considerably higher level than the other, and a hole runs from a corner of the lower floor under that of the upper, in which a man sits to tend the fire' (Wilson 1842, 2).

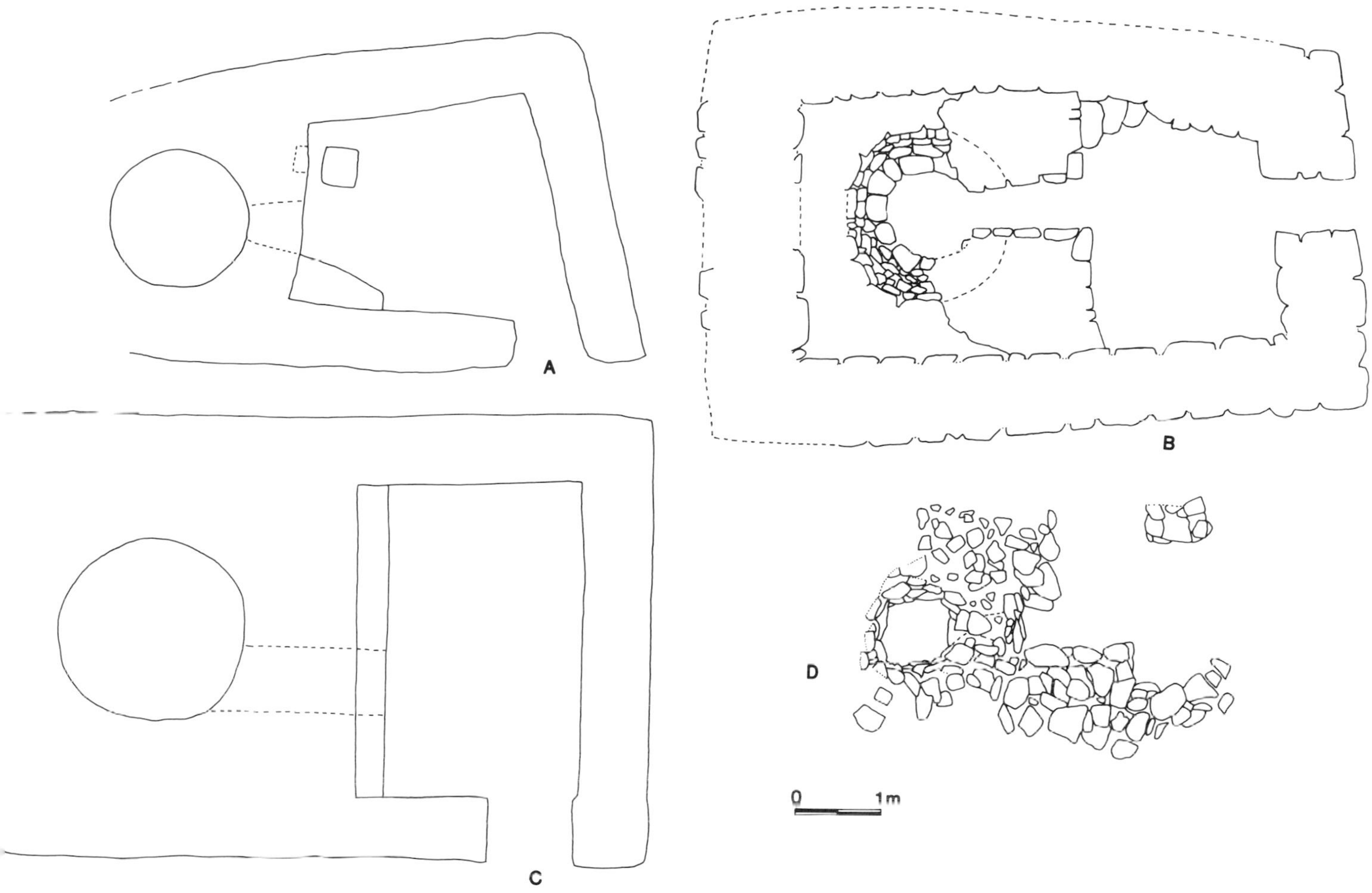

FIG. 81
Corn drying kilns: A — Allt a' Bhurg, Caithness; B — Forrester's Lodge, Isle of Man (after Cubbon and Megaw 1969); C — Port Henderson, Wester Ross (after SSS BV 29d3 6423); D — Rosal, Sutherland (after Fairhurst 1969)

PLATE 22
The bottle-shaped kiln and barn at Dunrossness, Shetland

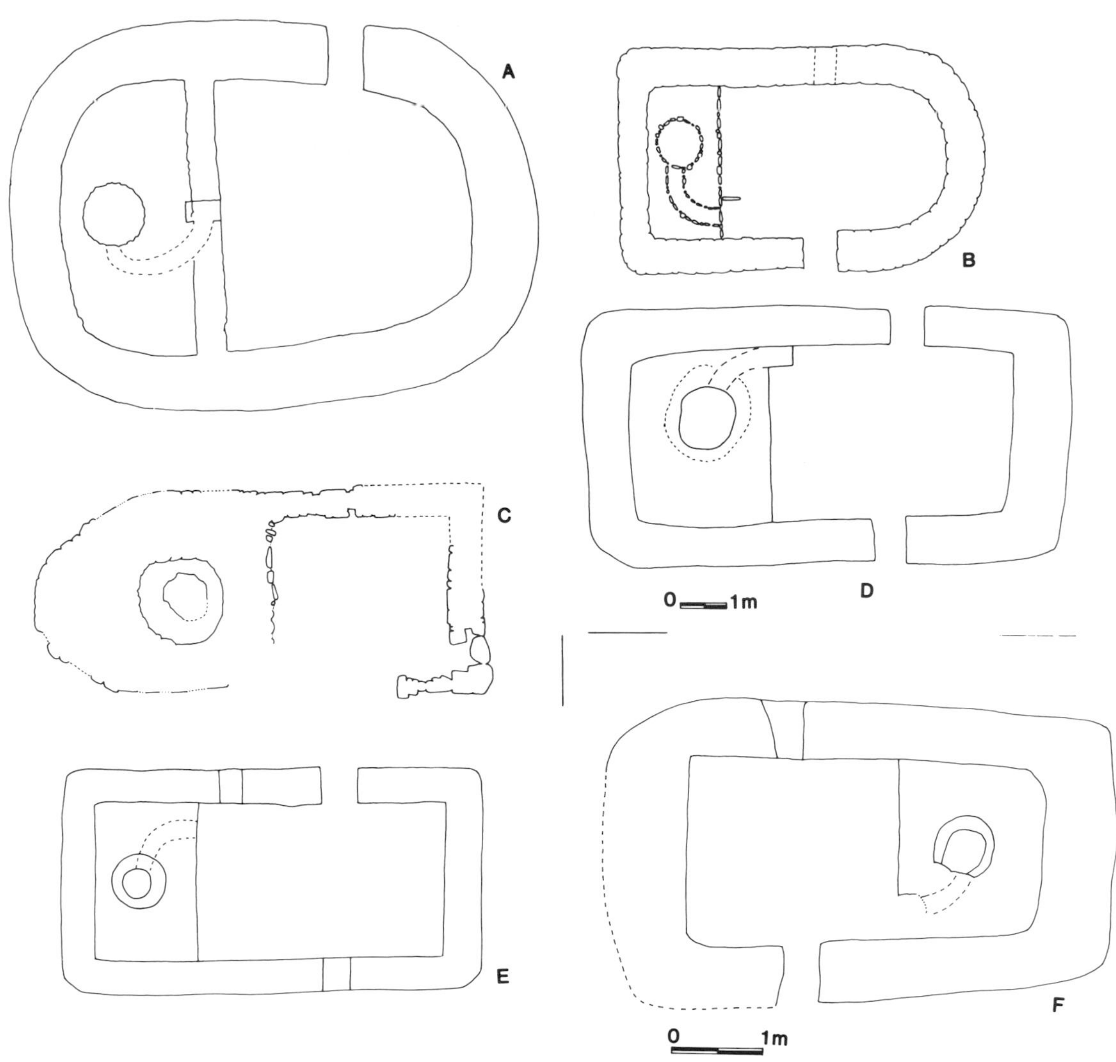

FIG. 82
Corn-drying kilns: A — Peninerine, South Uist (after Whitaker 1957); B — Griminish, North Uist (after Whitaker 1957); C — Ardmaleish, Bute (after Milligan 1963); D — Hougarry, North Uist (SSS BV 33d3 6462-3); E — Sollas, North Uist (M. Harman); F — Heisker (M. Harman)

In Lewis, a central beam was laid across the bowl, sometimes in line with the flue. In Scottish Gaelic it was known as a *maide suirn* or *druim suirn* (Whitaker 1957, 166), and was equivalent to the Sutherland *simearain* (Cheape 1984, 9); Shetland kiln *simmer* (Fenton 1978a, 381); Orcadian kiln *laece* (Firth 1974, 19); the kiln *kebbars* of Aberdeenshire (Gregor 1892–5, 125); Welsh *Marchbren odyn* (Britnell 1984, 193); and Irish *na taobhain* (Gailey 1970, 64). On this was laid sticks (Scottish Gaelic *ciuthlein slinnteach, stitigean*; Aberdeenshire *stickles*; Irish *beamabhac*) and a straw cover (Scottish Gaelic *cnodach*; Aberdeenshire *beddin*; Irish *sgri(o)bh*), cloth or even metal sheeting. This formed a surface for the grain. On St Kilda the cut ears were laid out to dry, though elsewhere it was usually just the grain. At Kirtomy kiln in Sutherland the load was 12–14 bushels of grain, laid in a circular pattern, while at Arnol in Lewis it was 3 bagfuls laid to a depth of around 300mm (Fenton 1978b, 44). At Abercairny, in Perthshire, the 11th-century charred cereal grain comprised 60% of lax 6-row hulled barley, *Hordeum vulgare* (syn *H. polystrichum*), and 40% oats either *Avena strigosa* or *A. fatua* (Gibson 1989, 227). At Capo in Kincardineshire, the 13th-century cereals consisted of 80% oats and 11% lax 6-row hulled barley (Gibson 1989, 228). At Chapelton kiln in Angus, the grain recovered in excavation was wheat (Pollock 1987, 367), while at Machrins, Argyll, barley (*Hordeum vulgare* L. Emend) and some oats (*Avena fatua* L. or *A. strigosa* Schreb) was extracted by flotation technique (Ritchie 1981, 528). Cheape has recorded oral testimony for the drying of bere barley first, before the laying of the oats, in Sutherland (Cheape 1984, 9).

The fire would either be lit at the start of a flue which was wholly contained within the platform or *sorn*, like the *munnhella* of Faroese kilns (Williamson 1948, 209), or at the end of a covered flue which projected beyond the *sorn*. The positioning of the flue could vary from kiln to kiln. On Hirta it entered the bowl from the south-east (i.e. from the right), as was the case at South Galson (Lewis); Heisker, Sollas and Hougarry (North Uist). Elsewhere, kiln flues entered from the left, as at Griminish (North Uist) and Creag an Starraig, Lewis. Alternatively, the flue ran straight in from the centre. This happened at Eilean An Naoimh and Fiola Meadhonach, Lunga. At Peninerine (South Uist) the flue curved from the central fire until it reached the bowl, and this happened to a lesser

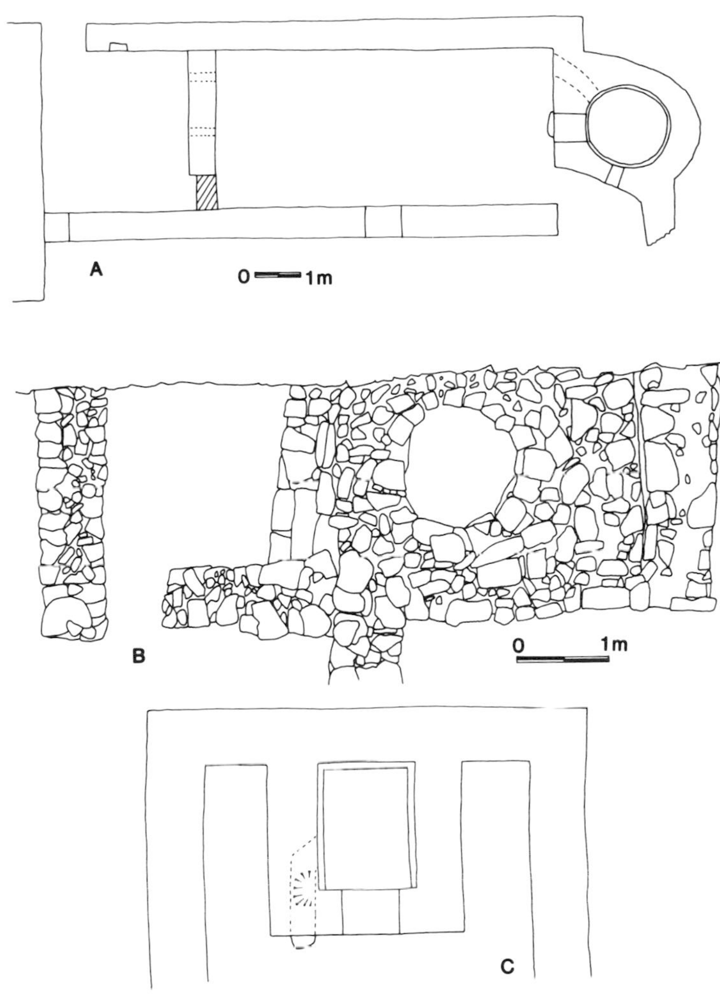

FIG. 83
Corn-drying kilns: A — Skaill, Rousay, Orkney; B — Kebister, Shetland (after Owen 1987); C — Northside, Orkney

PLATE 23
The internal face of a corn-drying kiln on Mousa, Shetland

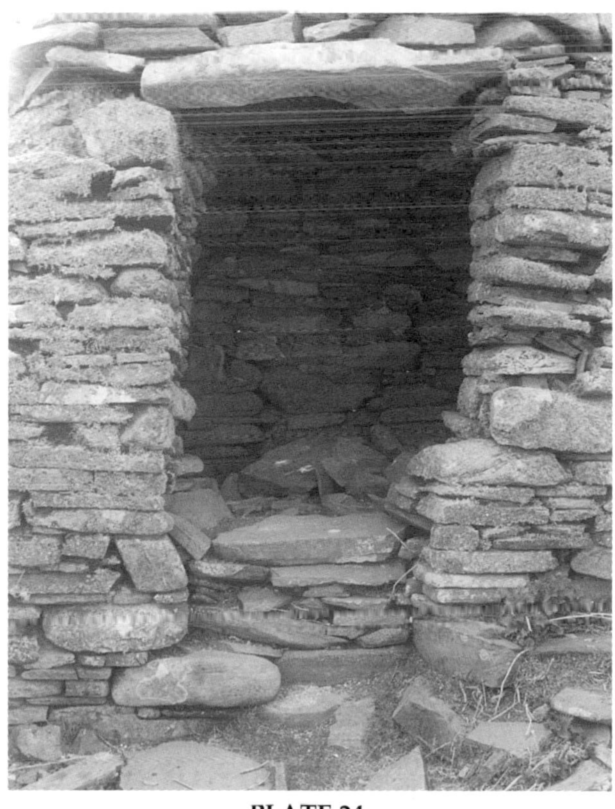

PLATE 24
The loading door of the Mousa kiln

PLATE 25
The capped flue of the Mousa kiln

extent at Garbh Eileach, The Garvellachs. The centrally placed fire area at the kiln face, with a direct flue leading to the bowl, was also used on the Isle of Man, where an example has been excavated at Forrester's Lodge, in the Sulby Glen (Cubbon and Megaw 1969, 113–14).

A drying — *cruadhachadh* or *tioradh* — took from 6 to 8 hours at Arnol, and there were often three dryings carried out in a day. At other kilns, like Creag an Starraig and Kirtomy, it was usually 12 hours for a drying; the grain being tested between the teeth.

Rev. Neil Mackenzie said that on St Kilda after drying 'they beat off the grain from the straw, and winnow it from the chaff in the breeze' (Mackenzie 1911, 9); and Wilson further notes that it was threshed on the lower floor (Wilson 1842, 2). These floors were generally of hard clay or beaten earth. In Orcadian kiln-barns there were often two opposing doors to allow a through draught for winnowing. On St Kilda, and at other Hebridean kilns, there was often only one door, and a hole or vent in the opposite wall (*feadan a' chathaidh*).

The threshed and winnowed grain was taken from the kiln on Hirta and stored ready for use, and would then be ground by means of a quern. If necessary, the stored grain could be further dried before use by placing it in a straw tub in which were placed heated stones (Mackenzie 1911, 10). This technique of drying was also used in the Northern Isles, and in Norway in the 19th century (Fenton 1982, 91). Pot drying was traditionally used by poor people in times of scarcity in Aberdeenshire (Gregor 1892–5, 125).

PLATE 26
The corn-drying kiln and loading area, Kebister, Shetland

CHAPTER 5

A Viscera/Rubbish Pit

5.1 Survey and Excavation Area (Figs 84–6)

A rubbish pit lying to the rear of House 7 and Blackhouse G was excavated in 1989–90, and designated as 'Area 6' (Fig. 84, Pl. 27). A contour survey was undertaken (Fig. 85), and the area within the pit and the immediate surrounding area was examined botanically before excavation. Species were plotted directly to indicate the approximate cover of each plant (Fig. 86). A detailed record was also made of a gridded one metre square area, where dominant species, ground-cover species, and other plants were recorded in each 200mm square.

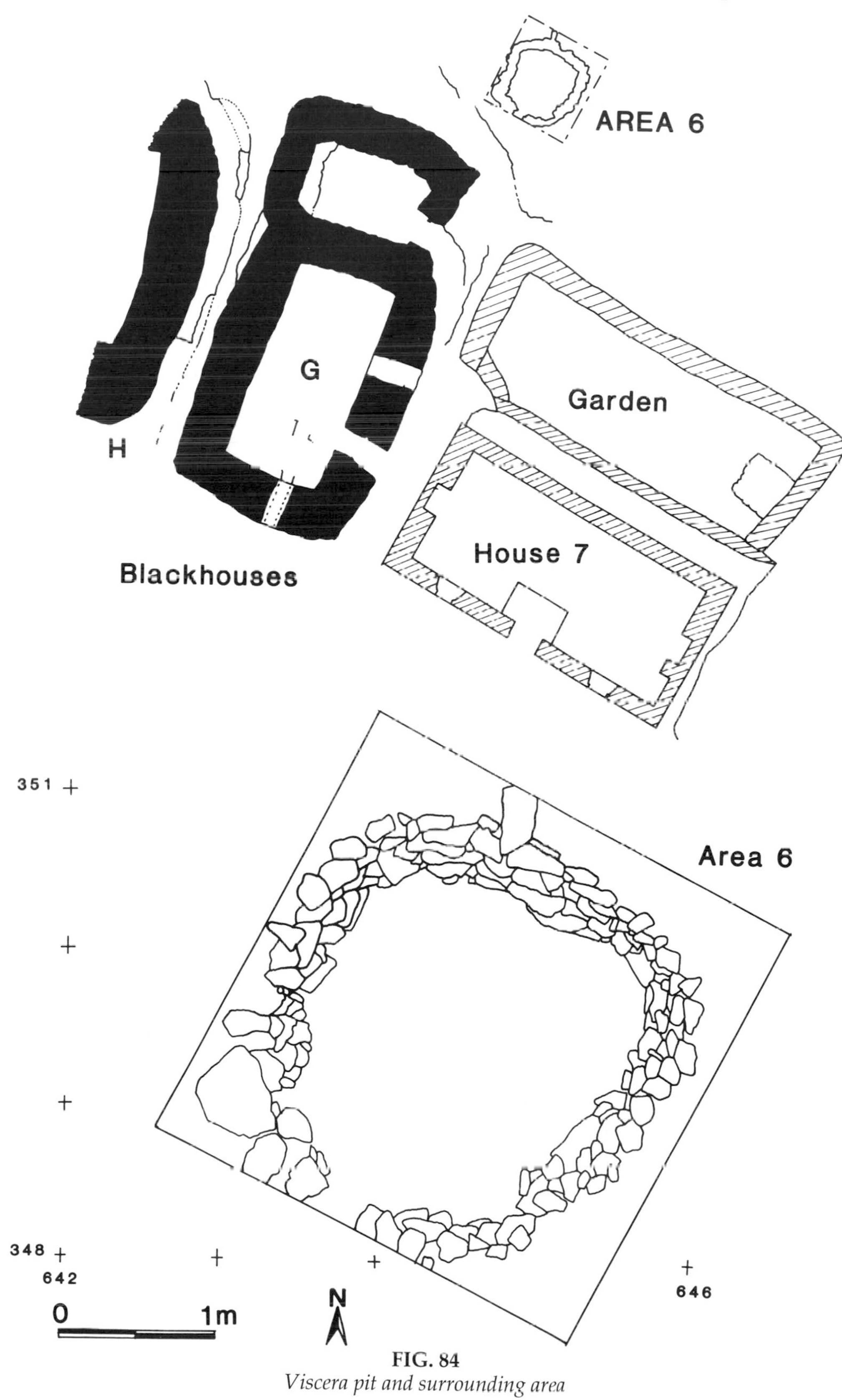

FIG. 84
Viscera pit and surrounding area

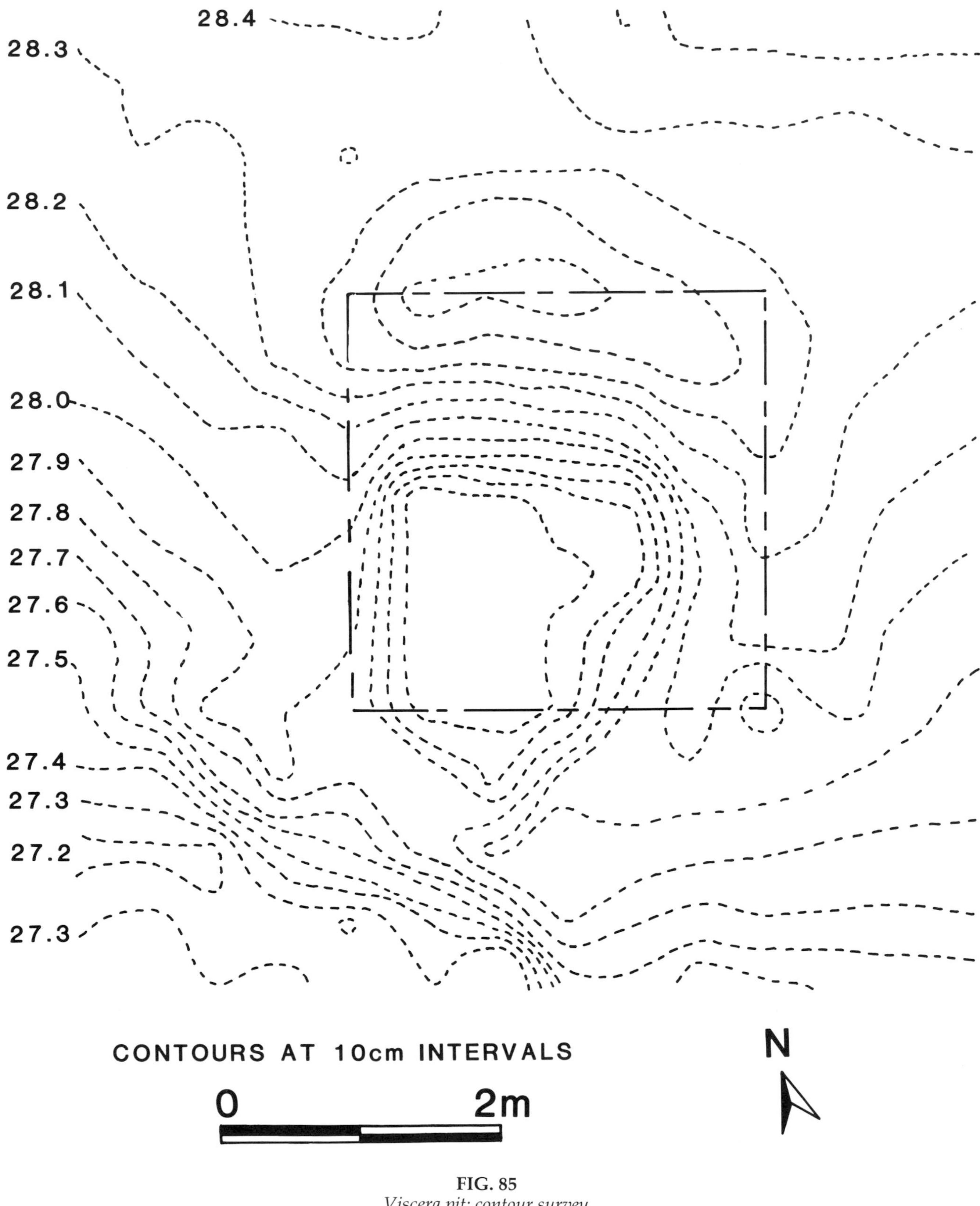

FIG. 85
Viscera pit: contour survey

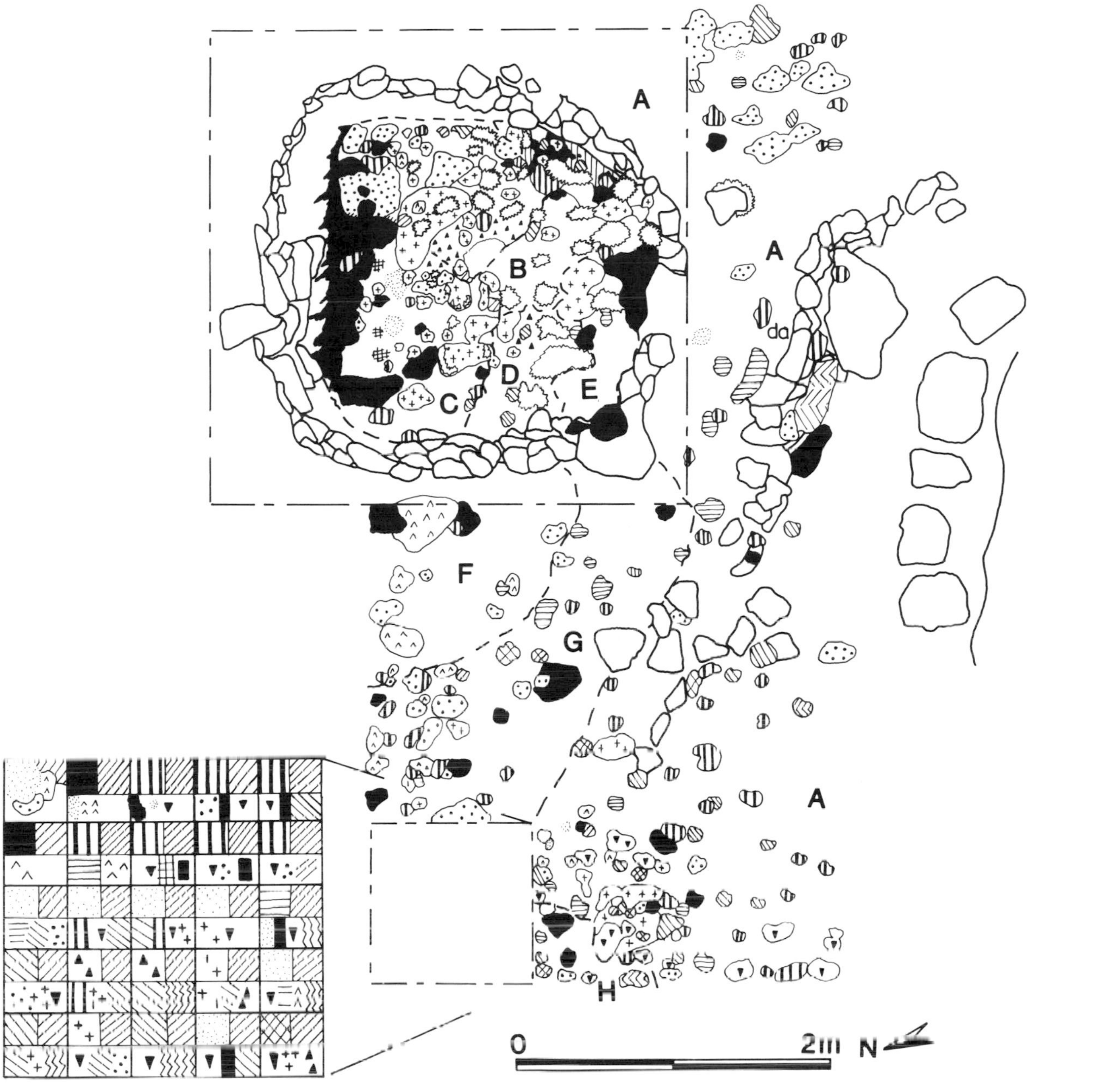

Dominant grass communities

A., D. *Anthoxanthum/Agrostis* B. *Agrostis/Poa annua/Deschampsia*
C. *Agrostis/Poa annua* E. *Agrostis tenuis* F. *Anthoxanthum odoratum*
G. *Holcus/Anthoxanthum* H. *Deschampsia flexuosa*

Species

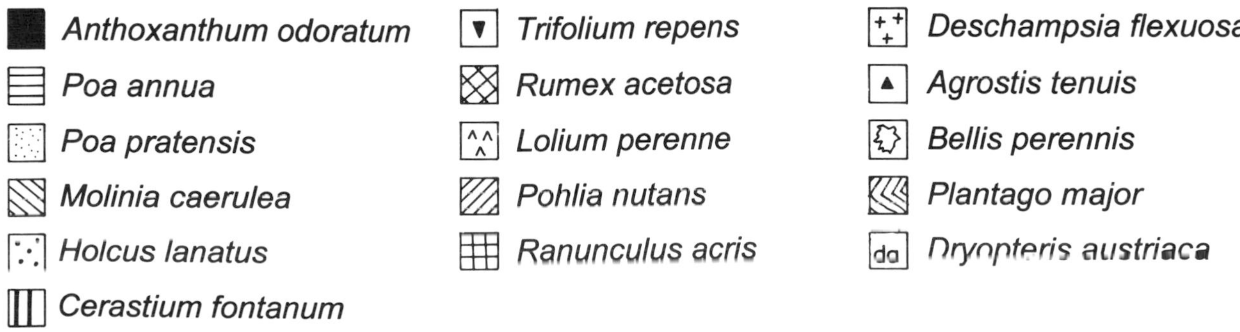

1 2 3 **Inset metre square survey**

1. Dominant species 2. Undercover 3. Other species

FIG. 86

Viscera pit: vegetation survey

PLATE 27
The viscera/rubbish pit before excavation, looking north

An area 3 x 3m was opened up, with work concentrating on the interior of the pit, and not extending beyond it. The stone facing of the pit was not removed.

5:2 The Vegetational Survey (S.J. Mason)

The pit (Fig. 86) is encircled by lush-growing flowering vernal grass *(Anthoxanthum odoratum),* whereas the centre appears to have been grazed quite heavily, and thus well trampled, hence a greater preponderance of daisy *(Bellis perennis),* which is disturbance tolerant. Similarly the vegetation around the stones of the pit structure is much lusher than that which is exposed. Within the pit *Agrostis* is found everywhere. *Deschampsia flexuosa* (wavy hair grass) appears where the area has been cropped more closely.

The pit appears to provide a wider range of habitat than the open ground, because of the complex of shelter, bare rock and underlying soil differences, and it seems that this is shown in relatively greater species diversity. Grazing is an important factor which will limit a species extent. The following is a short-list of habitat requirements for the grass species present:

Sweet vernal grass *(A. odoratum)*
Great variety of habitats; heaths, moor, hill-grassland, old pastures, meadows. At all moisture levels, from sands to clays. Not very palatable to stock.

Annual meadow grass *(P. annua)*
On cultivated and waste land; frequently in short grassland, paths, damp and dry places. Open and partial shade. Wide range of soil types. Abundant in shaded and closely mown turf.

Smooth meadow grass *(P. pratensis)*
Great variety of habitats; old meadows, pasture, waste land, walls and shaded places. Mainly on well-drained, sandy, gravelly and loamy soils.

Purple moor grass *(Molinia caerulea)*
Found in wet and damp peaty areas. Leaves are eaten by stock only when young.

Yorkshire fog *(Holcus lanatus)*
On sandy and peaty soils, dry places, moor and heath.

Common bent *(Agrostis tenuis)*
All habitats, under a range of soils.

Outside the pit lush vegetation is found, consisting primarily of *A. odoratum* and *H. lanatus.* Large amounts of chickweed are found within the perimeter area. There are bare areas of *Deschampsia*/clover, that appear to be heavily grazed. Some plantains are found in disturbed areas close to the path.

5:3 The Stratigraphic Sequence

Phase 1 (Fig. 87)

The southern sloping weathered bedrock (17) formed the primary surface on the site.

Phase 2 (Fig. 87)

Over the rock was a general deposit of gritty brown soil (16). Some charcoal flecks were found in the soil, and 23 fragments of coarse pottery (sfs 83–100, 104–5, 107–9); a piece of ?iron (sf. 101); a pebble flake (sf. 102); a piece of gneiss (sf. 103); and a fragment of granite (sf. 106) were recovered.

A hard crust or pan had formed at the top of this layer, possibly through dampness and the effects on the mineral salts in the soil.

Phase 3 (Fig. 87)

A rubbish pit was dug, and its sides lined with medium to very large granite fragments (13). It was sub-rectangular in shape, 2.14m north-south, and 1.94m east-west, with the facings sloping slightly out towards the top.

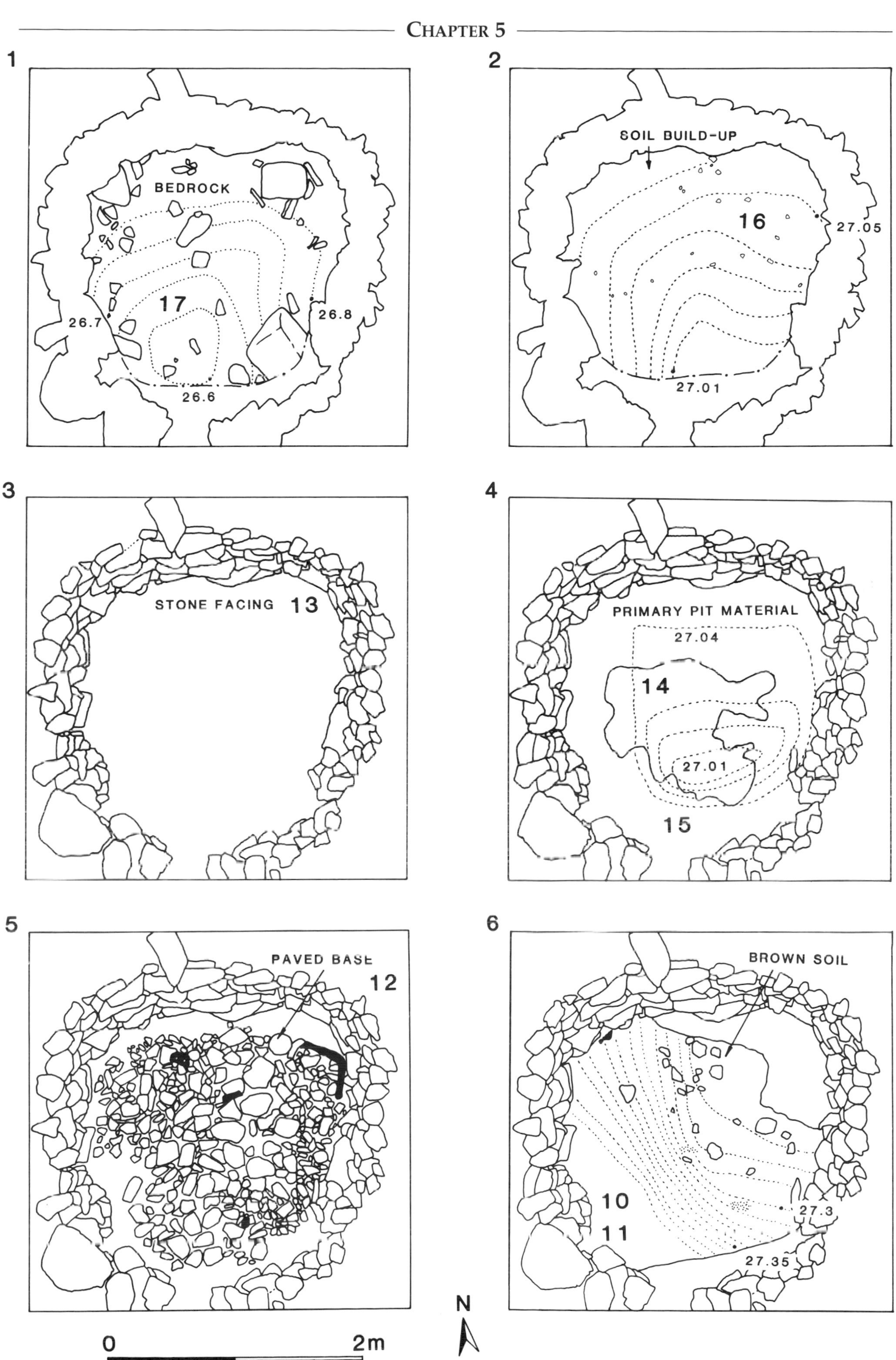

FIG. 87
Viscera pit: Phases 1–6

Phase 4 (Fig. 87)

Within the confines of the stone lining, and over the 'pan', was a deposit of brown gritty soil (15). Some bones, three small pieces of crockery, a fragment of glass, and a small quantity of coal and cinder were found. The layer was covered by a patch, roughly in the centre, of sticky dark brown soil (14). This material also produced small quantities of crockery, bone, coal, a piece of slate, and a club sauce-type stopper.

In part these layers were below the base of the stone lining, but it appeared that during its early use the pit had been cleaned out at various times, and the base partly re-cut.

Phase 5 (Fig. 87)

At a later stage, the base of the pit was paved with medium to large angular and sub-angular fragments of granite (12 — Pl. 28). A number of objects were located with the stones, but may well represent items from the lowest fill of the pit. They include four fragments of coarse pottery (sfs 71–2, 75, 82); stone tools (sfs 73, 79–81); flints (sfs 76, 78); a bone button (sf. 74); textile with copper alloy (sf. 77); and glass.

Phase 6 (Fig. 87)

Immediately over the paving was a layer of gritty brown soil (11), containing a tiny red bead (sf. 10), a bone button (sf. 70), small quantities of bone, coal, glass, iron, zinc roofing sheet, linoleum and organic material. It was covered by a similar, but mottled, brown soil with less grit (10). This produced textiles (sfs 8–9, 20–53), leather (sfs 29, 59–68), a papier-mâché button (sf. 11), a metal button (sf. 69), crockery, glass, iron, linoleum, tar, membrane, and synthetics.

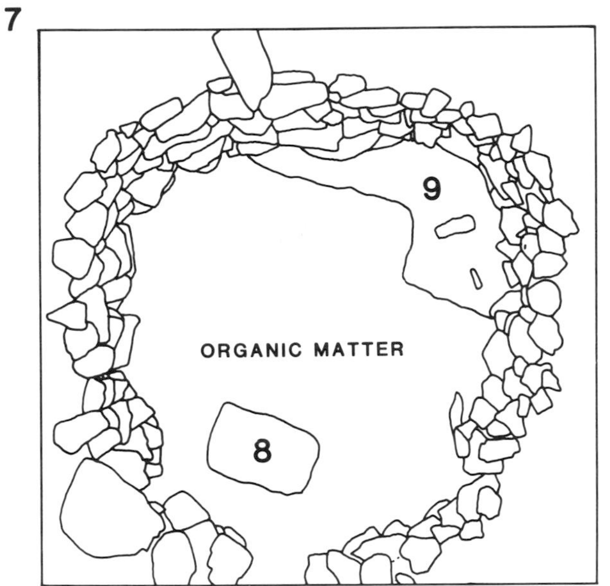

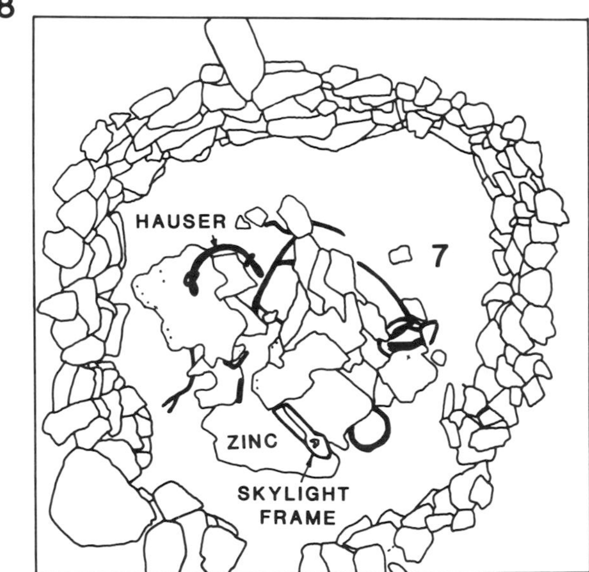

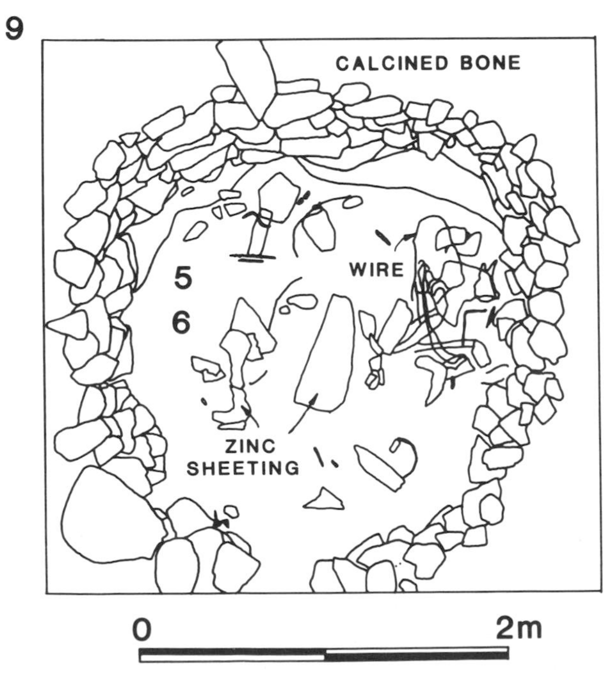

FIG. 88
Viscera pit: Phases 7–9

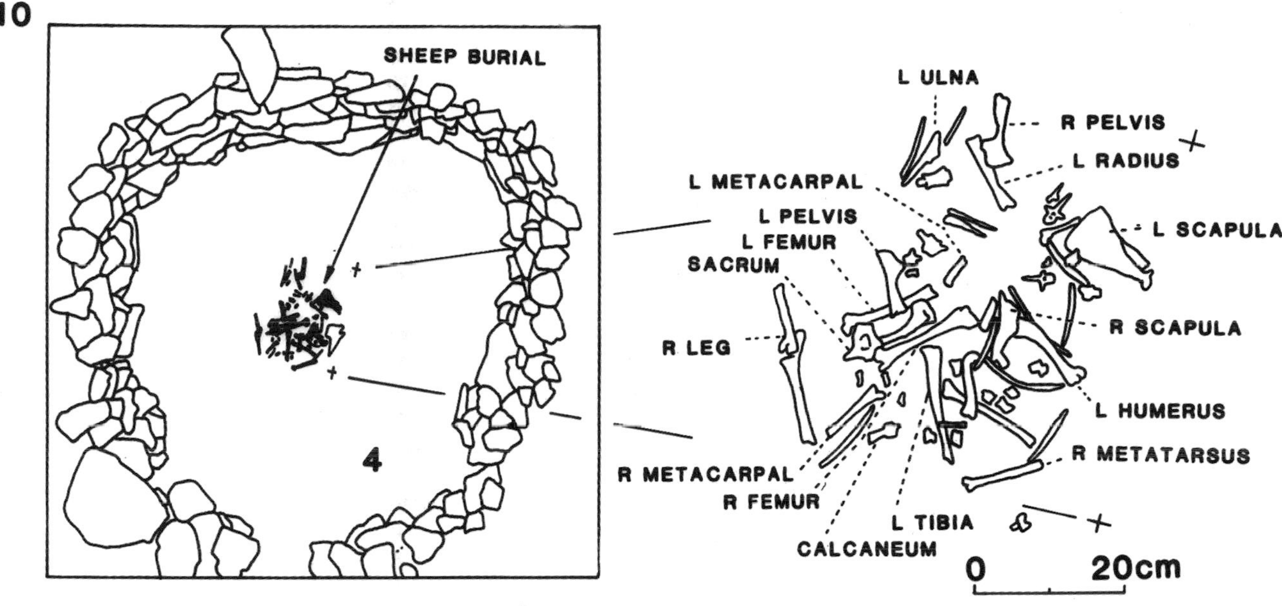

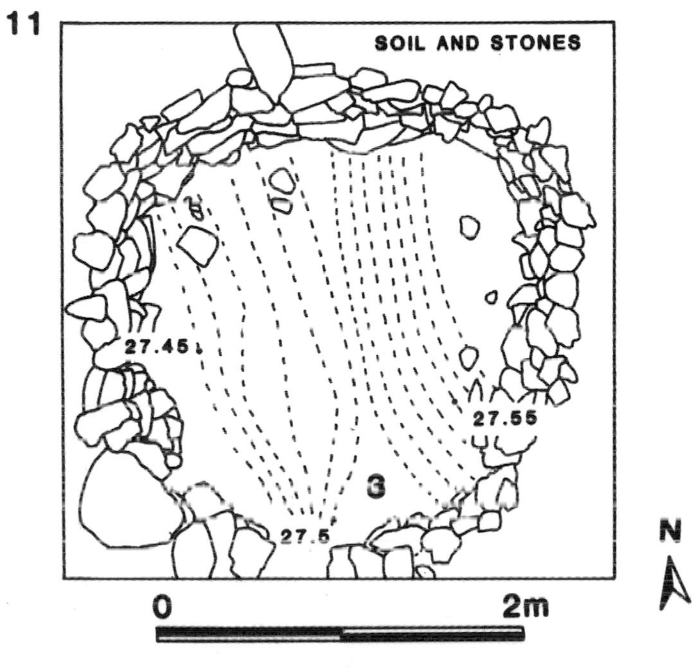

FIG. 89
Viscera pit: Phases 10–11

Phase 7 (Fig. 88)

More brown gritty soil (9) was found by the north-east edge of the pit. Also dumped into the pit was a rich organic deposit (8), probably byre litter. It contained matted straw, grass, scraps of textile (sfs 18–19), three strips of leather (sf. 58), ?cattle hair, insect remains, and seeds.

Phase 8 (Fig. 88)

The organic fill was covered by a later dump of cleared refuse (7 — Pl. 29), which included paint tins, a copper-alloy beaker, cap, a bulb, glass vessels, stoneware jars, a large quantity of iron (bands, straps, tubes, etc.), a small lamp burner (sf. 110), textiles (sfs 13–17), leather (sfs 56–7), linoleum, electric cable, and lead. Overlying this dump were several layers of scrap or folded zinc roof sheeting.

Phase 9 (Fig. 88)

Over the cleared rubbish was a brown soil (6) containing small amounts of glass, a collar stud, zinc sheet, lead, iron and pieces of textile (sf. 12).

It was used as a surface for the cremation of sheep carcases. Amongst the ash (5) was a metal sheep ear tag (sf. 7), and glass, copper wire and lead.

Phase 10 (Fig. 89)

At a later stage, a hollow was scooped into the underlying layer, and sheep bones were dumped into it (4). A lemon and white plastic ear tag (sf. 6) was also recovered.

Phase 11 (Fig. 89)

The bones were covered by a homogenous mixture of brown turf soil, small stones, and lumps of mortar (3). The disturbed finds from this cover include a Victorian

PLATE 29
A dump of refuse in the pit (Phase 8)

PLATE 28
The paved base of the pit (Phase 5)

penny (sf. 1), a bone button (sf. 2), three fragments of coarse pottery (sfs 3–5), glass, copper alloy, iron and zinc sheet. The area was finally covered by turf and topsoil (1, 2), in which were found three pieces of leather upper (sfs 54–5), glass, lead and chalk.

5:4 The Artefactual Evidence

5:4:1 Coarse Pottery (A. MacSween)

Thirty sherds of coarse pottery were recovered from Area 6 and, with one exception (sf. 83), a basal sherd, all are body fragments. The majority are small and abraded and show signs of secondary burning. The pottery is all undecorated, and there is no indication of any surface treatment.

From microscopic examination, the fabric appears very similar to that from the House 8 site, where thin-section analysis indicated local production. The proportions of large inclusions present in the sherds are so small that temper addition is not suspected.

The only sherd from which it is possible to suggest parallels is the basal sherd (sf. 83). It is possibly from a 'corrugated vessel' of the type associated with the blackhouse phase of the House 8 site.

Catalogue

Only the illustrated sherd is described. See Table 28 for summary details of the pottery found from this area. In the table the pottery has been grouped by the phase to which it relates. If a vessel comprising sherds from different phases is represented, it is included in the phase in which the majority of finds were made. If there were the same number of finds from each phase, the vessel is included with the earliest phase represented.

Phase 2 (context 16)

sf. 96. 1 body sherd. Grey with brown exterior surface. Fabric — hard; large quartz inclusions to 3mm diameter — natural. Exterior and interior sooted. Organic (grass) impressions on exterior and interior. Th. 8mm, wt 19g. Fig. 90.

Phase 2

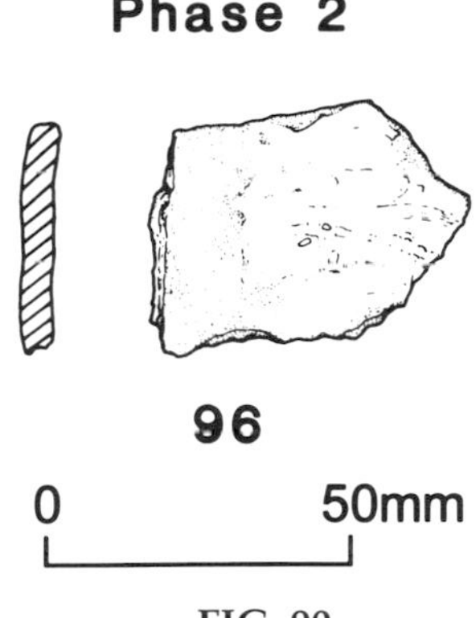

FIG. 90
Viscera pit: coarse pottery (Phase 2). Scale 1:2

5:4:2 Crockery (H. Kelly)

The assemblage displays one or two peculiarities. The first is the scarcity of slip-trailed red earthenware in the sample. The assemblages from the other excavated areas have contained a good deal of the sort of red earthenware usually associated with dairy work.

The second anomaly is the great scarcity of transfer-printed material from the area. What little there is seems to occur on china, and that is of the cheapest sort which was manufactured in Staffordshire in

FN	No.	F	M	T	R	BY	BS	D	S	FAB	MAN	SOOT
Phase 2												
83	1			*		c					cl	
84	1		*									
85	1		*									*
86	1			*								*
87	1											*
88	1		*									
89	2		*								cl	*
90	1			*							cl	*
91	1			*								*
93	3			*								*
94	1			*								*
95	1			*								*
96	1		*							or		*
97	1			*								*
98	1		*									*
99	1			12								
100	1		*									
104	1		*									*
107	1	*										*
Phase 5												
71	2			*							cl	
75	1		*									*
82	1			*								*

KEY

FN	–	finds number of catalogue entry
No.		number of sherds represented
F	=	fine; sherds less than 4mm thick
M	=	medium; sherds between 5–9mm thick
T	=	thick; sherds over 10mm thick
R	=	Rim type: p — plain; f — flattened; e — everted; i — inward sloping; o — outward sloping
BY	=	Body: g — globular; c — corrugated; s — straight sided; n — necked
BS	=	Base: pa — plain, angled; fa — footed, angled; pr — plain, rounded
D	=	Decoration: co — undecorated cordon; dc — decorated cordon; ca — carination; r — rilling
S	=	Surface finish: b — burnished; s — smoothed; p — perforated
FAB	=	Fabric: a percentage indicates the presence of organic tempering
MAN	=	Manufacture: cl — coil (type undetermined); n — N-shaped coil; u — U-shaped coil; sl — slab-built
SOOT	=	* indicates that either the exterior, interior, or both surfaces of a sherd are sooted

TABLE 28
Viscera pit: summary of coarse pottery

the second half of the 19th century, as an answer to cheap foreign imports. These sherds are quite useful for dating, since they almost certainly date from the fourth quarter of that century.

Some of the stoneware sherds look even later, for example the SCWS-marked (Scottish Co-operative Wholesale Society) sherds. These should date from the early 20th century, but they are less helpful than one would think from the name in fixing on a place of origin, since the Co-operative movement tended to have its pottery made wherever the prices were cheapest at the time and not necessarily in its own area, nor indeed from its own potteries.

The presence of the 'Grecian' pattern among the sponge-printed wares confirms this dating, but again is of little help in fixing on a provenance since the pattern was widely distributed amongst known makers and there is a large number of unknown makers to take into consideration. The light blue colour in the sponge-printing is undoubtedly from *c.* 1900.

Creamware was a type of body invented in England in the 18th century and brought to perfection by Wedgwood and, above all, by the Leeds Pottery. It was eventually manufactured widely in all parts of Britain where there were commercial potteries, including Glasgow. The (probably) one piece of creamware found is very atypical. It is so heavy as to lead one to suspect that the body has added inclusions to strengthen it. The mark was revealed by X-ray to be that of the Mehlem Pottery at Poppelesdorf, near Bonn, Germany, and the piece certainly dates from after 1836 when the pottery was founded. It could be the earliest piece in the collection. It is difficult to be dogmatic about this as the piece is so atypical, and most studies have been done on early creamware since this is the type most collected. The piece could represent a broken heirloom or a gift from the laird (who might even have been getting rid of a broken dinner service).

The fragments of Rockingham glazed teapots do not display enough characteristics to allow them to be identified, but their dating falls within the range of the pottery referred to above.

Some fireclay sherds look as if they came from drainpipes and could be evidence of some sort of drainage of the land.

Most of the sherds could have been made in Scotland from *c.* 1875 to *c.* 1910, but the red transfer-printed china is almost certainly from Staffordshire and would itself agree with this dating, since between 1880 and 1920 many of the Glasgow potteries closed down and sources would have had to be found elsewhere. The German creamware is almost certainly of an earlier date and must be accounted for as a 'treasure' that had been kept largely for display.

5:4:3 Glass

The glass from Area 6 has, where possible, been catalogued by type and function. They have been categorised as a bead, containers, closures, lighting, sheet glass, melted glass, and unidentified fragments and flakes. The containers have been further divided into bottles for alcohol and other beverages, pharmaceutical products, and jars. It should be noted again that although some containers may have been designed for a particular product, others could have taken a range of substances. While a vessel may have had its contents consumed on the island, it could then have been used to contain a number of substances or even objects. Equally, the vessel may have arrived at St Kilda empty, or containing a substance for which it was not originally designed.

Bead

Phase 6

sf. 10. Red standard cylindrical type, with a black core.

Bottles for alcohol and other beverages (69 items)

Three whisky bottles were found in Phases 8–9.

Phase 8

gf. 7/8. Complete round-sectioned dark green bottle with slightly indented base, embossed 'PETER DAWSON LTD DISTILLERS'. Rounded shoulder and lower half of body are decorated with pattern of moulded bosses and circular hollows; there is a two-part finish with bulging neck and string rim. Continuous mould lines run up sides and on top of lip, which originally took a cork. Machine-made. Fig. 93A.

gf. 7/8. Incomplete square clear glass bottle with embossed base 'WALKER'S/S/KILMARNOCK/WHISKY/26A'. Mould scars extend up to neck finish, with two-part finish containing a pierced cork. Exterior is blackened and tar-stained, with white paint on shoulder. Fig. 93B.

Phase 9

gf. 6/9. Complete round-sectioned light green bottle, having dished base with embossed central '2'. Mould seams run up side of bottle; there is a two-part applied finish with string rim. Faint traces of a parallel 'ghost' seam on body. Machine-made. Fig. 94A.

Dawson established a distillery at 82 Great Clyde Street, Glasgow, by the Custom House Quay, between 1878 and 1893. It operated throughout the 1920s, but had ceased business by 1931–2 (Slater and Co. 1893, ii, 316). The Walker's whisky bottle is of a type produced between 1950 and 1965, most probably in the latter part of that period (G. Burnet, United Distillers Co. Ltd, pers. comm.).

Three bottle fragments may have been used for carbonated drinks. One (gf. 3/11) is a highly embossed decorated body fragment, while the other two are from the upper half of bottles; gf. 7/8 having a champagne-form shoulder and neck, with blob top (Fig. 93C), while gf. 2/11 is a part of a blob top. Carbonated drinks took off after stamp duty was removed in 1833, and a variety of bottles were designed for it (Talbot 1974). In America the champagne shape was in use by the 1840s and '50s, but in Britain it seems to have appeared about 20 years later.

Sixty-three further fragments derived from bottles were also recovered from contexts 3, 5 and 7 — Phases 11, 9 and 8.

Pharmaceutical products (17 items)

Remains of six bottles were found which may have contained pharmaceutical preparations.

Phase 8

gf. 7/8. The most obvious is a complete 'flat', with mould lines running up to string rim of a two-part finish. Embossed with product label '"Anderson Gratton's"/"Embrocation"'. Fig. 93E.

gf. 7/8. Seven conjoining fragments of a bottle of basically ovoid shape with flat back, faceted sides, fluted shoulder-neck finish, and prescription lip. Facet embossed with '6', and base with the letters 'IXL'. Fig. 93F.

gf. 7/8. Indented base of small rectangular bottle with rounded corners. Embossed with a '2'.

gf. 7/8. Base of small rectangular bottle with rounded corners.

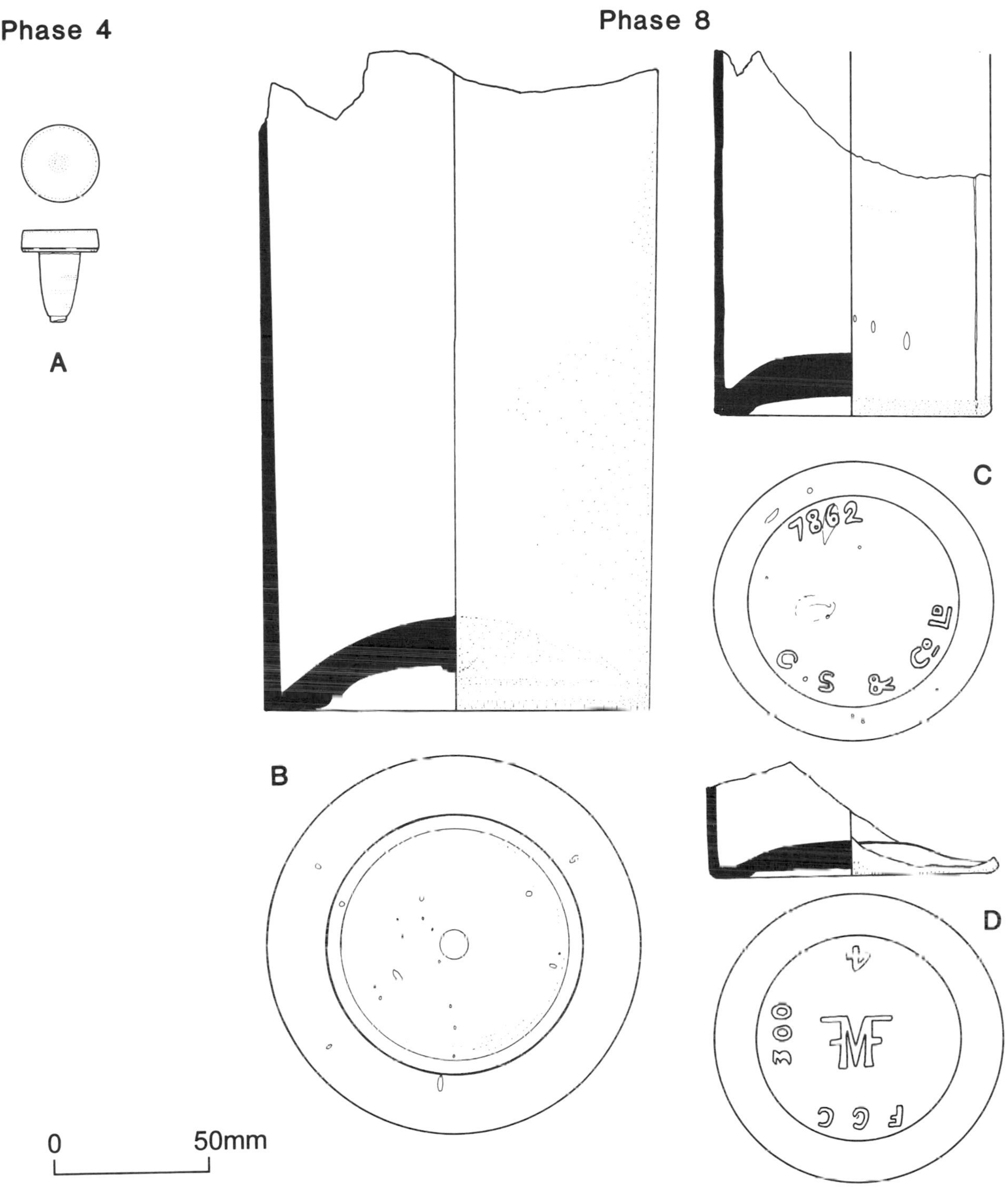

FIG. 91
Viscera pit: glass (Phase 4). Scale 1:2

Phase 9

gf. 5/9. Burnt fragment of thick white glass base of square bottle. Embossed on two sides '...'S' and '...s'. White glass, which was particularly popular from the 19th century, was produced by adding tin or zinc to the melt.

Phase 11

gf. 3/11. Fragment of a bottle with flat chamfered corners.

Fragments of tubes or phials, perhaps for small quantities of medicine or tablets, were recovered (gfs 10/6, 1/11). They were exceptionally fine, and extremely delicate.

Jars (54 items)

Two principal types were found — round and square-based. The former could be divided into those used for bottling, storage and preserving foods, and those normally containing products with a relatively limited shelf life. A third type was a more specialised form for a particular product.

Type 1: Round-based jars

Forty-one pieces belonged to this group.

Two conjoining fragments of the shoulder, neck and finish of a jar (gf. 7/8 — Fig. 92E) represent a

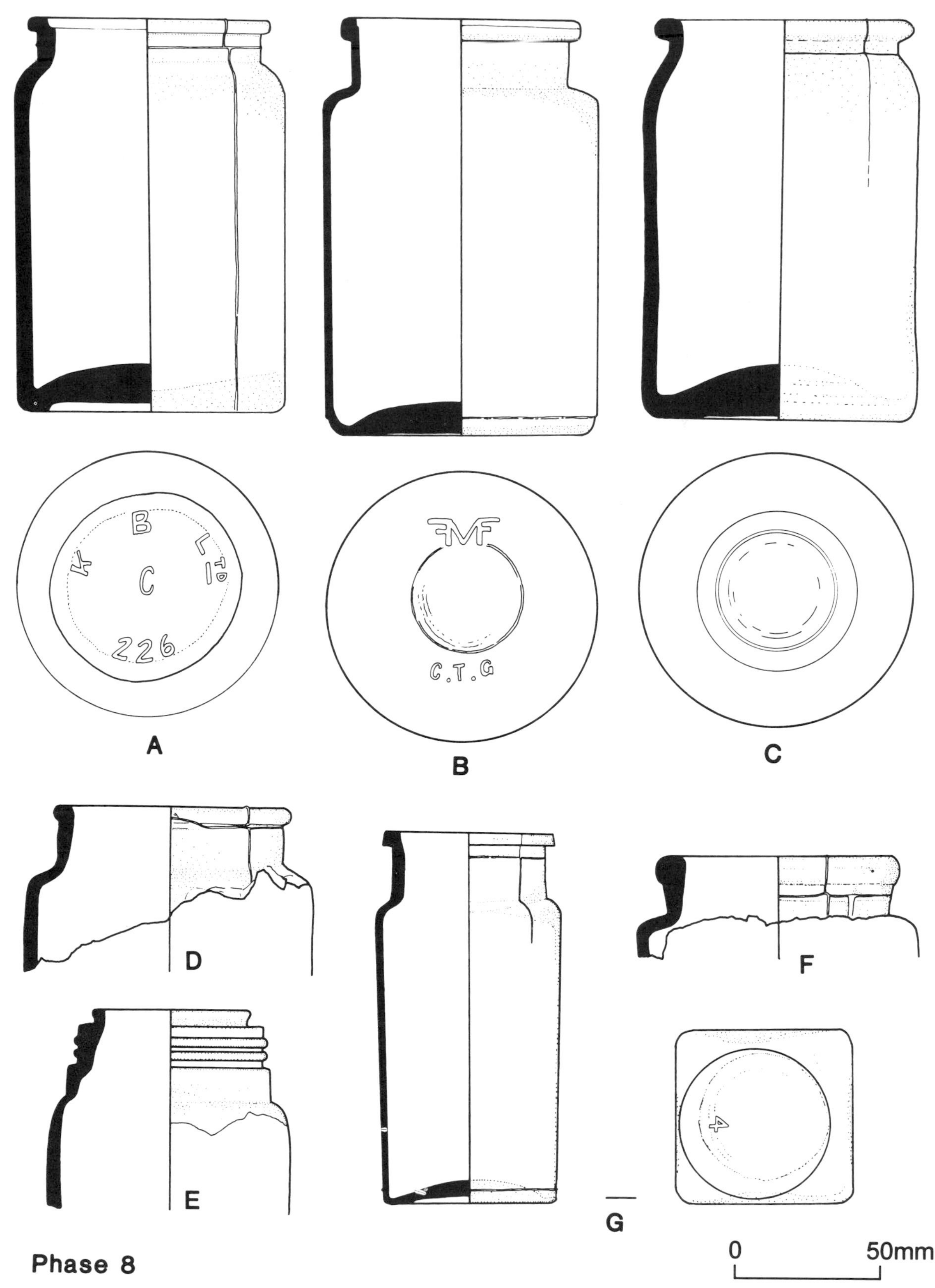

FIG. 92
Viscera pit: glass (Phase 8). Scale 1:2

distinctive form of vessel for storage of foods ranging from dry goods to bottled fruit. The fragments have an external screw thread and a seat designed to take a glass cap, secured in place with a metal screw band. The original design was patented by Mason in 1858, with a glass liner patented by Boyd in 1869. Several jar makers used variations, particularly the Kilners.

The jars, which were originally designed for preserves and pickles, range in diameter from 3⅗" (92mm) to 3¾" (95mm), though one huge, incomplete, vessel was 5" (127mm) in diameter (Fig. 91B). Generally the jars' height are from 4⅘" (120mm) to 5½"

FIG. 93
Viscera pit: glass (Phase 8). Scale 1:2

(140mm), with a capacity of around 20fl. oz (560ml). The glass is clear, sometimes with a slight copper-green hue. The bases have varying widths of resting point, and generally a shallow, flat push-up. The 5" jar has a dished push-up and mamelon. Embossed base marks include — 'K B Ltd/226/C' (Fig. 92A); 'C.S & Co Ld/7862' (Fig. 91C); '. . . C & S/P/180'; 'C.T.G' and an 'M' flanked by 'F's' (Fig. 92B); 'FCC/300/4' an 'M' flanked by 'F's' (Fig. 91D); and a triangle enclosing the numbers 628(?). The heel is usually low and rounded, sometimes with a horizontal mould line. The body sides are vertical, with short rounded, or sloped-down shoulders. The sides are marked by vertical mould scars extending to half the height of the neck. A horizontal scar separated it from the upper neck half and the finish (gf. 6/9 — Fig. 91D). The vertical mould lines continue up this part of the container, extending to the top of the lip. Sometimes a parallel scar is seen (gf. 7/8 — Fig. 92F). The lip itself is generally beaded, with varying flatness on top, and the excrescences produced by the mould on the lip top have either been left (Fig. 92D), or else have been polished off. One bore exhibits a seat for a disc or cap. These jars would all appear to have been machine-made.

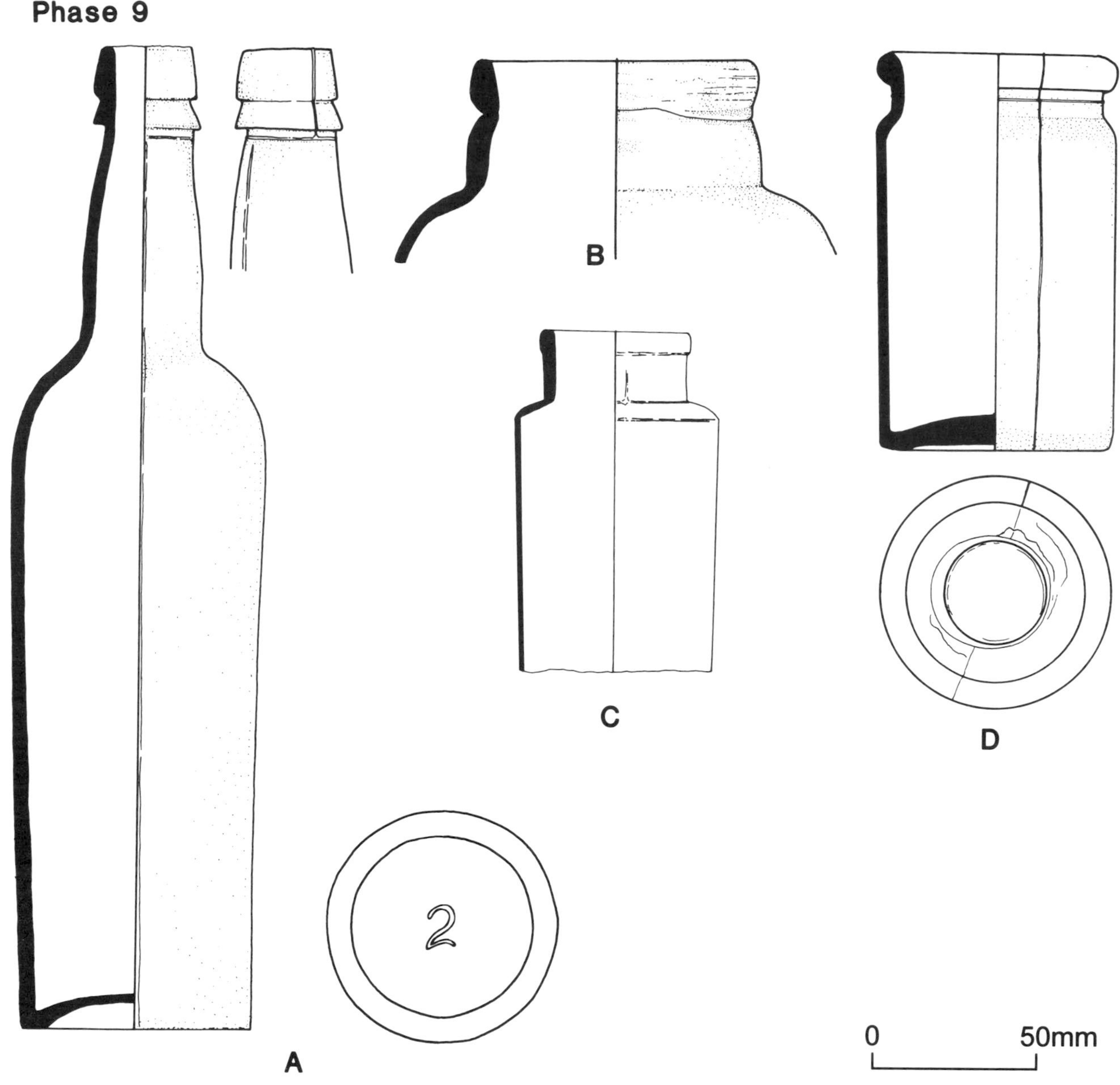

FIG. 94
Viscera pit: glass (Phase 9). Scale 1:2

One incomplete upper jar section, with a bulging neck (Fig. 94B), was discovered in thirteen fragments spread through contexts 6 and 7 (Phases 8 and 9). The neck has an applied lip, the molten glass having run slightly.

Type 2. Square jars
One square clear glass jar was found (gf. 7/8 — Fig. 92G), and was probably used for containing 10oz of preserves or pickles. Mould seams near two corners extend from the upper part of the body-shoulder to the lip top. The neck is vertical, with a flat-topped lip, and probably accommodated a metal cap with a rubber washer. The slightly dished base is scored with a circular scar enclosing an embossed '4'. Machine-made.

Type 3. Specialised jar form
This is a square-ended kidney-sectioned jar with an external screw thread, of the type used for 5oz of 'Very superior boiled assorted flavour sugar drops' (gf. 7/8 — Fig. 93D, Pl. 30). The curved body bears the embossed palm tree logo and lettering of 'TERRY YORK'. Terry's sold sweets in this type of jar from 1930–35, first at 9d and later at 8d (M. Pattison, Packaging Dept., Terry's of York, pers. comm.).

Closures
Two examples of stoppers were recovered: the top of a club sauce type, with a slight depression in the centre of the 1" (26mm) finial top (gf. 12/5); and a complete club sauce type, 1⅒" (29mm) high with a 1" (26mm) round flat finial (gf. 14/4 — Fig. 91A).

Lighting
Three fragments of very fine clear glass (gfs 12/5, 7/8, 3/11) may have been from light bulbs, lamp chimneys or, conceivably, glass phials.

Nineteen fragments of an incandescent domestic lamp (gf. 7/8) were also recovered. It comprises a

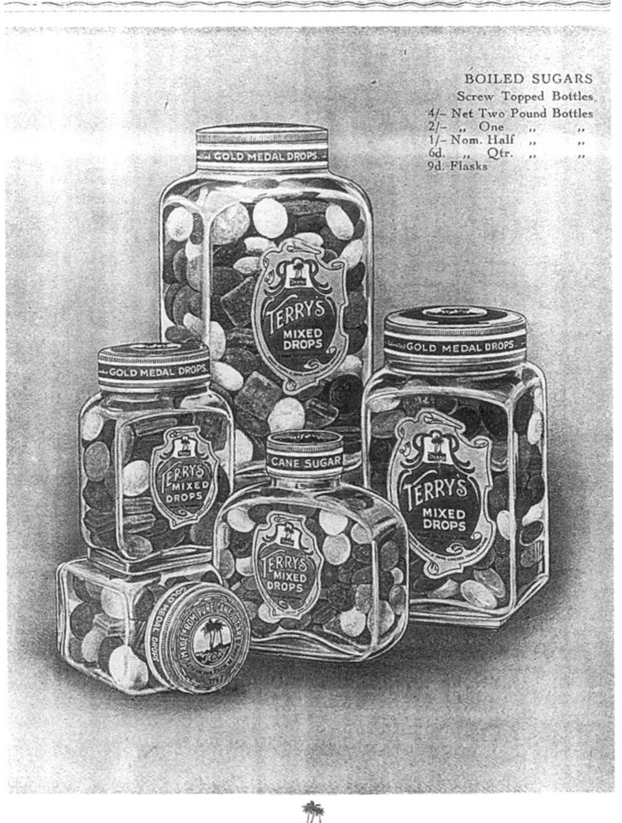

PLATE 30
Terry's advert for boiled sweets, with the excavated jar type (gf. 7/8) shown in the front centre (see also Fig. 93D)

bayonet type base with two metallic contacts; a glass foot with tall node; two wire supports, originally holding the filament, which is now lost; and the remains of the internally glazed glass bulb. Internal glazing and automatic production of bulbs began in the mid- to late 1920s. This bulb, however, must date from 1937 or later. Ht 111mm.

Two small incandescent lamps (gf. 2/11) are from a vehicle or electrical appliance. They both have a looped filament on two rods. The bulb is largely encased in a copper-alloy cap with a base band. There are traces of inked numbering, ?29/18, on the cap.

Sheet glass
Seventy-five fragments were found (1 in 11/6, 2 in 7/8, 27 in 2/11 and 45 in 3/11). The glass is clear, though sometimes having a slight green or turquoise hue. It ranges in thickness from 1mm to 4mm.

Melted glass
Eleven pieces of glass (gfs 7/8, 5/9, 6/9, 2/11, 3/11) exhibit distortion due to heat, resulting in alterations to colour, patination, stretching and twisting, and sometimes reduction to viscous lumps. The pieces had originally been clear and green glass vessels.

Unidentified
This group comprises 85 fragments and tiny flakes. Although eleven fragments probably come from bottles, it was not possible to categorise them more closely. The majority are body fragments, principally of clear glass, though a small number of flakes of light green and amber glass were recovered. Three pieces show remnants of decoration — an amber sherd with external boss decoration (gf. 2/11), and a ?bowl fragment in clear glass with an etched leaf design (gf. 3/11).

5:4:4 Coin

Phase 11

sf. 1. A penny of Victoria in very poor condition, with no graining and the reverse blank. It would appear to be a young head, apparently crowned, *c.* 1860–95.

5:4:5 Copper Alloy

Catalogue

Phase 7
gf. 9/7. Round-headed nail with tapering shank. L. 51mm (2").

Phase 8
sf. 110. Small vertical wick lamp burner, with ¾" (19mm) wick tube; perforated vapour plate; thumb wheel marked 'E M & Co'; decorative gallery on chimney seating; remnants of deflector. Fig. 95C.

gf. 7/8. Lightweight screw-top beaker, possibly from military water-bottle. Fig. 95B.

gf. 7/8. Flat-topped cap with central hole, milled edge, and three side slits for attachment, possibly from electrical appliance. Fig. 95A.

gf. 7/8. Insulated 2-strand cable, each strand comprising three copper wires.

Phase 9
gf. 5/9. Fifteen lengths of copper wire, where identifiable they are of 7-strand, either made up of single or multiple fine wires. ⅛" (3mm) wide.

gf. 6/9. Collar stud with bone setting; decorated, hinged, end plate. Stud shows traces of gilding. Fig. 95D.

Phase 11
gf. 3/11. 1" (26mm) boat rivet.

gf. 3/11. ¾" (20mm) small wood screw.

gf. 3/11. Seven lengths of wire cable, one clearly of 7 strand type.

5:4:6 Iron and Steel

A total of 829 items of iron were recovered from Phases 6–11.

Catalogue

Phase 6
Thirty items, comprising a corroded iron button (sf. 69), diam. 16mm, th. 6mm; a heavily corroded ring; nineteen nails (two cut, nine wire, one 'nail' with splayed ends — Fig. 96A, and seven corroded fragments); and eight indeterminate lumps.

Phase 7
One corroded nail shank.

Phase 8
A total of 240 items, comprising household fittings (4), part of a fanlight (1), containers (98), sheet metal fragments (85), fasteners and other connecting media (51), and an indeterminate lump were found in context 7.

The household fittings comprise part of a bedstead, including a pinned-together two-part angle, with a socket to take the leg; remnants of the side bars; a

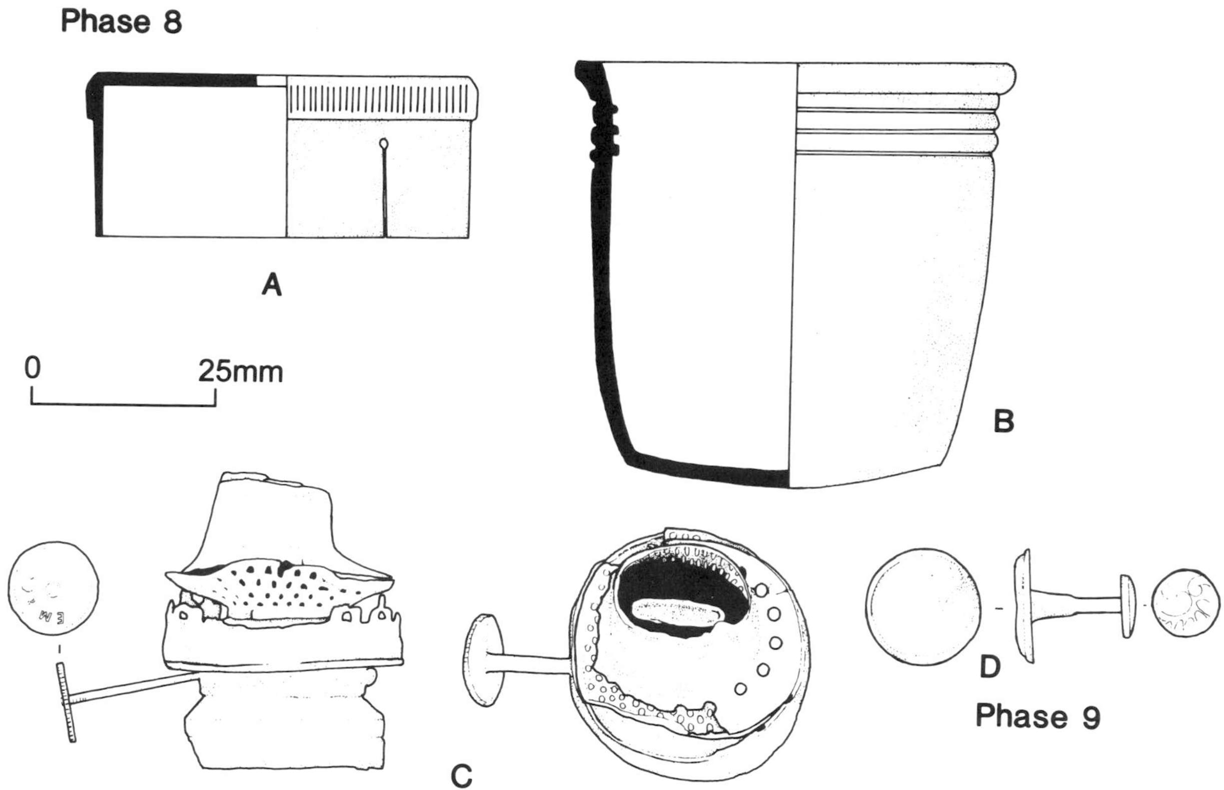

FIG. 95
Viscera pit: copper alloy (Phases 8–9). Scale 1:1

recess to accommodate the wired frame for the mattress; and elements of the framework of the head or foot end, consisting of a cast decorative socket for a cross-tube, attached straps of a curved-sided diamond pattern, moulded end pieces and a finial.

A side strap and loop attachment, partly painted with tar, was probably part of a fanlight used to light the small back closet of one of the houses.

The container types comprise large items, including a 1' (305mm) diameter, No. 14, cast-iron cooking pot, with a rod suspension handle looped through simple lugs (Fig. 96D); flat base fragments of two 1'1" (330mm) diameter containers, with outer riveted strengthening hoops, which had been used to contain white paint; and eleven body fragments, possibly from buckets, which had, during their final use, also contained paint.

Ten body fragments with a simple handle are from an enamelled cup or bowl. A variety of kitchen utensils, of both tin and iron, were enamelled in Britain, particularly during the latter half of the 19th century, and an extensive range of such kitchenware still survives in Captain Scott's Cape Evans Hut at McMurdo Sound, Antarctica (set up in 1911), with cups, mugs, plates, dishes, colanders, jugs and funnels in white and blue enamelling (see photograph in Flegg *et. al* 1990, 50–51). On St Kilda there is photographic evidence (Quine 1988, 37) certainly for the use of enamelled mugs before the Evacuation, though it is possible that the recovered fragments may have been used by the military.

Seventy-four heavily corroded fragments are from tin cans. Where identifiable they are 3" (76mm) in diameter and have locked ends and side seams of the 'sanitary can' type, which superseded the 'hole and cap' can in popularity around the 1920s (Busch 1981, 98). They probably had a paper label, as metal lithography normally occurred on containers which were not hermetically sealed. One top has clearly been pierced by a can punch, which may suggest that the tin contained condensed milk.

Eighty-five corroded metal sheet or plate fragments probably, in part, represent remains of containers; 33 of the pieces are coated on one side with solidified white or yellow-green paint.

Fasteners comprise twelve corroded 2" (51mm) wire nails; nine corroded nail fragments; a 1" (26mm) notched and countersunk wood screw; a hook or staple; a wire loop, possibly a hook (Fig. 96C); seven hoops or strengtheners; two 1' (305mm) diameter tub hoops with lapped and riveted ends; eleven straps or roof stays, 23mm and 32mm wide, accompanied by five cut rose-headed nails; an L-sectioned edging bar; and a T-hinge fragment (Fig. 96B). A length of ⅝" (15mm), broad, 6-strand wire rope was also found, looped and almost knotted at one end. It may have come from the supports of the telegraph aerial, or been spare hawser.

Phase 9

A total of 323 items were recovered from this phase.

Household fittings include six elements of a bedstead of the same form as those in Phase 8, including a moulded finial (Fig. 97H); an angle; two decorative straps from the diamond pattern within the framework of the head or foot end of the bed (Fig. 97C); along with two finials with brass caps from the top of the bed posts (Fig. 97B). The incomplete bow and stem of a key was also found (Fig. 97E).

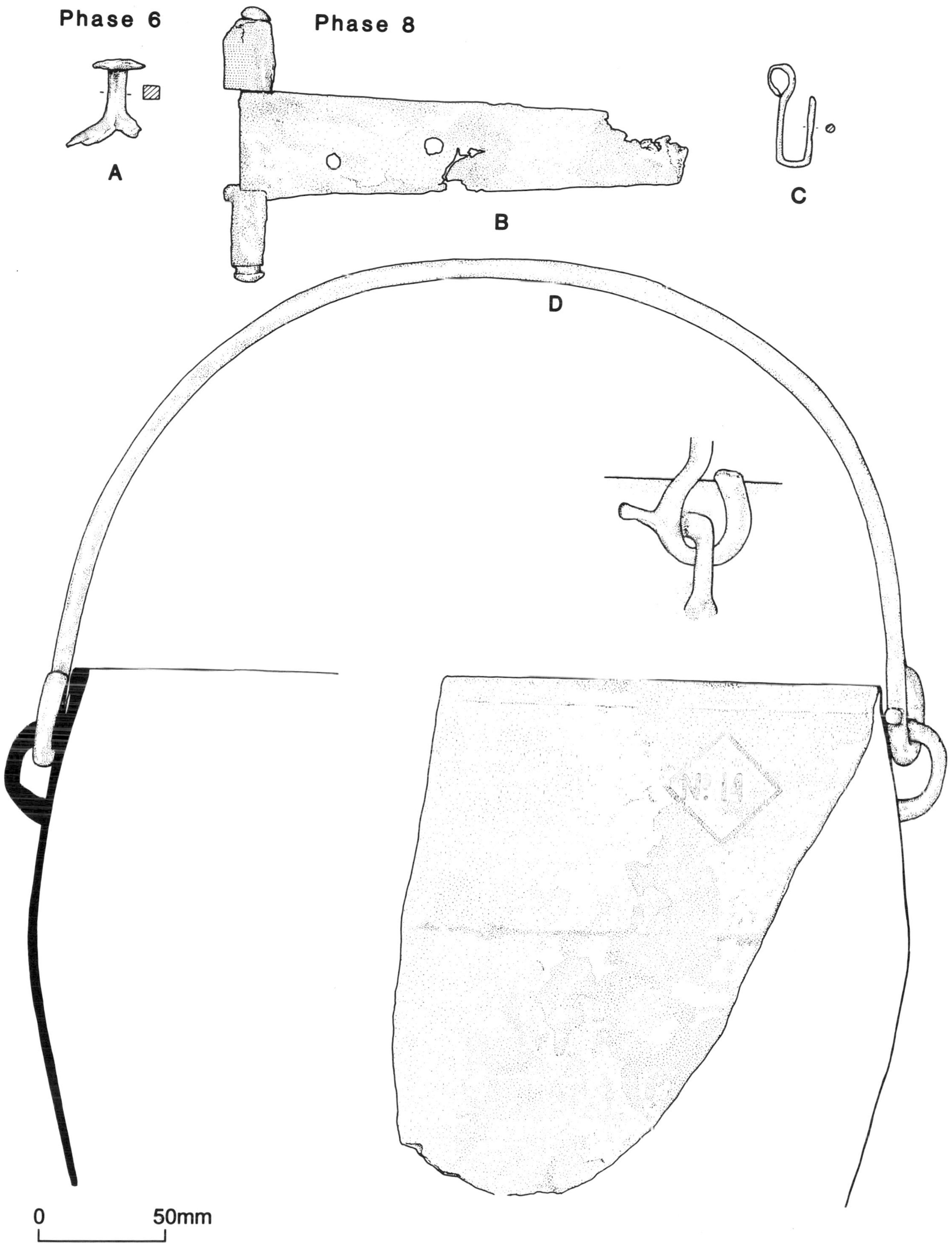

FIG. 96
Viscera pit: iron (Phases 6 and 8). Scale 1:2

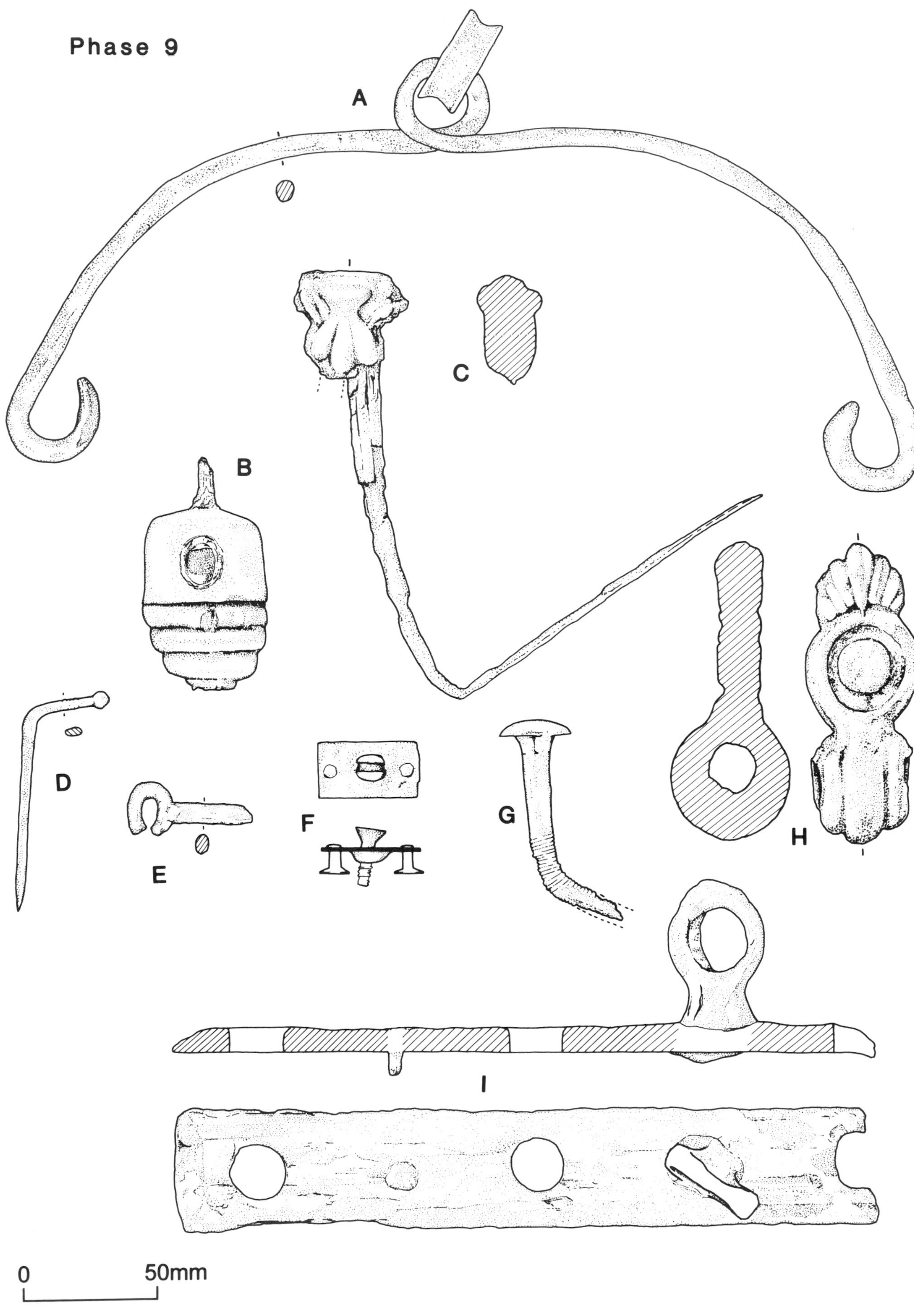

FIG. 97
Viscera pit: iron (Phase 9). Scale 1:2

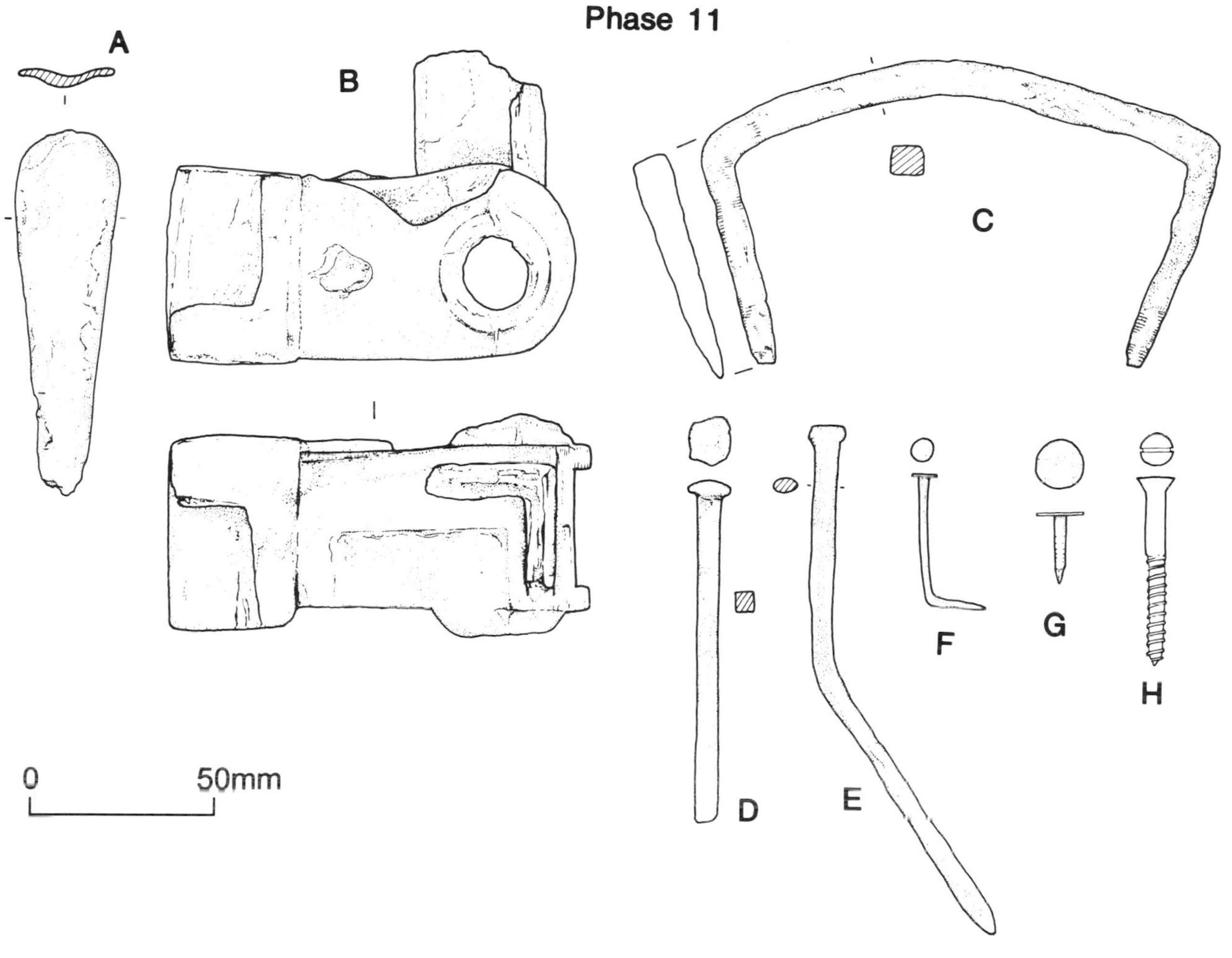

FIG. 98

Viscera pit: iron (Phase 11). Scale 1:2

Large household containers are represented by a 260mm (10¼") high cooking pot handle with hooked ends, from a vessel 324mm diameter, with looped triangular attachment plates; and another pot handle with twisted central loop, attached ring, and hooked ends (Fig. 97A). Thirteen fragments of tin can were also found, along with two fine shavings, possibly from a tin.

Twelve fragments of sheet metal were found.

Although there are six cut nails or fragments, including the rose-head type, the majority (128) are wire nails. They are of standard imperial sizes — 1¾" (1), 2" (86), 2½" (18), 3" (1), 4" (7 — Fig. 97D) and 6" (15). One hundred and twenty-four nail fragments, principally wire type, were also recovered. The collection seems to be a dump of scrap nails, many of them bent, particularly near the point.

Ten complete or fragmentary screws are of both fine and heavy gauge, 1½–2" long. Three 25mm diameter, dome-headed bolts, 90mm long, are similar to coach bolts (Fig. 97G).

One 1" rectangular wire staple is of the type used on lightweight boxes and packing cases, securing battens or sheet boarding to a frame.

Other fittings and fastenings include two heavy spikes, 67 x 9 x 9mm; an incomplete 3mm diameter curved rod; a fragment of a cast-iron pipe; two incomplete pieces of tube, 20mm and 22mm diameter; four small rectangular plates with a pierced, domed centre containing a screw on one face, and two projecting flat, round-headed copper rivets on the other (Fig. 97F); and a rod hoop, possibly a strengthener.

Straps include a piece of iron attached to a strip of zinc; an incomplete heavy 45mm wide ridged plate, pierced by large holes, and with a fixed loop on the ridge (Fig. 97I); and bent roof stays, 26mm and 32mm wide, pierced for attachment, and still retaining both wire and cut nails.

Phase 11

A total of 232 items were found.

Household fittings comprise a bedstead angle (Fig. 98B), and a fragment of an enamelled spoon (Fig. 98A).

One container was recovered — the base of a tin can, with traces of paint coating.

One hundred and eight fragments of sheet metal were of uncertain use, while four elements of a grid frame could have been some form of cover.

Fasteners comprise 82 complete and fragmentary nails — eight cut, nine wire and 65 corroded fragments. Amongst the cut nails is a 4" galvanised rose-head (Fig. 98D), and a ¾" rose. The wire nails are imperial 1½" (1), 1¾" (1), 2" (6 — Fig. 98F) and 6" (1 — Fig. 98E). A ¾" clout (Fig. 98G) had been used to attach felt to sarking board.

Five screws, a 2" (Fig. 98H), 4", and three fragments, were also recovered, along with a staple 146mm long and 9mm wide (Fig. 98C). The largest item is a heavy tie rod or bolt, 312mm long and 15mm diameter, with screw ends and an attached hexagonal nut and washer. A 2–pronged item, 138mm long, may have been a clamp.

Fittings comprise a ridged strap, part of that found in Phase 9; and a length of 11mm diameter wire rope.

One tool was found, a heavy bar, 502mm long and 22mm diameter, with a round splayed head and blunt end. Twenty-three indeterminate lumps were also recovered.

5:4:7 Lead

Solidified lumps of lead or solder were found in Phases 8 (gf. 7, 4 pieces), 9 (gf. 5, 6 pieces) and 11 (gf. 1, 1 piece). Phase 9 also produced two bundles of lead-insulated, 2-strand copper wire, which may have come from the telegraph station.

5:4:8 Zinc

Remnants of zinc roof sheeting were found in Phases 6–9 and 11, the largest surviving pieces being dumped into the pit in Phase 8. The latter indicated that sheets were 3' (0.91m) wide, and at least the same in length. Certainly in the late 19th century zinc was normally sold in sheets 7' (2.13m) and 8' (2.44m) in length by 3' and 2'8" (0.81m) in width. There is no obvious evidence for roll joints. Many of the sheet fragments had been punctured by nails, usually round, ranging in diameter from 10–50mm; and numerous examples show evidence for folding or occasional splashes of tar. This would suggest that they had been re-used after removal from the cottage roofs, possibly onto the old blackhouses when they were used simply as byres and store-places, before final disposal in the pit.

5:4:9 Tar (A. Crawshaw)

A sample (gf. 10/6) was treated with chloroform. The solution was filtered and evaporated onto salt plates. The infra-red spectra indicated that it is coal tar.

5:4:10 Stone (J.R. Senior)

Catalogue

Phase 2

Three items were specially recorded.

sf. 102. A fire-shattered porphyritic gabbro from the Western Gabbro Complex.

sf. 103. Foliated amphibolite schist, imported either by glacial action or by man.

sf. 106. A piece of smoke-blackened drusy Conachair-Oiseval granite with quartz feldspar crystal-filled cavity.

Phase 4

A piece of imported crenulated Ballachulish Slate.

Phase 5

Six items were recovered.

sf. 73. Medium-grained micaceous sandstone with four worked faces, probably Upper Carboniferous from mainland Scotland. Fig. 99A.

sf. 76. Tiny struck flint core. Fig. 99D.

sf. 78. ?Struck flake of flint, imported or of glacial origin. Fig. 99B.

sf. 79. Large rounded boulder, essentially natural, including peripheral impact points by collision. Grey-green porphyritic dolerite from the Mullach Sgar Complex.

sf. 80. Grey-green fine-grained dolerite from the Mullach Sgar Complex. Possibly a dressed flake but very weathered. Fig. 99C.

sf. 81. L-sectioned porphyritic basic igneous rock; smoke blackened.

Phase 6

gf. 11. Piece of chalk (calcium carbonate, not tailors' chalk), imported by man or ?by glacial action.

Phase 11

gf. 2. Blue chalk (gypsum) imported for school use.

5:4:11 Bone Objects

Three bone buttons, of the 4-hole, sew-through type, were located (sfs 2, 70 — Fig. 100, 74 — Fig. 100). The

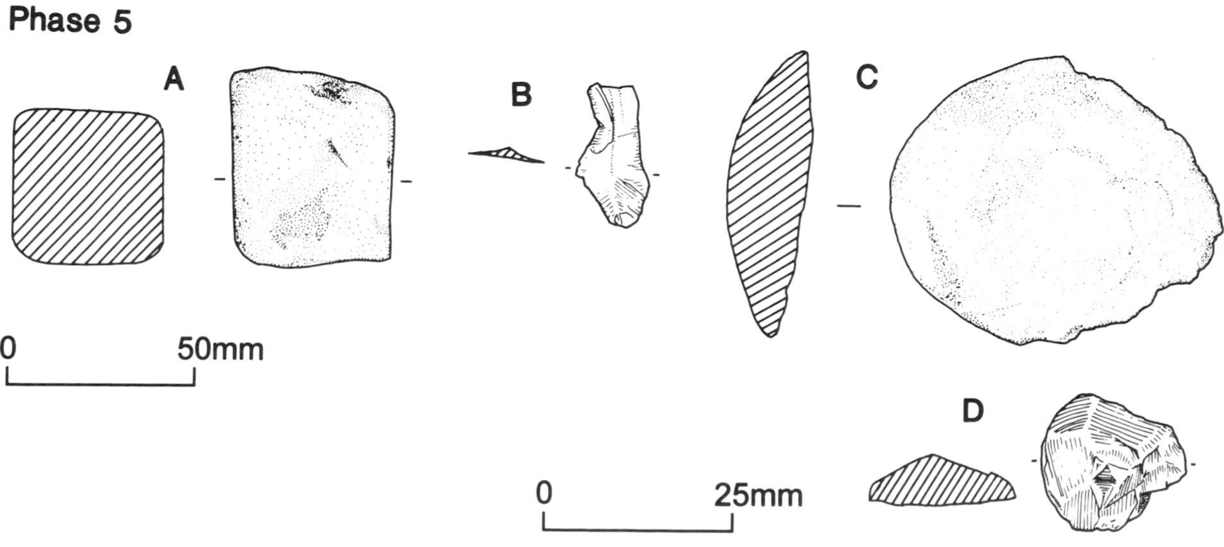

FIG. 99
Viscera pit: stone (Phase 5). Scale 1:2; D 1:1

material was examined by Sonia O'Connor of York Archaeological Trust's Conservation Laboratory using low and high-power microscopy. They were found to be dense compact tissue probably cut from cattle longbones.

5:4:12 Leather (C. Thomas)

This group of leather consists chiefly of offcuts (37), plus three shoe fragments, eight miscellaneous stitched fragments and four scraps. Some of the offcuts are typical of shoe-working waste.

Most of the leather came from Phase 6, with small quantities from Phases 7, 8 and 11. A full discussion of this assemblage and all the leather from the excavations is given after the catalogue.

Shoes

Phase 6

sf. 62. Upper fragment with lace holes, and facing.
a. Small fragment of upper of boot with three lace holes, with impressions from eyelets. Two holes are 8mm apart (edge to edge). Third is 23mm from the second hole. Parallel to first two holes, grain to flesh stitching channel, set in 2.5mm from edge. Stitch length 3mm. Grain to flesh stitching channel at 66° from edge, between second and third lace holes. *c.* 58 x 15 x 2mm.
b. Smaller fragment is facing, fitting on inside of above fragment, matching first and second holes and stitching. Grain worn. *c.* 40 x 14–17 x 0.75mm. Fig. 100.

Phase 8

sf. 57. Seat of sole, riveted construction.

Fragment of seat of sole, with round holes, diameter 1.5mm, most probably for brass rivets (not big enough for iron hobnails); if for stitching would have been stretched. Very worn and fragile, delaminated. Iron stain on underside. L. *c.* 65mm, w. 57mm. Fig. 100.

Phase 11

sf. 55. Fragment of upper, with lasting margin, with grain to flesh stitching channel, stitch length 5.5mm. Oval stitch holes, *c.* 2.5 x 1mm. Also side seam with pair of grain to flesh stitching channels, 2mm apart, stitch length 1mm, hole diam. *c.* 0.25m — machine-sewn. *c.* 55 x 33 x 0.75mm.

Other fragments with stitching

Phase 6

sf. 59. Four small scraps with faint traces of stitching. Very fragile and delaminated.

Phase 11

sf. 54. Four irregularly shaped fragments with stitch holes.
a. Approximately trapezoidal, with one slightly curved edge. Two parallel grain to flesh stitching channels on one long and one short edge. Stitching channels 3.5mm apart, stitch length 3.5mm. Stitching channels set *c.* 8mm in from edge on long side, but only 6.5mm on short side, tapering till stitch holes meet edge. Stitching channels overlap in shared corner. Single grain to flesh stitching channels, stitch length 3mm, set 3–4mm in from other two sides. Worn and torn. Probably delaminated. *c.* 160 x 80 x 1mm.
b. Smaller fragment, mostly torn, but with one cut edge with pair of stitching channels as on a., set 8–9mm in from edge; edge now folded — ?hem. Delaminated. Possibly part of flesh layer of a. *c.* 95 x 70 x 1mm.
c. Small fragment, curled up, worn and mostly torn but with two cut edges, one with single stitching channel, one with double stitching channel, as on a. *c.* 70 x 37 x 1mm.
d. Tiny fragment, worn and torn, with one edge with pair of stitching channels, as on a. Possibly delaminated part of a. *c.* 25 x 15 x 1mm.

Offcuts

Phase 6

sf. 60. Ten offcuts. Five triangular: 16 x 40 x 5mm, 25 x 37 x 5mm, 8 x 30 x 3mm, 12 x 21 x 4mm, and 21 x 30 x 4mm, with one curved edge. Four strips: 52 x 4 x 4mm, 4 x 60 x 5mm, 38 x 5 x 3mm, 29 x 3 x 3mm. Approximately rectangular offcut 38 x 7–9 x 5mm.

sf. 61. Eight offcuts. Four triangular: 18 x 40 x 4mm, 16 x 60 x 3.5mm, 16 x 10 x 3mm, 37 x 8 x 4mm. Rectangular strip 75 x 6–9 x 4mm. Strip 55 x 2 x 5mm. Fragment with one curved edge 36 x 24 x 5mm. Small fragment 8 x 4 x 3mm.

sf. 63. Two round fragments. Diam. *c.* 12mm, th. 0.5mm. Fig. 100.

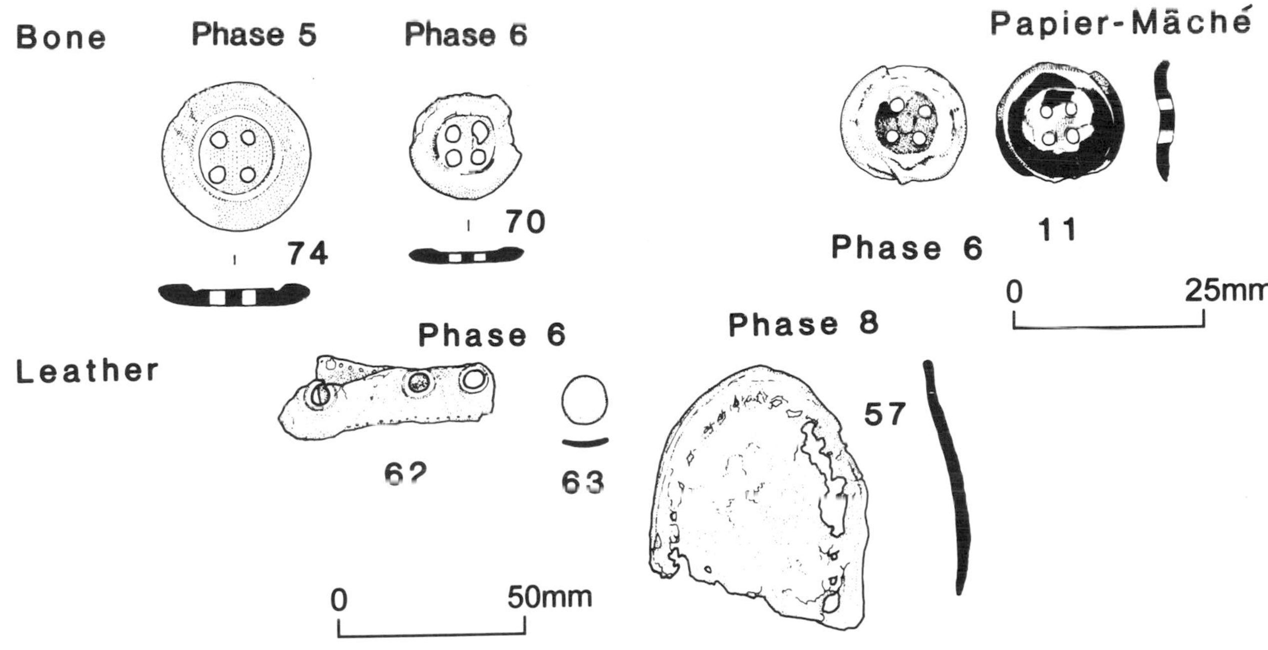

FIG. 100
Viscera pit: bone (Phases 5–6), leather (Phases 6 and 8) and papier-mâché (Phase 6). Scale 1:1; sfs 57, 62, 63 1:2

sf. 64. Three offcuts: *c.* 30 x 4 x 4mm, 25 x 5 x 4mm, 15 x 5 x 4mm.

sf. 65. Five offcuts. Three triangular: 21 x 14 x 3mm, 20 x 31 x 6mm with curved edge, 15 x 31 x 5mm. Strip 39 x 3 x 3mm. Irregularly shaped fragment 10 x 30mm, delaminated.

sf. 68a. Triangular offcut, *c.* 17 x 29 x 4mm.

Phase 7

sf. 58. Three offcuts. One triangular, 60 x 7 x 4mm. Two strips: 66 x 6 x 3mm, 50 x 6 x 3mm.

Phase 8

sf. 56. Five offcuts. One triangular, 26 x 27 x 5mm. Two strips: 75 x 2–14 x 4mm, 55 x 5 x 4mm. A rectangle, 20 x 15 x 6mm. A parallelogram-shaped piece, 8–20 x 29 x 4mm.

Scraps

Phase 6

sf. 66. Scrap, *c.* 22 x 3 x 3mm.

sf. 67. Two tiny scraps, *c.* 16 x 19 x 1mm, 9 x 14 x 1mm.

sf. 68b. Scrap, *c.* 20 x 31 x 2mm.

Discussion of leather from all excavated areas

The leather consists mainly of shoes, with significant portions of 14 shoes, plus 30 other shoe fragments. The rest of the assemblage is made up of 2 strap-loops, 11 miscellaneous stitched pieces, 60 offcuts and 27 scraps.

Shoes

At least fourteen shoes or boots are represented; these mostly comprise ankle boots with central lacing and with toe-caps separate from vamps. Except for one example, brass rivets were used to hold sole and upper together, while outer soles were frequently reinforced by iron hobnails.

Construction

Riveted

All but one shoe are of riveted construction, in which insole, mid-sole, sole and upper were fastened together by brass rivets; the lasting margin of the upper being sandwiched between insole and mid-sole. Rivets or rivet holes survive on at least 27 shoe fragments (Blackhouse W: sfs 68, 78, 82, 87–8; House 8: sfs 256, 419, gfs 2/13a–d, 11/13, 12/13, 1/14a, 1/14c–j, 1/14l–n, 1/14p; Rubbish pit: sf. 57).

Some sole fragments also have grain to flesh stitching channels, possibly used to hold the sole unit together prior to riveting (Blackhouse W: sf. 88; House 8: sf. 256, gfs 2/13c–d, 12/13, 1/14g, 1/14i, 1/14p–q).

The soles are composite, comprising (outer) sole, mid-sole and insole. The mid-soles vary. One, for instance, only occurs in the forepart area, and was reinforced with wood and a second, smaller piece of leather (House 8: gf. 1/14a). In another example, at least three leather scraps had been used to form the forepart mid-sole, while wood had been used in the waist and seat (House 8: gf. 12/13).

Five heels or top-pieces survive (Blackhouse W: sfs 82, 88; House 8: sfs 256, 419, gf. 12/13). They consist of several lifts of leather, held together by iron hobnails, except for one example where brass rivets appear to have been used. However, the evidence is not certain, as the outer layer is missing (Blackhouse W: sf. 82).

Iron hobnails, or traces of, were also found on other sole parts. Two nailing patterns emerge: (i) a single row round the outside of the sole, plus three nails in the centre forepart (e.g. House 8: sf. 419); and (ii) a double row on the outside, one large nail in the front centre forepart, three short rows in the rear of the forepart (e.g. House 8: gf. 12/13). These hobnails, apart from those used for clump soles (see REPAIRS), were intended to protect the boot, to make it last longer, and to give the wearer an improved grip (see Fig. 57A–B).

The upper fragments were sewn to each other with lapped grain to flesh stitching channels, usually in two or three rows. On two examples decorative patterns were incorporated in the seam joining toe-cap to vamp. These comprised a repeated motif: (i) a larger and a smaller hole (House 8: sf. 419 — Fig. 58); (ii) one larger and two smaller holes (House 8: sf. 256).

Welted

One example of welted construction survives (Blackhouse W: sf. 20). In this method, the upper and insole are stitched together to the welt, a narrow strip of leather, which is in turn stitched to the outer sole. No outer sole survives in this example, but vamp, welt and insole do. Both the insole and the lasting margin of the vamp have a double grain to flesh stitching channel, forming tunnel stitches. The welt has two grain to flesh stitching channels, one for attachment to upper and insole, the other for the outer sole. Traces of leather thong survive in the stitch holes of the welt and of the upper, suggesting that the seam might have been sewn, or more probably repaired, with a thong. The stitch holes, especially those of the welt's outer stitching channel, are rather irregular, suggesting that this shoe may have been stitched by hand. Similarly, the seam on the toe-cap of this shoe, although neat, lacks the precise regularity of the stitching channels on the other uppers, and was also probably hand-sewn.

Repairs

A few of the shoes appear to have been repaired. Clump soles had been added to two soles. The corresponding part of the vamp of one is torn; small holes around the worn area suggest that it may also have been patched. The nature and position of the wear indicates that the wearer may have had a bunion (House 8: sfs 256, 419 — Fig. 58). There are also traces of stitching near a worn patch on another upper (House 8: gf. 1/14a). It is possible that brass rivets were used to secure a patch on a third upper (Blackhouse W: sf. 68). As mentioned above, the use of a thong on the welted shoe suggests repair work, as do irregularly spaced stitch holes on the welt's outer stitching channel (Blackhouse W: sf. 20).

Style

Insufficient survives of the welted shoe to indicate anything about the style, apart from the fact that it may have had a toe-cap.

The riveted shoes appear to be high ankle boots with lace holes for a central fastening. The best-preserved example has fourteen lace holes, with metal eyelets. The vamp has a separate toe-cap attached to it, with decorated seam, as described above (House 8: sf. 419 — Fig. 58).

Strap loops

Two items are most probably fixed loops or keepers, used to secure a belt or strap, as, for instance, on a suitcase (Blackhouse W: sfs 74, 83b).

Offcuts and scraps

The leather includes 60 offcuts and 27 scraps. Nineteen are definitely triangular; their shape, size and thickness suggest leatherworking — possibly shoe manufacture, but more probably repair (e.g. House 6: sfs 18, 34–5, 37). Some of the other offcuts, especially from Blackhouse W, are quite large and irregularly shaped. Three fragments have noticeably well-preserved grain surfaces, suggesting that the leather has been little if at all used. This suggests that they may be waste from cutting of new leather — possibly the outer edges of hides (Blackhouse W: sfs 67, 69–70). The other, more worn fragments, may have been cut from other items for re-use.

Other stitched fragments

The other stitched fragments include an oblong fragment stitched on all four sides (Blackhouse W: sf. 31 — Fig. 78). It is almost certainly part of a larger item, possibly some sort of container.

Condition

The leather is noticeably worn and fragmentary, and had presumably been abandoned, thus explaining its occurrence among other household rubbish.

Discussion

Boots of riveted construction, with laced fronts and iron hobnails, are typical examples of inexpensive working wear of the late 19th to early 20th century.

Riveted construction dates from Cricke's patent of 1853 (Swann 1986, 130). 'There were huge quantities produced for cheap working wear from the late 1850s, and especially the '60s when there were machines to drive them, through to the early 1920s.' They were at their most common from the 1880s until World War I (Miss J. Swann, pers. comm.).

Although it is possible that the boots could have been made on the island, it is more probable that they were produced in a factory on the mainland. Suitable Singer sewing machines, required for the uppers, were available from 1857 and were used by most shoe repairers. However, given the poverty of the islanders, it is most unlikely that they would have possessed such a machine. It is more likely that they were ordered through the factor or through trawler men, or else that they were bought by islanders on visits to the mainland. They could even have been handed down by incomers, for instance, the minister.

It is possible that the welted shoe was made on the island. Reverend Mackenzie refers to the manufacture of shoes from cattlehide tanned on the island. These were sewn together with sheepskin thongs (see below). The welted shoe cannot, however, be dated as closely as the riveted ones, as welted construction came into use *c.* 1500, and is still employed.

Several writers refer to tanning of leather and shoe manufacture on the island, especially to the use of tormentil root for tanning (Martin 1753, 56; Macaulay 1765, 189). Mackenzie states that they used tormentil to tan cattlehide, but Sands believed that they only tanned sheepskins, buying their leather (presumably cattlehide) from the factor (Mackenzie 1911, 12–13; Sands 1878a, 191). Martin also describes the use of the neck of the solan goose for a temporary boot, which only lasted a few days (Martin 1753, 57).

Mackenzie, who was minister on St Kilda between 1829 and 1843, records the making of leather shoes, using home-produced leather:

> With the root of the tormentil they tan the hides of their cattle into leather, and while the supply of leather last the men make of it shoes for the family. These, which are sewed together with thongs of sheep-skin, are very badly shaped, but are always made with plenty of room. One peculiarity of their manufacture is that they have always a band of leather round them over both sole and upper. This they do to give a better grip on the rocks. (Mackenzie 1911, 12–13)

Possibly these are the same shoes which Sands called 'turned shoes . . . made without welts' and which he refers to as 'universal until within a few years. Specimens are still to be seen' (Sands 1878a, 191).

There are also references to the import of leather for shoe manufacture. In 1877 MacDiarmid went to St Kilda on *HMS Flirt* to distribute a gift of supplies from the Austrian government, given as thanks to the islanders for helping some of its shipwrecked sailors. The supplies included '1 bale leather, for shoes'. MacDiarmid also records the prices charged by the factor for imports: 'leather, 2/- per lb for sole, 2/3 for upper' (MacDiarmid 1878, 233, 249).

Photographic evidence also survives but, unfortunately, with little detail. Three photographs of 1886 show heavy boots with front lacing. None of the boots appear to have separate toe-caps. In one photograph a young man is wearing a somewhat unusual pair of boots, with long narrow toes, perhaps locally produced (Buchanan 1983, 28). Other photographs, showing men, women and children in heavy front-laced boots, date from *c.* 1900 until 1930 (Buchanan 1983, 18, 33, 41, 50, 51, 58, 64, 72). Cockburn's 'Three Generations of Gillies' photograph, taken *c.* 1927, shows the eldest Gillies wearing heavy front-laced boots with toe-caps, with decorative bands on the toe cap/vamp seam. A 1930 photograph shows one of the MacKinnon girls wearing something quite different — a pair of side-buttoned boots (Buchanan 1983, 60, pl. 56).

Conclusion

As discussed above, most of the shoes were front lacing ankle boots of riveted construction. They date most probably from *c.* 1880 to World War I, and were almost certainly made in a factory on the mainland, and imported, via either the factor or the trawler men.

The welted shoe could, however, have been home-made. The presence of the offcuts suggests some domestic working of leather, possibly repair work.

5:4:13 Textiles (P. Walton)

Most of the textiles and fibre from Area 6 (T39–40, 48–9, F8, T51–6, 60–105, F9) are from Phase 6, the early fill of a rubbish pit. A few fragments were contemporary with a layer of byre litter from Phase 7 (T46–7, F12); and the remainder were later finds from Phases 8 and 9 (F6–7, T41–2, 44–5, F10–11). The textiles therefore range in date from the late 19th to the mid-20th century.

Almost all the textiles are of wool, with one example of cotton (T76) and a single example of light, gauzy silk fabric (T49). This last, from Phase 6, is a slightly later piece than the silk bow (T38) and the fragment of silk satin (T21) found at the House 8 site in levels contemporary with its construction (Phase 12). Silk was always an expensive fibre and it is interesting to see that some luxuries, though rare, were available to the St Kildans.

Most of the fabrics have been woven on a loom, as was the case with the House 8 textiles, and the weaves are in general similar to those in that group, although the pit textiles seem to have fewer fancy weaves. There are also nine examples of knitted fabrics, varying in quality from very fine to extremely coarse; some are in stocking stitch and some in rib. One group of woven pieces appear to be related to each other and the evidence of cutting and stitching suggests that they are part of a jacket (T71/T735/T77/T81/T85/T88/T96/T100–02). Another group are more fragmentary, but are clearly all from the same cloth, which is similar to the jacket group: these may represent a second jacket (T46/T48/T51/T53–5/T65).

The dyes examined by Dr G.W. Taylor (Textile Research Associates, York) were similar to those in the House 8 textiles, being largely dark colours based on synthetic dyes and indigo (see above, 3:3:17, colour). The first synthetic dye, mauveine, was introduced in 1856, and new dyes were added at the rate of at least one a year until a considerable range was available. Aniline black, tentatively identified in T39, was invented in 1863. Indigo was finally synthesised in 1880.

Raw fibre

The seven examples of raw fibre (F6–12) were mostly wool and included full-length staples similar to those from House 8. A single example from the layer of byre litter seemed different from the rest and H.M. Appleyard, a specialist in animal coat fibres, has suggested it may be goat hair.

Catalogue

It is planned to publish a more detailed catalogue and report elsewhere.

Notes:
For textiles
'coarse' = less than 10 threads per cm in warp and weft
'medium' = 10–20 threads per cm
'medium-fine' = 20–30 threads per cm
'fine' = more than 30 threads per cm

For knitted fabrics
'coarse' = less than 2 stitches per cm
'medium' = 3–6 stitches per cm
'fine' = 7 or more stitches per cm.

Phase 6

sf. 8 (T39). Medium weight black wool knitting, worked in stocking stitch with plied yarn; tattered and thin from wear.

sf. 9 (T40). Medium black wool twill in 3/2 structure, slightly matted, perhaps fulled.

sf. 20 (T48). Medium wool twill in 3/2 structure; probably the same as T46.

sf. 21 (T49). Small fragment of very fine light brown silk in tabby weave; an open, 'gauzy' fabric.

sf. 21 (F8). Small tuft of raw wool fibre 20mm long.

sf. 22b (T51). Medium wool twill in 3/2 structure, as T46.

sf. 23 (T52). Medium brown wool twill in 2/2 structure.

sf. 24 (T53). Medium wool twill in 3/2 structure, as T46.

sf. 25 (T54). Ditto.

sf. 26 (T55). Ditto.

sf. 26 (T56). Fine light brown wool knitting made in stocking stitch from single yarn.

sf. 27 (T60). Medium or medium-coarse brown wool twill in 2/2 structure.

sf. 28 (T61). A pad of plied wool threads, matted together; possibly originally woven.

sf. 29a (T62). Fine light brown wool knitting worked in rib stitch from plied yarn.

sf. 29b (T63). Fine light brown wool knitting worked in stocking stitch from single yarn; finer than T62.

sf. 29c (T64). Medium-fine dark brown wool textile in double weave (one face twill, the other tabby); thick, solid fabric.

sf. 30 (T65). Medium wool twill in 3/2 structure, as T46.

sf. 31 (T66). Loose loops of wool fibre, probably the remains of coarse knitting.

sf. 32 (T67). Poorly preserved remains of coarse wool knitting, perhaps in stocking stitch.

sf. 33 (T68). Medium grey-brown wool knitting worked in stocking stitch from plied yarn.

sf. 34a (T69). Tattered remains of medium checked wool twill in 2/2 structure; bands of varying width, dark brown on pale ground; third colour represented by missing threads.

sf. 34b (T70). Medium-coarse dark brown wool twill in ?2/2 structure; one system of threads (warp or weft) less well preserved than the other.

sf. 35a (T71). Medium black wool twill in 3/2 structure, slightly matted, perhaps from fulling.

sf. 35b (T72). Medium brown wool twill in 2/2 structure.

sf. 36 (T73). Remains of jacket front with button holes; made with medium black wool twill, probably the same as T71.

sf. 37 (T74). Remains of jacket opening with front collar; made from medium black wool twill, probably the same as T71.

sf. 38 (T75). Remains of jacket with front opening; made from medium black wool twill, probably the same as T71.

sf. 39a (T76). Fine black cotton twill in 4/1 structure.

sf. 39b (T77). Medium brown-black wool twill in 3/2 structure; fulled; probably more of T71.

sf. 39c (T78). Medium-fine reddish brown wool twill in 3/3 structure.

sf. 39d (T79). Medium blue wool twill in 2/2 structure.

sf. 39e (T80). Medium or medium-coarse pale brown wool twill in 2/2 structure; very tattered and compacted together with T79.

sf. 40a (T81). Medium wool twill in 3/2 structure; probably more of T71.

sf. 40b (T82). Medium or medium-coarse wool twill in 2/2 structure; probably more of T80.

sf. 40c (T83). Medium-fine dark brown wool textile in double weave (twill on one face, tabby on the other); probably more of T64.

sf. 40d (T84). Medium-fine reddish brown wool twill in 3/3 structure; probably as T78.

sf. 41a (T85). Medium black wool twill in 3/2 structure; probably more of T71.

sf. 41b (T86). Medium brown wool twill in 2/2 structure; yarn is smooth, worsted type; a light, flimsy fabric.

sf. 41c (T87). Medium blue wool twill in 2/2 structure; similar to T79; adhering to T86 and perhaps a lining to it.

sf. 42a (T88). Medium black wool twill in 3/2 structure; probably more of T71.

sf. 42b (T89). Medium brown wool twill in 2/2 structure; very like T86.

sf. 42c (T90). Medium blue wool twill in 2/2 structure; probably more of T79.

sf. 42d (T91). Coarse blue-brown wool twill in 2/2 structure; tweed-like quality.

sf. 43a (T92). Coarse blue-brown twill in 2/2 structure; similar to T91.

sf. 43b (T93). Medium brown wool twill in 2/2 structure; possibly more of T86.

sf. 44 (T94). Tiny fragment of reddish wool textile, probably twill.

sf. 45a (T95). Medium checked wool twill in 2/2 structure; bands of varying width, dark brown on pale ground; third colour represented by missing threads; probably more of T69.

sf. 45b (T96). Medium black wool twill in 3/2 structure, slightly matted, perhaps from fulling; possibly more of T71.

sf. 46 (T97). Medium reddish wool twill in 2/2 structure.

sf. 48 (T98). Medium or medium-coarse light brown wool twill in 2/2 structure; possibly more of T80.

sf. 49 (T99). Medium brown wool twill in 2/2 structure; dark and light threads in one system, light only in the other.

sf. 50 (T100). Medium black wool twill in 3/2 structure, slightly matted, perhaps from fulling; probably more of T71.

sf. 51 (T101). Medium black wool twill in 3/2 structure, slightly matted, perhaps from fulling; tattered remnant of T71.

sf. 52a (T102). Medium black wool twill in 3/2 structure, slightly matted, perhaps from fulling; perhaps more of T71.

sf. 52b (T103). Medium brown wool twill in 2/2 structure.

sf. 52c (T104). Medium brown wool twill in 2/2 structure; a light and flimsy fabric; probably more of T86.

sf. 53 (T105). Medium reddish brown wool twill in 2/2 structure; felted; an offcut.

gf. 10/6 (F9). Two pads of compacted raw wool fibre; no intact staples present.

Phase 7

sf. 18 (T46). Medium wool twill in 3/2 structure; twill pattern emphasised by differently coloured yarn in warp and weft; worn and matted, perhaps fulled.

sf. 19 (T47). Coarse brown-black wool twill in 2/2 structure.

gf. 8/7 (F12). Pad of compacted fibre, identified as goat hair from the surface scale pattern on the fibres.

Phase 8

sf. 13 (F7). Raw wool staples, 50mm long, wavy.

sf. 14 (T41). Fine brown wool knitting, knitted in stocking stitch with a ribbed border; made from plied yarn.

sf. 15 (T42). Medium-quality checked wool twill in 2/2 structure; check pattern made from narrow brown bands on a light ground.

sf. 16 (T44). Coarse brown wool (or possibly goat hair) knitting made from plied yarn; very loosely made, in ?stocking stitch.

sf. 17 (T45). Medium brown wool chevron twill in 2/2 structure; chevron formed by reverses in twill after every 20 threads.

gf. 7/8 (F10). Pad of compacted raw wool fibre; no intact staples present.

gf. 7/8 (F11). Ditto.

Phase 9

sf. 12 (F6). Compacted raw wool fibre; in a layer, but too uneven to be felt.

5:4:14 Miscellaneous

A button from Phase 6 (sf. 11 — Fig. 100) was examined by Sonia O'Connor at York. It was found to be a brown fibrous material coated with black varnish. The edges of the button show the laminated nature of the fibrous material. A small fragment (smaller than a pin-head) was detached and disassociated in boiling water. A microscope slide was prepared from the resultant suspension.

Examination under high magnification and polarised light showed heavily processed fragments of vegetable material and small crystals which were probably the filler or binder of the paper pulp. Buttons were made of papier-mâché from the latter half of the 18th century.

5:5 The Ecofactual Material

5:5:1 Plant Remains (Jacqueline P. Huntley)

The sampling and processing methods follow those for the other areas (see 2:4:1).

Description of samples (Table 29)

Phase 2

Context 16 (flot 16). Other than a few modern roots this flot consisted of charcoal fragments. Many of these were from coniferous wood and it is suggested that this was the burnt remains of driftwood or, maybe, waste building material. Very few waterlogged seeds were present but there were seven carbonised, hulled barley grains and one oat grain.

Phase 4

The initial phase of infill of the rubbish pit.

Context 14 (sample 14 — wet sieved). This was a layer of sticky brown soil overlying context 15. There were quite a few bone fragments and many worm egg cases and fly puparia in this sample. Although there were no carbonised plant remains, waterlogged ones were abundant. These were predominantly sorrel and sheep's sorrel, with a variety of other

Area No.	6	6	6	6	6	6	6	6	6	6
Context No.	16	14	15	12	10	11	8	9	5	3
Phase	2	4	4	5	6	6	7	7	9	11
Carbonised:										
[c]*Avena* grain (oats)	1		3							
[c]*Cerealia* undiff.			2							
[c]*Hordeum* hulled (barley)	7		3			2				
[c]*Hordeum* indet.			2	1						
[c]*Hordeum* straight hulled			1							
[c]*Hordeum* twisted hulled						1				
[e]*Vitis vinifera* (grape)			1							
[r]*Cirsium* sp(p). (thistle)						1				
[w]*Carex* (trigonous) (sedges)						1				
[x]*Cerastium* undiff. (sedges)						1				
[x]Gramineae <2mm (small grasses)			2	1						
Waterlogged:										
[a]*Aphanes arvensis* (parsley piert)					2		1			
[a]*Chrysanthemum segetum* (corn marigold)		2		1		1	1			
[a]*Stellaria media* (chickweed)	+	+	+	5	1	+	1	+	+	+
[e]*Ficus carica* (fig)					1					
[e]*Vitis vinifera* (grape)				1						
[g]Gramineae 2-4mm (medium grasses)		+		1		2				
[g]*Rumex acetosa* (sorrel)		***	++	***	***	***	++	+		+
[r]*Polygonum aviculare* (knotgrass)			1			+				
[r]*Polygonum persicaria* (redshank)				1						
[r]*Rumex acetosella* (sheep's sorrel)		++	+	3	+	++	++			
[r]*Urtica dioica* (nettle)								1		
[t]*Fragaria vesca* (strawberry)		2		1		4				
[t]*Rubus fruticosus* (blackberry)		+	1	+	1	+		2		
[w]*Carex* (lenticular) (sedges)			1	1	1		+			
[w]*Carex* (trigonous) (sedges)		2	1			+	+			
[w]*Eriophorum latifolium/angustifolium* (cotton grass)			1							
[w]*Eriophorum vaginatum* (cotton grass)								1		
[w]*Lychnis flos-cuculi* (ragged robin)				1						
[w]*Montia font.* ssp. *chondr.* (blinks)		+	+	1	++	***	***	++	+	+
[w]*Sphagnum* sp(p). (bog moss)				+						
[x]*Cerastium fontanum* (mouse-eared chickweed)			1							
[x]*Cirsium* sp(p). (thistle)						1				1
[x]Gramineae <2mm (small grasses)				1	++		++			
[x]*Potentilla*-type (tormentil-type)		1		1	1	+				
[x]*Ranunculus repens*-type (buttercup)			1	+	1	2	2			
[x]*Viola* sp(p). (violet)		1	1			2				

TABLE 29

Viscera pit: plant remains

KEY

The taxa have been put into broad ecological category. The latter was subjectively derived and the prefix codes are as follows:

a = arable weeds   c = cereal grain   e = exotic   g = grassland   r = ruderals/disturbed ground
t = scrub/woodland   w = wet ground   x = broad, unclassified

For the waterlogged taxa up to five individuals were counted and then further quantities estimated thus:
+ = a few being present   ++ = moderate numbers   *** = extremely large numbers

weedy taxa. Some quantities of blackberry were present, suggesting use of a locally growing (even if imported and being grown in gardens) soft fruit.

Context 15 (sample 17, flot 3, flot 17 and second sample 17). This layer was a deposit of brown gritty soil lying immediately over an iron-pan formed at the base of the pit. The first sample was a large flot compared with many for this site. It consisted of modern roots and some coarse, organic debris. There were tiny pieces of fragmented charcoal, some fly puparia, bone fragments and earthworm egg cases present. Moderate numbers of waterlogged sorrel, chickweed and blinks seeds, and one well-preserved carbonised oat grain with a single poorly preserved carbonised barley grain were recorded. In the second sample were a number of carbonised cereal grains — three hulled barley, one oat, two undifferentiated barley and one indeterminable cereal. The remainder of the flot consisted of very similar material to the first sample. The third tub examined from this context consisted of a mixture of carbonised fragments, mineral fragments and organic debris. It contained the usual mixture of waterlogged seeds and a moderate number (for this site) of carbonised seeds — hulled straight barley, oats, grass and a single grape pip. This is interesting in itself, since it is one of only two records for the whole site of definite import of food species other than, perhaps, some of the cereal grains. It is, of course, pure speculation as to whether it was brought in as a bunch of grapes or, more likely, as raisins/sultanas.

Phase 5
During this stage the pit was paved with granitic fragments.

Context 12, (flot 12). This is the flot from these granitic fragments. It contained quite a few bone fragments and some fly puparia. There were large numbers of waterlogged seeds from a variety of taxa. These were the expected sorrel and chickweed but there were indications of more varied habitats being represented. For example, there were sedge seeds and *Sphagnum* leaves with the seeds of ragged robin together indicating a mire community; and there was some indication of cultivation on acidic, drier soils with the presence of corn marigold and parsley piert. There were considerable numbers of blackberry pips here — could this represent faecal material or simply a few odd, rotten fruit. This was another context containing one grape pip, but this time it was preserved through waterlogging and the question always remains as to its age.

Phase 6
This was a phase during which a wide variety of objects and rubbish were dumped into the pit.

Context 10 (sample 8, flots 1 and 2). This was a mottled brown soil overlying layer 11 (described below). The first was a large flot containing many earthworm egg cases but very few monocot. fragments or charcoal. There was the usual abundance of sorrel and blinks seeds, and there was one fig pip. This is the second exotic species recorded from the island. The second flot contained abundant worm egg cases, too, with Gramineae nodes and fly puparia. It contained large numbers of small grass and blinks seeds but very few chickweed or sorrel seeds. Its botanical assemblage is, in fact, more similar to that from context 8 (below) than the remainder of context 10.

Context 11 (flots 10 and 11). This was a gritty brown soil immediately over the granitic paving of Phase 5. The first flot contained more or less only sorrel seeds with some worm egg cases and the odd fly puparia and bone fragments. There were the usual mixture of waterlogged seeds from taxa of disturbed ground. The second tub of flot was similar to the first although slightly fewer taxa were present. There were fragments of coniferous charcoal in it as well as a few fragments of grass. Flot 11 was large and contained abundant worm egg cases with modern roots and waterlogged seeds. There was a little charcoal and a few fly puparia and bone fragments. There were the usual mixture of waterlogged seeds and a few carbonised ones — one sedge and three hulled barley grains, one of which showed a twisted embryo.

Phase 7
This phase contained a rich organic layer which could have been byre litter. Detailed insect analyses were carried out at York (see 5:5:6).

Context 8 (flot 3 and wet sieved sample). Flot 3 was very large and dominated by worm egg cases. It consisted principally of grass fragments with a few fly puparia and odd fragments of insect. The seeds were mainly from grasses or sorrel with some buttercups, corn marigold and chickweed. The second tubful of flot examined contained very high numbers of blinks seeds, with sheep's sorrel seeds the next most abundant. Grass and sedge seeds were common but there were a few sorrel seeds. This indicates either hay or animal dung. The wet-sieved material consisted principally of monocot. fragments although, surprisingly, grass seeds were not that abundant. The only seeds in any abundance were those from docks, along with the perianths (the flower segments). It is interesting to note that one of the weevils found (*Apion cruentatum*) lives on sorrel (see 5:5:6).

Context 9 (flot 4). This layer was classed as a brown gritty soil and was found near to the north-east edge of the pit. After flotation it consisted of more or less pure charcoal — some of which was coniferous — and a few worm egg cases and monocot. fragments. Only waterlogged seeds were recovered, and these indicated the expected disturbed and wet ground conditions with some slight evidence of nutrient enrichment with the presence of nettle seeds.

Phase 9
This phase consisted of the layers of soil dumped over the rubbish and used as a surface upon which to cremate sheep.

Context 5 (sample 2, wet sieve). The sample was predominantly coniferous charcoal and clinker with very few seeds. It is in accord with the archaeological interpretation of a levelling dump presumably using hearth waste. Some of the burnt material may have been from the cremation pyre. No carbonised seeds were recovered.

Phase 11
This consists of the layers of soil dumped over the burnt sheep carcases.

Context 3 (sample 1, A3; flot 1). This context was apparently lumps of mortar. The flot was mostly chunks of charcoal with some burnt bryophytes. Few waterlogged seeds were recovered, the expected chickweed, blinks and sorrel. Other than containing one seed from a thistle, the second sample was very similar to the first.

Discussion
Undoubtedly this rubbish pit contains the most botanical remains of any site so far investigated on St Kilda, although the bulk of the seeds are waterlogged and their contemporaneity must remain slightly in doubt. However, given that the feature is a pit, modern contamination is less likely. The carbonised material is sparse and predominantly from the earlier phases of deposition. It consists of a mixture of barley and oat grains as is usual for the island. It is suggested that they were simply swept up from cottage floors following minor domestic accidents. They are concentrated in Phase 4 when other taxa are relatively scarce too. The main interest in any rubbish

pit is in its potential to provide evidence for the diet of the local inhabitants. Although faecal material, as demonstrated by the presence of cereal bran, cannot be shown here (possibly as a result of poor preservation), there is limited evidence of diet, namely grapes and figs. In addition, they give indications of outside communication. Other indications of food plants are the blackberry (possibly including raspberry) and strawberry pips — such plants are quite likely to have been grown in a sheltered plot.

The majority of the waterlogged seeds were found in Phase 6 material and indicated damp and disturbed ground, perhaps with some compaction, thus allowing large amounts of blinks to flourish in the near vicinity. The very high numbers of sorrel seeds probably indicate that these plants had been established for some time too, although any individual sorrel plant does produce large numbers of seeds. Although it is the main period of dumping, it is suggested that much of the plant material represents vegetation growing around the pit. The high numbers of seeds reflecting that the pit was, indeed, open for some considerable time.

The dump of possible byre waste during Phase 7 demonstrates a different seed assemblage with far fewer representatives of disturbed ground and more of wet grassland. That the deposit was originally grass is not in doubt. The lack of grass seeds suggest that the sward was either cut young before the flowers had developed or that it was grazed, thus preventing flower development. If the docks *(Rumex)* are indeed part of the same community it would suggest, perhaps, that this is the remains of a rather rank, grazed grassland with docks being nibbled occasionally. The docks may, however, have been thrown into the pit as a separate entity or may have been growing around the pit. Overall, it is suggested that the deposit is from grass-grazed animals. If it had been hay more flowers and seeds would probably be expected, although the climatic and edaphic conditions of the island may preclude the production of even small areas of the flower-rich hay meadows that we associate with, for example, parts of extreme northern Scotland and the Pennines. The hay was more likely to have been cut from specially seeded fields, in the later stages of occupation, or from the somewhat base-rich mires and heavily grazed remnants which survive today. The overlying material simply reflects material dumped to level the site, and then fuel used to dispose of dead sheep.

During excavation, a vegetation study was undertaken (see 5:2), which describes in detail what was growing on and around the site of this rubbish pit. Although vegetation cover was not great, the majority of species were grasses. This is not reflected in the archaeological material. One reason may be that the grass seeds are not preserved for any length of time and would not be expected to be present in any other than the surface deposits. For example, even in modern seed bank studies from the Orkneys grass seeds are rare even where the present vegetation is a grass-rich sward (Huntley 1990). A second reason may well be that the vegetation today is not the same as that during the time from which the sampled deposits originate, and that grasses were not then common in this area. With respect to the other taxa in these modern studies, sorrel is abundant but blinks and chickweed are absent. This suggests that the ground today is drier and probably less used thus allowing other taxa, the grasses, to colonise which then out-compete the chickweed in particular. Today chickweed flourishes right up against the cleit walls but only in a narrow band; this is clearly an area of high nutrient input from the sheep but subjected only to limited trampling.

This pit has provided evidence for selected parts of the diet of the locals, and of some of their imported foods, as well as indications of some of the plants that they probably grew. Although principally a rubbish pit, it has provided evidence of the vegetation growing around it whilst in use and, compared with the modern vegetation work, has shown how this has changed through time. It has also provided evidence for possible animal husbandry in terms of the layer of byre waste. It demonstrates the great potential that rubbish pits have for the archaeobotanist.

5:5:2 Mammal and Bird Bones (M. Harman)

All the bones recovered were examined, with the exception of the calcined bones from context 5 (Phase 9). The condition varies, some being well preserved and robust, while many of those from the lower layers are more fragile and incomplete. The bones from contexts which were definitely deposited after the Evacuation are dealt with summarily here.

The mammal bones

All the bones recovered are from sheep. Most of them are from post-1930 deposits and are of a size indicating that they are bones of Soay sheep, which were introduced to the main island from Soay in 1932. Contexts 1–3 of Phase 11 contained 1, 14 and 54 bones respectively, a few of them probably belonging to context 4 (Phase 10) which was a burial of a sheep carcase. The skeleton is almost complete, but lacks one scapula, one metatarsal, a few small bones, the tail and the head. It is a ewe of more than 3 years old (Clutton-Brock *et al.* 1990, 34; Silver 1963, 252–3). With these bones there was a two-part plastic ear tag, in lemon and white (sf. 6). If this belonged to the skeleton, as seems likely although the head was missing, it indicates that the sheep was tagged as a lamb in 1961 (P.A. Jewell, pers. comm.). When horn cores and hoof bones were recognised among the calcined bones below this burial, and later a metal ear tag (sf. 7), the deposit was recognised as being post-1959. It seems that it is the result of a large sheep cremation pyre constructed by veterinarians studying the sheep in 1964 (Gulland and Jewell, pers. comm.). An assessment of the number of sheep involved was made by counting astragali, which are easily recognisable and were often complete.

Together with calcined astragali in overlying and underlying contexts, there are, in total, 52 left and 54 right bones representing at least 53 adult or well-grown sheep, two young lambs and one very young lamb. No attempt was made to count or list the rest of the calcined bones, many of which are recognisable. In addition to these there are 82 unburnt bones which probably belong with the deposits above and below. The 'tidying up' contexts preceding this, but probably post-1956, include fifteen sheep bones.

Only the lowest levels contained bones which were certainly deposited before the Evacuation. These are listed in Table 30. Most of them are either single small bones such as teeth, or fragments of bones; but two, the skull fragment and the

Bone	Phase 4	5	6
Skull			1
Mandible			1
Tooth	6	1	1
Vertebra	2		
Rib		1	
Scapula			1
Radius	1		1
Femur	2		
Metatarsal			1

TABLE 30
Viscera pit: sheep bones and fragments of bone from pre-1930 contexts

metatarsal from Phase 6, are large enough to show that they are from a sheep larger than a Soay, and must be from the stock carried in the hundred years or so before the Evacuation. The few bones are from both waste and meat-bearing parts of the animal. Had cattle been present they may have survived better, and their total absence suggests that beef was not often eaten.

The bird bones

There are very few bird bones from post-1930 contexts; no more than ten altogether from gannet, fulmar, puffin, guillemot and oyster catcher. Tables 31–33 show the numbers of bones from different species from Phases 4–6. Two things are immediately clear from these tables: the limited range of species represented, with a strong emphasis on fulmar; and the distribution of the bones about the body, almost all being from the wing and foot: the parts with no meat on them. Most of the fulmar bones are from full-sized but immature birds, and probably represent fat young, taken in the late summer. These groups of bones are just what might be expected in a rubbish pit and can usefully be compared with the refuse deposits of the blackhouse beside House 8. The comparatively small number of gannet bones is interesting: it is possible that these larger birds were 'processed' near the shore where they were landed after being brought back from Boreray or the stacks, and the waste discarded nearby; some gannet wings were kept for household use, as the bones in House 8 testify (3.4.2). There are also very few auk bones, but possibly there was some difference in the disposal of birds whose feathers were used and those which were not plucked; aromatic fulmar feathers may not have sold so well. Alternatively, the emphasis on fulmar bones may reflect their popularity with the family using the pit, or the season when the deposits accumulated in the pit. It is interesting to see how different the proportions of species are from those in the earlier refuse deposits in the blackhouse beside House 8, where the puffin accounted for about half the bones, followed by fulmar, guillemot, gannet and razorbill. While this could reflect a temporal change in fowling, there are other possible explanations.

5:5:3 Fish Bones (R. Nicholson)

Two bones came from context 12, Phase 5.
1 large *Gadidae* brachiostegal ray.
1 fragment of a vertebral centrum, unidentified.

Bone	Gannet L	Gannet R	Fulmar L	Fulmar R	Guillemot L	Guillemot R	Puffin L	Puffin R
Skull			1					
Maxilla			1					
Mandible				2				
Humerus			12	5	1			
Ulna	2		2	6				
Radius			2	6				
Carpometacarpus			5	10			1	
Wing 1st phal.			2	2				
Tarsometatarsus			2	3				
Total	2		61		1		1	

Also: 8 unspecified foot phalanges

TABLE 31
Viscera pit: bird bones from Phase 4

Bone	Gannet L	Gannet R	Fulmar L	Fulmar R	Puffin L	Puffin R
Skull	1		1	1		
Mandible			7	8		
Coracoid				1		
Humerus	2		8	11	3	
Ulna			10	10	1	1
Radius			4	4		1
Carpometacarpus	1		10	13	1	
Wing 1st phal.		2	9	7		
Femur				1		
Tibiotarsus						1
Tarsometatarsus			15	6		
Total	6		126		8	

Also: 10 unspecified foot phalanges

TABLE 32
Viscera pit: bird bones from Phase 5

Bone	Gannet L	Gannet R	Fulmar L	Fulmar R	Guillemot L	Guillemot R	Puffin L	Puffin R
Maxilla			2					
Mandible			2	1				
Humerus	1	1 2	21	20			10	9
Ulna	2		16	14	1		6	8
Radius		1	12	11			2	1
Carpometacarpus		1	13	10			1	3
Wing 1st phal.			7	4				
Femur			1				1	
Tibiotarsus			2	2				1
Tarsometatarsus	1		18	16				
Total	9		172		1		42	

Also: 28 unspecified foot phalanges

TABLE 33
Viscera pit: bird bones from Phase 6

5:5:4 *Egg*

Nine fragments of egg membrane were found in the mottled brown soil (10) of Phase 6. The species could not be identified.

5:5:5 *Molluscs*

Only one apex of a limpet *(Patella vulgata)* was recovered, from context 12, Phase 5.

5:5:6 *Insect remains (E.P. Allison and H.K. Kenward)*

A sample of raw sediment from context 8 (Phase 7) was submitted to the Environmental Archaeology Unit at the University of York. After subjective description of the raw sediment, a 2.45kg sample was disaggregated in water, washed to 300 microns and then subjected to paraffin flotation for extraction of insect remains, following the methods described by Kenward *et al.* (1980). A small amount of raw sediment was retained as a 'voucher'. Detailed identification was carried out only on beetles (Coleoptera) and bugs (Hemiptera). The methods used for the analysis of these groups were as described by Kenward (1978), with some modifications. The recording of some taxa was semi-quantitative (Kenward, Engleman *et al.* 1986), although it is highly likely in this case that the estimated numbers correspond closely to the actual numbers of individuals present in the sample. The assemblage was divided into broad ecological groupings as described by Kenward, Hall and Jones (1986). An index of diversity (alpha) was calculated for the whole assemblage, and for components within it, following Fisher *et al.* (1943). A full list of invertebrate taxa recorded is given in Table 34.

Results and discussion

The raw sediment was a dark grey-brown, moist, plastic to crumbly, slightly sandy, slightly silty, amorphous organic material, with much fine and coarse herbaceous detritus. An articulated radius and ulna of a fulmar *(Fulmarus glacialis)*, and a cinder were the only inclusions noted.

Oligochaeta egg capsules
Dermaptera sp.
Psocoptera sp.
Mallophaga:
Damalinia bovis (Linnaeus)
Damalinia ovis (Schrank)
?*Cuclotogaster heterographus* (Nitzsch)
Hemiptera:
Aphrodes flavostriatus (Donovan)
Auchenorhyncha spp.
Thysanoptera sp.
Diptera:
Melophagus ovinus (Linnaeus)
Diptera spp. (puparia and adults)
Siphonaptera sp.
Hymenoptera:
Parasitica spp.
Coleoptera:
Pterostichus nigrita (Paykull)
Pterostichus sp.
Calathus fuscipes (Goeze)
Carabidae sp.
Helophorus spp.
Cercyon analis (Paykull)
Cercyon haemorrhoidalis (Fabricius)
Cercyon terminatus (Marsham)
Cercyon unipunctatus (Linnaeus)
Megasternum obscurum (Marsham)
Ptenidium nitidium (Heer)
Acrotrichis spp.
Catops sp.
Megarthrus sp.
Arpedium brachypterum (Gravenhorst)
Omalium ?rivulare (Paykull)
Omalium sp.
Xylodromus concinnus (Marsham)
Xylodromus depressus (Gravenhorst)
Syntomium aeneum (Muller)
Anotylus nitidulus (Gravenhorst)
Anotylus rugosus (Fabricius)
Anotylus tetracarinatus (Block)
Oxytelus sculptus (Gravenhorst)
Stenus spp.
Lathrobium sp.
Othius punctulatus (Goeze)
Othius sp.
Xantholinus sp.
Philonthus ?politus (Linnaeus)
Philonthus spp.
Quedius boops group
Staphylininae sp.
Tachyporus sp.
Tachinus laticollis or *marginellus*
Tachinus signatus (Gravenhorst)
Aleochara spp.
Aleocharinae spp.
Aphodius rufipes (Linnaeus)
Clambus pubescens (Redtenbacher)
Hypnoidus riparius (Fabricius)
Elateridae sp.
Tipnus unicolor (Piller and Mitterpacher)
Ptinus tectus (Boieldieu)
Cryptophagus spp.
Atomaria ?nigripennis (Kugelann)
Atomaria sp.
Orthoperus sp.
Mycetaea hirta (Marsham)
Lathridius minutus group
Corticaria sp.
Longitarsus spp.
Apion cruentatum (Walton)
Sitona lepidus (Gyllenhal)
Rhinoncus pericarpius (Linnaeus)
Ceuthorhynchinae sp.
Aranae spp.
Acarina spp.

TABLE 34
Viscera pit: invertebrate taxa, Nomenclature follows Kloet and Hincks (1964; 1977)

A very substantial arthropod assemblage was recorded in the flot. Fly puparia were particularly abundant and it was estimated that several thousands were present. The remains of adult flies, beetles, bugs, mites, parasitic Hymenoptera, insect larvae, earthworm egg capsules, spiders, fleas, lice, thrips, psocids (booklice), and earwigs were also present.

An estimated 440 individuals of 81 beetle and bug taxa were recorded. The concentration of remains per kilogram of sediment was thus 179.6. This is in the higher range observed, for example, in Anglo-Scandinavian deposits at 16–22 Coppergate in York (Kenward and Hall, forthcoming). The diversity of the beetle and bug assemblage as a whole was moderately low (alpha = 29, SE = 2).

Conditions at the point of deposition are indicated by the decomposer component, which was very large in absolute terms and accounted for 68% of the assem-blage. Most of the 29 uncoded taxa (a further 25% of the assemblage) probably also belong to this group. Diversity of the decomposers was very low (alpha RT = 10, SE = 1), so they clearly lived *in situ*. This low diversity is particularly striking since the decomposer component was ecologically rather mixed. A range of species *(Lathridius minutus* group, *Atomaria* spp., *Cryptophagus* spp., *Mycetaea hirta, Ptinus tectus* and *Tipnus unicolor),* which are usually only found in large numbers in relatively clean and only slightly damp decomposing material, were well represented, accounting for 34% of the decomposers and 23% of the whole assemblage. These 'dry' decomposer taxa and *Xylodromus concinnus* are very typical of assemblages found in humble structures of Roman, Viking and medieval date elsewhere in Britain. Such assemblages have been given the name 'house fauna' although the term does not necessarily imply a human dwelling. *Xylodromus depressus* is recorded occasionally in archaeological deposits but *X. concinnus* is much more common. In this deposit, however, *X. depressus* was in the majority. One species, the spider beetle *(Ptinus tectus)*, represented by seventeen individuals, provides evidence for the date of the deposit. It is only a relatively recent introduction into Britain, being first recorded in 1901 (Hinton 1941), and clearly shows this deposit to be 20th century in date, or to contain 20th-century material.

The presence of fouler matter in the deposit was indicated by 49 individuals of four decomposer taxa associated with foul conditions. The most common of these was *Cercyon haemorrhoidalis* (39 individuals), a species which is mainly found in cow, horse and sheep dung, and also in rotting plant debris (Hansen 1987, 147). *Cercyon terminatus,* represented by six individuals, is found in very similar habitats. It is often abundant in barn manure and other debris around farm buildings (Hansen 1987, 154). *Cercyon unipunctatus* (two individuals) is a distinctly synanthropic species, again found in organic accumulations such as manure and compost heaps around farm buildings (Hansen 1987, 152). Two individuals of the dung beetle *Aphodius rufipes* were also recorded. *Philonthus politus* (seven individuals), although uncoded, probably also belong to this 'foul' group. It includes manure among its main habitats (Hansen 1952, 51). The remainder of the decomposer taxa could not be categorised as either 'foul' or 'dry' species. *Anotylus tetracarinatus,* for example, the most common species in the assemblage (52 individuals), is a very eurytropic species found in decaying matter ranging from foul dung right through to rather open-textured, compost-like material.

The 'outdoor' component (i.e. those species demanding an open-air habitat, or unable to live and breed successfully inside buildings or in large accumulations of decaying matter) was absolutely quite large, consisting of 34 individuals of 20 taxa, although this only accounted for a small proportion (8%) of the whole assemblage. For an 'outdoor' component, diversity was low (alpha OB = 21, SE = 7), possibly reflecting the availability of only a very restricted range of habitats. Six individuals of *Rhinoncus pericarpius* and a single *Apion cruentatum* indicate the presence of docks (*Rumex* spp.). The *Apion* is generally found on *Rumex acetosa* in Britain (Morris 1990, 43). *Sitona lepidus,* represented by three individuals, is very common on leguminous plants, especially *Trifolium* (Larsson and Hansen 1965, 86). Five individuals of two species of the highly migratory *Helophorus* were the only aquatic beetles present, but the froghopper *Aphrodes flavostriatus* and the ground beetle *Pterostichus nigrita* are found in damp places, usually near water (Le Quesne 1965, 58; Lindroth 1974, 73). The click beetle (*Hypnoidus riparius*) is found under stones and plant remains by water (Henriksen and Hansen 1966, 89). *Syntomium aeneum* is found in moss, especially in rather damp places (Tottenham 1954, 38). In contrast to these, another ground beetle, *Calathus fuscipes,* suggests a moderately dry, rather open grassland habitat. The record of *Arpedium brachypterum* is worthy of note. It is a very typical boreal species, found in wet moss and at the roots of heather in the more mountainous districts of the northern and western British Isles (Tottenham 1954, 31).

Among the other orders of insects recovered were the remains of a number of ectoparasites: two keds *(Melophagus ovinus:* a wingless fly that lives on sheep), two lice, *Damalinia ovis* (also found on sheep), three *Damalinia bovis* (found on cattle), and three individuals of a bird louse, possibly *Cuclotogaster heterographus,* found mainly on domestic fowl (Séguy 1944, 186). Parts of two flea abdomens were also recovered. They were not the human flea, *Pulex irritans,* but could not be identified further.

By comparison with insect assemblages obtained from a range of Roman through to medieval deposits on many other sites, this deposit would overall be interpreted as mainly being litter from the floor of a structure containing some foul matter, probably including herbivore dung. There were no human lice or fleas, only ectoparasites of animals, so the structure might perhaps have been a byre, with conditions on the floor ranging from foul to relatively dry, unless the 'dry' decomposers originated in the structure of the building or in nests or stored materials. The 'outdoor' fauna may have become incorporated into the deposit in any of several ways: with cut vegetation either strewn on the floor as animal bedding or brought for fodder; the structure may have been well ventilated, or even open or perhaps left unroofed for a time, thus allowing access to 'outdoor' taxa.

It is also possible that docks grew round the pit into which the litter was dumped and that insects living on them, and other 'background' fauna, became incorporated into the deposit at this stage. The arrival of the fauna in animal guts seems unlikely since the insect remains were very well preserved, most sclerites being complete. The presence of *Ptinus tectus* suggests that the use of the structure in which the litter built up was in, or continued into, the 20th century. Post-depositional invasion of dumped litter by some taxa is also a possibility, but it is unlikely that *P. tectus* would have entered moist, compressed material.

5:6 Discussion

The soil which had developed over the weathered bedrock, like similar layers in Areas 1–3 and 7, produced coarse pottery, though, unfortunately, the pieces were too small and abraded to be used for thermoluminescence dating, nor was their form and style diagnostic of date.

Subsequently, and probably during the period contemporary with the use of the blackhouses, the ground was dug into and lined with stone to serve as a pit for the disposal of viscera and other refuse.

The sanitary disposal of domestic waste in the pre-1830s dwellings has received little, if any, attention. Reverend Mackenzie gives a graphic description of the problem in his account of a house-call he made —

> "Owing to the great thickness of the wall the house door was at the end of a tunnel, and owing to the lowness of the door space one could not stand upright. In front of the doorway, and extending well into the tunnel, was a hollow into which were thrown all the portions of the birds not used for food, the entire carcases of those not edible, and all and every abomination you can think of." (Mackenzie 1911, 20)

With the building of the 'improved' blackhouses, the practice of spreading ash and rubbish on the floor to produce manure for spreading on the fields was discontinued; and through pressure from MacLeod the rubbish pit at the door was abolished. It seems likely that the practice of using prepared pits, away from the house, followed these measures. The majority lie behind the dwellings, but one, near Blackhouse V, lies south of The Street.

The accumulated waste would have been cleared out when necessary, and strewn on the fields. Initially the pit did not have a base, but was later paved. Brown soil, still containing remains of egg membrane, was found at the lowest level of the paved pit, and rich organic waste had then been dumped onto it. The plant remains and insect assemblage present in the pit presumably came from an old blackhouse, and many of the details revealed by this ecofactual material may be compared with documentary accounts, photographic evidence, and the oral testimony of Lachlan McDonald (Quine 1988, 118) for the later functions of these buildings. Wooden partitions divided the blackhouses into two main units. The northern, upper, end was used as a threshing floor and store-place. Atkinson, eight years after the Evacuation, noted that the area contained:

> "... old ropes, packing cases, wood, sacks, boots and bottles. There were many cauldrons, tubs and barrels filled with an unknown liquid, thick, dark brown and stinking. The iron cauldrons had been used for boiling up crotal, the lichen used by Hebrideans for dyeing wool, and for other, nameless brews. There were interesting miscellanea: a complete cradle, wooden hay rakes, flails (a wooden staff attached by a leather thong to a foot length of very stout rope), spades and forks, scythes and sickles, the balloon-like sheepskin floats of authentic St Kilda mail boats. There were piles of fulmars' feathers in many of the byres, which even after eight years kept their fulmar smell." (Atkinson 1949, 237)

PLATE 31
The interior of a blackhouse in 1938 (R. Atkinson)

The loom was often kept in the blackhouse. Plate 31 shows the upper end of a blackhouse in 1938.

Grass without seed, possibly cut as hay at the end of summer, was present in the recovered soil sample, and there is evidence for docks — as plant remains, and in the presence of *Rhinoncus pericarpius* and *Apion cruentatum*. Docks may have grown by the pit and entered the deposit, or been thrown in from elsewhere, but it is also known that docks were collected for the cattle, and they were certainly taken over to Gleann Mhor during the shieling period of the year to feed the cattle while milking (Kearton 1897, 19). Fodder was kept in the northern, store, end.

The southern end housed the cattle from October to spring, both milk cows and bullocks. They were said to be bedded on straw spread over the clay floor, and there was a box for the bullocks' feed. The ectoparasites of cattle survived, as did sheep keds, so it may be that sheep or lambs were housed in the byre at particular times. The domestic bird louse is presumably from hens, which probably spent some of their time roosting and foraging in the building. There were no human parasites present in the vegetative matter as there had been in the byre litter plastered onto the wall of Blackhouse H (3:4:8).

The presence of *Ptinus tectus*, an import from Australia, could suggest that this is a late cache of organic waste, possibly dumped sometime in the first 30 years of this century.

The pit, then, received a collection of glass vessels and a range of metal items. Although one container — the Dawson's whisky bottle — seems to pre-date the Evacuation, the Terry's sweet jar tends to indicate a presence on the island soon after 1930, and before about 1935. Colin Hamilton, an auctioneer, was on the island in 1930, just after the Evacuation (Hamilton 1990, 15); in the summer of 1931 six scientists from the Universities of Oxford and Cambridge were on Hirta undertaking botanical and other surveys; in 1932, A.G. Ferguson went to transfer Soay sheep from Soay to Hirta; and in 1933 Lord Dumfries visited his new possession with a party which included several islanders (Quine 1988, 171–3). Tourists also continued to visit, on Callum Orme Company vessels *Hebrides* and

Dunara Castle up until 1939. The tins, paint, light bulb and Walker's whisky bottle, however, are several decades younger, probably from the late 1950s or early 60s, and this would suggest that they may well be associated with activity around the time of the *Hard Rock* landing and the establishment of the military installations. Whether they were cleared up and dumped in the pit by troops, or by members of early National Trust for Scotland work parties cannot be deduced.

The collection was covered by zinc sheeting, a medium which had been superseded as a roof cover in the very late 19th century, but which continued to be used on the old blackhouse roofs up until the Evacuation. Clearly this too must have been part of the disposal of older items considered as rubbish.

The remains of several sheep, over the dump, in Phase 9, was not food waste but a deliberate and effective burning of carcases, for phalanges and horn cores were also present. The presence of a metal ear tag, an early type used by the Cambridge University Soay sheep survey, with the cremated sheep bones indicates a date some years after 1959. The later deposit of unburnt sheep bones showed that there was no skull present. It seems to have been a partly decayed carcase placed into a hollow, for some of the bones were articulated. The plastic ear tag found with the remains dates from around 1965.

CHAPTER 6

Overall Discussion

Prehistoric activity

The earliest human presence revealed by archaeological excavation is in the vicinity of the House 8 site, indicated by the pottery fragments from Phase 2. The thermoluminescence date for one sherd covers a broad time span — AD 190 ± 360 — from the Scottish Iron Age into the Dark Ages. The pottery form and decoration suggests either a Bronze Age or Iron Age date. Pottery at a similar stratigraphic level in Areas 6 and 7, in the soil immediately over the bedrock, may have represented a further spread of early occupation to the east, although it was not possible to carry out thermoluminescence dating on the small abraded sherds recovered from these areas.

Stone tools were recovered at all sites investigated, though the majority were of local rock types, and include examples used as hammers, which could be of any date. The 'blades' recovered from Area 7 (sfs 200, 220) and perhaps from disturbed contexts in Areas 4–5 (sfs 38, 49–50, 55, 57) are heavy flat rectangular stones, shaped to a roughly rounded blade at one end, and flat or broken at the other. They are known from the Neolithic site at Scord of Brouster in Shetland (Rees 1986, 81), but have also been found during the excavations of the earth-house, *Tigh an t' sithiche,* on Hirta, where Iron Age pottery was also recovered (Sands 1878a, 187).

Possible prehistoric remains were found on St Kilda during the period of blackhouse building and agricultural improvements in the 1830s and 1840s. Rev. Mackenzie reported numerous grassy mounds, or *gnocan sithichean,* which, when cleared, were found to be composed of earth and stones overlying stone cists (Mackenzie 1911, 6–7). There were apparently two types: four side-stones with a cap, and the same form made up of more stones. Some contained bones and coarse pottery. Also, near the centre of the glebe land, and below Oiseval, Rev. Mackenzie found a scatter of ashes on a flat stone, lying just below the surface. Under the stone was a cavity, though the minister did not explore it. Another stone-capped cavity can still be seen near the seaward end of the consumption dyke between Houses 7 and 8 (Stell and Harman 1988, 49).

The poetess, Euphemia MacCrimmon, mentioned that while preparing the foundations for a black-house, a chamber, apparently an earth-house, was found, with cavities (croops) in the wall (Kennedy 1875, 703). The *Tigh an t' sithiche* earth-house was found near the present burial ground, and was excavated on several occasions. Near it was a midden which contained limpet shells, bone and two stone implements (Sands 1878a, 187). Sands recorded that: 'The men told me they had often found small vessels of clay in the earth, but had never seen any pottery made, nor heard that it had ever been made on Hirta' (Sands 1878a, 186). Donald MacDonald, when giving evidence to the Napier Commission, also said that coarse pottery had been found in the Village Bay area — 'little crocks made of clay. I have seen them myself. I have seen such found where we were digging, of the size of little bowls' (Report 1884, 27, answer 13648). He also said that arrowheads had been found.

The early stream in Area 1 may have brought down with it material from activity further up-slope, including the possibility of objects washed out from earlier sites. The potential for the disturbance and mixing of items of different dates by water action is a serious problem. The accumulation of silt and grit in the channel may also have taken many years to collect.

The deposits from Area 1 contained a range of objects, principally of stone and pottery. The two disc edge flakes (sfs 758, 760), split from pebbles, are reminiscent of the 'Skaill knives' found at the type site of Skara Brae in Orkney (Childe 1931, 114). They have been found at the Knap of Howar (Ritchie, A. 1984, 82), Pierowall Quarry, Westray (Clarke 1984, 101–102), and the Calf of Eday (Calder 1939, 180–81) in Orkney; Jarlshof in Shetland (Hamilton 1956, 12); and four possible examples have been located at Freswick Links, Caithness (Batey 1987, 167, 187). They are usually found in Neolithic contexts, though the knives from the Calf of Eday were apparently associated with Iron Age structures. Pebble flakes could, of course, be fortuitous features, accidentally produced, or they could be designed for a specific function, and be of any date. Flaked stones were, for instance, also found in Phase 5 of the House 8 site (gf. 176).

Scandinavian connections

The steatite from the channel fill is more diagnostic. Steatite, or soapstone, was quarried in Norway (Ritchie, P.R. 1984), with a high peak of production in the Viking period (Skjölsvold 1961, 15). With the colonisation of Shetland, outcrops were worked at Catpund, Cunningsborough, Mainland (Hamilton 1956, 206–10), and on the islands of North Roe, Fetlar and Unst (Butler 1989). Worked steatite, in the form of vessels and other objects, was exported to Orkney, Caithness, the Western Isles, and to Scandinavianised settlements, including York (MacGregor 1978, 37–9). There is no steatite outcrop on St Kilda, and thin-sectioning reveals its most likely source to be Shetland.

The body sherds appear to be from hemispherical vessels, a form found on many Viking sites. Round vessels were found at Da Biggins, Papa Stour, Shetland, along with square-sided vessels, but the evidence from Jarlshof suggests that the square form was becoming more popular by the late Norse phase.

The steatite spindle whorl (sf. 325), apparently disturbed, and located in a context of Phase 10, is a disc type, with straight sides and rounded edges, and of a form which could be considered Viking. Steatite examples have been found in various parts of Britain occupied by Scandinavians, and examples of a similar size and shape in chalk have also been found in late 10th to mid-11th-century contexts at 16–22 Coppergate, York (P. Walton, pers. comm.). There was a tendency for hemispherical or conical forms to take over in popularity from the flat disc type by the late Norse period.

The plate-like fragment of actinolite schist (sf. 789), possibly from Shetland, was unburnt, but could conceivably be part of a baking plate. Stone baking plates are known from Norway and her colonies. Production of steatite plates in the homeland has been discussed by Weber (1984) and Natterstad (1984), and excavated examples have come from urban sites, such as Bergen (Bryggens Museum 1978, 61) and Trondheim (Long 1975, 25) in Norway. Steatite plates have also been found in Orkney and Shetland. Because of its structure, schist was easier to split than steatite, though the site at Sandwick in Shetland has produced both steatite and 'slate' examples. Baking plates are generally considered to be utensils used in the 'Late Norse' period, but appear to have a long history of use. At Da Biggins, Papa Stour, Shetland, a steatite plate fragment was found in association with a 15th-century hearth (Crawford 1985, 147), and in Norway they continued to be used possibly up to 1700 (Weber 1984, 160).

The objects may be linked to a number of others found previously on Hirta, which indicate a Scandinavian presence or influence. Between 1829 and 1843 a mound on the glebe land was cleared. Although no skeleton is reported, an iron sword, spearhead, large whetstone and a number of irregular pieces of iron were found (Mackenzie 1905, 397). The sword may be that reported by Goodrich-Freer (1897, 61). Another spearhead was found by the Keartons while carrying out excavations at the earth-house, *Tigh an t' sithiche* (Kearton 1897, 13). It was 0.356m long, with a simple leaf-shaped blade, slightly less than a third of its length, and a cleft socket. This site had initially been investigated by Sands (1878a, 186–7); and during the Keartons' exploration they also found coarse pottery, fire-shattered stones, querns, stone lamps, and net-sinkers or loom-weights. These objects, and the spearhead, were given to MacLeod of MacLeod, who presented them to the National Museum of Antiquities of Scotland in Edinburgh (Soc. Antiq. Scotl. 1897), though the spearhead later seems to have been destroyed. There is no evidence here that the spearhead was associated with a human burial.

Perhaps at some time around that of the discovery of the sword, and before the mid-1840s, two oval brooches were also found on the island. The precise location is not recorded, and there is no account of any skeletal remains, or other objects. They were sent to the Andersonian Museum in Glasgow (Anderson 1875, 555–6), and in 1872 one of them was illustrated by Worsaae (Taylor 1969, 135). Unfortunately they were later lost or stolen, although one seems to have gone to Copenhagen. Grieg defined the illustrated brooch as a Rygh 649 type of the 9th century (Grieg 1940, 78), but R.B.K. Stevenson later identified it as a type 652/4 of the 10th century (Taylor 1969, 134–5). The brooches may have reached St Kilda at that time, though it is possible that they may have been heirlooms when they were deposited. A number of female graves with oval brooches have been found in the Western Isles, including examples from Islay, Oronsay and Tiree, and Batey has noticed similarities in form between the St Kilda brooch and a 10th-century example found recently at a grave at Kneep on Lewis (Welander *et al.* 1988, 168–71). The brooches may represent booty, or the presence of a woman on Hirta, which may suggest a colony rather than a base for pirates. The discovery of the spindle whorl at the House 8 site, furthermore, implies a fairly settled existence.

Two incised crosses, one on a stone built into House 16, and another in the roof of cleit 74, probably came from Christ's Church, close to the present graveyard, and Harman suggests that they may 'be the work of a Norse-dominated population, influenced by a tradition acquired elsewhere in the Celtic Christian area' (Harman 1979).

There are a number of place-name forms indicative of Scandinavian influence on St Kilda (Taylor 1969, 124–9). There are no instances of farm or shieling names, like *—staðir, —bólstaðir,* and *—setr,* they are confined to topographical names. Taylor considered that some of the names were similar to examples on Harris, and he suggested that St Kilda had been settled by people from that island.

The thermoluminescence date of the coarse pottery fragment from Area 1, Phase 4 — AD 1135 ± 170 places this item well after the 'Lochlannaibh' had first devastated Iona and plundered elsewhere in the Hebrides (AD 795, AD 798). The islands were used extensively as bases for raiding and land seizure from the 9th century, and by the middle of the 10th century Crawford notes that all the Northern and Western Isles were Norse colonies (Crawford 1987, 62).

Medieval administration

In terms of historical administration, it is clear that Godfred Crovan, probably a Hebridean, had brought the Suðreyar and Man together as a unified kingdom, under the overlordship of the Norwegian crown, by the time of his death in 1095 (Kinvig 1975, 59–61). The Isle of Man served as the centre of power, with the Hebridean islands divided into two main groups at a line through Ardnamurchan Point, and further subdivided into the four units of Lewis and Skye in the north, Mull and Islay in the south (Kinvig 1975, 59). Presumably St Kilda was included in the northern or Out Isles. During the 12th century violent conflict broke out between various factions in the area, with the Manx rising against Godred, the grandson of Godfred Crovan. Somerled of Argyll, who sided with the Manx, took as his spoil the Mull and Islay units (Duncan and Brown 1959), as well as the Uists, and perhaps St Kilda, in the 12th century. Godred retained Man, Lewis and Skye, as did his son, Olaf II, during whose lifetime Leod, son of Olaf the Black, succeeded his foster-father Paul Baalkeson as heritable sheriff of Skye. Magnus, Godred's grandson, held overall control of Skye, Lewis, and their 'pertinents' up until the battle of Largs in 1263. This, and the Treaty of Perth in 1266, marked the end of Norse dominion in the Hebrides, and the increasing influence of the Scots under Alexander III. A number of island barons, particularly Angus Mor MacDonald of Islay, supported the king. John MacDonald, Lord of the Isles, Angus' grandson, succeeded to the estate around 1330, and before his death in the 1380s, granted certain islands, including St Kilda, either to his son Reginald, or to a brother, Godfrey. One of them granted St Kilda to the laird of Harris. By 1594, Donald Munro, High Dean of the Isles, reported that 'McCloyd of Herray' sent his steward and a chaplain to St Kilda once a year (Munro 1818, 142). In 1595 Ian, 15th clan chief of the MacLeods died, and was succeeded by Ruari Mor, who was later knighted by James VI in London. In 1615 Colla Ciotach Macghilleasbuig went to St Kilda, and it is made clear that the archipelago then belonged to Ruari (Black 1976, 208).

Although St Kilda was the possession of the clan chief, it was held by a kinsman of MacLeod, as tacksman or 'Steward of the Isle'. Dean Munro reported that 'The said Stewart receives thir dewties in miell and reistit mutton, wyld foullis reistit, and selchis' (Munro 1818, 143). The economy was a mix of agriculture and hunter-gathering. Cultivation of around 80 acres of arable land was by run-rig, with ten major divisions split into strips, from the late 17th century onwards, with the grass divided into plots. Macaulay said of the arable land that:

> "Originally it was covered and lined with a vast number of stones, which have been cleared away by the inhabitants in some former period. All the arable is divided out into a great many unequal plots, and each one of these is in a manner inclosed and kept invariably within the same bounds, by the help of the stones just now mentioned: These serve for boundaries, and are not to be removed or any how violated . . ." (Macaulay 1765, 28)

Martin and Macaulay both refer to the naming of the plots, often with the name of a dead islander, though other non-Gaelic names were apparently used. It is possible that the stone lines found in Area 1, Phase 6, of 17th/early 18th-century date, and linked with evidence of cultivation, may be associated with these land divisions. The dumping of rubble in that area, and the development of gritty soils over the stone lines, indicates that by the early 19th century they had gone out of use.

The presence in the subsequent gritty layers of Areas 1–2, Phase 7, of burnt seaweed is intriguing. *Phaeophyceae* (brown seaweeds) occur in both bays, and it may be that some had been spread on the fields. MacDiarmid records some being gathered in the late 19th century, but he pointed out that there were only limited supplies (MacDiarmid 1878, 243). It was certainly used elsewhere in the Hebrides, and on ground planted with barley or rye, for instance, gave a good yield; while in Ayrshire a main crop of wrack was ploughed into fields used for growing early potatoes, but here around 20 tons was used per acre, and it was not burnt (Noble 1975). On Heisker in the 17th century, because of limited fuel sources, seaweed was burnt, and it was found that 'Bread baked by the Fuel of Sea-ware, relishes better than done otherwise' (Martin 1716, 60). On North Uist it was also the practice at this time to preserve mackerel in burnt seaweed ash (Martin 1716, 56). Perhaps activities like these, where a limited amount of seaweed was burnt, may be an explanation of its presence.

The 1830s 'improved' blackhouses

In the years around 1800, largely due to economic pressure, many landowners in the Highlands and Western Isles began to transform their estates from run-rig into farms and crofts. By the 1830s changes were also occurring on St Kilda. The whole community had to be persuaded to move from their traditional homes and build new houses farther down-slope, and also to change their long-accepted agricultural system. In part this was carried out with the help of a grant from Sir Thomas Dyke Acland, but it is perhaps surprising to see the sheer extent of the involvement of the minister, Rev. Neil Mackenzie, in this transformation of MacLeod's possession. A new linear village was laid out, with each 'improved' blackhouse set in its own plot of ground.

The slope of the ground in the vicinity of Areas 1 and 2, and the flow of water from Tobar Childa, necessitated an effective drainage system at the site of the new blackhouse, and measures were taken to deal with this in Phase 9. One of the capstones, a muscovite biotite schist, probably Moinian, seems to have come from mainland Scotland. The drains were not just a requirement in this area, the possible remains in Area 7 (Phase 3) may have formed part of this system; Quine also noted a drainage system at Blackhouse U, at the west end of the village (Quine 1983, 41); and Fenton records similar care in drainage at Blackhouse no. 42 at Arnol, Lewis (Fenton 1978b, 24), where one drain was found to run out under the front door, and another underlay the hearth.

John MacDonald's blackhouse in Areas 1–2 would have been almost rectangular internally, with broad walls, rounded at the external corners. The walls were of typical form with heavy rubble facings and an earth and stone core. The roof timbers would have been set at a low pitch, laid on the inner face of the wall, like most other 19th-century Outer Hebridean blackhouses. The cover was barley straw thatch, held down with ropes *(simmens)* tied to large stones *(acairiachean)*. It was entered by a single east door.

Internally the building was a single main cell, divided into living quarters and byre by a stone partition or *talan*. It was, then, unlike many of the blackhouses on Lewis, particularly those on the west side, which had developed attached but distinct units, like a projecting porch, a back barn, or a built-in kiln.

The living area of the excavated blackhouse was *c*. 13.9m^2, or 12.9m^2 excluding the hearth. This clay-floored area, theoretically, accommodated up to eight members of the MacDonald family. It continued the open-hearth tradition, though the box form was different from the flat slabs, often laid in a circle, found elsewhere in the Hebrides. A development was the insertion of a glazed window, providing a little light to the living area, and certainly more than that provided by the occasional slit or the *fairleus* in the thatched roofs of other Hebridean blackhouses.

Captain Thomas, who visited one of the St Kildan blackhouses with a crub bed, referred to the *talan* as 'a most inhuman stone wall shoulder high, effectively cutting off crummie from a view of the fire, unless when standing on her hind legs' (Thomas 1870, 158). Such a division was not universal in Hebridean blackhouses. Some had no division at all, and measures drawn up to separate the cow from the humans in houses on Lewis were not popular. In other houses, including examples on Skye, there was a wooden partition.

There would seem to have been a tendency for the door to be just to the south of the *talan*. A plan published in 1867 (Thomas 1870, pl. xxviii) shows that this was certainly the case in Blackhouse K, the home of the 'Queen of St Kilda', Betty Scott.

The byre at the southern end would have accommodated the milk cow over winter, and perhaps other beasts and hens when the weather was bad. The cow would have been tethered by the horns, and there would have been a channel through the wall to drain away the slurry, probably into a collecting pit (Seton 1878, 124). The St Kildans followed the general Hebridean tradition of not cleaning the byre out over the winter, but let the dung accumulate until the spring when it was collected in wooden containers or baskets for manuring the fields.

By the early 19th century it seems that there was also a determined move to keep offal and other domestic waste away from the house, and to compost it in a pit, like that in Area 6, before spreading it on the fields to fertilise them.

The blackhouses were set in their own strips of land. The boundaries of the plots were marked by consumption dykes, which stretched from near the shore to the newly constructed head-dyke, the division between the infield, and the hill grazing. There were openings for access between the two areas.

The excavated pit in Area 7, is recorded by Sharbau as a 'cabbage enclosure' (SRO 1858/1860 RHP), although this could not be corroborated by archaeology due to the lack of survival of any botanical evidence from the pit fill. It may have been associated with the walled enclosures found on strips within the head-dyke (Pl. 32). They are comparable to the somewhat larger 'planticrues' found in the Northern Isles. In Shetland they can be found from Mainland to Unst, and some, like those in the Catpund area of Cunningsborough parish, are still used (Pl. 33). Planticrues were normally used for raising kail, before transplanting, with the seed planted on a bed of fresh turf. When necessary this would be dug out and replaced, to avoid exhausting the soil (Fenton 1978a, 104). In Faroe, walled raising beds are also known. Some in Borðoy are rectangular, in which *Archangelica officinalis* (angelica) was grown as a vegetable (Uldall 1980, 18).

Cleitean

The cleitean (Pl. 34), of which remnants were found in Area 2, have already been noted as having similarities with the 'skeos' of the Northern Isles (see 3:5), but they also form part of a much wider practice of food storage in buildings constructed in such a way as to allow a passage of air through the storage area. The part-stone, part-slatted wood sheds of Faroe (Pl. 35), the stone fish-drying sheds of the Vestmannaeyjar, and the slatted wooden sheds of Iceland (Pl. 36) — the hjallur — form part of this basic principle, as do the drystone 'skemma' of Greenland (Gad 1970, 83–4). In Iceland and Faroe the slatted sheds are used for hanging fish, sheep and pilot whale meat, and also as stores for fowling nets, creels, whale spears and barrels. On the sides of Isafjorður in north-west Iceland the small rectangular slatted wooden sheds used for drying fish are spaced out some distance from the settlements (C. Richardson, pers. comm.).

Seabirds — the mainstay of the economy

The cleitean were, amongst other things, used for the storage of the islanders' seabird catch and eggs. The huge numbers of seabirds resident in or visiting St Kilda provided an invaluable resource for the islanders, and the techniques used to catch the birds, comparable with methods used elsewhere in the North Atlantic islands (Baldwin 1974), are referred to in published sources from the 17th century onwards. There were also established rules concerning the allocation of cliff fowling areas, and the arrangements for working cliffs and stacks.

The cliffs of Hirta were clearly divided up for the catching of seabirds from at least the 17th century, for

PLATE 32
A walled raising bed within the head-dyke, Hirta

PLATE 33
A planticrue in use at Catpund, Shetland

PLATE 34
Cleit 87, south of House 8, looking west

PLATE 35
A foodstore at Viðerejde, Viðoy, Faroe

PLATE 36
A lattice-work fish drying shed, West Reykjavik, Iceland

when Martin visited the island he noted that 'cuddiche' was paid proportionately to the steward by the islanders 'with regard to their respective portions of land and rocks' (Martin 1753, 48). At that time Stac Lee was worked in common because the gannets were so numerous and could not be easily divided up. The drawing of lots decided who would go over to take birds from the stack for communal use, and drawing lots was also used for dividing into sections the birds' breeding places on the cliffs, which would then be worked by four or five men. By the 19th century the islanders paid a pound for the rocks, the same as for the land, but Donald MacDonald recalled that after complaints, the laird took off the charge for the rocks, and placed it, instead, for the use of Boreray (Report 1884, 27).

The bone and membrane evidence from the excavations, along with documentary sources, indicate that puffin, fulmar, gannet and some other seabirds were taken, along with their eggs. The gannets arrived in mid-March and left around October; puffins came in late March or early April; while the fulmar was largely resident, only flying out to sea in September and October.

While snaring of puffins was carried out by women and children, the descent of cliffs and the scaling of the sea stacks to take birds and eggs were tasks invariably undertaken by men, and, in the British Isles, this work is still carried out by men from Ness in Lewis, who usually take around 3000 gugas on Sula Sgeir. MacDiarmid said that the fowler 'is looked upon as the greatest hero who succeeds in capturing the largest number of birds at a time; and a young man was pointed out to me who, in a single night last year, bagged six hundred' (MacDiarmid 1878, 252). Fisher has suggested that never more than 5000 gannets were taken in a year (Fisher 1952, 139), whereas between 1860 and 1910 the annual catches of fulmar ranged from 7500 to 9600, and, on Sands' figures, 89,600 puffins were harvested in the year 1876.

Women and children often waited on the cliff tops to receive the carcases from the catchers, and the whole community plucked them. Although there is no apparent record of any adverse effects to the islanders, particularly the women, from doing this, in Faroe psittacosis from feathers of diseased birds caused 'September Sickness', which could lead to death (West 1986).

Fledgling and older birds were taken at accepted times — old gannets as they came in, gugas when they were fully fledged in early August. Young fulmar were taken before they could fly, on or after the 12th of August (Fisher 1952, 130), while older birds were caught in the spring and around June. Eggs were taken in vast quantities. Fulmar eggs were taken in May. Gannets laid one egg, but if it was taken, they tended to lay another. In the case of guillemots, up to 10,000 eggs might be taken.

The birds themselves were taken either by climbing up to roosting ledges, as on the stacks, or down the cliffs on ropes, a practice also employed by Faroese fowlers on the Mykinesholmur gannetry (Williamson 1945, 256–7). In some areas, like the Vestmannaeyjar, leather ropes were used by fowlers, but on St Kilda up until the 1870s horsehair rope was used. In the 17th century the islanders had three 24-fathom communal ropes.

Martin and later writers refer to the night raids on the stacks, the killing of the 'sentinel', and the catching of the nesting gannets. Martin refers to fowlers hitting the birds on the head during these raids (Martin 1753, 23), and hammers with horsehair wrist loops were certainly used by fowlers in the Myrdal area of Iceland for that purpose (examples in Skógar Folk Museum), but many were simply taken by hand, by breaking the bird's neck. Fulmar were taken by hand or by means of a fowling rod with a noose at the end. These nooses were carefully slipped over the bird's head and pulled quickly. Great care was taken to go behind the bird when catching by hand, and seizing its beak so that it could not squirt oil. Dogs would sometimes be used to locate puffin burrows, and these birds would either be caught by rod or horsehair snare. The snares were made from a cord with up to 40 nooses along its length, each noose about an inch in diameter, spaced about four inches apart. These were laid across a rock and secured. Puffins attracted to it tended to get their feet caught in a noose and were then taken. Guillemots were either taken by rod, or by means of a lure (Mackenzie 1911, 51). Fleygg nets (like butterfly nets) were apparently never used on St Kilda.

The fulmar carcases were drained of their oil, which was stored in a gannet stomach, while puffins were 'plucked, split open like kippers, cured and hung up to dry on strings stretched across the cottages' (Kearton 1897, 113). 'One of these mummified puffins, grilled in the ashes, ranks amongst the few dainties these bleak and lonely islands can afford' (Seebohm 1885, 368). Feathers were retained for rent payment.

1860 onwards — new housing

The effects of the storm of 1860 led to the gradual process of constructing the sixteen new houses. Though most of the other islanders still had their damaged homes to shelter in during the construction process, MacDonald's blackhouse was demolished.

The building of mainland-type houses in the 1860s introduced a new, alien form of dwelling. The cottage was lime-mortared, had squared corners and chimneys, features not normally found on blackhouses, and was purely for human habitation, thus breaking the long tradition of man sharing his home with his animals. A report into housing in 1885 noted that 'white houses' did occur in certain parts of the Western Isles, but were more common in East Scotland and the Northern Isles —

> "They differ from the blackhouses, being built partly with skilled labour, and with materials imported from other districts. In appearance they resemble a common description of a cottage in the Lowlands, though the materials are more perishable, and the roof more defective in material. They have chimneys at the gables, and windows; the walls are built with mortar, the floors are made with boards, earth or flags; the partitions and ceiling are of wood and clay roughly put together; the roofing is of boards covered with thatch, or felt and tar, and occasionally slated." (Report 1885, 9–10)

For such an isolated Hebridean island as Hirta, the new housing was an incredible improvement; for even in 1919, in the whole of Lewis, there was only one *tigh geal* to every three *tighean dubha* (Gibson 1925, 365).

The internal layout of the St Kildan cottage, with a main room either side of a lobby and back closet, can be seen elsewhere in western Scotland, like 12 Lower Ardelve, Lochalsh, which still has rounded corners and a hipped thatched roof (Souness 1987, 17); or in a modernised blackhouse at Carbost, Skye, with the interior divided up into the units by wooden partitions, and where the fire has been moved from the floor to a central wall (Walton 1957, 156). Throughout, it would appear that the flooring of the St Kildan cottages was of earth and clay, and only in the late 19th century was it renewed with timber and, probably in the 1920s, with concrete.

The building materials, fittings and furnishings of the cottages were largely imported. Virtually all cement used on the Scottish mainland and islands during the period 1850–1930 came from cement works along the east coast of England (e.g. Hull/Humberside) and was traded by various groupings of Scottish merchants (W. Brannan, pers. comm.). Metal sheet roof covering was extensively used in the 19th century. John Spencer's patent for corrugating iron sheeting in 1844 led to its use as a roof cover, and as a cladding, while rolled zinc sheets became increasingly popular in the latter half of the century. Roofers used zinc nails (which cost about 8d per pound) when laying sheeting, as iron nails reacted with the zinc. It is possible that the sheets may have come from zinc smelt works in Glasgow. The later felt cover to the roof was coated with coal tar — a product of the destructive distillation of coal, either from a gas works or from by-product coke ovens; while the covering of floorcloth was probably from Kirkcaldy in Fife.

The blackhouses became simply byres, with storage space. Blackhouse H, which had faced MacDonald's old blackhouse, continued to be thatched, but after 1884 the end walls were built up to take a gabled roof with a tarred felt cover, as happened elsewhere in the village. There was a drain in the southern end, and a tethering ring in the east wall. Atkinson, during his visit to Hirta, had noted that the blackhouses were 'sometimes plastered in the common mud-pie style of peasantry; in this case cow manure slapped into the chinks and still showing the plasterer's fingerprints' (Atkinson 1949, 235). Such material was found in the south wall of Blackhouse H, with traces of human excrement. The lower end of the threshing barn, in Area 5, was converted into a tiny dwelling with built-up gables, but it, too, ultimately became a byre on the death of the occupant.

Living conditions and economy in the later 19th century

Living conditions improved — MacLeod said that 'The inhabitants are well-fed, well-clothed, and, for a Hebridean peasantry, particularly well housed' (MacLeod 1871). Limited medical care was provided with the appointment of a nurse in the 1890s, a period which saw the eradication of the scourge of neonatal tetanus (Turner 1895; Collacott 1981; 1985; Holohan 1985). The island children were being educated, and, to an increasing extent, in the language of the outside word — English. In 1822 only one islander could read, and there was only limited instruction up to 1851, when a teacher was sent for two years. In 1867 'none can read anything worth noticing in English; a few of the young men can sign their names with difficulty; the whole adults can read Gaelic, and are well informed in Scripture' (Report 1867, 812). The establishment of a more formal system of education in 1884 and the building of a school onto the church in 1898–9 (Heathcote 1900, 92–7) changed things. By 1901, 32 of the 77 islanders could speak both Gaelic and English (Report 1901, 288). Fragments of the children's school slates were found in the excavations.

The late 19th century saw a decline in the importance of fowling and agriculture in the economy of St Kilda. The seabirds still provided flesh, feathers, eggs, and proventricular oil, while their wings served as fire-side brushes (Atkinson 1949, 238). Feathers had been used as rent payment, as they had been on North Rona (Nisbet and Gailey 1962, 91), and were sent to Liverpool for use in bedding, though the market gradually declined. The *giben* (oil) was a popular medicine in parts of the Hebrides at one time, but was later used as a mix with tar for sheep marking in Skye. Bird and egg collection continued into the 20th century, but it was also being undertaken as a display for visitors, or to provide eggs for sale to tourists.

The rise of fishing

In the late 18th century it was said that the islanders had more food than they could consume (Buchanan 1793, 129). Their stock included sheep, cattle, and some hens, with crops of 6-row bere barley, oats, potatoes, turnips and cabbage. The blades, or *ceabannan*, found in excavation indicate the use of the cas-chrom, the long spade and lever ideal for the poorer and rocky soils of the Highlands and Islands. Fenton has suggested it was in use on St Kilda from the first half of the 19th century (Fenton 1974, 132), and Sands noted 'a casschrom or two put away on the rafters of barns' (1878a, 190). The potato blight, which so seriously affected Ireland and the western highlands, also hit St Kilda. By the late 1870s the return from the tilled land generally was said to be 'miserable' (MacDiarmid 1878, 242), partly due to blight and the stripping of turf for fuel, but also due to overworking the land, and poor planting practice. Botanical remains indicate that 6-row hulled barley and oats were grown and dried at the kiln, while the remains from the House 8 site showed that bere had been the principal crop, though there was some increase in oat production during and following Phase 9. However, by the latter half of the 19th century documentary evidence indicates that bere production was down, local oat seed corn was avoided because of its poor quality, and the root crops had declined markedly.

The starvation and destitution in Scotland caused by the potato blight in the 1840s led to a range of measures designed to alleviate some of the suffering. The establishment of fishing stations was one of these economic projects. Martin Martin, in the 17th century, referred to the plentiful stocks of cod, ling, saithe, mackerel, herring, turbot, coalfish and conger eel around St Kilda. Limpet-baited hook and line was used, though, at that time, there were no nets or longlines. Macaulay suggested that a fishery could be established (Macaulay 1765, 217–25), and by the first half of the 19th century some fish was being caught, but it was not a popular food, for the islanders believed it caused skin infections. Very few fish bones were found in the excavations, those in Areas 1–3 were no earlier than the blackhouse phase (Phase 10). The stacked shells dumped following demolition of the blackhouse and cleit (Phase 11) may have been a food resource, but they may also have been used as bait for craig fishing. In the Northern Isles it was common to parboil limpets for use on the hook, or chewed and spread as ground-bait (Fenton 1973, 73–4). In the 17th century, St Kilda limpets were also parboiled and used as bait, sometimes with puffin flesh (Martin 1753, 19), and there were ten craig seats in 1758 (Macaulay 1765, 223).

The caught fish were generally exported, and the dogs ate the remainder. However, around the 1860s, the younger men began deep-water fishing (Seton 1878, 103). By the 1870s they had two boats, which increased to four, and owned their own long-lines — 50 fathoms or more, with hooked snoods. One hook, found in the excavations, may be a Harwich type (see Muus and Dahlstrom 1988, 215). These lines were ideal for catching cod and ling, and conger eel, which was used as bait. Bream, probably red sea bream, is also known to have been caught by craig fishing. The boat catch was normally prepared on the rocks, and salted in barrels for sale to the factor.

Home industries

Other projects included the development of home industries. Tweed had been made in the Hebrides for household use or for a very local market for many years, but in 1844 the Harris tweed industry was established, with an extended range of markets. The industry expanded to other districts and, once organised, it was taken up on St Kilda. In 1875 the islanders exported 227 yards of cloth and 403 yards of blanketing, totalling in value £62/8s/4d. By 1879 annual production was 800–1000 yards, 'and this quantity was generally booked as sold before its arrival from St Kilda' (Report 1914, 88). Stocking knitting was also established in Harris, South Uist, and on Skye, where MacLeod of MacLeod started the project. Probably in the 1830s stocking knitting began on St Kilda, to supply the tourist trade (Mackenzie 1911, 14) (Pl. 37).

From the excavated sites, the recovered textile finds were predominantly woven on a loom, with some fancy weaves in the collection from Areas 1–3. Fewer examples were found in the other areas, but there are some patterned fabrics such as coloured chevron twills and checked fabrics of various designs. There is, however, no satin weave, nor anything comparable with the sophisticated weave of the lightweight ribbed dress fabric from House 8. There are correspondingly more simple twills from the other areas, some of which probably represent the locally made tweed. No hand-knitting was recorded in the House 8 samples, but it was found in the pit, varying considerably in quality from very fine to extremely coarse, some in stocking stitch and some knitted in rib. Linen-wool union cloths were represented at House 8, but not at the other excavated areas.

Changes in material culture

Coarse pottery and stone tools appear to have continued in use into the 19th century, but the dumping of eighteen stone tools in the blackhouse ruins in Areas 1–2, seems almost like a deliberate move to dispose of primitive tools before the new cottage was built, for by the 1870s, apart from querns, stone tools were not commonly used (Sands 1878a, 187).

The impact of a different material culture began, perhaps most noticeably, in the 1830s, when Rev. Mackenzie went to the mainland and purchased 'windows, tables, bedsteads, kitchen dressers, chairs, stools, and crockery' for the new blackhouses (Mackenzie 1911, 22). As Britain became the 'workshop of the world', producing goods for a developing consumer society, so the range of items and materials increased, particularly with the appearance of more exotic goods from continental Europe and the expanding empire. The development of the rail network to the west in the 1860s–80s, and increasing steamer routes, brought these goods to the Hebrides. Products from various parts of the country, including the emporium of Glasgow, increasingly came to be used on St Kilda, and the remnants of this contact were found most particularly in the accumulated dumps of Phase 7 in Area 6, Phase 13 at House 8, and Phase 7 at the kiln.

External influences can be seen, for instance, in the islanders' diet. Although they ate traditional porridge, mutton and fulmar flesh, some of the preserved grain indicates that wheat was being imported, and documentary sources record that by the 1880s some families were buying eight to twelve bolls of meal a year from the mainland because the island could not produce enough (Report 1884, 25). On other Hebridean islands, like Tiree, factory-made bread began to appear in the latter half of the 19th century with the development of scheduled steamer services with rail connections (Banks 1977, 95). By the 1870s the St Kildans were drinking tea and were purchasing sugar. Bottled chicory, probably in the form of coffee essence, like Camp Coffee, was used. This drink was produced from the 1880s, particularly by Pattersons of Glasgow. Sauce began to be produced and bottled by a number of firms around the 1830s and this too reached the island, probably after the 1880s (Ross 1893, 83). An excavated stoneware jar from House 8, made at Portobello, Edinburgh, would have been filled with preserves, either in Dundee, or possibly Paisley. Other consumables included tobacco, which was often begged from passing trawlermen. Excavated clay pipes were made in Manchester and probably Glasgow. Alcohol was also shipped across, though it was used sparingly for medicinal purposes. One whisky bottle, made between 1900 and 1910, originally came from Kilmarnock. Medicines and cure-alls came from chemists in Glasgow. The imported foods came in perishable packaging, glass containers and pottery jars.

Crockery eventually took precedence over coarse pottery, though the vessels were generally of the cheapest forms. There is a predominance of sponge-printed, hand-painted and transfer-printed bowls over plates, the latter including a few pieces of fine Bell's 'Corea' pattern. There are one or two punch or toddy bowls, one of them dating from around the 1870s, but there is, unusually, only one jug fragment — a spout sherd from a yellow ware cream jug. Several examples of brown teapot were recovered — they have a long lifespan from *c.* 1850 into this century.

The pottery types, none of which appear to pre-date about 1840, include slipware, spongeware,

PLATE 37
A girl knitting (SSS D11 3.9 7923)

stoneware, transfer-printed ware, hand-painted ware and creamware.

The red earthenware types with a slip cover are fairly large bowls, and storage jars that on the mainland were used for dairy work. A finer type, popular in the 1840s and '50s, was possibly made at Robert A. Kidston & Co's Verreville Pottery in Glasgow, though the shape was also produced in Stockton and North Staffordshire. Many of the St Kilda spongeware sherds can be paralleled with pieces from Glasgow and Bo'ness. The post-1860 stoneware consists mainly of jam jars and 'meat loaf jars', with at least one whisky jar, and the knob from a hot water bottle. The transfer-printed material, dating from about 1840–1910, is certainly English; while the sherds with 'chrysanthemums' were extensively produced in Britain in the 1840s and '50s. One apparently Scottish piece of Egyptian black basalte was found, while a piece of creamware is from the Mehlem pottery at Popplesdorf near Bonn, dating from after 1836. Some green 'fancy edge' decoration and Japanese patterns also form part of the collection.

The glass forms found on the island are predominantly containers — commercial bottles for foods, alcohol, soft drinks and medicines; and jars, either empty, pre-packed, or for canning purposes. There are a few closures, some fine glass, possibly from phials or lighting devices, and flat glass for windows. Items of table ware or decorative pieces form a very small part of the collection. Although fragmentary, the range shows evidence of the developments in glass manufacture in the 19th and early 20th century, with mould-blown containers, using 2- or 3-part moulds, with semi and fully automatic machine products, embossing using lettered plates, blob tops, string rims, patent lips and screw threads.

In the case of the glass from lighting devices, the development of the American oil fields brought plentiful supplies of cheap paraffin onto the market around the 1860s, providing an improved lamp fuel. By the turn of the century paraffin lamps had taken over from the old crusies with their fulmar oil fuel on St Kilda. The recovered copper-alloy lamp fragments all come from vertical wick lamp burners, and show the extent of standardisation achieved by the latter half of the century, in the size of wicks and their tubes, burners and chimneys, and the screw collar mounts to the reservoir or font (see Woodhead *et al.* 1984, 50).

There is documentary evidence for some types of metal container being used on St Kilda, like canisters for holding bread and other provisions, which were carried by fowlers on their trips to Boreray in the late 1920s (Gordon 1933, 106–7); tins used for storing fat from boiled fulmar, which was used to oil wool before it was carded (MacGregor 1931, 252); and treacle tins (MacGregor 1931, 257), but there is little surviving evidence for metal containers, particularly for canned food, in the excavated deposits. The long life and ease of transport of such foods led to their use by the Royal Navy, and by polar expeditions — a number of 19th-century caches and rubbish dumps containing tins have been found in the High Arctic islands (Phillips 1985). Developments in manufacture and cooking methods had led, by the early decades of the 20th century, to machine-stamping of tins, automatic soldering, acid cleaning and tin coating on a factory scale. Perhaps because of soil conditions there is little evidence for such tins; the only metal packages which have been found in the excavations include a tin of Andrews Liver Salts, part of a boot polish tin, and the base-resting point of a tin of uncertain content. It seems, from the late deposits in the pit of Area 6, that it was not until after the Evacuation that tins were brought over in any quantity, and survived in the archaeological record.

Clothing was traditionally home-made. Rev. Neil Mackenzie said of the men that they are all 'able to act as tailors, dressmakers, and shoemakers for their own families' (1911, 12); a triangular piece of tailors' chalk was recovered from the soil (House 8, sf. 29). Yet other clothing was being imported — cotton shirts, vests and handkerchiefs, possibly from the factories of central and south-west Scotland; silks, women's *soubach* caps, brilliant coloured petticoats, Rob Roy plaids, and Glengarry bonnets. By the 1880s the women were also wearing 'Turkey red' cotton napkins as head-scarves. Dyeing with this colour was begun in Glasgow by David Dale and George MacIntosh. The old bone and wooden buttons were replaced by a range of new types, many made in Birmingham (see Ross 1893, 89). Other fasteners include a Parisian buckle, and an American-style hook and eye. Their work boots were machine-sewn in mainland factories, and by 1909 some of the men were wearing wooden clogs made on the Scottish mainland, possibly in Dumfriesshire. The clothing worn by the St Kildans had often been modelled on fashions prevailing in other parts of the Hebrides; in the early 19th century, for instance, their clothes were similar to those worn on Harris, but by the late 19th century their dress was virtually indistinguishable from the Ness fowlers of Lewis or the crofters of Shetland.

A wide range of tools was imported. MacDiarmid noted in 1877 that 'They have axes and hammers, and in one house there was a large box of joiners' tools. They are rather scarce of nails, which are always of use to them in the case of accidents to their boats' (MacDiarmid 1878, 242). The excavations have revealed agricultural tools — cas-chrom blades, remnants of spades, a byre graip, a scythe and sickle; while carpenters' and smiths' tools, including an adze, brace, chisels, claw hammer, hatchets, sledge hammers, anvil, bellows and tongs, have been found on the island in the recent past.

Other imported materials include the fowling ropes. The increasing export of hemp from the Philippines in the third quarter of the 19th century led to a greater demand for this stronger form of cordage in Britain. Horsehair had often been sent over for the islanders to make ropes, but around the 1870s they were being replaced by rope made from Manila hemp (Sands 1878a, 192).

Even the locks on their doors changed. The blackhouses had wooden tumbler locks (Allen 1880; Hay 1972) of such an intricate form that it would 'have honoured a Chubb or a Chinaman' (Muir 1858, 13). However, with the new cottages came new doors and locks with iron keys, and padlocks also appeared, until the wooden lock became simply an item of antiquarian curiosity.

Some of these goods were brought over by the factor, or sent by friends and relations on the mainland, while others came from the government and public in Britain during times of shortage on the island. Occasional Jewish pedlars brought over gaudy items (Kearton 1897, 23), but many essential supplies came from passing trawlers and whalers.

Events leading to the Evacuation

The late 19th century, and the beginning of the 20th century, saw significant changes and developments in the British fishing industry, with the creation of steam trawler fleets, and a wider ranging search for fish, as far north as the Iceland Banks; a move which was also linked to the gradual decline in the number of British vessels hunting in the North Sea (Gray 1978). St Kilda lies on the Hebrides shelf, surrounded by water with salinity levels indicative of true Atlantic origin, unaffected by river run-off, containing plankton species typical of the north-east Atlantic. Consequently, the Hebrides area is the main spawning ground for a number of fish species. Saithe, for instance, spawn in the St Kilda area in January to March, and spend some time inshore before swimming to deep water. Haddock spawn to the north of Lewis in March to mid-May, while cod spawn in the area from Lewis to Cape Wrath. Consequently, Scottish companies, like David MacBrayne of Glasgow, the Fraserburgh and North Scotland Steam Trawling Co. Ltd, J.H. Irvine, the North British, and the Aberdeen-Icelandic Steam Fishing companies worked off the west coast. They trawled and fished with lines, sometimes illegally within the 3-mile limit, around Boreray, the Soay Banks and out to Rockall, for cod and halibut. With the decline of these species through overfishing, English boats like those of the Dodds, and the Northumberland steam fishing companies of North Shields; the Palatine, and the Atlas companies of Grimsby; the City, Kingston, and National steam trawling companies of Hull; and the Fleetwood Steam Fishing Co. Ltd, began to hunt dogfish, suitable for the fried fish trade (MacKay 1963, 19), and later ling, hake, codling, grey skate, gurnets and roker. Their boats often came into Village Bay for shelter, and their skippers were particularly kind to the islanders, one Hull crew giving 'coal, paraffin, medicine for the sick men, jam, butter, string, lamp glasses, and everything they needed — biscuits, bread etc.' (Quine 1988, 71–2).

1904 saw the establishment of Norwegian Antarctic whaling from South Georgia (Headland 1986, 10–11), and the creation of land-based stations in the Northern and Western Isles of Scotland. The Bunavoneader Company, apparently Icelandic under the Danish flag, but with a noticeable Norwegian connection, was established on Harris to carry out whaling in the North Atlantic (Report 1904, 453; Jackson 1978, 165). A number of Christiania (Oslo) registered harpoon whalers hunted sei, fin, and blue whale, bringing their catches into Village Bay for temporary storage, before transfer to the flensing plans (the angled surface on which the whale is cut up) of West Loch Tarbert. In 1907 there had been plans to establish a Norwegian station on Hirta, but it was never carried through (Quine 1988, 81). In 1922 Lever Brothers took over the hunting operation, forming the Harris Whaling and Fishing Co., using Antarctic boats, but the number of whales had been seriously depleted, and within six years the company went into liquidation (Jackson 1978, 209). The whaling season was from May to September, and during this period the vessels brought supplies, tons of coal, and mail to St Kilda, and also gave lifts.

Tourism

The arrival of tourist boats in 1877 (MacGregor 1931, 164) also affected the islanders and their economy. The increasing reliance on supplies from outside led to shortages when vessels could not reach the island. In addition, the problem of communicating with the mainland, for supplies or medical assistance, made their isolated position increasingly precarious. Knowledge of the outside world began to draw the islanders away. In the 1850s the Emigration Society assisted many islanders, particularly from Skye, Harris and North Uist to leave for Australia (Richards 1982, 11), and in 1852, 36 St Kildans left for Australia. Fraser Darling later wrote that the:

> "Rapid decrease in population without complete evacuation involves a people in psychological troubles which both further the course of decline and foster a certain hopelessness which is not understood by the neighbouring people in a different environment." (Darling 1955, 69)

The military

The establishment of a military unit on the island during the First World War allowed the islanders prolonged direct contact with mainlanders. Their influence, the problems of isolation, the attractions of mainland life and opportunities, and demographic change, made evacuation inevitable. The depopulation of St Kilda was only one example in a list of island desertions, particularly from the smaller and more isolated islands. The sentiments of the islanders of Inishbofin, off the north-west of Ireland, surely echo those of the St Kildans in many ways. In 1968 the population was 128, in 1984 there were only three. A member of the older generation remaining on the island said 'I like to live where I was brought up. I think it's the best place in the world', but younger people who had left the island said 'We came to the comfort of the mainland as we saw little future on the island. The thought of being alone in a time of emergency was too much' (Davenport 1984).

Post-Evacuation

Within eight years of the evacuation many of the cottages were in an advanced state of decay. Most of the roof cover of Houses 6 and 8 had gone by that stage, as had much of the wooden partitioning and wainscotting. In House 8, of furnishings, only the beds were left in the east bedroom and closet, with a dresser in the living room. In part the decay was due to the elements, but there is also evidence of plundering by visiting trawler crews (Parliamentary Debates 1931, 1051). Since 1957 the cottages have been consolidated, and remain as a memorial.

Conclusion

St Kilda has long been noted for its isolation, but only in the human mind, for its location in the North Atlantic was a major influence in establishing it as a great seabird breeding colony, and it was the seabirds, along with areas of exploitable land and fresh water, which drew man to it. Documentary sources and the archaeological excavations have indicated the long span of human settlement there — a world influenced by the weather, sea state, and particularly the life cycles of a distinctive group of seabirds. While it may seem bizarre, if not reckless, to modern eyes to scale cliff faces or sea stacks to kill birds and collect eggs, and to pay rent in feathers, the birds, livestock and crops maintained the people as a viable, but always fragile, community for centuries. There was clearly contact with other Hebridean islands throughout the settlement period, influencing the gene pool, but always on a limited scale, and within a culturally comparable environment. The contact with the outside world from the 19th century onwards was both intrusive and culturally alien, and affected the delicate social balance with disastrous consequences. The excavations have illustrated the historical sequence of settlement, but the structural evidence, and particularly the artefacts recovered, have shown the changes to the material culture of the islanders, which was part of the dominating outside influences on their lives, influences which ultimately led to the Evacuation and the dispersal of the population, an event which is 'part of the national consciousness' (Ancrum 1985, 16).

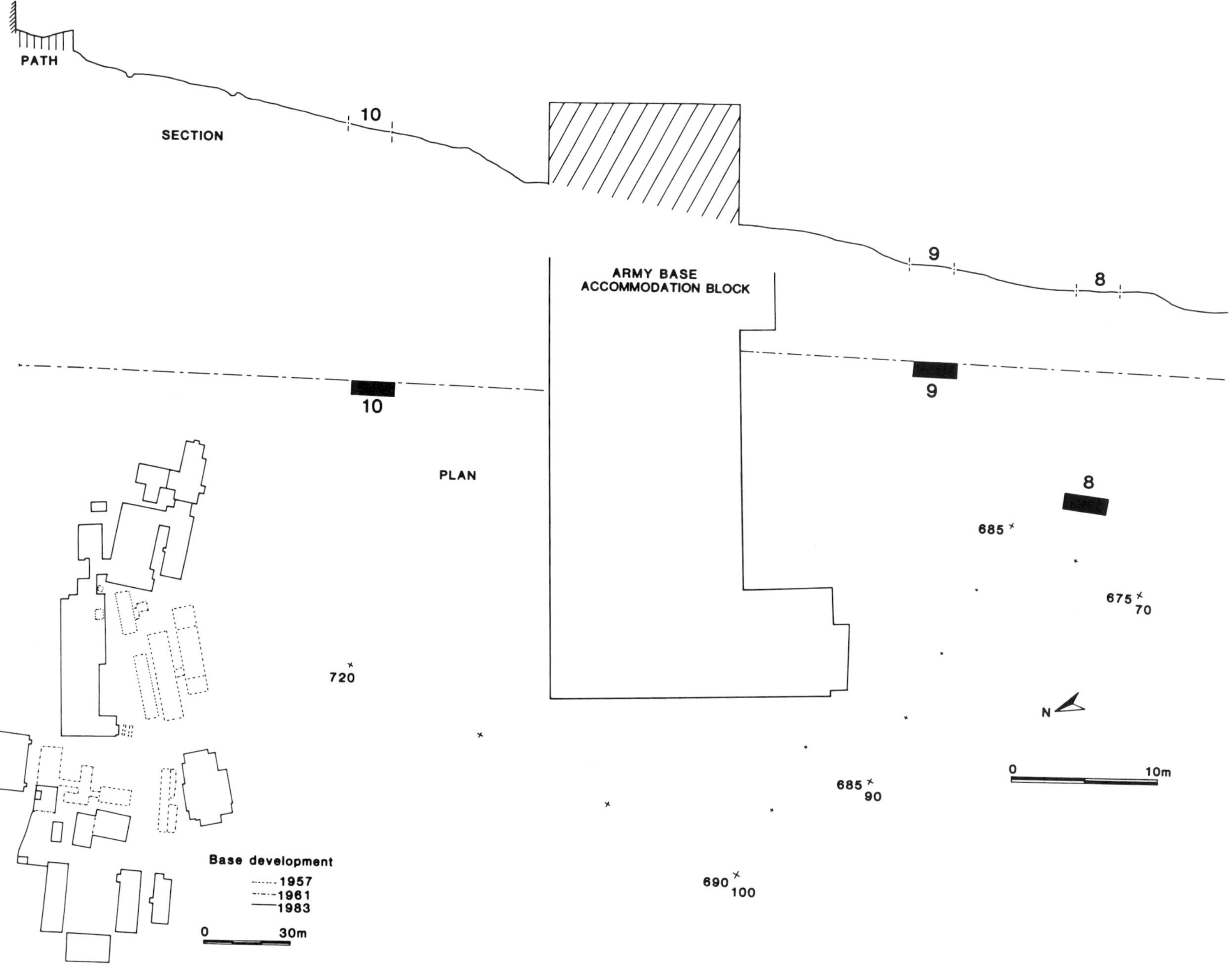

FIG. 101
The army base: location of excavation areas and base development

APPENDIX A

Rescue Excavations at the Army Base

A:1 Reasons for Excavation

In 1987–8 the Ministry of Defence undertook re-development work on the radar facilities on Mullach Mor and Mullach Sgar. Linked to the upgrading of facilities were proposals to replace the existing army base with new accommodation. Nineteenth-century references to the discovery of cists and Viking burials in the general area of the base necessitated the carrying out of exploratory archaeological work in the likely area of redevelopment. Trenches were dug to assess the stratigraphy, the state of any surviving archaeological remains, and the extent of contamination through recent activity.

A:2 Excavation Areas (Fig. 101)

Three trenches were opened up — Areas 8 and 9 south of the main accommodation block, and Area 10 to the north.

A:3 The Stratigraphic Sequence (Fig. 102)

Area 8

A 3m x 1m trench, aligned roughly north-east/south-west, was opened up 22m south of the accommodation block. Overlying the granite bedrock (8003, Phase 1) was a friable compact dark greyish-brown sandy silt (8002, Phase 2), containing small to medium pieces of granite, brick fragments, two tiny sherds of crockery, some window glass, a ?nail, scraps of cable covering, paint, and man-made floor surfacing. Over this was a mixed layer of dark greyish-brown friable sandy silt (8001, Phase 3), containing synthetics, glass, tar and mortar. The deposits were sealed by turf and topsoil (8000, Phase 4).

It seems likely that the soil of Phase 2 represents a ground surface, but that the material found in it, and the overlying layer, represent modern clearance activity

Area 9

A further trench, 3m x 1m, was dug on slightly higher ground, 12m south of the accommodation block, east of Area 8.

The primary surface comprised weathered granite and a gritty deposit (9004, Phase 1). Over it was a dark brown friable sticky silty sand (9003, Phase 2), which was quite humic, and appears to represent a soil build-up over the primary surface. This soil was covered by some large rounded stones at the southern end of the trench, along with concrete and Newton bricks, and would appear to represent the foundations of a structure or the demolished base of a military building (9002, Phase 3). Over this was a dark greyish-brown sandy silt containing small to medium-sized granite pieces and fragments of brick (9001, Phase 4), representing levelling of the demolished material. This debris was sealed by a topsoil of dark brown humic sandy silt (9000, Phase 5), containing brick fragments, drain pipe, a button, a ?fire extinguisher nozzle, and a ring-pull.

Area 10

A 3m x 1m trench was also dug on the higher ground 10.5m north of the accommodation block.

The primary surface was granite, with a gritty soil (1006, Phase 1), producing no finds. Over this surface was a light brownish-grey sticky compact sandy silt (1005), which may have been part of the natural soil build-up. It produced scraps of bone and a 6" nail. Apparently overlying it was a scatter of stones (1003), particularly dense at the northern end of the trench, which appeared to be natural boulders, although there was some suggestion that one cluster had a linear pattern. Overlying them was a spread of soil (1002, Phase 2), similar to that on the primary surface. It produced a slate pencil (sf. 1), an iron tent peg (sf. 2), a scrap of slate, and some concretion. The peg is presumably associated with the 1950s camp. Associated with the layer was a spread or dump of small to medium-sized stones (1004) in the south of the trench. These deposits were covered by a loose light brown gritty sandy silt (1001, Phase 3). It contained plastic sheeting, wood, nails, and a tiny fragment of crockery, and would appear to represent a level, or levelled, surface containing material associated with military activity. The layer was sealed by topsoil (1000, Phase 4).

A:4 The Artefactual Evidence

A:4:1 Crockery (H. Kelly)

The sherds from Area 8 show, in the main, very marked abrasion so that it is impossible to obtain any definite information from them. They would, however, all fit into a late 19th or early 20th-century context.

The abrasion exhibited by these sherds is in marked contrast to the material from the other excavated areas. Although the sherds from the other areas had certainly been disturbed, perhaps repeatedly, they show very little sign of damage apart from breakage.

A:4:2 Glass

Area 8

Thirty-six fragments of glass were recovered.

Phase 2

Six fragments of 3mm clear window glass.

Phase 3

Fourteen fragments of 3mm clear window glass.
One clear glass flake.

Phase 4

One fragment of 4mm clear window glass.
Seven fragments 3mm window glass.
Seven fragments 3mm window glass, with one surface ribbed.

Area 9

Thirty-six fragments of glass were recovered.

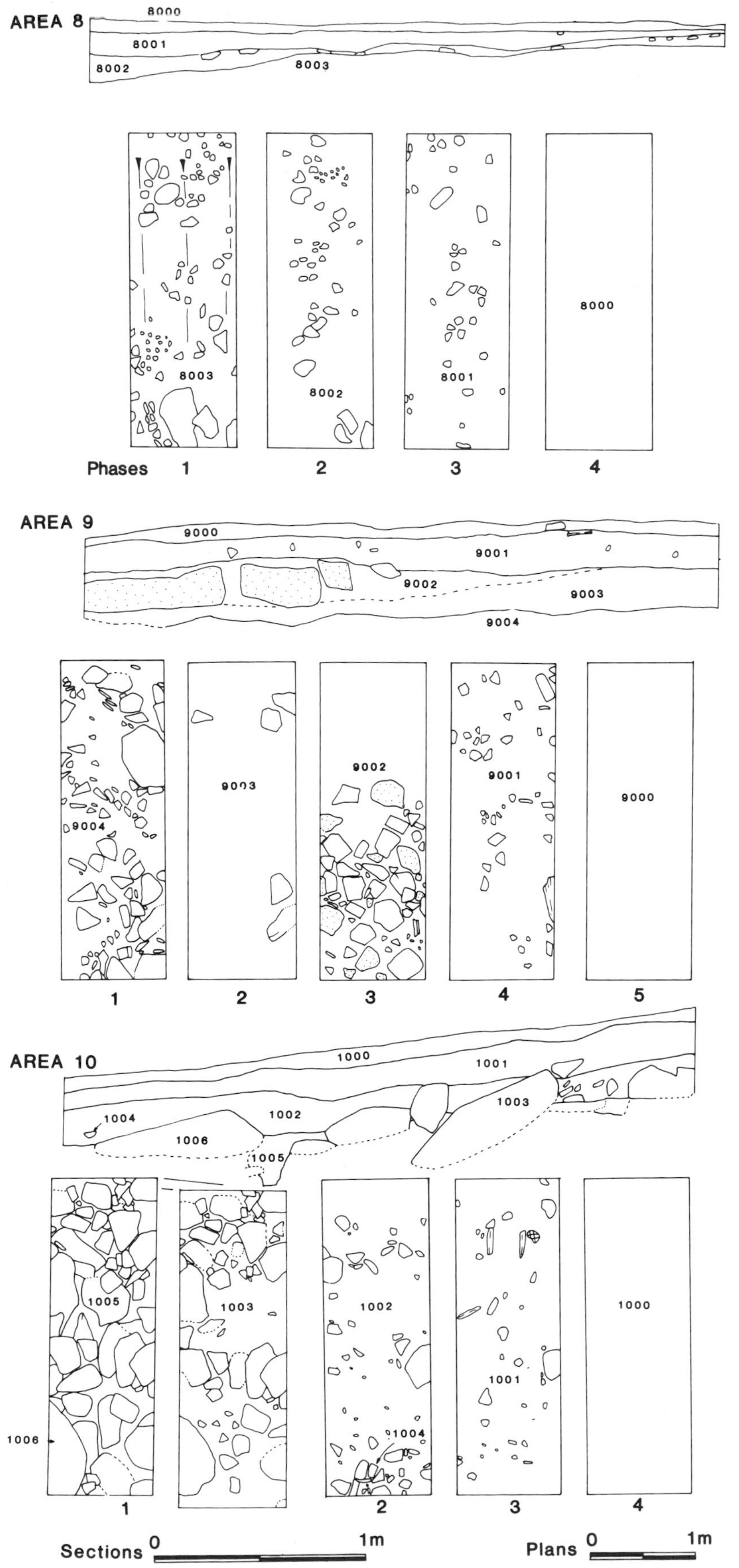

FIG. 102
The army base: excavation areas and phases

Phase 4
Five fragments clear vessel glass.
Two very fine clear fragments, possibly from a phial.
Three fragments of 6mm wired window glass with a moulded surface. Although wired window glass was developed in the 1880s, this is more likely to be associated with a military structure.
Fifteen fragments of 3mm window glass.
One fragment 2mm window glass.

Phase 5
Four fragments of 3mm clear window glass.
One fragment of 3mm window glass with one surface moulded.
One fragment 2mm clear window glass.
Two fragments clear sheet glass with white backing.
One fragment clear vessel body fragment.
One clear flake.

A:4:3 Iron and Steel

Area 8
gf. 8002/2. ?Nail fragment.

Area 9
gf. 9000/5. ?Fire hose nozzle.

Area 10
sf. 2. A T-sectioned, 1' (304mm) long tent peg.

gf. 1005/2. 6" (152mm) wire nail.

A:4:4 Stone (J.R. Senior)

Area 10
sf. 1. Soft school slate pencil.

A:4:5 Miscellaneous

Area 8
Phase 2
Pieces of cable cover, paint and linoleum.

Phase 3
A roof felt tab, asbestos and tar.

Phase 4
Coal, linoleum and a paint flake.

Area 9
Phase 5
Roof felt; a 4-hole, sew-through, matt dark green plastic coat button (¾" (19mm) diam.); a white paint flake; and a drinks can ring-pull (ring pulls were introduced in the mid-1960s).

Phase 5
Cream linoleum, asbestos, red asphalt floor surfacing, and two lengths of plastic-coated wire.

Area 10
Phase 3
Thin, clear plastic sheeting.

A:5 The Ecofactual Material

A:5:1 Mammal and Bird Bones (M. Harman)

Area 9
Context 9000/5. Sheep pelvis — most of the L. ilium, not fused, and nearly full size. Too robust to be a Soay.

Area 10
Context 1005/1. Sheep longbone fragment, probably a femur shaft, towards the distal end.
Small fragment of calcined bone, possibly a thin-walled longbone.

A:6 Discussion

During Churchill's post-war government a British atomic weapons programme was undertaken, with testing on Monte Bello Island off the western coast of Australia, and with V-bomber production. This air-dropped system was brought into operation in 1955, but there was increasing involvement in missile technology, particularly during the Eden and MacMillan ministries, with 'Blue Streak'.

In 1955 there were proposals to establish a missile test range in the Hebrides, and to ensure control of the sea area to the west a party from *HMS Vidal* landed and formally claimed Rockall (Fisher 1956, 149). In the House of Commons, during the 'Air Estimates 1957–8, Vote on Account', Charles Orr-Ewing, the Under-Secretary of State for Air, gave details of a site chosen for the missile test range in the Hebrides (Parliamentary Debates 1956–7, 566, 647–50). The area had been chosen because it could provide for a range head on South Uist, with airstrip facilities on North Uist and Benbecula. There was also a good sea area in which to test fire missiles, but an island out beyond the range was also needed as a radar plotting station. St Kilda was ideal for this purpose.

In April 1957, about 40 men of 5004 Airfield Construction Squadron were moved from RAF Wellesbourne Mountford, near Stratford on Avon, to Lochboisdale, and by tank landing craft to Hirta (Williamson and Boyd 1960, 34). The party increased to about 100, to make initial preparations before the arrival of around 240 more men throughout May, to erect the radar facility.

While the manse was re-occupied, and the church repaired, the main camp was initially in tents, spread throughout the fields of The Street. It is presumably from a tent of this phase that the excavated peg belongs. Some land was prepared, and a roughly H-shaped block of Nissen huts was erected as canteens, etc.

Once the radar had been established the man-power was reduced, and a permanent army garrison took their place in 1958. Some time between 1957 and 1963 an additional Nissen hut was erected parallel to the other two, and REME workshops and garages were built further to the west (Williamson and Boyd 1963, pl. 12). The group of three Nissen huts was replaced in 1969 (Steel 1977, 240–41) by the present military base, with offices, accommodation block, officers' mess (the sergeants' mess is in the old manse), bar, medical and recreational facilities, and power station. Much of the debris found in the rescue trenches probably relates to the camp of Nissen huts, its removal, and the construction of the present camp.

APPENDIX B

Excavation and Basic Artefact Data

A. Excavation Data

1 House 6 (Area 7)

1:1 Context/Phase list (C - context, P - phase)

C	P	C	P	C	P	C	P	C	P
1	9	14	6	27	4	40	4	53	4
2	7	15	5	28	4	41	1	54	4
3	8	16	5	29	4	42	1	55	5
4	8	17	4	30	5	43	1	56	3
5	8	18	5	31	5	44	5	57	3
6	4	19	2	32	5	45	4	58	3
7	4	20	5	33	5	46	4	59	5
8	4	21	5	34	5	47	4	60	3
9	4	22	1	35	4	48	4	61	4
10	4	23	5	36	6	49	5	62	3
11	4	24	5	37	5	50	5	63	3
12	8	25	4	38	4	51	5	64	4
13	6	26	4	39	5	52	5	65	3

2 House 8 (Areas 1–3)

C	P	C	P	C	P	C	P	C	P
1	14	44	9	87	12	130	8	173	11
2	13	45	9	88	10	131	9	174	9
3	14	46	12	89	10	132	1	175	7
4	12	47	12	90	11	133	14	176	5
5	12	48	11	91	11	134	12	177	7
6	12	49	10	92	8	135	12	178	7
7	12	50	11	93	12	136	12	179	7
8	13	51	12	94	12	137	14	180	11
9	12	52	12	95	10	138	12	181	6
10	12/13	53	13	96	12	139	11	182	6
11	13	54	11	97	12	140	12	183	6
12	13	55	8	98	10	141	12	184	6
13	12	56	10	99	11	142	12	185	11
14	12	57	9	100	10	143	12	186	4
15	10	58	12	101	13	144	9	187	11
16	10	59	10	102	8	145	9	188	11
17	13	60	12	103	10	146	8	189	5
18	13	61	11	104	11	147	12	190	9
19	13	62	12	105	11	148	9	191	9
20	10	63	12	106	11	149	9	192	14
21	10	64	11	107	11	150	9	193	12
22	13	65	10	108	7	151	9	194	11
23	10	66	10	109	7	152	9	195	12
24	11	67	10	110	8	153	9	196	10
25	10	68	10	111	6	154	9	197	8
26	11	69	10	112	11	155	9	198	6
27	11	70	12	113	13	156	9	199	9
28	11	71	11	114	7	157	9	200	10
29	10	72	13	115	8	158	10	201	4
30	9	73	14	116	11	159	9	202	2
31	9	74	12	117	11	160	10	203	9
32	9	75	12	118	7	161	10	204	9
33	11	76	10	119	7	162	9	205	9
34	10	77	13	120	7	163	10	206	9
35	11	78	10	121	7	164	7	207	10
36	11	79	12	122	6	165	7	208	9
37	11	80	13	123	6	166	10	209	11
38	10	81	10	124	7	167	10	210	nu
39	10	82	12	125	11	168	11	211	6
40	8	83	10	126	10	169	10	212	6
41	11	84	10	127	8	170	11	213	6
42	11	85	9	128	9	171	11	214	9
43	8	86	12	129	9	172	7	215	9

2 House 8 (Areas 1–3)—continued

C	P	C	P	C	P	C	P	C	P
216	11	229	9	242	12	255	1	268	3
217	11	230	4	243	4	256	10	269	4
218	6	231	10	244	11	257	9	270	4
219	6	232	4	245	12	258	4	271	9
220	6	233	12	246	2	259	4	272	4
221	6	234	4	247	11	260	9	273	1
222	6	235	5	248	11	261	9	274	2
223	6	236	9	249	11	262	9	275	2
224	4	237	9	250	4	263	6	276	9
225	9	238	9	251	4	264	6	277	9
226	9	239	9	252	9	265	7	278	9
227	9	240	9	253	4	266	4	279	1
228	9	241	12	254	4	267	3		

(nu = not used)

3 Blackhouse W (Areas 4–5)

3:1 Context/Phase list (C - context, P - phase)

C	P	C	P	C	P	C	P	C	P
1	9	36	6	71	3	105	5	139	1
2	9	37	6	72	3	106	5	140	3
3	4	38	4	73	3	107	5	141	3
4	4	39	8	74	3	108	5	142	3
5	7	40	7	75	4	109	5	143	3
6	7	41	3	76	nu	110	5	144	3
7	4	42	7	77	7	111	5	145	3
8	4	43	9	78	4	112	2	146	3
9	4	44	6	79	7	113	2	147	3
10	4	45	7	80	3	114	1	148	3
11	7	46	7	81	2	115	2	149	3
12	7	47	5	82	7	116	3	150	3
13	4	48	7	83	4	117	2	151	3
14	4	49	6	84	3	118	4	152	1
15	4	50	5	85	2	119	5	153	2
16	4	51	6	86	2	120	2	154	3
17	7	52	6	87	3	121	4	155	3
18	4	53	4	88	5	122	4	156	2
19	9	54	4	89	5	123	4	157	2
20	6	55	4	90	5	124	5	158	3
21	6	56	4	91	5	125	4	159	3
22	4	57	4	92	3	126	4	160	3
23	4	58	6	93	3	127	5	161	4
24	4	59	6	94	3	128	5	162	2
25	4	60	4	95	3	129	3	163	2
26	4	61	4	96	3	130	3	164	5
27	4	62	4	97	3	131	3	165	4
28	9	63	4	98	3	132	3	166	2
29	6	64	6	99	3	133	2	167	2
30	7	65	7	100	3	134	4	168	6
31	7	66	2	101	6	135	2	169	3
32	7	67	3	102	4	136	2	170	3
33	4	68	6	103	4	137	2	171	3
34	7	69	3	104	4	138	1	172	3
35	8	70	5						

(nu = not used)

4 Viscera/Rubbish Pit (Area 6)

4:1 Context/Phase list (C - context, P - phase)

C	P	C	P	C	P	C	P	C	P
1	11	5	9	9	7	12	5	15	4
2	11	6	9	10	6	13	3	16	2
3	11	7	8	11	6	14	4	17	1
4	10	8	7						

B. Artefact Data

1 House 6 (Area 7)

1:1 Numerical check-list of small finds

No.	Material	C	P
1	Textile	2	7
2	Lead weight	1	9
3	Lead sheet	1	9
4	Cu lamp	1	9
5	2 clench bolts	1	9
6	Plastic comb	12	8
7	Bottle	12	8
8–9	Bottles	1	9
10	Bone button	1	9
11	Mother of pearl button	2	7
12	Cu button	2	7
13	Fe caster	2	7
14	Fe button	2	7
15	Whetstone	2	7
16	Kettle lid	2	7
17	Fe metal strap	2	7
18	Leather offcut	2	7
19	Cu boat nail	2	7
20	Fe padlock	2	7
21	Mother of pearl button	2	7
22	Fe spoon	2	7
23	Fe key	2	7
24	Fe nail & zinc	2	7
25	Fe nail shank	2	7
26–31	Nails	2	7
32	Fe nail	2	7
33	Zinc nail	2	7
34–5	Leather offcuts	1	9
36	Fe knife handle	2	7
37	Leather offcut	1	9
38	Textile	2	7
39	Mother of pearl button	2	7
40	Zinc nail	2	7
41–2	Nails	2	7
43	Zinc nail	2	7
44–6	Nails	2	7
47	Zinc nail	2	7
48–54	Nails	2	7
55	Cu fitting	2	7
56–8	Nails	2	7
59	Fe spike	2	7
60	Fe vessel rim	2	7
61	Fe nail	2	7
62	Looped fe rod	2	7
63	Fe nail	2	7
64	Fe rod	2	7
65–7	Fe nails	2	7
68	Bottle	2	7
69–72	Nails	2	7
73	Fe handle	2	7
74	Plate & spike	2	7
75–7	Nails	2	7
78	Zinc nail	2	7
79	Cu nail	2	7
80	Fe nail	2	7
81	Fe loop	2	7
82–3	Fe nails	2	7
84	Zinc nail	2	7
85	Nail (2)	2	7
86–8	Wooden peg	2	7
89–90	Nails	2	7
91	Zinc nail	2	7
92	Wooden peg	2	7

No.	Material	C	P
93	Nail (2)	2	7
94	Wooden peg	2	7
95–6	Zinc nail	2	7
97–100	Nails	2	7
101	Fe fitting	2	7
102	?Nail	2	7
103	Fe band	2	7
104	Cu screw	2	7
105	Fe band	2	7
106	Cu nail	2	7
107	Bone button	2	7
108	Fe ?shank	2	7
109	Fe cold chisel	2	7
110–12	Nails	2	7
113	Wood	2	7
114	Plaster	2	7
115	Fe ?ring	2	7
116–7	Nails	2	7
118	Zinc nail	2	7
119	Fe rod	2	7
120	Wood	2	7
121–2	Fe nails	2	7
123	Stone tool	2	7
124	Zinc nail	2	7
125	Fe rod	2	7
126	Wooden ?rod	2	7
127	Plastic comb	2	7
128–30	Zinc nails	2	7
131	Fe fragment	2	7
132–3	Fe fragments	2	7
134	Wooden peg	2	7
135	Nails and zinc nail	2	7
136–8	Fe rods	2	7
139	Fe spike	2	7
140	Fe band	2	7
141	Fe band and spike	2	7
142	Cu boat nail	2	7
143	Fe strip	19	2
144	Fe wire	2	7
145–7	Nails	2	7
148	Textile	2	7
149	Cu lamp	2	7
150	Cu nail	38	4
151	Nail and tar	2	7
152	Zinc nail	2	7
153	Cu button	2	7
154	Fe nail	2	7
155	Zinc nail	2	7
156	Cu ring/band	2	7
157–8	Nails	2	7
159	Zinc nail	2	7
160–61	Nails	2	7
162	Zinc nail	2	7
163	Wooden peg	2	7
164–7	Nails	2	7
168	Zinc nail	2	7
169–70	Nails	2	7
171	Zinc nails	2	7
172	Cu and Fe nails	2	7
173	Cu knife scale	2	7
174	Fe fork	2	7
175–6	Nails	2	7
177	Cork	37	5

1 House 6 (Area 7)—*continued*

No.	Material	C	P
178	Wood/paint	37	5
179	Cu nail	18	5
180	Cu washer	46	4
181	Nail	17	4
182	Lino	46	4
183	Cu nail	46	4
184	Lino	46	4
185–6	Cu pins	34	5
187–8	Quern fragments	40	4
189	Fe spike	2	7
190	Fe plate	2	7
191	Fe loop	2	7
192	Cu nail	38	4
193	Clay pipe	61	4
194	Clay pipe	28	4
195–9	Coarse pot	62	3
200	Stone tool	62	3
201–4	Coarse pot	62	3
205–6	Stone	54	4
207–8	Fe nails	19	2
209	Stone, burnt	19	2
210	Stone flake	19	2
211	Pebble tool	19	2
212–15	Pebble fragments	19	2
216	Coarse pot	19	2
217–19	Stone ?tools	19	2
220	Stone tip	19	2
221	Coarse pot	19	2
222–3	Pebble fragments	19	2
224	Coarse pot	19	2
225	Coarse pot	12	8
226	Cu disc	19	2
227–8	Pebble fragments	19	2
229	Coarse pot	19	2
230	Pebble fragment	19	2
231	Coarse pot	19	2
232–3	Pebble flakes	19	2
234	Stone	19	2
235–9	Pebble fragments	19	2
240–41	Coarse pot	19	2
242	Cu lamp	2	7
243	Cu lamp fragment	1	9
244	Cu escutcheon	2	7
245	Lead sheet	2	7
246	Cu lamp	1	9
247	Cu bar	2	7
248	Tinned iron	2	7

2 House 8 (Areas 1–3)

2:1 Numerical check-list of small finds

No.	Material	C	P
1	Quern	2	13
2–3	Coarse pot	12	13
4–7	Coarse pot	17	13
8	Coarse pot	2	13
9–10	Coarse pot	17	13
11	Coarse pot	12	13
12	Coarse pot	19	13
13	Pot whorl	19	13
14	Coarse pot	19	13
15	Bone	20	10
16	Coarse pot	17	13
17	Cu nail	26	11
18	Coarse pot	18	13
19	Coarse pot	37	11
20	Whetstone	37	11
21	Coarse pot	40	10
22	Cartridge	12	13
23	Slate pencil	1	14
24–5	School slate	1	14
26	Glass button	28	11
27	Button	2	13
28	Button	1	14
29	Tailors' chalk	17	13
30	Doll fragment	2	13
31	Zinc nail	2	13
32–3	Fe	47	12
34	Coin	10	12/13
35–8	Fe	10	12/13
39–41	Fe	8	13
42	Coarse pot	1	14
43	Fe	47	12
44	Leather	8	13
45	Tar	47	12
46	Fe	47	12
47	Glass	20	10
48	Crockery	20	10
49	Cu	10	12/13
50	Wood	47	12
51	Fe	20	10
52	Glass	20	10
53	Fe	55	8
54	Fe	10	12/13
55	Leather	10	12/13
56	Glass	10	12/13
57	Fe	10	12/13
58	Coarse pot	43	8
59	Not used		
60	Fe	43	8
61	Coarse pot	20	10
62	Fe	8	13
63–4	Zinc	10	12/13
65	Fe	10	12/13
66	Leather	10	12/13
67	Button	10	12/13
68	Fe	10	12/13
69	Bead	10	12/13
70	Bone	10	12/13
71	Fe	10	12/13
72	Glass	55	8
73	Crockery	43	8
74	Fe	10	12/13
75	Wood object	10	12/13
76–7	Fe	10	12/13
78	Lead	10	12/13
79	Fe	20	10
80	Lino	47	12
81	Coarse pot	1	14
82–3	Coarse pot	62	12
84	Shell	47	12
85	Fe	47	12

2 House 8 (Areas 1–3)—*continued*

No.	Material	C	P
86	Concretion	58	12
87	Fe nail	58	12
88	Bone	58	12
89–91	Coarse pot	62	12
92	Flint	62	12
93	Cu button	47	12
94	Wood	58	12
95	Fe nail	58	12
96	Wood	58	12
97	Fe	58	12
98	Wood	58	12
99	Fe nail	58	12
100–01	Wood	58	12
102	Fe nail	58	12
103	Wood	58	12
104	Plant	58	12
105	Coarse pot	62	12
106	Wood	58	12
107	Cu button	58	12
108–9	Fe nails	58	12
110–11	Coarse pot	62	12
112	Glass	10	12/13
113	Fe	10	12/13
114	Coarse pot	64	11
115	Bone button	64	11
116–17	Fe	64	11
118	Coarse pot	64	11
119–21	Fe	10	12/13
122	Zinc	10	12/13
123–5	Fe	10	12/13
126	Bead	10	12/13
127	Coarse pot	36	11
128	Coarse pot	48	11
129	Bottle	10	12/13
130	Slate pencil	10	12/13
131	Stone	64	11
132	Fe	10	12/13
133	Bead	10	12/13
134	Fe	10	12/13
135	Cu/Leather	10	12/13
136	Zinc	10	12/13
137	Collar stud	10	12/13
138	Fe	10	12/13
139	Wood object	69	10
140	Bead	55	8
141	Coarse pot	80	13
142–3	Fe	10	12/13
144	Clay pipe	10	12/13
145	Wood	24	11
146	Fe	10	12/13
147	Leather	10	12/13
148	Cu	10	12/13
149	Glass	10	12/13
150	Zinc	10	12/13
151–2	Fe	10	12/13
153	Crockery	10	12/13
154	Plaster	10	12/13
155	Comb	10	12/13
156	Coin	10	12/13
157	Pencil lead	10	12/13
158	Coin	10	12/13
159	Fe	10	12/13
160–61	Cu	10	12/13
162	Fe	10	12/13
163	Textile	10	12/13
164	Comb	10	12/13
165	Glass	10	12/13
166–7	Fe	10	12/13
168	Glass	10	12/13
169	Medallion	10	12/13
170	Textile	10	12/13
171	Coin	10	12/13
172	Tin	10	12/13
173	Bead	24	11
174–5	Coarse pot	80	13
176	Coarse pot	81	10
177	Fe	81	10
178	Coarse pot	80	13
179	Clay pipe	81	10
180–82	Fe	24	11
183	Slate pencil	64	11
184	Glass stopper	24	11
185	Coarse pot	24	11
186	Bead	24	11
187	Bone button	24	11
188	Coarse pot	64	11
189	Coarse pot	24	11
190	Fe	24	11
191	Coarse pot	64	11
192	Cu	10	12/13
193	Fe	10	12/13
194	Mortar	27	11
195	Stone	97	12
196	Zinc	24	11
197	Coarse pot	90	11
198	Fe	96	12
199	Coarse pot	104	11
200	Coarse pot	88	10
201	Stone	80	13
202	Fe	92	8
203	Stone	92	8
204	Crockery	92	8
205	Iron	92	8
206	Crockery	92	8
207	Fe	92	8
208	Crockery	88	10
209	Coarse pot	92	8
210–11	Crockery	92	8
212–15	Coarse pot	80	13
216	Coarse pot	86	12
217	Fe	92	8
218–21	Coarse pot	86	12
222	Coarse pot	92	8
223	Glass	92	8
224	Stone	80	13
225	Clay pipe	55	8
226	Fe	55	8
227	Coarse pot	55	8
228	Coarse pot	104	11
229a	Coarse pot	24	11
229b	Coarse pot	104	11
230	Coarse pot	102	8
231	Coarse pot	104	11
232	Fe	102	8
233	Not used		
234–7	Coarse pot	116	11
238	Coarse pot	92	8
239	Wood	92	8
240	Coarse pot	92	8
241	Coarse pot	88	10
242–3	Stone	88	10
244–5	Coarse pot	88	10

2 House 8 (Areas 1–3)—*continued*

No.	Material	C	P
246	Coarse pot	92	8
247	Not used		
248	Stone	124	7
249–50	Coarse pot	124	7
251–2	Coarse pot	102	8
253	Coarse pot	124	7
254	Stone	124	7
255	Coarse pot	124	7
256	Leather	113	13
257	Stone	Unstrat.	
258	Stone	72	13
259	Stone	80	13
260	Stone	69	10
261	Coarse pot	88	10
262	Coarse pot	92	8
263–5	Coarse pot	104	11
266	Coarse pot	113	13
267–8	Cu	73	14
269	Burnt material	131	9
270	Crockery	131	9
271	Coarse pot	145	9
272–3	Wood	141	12
274	Fe	141	12
275	Mortar	137	14
276	Coarse pot	142	12
277–9	Fe	143	12
280	Coarse pot	142	12
281	Coarse pot	141	12
282–6	Fe	143	12
287	Fe	142	12
288–9	Fe	143	12
290	Leather	142	12
291	Fe	147	12
292–3	Fe	142	12
294	Zinc	142	12
295	Coarse pot	147	12
296	Coarse pot	142	12
297	Quartz	164	7
298–300	Coarse pot	165	7
301	Concretion	165	7
302–5	Coarse pot	165	7
306	Stone	165	7
307	Tile	146	8
308–9	Coarse pot	165	7
310	Coarse pot	160	10
311	Stone	124	7
312	Stone	168	11
313	Fe	168	11
314	Shell	168	11
315–17	Stone	168	11
318	Fe	168	11
319–21	Coarse pot	168	11
322–4	Coarse pot	124	7
325	Whorl	39	10
326	Coarse pot	124	7
327	Coarse pot	120	7
328	Coarse pot	39	10
329	Coarse pot	168	11
330–32	Stone	168	11
333	Fe	168	11
334–7	Stone	168	11
338	Coarse pot	168	11
339	Fe	168	11
340–42	Fe	171	11
343	Coarse pot	168	11
344	Bone	168	11

No.	Material	C	P
345	Whale bone	168	11
346	Stone	168	11
347	Coarse pot	168	11
348	Fe	168	11
349	Coarse pot	172	7
350	Coarse pot	120	7
351	Textile	Unstrat.	
352	Coarse pot	124	7
353–4	Coarse pot	39	10
355	Coarse pot	120	7
356	Fe	171	11
357–8	Coarse pot	171	11
359	Coarse pot	115	8
360–61	Coarse pot	116	11
362	Coarse pot	Unstrat.	
363	Bone button	Unstrat.	
364	Coarse pot	168	11
365	Whale bone	170	11
366	Coarse pot	165	7
367	Coarse pot	124	7
368–76	Coarse pot	168	11
377	Coarse pot	115	8
378	Stone	39	10
379	Coarse pot	39	10
380	Stone	175	7
381	Coarse pot	166	10
382	Coarse pot	178	7
383	Quern fragment	168	11
384–5	Coarse pot	168	11
386–7	Coarse pot	139	11
388	Membrane	185	11
389	Whale bone	168	11
390	Coarse pot	139	11
391–2	Membrane	185	11
393	Coarse pot	39	10
394	Fe nail	39	10
395	Coarse pot	201	4
396	Crystal	124	7
397	Coarse pot	175	7
398	Coarse pot	39	10
399–400	Stone	39	10
401–2	Coarse pot	124	7
403	Cu	139	11
404	Membrane	185	11
405	Coarse pot	139	11
406	Membrane	185	11
407	Coarse pot	117	11
408	Quern fragment	171	11
409	Coarse pot	187	11
410	Stone	117	11
411	Stone	116	11
412	Coarse pot	Unstrat.	
413	Coarse pot	175	7
414–18	Coarse pot	174	9
419	Leather	2	13
420	Coarse pot	174	9
421	Coarse pot	176	5
422	Stone	176	5
423	Coarse pot	185	11
424	Coarse pot	Unstrat.	
425–6	Coarse pot	116	11
427	Whale bone	170	11
428–31	Coarse pot	170	11
432	Wood	170	11
433	Coarse pot	179	7
434–6	Coarse pot	170	11

2 House 8 (Areas 1–3)—*continued*

No.	Material	C	P
437	Coarse pot	117	11
438–40	Coarse pot	185	11
441	Coarse pot	170	11
442	Bone	170	11
443	Coarse pot	103	10
444	Coarse pot	170	11
445–6	Stone	196	10
447–53	Coarse pot	170	11
454	Coarse pot	176	5
455	Coarse pot	179	7
456	Stone	176	5
457	Stone	123	6
458	Stone	176	5
459	Fe	178	7
460	Stone	176	5
461–5	Coarse pot	176	5
466–9	Coarse pot	170	11
470	Stone	103	10
471–3	Coarse pot	196	10
474–5	Coarse pot	170	11
476–8	Coarse pot	188	11
479	Membrane	187	11
480	Coarse pot	196	10
481–2	Coarse pot	170	11
483	Membrane	170	11
484–5	Coarse pot	170	11
486–93	Coarse pot	176	5
494	Stone	176	5
495	Coarse pot	176	5
496	?Peat	176	5
497–502	Coarse pot	170	11
503	Coarse pot	196	10
504	Fe	205	9
505	Charcoal	206	9
506	Coarse pot	170	11
507	Coarse pot	206	9
508–10	Coarse pot	196	10
511	Membrane	170	11
512	Coarse pot	196	10
513	Coarse pot	170	11
514	Membrane	170	11
515	Coarse pot	216	11
516	Coarse pot	196	10
517–19	Coarse pot	176	5
520	Cu	201	4
521	Coarse pot	201	4
522–3	Coarse pot	176	5
524	Stone	176	5
525	Coarse pot	213	6
526	Flint	212	6
527	Flint	176	5
528	Flint	213	6
529	Coarse pot	201	4
530	Coarse pot	176	5
531	Coarse pot	201	4
532–9	Coarse pot	176	5
540–44	Coarse pot	230	4
545	Steatite	230	4
546–50	Coarse pot	230	4
551	Coarse pot	216	11
552	Textile	233	12
553	Metal	233	12
554	Coarse pot	216	11
555–8	Coarse pot	196	10
559	Coarse pot	216	11
560	Fe knife	233	12

No.	Material	C	P
561	Quartz	170	11
562	Coarse pot	196	10
563	Coarse pot	170	11
564	Bottle	233	12
565	Coarse pot	216	11
566	Bead	233	12
567–8	Coarse pot	216	11
569	Coarse pot	196	10
570	Coarse pot	233	12
571	Coarse pot	230	4
572	Coarse pot	176	5
573–86	Coarse pot	201	4
587	Coarse pot	216	11
588	Coarse pot	196	10
589	Coarse pot	216	11
590–602	Coarse pot	196	10
603	Coarse pot	187	11
604	Stone tool	187	11
605–6	Coarse pot	187	11
607–13	Coarse pot	201	4
614–15	Coarse pot	216	11
616–18	Coarse pot	196	10
619	Conglomerate	196	10
620–22	Coarse pot	196	10
623	Coarse pot	216	11
624–7	Coarse pot	196	10
628	Fe	243	4
629	Coarse pot	245	12
630	Coarse pot	216	11
631	Coarse pot	233	12
632–3	Coarse pot	196	10
634–5	Coarse pot	201	4
636–8	Coarse pot	230	4
639–40	Coarse pot	176	5
641	Coarse pot	230	4
642	Steatite	230	4
643	Coarse pot	230	4
644	Coarse pot	196	10
645	Fe	196	10
646–50	Coarse pot	196	10
651	Coarse pot	205	9
652	Coarse pot	252	9
653–6	Coarse pot	216	11
657	Coarse pot	196	10
658	Coarse pot	252	9
659	Coarse pot	208	9
660	Coarse pot	196	10
661	Coarse pot	252	9
662	Coarse pot	170	11
663	Coarse pot	252	9
664	Coarse pot	202	2
665–71	Coarse pot	230	4
672	Steatite	230	4
673–8	Coarse pot	230	4
679	Stone	230	4
680–82	Coarse pot	196	10
683–5	Coarse pot	252	9
686	Stone	170	11
687	Coarse pot	170	11
688–93	Coarse pot	196	10
694–5	Coarse pot	170	11
696–7	Coarse pot	196	10
698–9	Coarse pot	204	9
700–01	Coarse pot	230	4
702–5	Coarse pot	246	2
706	Coarse pot	196	10

2 House 8 (Areas 1–3)—*continued*

No.	Material	C	P
707	Coarse pot	170	11
708–9	Coarse pot	196	10
710	Coarse pot	231	10
711–12	Coarse pot	196	10
713	Coarse pot	170	11
714–15	Coarse pot	196	10
716	Coarse pot	252	9
717	Coarse pot	196	10
718	Membrane	245	12
719	Coarse pot	196	10
720–21	Coarse pot	257	9
722	Bone	245	12
723	Coarse pot	256	10
724–5	Coarse pot	257	9
726	Coarse pot	230	4
727	Coarse pot	232	4
728	Coarse pot	196	10
729–34	Coarse pot	216	11
735–6	Coarse pot	196	10
737–9	Coarse pot	216	11
740	Coarse pot	196	10
741	Coarse pot	252	9
742	Coarse pot	216	11
743–4	Coarse pot	170	11
745–6	Coarse pot	208	9
747	Coarse pot	243	4
748–50	Coarse pot	232	4
751	Coarse pot	259	4
752	Flint	232	4
753–7	Coarse pot	232	4
758	Stone	232	4
759	Coarse pot	176	5
760	Stone	230	4
761–8	Coarse pot	230	4
769	Steatite	230	4
770	Stone	230	4
771	Coarse pot	230	4
772–8	Coarse pot	202	2
779	Slate pencil	195	12
780	Coarse pot	202	2
781–3	Coarse pot	269	4
784	Fe	196	10
785	Steatite	243	4
786	Coarse pot	243	4
787–8	Coarse pot	269	4
789	Steatite	243	4
790	Coarse pot	256	10
791–800	Not used		
801	Coarse pot	202	2
802–5	Coarse pot	274	2
806	Whetstone	196	10

3 Blackhouse W (Areas 4–5)

3:1 Numerical check-list of small finds

No.	Material	C	P
1–2	Coarse pot	1	9
3	Fe	1	9
4	Glass button	1	9
5	Coarse pot	1	9
6–7	Coarse pot	13	4
8	Bead	11	7
9	Coarse pot	1	9
10–11	Fe	30	7
12	Slate pencil	2	9
13	Stone	40	7
14	Stone	31	7
15	Byre fork	1	9
16	Textile	11	7
17	Slate	11	7
18	Stone tool	11	7
19	Stone tool	40	7
20	Leather	17	7
21	Stone tool	31	7
22	Textile	2	9
23	Stone tool	32	7
24	Stone	34	7
25–6	Stone	32	7
27	Stone tool	1	9
28	Coarse pot	17	7
29	Crockery	17	7
30	Textile	11	7
31	Leather	29	6
32–4	Coarse pot	17	7
35	Stone	65	7
36–7	Coarse pot	34	7
38	Stone	85	2
39	Fe	109	5
40–41	Crockery	111	5
42	Fe	126	4
43	Stone	126	4
44	Crockery	124	5
45	Crockery	114	1
46	Coarse pot	86	2
47	Stone tool	86	2
48	Fe	167	2
49–50	Stone tool	53	4
51	Glass	140	3
52	Crockery	142	3
53	Wood	133	2
54	Coarse pot	133	2
55	Stone tool	51	6
56	Wood	161	4
57	Stone tool	21	6
58–9	Crockery	21	6
60–61	Crockery	117	2
62	Stone	166	2
63	Textile	11	7
64–5	Textile	1	9
66	Textile	17	7
67–76	Leather	1	9
77–9	Leather	2	9
80–83	Leather	11	7
84–6	Leather	13	4
87–8	Leather	17	7
89	Leather	28	9
90–95	Leather	35	8
96	Leather	43	9
97–8	Leather	44	6

4 Viscera/Rubbish Pit (Area 6)

4:1 Numerical check-list of small finds

No.	Material	C	P
1	Coin	3	11
2	Bone button	3	11
3–5	Coarse pot	3	11
6	Plastic ear tag	4	10
7	Metal ear tag	5	9
8–9	Textile	10	6
10	Bead	11	6
11	Button	10	6
12	Textile	6	9
13–17	Textile	7	8
18–19	Textile	8	7
20–53	Textile	10	6
54	Leather	1	11
55	Leather	2	11
56–7	Leather	7	8
58	Leather	8	7
59–68	Leather	10	6
69	Fe button	11	6
70	Bone button	11	6
71–2	Coarse pot	12	5
73	Whetstone	12	5
74	Bone button	12	5
75	Coarse pot	12	5
76	Flint	11	5
77	Textile	12	5
78	Flint	12	5
79–81	Stone	12	5
82	Coarse pot	12	5
83–100	Coarse pot	16	2
101	?Slag	16	2
102–3	Stone	16	2
104–5	Coarse pot	16	2
106	Stone	16	2
107–9	Coarse pot	16	2
110	Lamp burner	7	8

5 Army Base (Area 10)

5:1 Numerical check-list of small finds

No.	Material	C	P
1	Slate pencil	1002	2
2	Tent peg	1002	2

Bibliography

Acland, A. 1981. *A Devon Family: The Story of the Aclands* (London)

Allen, J.R. 1880. 'Notes on wooden tumbler locks', *Proc. Soc. Antiq. Scotl.*, **14** (1879–80), 149–62

Ancrum, M. 1985. *Nomination of St Kilda for inclusion in the World Heritage List* (Edinburgh)

Anderson, J. 1875. 'Notes on the relics of the Viking period of the Northmen in Scotland, illustrated by specimens in the Museum', *Proc. Soc. Antiq. Scotl.*, **10** (1872–4), 536–94

Atkinson, R. 1949. *Island Going* (London)

Baldwin, J.R. 1974. 'Sea bird fowling in Scotland and Faroe', *Folk Life*, **12,** 60–103

Banks, N. 1977. *Six Inner Hebrides* (Newton Abbot)

Banks, S. 1978. *The Magpie's Companion* (London)

Barclay, G.J., Brooks, M. and Rideout, J.S. 1982. 'A corn-drying kiln at Barbush Quarry, Dunblane, Perthshire', *Proc. Soc. Antiq. Scotl.*, **112,** 583–6

Batey, C.E. 1987. *Freswick Links, Caithness — A Re-Appraisal of the Late Norse Site in its Context.* Br. Archaeol. Rep. (Br. Ser.), **179**

Batey, C.E. (forthcoming). 'The finds', in Morris, C.D. *Excavations and Survey in Birsay Village, Orkney. The Birsay Bay Project.* Durham Univ. Monogr., **2**

Batey, C.E. and Heggie, G. (forthcoming). 'The finds from the Brough of Birsay' in Morris, C.D. *Brough of Birsay, Orkney. Excavations 1974–81. The Birsay Bay Project.* Durham Univ. Monogr., **3**

Beattie, O. and Geiger, J. 1987. *Frozen in Time: The Fate of the Franklin Expedition* (London)

Beresford, G. 1979. 'Three deserted medieval settlements on Dartmoor: a report on the late E. Marie Minter's excavations', *Medieval Archaeol.*, **23,** 98–158

Beveridge, E. 1931. 'Excavation of an earth-house at Foshigarry, and a fort, Dun Thomaidh, in North Uist', *Proc. Soc. Antiq. Scotl.*, **65** (1930–31), 299–317

Black, R. 1976. 'Colla Ciotach', *Trans. Gaelic Soc. Inverness*, **48** (1972–4), 201–43

Britnell, W.J. 1984. 'A 15th-century corn-drying kiln from Collfryn, Llansantffraid Deuddwr, Powys', *Medieval Archaeol.*, **28,** 190–94

Brown, S.G.G. 1976. 'Modern whaling in Britain and the north-east Atlantic Ocean', *Mammal Rev.*, **6,** 25–36

Bryggens Museum. 1978. *Handbook to the Cultural History of the Middle Ages* (Bergen)

Buchanan, J.L. 1793. *Travels in the Western Hebrides: from 1782 to 1790* (London)

Buchanan, M. 1983. *St Kilda: A Photographic Album* (Edinburgh)

Busch, J. 1981. 'An introduction to the tin can', *Hist. Archaeol.*, **15** (no. 1), 95–104

Butler, S. 1989. 'Steatite in Norse Shetland', *Hikuin*, **15,** 193–206

Calder, C.S.T. 1939. 'Excavations of Iron Age dwellings on the Calf of Eday in Orkney', *Proc. Soc. Antiq. Scotl.*, **73** (1938–9), 167–85

Cameron, A.D. 1986. *Go Listen to the Crofters* (Stornoway)

Campbell, K. 1984. 'Co. Louth: Drogheda, South Quay', *Medieval Archaeol.*, **28,** 256

Celoria, F. 1966. 'St Kilda'. Keele University Expedition. Ms. report to NTS, Edinburgh

Cheape, H. 1983. 'Crogans and Barvas Ware pottery in the islands', *Stornoway Gazette and West Coast Advertiser*, week ending 22 January

Cheape, H. 1984. *Kirtomy Mill and Kiln.* Scott. Vernacular Build. Working Group

Childe, V.G. 1931. *Skara Brae. A Pictish Village in Orkney* (London)

Clarke, A. 1984. 'Stone tools', in Sharples, N.M. 'Excavations at Pierowall Quarry, Westray, Orkney', *Proc. Soc. Antiq. Scotl.*, **114,** 101–5

Clarke, E.D. 1824. *The Life and Remains of Edward Daniel Clarke* (ed. W. Otter) (London)

Clegg, E.J. 1977. 'Population changes in St Kilda during the 19th and 20th centuries', *J. Biosoc. Sci.*, **9,** 293–307

Clipson, J. 1980. 'Back Silver Street, Durham, 1975–6 excavations', *Archaeologia Aeliana*, **8** (5th ser.), 109–26

Close-Brooks, J. 1981. 'Excavations in the Dairy Park, Dunrobin, Sutherland, 1977', *Proc. Soc. Antiq. Scotl.*, **110** (1978–80), 328–45

Clutton-Brock, J., Dennis-Bryan, K., Armitage, P.L. and Jewell, P.A. 1990. 'Osteology of the Soay sheep', *Bull. Br. Mus. Nat. Hist. (Zool.)*, 56 (1), 1–56

Collacott, R.A. 1981. 'Neonatal tetanus in St Kilda', *Scott. Med. J.*, **26,** 224–7

Collacott, R.A. 1985. 'Medical and nursing services to St Kilda', *Scott. Med. J.*, **30,** 181–3

Connell, R. 1887. *St Kilda and the St Kildians* (London)

Cottam, M.B. 1973. 'St Kilda Archaeological Survey'. Ms. report to NTS, Edinburgh

Cramp, S. and Simmons, K.E.L. 1977. *The Birds of the Western Palearctic*, **I** (Oxford)

Cramp, S. and Simmons, K.E.L. 1985. *The Birds of the Western Palearctic*, **IV** (Oxford)

Crawford, B. 1985. 'The Biggings, Papa Stour — A multi-disciplinary investigation', in Smith, B. (ed.) *Shetland Archaeology: New Work in Shetland in the 1970s* (Lerwick), 128–58

Crawford, B.A. 1987. *Scandinavian Scotland* (Leicester)

Crawford, I.A. 1967. 'Whale bone artifacts and some recent finds in Berneray, Harris', *Scott. Stud.*, **11,** 88–91

Crawford, I.A. 1976. 'Western Isles (Inverness-shire): N. Uist, Coileagan An Udail (The Udal)', in Webster, L.E. and Cherry, J. 'Medieval Britain in 1975', *Medieval Archaeol.*, **20,** 176

Cubbon, A.M. and Megaw, B.R.S. 1969. 'Corn drying kilns in the Isle of Man', *J. Manx Mus.*, **7** (no. 85), 113–16

Curle, C.L. 1982. *Pictish and Norse Finds from the Brough of Birsay 1934–74.* Soc. Antiq. Scotl. Monogr. Ser., **1**

Curwen, E.C. 1938. 'The Hebrides: a cultural backwater', *Antiquity*, **12,** 261–89

Darling, F.F. (ed.) 1955. *West Highland Survey* (Oxford)

Davenport, H. 1984. 'Post Office writes an island's epitaph', *The Observer*, 25 November

Devine, T.M. 1988. *The Great Highland Famine: Hunger, Emigration and the Scottish Highlands in the Nineteenth Century* (Edinburgh)

Donaldson, A.M., Morris, C.D. and Rackham, D.J. 1981. 'The Birsay Bay project: preliminary investigations into the past exploitation of the coastal environment of Birsay, Mainland, Orkney', in Brothwell, D.R. and Dimbleby, G.W. (eds) *Environmental Aspects of Coasts and Islands*. Br. Archaeol. Rep. (Int. Ser.), **94,** 65–85

Dorchester Excavation Committee. 1973. 'Dorset: Dorchester, Poundbury Camp', in Webster, L.E. and Cherry, J. 'Medieval Britain in 1972', *Medieval Archaeol.*, **17,** 138–40

Duncan, A.A.M. and Brown, A.L. 1959. 'Argyll and the Isles in the Earlier Middle Ages', *Proc. Soc. Antiq. Scotl.*, **90** (1956–7), 192–220

Emery, N. 1985. 'Changing patterns of farming in an Isle of Man glen', *Post-Medieval Archaeol.*, **19,** 1–11

Evans, J.G. 1972. *Land Snails in Archaeology* (London)

Fairhurst, H. 1969. 'Rosal: a deserted township in Strath Naver, Sutherland', *Proc. Soc. Antiq. Scotl.*, **100** (1967–8), 135–69

Fenton, A. 1973. 'Craig-fishing in the Northern Isles of Scotland', *Scott. Stud.*, **17,** 71–80

Fenton, A. 1974. 'The cas-chrom: a review of the Scottish evidence', *Tools and Tillage,* **2,** 131–48

Fenton, A. 1975. *Traditional Elements in the Diet of the Northern Isles of Scotland.* Ethnologische Nahrungsforschung: Vortrage des Zweiten Internationalen Nahrungsforschung (Helsinki)

Fenton, A. 1978a. *The Northern Isles: Orkney and Shetland* (Edinburgh)

Fenton, A. 1978b. *The Island Blackhouse* (Edinburgh)

Fenton, A. 1982. 'Net-drying, pot-drying and graddaning: small-scale grain drying and processing techniques'. *Saga och Sed* (Uppsala), 85–106

Firth, J. 1974. *Reminiscences of an Orkney Parish* (Stromness)

Fisher, J. 1952. *The Fulmar* (London)

Fisher, J. 1956. *Rockall* (London)

Fisher, R.A., Corbet, A.S. and Williams, C.B. 1943. 'The relation between the number of species and the number of individuals in a random sample of an animal population', *J. Anim. Ecol.*, **2,** 42–58

Flegg, J., Hoskings, E. and Hoskings, D. 1990. *Poles Apart. The Natural Worlds of the Arctic and Antarctic* (London)

Gad, F. 1970. *The History of Greenland,* **I** (London)

Gailey, A. 1970. 'Irish corn-drying kilns', *Ulster Folk Life,* **15,** 52–71

Gallagher, D.B. 1987. 'Tobacco pipemaking in Glasgow 1667–1967', in Davey P. (ed.) *The Archaeology of the Clay Tobacco Pipe, X, Scotland.* Br. Archaeol. Rep. (Br. Ser.), **178,** 35–109

Garbett, G. and Skelton, I. 1987. *The Wreck of the Metta Catherina* (Truro)

Gardner, K.S. 1968. 'Devonshire: Lundy Island', in Wilson, D.M. and Hurst, D.G. 'Medieval Britain in 1966', *Medieval Archaeol.*, **11** (1967), 301–2

Gauld, T., Bagenal, T.B. and Connel, J.H. 1953 'The marine fauna and flora of St Kilda, 1952', *Scott. Nat.*, **65,** 29–49

Gelling, P.S. 1971. 'A Norse homestead near Doarlish Cashen, Kirk Patrick, Isle of Man', *Medieval Archaeol.*, **14** (1970), 74–82

GROS. 1871. CEN/1871/111 3. St Kilda. Census Enumerators Returns, 1871 (General Register Office for Scotland)

GROS. 1891. CEN/1891/111 4. St Kilda. Census Enumerators Returns, 1891 (General Register Office for Scotland)

GROS. OPR 111/2. St Kilda. Registers of Baptisms, Marriages and Deaths (General Register Office for Scotland)

Gibson, A. 1989. 'Medieval corn-drying kilns at Capo, Kincardineshire and Abercairny, Perthshire', *Proc. Soc. Antiq. Scotl.*, **118** (1988), 219–29

Gibson, G. 1925. 'The blackhouses of the Outer Isles', *Caledonian Med. J.*, **12,** 364–72

Gilchrist, D.W. 1966. *An Agricultural Geography of Great Britain* (Oxford)

Goodrich-Freer, A. 1897. 'The Norsemen in the Hebrides', *Saga Book,* **2,** 51–74

Gordon, S. 1933. *Islands of the West* (London)

Grant, S., Macdonald, J., Swanson, C. and Wood, J.S. 1983. 'A survey of two deserted settlements at Braleckan and Brenchoillie, Argyll', *Glasgow Archaeol. J.*, **10,** 143–56

Gray, M. 1978. *The Fishing Industries of Scotland, 1790–1914* (Oxford)

Gregor, W. 1892–5. 'Kilns, mills, millers, meal and bread', *Trans. Buchan Field Club,* **3,** 125–59

Grieg, S. 1940. 'Viking antiquities in Scotland', in Shetelig, H. (ed.) *Viking Antiquities in Great Britain and Ireland* (Oslo)

Grieve, S. 1885. *The Great Auk or Garefowl* (London)

Gwynne, D., Milner, C. and Hornung, M. 1974. 'The vegetation and soils of Hirta', in Jewell, P.A., Milner C. and Boyd, J.M. *Island Survivors: The Ecology of the Soay Sheep of St Kilda* (London), 36–87

Hamilton, A.B. 1966. 'Sussex: Streatham', in Wilson, D.M. and Hurst, D.G. 'Medieval Britain in 1964', *Medieval Archaeol.*, **9** (1965), 204

Hamilton, A.Y. 1990. 'Colin Hamilton — auctioneer', *St Kilda Mail,* **14,** 15

Hamilton, J.R.C. 1956. *Excavations at Jarlshof, Shetland* (Edinburgh)

Hansen, M. 1987. *The Hydrophiloidea (Coleoptera) of Fennoscandia and Denmark.* Fauna Entomologica Scandinavica, **18**

Hansen, V. 1952. *Biller 16. Rovbiller 2.* Danmarks Fauna, **58**

Harbottle, L.B. 1974. 'Northumberland: Belling Mill', in Cherry, J. 'Post-medieval Britain in 1973', *Post-Medieval Archaeol.*, **8,** 135

Harcourt, R.A. 1974. 'The dog in prehistoric and early historic Britain', *J. Archaeol. Sci.*, **1,** 151–75

Harding, R.R., Merriman, R.J. and Nancarrow, P.H.A. 1984. *St Kilda: An Illustrated Account of the Geology.* Rep. Br. Geol. Surv., **16** (no. 7)

Harman, M. 1979. 'An incised cross on Hirt, Harris', *Proc. Soc. Antiq. Scotl.*, **108** (1976–7), 254–8

Harris, M.P. and Murray, S. 1978. *Birds of St Kilda* (Cambridge)

Harvie-Brown, J.A. and Buckley, T.E. 1888. *A Vertebrate Fauna of the Outer Hebrides* (Edinburgh)

Hay, G.D. 1972. 'Scottish wooden tumbler locks', *Post-Medieval Archaeol.*, **12,** 125–7

Headland, R. 1986. *The Island of South Georgia* (Cambridge)

Heathcote, N. 1900. *St Kilda* (London)

Henriksen, K. and Hansen, V. 1966. *Biller 23. Smaeldere og Pragtbiller Larverne.* Danmarks Fauna, **74**

Hinton, H.E. 1941. 'The Ptinidae of economic importance', *Bull. Entomol. Res.*, **31,** 331–81

Holleyman, G.A. 1947. 'Tiree Craggans', *Antiquity*, **21,** 205–11

Holohan, A.M. 1985. 'St Kilda: childbirth and the women of Main Street', *Scott. Med. J.*, **30,** 50–53

Holohan, A.M. 1986. 'St Kilda: emigrants and disease', *Scott. Med. J.*, **31,** 46–9

Hudson, G., Towers, W., Biddy, J.S. and Henderson, D.J. 1982. *Soil Survey and Land Capability for Agriculture: The Outer Hebrides.* Soil Survey of Scotland (Edinburgh)

Hunter, J.R. (ed.) 1984. *Fair Isle Survey: Interim 1984.* Bradford Univ. School Archaeol. Sci. Physics Occas. Pap., **5**

Hunter, J.R. 1986. *Rescue Excavations on the Brough of Birsay 1974–82.* Soc. Antiq. Scotl. Monogr. Ser., **4** (Edinburgh)

Huntley, J.P. 1986. 'Analysis of carboniferous plant remains from Freswick Links, Caithness'. Palaeoenviron. Stud. Serv. Rep., Dept. Botany, Durham Univ.

Huntley, J.P. 1990. 'The arable weed communities of Mainland Orkney' (Interim report submitted to the British Ecological Society)

Hurley, M. 1983. 'Co. Kilkenny: Kilferagh', in Youngs, S.M, Clark, J. and Barry, T.B. 'Medieval Britain in 1982', *Medieval Archaeol.*, **27,** 218

Hurst, D.G. and Hurst, J.G. 1971. 'Excavations at the medieval village of Wythemail, Northamptonshire', *Medieval Archaeol.*, **13** (1969), 167–203

Jackson, G. 1978. *The British Whaling Trade* (London)

Jope, E.M. 1958. 'Excavation of a medieval settlement at Beere, North Tawton, Devon', *Medieval Archaeol.*, **2,** 112–40

Kearton, R. 1897. *With Nature and a Camera* (London)

Keepax, C.A. 1981. 'Avian egg-shell from archaeological sites', *J. Archaeol. Sci.*, **8,** 315–35

Kennedy, A. 1875. 'Letter from St Kilda by Miss A. Kennedy communicated with notes by Capt. F.W.L. Thomas', *Proc. Soc. Antiq. Scotl.*, **10** (1872–4), 702–11

Kenward, H.K. 1978. *The Analysis of Archaeological Insect Assemblages: A New Approach.* The Archaeology of York, **19/1**

Kenward, H.K., Engleman, C., Robertson, A. and Large, F. 1986. 'Rapid scanning of urban archaeological deposits for insect remains', *Circaea*, **3,** 163–72

Kenward, H.K. and Hall, A.R. (forthcoming). *Biological evidence from Anglo-Scandinavian deposits at 16–22 Coppergate.* The Archaeology of York, **14/7**

Kenward, H.K., Hall, A.R. and Jones, A.K.G. 1980. 'A tested set of techniques for the extraction of plant and animal macrofossils from waterlogged archaeological deposits'. *Sci. Archaeol.*, **22,** 3–15

Kenward, H.K., Hall, A.R. and Jones, A.K.G. 1986. *Environmental Evidence from a Roman Well and Anglian Pits in the Legionary Fortress.* The Archaeology of York, **14/5**

Kinvig, R.H. 1975. *The Isle of Man: A Social, Cultural and Political History* (Liverpool)

Kloet, G.S. and Hincks, W.D. 1964. *A Checklist of British Insects. Part 1: Small Orders and Hemiptera.* Handbooks for the Identification of British Insects, **11 (1)** (2nd ed.). R. Entomol. Soc. (London)

Kloet, G.S. and Hincks, W.D. 1977. *A Checklist of British Insects. Part 3: Coleoptera and Strepsiptera.* Handbooks for the Identification of British Insects, **11 (3)** (2nd ed.). R. Entomol. Soc. (London)

Larsson, Sv.G. and Hansen, V. 1965. *Biller 21. Snudebiller Larverne.* Danmarks Fauna, **69**

Lawson, W.M. 1981. 'Families of St Kilda', *St Kilda Mail*, **5,** 38–43

Le Quesne, W.J. 1965. *Hemiptera (Cicadomorpha).* Handbooks for the Identification of British Insects, **2 (2a).** R. Entomol. Soc. (London)

Lindroth, C.H. 1974. *Coleoptera: Carabidae.* Handbooks for the Identification of British Insects, **4 (2).** R. Entomol. Soc. (London)

Long, C.D. 1975. 'Excavations in the medieval city of Trondheim, Norway', *Medieval Archaeol.*, **19,** 1–32

Low, G. 1879. *A Tour Through the Islands of Orkney and Shetland* (Kirkwall)

Macaulay, K. 1764. *The History of St Kilda* (London)

Macaulay, K. 1765. *A Voyage to, and History of, St Kilda* (Dublin)

MacCulloch, J. 1824. *The Highlands and Western Isles of Scotland*, **IV** (London)

MacDiarmid, J. 1877. *St Kilda and its inhabitants* (Edinburgh)

MacDiarmid, J. 1878. 'St Kilda and its inhabitants', *Trans. Highland Agric. Soc.*, **10** (4th ser.), 232–54

MacDonald, D. 1984. *The Tolsta Township* (Tolsta, Lewis)

McGavin, N.A. 1983. 'Excavations in Kirkwall 1978', *Proc. Soc. Antiq. Scotl.*, **112** (1982), 392–436

MacGregor, A. 1975. 'The Broch of Burrian, North Ronaldsay, Orkney', *Proc. Soc. Antiq. Scotl.*, **105** (1972–4), 63–118

MacGregor, A. 1978. 'Industry and commerce in Anglo-Scandinavian York', in Hall, R.A. (ed.) *Viking Age York and the North.* Counc. Br. Archaeol. Res. Rep., **27,** 37–57

MacGregor, A.A. 1931. *A Last Voyage to St Kilda* (London)

MacKay, J.A. 1963. *St Kilda, its Posts and Communications* (Edinburgh)

Mackenzie, J.B. 1905. 'Antiquities and old customs in St Kilda, compiled from notes made by Rev. Neil Mackenzie, minister of St Kilda, 1829–43', *Proc. Soc. Antiq. Scotl.*, **39** (1904–5), 397–402

Mackenzie, J.B. 1911. *Episode in the life of the Rev. Neil Mackenzie at St Kilda from 1829 to 1843* (privately publ.)

MacLaren, A. 1974. 'A Norse house on Drimore Machair, South Uist', *Glasgow Archaeol. J.*, **3,** 9–18

McLellan Mann, L. 1908. 'Notices — (1) of a pottery churn from the island of Coll, with remarks on Hebridean pottery; and (2) of a workshop for flint implements in Wigtownshire', *Proc. Soc. Antiq. Scotl.*, **42** (1907–8), 326–9

MacLeod, J.M. 1871. 'St Kilda: Letter to the Editor', *The Times*, 26 August, 10

MacSween, A. 1984. 'Neutron activation analysis of Barvas Ware: handthrown pottery of the Hebrides'. Unpubl. MA Diss., Univ. Bradford

Mahany, C. 1967. 'Northamptonshire: Grafton Regis', in Wilson, D.M. and Hurst, D.G. 'Medieval Britain in 1965', *Medieval Archaeol.*, **10** (1966), 202–3

Marshall, D.N. and Taylor, I.D. 1979. 'The excavation of the chambered cairn at Glenvoidean, Isle of Bute', *Proc. Soc. Antiq. Scotl.*, **108** (1976–7), 1–39

Martin, M. 1698. *A Late Voyage to St Kilda* (London)

Martin, M. 1716. *Description of the Western Isles of Scotland* (London)

Martin, M. 1753. *A Voyage to St Kilda* (4th ed.) (London)

Mathieson, J. 1928a. 'The antiquities of the St Kilda group of islands', *Proc. Soc. Antiq. Scotl.*, **62** (1927–8), 123–32

Mathieson, J. 1928b. 'St Kilda', *Scott. Geogr. Mag.*, **44,** 65–90

Megaw, J.V.S. and Simpson, D.D.A. 1963. 'A short cist burial on North Uist and some notes on the prehistory of the Outer Isles of the second millennium BC', *Proc. Soc. Antiq. Scotl.*, **94** (1960–61), 62–78

Mercer, J. 1972. 'Roomed and roomless grain-drying kilns: the Hebridean boundary', *Trans. Anc. Monuments Soc.*, **19,** 27–36

Milligan, I.D. 1963. 'Corn kilns in Bute', *Trans. Buteshire Nat. Hist. Soc.*, **15,** 53–9

Milne, G. 1979. 'Yorkshire, North (Yorkshire E. Riding): Wharram Percy', in Webster, L.E. and Cherry, J. 'Medieval Britain in 1978', *Medieval Archaeol.*, **23,** 272–3

Morales, A. and Rosenlund, K. 1979. *Fish Bone Measurements* (Copenhagen)

Morris, M.G. 1990. *Orthocerous Weevils. Coleoptera: Curculionoidea (Nemonychidae, Anthribidae, Urodontidae, Attelabidae and Apionidae).* Handbooks for the Identification of British Insects, **5 (16).** R. Entomol. Soc. (London)

Muir, A. 1956. *Nairns of Kirkcaldy: A Short History of the Company (1847–1956)* (Cambridge)

Muir, T.S. 1858. *St Kilda, A Fragment of Travel* (Edinburgh)

Munro, D. 1774. *A Description of the Western Isles of Scotland* (Edinburgh)

Munro, D. 1818. *Description of the Western Isles of Scotland called Hybrides, by Mr. Donald Munro, High Dean of the Isles, who travelled through most of them in the year 1594.* Misc. Scotica, **2**

Murray, G. 1886–7. 'St Kilda Diary of George Murray'. NTS, Edinburgh, Bute Box

Murray, S. and Wanless, S. 1986. 'The status of the gannet in Scotland 1984–5', *Scott. Birds,* **14,** 74–85

Muus, B.J. and Dahlstrom, P. 1988. *Sea Fishes of Britain and North Western Europe* (London)

Natterstad, J. 1984. 'Den geologiske bakgrunn for bakstehelle-industrien vet Kvitebergvatnet i Hardanger', *Viking,* **47** (1983), 161–4

Nicholson, R.A. 1991. 'An investigation into variability within archaeologically recovered assemblages of faunal remains: the influence of pre-depositional taphonomic processes'. Unpubl. D.Phil. thesis, Univ. York

Nicholson, R.A. 1992. 'Bone survival: the effects of sedimentary abrasion and trampling on fresh and cooked bone', *Int. J. Osteoarchaeol.*, **2:1,** 79–90

Nisbet, H.C. and Gailey, R.A. 1962. 'A survey of the antiquities of North Rona', *Archaeol. J.*, **117** (1960), 88–115

Noble, R.R. 1975. 'The end to "wrecking": the decline in the use of seaweed as a manure on Ayrshire coastal farms', *Folk Life,* **13,** 80–83

Norwegian Folkmuseum. 1975. *Guide to the Open Air Museum* (Oslo)

Opie, R. 1987. *The Art of the Label* (London)

Oswald, A. 1975. *Clay Pipes for the Archaeologist.* Br. Archaeol. Rep. (Br. Ser.), **14**

Owen, O. 1987. 'Interim report on the survey and excavations undertaken at Kebister, Shetland'. Central Excavation Unit and Ancient Monuments Laboratory Annual Report (Edinburgh)

Parliamentary Debates. 1931. Official Reports, House of Commons (5th ser.), 254, col. 1051, 34

Parliamentary Debates, 1956–7. Official Reports, House of Commons (5th ser.), 566, 647–50

Peacock, P. 1978. *Discovering Old Buttons* (Aylesbury)

Perring, F.H. and Walters, S.M. 1976. *Atlas of the British Flora.* Botanical Society of the British Isles

Perrins, C. 1987. *Birds of Britain and Europe* (London)

Pfleger, V. and Chatfield, J. 1988. *A Guide to Snails of Britain and Europe* (London)

Phillips, C. 1985. 'The camps, cairns and caches of the Franklin and Franklin search expeditions', in Sutherland, P.D. (ed.) *The Franklin Era in Canadian Arctic History.* Nat. Mus. Man, Mercury Ser., Archaeol. Surv. Canada Pap., **131**

Pollock, D. 1987. 'The Lunan Valley project: medieval rural settlement in Angus', *Proc. Soc. Antiq. Scotl.*, **115** (1985), 357–99

Quine, D.A. 1988. *St Kilda Portraits* (Frome)

Quine, T.A. 1983. 'Excavations in Village Street, Hirta, St Kilda 1983'. Ms. report to NTS, Edinburgh

Rahtz, P.A. 1971. 'Herefordshire, Hereford, Victoria Street', in Wilson, D.M. and Hurst, D.G. 'Medieval Britain in 1968', *Medieval Archaeol.*, **13** (1969), 233

Ramm, H.G., McDowall, R.W. and Mercer, E. 1970. *Shielings and Bastles.* R. Comm. Hist. Monuments (England) (London)

Rees, S. 1986. 'Stone implements and artifacts', in Whittle, A.W.R. *Scord of Brouster: An Early Agricultural Settlement on Shetland.* Oxford Univ. Comm. Archaeol. Monogr., **9,** 75–91

Renfrew, J. 1973. *Palaeoethnobotany* (London)

Report. 1867. *Report on the State of Education in the Hebrides. Education Commission (Scotland).* PP 1867 (cd. 3845–iv), **25,** 812

Report. 1884. *Report of Her Majesty's Commissioners of Inquiry into the Condition of the Crofters and Cottars in the Highlands and Islands of Scotland.* PP 1884 (cd. 3980), **34,** 18

Report. 1885. *Second Report of Her Majesty's Commissioners for Inquiry into the Housing of the Working Classes: Scotland.* PP 1884–5 (cd. 4409), **41,** 9–10

Report. 1901. *Eleventh Decennial Census of the Population of Scotland.* PP 1901 (cd. 1257), **129,** 288

Report. 1904. *Report of the Departmental Committee on Whaling and Whale-curing in the North of Scotland.* PP 1904 (cd. 2138), **42,** 449

Report. 1914. *Report to the Board of Agriculture for Scotland on the Home Industries in the Highlands and Islands.* PP 1914 (cd. 7564), **32,** 88, app. ix, 224

Richards, E. 1982. 'Highland emigrants to South Australia in the 1850s', *Northern Scotl.*, **5** (no. 1), 1–29

Ritchie, A. 1979. 'Excavation of Pictish and Viking-age farmsteads at Buckquoy, Orkney', *Proc. Soc. Antiq. Scotl.*, **108** (1976–7), 174–227

Ritchie, A. 1984. 'Excavation of a Neolithic farmstead at Knap of Howar, Papa Westray, Orkney', *Proc. Soc. Antiq. Scotl.*, **113** (1983), 40–121

Ritchie, J.N.G. 1981. 'A kiln at Machrins, Colonsay, Argyll', *Proc. Soc. Antiq. Scotl.*, **110** (1978–80), 528–30

Ritchie, P.R. 1984. 'Soapstone quarrying in Viking lands', in Fenton, A. and Palsson, H. (eds) *The Northern and Western Isles in the Viking World* (Edinburgh), 59–84

Ross, A. 1893. 'A visit to the island of St Kilda', *Trans. Inverness Sci. Soc. Field Club*, **3** (1883–8), 72–91

Ross, J. *c.* 1890. 'St Kilda'. Ms. account. NTS, Edinburgh, Bute Box

Ross, L. 1983. 'The stone objects', in McGavin, N.A., 'Excavations in Kirkwall 1978', *Proc. Soc. Antiq. Scotl.*, **112** (1982), 418–19

RCAHMS. 1971. *Argyll Volume 1: An Inventory of the Ancient Monuments of Kintyre.* R. Comm. Anc. Hist. Monuments Scotl.

RCAHMS. 1980. *Argyll Volume 3. An Inventory of the Monuments, Mull, Tiree, Coll and Northern Argyll.* R. Comm. Anc. Hist. Monuments Scotl.

Ryder, M.L. 1968. 'The origin of spinning', *Text. Hist.*, **1.1,** 73–82

Sands, J. 1878a. 'Notes on the antiquities of the island of St Kilda', *Proc. Soc. Antiq. Scotl.*, **12** (1876–8), 186–92

Sands, J. 1878b. *Out of the World; or, Life in St Kilda* (Edinburgh)

SSS — BV 29d3 6423. Plan of kiln, Port Henderson, Wester Ross (School of Scottish Studies)

SSS — BV 33d3 6462–3. Plans of kilns at Hougarry, N. Uist (School of Scottish Studies)

SSS. 1909. DII 3.9b 7930 — Photograph by R.M.R. Milne (School of Scottish Studies)

SSS. 1909. DII 3.9b 7932 — Group photograph by R.M.R. Milne (School of Scottish Studies)

SSS. 1938. S265 — R. Atkinson photograph looking into House 8 (School of Scottish Studies)

SSS. 1938. S290 — R. Atkinson photograph of a barrel in House 5 (School of Scottish Studies)

Scott, L. 1951. 'Corn-drying kilns', *Antiquity*, **25,** 196–208

SRO. 1858/1860. RHP 6778 — St Kilda from a survey by Mr H. Sharbau (Scottish Record Office)

Seebohm, H. 1885. *A History of British Birds*, **3** (London)

Séguy, E. 1941. *Insectes Ectoparasites. (Mallophages, Anoplures, Siphonapteres).* Faune de France, **43**

Seton, G. 1878. *St Kilda Past and Present* (Edinburgh)

Silver, I.A. 1963. 'The ageing of domestic animals', in Brothwell, D.R. and Higgs, E.S. (eds) *Science in Archaeology*, 250–68

Skjölsvold, A. 1961. *Klebersteinsindustrien i vikingetiden* (Oslo)

Slater & Co. 1893. *Slater's Royal Commercial Directory of Scotland* (Edinburgh)

Small, A. 1967. 'Excavations at Underhoull, Unst, Shetland', *Proc. Soc. Antiq. Scotl.*, **98** (1964–5 and 1965–6), 225–48

Soc. Antiq. Scotl. 1897. 'Donations to the museum and library', *Proc. Soc. Antiq. Scotl.*, **31** (1896–7), 153–5

Souness, J.R. 1987. 'Re-thatching at 12 Lower Ardelve, Lochalsh', *Vernacular Build.*, **10** (1986), 17–24

Steel, T. 1977. *The Life and Death of St Kilda* (Glasgow)

Stell, G.P. and Harman, M. 1988. *Buildings of St Kilda.* R. Comm. Anc. Hist. Monuments Scotl. (Edinburgh)

Stewart, J.H. and Stewart M.B. 1989. 'A highland longhouse — Lianach, Balquhidder, Perthshire', *Proc. Soc. Antiq. Scotl.*, **118** (1988), 301–17

Stone, J.C. 1988. 'The St Kilda archipelago', *St Kilda Mail*, **12,** 4–7

Swann, J. 1986. *Shoes.*

Sutherland, D.G., Ballantyne, C.K. and Walker, M.J.C. 1984. 'Late Quaternary glaciation and environmental change on St Kilda, Scotland, and their palaeoclimatic significance', *Boreas*, **13,** 261–71

Talbot, O. 1974. 'The evolution of glass bottles for carbonated drinks', *Post-Medieval Archaeol.*, **8,** 29–62

Tasker, M.L., Moore, P.R. and Schofield, R.A. 1988. 'The seabirds of St Kilda 1987', *Scott. Birds*, **15,** 21–9

Taylor, A.B. 1969. 'Norsemen in St Kilda', *Saga Book*, **17** (1966–9), 116–44

Taylor, S.J. 1972. 'Warwickshire: Nuneaton, Bermuda, Templars' Manor', in Wilson, D.M. and Moorhouse, S. 'Medieval Britain in 1970', *Medieval Archaeol.*, **15** (1971), 168

Thomas, F.W.L. 1870. 'On the primitive dwellings and hypogea of the Outer Hebrides', *Proc. Soc. Antiq. Scotl.*, **7** (1866–8), 153–95

Tottenham, C.E. 1954. *Coleoptera: Staphylinidae. (a) Piestinae to Euaesthetinae.* Handbooks for the Identification of British Insects, **4 (8a).** R. Entomol. Soc. (London)

Turner, C.A. 1895. 'The successful preventative treatment of the scourge of St Kilda (*Tetanus neonatorum*), with some considerations regarding the management of the cord in the newborn infant', *Glasgow Med. J.*, **43,** 161–74

Uldall, K. 1980. *Frilandsmuseet* (Copenhagen)

Walton, J. 1957. 'The Skye house', *Antiquity*, **31,** 155–62

Ward, S. 1980. 'Cheshire: Chester, Princes Street/Hunter's Walk', in Webster, L.E. and Cherry, J. 'Medieval Britain in 1979', *Medieval Archaeol.*, **24,** 219

Weber, B. 1984. '"I Hardanger er Qverneberg og Helleberg . . . og Hellerne, det er tyndhugne Steene, bruger man til at bage det tynde Brød flatbrød paa . . ."', *Viking*, **47** (1983), 149–60

Welander, R.D.E., Batey, C.E. and Cowie, T.G. 1988. 'A Viking burial from Kneep, Uig, Isle of Lewis', *Proc. Soc. Antiq. Scotl.*, **117** (1987), 149–74

West, J.F. 1986. 'Only the men go chasing the chicks', *The Guardian*, 30 August

Wheeler, A.C. 1978. *A Key to the Fishes of Northern Europe* (London)

Whitaker, I. 1957. 'Two Hebridean corn-kilns', *Gwerin*, **1** (no. 4), 161–70

White, D.P. 1977. 'The Birmingham button industry', *Post-Medieval Archaeol.*, **11,** 67–79

Wiglesworth, J. 1903. *St Kilda and its Birds.* Reprinted from the Trans. Liverpool Biol. Soc. (Liverpool)

Williams, J.H. 1979. *St Peter's Street, Northampton. Excavations 1973–6.* Northampton Archaeol. Monogr., **2**

Williamson, K. 1945. 'The economic importance of sea-fowl in the Faroe Islands', *Ibis*, **87,** 249–69

Williamson, K. 1948. *The Atlantic Islands: Study of the Faroe Life and Scene* (London)

Williamson, K. and Boyd, J.M. 1960. *St Kilda Summer* (London)

Williamson, K. and Boyd, J.M. 1963. *A Mosaic of Islands* (Edinburgh)

Wilson, J. 1842. *A Voyage round the Coasts of Scotland and the Isles*, **II** (Edinburgh)

Woodhead, E.I., Sullivan, C. and Gusset, G. 1984. *Lighting Devices in the National Reference Collection, Parks Canada* (Ottawa)

Young, A. 1958. 'Excavations at Dun Cuier, Isle of Barra, Outer Hebrides', *Proc. Soc. Antiq. Scotl.*, **89** (1955–6), 290–327

Index

Compiled by Lesley Adkins

Where several page references are made, main entries are given in **bold**.

Printed in Scotland for HMSO by (3808)
Dd 0293251 C10 07/96